Contemporary Challenges for Agile Project Management

Vannie Naidoo
University of KwaZulu-Natal, South Africa

Rahul Verma
Delhi University, India

A volume in the Advances in Logistics, Operations, and Management Science (ALOMS) Book Series

IGI Global
PUBLISHER of TIMELY KNOWLEDGE

Published in the United States of America by
IGI Global
Business Science Reference (an imprint of IGI Global)
701 E. Chocolate Avenue
Hershey PA, USA 17033
Tel: 717-533-8845
Fax: 717-533-8661
E-mail: cust@igi-global.com
Web site: http://www.igi-global.com

Library of Congress Cataloging-in-Publication Data

Names: Naidoo, Vannie, 1972- editor. | Verma, Rahul, 1989- editor.
Title: Contemporary challenges for agile project management / Vannie Naidoo and Rahul Verma, editors.
Description: Hershey, PA : Business Science Reference, [2022] | Includes bibliographical references and index. | Summary: "This book investigates agile project management, a modern flexible approach to project management, as it pertains to international business/trade within the context of globalization by offering concepts to help organizational teams to adapt to change quickly and deliver work fast"-- Provided by publisher.
Identifiers: LCCN 2020052128 (print) | LCCN 2020052129 (ebook) | ISBN 9781799878728 (hardcover) | ISBN 9781799878735 (paperback) | ISBN 9781799878742 (ebook)
Subjects: LCSH: Project management. | International trade. | International business enterprises. | Organizational change.
Classification: LCC HD69.P75 C757 2022 (print) | LCC HD69.P75 (ebook) | DDC 658.4/04--dc23
LC record available at https://lccn.loc.gov/2020052128
LC ebook record available at https://lccn.loc.gov/2020052129

This book is published in the IGI Global book series Advances in Logistics, Operations, and Management Science (ALOMS) (ISSN: 2327-350X; eISSN: 2327-3518)

British Cataloguing in Publication Data
A Cataloguing in Publication record for this book is available from the British Library.

Advances in Logistics, Operations, and Management Science (ALOMS) Book Series

John Wang
Montclair State University, USA

ISSN:2327-350X
EISSN:2327-3518

Mission

Operations research and management science continue to influence business processes, administration, and management information systems, particularly in covering the application methods for decision-making processes. New case studies and applications on management science, operations management, social sciences, and other behavioral sciences have been incorporated into business and organizations real-world objectives.

The **Advances in Logistics, Operations, and Management Science** (ALOMS) Book Series provides a collection of reference publications on the current trends, applications, theories, and practices in the management science field. Providing relevant and current research, this series and its individual publications would be useful for academics, researchers, scholars, and practitioners interested in improving decision making models and business functions.

Coverage

- Organizational Behavior
- Risk Management
- Production Management
- Networks
- Marketing engineering
- Finance
- Information Management
- Operations Management
- Services management
- Political Science

IGI Global is currently accepting manuscripts for publication within this series. To submit a proposal for a volume in this series, please contact our Acquisition Editors at Acquisitions@igi-global.com or visit: http://www.igi-global.com/publish/.

The Advances in Logistics, Operations, and Management Science (ALOMS) Book Series (ISSN 2327-350X) is published by IGI Global, 701 E. Chocolate Avenue, Hershey, PA 17033-1240, USA, www.igi-global.com. This series is composed of titles available for purchase individually; each title is edited to be contextually exclusive from any other title within the series. For pricing and ordering information please visit http://www.igi-global.com/book-series/advances-logistics-operations-management-science/37170. Postmaster: Send all address changes to above address.

Titles in this Series

For a list of additional titles in this series, please visit: www.igi-global.com/book-series

Handbook of Research on Current Trends in Asian Economics, Business, and Administration
Bülent Akkaya (Manisa Celal Bayar University, Turkey) Kittisak Jermsittiparsert (Henan University of Economics and Law, China) and Ayse Gunsel (Kocaeli University, Turkey)
Business Science Reference • © 2022 • 497pp • H/C (ISBN: 9781799884866) • US $295.00

Logistics and Supply Chain Management in the Globalized Business Era
Lincoln C. Wood (University of Otago, New Zealand) and Linh N.K. Duong (University of the West of England, Bristol, UK)
Business Science Reference • © 2022 • 325pp • H/C (ISBN: 9781799887096) • US $225.00

Managerial Issues in Digital Transformation of Global Modern Corporations
Thangasamy Esakki (Poompuhar College (Autonomous), India)
Business Science Reference • © 2021 • 323pp • H/C (ISBN: 9781799824022) • US $195.00

Reviving Businesses With New Organizational Change Management Strategies
Nuno Geada (College of Business Administration, Polytechnic Institute of Setúbal, Portugal) and Pedro Anunciação (College of Business Administration, Polytechnic Institute of Setúbal, Portugal)
Business Science Reference • © 2021 • 356pp • H/C (ISBN: 9781799874522) • US $225.00

Handbook of Research on Decision Sciences and Applications in the Transportation Sector
Said Ali Hassan (Cairo University, Egypt) and Ali Wagdy Mohamed (Cairo University, Egypt)
Business Science Reference • © 2021 • 419pp • H/C (ISBN: 9781799880400) • US $285.00

Handbook of Research on Management Techniques and Sustainability Strategies for Handling Disruptive Situations in Corporate Settings
Rafael Perez-Uribe (Universidad Santo Tomas, Bogotá, Colombia) David Ocampo-Guzman (EAN University, Colombia) Nelson Antonio Moreno-Monsalve (EAN University, Colombia) and William Stive Fajardo-Moreno (EAN University, Colombia)
Business Science Reference • © 2021 • 616pp • H/C (ISBN: 9781799881858) • US $295.00

Digitalization of Decentralized Supply Chains During Global Crises
Atour Taghipour (Normandy University, France)
Business Science Reference • © 2021 • 254pp • H/C (ISBN: 9781799868743) • US $225.00

IGI Global
PUBLISHER of TIMELY KNOWLEDGE

701 East Chocolate Avenue, Hershey, PA 17033, USA
Tel: 717-533-8845 x100 • Fax: 717-533-8661
E-Mail: cust@igi-global.com • www.igi-global.com

Editorial Advisory Board

Table of Contents

Detailed Table of Contents

The agile revolution and increasing cross-functionality nature of project teams imply an increasing need for effective and results-orientated project leadership. Irrespective of one's role in a project, there is a need for self-examination and self-reflection regarding how members relate during the various phases of project implementation. This chapter focuses on a theoretical review of the various elements necessary for effective agile project leadership. Through a synthesis of both old and more recent literature, the chapter identifies and conceptualizes ten determinant factors of effective agile project leadership and proposes a self-reflection framework for each of the ten project leadership competency areas. The chapter concludes by proposing a personal agile project leadership development plan (PAPLDP) template with an agility component that can be adopted for improvement and growth. This chapter challenges project managers and/or project team leaders to define their own value-based leadership competence and continuously reflect, evaluate, and improve themselves.

Software engineering is used in order to develop larger and complex software products. As software product is needed in almost all the industries, software engineering becomes really important. Software development can be done through various software development life cycle (SDLC) models like waterfall model, agile model, spiral model, prototype model, etc. SDLC is a framework that defines the tasks that to be performed at each step in the development process. Authors are mainly focusing on two models (i.e., waterfall and agile model). Waterfall model is a serial model which follows a strict sequence. Agile methodology can be divided into scrum methodology and extreme programming. Scrum methodology mainly focuses on how to manage tasks in a team-based environment. Scrum consists of three main roles. They are scrum master, product owner, and scrum team. While comparing both the models, the main difference obtained is waterfall does not allow any customer involvement while agile does allow it.

Project management is a term for which there are endless books professing the right way to conduct it. Project management is the systematic application of a standardized approach to conducting a project that increases that project's chances of success. It is known that IT projects are some of those projects most likely to fail, and e-learning projects are no different. The aim of this chapter is to explain how it might be possible to develop a toolkit that could allow e-learning systems of any scale to be developed by those who often have to deliver learning, but may not necessarily have skills in project management or ICT development. It is intended that the proposed toolkit would be valued by other internationally focussed organisations where learning and teaching are a core part of the activities that it conducts, but on a smaller scale. To achieve this, research is proposed at the University of Gloucestershire and Crocels Community Media Group. A pilot study is conducted, and the questionnaire for the study proves to be reliable.

Agile software development methodologies are attracting attention from academics and practitioners for planning and managing software projects. The eXtreme Programming (XP) challenges conformist wisdom regarding software system development processes and practices as agile methodologies. To work efficiently in the current software development practice, characterized by requirements fuzziness, XP moves away from document-centric operations into people-centric management. In the XP-based software project, the customers play an essential role, having multiple responsibilities such as driving the project, gathering requirements ('user stories'), and exercising quality control (or acceptance testing). Besides, the customers must liaise with external project stakeholders (e.g., funding authorities, end-users) while maintaining the development team's trust and the wider business. The success of such software project management practices relies on the quality result of each stage of development obtained through rigorous testing. This chapter describes three characteristics of XP project management: customer role, software testing feedback, and learning.

It is the total sum of money allocated for the specific project for a specific period of time. The goal of the project budget is to cost control. The objective of this chapter is to give the implication of budgeting on contemporary project management. The main focus of this chapter is to discuss the introduction, history, agile approach, etc. It has a direct impact on the company's financial feasibility. The research would discuss the approaches for the projects budget estimation and various steps for cost control. There are two types of reserves against risks: one is the contingency reserve for identified risk, and the other is the management reserve for unidentified risks. The project manager needs to be aware of existing resources acquisition policies, guidelines, and procedures. The author discusses the procedures for project budgeting and methods for evaluation of project budgeting.

With projects becoming more complex and multifaceted than before, there arises a need for agile efficient project management. This chapter seeks to define project management efficiency. The chapter explores the five variables that influence project management efficiency. It also delves into the importance of project management efficiency. Finally, the chapter breaks down the challenges to project management efficiency and gives solutions to counter the challenges. The variables explained in this chapter are project scope, cost, time, resources, and quality. As evidenced here, each variable has a role in enhancing efficiency in managing projects. The benefits of efficiently managed projects examined are quality control, customer satisfaction, risk identification and evaluation, consistent communication, and on-schedule project delivery. The challenges expounded in the chapter are inadequate skillset, undefined goals, impossible deadlines, scope creep, resource deprivation, and poor communication.

Mega-projects are crucial as they strive to provide infrastructural development and support growth and sustainability of a country's economy. Scheduling is an integral part of mega-projects, and special attention needs to be given to the planning of this activity. It is important that an experienced person in the project team be responsible for scheduling activities for the mega-project. In 2020, COVID-19 appeared and had devastating consequences on the world and all sectors of society including business, industry, and the economy. Mega-projects were also affected by COVID-19, a deadly pandemic that has caused a loss of millions of lives worldwide. The scheduling of mega-projects during lock-down proved problematic, causing major delays, backlogs, and additional cost and rescheduling of activities in the project. Disasters are also another factor that can hinder project performance. This chapter will unpack scheduling in mega-projects and how it is affected by COVID-19 and other disasters.

People work in software development projects to bundle the human resources and use the systematic approach to share system development knowledge. One can view knowledge as personalized related to facts, procedures, concepts, interpretations, ideas, and judgments. This way, knowledge is the outcome of the cognitive processing of information. Knowledge can be transferred from a source to a receiver. The collaborative knowledge-sharing mechanism is known as knowledge management (KM) in the software industry. The software developers can communicate with, learn from, and solve problems with other participating team members. The organizational culture is an essential factor in knowledge management success since it influences how team members learn and share knowledge. This chapter presents a case study that aimed to compare, in practice, the relationship between the KM cycle (SECI – socialization, externalization, combination, and internalization model) and the organizational culture through the competing values framework (CVF).

Foreword

The complex environments businesses have to operate in have changed considerable over the last decade. This in essence has implications on the functional areas of the project manager and his team. The area of Project management which is the focus of the book has evolved over the years. As the business environments have become more complex, the area of project management has also become more dynamic and complex. This is a unique interdisciplinary book that focuses on agile project management and the various contemporary issue faced in Project management.

To keep abreast of the 4th industrial revolution the area of project management also had to adapt. By adapting to these technologies, meant faster more efficient and smooth systems and software used in project management that cut costs, limit production delays, streamline quality and completion of projects within the necessary scheduled time frames. In the short term these technologies have cost companies millions, however the in the long term it has provided great benefits that far outreach the initial costs incurred.

Agile project management is a more recent aspect of Project management. It is important to note that tradition and agile project management is unpacked and reasons to use them in specific circumstances will be outlined in the book. Software projects found it highly beneficial to use the agile methods. Agile principles have also provided added benefits to the area of project management. According to Larson and Grey, these principles include, focus on customer value, interactive and incremental deliver, experimentation and adaption, servant leadership and continuous improvement. Waterfall and scrum are common terminologies associated with agile methodology. Although scrum is a method most popular that is used for small projects it can also be adapted to larger projects.

Other contemporary issues that have been raised as that cause major impacts on agile project management systems are terrorism, knowledge management, COVID-19 and pandemics, natural disasters, E-learning, and Organizational culture.

This unique book has contributions by authors from various countries who conduct research in engineering, project management, management and other various contemporary research areas that shape the area of project management.

Faiza Mohamed Osman
Association of African Universities, Ghana

Preface

Cross functional collaboration is a group of people with different functional expertise coming together to work toward a common goal. Cross-functional collaboration occurs when people from different operational developers working together to deliver an improved ecommerce experience. Cross-functional collaboration is bringing people from various spheres, bringing together their knowledge, expertise, and experience. The major point is work. A cross-functional team is a group of people with different functional expertise working toward a common goal. It may include people from finance, etc. In a cross-functional team, team members from various departments with different skill sets come together to work on a project or reach for a common goal. A team is a group of people who work together toward a common goal. Cross-functional teams utilize a wide variety of unique skill sets to build teams. In a nutshell, cross-functional collaboration is when people from within a company join forces to work on a common goal or project. Cross-functional collaboration is when a group of people with different functional expertise come together to work on a goal or project. The simplest definition of building a cross-functional team is to put together a group of people with different functional expertise.

In many cases, the team is simply a group of people from the different departments across a business working on solving a specific problem or a set of problems. In a business setting most work is accomplished by teams of individuals. A cross-functional team is a group of people from different departments. Many of the problems organizations find most challenging involve the moments when work passes from one department or team to another. That's why organizations often create cross-functional teams on a temporary basis to function as a unit for the duration of a specific project, existing from the start. A cross-functional team is a group of people with different functional expertise working toward a common goal. It may include people from finance, etc. The most simple definition of cross-functional teams (or CFTs) is bringing people together from different disciplines can improve problem solving. The difference between teams that perform and other groups that don't is a subject to which most of us pay far too little attention. In a cross-functional team, team members from various departments with different skill sets come together to work on a project or reach for a common goal. Cross-functional teams consist of various employees with different functional expertise working on a common goal. A cross-functional team is simply a team made up of individuals from different functions or departments within an organization. Teams like this are useful.

Agile project management is a modern, flexible approach to project management that allows a team to break large projects down into more manageable tasks, which are tackled in short iterations or sprints thus enabling a team to adapt to change quickly and deliver work fast. This definition explains what Agile Project Management is and how it works. It stresses customer satisfaction and uses available teams to fast-track software development at every stage. The ultimate value in agile development is that it enables teams to deliver value faster, with greater quality and predictability, and greater aptitude. That's why, instead of producing one big batch of work, agile focuses on an iterative approach where teams break down their projects and continuously deliver. Agile project management is an approach based on delivering requirements iteratively & incrementally. Agile, in a nutshell, is an iterative and incremental approach to project management that helps teams keep up with the demands of the modern. Now agile methodologies-which involve new values, principles, practices, and benefits and are a radical alternative to command-and-control-style management. The Agile methodology in project management breaks projects up into several stages called "sprints".

Given the pace at which project management must be conducted these days in an era of global hyper-competition, examining the profession within the contexts of international trade and globalization is a must for academics and practitioners alike. International trade and competition are consistent themes in the business literature. Globalization is reshaping global value chains through rising demand and new industry capabilities in the developing world as well as this wave shows that over the last hundred years of economic growth, there has been more than proportional growth in global trade. They also created regional custom and trade agreements and unions to facilitate economic interdependence. The most important of these organizations, treaties, etc. in the era of entrepreneurial universities is to foster. Time as audiences face a world awash with content and information, the profession best skilled and most dedicated to help them make sense of the deluge.

ORGANIZATION OF THE BOOK

The book is organized into 14 chapters. A brief description of each of the chapters follows:

Chapter 1, "Using Technology and Innovation to Streamline Agile Project Management," establishes that Agile project management has transformed due to the rapid advancements in technologies. The authors of this chapter contend that this is a key contributor to successful Agile Project Management.

Chapter 2, "Agile Project Management in International Logistics Operations," discusses a Business Model (BM) perspective as an innovating practice to analyse the transition of the EuroPacific LL Company (EuroPacific) from regional logistic operator to domestic logistic operator or Third-Party Logistic Provider (3PL) for Asian companies.

Chapter 3, "Agile Project Management: Experience and Adoption," presents the notion of 'Agile Project Management' and identifies the existing challenges in the Agile Project Management in the new millennium. It sets the scene for discussions presented by various authors too. In particular the chapter identifies the Experience and the related problems with Agile Project Management. It also identifies the importance of adoption of Agile Project Management and debates about the measure of Agility.

Chapter 4, "Project Success Criteria, Critical Success Factors (CSF), and Agile Projects," reviews the concept of project success, project success criteria, and CSF by narrowing the focus from generic projects to IT and then agile projects. The review revealed that client satisfaction has a critical role in the perceived success of the project, along with iron triangle (cost, budget, scope). It is widely accepted that some CSF are dependent on the context of the project.

Chapter 5, "Machine Learning and Data Science Project Management From an Agile Perspective: Methods and Challenges," aims at discussing methods and challenges according to the background information and practice areas of Machine Learning (ML), Data Science (DS), and Agile Project Management (APM). This study can be viewed as an initial attempt to enhance these knowledge and practice domains in view of Agile Project Management.

Chapter 6, "Effective Agile Project Leadership Through Competency-Based Self-Reflection: A Synthesis of Literature," focuses on a theoretical review of the various elements necessary for effective agile project leadership. Through a synthesis of both old and more recent literature, the chapter identifies and conceptualises ten determinant factors of effective agile project leadership and proposes a self-reflection framework for each of the ten project leadership competency areas.

Chapter 7, "A Quantitative Study of Waterfall and Agile Methodologies With the Perspective of Project Management," focuses on two models i.e. Waterfall and Agile Model. Waterfall model is a serial model which follows a strict sequence and agile methodology can be divided into Scrum methodology and Extreme programming. While analysing and comparing both the models the main difference obtained is waterfall does not allow any customer involvement while agile does allow.

Chapter 8, "The Role of an Agile and Lean Project Management Toolkit for Assisting E-Learning Project Management Teams in Multi-National Organisations: Accounting for Inter-Organisational Architecture, Culture, Agility, and Change in Legacy Systems," aims to explain how it might be possible to develop a toolkit that could allow e-learning systems of any scale to be developed by those who often have to deliver learning, but may not necessarily have skills in project management or ICT development. The authors intend that the proposed toolkit would be valued by other internationally-focussed organisations where learning and teaching are a core part of the activities that it conducts, but on a smaller scale.

Chapter 9, "Customers Role in Software Development Under Agile, Extreme Programming Projects," establishes that agile software development methodologies are attracting attention from academics and practitioners for planning and managing software projects. The authors also suggest that eXtreme Programming (XP), part of agile methodologies, is challenging conformist wisdom regarding software system development processes and practices.

Chapter 10, "Implication of Budgeting on Contemporary Project Management," reviews the implication of budgeting on Contemporary Project Management. The main focus of this chapter is to discuss the introduction, history, agile approach etc. It has a direct impact on the company's financial feasibility. The author systematically reviews the approaches for the projects budget estimation and various steps for cost control. The author also discusses the procedures for project budgeting and methods for evaluation of project budgeting.

Chapter 11, "Exploring the Broad Underlying Principals That Govern Project Management," seeks to define project management efficiency. The chapter explores the five variables that influence project management efficiency. It also delves into the importance of project management efficiency. Finally, the authors break down the challenges to project management efficiency and gives solutions to counter the challenges.

Chapter 12, "The Effects of COVID-19 and Disasters on Scheduling Function in Mega-Projects," unpacks scheduling in Mega-projects and how it is affected by COVID-19 and other disasters. In 2020 COVID-19 appeared and had devastating consequences on the world, and all sectors of society including business, industry and the economy. Mega-projects were also affected by COVID-19, a deadly pandemic that has caused a loss of millions of lives world-wide.

Chapter 13, "A Case Study of Knowledge Management and Organizational Culture in an Undergraduate Software Development Team Project," presents a case study that aimed to compare, in practice, the relationship between the Knowledge Management cycle (SECI – Socialization, Externalization, Combination, and Internalization model) and the organizational culture through the Competing Values Framework (CVF).

Chapter 14, "How Does Terrorism Change the Business Landscape for Firms? A New Framework for Analysing Risks," introduces a new framework for understanding firm creation and firm behaviour in the face of terrorism and its ensuing risks such as institutional disruption.

Acknowledgment

The editors would like to acknowledge the help of all the people involved in this project and, more specifically, to the authors and reviewers that took part in the review process. Without their support, this book would not have become a reality.

First, the editors would like to thank each one of the authors for their contributions. Our sincere gratitude goes to the chapter's authors who contributed their time and expertise to this book.

Second, the editors wish to acknowledge the valuable contributions of the reviewers regarding the improvement of quality, coherence, and content presentation of chapters. Most of the authors also served as referees; we highly appreciate their double task.

Vannie Naidoo
University of KwaZulu-Natal, South Africa

Rahul Verma
Delhi University, India

Chapter 1
Using Technology and Innovation to Streamline Agile Project Management

Vannie Naidoo
https://orcid.org/0000-0001-8435-4348
University of KwaZulu-Natal, South Africa

Thokozani Ian Nzimakwe
https://orcid.org/0000-0001-5817-9910
University of KwaZulu-Natal, South Africa

ABSTRACT

Agile project management has transformed due to the rapid advancements in technologies. Digitisation of work processes has also contributed to increased efficiencies and lowering of costs within companies and organisations worldwide. This is essential in agile project management as managing and maintaining schedules and budgets are imperative for a successful project completion. The employees' drive, confidence, job meaningfulness, autonomy in job, and mastery of skills, or psychological empowerment as they often referred to in literature, are instrumental in nourishing employees' innovative work behaviour. This is a key contributor to successful agile project management.

INTRODUCTION

The area of agile project management is dynamic and constantly changing. Technology has had major impact on all functional areas of project management. Technological advancements have in fact made the world of work in agile project management more streamlined, efficient and has improved the overall performance of the project. Since project management is a multi - dollar or billion dollar industry technology has aided in creating competitive advantage in this industry. The area of innovation is a key aspect in ensuring competitive advantage in this sector. A strong project management team that is highly driven and innovative can add value to the project in terms of its performance and ensuring its' final comple-

DOI: 10.4018/978-1-7998-7872-8.ch001

tion is on time as well as within the budgeted norms. In this chapter themes associated with technology and innovation will be outlined and discussed as it impacts on the efficient and high performance of a project towards final completion.

BACKGROUND

Agile project management is essential. It drives projects that develops a country's economy and enhance its' future sustainability. The project management sector is a Multi - billion dollar industry. The industry is fast moving, complex and continuously changing. Cohen et al. (2004) argue that agile project management or "agile methods" represents a team management approach and a productivity framework that supports continuous and incremental progress on work priorities, even in the face of changes. This method is recognised as superior by many in the industry and has its origins in the agile processes of software development, such as Scrum, XP, DSDM, Cristal, which are programming methodologies based on adaptability to any change as a means to increase the chances of success of a project. Agile project management is very versatile and can be used in projects in different industries not only the software industry. According to Stare (2014) analyses have been conducted on the implementation of agile management in product development, educational projects (Grimheden, 2013), construction projects (Demir & Theis, 2016), venture capital groups (Sutherland & Altman, 2009), innovation processes (Hannola et al., 2013) and the management of projects in libraries (Niemi - Grundström, 2014). The chapter will highlight how technology and innovation has streamlined agile project management. Keegan & Turner (2002) analysed the management of innovation in project - based firms along three dimensions - context supportive for innovation, slack resources and perception of innovation as being useful or not. The authors observe that the interplay between innovation and projects is dominated by the ideas on how to correctly manage projects, rather than how to effectively manage innovation. In other words, the attitude towards managing innovation projects remains mechanical in nature as traditional project management approaches are applied to innovation projects. Rycroft & Kash (1999) posit that emerging industries (ICT, biotechnology) are increasingly adopting project - based forms. New forms of organisation (such as projects) are used in order to cope with increasing complexity of production, communication and technology.

MAIN FOCUS OF THE CHAPTER

In the main focus of the chapter the discussion will begin with defining agile project management. The next area under discussion will be to discuss successful agile project management from companies in industry. The discussion will then highlight innovation in project management. Agile methodologies will then be outlined and discussed in detail, as this is crucial area to unpack. The discussion thereafter will elude to highlighting Psychological empowerment and how it improves work tasks and innovation by employees.

Defining Agile Project Management

There are divergent views on the definition of agile project management. Highsmith (2004) understood agility in terms of five key objectives: continuous innovation, product adaptability, reduced delivery times, people and process adaptability, and reliable results.

Agile Project Management is defined as a conceptual framework which responds quickly to changes, collaborates with the client frequently and covers minimum amount of document needs. Agile methods facilitate the software development by performing incrementally and iteratively and thereby minimising the risk (Madampe, 2017).

Basic condition of agility in the context of the development of the project is the ability to change an entry in project development. Antlova (2014) states that the customer then has the option to modify requirements during running project, without a massive re - engineering of work already carried out, and the unnecessary waste of time and resources for all involved. Agile methodology arose in the mid - 1990 years of the last century as a response to difficult traditional methodology, which has been criticized for bureaucracy, rigidity and inability to respond flexibly to changes.

Agile has becoming more popular method in a software development process among the software development community. With agile, the development process becomes simpler and easier. Most of the researchers agreed that agile provides simple steps and much easier compared to the traditional method. In general, agile provides more customer's involvement, earlier testing, quick delivery and active requirements (Mansor et al., 2011).

Agility is characterized by the breakdown of work in short, regular and frequent cycles of finished tasks, involvement of the customer in the process of planning and, of course, the organization of the team. One of the most innovative agile approaches is Scrum process, whose aim is to break down large and complex projects, that it is hard to comprehend at once. Scrum divides large areas into smaller units and sets out the priority of each task (Antlova, 2014).

According to Bunsiri & Kumpron (2016), agile was created in 2001 by group of the expert software development as Agile Alliance. It is one of the fastest - growing management techniques since the traditional project management was not suitable in the age of highly competitive business and rapid change. Moreover, today business processes are more complex and interconnected than ever before. Many projects failed to deliver and to meet their objectives in terms of cost, time and features and traditional project delivery frameworks cannot deliver as fast as changes and highly uncertain environments. Agile project management allows team to deliver the product with product feature which is the most important element for business, on time

Agile project management is an iterative way of planning and guiding a project. Figure 1 shows the life cycle of agile. At the beginning the stakeholders determine the features which are going to be developed in the project. Product owner who is a key stakeholder write epics (large user stories) which require to be broken in to smaller pieces of work. Once an epic is broken into user stories, the user stories are prioritized and stored in a backlog. With regard to software development, agile software development is where the software is developed in iterative cycles, where all the phases are connected together and each phase being a feedback to the other phases (Madampe, 2017).

Agile is a project management approach developed as a more flexible and efficient way to get products to market. The word 'agile' refers to the ability to move quickly and easily. Therefore, an agile approach enables project teams to adapt faster and easier compared to other project methodologies (WRIKE, 2020).

Figure 1. Life cycle of agile
Source: Madampe, 2017

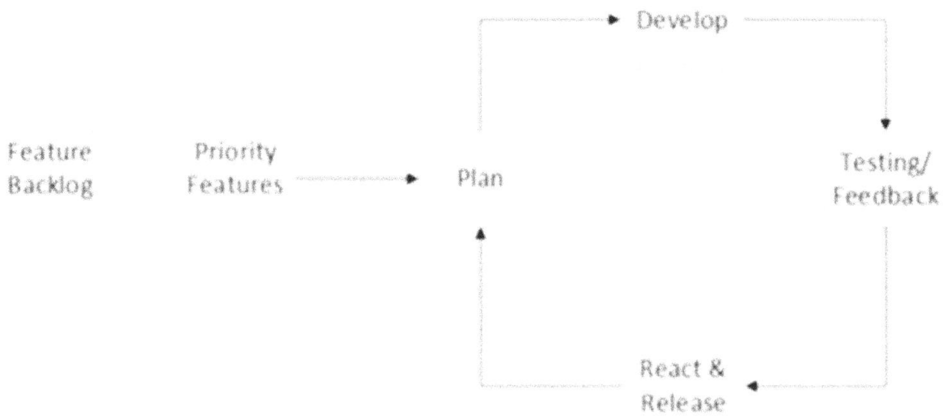

Agile project management is an iterative development methodology that values human communication and feedback, adapting to change, and producing working results. Agile project management is all about efficient communication over documentation, convoluted email chains, or excessive meetings.

What Is Agile Methodology?

Agile methodology is an approach to project management that uses four values and 12 principles to organise projects (WRIKE, 2020). Agile is a methodology in which an association engages its people to work where, when and how they choose with greatest adaptability and least requirements to optimise their execution and convey best in class esteem and customer administration (Raj & Sinha, 2020). It utilizes communication and information technology to empower individuals to work in ways, which best suit, their requirements without the traditional limitations of where and when errands must be performed. The Agile Manifesto gives a breakdown of Agile Methods' intention.

The four values of the Agile Manifesto are (Raj & Sinha, 2020):

- Individuals and interactions over processes and tools;
- Working software over comprehensive documentation;
- Customer collaboration over contract negotiation; and
- Responding to change over following a plan.

The agile method works in ongoing sprints of project planning and execution, enabling you to continuously adapt and mature your plan, scope, and design throughout the project. Agile projects require an iterative approach, which supports incremental, frequent, and consistent delivery of workable products to your customer or client. This innovative approach ensures your project team can consistently deliver concrete products without being delayed by changes and evolving requirements. Agile has a high level of customer involvement and includes frequent reviews of progress with both the project team and the customer (WRIKE, 2020).

Agile project management is, by definition, ever evolving and changing. Successfully completed projects point to need for the new approaches towards the customer, flexibility and the appropriate management of the customer's requirements. These claims comply with agile approaches.

Agility Attributes

In the core of agile project management lies the word "agility", which means "mobility, nimbleness", as well as from the Latin "agere: keep in movement". This signifies the ability to move something forward in a quick way that allows easy changes of direction (Kanbanize, 2019). For the purposes of organizations, agility is usually referred to in terms of timeliness and flexibility. Agility can be defined as the ability to respond and execute to a business - scenario change quickly and at a low cost. However, this does not provide or give a measure of what quickly is (Baweja & Venugopalan, 2015).

According Eschenbach et al. (2015), for decades, as Information Technology (IT) projects grew bigger and more complex, project failures seemed to become increasingly common, in spite of intense efforts to apply traditional project planning. Those traditional planning tools focused on balancing the triple constraints of cost, schedule, and scope to create a plan. Then those tools unsuccessfully focused on delivering the planned scope within the planned cost and schedule. In 2001 the "agile project manifesto" pointed the way to better manage projects having a flexible scope in an uncertain environment. Since then agile project management in IT has matured and proven itself for large and small IT projects.

So, in terms of project management, "agility" has five essential attributes that form the building blocks of the agile process, as indicated in Figure 2. Those are: Transparency; Customer focus; Adaptability; Sense of Ownership (Effective Leadership); and Continuous Improvement (Kanbanize, 2019). Combined together, they are what make a project agile.

Figure 2. Agility attributes
Source: Kanbanize, 2019

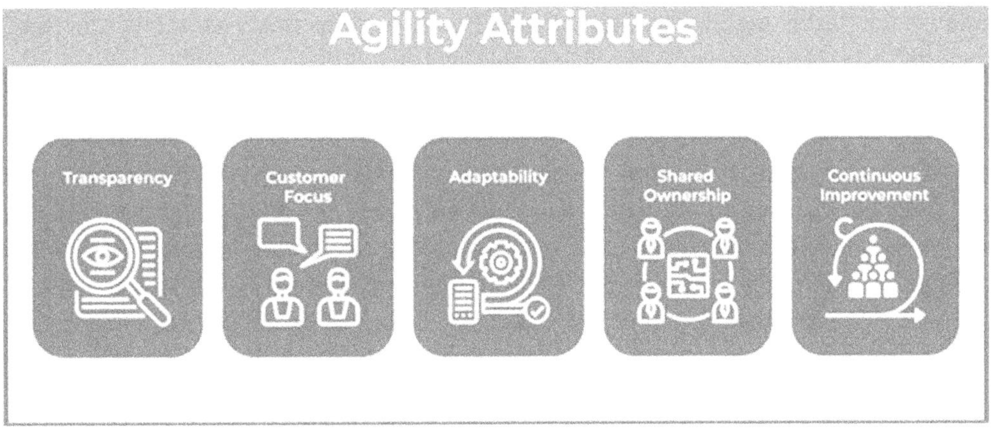

Kloppenborg et al. (2019) argue that while much has been written about Agile, starting with the Agile Manifesto, a simplified version of the mind - set needed to successfully plan and manage agile projects boils down to four key ideas:

- Satisfy the customer by placing emphasis on outputs that fulfil their needs;
- Engage all participants through empowerment, co - operation and knowledge sharing;
- Facilitate that engagement through servant leadership and visible and continual communication; and
- Keep things simple with a sustainable pace and emphasis on process improvement.

Successful Agile Project Management from Industry

Agile methods are developed as a reaction to the traditional project management which is plan - driven. In case of software development, when following traditional project management due to the plans to be followed slows down the software development, Therefore agile methods have become prominent as a group of software development methodologies which are adaptive rather than predictive and are people - oriented rather than process - oriented. Agile software development method is incremental, cooperative, straightforward and adaptive. Incremental is small software releases are done in rapid development cycles. Cooperative is the close relationship between the development team and the client. Straightforward refers that this method can be easily learnt and easy to modify. Adaptive implies the ability to respond to any changes produced at any moment (Madampe, 2017).

In a survey conducted in Czech companies during 2013, the results of the survey showed that agile approaches are still used in most projects, software, and Internet organizations. Antlova (2014), point out that here the project managers also have the greatest knowledge of agile principles. However, it is essential that organizations must have corporate culture, which allows the greatest possible extent an appropriate communication of team project members and also to communicate with the customer. It is also essential that the members of the project teams were constantly acquainted with new trends in project management. Agile methods are a set of best practices and recommendations, but like any other methodology must be taken not dogmatically. In agile approach very close and often communication with customers or users requires effort and can be seen as time consuming. Therefore it is necessary that both sides have to agree with this communication. These problems could be solved by using of information and communication technologies. From this point of view, these methods are rather loose philosophy that is supported by corporate culture rather than strict rules.

In the Czech ICT companies the knowledge of agile approaches is much greater than in the other companies (8 project managers agile approaches used). Also all the organizations in the area of project management from car industry used project management methods (especially by the standards of Prince2, IPMA, and PMBOOK), 5 project managers has some awareness of agile approaches. The situation is worse in organizations from the construction industry, where only larger companies - 3 are using the principles of project management, in terms of agile approaches - there are unknown. In the six logistics companies, project management is used (in 2 companies it is used a standard methodology, the others have their own design rules), only 2 project managers are familiar with the concept of the agile approach. In the remaining 11 organizations in the area of services it is used just project management in five major companies. Agile approaches are also not known to project managers (Antlova, 2014).

The benefits of agile project management are many, particularly for the following organizations and project types (WRIKE, 2020):

- Any project that evolves or does not have clear scope and requirements at the start;
- Organizations that work in a fast - changing environment, such as technology;

- Organizations that need to work closely with their customers and other external parties throughout the life of the project;
- Companies that emphasize process and product improvement and are constantly looking to innovate;
- Projects with many interdependent tasks, where the team needs to work closely and frequently communicate to ensure success;
- Companies that need to create a prototype before building the final project outcome; and
- Projects that require rapid feedback from stakeholders about each product iteration before moving on to the next version or draft.

Eschenbach et al (2015), state that IT projects have demonstrated many times that success does not always come through better planning. IT projects were also the test bed for developing agile PM which is a clearly superior project management method for this environment. Academia has aspects in common with IT that make agile PM a viable choice for managing activities. Because academics are always juggling multiple projects over an academic year (or day), agile management of project scope is very likely to work better than better planning to execute the current scope.

The 12 Agile Principles

Globalisation, increasing complexity, dynamic markets, technical and ecological changes are the most frequents trends of the past few years. They reveal the background of the social paradigms shift and bring new visionary ideas about the future direction of the contemporary society and modern organizations. For most organisations it is necessary to be able to respond to these changing conditions. One of the possible solutions how to react quickly, is to carry out a variety of activities and changes in the organisations through the projects. This means that it is clearly defined target with a specific effort. This effort will define the time schedule and the necessary material, technical, personnel and financial resources, and all the coordinates, so that the resources have maximum benefit. Antlova (2014) states that the application of project management generates several fundamental advantages: accurate business planning resources (finance, personnel, material, and technical base), streamlining and simplification of internal procedures and a substantial supply chain management subscription, and identification of business strategies and changes.

The Manifesto for Agile Software Development outlines 12 agile principles that all projects should follow. These are (WRIKE, 2020; Bunsiri & Kumpron, 2016):

- The highest priority is to satisfy the customer through early and continuous delivery of valuable software.

The first principle of agile methodology states that customers should receive project deliverables or iterations across regular intervals throughout the project's life cycle, rather than just one product delivery at the end.

- Welcome changing requirements, even late in development. Agile processes harness change for the customer's competitive advantage.

The authors of Agile Manifesto found that, with traditional project management, it was difficult to accommodate last - minute change requests. This principle ensures that agile projects can adapt to any changes, no matter how late in the game, with minimal delay.

- Deliver working software frequently, from a couple of weeks to a couple of months, with a preference for shorter timescales.

Agile projects plan for frequent, short project timelines that allow for a fast turnaround of workable products. Teams will often break agile projects into one to four week - long sprints or project intervals, each one ending in the delivery of a product.

- Business people and developers must work together daily throughout the project.

This Agile principle states that regular communication with all stakeholders is critical to the project's success. Commonly, this involves a short daily meeting with both the project team and any other key stakeholders.

- Build projects around motivated individuals. Give them the environment and support they need, and trust them to get the job done.

A central concept of the agile project management methodology is that the right people need to be placed in the right positions and given the autonomy required to do their jobs well. It's essential to design a project team based on capabilities rather than job positions or titles. The project manager's focus should be on motivating the project team and supporting them, rather than micromanaging them.

- The most efficient and effective method of conveying information to and within a development team is face - to - face conversation.

The Agile Manifesto emphasizes the importance of co - locating teams and stakeholders whenever possible, as face - to - face communication is more effective than email or phone. If your team cannot be co - located, video conferencing is an option that can still capture the value of non - verbal cues.

- Working software is the primary measure of progress.

The Agile methodology aims to provide complete, working deliverables. This goal should always take priority over any additional requirements, such as project documentation. Other metrics, such as hours spent or time elapsed, are not considered as important as delivering working products.

- Agile processes promote sustainable development. The sponsors, developers, and users should be able to maintain a constant pace indefinitely.

According to this principle, agile projects should have a consistent pace for each iterative cycle or sprint within the project. This breakdown should eliminate the need for overtime or crashing schedules while promoting frequent output of workable products. It should also create a repeatable cycle that the team can continuously follow for as long as necessary.

- Continuous attention to technical excellence and good design enhances agility.

An Agile project's primary focus should be on improving the end product and achieving advancements consistently over time. Each iteration should always improve on the previous one, and the team should always be looking to innovate.

- Simplicity - the art of maximizing the amount of work not done - is essential.

An Agile project aims to get just enough done to complete the project and meet the requested specifications. Any additional documentation, steps, processes, or work that does not add value to the customer or enhance the project outputs should be avoided or eliminated.

- The best architectures, requirements, and designs emerge from self - organizing teams.

Agile is based on the belief that you need motivated, autonomous, and skilled teams to deliver the best results and products. Teams should be empowered to organize and structure themselves as required. They should have the freedom to collaborate and innovate as they see fit, without being hampered by too much oversight.

- The team discusses how to become more effective at regular intervals, then tunes and adjusts its behaviour accordingly.

A successful, self - motivated team requires a strong focus on advancing their skills and processes to grow and improve. The team should have regular reviews on their performance and outcomes, including discussions on improving as they move forward.

Best Practices to be Followed to Adopt Agile Project Management

The traditional concept of a project manager's role has to be altered as a leader and a coach who shows the correct direction to the team in a very innovative and creative way. According to Madampe (2017), in agile project management the resources may be distributed over different geographical locations and the team may be a virtual one. So the team members including the project manager should be able overcome the issues coming across and maintain the agile practices. An organization's readiness for agile project management has to be assessed. Importantly the degree to which the organization is willing to face the risks, accept the changes, value the deliverables than the procedures have to be assessed.

When starting with agile project management, it is always encouraged to start with a small project rather than going for a complicated one. The reason is since this is the first time of applying the knowledge and first time of practicing, the risk of failing the project should be mitigated. In order to do that a simple small project which covers almost all the aspects of agility can be used. Thereby after obtaining the experience of how to work in an agile environment, with the time the organization will be able to practice agile very successfully.

Kloppenborg et al (2019) contend that an agile project should start with a charter, as any other project should. This high - level agreement between the product owner, scrum master, and empowered team will help share the compelling project vision, create commitment, uncover risks, identify stakeholders, ensure common understanding of success criteria, and establish working agreements and ground rules as needed. Often, the iteration is used to determine the product to be built and prioritise the most valuable work for the next iteration.

Innovation in Agile Project Management

Innovation is a very crucial aspect in agile project management. In order for the company involved in agile project to have competitive advantage over its competitors it needs to have innovation and a project team that can drive innovative processes. Highsmith & Cockburn (2001) argue that innovation and creativity has been highlighted as a pivotal strength underpinning agile methods. Companies or other organizations (including those in the project management sector) combine incremental innovation activities with increasingly successful or even disruptive innovation projects to create value in uncertain environments (Morris et al., 2014).

There are various innovation approaches or models used in project management. However one needs to bear in mind the uniqueness and complexity of project, so there is no one size fits all mentality that can permeate the agile project management industry. Project managers and their teams need to be flexible in their approach and adapt innovation approached that best fits their unique needs on their specific project. This is best practice. Also Preez & Louw (2008) support this line of argumentation and stated that: “there are just too many variables impacting on the innovation and design process for one framework to provide a “one - size - fits - all” solution” (Preez & Louw 2008).

In the discussion below a few innovation approached used in projects will be outlined and discussed. Micheal Porter who argues that “companies achieve competitive advantage through acts of innovation” (Porter 1990). Cooper introduced, during the 1980s and 1990s, his new tool for managing new products, namely the Stage - Gate system. In fact, the Stage Gate is very applicable to use in the manufacturing sector. The focus within developing innovations has shifted towards an efficient oriented process. Therefore, the third generation evolved and includes four F’s, namely Fluidity, Fuzzy gates, Focused, and Flexibility. Fluidity stands for overlapping stages, whereby certain activities are brought forward. Fuzzy gates mean conditional go decisions that are dependent on the context situation. Focused is being created by integrating various prioritization methods, which look at the entire project portfolio. At last, the third generation system is still a framework and requires a certain degree of flexibility in order to adapt to project type (Cooper, 1994). When it comes to software development, Winston Royce introduced “the waterfall method” in 1970. This approach assumes that complex software systems can be built in one single proceeding. The proceeding is visualized in a sequential manner without going back and revisiting conditions (Royce, 1970). According to previous software projects studies, results revealed that only nine to sixteen percent of the projects which used the Waterfall method were on time and within budget (Clancy, 2014).

Another very useful innovation came into being that of the agile approach. In the agile approach, software is developed by using design - code - test loops. In this way, the company is able to adapt directly to the changing requirements with limited costs involved (Szalvay 2004) The Standish Group International Inc. shows in their CHAOS report that the success rate of software projects which used the Agile approach was increased towards 34 percent (The Standisch Group International, 2003). A particular strength of the agile approach is that they move away from 'introverted' development where the team building the system are detached from the customer. Instead, agile approaches continually involve the customer in the development process, supposedly leading to the development of a more innovative and hence more valuable information system.

Cooper (2014) named the new generation of his Stage - Gate model: The Triple a System. The Triple A stands for: Adaptive & flexible, Agile, and Accelerated. In other words, leading firms try to adapt themselves to the context of the particular project. Agile purpose that various sprints are made by the project team to get a product in front of the client. Accelerated stands for that activities and even stages are done in a parallel fashion. Given that sense, the concept Stage is less relevant in this approach (Cooper, 2014). There is a belief that Stage - Gate contributes to a rigid and fixed mindset, which is often not desirable in a dynamic project management sector.

Another Hybrid approach introduced was the Fugle Innovation Process of Preez & Louw (2008). The Fugle approach reflects the whole innovation process from idea to exploitation. Preez & Louw, (2008) further adds that the gates in the first part (the funnel) of the innovation process bear another name, namely filters. This name represents the split function of the attractive and less attractive ideas and concepts. Based on the previous mentioned characteristics, it can be concluded that the Fugle approach also contains and combines various aspects of the linear (StageGate / Waterfall) and the iterative (Agile) project management concepts. Stage - gate system arises from the PPP approach and therefore the Stage - Gate has to be seen as the second - generation tool for guiding product innovation (Cooper 1994). Karlström & Runeson (2006) argue that: "software development projects are not isolated activities. They usually exist as subprojects in an environment composed of hardware development, marketing, production planning, et cetera. All the sub - projects must be managed and coordinated concurrently [A Stage - Gate system] gives support not only for the communication within the project, but also for decision makers sponsoring the project or acquiring the outcome of the project" (Karlström & Runeson, 2006).

Psychological Empowerment and How it Improves Work Tasks and Innovation by Employees

Agile is a set of methodologies created for the development of new software products; it is based on the Agile Manifesto crafted by IT industry leaders in 2001 - a set of rules and guidelines for how to best develop new software code (Beck et al., 2001). The twelve supporting principles are of the agile methodologies is: (1) early and continuous delivery of valuable software; (2) embracing changing requirements, even late in development; (3) frequent delivery of working software; (4) daily interaction of business people and developers; (5) motivated individuals; (6) face - to - face interaction; (7) working software as the primary measure of progress;(8) sustainable development, ability to maintain a constant pace;(9) continuous attention to technical excellence and good design; (10) simplicity; (11) self - organizing teams; and (12) regular reflection and adaptation (Edwards et al., 2019). According to Conforto et al. (2014) Agile project management practices include: (1) the use of the "project vision" concept, (2) simple communication tools and processes, (3) iterative planning, (4) developing activities via self - managed and self - directed teams, and (5) frequently applying project plan monitoring and updating activities.

In 1986, Takeuchi and Nonaka called for a "rugby approach" to managing new product development, where the team meets for scrummage (much like a huddle in North American football) to decide their next moves (Takeuchi & Nonaka, 1986). The Scrum Master, therefore, performs the role traditionally assumed by a project manager or team leader and, in this case, is responsible for implementing scrum values and practices, as well as removing impediments (Cervone, 2011). Whether via physical or digital tools, the Kanban board infuses the agile development process with high visibility - providing a means of displaying the work assignments of the team, communicating priorities, making it easier to highlight bottlenecks, and helping to optimize efforts (Cocco et al., 2011). Whether following the scrum methodology or more "light" and simple aspects of the APM framework, the adoption of a Kanban board is useful for its practicality and for tracking implementation on a daily basis (Anderson et al., 2012).

According to Hannola et al. (2012) and Cooper & Sommer (2018), the main components of the agile process are:

- Sprint planning meeting: At the beginning of each sprint, the development team meets to agree on what it can accomplish in the sprint and creates a task plan.
- Daily stand - up meetings: During the sprint, the team meets every morning to ensure that work is on course to accomplish the sprint goals, review what has been accomplished in the last 24 hours and what should be done in the next 24, and resolve problems; these meetings are also sometimes called scrums.
- Demo: Towards the end of each sprint, product increments or new features developed in the sprint are demonstrated and validated with stakeholders, including both management and customers.
- Retrospective meeting: At the end of each sprint, the team meets to review how team members worked together and how the team can improve.

According to Sommer et al. (2015) the study of Danish manufacturing firms that implemented Agile - Stage - Gate identified the following major benefits in the hybrid model and the results indicated that:

- Increased design flexibility;
- Improved productivity, communication, and coordination among project team members;
- Drove better focus on projects, resulting in better prioritization of time and effort; and
- Raised team morale.

The flexibility that Agile - Stage - Gate offer can only be obtained if relevant technical and managerial skills are available to support the innovation project (Judi & Beach, 2010). Therefore, the methods, tools and processes offered by Agile - Stage - Gate will have most impact if the employees and managers understand and commit to its grounding principles (Walters et al., 2006). An investigation based on case studies of software projects, where agile methods were combined with Stage - Gate, provide successful illustrations of the hybrid model in practice in the IT world (Karlstrom & Runeson, 2006). Schmidt et al. (2018) argued that in a recent study German study carried out on a large - sample the following major difficulties were cited in the use of Agile - Stage - Gate in the following areas:

- Embedding agile teams into the classic organizational structure,
- Interpreting Agile practices for physical products, and
- Modularizing the product or project (breaking the project into increments that could be undertaken within a single sprint).

Conforto et al. (2014) argue that among the most frequently applied Agile project management practices researchers found could be seen in, small cross - functional teams, customer integration, frequent face - to - face meetings, empowering the team with autonomy to make decisions, test - driven development, and frequent updates to the project plan. Hilt et al. (2016) analysed the adoption of APM methodologies in predevelopment of new products and technologies in a large automotive company. They did not manage to implement a fully agile project, but they showed that many APM practices are easily adoptable and can help developers in the early stages. Serrador & Pinto (2015) found that 65% of the surveyed projects have at least some agile component, and that implementing APM practices positively impacts project success.

Psychological Empowerment and How It Improves Work Tasks and Innovation by Employees

Agile project management like any other industry needs skilled and experienced staff to carry out the projects efficiently. Psychological empowerment is an important area to discuss as it is imperative for motivating high powered personnel in agile management industry that work in volatile environments. Psychological empowerment according to Buckle (2003) is a motivational process by which an individual experiences a sense of enablement, as well as provide an effective buffer against the adverse effects of stress.

Rawat (2011) argues that feelings of empowerment have been proposed and found to facilitate workers' commitment to the organization. Lot of research has supported the contention that psychological empowerment is related to employee performance and job satisfaction (Liden et al., 2000). West & Bogers (2017) believe that the open innovation of an enterprise is explained, decided and implemented by employees. Spreitzer & Janasz (1999) add that for the authorized leaders, how employees understand and perceive the empowerment behaviour of the authorized leaders, forming the construction of the empowerment behaviour directly affects the behaviour of employees. Psychological empowerment is a synthesis of individual experience of the empowerment behaviour, including four dimensions of meaning, self - efficacy, self - determination and influence. According to Vardi (2000) empowerment is considered important because of the potential benefits that can result from it, including increased commitment, better decisions, improved quality, more innovation and increased job satisfaction. Many theorists of peer - reviewed papers and other empirical studies highlight the benefits of adopting agile methods. Analyses have been conducted on the implementation of agile management in product development (Lehnen et al., 2016; Stare, 2014), educational projects (Grimheden, 2013), construction projects (Demir & Theis, 2016), venture capital groups (Sutherland & Altman, 2009), innovation processes (Hannola et al., 2013) and the management of projects in libraries (Niemi - Grundström, 2014) and banks.

The agile project management industry is complex, dynamic and constantly changing. The fluid nature of the industry requires a special breed of project teams that can use their skills and knowledge and make necessary decisions that can benefit the performance of the project in the long run. These team members responsible for the project must be dedicated, highly driven and experienced and skilled so that they can perform in dynamic circumstances and complete the tasks that would assist in ensuring the final completion of the project. Cook (1994) argues that these empowered employees have complete knowledge about their work, so that they plan and schedule their work and are capable of identifying and resolving any obstacles for their performance.

Benefits of Technology and Innovation to Improve Agile Project Management

Though there are many agile methods available only few are used widely. Scrum and Extreme Programming are widely practiced and proven results have been shown regarding the success of the projects and the organizations which practiced them. Agile methodology has two popular methods which is SCRUM and Extreme Programming that are employed in its implementation in software development projects. Both of these procedures improve cooperation between individual disciplines involved in software project management, cost reduction and increase speed of system development time to send software modules that are ready. The changes from the traditional methodology to agile project management bring various advantages and good reflections to the way software development projects are run (Fahmi - bin - Ismail & Mansor, 2018).

Organizations produce work to their best when the project management processes are simple. Using non - bureaucratic project management processes enables organizations to respond to client's requirements faster and flexibly. Madampe (2017), argue that this allows the organizations to gain competitive advantage. Agile project management practices daily, weekly updates. This allows the clients to adjust their requirements in order to achieve their desired needs accordingly. Since the client is also considered as a part of the agile team, this creates high transparency and allows greater input from clients throughout the software development life cycle. Due to the presence of iterations if any problems occur, the problems are fixed early and it reduces the possibility of reworking later in the process. If anything is missed, these can be found at the time to time demonstrations and then the project team can take corrective measures. This makes to save the cost of the project by identifying missing components or correcting faults earlier.

Agile provides more advantages compared to the traditional method. Since it is an adaptive approach, it coped with the changes of requirements until the project is close. Project teams are actively accepted and responded to the customers' requirements from time to time, but once the project is closed, the requirements are no longer considered. Since the requirements are managed from time to time, therefore, the project team requires less time to deliver in the end of iteration. As mentioned earlier, agile implement time box which has a specific time and must be delivered on time. Thirdly, it involves active customers to give input (Mansor et al., 2011).

To realise the benefit for stakeholders, Madampe (2017) is of the view that due to the daily or weekly meetings with the stakeholders, it increases the relationship and it helps to focus developing the product together. And also since the agile team is cross functional it helps to solve issues quickly and interacts highly. Therefore the team becomes goal - oriented. This leads to make innovative and creative solutions. Benefits are not limited to the collective team. Also the team members get benefited individually by being able to interact with other team members who are specialized in multiple fields. Finally all these benefits lead to organizational benefits by increasing the productivity and producing high quality software products at the end.

Bunsiri & Kumpron (2016) have also highlighted the following benefits:

- **Benefits for Customer:** Agile project management definitely serves customer satisfaction. It needs user's involvement and product is developed based on the requirement taken from customer. The development team gives the product for user to use and improve by using iteration process, then customer gives feedback. Any changes and requirement are welcome at any stage of development by updating and prioritizing product backlog in order to ensure that they get the final high quality product and potential funding project.

- **Benefits for Project Management Team:** Agile methodology helps team member to learn new skills by teaching others. It allows member to be creative, innovative, and acknowledged. More than that it increases collaboration and ownership between the development team, the product owner, and the scrum master. The scrum master, who removes impediments and shields the development from external interference by daily scrum meetings, daily reviews, and visible progress chart, then, plays an important role in product development.
- **Benefits for Product:** Agile development methodology produces better quality product because of its frequent sprint retrospective, and continual improvisations through iteration. It also prevents product problems. Furthermore, the product turns result in hitting the market early as a result of the agile development methodology promotes the concept of early and regular roll out of the product through iterations and beta demonstrations.

SOLUTIONS AND RECOMMENDATIONS

Five Largest Benefits of Adopting an Agile Method (WRIKE, 2020):

- **Continuous Customer Contact:** Traditional project management methods generally only had the project team in touch with the customer at the start and end of the project. If customer requirements or expectations were not captured correctly in the beginning or changed over time, the project team had no idea until it was too late. With Agile, there's ongoing contact throughout the entire process and iterative deliveries to ensure your team is on track, so the end product will be exactly what the customer wants.
- **The Ability to Adapt:** What if your customer told you halfway through a project that they needed a scope change? Using a traditional approach to project management, this either could not be accommodated or likely involved significant increases to both the project cost and schedule. With Agile, you can incorporate changes with minimal effort, no matter how far along in the project.
- **Faster Delivery:** Agile incorporates a continuous development approach that ensures your team is continuously delivering workable products. Instead of waiting for six to 12 months or longer for an end product, your client is getting a working version of the product at much shorter intervals, typically every two to four weeks.
- **Lower Project Risk:** Your team is developing versions of the product regularly and getting customer feedback early on, minimizing the risk of a project failing. Breaking a large project into iterations reduces your risk of an iteration or draft failure. You're more likely to find small problems early that can be addressed quickly, rather than discovering a large issue only at the time of final testing before the end delivery. If later you encounter a problem or need to cancel the project, you'll have invested less time and money.
- **Ongoing Innovation:** Agile supports collaboration and continuous improvement, both of which can lead to innovation and the development of new products and features. Co - locating teams and having daily meetings encourages brainstorming and idea creation. Agile supports an "idea meritocracy" where the best idea wins out, no matter who it comes from. The project team, other stakeholders, and the customer can figure out functionality and features together.

Success Determinants in Agile Development Methodology

Agile project management is about human - to - human communication, adapting to changing conditions, and producing working results. The following are also the benefits of using agile project management (Mansor et al., 2011):

- **Time Allocation:** Agile methodology concerns punctuality in delivery. Agile introduced a process called time box in order to measure all the deliverable will release on time. Normally, each time box has limited time and is done iteratively. For each time box, the plan, development and review will be done for few times. In agile software development, time box is used to define a specific time a project should be completed. It helps software development community to be more focus in a software development project. Normally, a short iteration will enable high motivation, fast feedback, prioritization, good reflection and high creativity in a project. Therefore by fixing the time, a project team can amplify the productivity. In addition, time box also can be used to track the progress. At the end of the allocated time (or time box), the task is either considered 'done', or re - evaluated and therefore, more time will be provided.
- **Simplicity:** Agile offers simplicity in a process. The process is shorter compared to the traditional method. It helps the project team to complete the project in shorter duration because of the process is not that complex. There are three dimensions or faces to simplicity which are; do less, do better, and do swarms. 'Do less' means do fewer activities, produce fewer documents, and reduce management reports. Whereas, 'do better' has a particular flavour particularly when applied to design and 'do swarms' value simplicity for the complexity it generates.

Over and above the above indicated benefits, the success determinants in agile include: Customers Involvement, Minimum Changes of Requirements, Communication, Corporate Culture, Team Size, Active Testing, Customer's Collaboration, Code Review, and Effective Cost Management. The changes from the traditional methodology to agile project management bring various advantages and good reflections to the way software development projects are run.

FUTURE RESEARCH DIRECTIONS

The area of agile project management is still fairly recent. More studies need to be conducted on how innovation affects agile project management in developed countries compared to undeveloped countries. Other areas that need attention is unpacking differences between tradition project management and agile project management. The area of innovation and teams employing innovation in agile project management need to be further unpacked so that more knowledge can be added to this theme. Psychological empowerment and how it improves project teams and their tasks and innovation need to be investigated, so more light can be shed on this area. Research can also be conducted in Small and Medium enterprises and how they employ innovation and agile project management.

CONCLUSION

Agile project management has made tremendous in - roads in the last few years. It has contributed to projects in many industries. Technology and innovation has had a big part to play in streamlining agile project management operations and functional areas. Innovation is what drives high performance in projects and ensures their final completion is done on time and within the budgeted cost estimates. This chapter has indicated how versatile agile project management is in changing environments. Technology and innovation when added to the mix is a sure winner for successful project completions.

REFERENCES

Anderson, D. J., Concas, G., Lunesu, M. I., Marchesi, M., & Zhang, H. (2012). A comparative study of Scrum and Kanban approaches on a real case study using simulation. In *International Conference on Agile Software Development*. Springer.

Antlova, K. (2014). Agile approach in the project management of the Czech companies. *Procedia Technology., 16*, 929–933. doi:10.1016/j.protcy.2014.10.045

Baweja, S., & Venugopalan, N. (2015). Agility in Project Management. *PM World Journal., IV*(X), 1–14.

Beck, K., Beedle, M., van Bennekum, A., Cockburn, A., Cunningham, W., Fowler, M., Grenning, J., Highsmith, J., Hunt, A., Jeffries, R., Kern, J., Marick, B., Martin, R. C., Mellor, S., Schwaber, K., Sutherland, J., & Thomas, D. (2001). *Manifesto for Agile software development*. Agile Alliance. Available at: http://agilemanifesto.org/

Buckle, P. (2003). *Empowerment, organizational commitment and job satisfaction within a chemical organization* (Unpublished master's dissertation). Potchefstroom University, Vanderbijlpark.

Bunsiri, T., & Kumpron, T. (2016). Benefits of Agile Project Management. *Apheit Journal., 5*(1), 23–29.

Cervone, H. F. (2011). Understanding agile project management methods using scrum OCLC Syst. *Serv. Int. Dig. Libr. Persp., 27*(1), 18–22.

Clancy, T. (2014). *The Standish Group Report - CHAOS*. Academic Press.

Cocco, L., Mannaro, K., Concas, G., & Marchesi, M. (2011). Simulating kanban and scrum vs. waterfall with system dynamics. In *International Conference on Agile Software Development*. Springer. 10.1007/978-3-642-20677-1_9

Cohen, D., Lindvall, M., & Costa, P. (2004). An Introduction to Agile Methods. *Advances in Computers, 62*(1), 1–66.

Conforto, E. C., Salum, F., Amaral, D. C., da Silva, S. L., & de Almeida, L. F. M. (2014). Can agile project management be adopted by industries other than software development? *Project Management Journal, 45*(3), 21–34. doi:10.1002/pmj.21410

Cook, S. (1994). The cultural implications of empowerment. *Empowerment in Organizations., 2*(1), 9–13. doi:10.1108/09684899410054625

Cooper, R. G. (1994). Third generation new product processes. *Journal of Product Innovation Management, 11*(1), 3–14. doi:10.1111/1540-5885.1110003

Cooper, R. G. (2014). What's Next? After Stage - Gate. *Research Technology Management, 57*(1), 20–31. doi:10.5437/08956308X5606963

Cooper, R. G., & Sommer, A. F. (2018). Agile - Stage - Gate for manufacturers - Changing the way new products are developed. *Research Technology Management, 61*(2), 17–26. doi:10.1080/08956308.2018.1421380

Demir, S. T., & Theis, P. (2016). Agile design management - the application of scrum in the design phase of construction projects. *24th Annual Conference of the International Group for Lean Construction*, Boston, MA.

Edwards, K., Cooper, R. G., Vedsmand, T. & Nardelli, G. (2019). Evaluating the agile - stage - gate hybrid model: Experiences from three SME manufacturing firms. *Int. J. Innov. Technol. Manag., 16.*

Eschenbach, T., Lewis, N., Nicholls, G. M., & Schell, W. J. (2015). *Using Agile Project Management to Maximize You and Your Co - authors' Productivity. American Society for Engineering Education. 122nd ASEE Annual Conference & Exposition*, Seattle, WA.

Fahmi-bin-Ismail, M. & Mansor, Z. (2018). Agile Project Management: Review, Challenges and Open Issues. *Advanced Science Letters, 24*, 463 - 466.

Grimheden, M. E. (2013). Can agile methods enhance mechatronics design education? *Mechatronics, 23*(8), 967–973. doi:10.1016/j.mechatronics.2013.01.003

Hannola, L., Friman, J., & Niemimuukko, J. (2012). Application of agile methods in the innovation process. *International Journal of Business Innovation and Research., 7*(1), 84. doi:10.1504/IJBIR.2013.050557

Hannola, L., Friman, J., & Niemimuukko, J. (2013). Application of agile methods in the innovation process. *Int. J. Bus. Innov. Res., 7*(1), 84–98. doi:10.1504/IJBIR.2013.050557

Highsmith, J. (2004). *Agile Project Management: Creating Innovative Products*. Addison Wesley.

Highsmith, J., & Cockburn, A. (2001, September). Agile software development: The business of innovation. *Computer, 1*(1), 120–127. doi:10.1109/2.947100

Hilt, M. J., Wagner, D., Osterlehner, V., & Kampker, A. (2016). Agile Predevelopment of Production Technologies for Electric Energy Storage Systems - A Case Study in the Automotive Industry. In *Proceedings of the Procedia CIRP*. Elsevier B. V.

Judi, H. M., & Beach, R. (2010). Achieving manufacturing flexibility: The role of people, technology, innovation and continuous improvement. *International Journal of Innovation and Technology Management, 07*(2), 161–181. doi:10.1142/S0219877010001891

Kanbanize. (2019). *Agile Project Management: A Comprehensive Guide*. https://kanbanize.com/agile/project-management

Karlström, D., & Runeson, P. (2006). Integrating agile software development into stage - gate managed product development. *Empirical Software Engineering, 11*(2), 203–225. doi:10.100710664-006-6402-8

Keegan, A., & Turner, J. R. (2002). The management of innovation in project - based firms. *Long Range Planning*, *35*(4), 367–388. doi:10.1016/S0024-6301(02)00069-9

Kloppenborg, T. J., Anantatmula, V., & Wells, K. N. (2019). *Contemporary Project Management* (4th ed.). Cengage Learning.

Liden, R. C., Wayne, S. J., & Sparrowe, R. T. (2000). An examination of the mediating role of psychological empowerment on the relations between the job, interpersonal relationships and work outcomes. *The Journal of Applied Psychology*, *85*(3), 407–416. doi:10.1037/0021-9010.85.3.407 PMID:10900815

Madampe, M. A. K. G. (2017). Successful Adoption of Agile Project Management in Software Development Industry. *International Journal of Computer Science and Information Technology Research.*, *5*(4), 27–33.

Mansor, Z., Yahya, S., & Arshad, N. H. (2011). Towards the Development of Success Determinants Charter for Agile Development Methodology. *International Journal of Information Technology and Engineering.*, *2*(1), 1–7.

Morris, L., Ma, M., & Wu, P. C. (2014). *Agile Innovation: The Revolutionary Approach to Accelerate Success, Inspire Engagement, and Ignite Creativity*. John Wiley & Sons Ltd.

Niemi-Grundström, M. (2014). Developing, evaluating and managing library with agile methods. *Library Management*, *35*(6/7), 481–485. doi:10.1108/LM-02-2014-0022

Porter, M. E. (1990). The competitive advantage of notions. *Harvard Business Review*, *68*(2), 73–93.

Preez, N. D., & Louw, L. (2008). A framework for managing the innovation process. *PICMET '08 - 2008 Portland International Conference on Management of Engineering & Technology*. 10.1109/PICMET.2008.4599663

Raj, P. & Sinha, P. (2020). Project Management in Era of Agile and DevOps Methodologies. *International Journal of Scientific & Technology Research, 9*(1), 1024 - 1033.

Rawat, P. S. (2011). Effect of Psychological Empowerment on Commitment of Employees: *An Empirical Study. In International Conference on Humanities, Historical and Social Sciences*. Singapore: International Association of Computer Science & Information Technology.

Royce, W. W. (1970). Managing the development of large software systems. *Proceedings of IEEE Wescon*.

Rycroft, R. W., & Kash, D. E. (1999). *The Complexity Challenge: Technological Innovation for the 21st Century*. Pinter.

Schmidt, T. S., Weiss, S., & Paetzold, K. (2018). *Agile Development of Physical Products: An Empirical Study About Motivations, Potentials and Applicability: Report*. University of the German Federal Armed Forces.

Serrador, P., & Pinto, J. K. (2015). Does Agile work - A quantitative analysis of agile project success? *International Journal of Project Management*, *33*(1), 1040–1051. doi:10.1016/j.ijproman.2015.01.006

Sommer, A. F., Hedegaard, C., Dukovska-Popovska, I., & Steger-Jensen, K. (2015). Improved product development performance through Agile / Stage - Gate hybrids - The next - generation Stage - Gate process? *Research Technology Management*, *158*(1), 1–10. doi:10.5437/08956308X5801236

Spreitzer, G. M., Janasz, S. C. D., & Quinn, R. E. (1999). Empowered to lead: The role of psychological empowerment in leadership. *Journal of Organizational Behavior*, *20*(4), 511–526. doi:10.1002/(SICI)1099-1379(199907)20:4<511::AID-JOB900>3.0.CO;2-L

Stare, A. (2014). Agile project management in product development projects. *Procedia: Social and Behavioral Sciences*, *119*(1), 295–304. doi:10.1016/j.sbspro.2014.03.034

Sutherland, J., & Altman, I. (2009). Take no prisoners: how a venture capital group does scrum. In *Agile Conference, 2009. AGILE'09* (pp. 350 - 355). IEEE. 10.1109/AGILE.2009.29

Szalvay, V. (2004). An introduction to agile software development. *Danube Technologies*, 1 - 9.

Takeuchi, H., & Nonaka, I. (1986). The new product development game. *Harvard Business Review*, *64*(1), 137–146.

The Standisch Group International. (2003). *Latest Standisch Group CHAOS report shows project success rates have improved by 50%*. Author.

Vardi, Y. (2000). Psychological empowerment as a criterion for adjustment to a new job. *Psychological Reports*, *87*(1), 1083–1093. doi:10.2466/pr0.2000.87.3f.1083 PMID:11272748

Walters, A. T., Millward, H. U. W., & Lewis, A. (2006). Case Studies of Advanced Manufacturing Technology Implementation in Small Companies. *International Journal of Innovation & Technology Management.*, *3*(2), 149–169. doi:10.1142/S0219877006000752

West, J., & Bogers, M. (2017). Open innovation: Current status and research opportunities. *Innovation (North Sydney, N.S.W.)*, *19*(1), 43–50. doi:10.1080/14479338.2016.1258995

WRIKE. (2020). *Agile Methodology Basics*. https://www.wrike.com/project-management-guide/agile-methodology-basics

KEY TERMS AND DEFINITIONS

Agile Project Management: It is more flexible approach and promotes collaborative working with the customer.

Digitization: This requires a process of converting information into a digital format.

Innovation: It involves improvements on goods services. In agile, innovation is when you constantly adopt new processes to improve on efficiencies so that the project is completed on time whilst saving costs and time.

Psychological Empowerment: It refers to meanings that an employee places on his work and how he / she aligns this with one's work role and responsibilities, one's individual beliefs, values, and the standards one abides by.

Technology: It is the study of machines, tools, processes, and techniques created by humans. It is when humans use these tools and advancements to improve communications, efficiencies, and their lives.

Chapter 2
Agile Project Management in International Logistics Operations

Armand Faganel
https://orcid.org/0000-0002-3618-4986
University of Primorska, Slovenia

Aleksander Janeš
University of Primorska, Slovenia

ABSTRACT

The chapter discussed a business model (BM) perspective as an innovating practice to analyze the transition of the EuroPacific LL Company (EuroPacific) from regional logistic operator to domestic logistic operator or third-party logistic provider (3PL) for Asian companies. The company operates regionally in markets of Croatia, Hungary, Serbia, Slovakia, and Slovenia and globally in South Korea, India, and Singapore. The chosen long-term business vision of the company is based on the goal of becoming the key logistics provider of goods from the Far East directed to the European markets. The company was confronted with the first period of crisis from 2008 to 2010 and again with the second crisis started in 2020 when they realized that, although known as the crisis breaker, the company is not being exempted from market challenges, extraordinary situations like pandemic, and consecutive economic downturn effects.

INTRODUCTION

Transportation sector is fundamental for the economy of the European Union (EU) countries and acts as a generator in today's globalized and mobile society. EU's vision would be to support a more sustainable transportation industry that handles the requirements of the EU states and their population yet fighting the upcoming restrictions: oil shortage, increasing crowding and the urge to diminish toxic emissions like CO_2 and others, with the aim of improving the environmental conditions. In the next 30 years transport

DOI: 10.4018/978-1-7998-7872-8.ch002

sector must decrease the greenhouse gas emissions by 60% compared to 1990 and to cut dependence on imported oil (European Commission, 2018; European Union, 2019).

In the naval sector too, efforts are being made to mitigate the impacts of greenhouse gases and therefore reduce the effects of climate change underway: shipping as a whole emitted 1,036 million tons of CO2 in 2007, equal to 3.3% of global emissions. If we consider only maritime transport in international navigation, excluding cabotage and fishing, the estimate is 870 million tons, equal to about 2.7% of global CO2 emissions. International maritime transport is the only sector, among the main energy consumers, to have remained excluded from the implementation measures of the Kyoto Protocol, implemented by the European Union and by the main industrialized countries (with the exception of known, have not ratified the protocol). It is possible to work to increase energy efficiency in ship design but it must be remembered that the energy management of a fleet is extremely complex, as it requires huge resources and a systematic approach. In the maritime sector, there are essentially three areas of final consumption: the mechanical energy required for propulsion, the absorption of electricity and the need for thermal or cooling energy. While the port infrastructures can include handling systems for TEUs and accessibility to ports. Primary energy consumption does not depend only on the efficiency and management of the fleets in relation to the loads but also on the management of the navigation speed in relation to the waiting times at the terminals (Villani, 2011).

Economic logistics could be divided into two broad categories: 1) the study of logistic systems; 2) the study of the logistics services industry. The first should mainly deal with public and private networks and infrastructural systems (ports, airports, inter - ports, railway networks, platforms, distripark, etc.) and related problems of regulation, planning, programming, design, financing, monitoring and management (Forte, 2001a; Iannone, 2002a, 2002b). The infrastructural policies in fact guarantee the necessary pre - conditions to ensure physical circulation of products, assuming a central role in the structuring of logistic cycles and influencing the location choices and therefore also the selection of the privileged areas of settlement. It is therefore a question of optimizing the capacity and potential for use of infrastructures, mutually adapting them to each other and to the size of the flows, which express the dimension of demand understood as a component of the market, where capacity and potential make up the offer on a macro - territorial scale (Forte, 2003a). So, in addition to the continuous rationalization of the production and commercial chains, the attention of the logistic culture goes also and above all to the logistic strategies of country - system and the ability to reposition and logistical integration with other areas, in particularly with those in the developing world: South America, South Africa, Eastern Europe, South Asia, but also the Central Asia. The volume of exports to Asia has increased significantly due to policies export - oriented based on sea and air navigation (UN ESCAP, 2019; WTO, 2019). In this continent it is witnessed an acceleration towards the globalization of local economies and an increase in activities by multinational companies. The improvement of domestic transport activities in Asian countries, however, still represents a difficult objective to pursue, with notable repercussions on the full efficiency of globalized production and logistics systems. In particular, laws and regulations regarding the logistics sector are quite different in each country of the continent in question. Indeed, in most of them is missing a clear political direction for freight logistics, as well as for supporting scientific research (Ianone, 2003a).

Anyone who is familiar with the notion of sustainable development can agree on the fact that a phenomenon of growth continues within a limited system with difficulty can take on those connotations of sustainability to which, conversely, were we would like to direct the economic development of a region and of the planet more generally (Ianone, 2003b). The transport sector plays an essential role in the economy and in modern society, and not it should be surprising that there is a direct relationship between gross domestic product growth and growth of transport activities (Vickerman & Monnet, 2003). This correlation was, even, for many years identical, that is, a 1% GDP growth was followed by a 1% growth in transport demand. However, GDP growth accompanies a more than proportional growth in the demand for transport, with high private and social costs. However, this dispersion in terms of rates of change could tend to decrease in those economic systems where the logistic culture is more extensive, resulting in an increase of competitiveness (Forte, 2003a).

There is a question if sustainable logistics exists, and if it can be compatible with current economic needs. Aguiari (2013) believe both issues can be addressed, albeit with appropriate distinctions. In this chapter we propose a quick overview of the main issues to consider. Even if the tumultuous explosion of different and often conflicting problems affecting the various economies in recent years, it does not seem to outline clear strategies in this regard. By sustainable logistics, we still mean a logistics that aims to offer services and economic conditions required by the market, while seeking all the most appropriate solutions from the point of view of the environment and mobility, associated with the transport, delivery and recycling of products e of goods. Sustainable logistics ultimately wants to promote more efficient logistics and at the same time more respectful of the quality of life.

The Supply Chain Management (SCM) field has a built - in relation with the sustainable development; Winter & Knemeyer (2013) argue that the sustainability concept expands across the companies' profitability drivers and their connections with the society and its environment. Companies have begun to dedicate more attention and prioritize good environmental governance because of the increasing societal, political and economic pressures. Thanks to such development, environmental impact of the companies' operations is becoming one of the highest priorities. As much as 8% of the world energy - issued CO_2e - the equivalent in CO_2 of the global warming impact of all the greenhouse gases (GHGs) emissions is being produced by the freight transport (Kahn et al., 2007). According to the Council of Supply Chain Management Professionals (CSCMP), the company's logistics can contribute up to 75% of its carbon footprint (Dey et al., 2011; Makarova - Jørsfeldt et al., 2016). So the term Green Logistics was conceived to deal with this phenomenon, determined as the effort to weigh and reduce the environmental influence attributed to logistics activities (Rogers & Tibben - Lembke, 1998 as cited in Tacken et al., 2014).

Marchet et al. (2014) offer a thorough literature review of 72 papers published from 1994 to 2011 in international peer - reviewed journals tackling environmental sustainability in logistics and freight transportation: "Five key themes were examined: sustainability initiatives, reasons for adoption, benefits achieved following adoption, critical issues and barriers to adoption, and the evaluation and measurement of environmental initiatives. While many studies have addressed the issue of environmental sustainability within the supply chain as a whole, papers focusing specifically on environmental sustainability within logistics and freight transportation are fewer and relatively more recent. Although researchers have started to examine the decision - making process involved in environmental sustainability adoption in recent years, many themes, such as sustainability evaluation and measurement, and the level of adoption of sustainability initiatives in the context of the third - party logistics (3PL) industry are under - represented in the literature. As far as the methodology is concerned, our review revealed that many articles are either conceptual papers or empirical studies (i.e. mostly based on surveys or case studies), while simulation and analytical modelling have rarely been addressed."

EU regulations at the moment include directives on CO_2 emissions for new automobiles and vans only (European Commission, 2015). From 2030 on new automobiles will have to release on average 37.5% less CO_2 and new light vehicles will emit on average 31% less CO_2 compared to 2021 levels (Council of the EU, 2019). It's a fact that CO_2 emission from other types of vehicles is not regulated with the current legislation, but the strategic goals for the subsequent periods are formulated in the 'Transport white paper' and the 'Roadmap for moving to a competitive low carbon economy in 2050' (Makarova - Jørsfeldt et al., 2016).

Considerable focus is being applied by EU governments, to decouple this growth in carbon emissions from growth in gross domestic product. An important anxiety is about the freight transport, as the increase of energy used is growing at a higher rate than the energy consumed by cars and buses and is estimated to beat it until 2025 (World Business Council For Sustainable Development [WBCSD], 2004). Therefore, it is of great importance to investigate thoroughly how third - party logistic providers (3PLs) of services meet the issue of managing propitiously their emissions performance.

3PLs are self - standing companies that cooperate on contract basis with producer, dealer and buyer. They don't take the ownership of the service or product; they only overtake the responsibility for the supply in the name of their customer. Besides the traditional services of carriers and / or storage 3PLs offer diverse activities that add some value and provide different servicing as return of products, elaborating orders, tailored packaging, barcode/RFID, labelling, etc. (Modarress et al., 2009; Giri & Sarker, 2017; Gardas et al., 2019).

In this paper 3PL provider's strategy and practice are presented, discussed through a case study of the EuroPacific LL Company (EuroPacific), its BM innovation activity, ending with suggestions for further research, conclusions and limitations.

BACKGROUND

The logistics sector in general has greatly contributed to the welfare of societies and economies. Environmental sustainability has to be taken into consideration today also in logistics. Climate change is an important issue; the estimation is that 5 - 20% of global GDP shall be employed for climatic impacts (Stern, 2007). It is a fact that the logistic companies account as an important source of CO_2 emission (Gardas et al., 2019).

Globalization, together with the growth of competition and the increased concern for customers' satisfaction compelled companies to collaborate with external partners (Wang et al., 2015; Raut et al., 2018). The majority of supply chains worldwide are increasing their use of 3PLs services (Lam & Dai, 2015).

And if they want to change environmental issues into business opportunities, companies have to think out how they could integrate green perspectives into their service provision. Especially logistics service providers might be interested in such offer, as their basic business has already embodied an environmental impact (Isaksson & Huge - Brodin, 2013).

Diverse authors often examine regulatory pressures, customer pressures and competition pressures as representations of normative, forced and hidden pressures. It can be confirmed that customers' pressures embody a significant feature of green innovations from 3PL service providers. In contempt of the notion that the green innovation might be a risky venture, it could bring important competitive advantages on the long - term, on the green differentiation premise (Berrone et al., 2013; Dimaggio & Powell, 1983; Chu et al., 2018; Chu et al., 2019). Several authors consider 'competition' as a key leverage for 3PL providers that strive to develop environmentally friendly logistic systems (Mollenkopf et al., 2010 as cited in Tacken et al., 2014).

The innovations for the economist would not be constantly introduced in market but they concentrate in certain time periods, which, for this reason, are characterized by strong expansion. The expansive phases, however, are followed by the recessive ones, where the economy returns to the circular flow equilibrium due to the saturation of the market by the new product, until the resumption of further expansion due to the introduction of a different innovation. Schumpeter's theory of innovation is in a certain sense related to the cycles of Kondratieff (1925), in fact, showed that the long waves in production and prices, which went up until the last years of the eighteenth century, they belonged to the same dynamic process as the shorter cycles and were related to greater sectoral shifts in investments. Subsequently Schumpeter (1934) resumed the long wave model of Kondratieff and explained the turning point of the upward curve with the introduction on the market of an innovation. Therefore, according to Schumpeter's theory, the company must first know how to adapt to times and conditions in which it operates but in the second instance must absolutely foresee, anticipate and even direct the continuous social, technological, economic and productive, since huge opportunities (or equally significant threats) can derive to the company from the evolution of the company. So if the company desires to win a competitive advantage and maximize long - term profits, it needs to adopt an innovation (Ruggiero, 2014).

Aguezzoul (2014) offers a literature review on 3PL selection decision from the viewpoint of methods and criteria. He analysed 67 articles published within the 1994 - 2013 period, and found out that 3PL selection is empirical in nature and also: "related to a region/country, industrial sector, and logistics activities outsourced. In terms of 3PL selection criteria, 11 key criteria are identified; each one is defined by a set of attributes. Cost is the most widely adopted criterion, followed by relationship, services, and quality. In terms of methods for 3PL evaluation, they can be categorized in 5 groups, namely: MCDM techniques, statistical approaches, artificial intelligence, mathematical programming, and hybrid methods". Managing supply chain risks has emerged as an important area of research in the field of supply chain management (Aqlan & Lam, 2015). Additionally, it is a topic of great interest to those in charge of management, thus presenting itself as an important issue not only from an academic perspective but also from business practice (Colicchia & Strozzi, 2012). In fact, talking about risks without involving companies can be ineffective when considering the contribution of these works to the economic development of the regions.

Companies have a wide choice of partners, when looking for a 3PL provider and do not feel strongly connected to a single provider. Gürcan et al. (2016) argue that: "the third party logistic (3PL) provider selection problem was modelled by one of the most frequently used multi criteria decision making method, AHP, which takes into account both tangible and intangible criteria. As a result of AHP, best alternative for 3PL provider is determined. According to the results obtained by AHP method, second alternative (B Company) is favoured over other alternatives (A and C) with highest score 0.444. This superiority of the second company with respect to first and third companies can be explained by the experience of the company in 3PL sector, financial performance and the fact that it has a strong infrastructure of information technologies. The most important factor in firm selection was found to be Compatibility with a (47.15%) weight. It is followed by Financial Performance (25.49%), Reputation (16.52%) and Long - term Relationship (10.82%) respectively. The decision maker must not be misled by the fact that Long - term Relationship criterion has a relatively low importance. In fact, the provision of a firm with quality logistics service at the minimum cost is one of the prerequisites for achieving the compatibility between the company and the 3PL service provider. This indicates that long - term relationship criterion must not be overlooked".

Corporate risk can come from many sources, some related to internal production and distribution processes and other times from outside (Osorio et al., 2017). There are many ways to categorize the types of risk, but perhaps the most relevant in terms of the supply chain are: Risks external to the company but internal to the chain and external to the chain (Manners - Bell, 2014). Tang (2006) concludes that there are two types of risks in the supply chain; operational risks and disruptive risks. Operational risks refer to the inherent uncertainty about what happens daily in operations, such as uncertainty in consumer demand, uncertainty in supply and uncertainty about costs. For their part, disruptive risks are major disruptions caused by natural disasters or man - made disasters or economic crises. In most cases, the business impact associated with disruptive risks is much greater than that of operational risks (Tang, 2006). However, although operational risks have a relatively small impact on the supply chain, if they are not addressed correctly and in a timely manner, the risk will be amplified throughout the chain.

Chu et al. (2019) claim, that customer pressure affects green innovation in the context of 3PLs in China, and particularly the organizational culture in mediating this relationship. According to Tacken et al. (2014) there is a visible customers' influence upon the ecological conduct of German 3PLs. It could be said that green innovation importantly adds to flexibility orientation and financial performance, strengthening this contribution, opposite to control orientation that it leads to the weakening.

Pazirandeh & Jafari (2013) observe that almost every surveyed Swedish company that puts greening of their transportation in the spotlight presents sustainability as a company's strategic plan component. These companies had also a chance to advance their logistics performance, be it from effectiveness or efficiency perspectives, through greening of their logistic purchasing procedures (Ludvigsen, 1999; Evers et al., 1996). Eng - Larsson & Kohn (2012) researched shippers' opinions regarding the tendency of redirecting to an intermodal road - rail transport; they showed a potential interest but expressed scepticism that such solution might endanger logistics performance (Ludvigsen, 1999; Vannieuwenhuyse et al., 2003). It has been displayed by some shippers that it can be shifted from road to intermodal transport avoiding the performance degradation even if the conditions are not ideal for similar context. The disadvantages of such a solution can be overcome through improvements to the shipper's logistics services (Flodén, 2007; Kohn, 2008; Eng - Larsson & Kohn, 2012).

The concepts of green logistics or sustainable logistics, basically synonyms, as a key to improvement and innovation of products and processes along the supply chain, have now become common references afterwards having been considered a kind of weird in the early 2000s neologisms. Start a process and product transformation action according to a logic of sustainability in fact means reducing waste, optimizing consumption and favour reuse, with significant cost savings and interesting economic and image returns. Certainly, the transition to a company that is more sensitive to the ecosystem initially brings with it constraints and burdens, however, if this process is carefully managed, it can generate multiple opportunities and build a more balanced and transparent relationship with civil society and the environment. A need for the entire industry and in particular for logistics or supply chain processes, which by nature permeate the entire production flow from upstream downstream: from relations with suppliers, to process problems production, up to the final consumer and product recycling (Aguiari, 2013).

Examples of sustainable logistics include:

- The use of fuel - efficient transportation vehicles (Lin & Ho, 2011);
- The use of green materials (Evangelista, 2014) and;
- Strategic imperative (Green et al., 2012), differentiation advantage (Maas et al., 2014; Raut et al., 2018) and software for the environmental evaluation (Lieb & Lieb, 2010), to mention some of them.

Colicchia et al. (2011) provided the case of Nestle´: the company has developed multi - spring brands to bring production sites nearer to areas of consumption, in order to reduce travelled distances and road traffic. Hazen et al. (2011) found that consumers perceive products made via some Green Reverse Logistics (GRL) practices as following; remanufactured products and reused products to be of lesser quality than brand - new products; and products made with recycled materials were found to be perceived as being equal to brand - new products in terms of quality. The effects of strategies that are friendly to the environment have been analysed by Raut et al. (2018) and it has been proven that such strategies could provide 3PLs a substantive differentiation advantage. Pålsson & Johansson (2016) found three discerning elements affecting the shipper's objective of reducing transportation emissions: potential gains that are being perceived, the size of the company, and mode of shipper's organization. Organizations prone to reduce the emissions are 3PLs, bigger companies, and those that perceive larger potential of reduction.

Chu et al. (2018) argue that green innovation in 3PL research is still growing. It is also emphasized in the literature that green innovation influences the competitive advantage of shipping companies (Raut et al., 2018; Lam & Dai, 2015). Competitiveness is being increased by the green differentiation process, enabling the organizations enhance the company's image, allowing them to relish the advantage of the first mover (Chen et al., 2006).

Bask et al. (2018) performed a survey among Finnish 3PLs and advocate the adoption of environmentally sustainable practices in order to provide 3PL operators with a competitive advantage. From the recent research we can conclude that 3PL providers mostly adopt green initiatives because of customer pressure (Bask et al., 2018; Baz & Laguir, 2017; Chu et al., 2019). Berg & Langen (2016) argue that despite the existing image of shippers as being little concerned about the environment, 3PL customers seem to be more and more worried with responsible procurement, taking care about the damage in nature, caused by non - green practices in forwarding their goods.

This creates an opportunity for 3PLs to be proactive and meet these demands by considering environmental issues in their business models (BMs) and as a value adding service offer (Martinsen & Björklund, 2012; Janeš et al., 2017). Berg & Langen (2016) noticed that in the recent years 3PL customers increasingly express concerns about the environment. In order to emphasize similar customers' demands, 3PL providers try to develop innovative management practices. Therefore, definition of the green innovation represents a kind of green management practice, which the 3PL provider adopted without having previous experience with it (Chu et al., 2019; Large et al., 2013; Lin & Ho, 2008). The environmentally friendly and innovative service providers' practices, especially 3PLs, enhance unique opportunities and challenges for practicians, scholars, and researchers (Lieb & Lieb, 2010).

MAIN FOCUS OF THE CHAPTER

Sustainable Green Logistics: Issues and Problems

Building on an extensive literature review the following research question has emerged:

RQ1: What are the changes needed in the design of business model elements in the transition process of profiling for a domestic logistic operator (3PL)?

Studying the EuroPacific's BM and having in mind that both disruptive Information and Communication Technology (ICT) have to be mastered, it could be assumed that a Company has to incorporate and foster disruptive technologies successfully in some way (Alberti - Alhtaybat et al., 2019). The second research question is therefore:

RQ2: Which business model elements allow EuroPacific to address and incorporate disruptive technologies successfully?

To address these questions, a BM perspective, which allowed observing and identifying BM innovation (BMI) activities, was employed. This enabled to understand these activities as innovative tools to deliver the value across diverse channels and as innovative drivers of value creation and appropriation (Schneider & Spieth, 2013; Sorescu et al., 2011; Teece, 2010). They were studied through approaches that the company used to reach the desired changes (Jocevski et al., 2019).

Methodology

In the present study the interpretivist paradigm was pursued and applied an inductive narrative approach based on a single paradigmatic case study of a sustainable BM (Yin, 2014; Janeš et al., 2017). Geissdoerfer et al. (2016) describe BM 'as simplified representations of the elements and interactions between these elements that an organizational unit chooses in order to create, deliver, capture, and exchange value.' In presented case BM canvas has been adopted to function as a debate tool during interviews and research workshops, later filled with the acquired data from the workshops' participants. Gathered information's have been analysed through content analysis.

Executive management and the owner of the Company agreed to participate in the study through semi - structured interviews. They were carried out in two hours (Kvale, 2007), with three key employees of the Company. Themes that were discussed were the activities that might be defined as sustainable innovation, Company's business model, and carriers of sustainable development inside the business model.

In order to be acquainted and prepared the participants have been provided with the research overview by e - mail before the interviews. They have been asked about the history of the Company, their sustainable and innovative practices and the most important moments in the Company's life cycle. Sustainable and innovative practices as recognized by interviewees have been elaborated in depth. Based on the findings the business model map has been created and strategic knowledge investigated. To be able to research the strategic innovation of the company's business model, a plethora of questions must be answered, but the ground question to be answered is the reason why the company exists and what is their main goal. The next question was about the right moment when the business model should be redesigned. When the necessity for a business model innovation has been established, it should be acknowledged what are the features of the current business model. Bagnoli (2012) instructs that the questions should be formed and delivered according the business model key elements. These key elements are tackling the issues that provide an insight into the activities and roles of key stakeholders, company's key resources, business partners, company's business processes, their services and / or products, customers divided into clusters, and the core value proposition (Elkington, 1997; White, 2009; Bocken et al., 2013; Janeš et al., 2014; see Table 1).

The introductory interview has been organized to provide the visualization of the current company's circumstances ('as - is' BM) and used as the kick - off for the following interview that was thought for the wanted state development and alteration of the existing BM ('to - be' BM). Company's owner expressed explicit desire for a third interview to be implemented, to discuss the adoption and employment of company's management tools.

The follow - up analysis has been conducted between April and June 2020, based on the Company's openly accessible data, with published texts and videos, through data gathered with semi - structured interview with executive management, and also interviews with ex - employees (Alberti - Alhtaybat et al., 2019; Kobal & Dežjot, 2020) and members of management team.

It has been decided to include the Company's ex - employees because of their valuable insight when still working for the Company; selection was done upon their willingness to participate. They provided a more demanding and penetrating insight into the company and its activities; active employees served to avoid bias. Participants were classified as interviewees, to allow them full anonymity. Through semi - structured interview were addressed their perceptions of the introduced sustainable innovation activities at Company.

Recording of interviews was provided, to which the interviewees gave the approval, later have been transcribed and analysed (Easterby - Smith et al., 2007; Janeš & Biloslavo, 2013; Janeš & Trnavčević, 2014). To supplement the interviews, the researchers' participation and observation method have been used, together with collecting of documents (Angrosino & Mays de Pérez, 2000; Bocken et al., 2013; Alberti - Alhtaybat et al., 2019). The derived BM canvas has been analysed and debated as a singular case study and afterwards mailed to the interviewees for their approval (Janeš et al., 2014; Faganel et al., 2020).

SOLUTIONS AND RECOMMENDATIONS

University Ca` Foscari of Venice, Italy, developed a methodological model known as Competitive Knowledge Audit, which was used as the platform for the methodology, that has been developed during the project (Bagnoli, 2012; Know Us, 2013).

Strategic - cognitive maps were designed between January 2012 and May 2014 for 30 Slovenian companies, ranging from the construction, logistic, tourism, agriculture and food, and wood industry sectors. These maps have been conceived upon the innovative business model canvas, which has been introduced and tested along the project. Here described case study has been one of the companies' cases that partaken within the Know Us (2013) project and has been chosen and conferred due to its exceptional innovative logistic expertise (Yin, 2014; Janeš et al., 2014; Stake, 2000).

In the first period of financial crisis from 2008 to 2010, and again when the second (COVID - 19) crisis started in 2020 it could be noticed that despite been known as crisis breaker, the Company is not exempt to market changes, extraordinary situation like pandemic and consecutive economy down - turning effects. Amid the first crisis, they said farewell to their vital customer, Hyundai, from whom they gained most of their earnings. Management had to intensely cut down Company's costs, disinvest some of unnecessary assets and to lay off many of its employees. The Company has been co - financed with the family capital in 2010; management optimized their business processes, and minimized the costs until the lowest bearable limits of sustainability. The business focus has been sharpened and decisively oriented toward limited set of customers in South Korea, Israel and USA. Company's operations have been since then directed on customers regarded as partners, offering them complex and exhaustive logistics solutions. Such customer - oriented strategy allowed the Company to reorganize internally and diversify in the heavily competitive sector taking care of the Company's best interest on the long - term to create the ground for the existing and forthcoming business growth. Large financial investments and additional risk management was necessary to make this happen.

'We are the eyes and ears of the market! Assisting our customers in providing information from the marketplace that helps to improve the service and facilitate decisions is vital. The latter gives principals more time to do what they know best, i.e. adding value to their service in terms of efficiency and reliability' (interview with executive management). Company's activities are being performed acknowledging perceived cultural differences, as they service an international clientele across the globe. Crucial advantage offered to their Asian customers is the accessibility and responsiveness on a 24/7 basis. The introduced BM has been further upgraded with Lean, Agile, Resilient, and Green paradigms (do - Rosário - Cabrita et al., 2016), to preserve the stand of an authorized business partner to global companies such as Kia, Hyundai, Samsung, Tesco, Nokia, Philips, LG, Sony, etc. 'In 2017, Company continued to optimize processes, minimize costs and focus even more on core business. Investments have been made in units in Asia and Serbia, which will in the future contribute to a greater outflow of logistics services in region. The 2017 was a turning point for the Company which is now more focused on employees, providing them with additional training to help optimize business processes' (interview with executive management); these guidelines are in line with EuroPacific's original goals, so more focus is being put on core business and more aggressive approach in the market (Europacific.si, 2020).

Company's BM was adopted because of positioning as a domestic logistic operator for international corporations, but somehow missed the capital to build a larger logistics fleet. The new BM's swiftness, contention and adaptation ability in adopting the improved strategies are rare in the Slovenian and regional 3PL industry. It reflects knowledge that arises from the family tradition that has been gathered for more than forty years in innovating logistic business and creating a sustainable competitive advantage. 3PL organizations might create a position of local company or establish a globalized 3PL service to important companies and / or distributers. But usually they don't expand beyond the regional level and this is what differs the EuroPacific from competitors (Janeš et al., 2014; do - Rosário - Cabrita et al., 2016; Janeš et al., 2017; Alberti - Alhtaybat et al., 2019; see Table 1).

Company's business model using short list of assets conveys a large proportion of innovation and entrepreneurship which mirrors the firm character with innovation and entrepreneurship notes that penetrate the organizational design i.e. structures, processes and systems. Avoiding investments in costly assets, owners and managers built strong alliances network, concentrating on Euro 5 and 6 truck transport subcontractors. 'Innovation in technology is of a key importance to cultivate the asset - light BM and maintain the globalized network; rather than invest in infrastructure, partnership with domestic - focused logistics companies having strong local networks (e.g. Croatia, Hungary, India, Serbia, Singapore, Slovakia and Slovenia), knowledge and transportation solutions already in place for efficient and effective last - mile delivery was gained' (interview with executive management; Europacific.si, 2020; Table 1). Such innovative business model allowed them to develop a competitive strategic approach, as Company advocates it is represented by the agility, lean service and best - price - for - customer approach they provide by using the available logistic services, such as trucks and vans, at the best price possible, rather than keeping their own transportation fleet, rendering their services pricey. 'Technology is definitely not enough. Professional staff with extensive knowledge and experience of the shipping industry and local rules and regulations is a must for a successful business' (interview with executive management and interviewees).

Table 1. BM canvas innovation drivers

	Strategic themes for green sustainability			
Canvas element	**Lean service**	**Logistic expertise**	**Domestic logistic operator (3PL)**	**BM innovation activities**
stakeholders				Mutual property share acquisition with Samsung strategic partner; Employee participation and equity shares
business partners		Hyundai merchant marine; Port of Koper Ltd; Intereuropa Group Ltd; ZOLL - POLL transit guarantees in the amount of € 33.33 million; Gemini LLC;		Project with Hyundai merchant marine
key resources	Expert IS; Key account managers	Expertize of Asian business philosophy; Competence centre with partners	Expertize of Asian business philosophy	Establishment of a Competence centre with partners Port of Koper and Intereuropa Group; Key account managers; Euro 5 and 6 truck transport subcontractors
business processes	24/7 accessibility and responsiveness	Transport of products with high added value; Management system optimization	Transport of products with high added value	
products	Complete solutions of road, rail, sea and air transport	Domestic logistic operator for existing and new customers	Domestic logistic operator for existing and new customers; Consulting services; Complete solutions of road, rail, sea and air transport	Carbon footprint CO_2 measurement; Consulting services
customer segments			South Korean High - tech products; Emerging markets: India, Singapore; CMA - CGM Logistics; Israel; South - eastern markets	South Korean High - tech products; Emerging markets: India, Singapore; Business units opening in Croatia, Hungary and Serbia
value proposition	Project management; Just in time; IS for customer support at Traceability of goods	Trust based business networks	Strategy of domestic logistic operator for eastern markets	Traceability of goods with upgraded flexible IS

Note: Information System (IS); Compagnie Maritime d'Affrètement (CMA) and Compagnie Générale Maritime (CGM), which translate as Maritime Freighting Company and General Maritime Company (CMA - CGM)

Local networks are a concept of City Logistics (CL) which has emerged to reduce social, economic, and environmental impacts of last - mile freight distribution in urban areas (Mangano et al., 2019). Perboli & Rosano (2018) studied the collaborative transportation system offering traditional and green couriers in Turin (Italy), that could be quantified in terms of value chain efficiency (total end - to - end logistics cost), total system productivity, effectiveness (of asset utilization and customer service levels), combined data analysis, and environmental sustainability (minimize the overall carbon footprint), by which their competitive advantage shouldn't be compromised.

Another chosen strategy has been mutual property share acquisition and cooperation with South Korean Samsung strategic partner, which can grow their competitive advantage, in particular due to technological innovation, which is a repeated contemporary development. What makes EuroPacific's BM very agile and dynamic, is a long - term attained and matured knowledge of being an innovative 3PL provider, their domestic logistic operator's profile and the knowledge put in Information System (IS) for traceability of goods, that importantly increase the value and boost the sustainable competitive advantage creation (Chesbrough, 2007; Berman, 2012; Janeš et al., 2014; Denning, 2017; Alberti - Alhtaybat et al., 2019).

FUTURE RESEARCH DIRECTIONS

As it can be read in the literature, BMs can be generally understood as a way of performing business by the companies; with the goal to create, deliver and capture value (Augier & Teece, 2007; Zott & Amit, 2007, 2010; Teece, 2010; Demil et al., 2015; Österwalder & Pigneur, 201014; Chesbrough, 2007; Österwalder et al., 2005; Joyce & Paquin, 2016; do - Rosário - Cabrita et al., 2016), exploiting identified business opportunities and creating markets through established business models. Network partnering and companies' collaborating is one of the main leverages in changing the opportunities into business (Teece, 2010; Abrahamsson et al., 2018).

It lacks a straight interpretation what does it need to have a 'data - driven' business model, although every enterprise has a way how it handles data. This makes us conclude that the key differentiation's feature should be the term which describes the position of data as the main resource (Kühne & Böhmann, 2018). But the explicit conversion from a simple use of data to the treatment of data as the secret weapon has yet to be defined (Schüritz et al., 2017; Möller et al., 2020). Möller et al. (2020) suggest that two groups have been already identified categories were identified, both very important in the business models' field, for example the revenue model and the value proposition. Based on that have been outlined three clusters of data - driven BMs; visibility services exclusively, both visibility and optimization services and pure optimization services. A good example of the innovative, visibility and optimization services, approach of the Company is the setting of its own IS for customer support at traceability of goods, related to the Port of Koper's IS, allowing the control of containers' real - time processing. In such a way operator is being informed by the IS about the location and status of containers. Customers can use this application to monitor the movement of containers (Ellram & Cooper, 2014; Prajogo & Olhager, 2012). Goods are being continuously retraceable because of the IS and the shipment on the road is faster, as the truckers' waiting time is being shortened and operation costs optimized. Some interest has been expressed regarding the application's purchase, however the management decided not to monetize it, due to its importance for the Company's competitive advantage. Company's engagement in gathering information about customers, its exclusive BM that concentrates on building nontangible assets, e.g. technological development, human capital, and strategic alliances, differs importantly from competitive 3PLs (Kobal, Dežjot & Ventin, 2013a; 2013b; Kobal & Dežjot, 2020; Kim et al., 2008; Joyce & Paquin, 2016; Janeš et al., 2017; Alberti - Alhtaybat et al., 2019).

A specific challenge is being provided by the 3PL industry to the awareness of how customers assess diverse services' features, for example consumer to business and inter - organizational business. Crucial business features such as warehousing and transport are very structured, with built - in Information

Technology (IT), physical migration of products and personnel service cape. Performance is significantly affected by the material flow and information integration. The usage of ICT solutions in road freight transport exercises a positive influence on reduction of CO_2 emissions (Wang et al., 2015). ICT impact in freight transport for the CO_2 emission reduction has not been investigated in depth yet and its impact is largely unknown. Beside that Joyce and Paquin (2016) argue that the Triple Line BM canvas which include the three layers of how an organization generates multiple types of value, i.e. economic, environmental and social, should be used as a tool to help companies reinvent and plan the future organizational changes. Visually representing a business model through this canvas tool supports developing and communicating a more holistic and integrated view of a business model.

CONCLUSION

Presented chapter discusses the usability that the business model perspective offers, because of operations, logistics, and marketing aspects integration; in this way it can present an overall view to the analysis of every aspect of business transformations (Jocevski et al., 2019). As the analysis proved, transport system is being heavily congested by the advanced increase of vehicles and economy growth. Road transport's efficiency is being downsized, while the environmental pollution and oil consumption grow. That's why the rail transport must be revitalized, so as the rest of alternative transport solutions. Good practices are for example establishing intermodal transportation centres, to enact optimized payment systems for transport infrastructure customers, and to connect regional railway networks.

The motor of the transport sector development in the region where the Company is headquartered is the regional Port. Its activities leverage the growth of other logistic operations, i.e. maritime, rail, road and warehousing services. Company's activities are focused into development of bolstering its competitive advantage on the market, through network expansion and intensifying of partnership in logistic markets of Central and Eastern Europe and Asia, taking care of consumers' needs in a flexible manner.

Answers to research questions point to that EuroPacific succeeded in fulfilling the strategic theme (see Table 1, 4th column) and became domestic logistic operator or 3PL for Asian customers with the outstanding expertize of Asian business philosophy, complete solutions of road, rail, maritime and air transport of goods with high added value. For the successful implementation of disruptive technologies, i.e. IS for customer support at traceability of goods, the EuroPacific further developed and improved BM elements which are key resources, business processes, products and / or services and value proposition.

It's not possible to generalize the findings from the presented case study to the whole logistic industry, even though it presents an outstanding example. Determining the value of offered solutions, as they are being recognized in the eyes of companies' customers, remains the greatest challenge. Kano et al. (1984) already researched customers' preferences such as delighters, satisfiers, and dissatisfiers, and determined diverse categories: must be quality, one - dimensional quality, attractive quality, indifferent quality, and reverse quality of products and services. It is essential to remember, that chosen attributes inevitably drift over time from exciting to performance and then to essential attribute - must be. So, the companies have been on alert all the time (Alberti - Alhtaybat et al., 2019). And as Joyce and Paquin (2016) suggest, the Triple Line BM canvas should be used as a tool to help users reimagine the organizational changes in a more holistic and integrated view.

REFERENCES

Abrahamsson, J., Boter, H., & Vanyushyn, V. (2018). Business model innovation of international new ventures: An empirical study in a Swedish context. *Journal of International Entrepreneurship*. Advance online publication. doi:10.100710843-018-0238-3

Aguezzoul, A. (2014). Third - party logistics selection problem: A literature review on criteria and methods. *Omega*, *49*, 69–78. doi:10.1016/j.omega.2014.05.009

Aguiari, G. (2013). Che cosa intendiamo per logistica sostenibile? In G. Aguiari & R. Provedel (Eds.), *Logistica sostenibile: un'occasione di sviluppo & innovazione* (pp. 17–30). FrancoAngeli.

Alberti-Alhtaybat, L. V., Al-Htaybat, K., & Hutaibat, K. (2019). A knowledge management and sharing business model for dealing with disruption: The case of Aramex. *Journal of Business Research*, *94*, 400–407. doi:10.1016/j.jbusres.2017.11.037

Angrosino, M. V., & Mays de Pérez, K. A. (2000). Rethinking Observation. In N. Denzin & Y. Lincoln (Eds.), *Handbook of qualitative research* (pp. 673–702). Sage.

Aqlan, F., & Lam, S. S. (2015). A Fuzzy - based Integrated Framework for Supply Chain Risk Assessment. *International Journal of Production Economics*, *161*, 54–63. doi:10.1016/j.ijpe.2014.11.013

Augier, M., & Teece, D. J. (2007). Dynamic capabilities and multinational enterprise: Penrosean insights and omissions. *Management International Review*, *47*(2), 175–192. doi:10.100711575-007-0010-8

Bagnoli, C. (2012). Methodology of Analysis Canvas. Lecture at Faculty of Management, Koper.

Bask, A., Rajahonka, M., Laari, S., Solakivi, T., Toyli, J., & Ojala, L. (2018). Environmental sustainability in shipper - LSP relationships. *Journal of Cleaner Production*, *172*(1), 2986–2998. doi:10.1016/j.jclepro.2017.11.112

Baz, J. E., & Laguir, I. (2017). Third - party logistics providers (TPLs) and environmental sustainability practices in developing countries: The case of Morocco. *International Journal of Operations & Production Management*, *37*(10), 1451–1474. doi:10.1108/IJOPM-07-2015-0405

Berg, R. V. D., & Langen, P. W. D. (2016). Environmental sustainability in container transport: The attitudes of shippers and forwarders. *International Journal of Logistics: Research and Applications*, *20*(2), 146–162. doi:10.1080/13675567.2016.1164838

Berman, S. (2012). Digital transformation: Opportunities to create new business models. *Strategy and Leadership*, *40*(2), 16–24. doi:10.1108/10878571211209314

Berrone, P., Fsfuri, A., & Gelabert, L. (2013). Necessity as the mother of 'green' innovation: Institutional pressures and environmental innovation. *Strategic Management Journal*, *34*(8), 891–909. doi:10.1002mj.2041

Bocken, N., Short, S., Rana, P., & Evans, S. (2013). A value mapping tool for sustainable business modelling. *Corporate Governance*, *13*(5), 482–497. doi:10.1108/CG-06-2013-0078

Chen, Y. S., Lai, S. B., & Wen, C. T. (2006). The influence of green innovation performance on corporate advantage in Taiwan. *Journal of Business Ethics*, *67*(3), 331–339. doi:10.100710551-006-9025-5

Chesbrough, H. (2007). Business model innovation: It's not just about technology anymore. *Strategy and Leadership*, *35*(6), 12–17. doi:10.1108/10878570710833714

Chu, Z., Xu, J., Lai, F., & Collins, B. J. (2018). Institutional theory and environmental pressures: The moderating effect of market uncertainty on innovation and firm performance. *IEEE Transactions on Engineering Management*, *65*(3), 392–403. doi:10.1109/TEM.2018.2794453

Chu, Z., Wang, L., & Lai, F. (2019). Customer pressure and green innovations at third party logistics providers in China: The moderation effect of organizational culture. *International Journal of Logistics Management*, *30*(1), 57–75. doi:10.1108/IJLM-11-2017-0294

Colicchia, C., Melacini, M., & Perotti, S. (2011). Benchmarking supply chain sustainability: Insights from a field study. *Benchmarking*, *18*(5), 703–732. doi:10.1108/14635771111166839

Colicchia, C., & Strozzi, F. (2012). Supply chain risk management: A new methodology for a systematic literature review. *Supply Chain Management*, *17*(4), 403–418. doi:10.1108/13598541211246558

Council of the EU. (2019). *Stricter CO_2 emission standards for cars and vans signed off by the Council.* https://www.consilium.europa.eu/en/press/press-releases/2019/04/15/stricter-co2-emission-standards-for-cars-and-vans-signed-off-by-the-council

Demil, B., Lecocq, X., Ricart, J. E., & Zott, C. (2015). Introduction to the SEJ special issue on business models: Business models within the domain of strategic entrepreneurship. *Strategic Entrepreneurship Journal*, *9*(1), 1–11. doi:10.1002ej.1194

Denning, S. (2017). The age of agile. *Strategy and Leadership*, *45*(1), 3–10. doi:10.1108/SL-12-2016-0086

Dey, A., LaGuardia, P., & Srinivasan, M. (2011). Building sustainability in logistics operations: A research agenda. *Management Research Review*, *34*(11), 1237–1259. doi:10.1108/01409171111178774

Dimaggio, P., & Powell, W. (1983). The iron cage revisited: Institutional isomorphism and collective rationality in organizational fields. *American Sociological Review*, *48*(2), 147–160. doi:10.2307/2095101

Rosário Cabrita, M., Duarte, S., Carvalho, H., & Cruz-Machado, V. (2016). Integration of Lean, Agile, Resilient and Green Paradigms in a Business Model Perspective: Theoretical Foundations. *IFAC-PapersOnLine*, *49*(12), 1306–1311. doi:10.1016/j.ifacol.2016.07.704

Easterby-Smith, M., Thorpe, R., & Lowe, A. (2005). Raziskovanje v managementu [Research in management]. Fakulteta za management, Koper.

Elkington, J. (1997). *Cannibals with Forks: The Triple Bottom Line of 21st Century Business*. Capstone Publishing.

Ellram, L. M., & Cooper, M. C. (2014). Supply Chain Management: It's all about the Journey, Not the Destination. *The Journal of Supply Chain Management*, *50*(1), 8–20. doi:10.1111/jscm.12043

Eng-Larsson, F., & Kohn, C. (2012). Modal shift for greener logistics - the shipper's perspective. *International Journal of Physical Distribution & Logistics Management*, *42*(1), 36–59. doi:10.1108/09600031211202463

Europacific.si. (2020). *About Us*. https://europacific.si/en/about - us/

Europcan Commission. (2015). *A European Strategy for low - emission mobility*. https://ec.europa.eu/clima/policies/transport_en

European Commission. (2018). *Transport in the European Union*. https://ec.europa.eu/transport/sites/transport/files/2018-transport-in-the-eu-current-trends-and-issues.pdf

European Union. (2019). *Energy, transport and environment statistics*. https://ec.europa.eu/eurostat/documents/3217494/10165279/KS-DK-19-001-EN-N.pdf/76651a29-b817-eed4-f9f2-92bf692e1ed9,doi:10.2785/499987KS-DK-19-001-EN-C

Evangelista, P. (2014). Environmental sustainability practices in the transport and logistics service industry: An exploratory case study investigation. *Research in Transportation Business & Management*, *12*(1), 63–72. doi:10.1016/j.rtbm.2014.10.002

Evers, P. T., Harper, D. V., & Needham, P. M. (1996). The determinants of shipper perceptions of modes. *Transportation Journal*, *36*(2), 13–25.

Faganel, A., Biloslavo, R., & Janeš, A. (2020). Towards an innovative ecotourism business model framework. In L. C. Carvalho & L. Calisto (Eds.), *Strategic business models to support demand, supply, and destination management in the tourism and hospitality industry* (pp. 200–215). IGI Global. doi:10.4018/978-1-5225-9936-4.ch011

Flodén, J. (2007). *Modelling intermodal freight transport - the potential of combined transport in Sweden* [Unpublished doctoral dissertation]. Gothenburg University, Gothenburg School of Business, Economics and Law, Sweden.

Forte, E. (2003a). *Logistica economica ed equilibri spazio - territoriali* [Economic logistics and spatial - territorial balances]. Working paper presented at the seminar: I fondamenti concettuali della Logistica economica, Dipartimento di Architettura e Pianificazione, Politecnico di Milano.

Gardas, B. B., Raut, R. D., & Narkhede, B. E. (2019). Analysing the 3PL service provider's evaluation criteria through a sustainable approach. *International Journal of Productivity and Performance Management*, *68*(5), 958–980. doi:10.1108/IJPPM-04-2018-0154

Geissdoerfer, M., Bocken, N. M. P., & Hultink, E. J. (2016). Design thinking to enhance the sustainable business modelling process. *Journal of Cleaner Production*, *135*, 1218–1232. doi:10.1016/j.jclepro.2016.07.020

Giri, B. C., & Sarker, B. R. (2017). Improving performance by coordinating a supply chain with third party logistics outsourcing under production disruption. *Computers & Industrial Engineering*, *103*(1), 168–177. doi:10.1016/j.cie.2016.11.022

Green, K. W. Jr, Zelbst, P. J., Meacham, J., & Bhadauria, V. S. (2012). Green supply chain management practices: Impact on performance. *Supply Chain Management*, *17*(3), 290–305. doi:10.1108/13598541211227126

Gürcan, Ö. F., Yazıcı, İ., Beyca, Ö. F., Arsland, Ç. Y., & Eldemir, F. (2016). Third Party Logistics (3PL) Provider Selection with AHP Application. *Procedia: Social and Behavioral Sciences*, *235*, 226–234. doi:10.1016/j.sbspro.2016.11.018

Hazen, B. T., Cegielski, C., & Hanna, J. B. (2011). Diffusion of green supply chain management: Examining perceived quality of green reverse logistics. *International Journal of Logistics Management*, *22*(3), 373–389. doi:10.1108/09574091111181372

Iannone, F. (2002a). *Territorio e nodi logistici: dagli interporti alle piattaforme logistiche, ai distripark, ai city logistics centre* [Territory and logistic nodes: from interports to logistic platforms, distriparks, city logistics centres]. working paper, Dipartimento di Scienze Economiche e Sociali, Università degli Studi di Napoli Federico II.

Iannone, F. (2002b). *Possibili applicazioni di Teoria dei giochi al mercato dei servizi logistici e di trasporto* [Possible applications of Game Theory to the logistics and transport services market]. Working paper presented at the seminar: Logistica economica e strumenti di analisi, Dipartimento di Scienze Economiche e Sociali, Università degli Studi di Napoli Federico II, June 7, 2002.

Iannone, F. (2003a). *Aspetti pubblici e privati di un modello di logistica sostenibile* [Public and private aspects of a sustainable logistics model]. working paper presented at the seminar: Trasporti e politiche economiche, University of Palermo, Facoltà di Economia, VI Riunione Scientifica SIET. Palermo.

Iannone, F. (2003b). *L'esperienza del sito* logisticaeconomica.unina.it*: pianificazione, progettazione e comunicazione Web* [The experience of the logisticseconomica.unina.it site: planning, design and Web communication]. working paper presented at the seminar: I fondamenti concettuali della Logistica economica, Dipartimento di Architettura e Pianificazione, Politecnico di Milano.

Isaksson, K., & Huge-Brodin, M. (2013). Understanding efficiencies behind logistics service providers' green offerings. *Management Research Review*, *36*(3), 216–238. doi:10.1108/01409171311306382

Janeš, A., & Biloslavo, R. (2013). Preoblikovanje poslovnega modela za večjo uspešnost podjetij [Transform business model to improve company performance]. In Izzivi gospodarskega razvoja - Inovativni projektni management: zbornik prireditve, Ljubljana, GZS, Zbornica osrednjeslovenske regije.

Janeš, A., Biloslavo, R., & Faganel, A. (2017). Sustainable business model: A case study of Fonda.si. *Annales Series Historia et Sociologia*, *27*(1), 175–190.

Janeš, A., Bratkovič Kregar, T., Trnavčević, A., & Biloslavo, R. (2014). Projekt Know Us: primer povezovanja univerze in gospodarstva. In Soustvarjanje kompetenčnega znanja [Co - creation of competency knowledge] (pp. 93 - 125). Fakulteta za management, Koper.

Janeš, A., & Trnavčević, A. (2014). Dobre prakse Interreg Slovenija Italija: Projekt Know Us [Good practices Interreg Slovenia Italy: Know Us Project]. In Izzivi gospodarskega razvoja - Inovativni projektni management: zbornik prireditve, Ljubljana, GZS, Zbornica osrednjeslovenske regije.

Jocevski, M., Arvidsson, N., Miragliotta, G., Ghezzi, A., & Mangiaracina, R. (2019). Transitions towards omni - channel retailing strategies: A business model perspective. *International Journal of Retail & Distribution Management*, *47*(2), 78–93. doi:10.1108/IJRDM-08-2018-0176

Joyce, A., & Paquin, R. L. (2016). The triple layered business model canvas: A tool to design more sustainable business models. *Journal of Cleaner Production*, *135*(1), 1474–1486. doi:10.1016/j.jclepro.2016.06.067

Kahn, R. S., Kobayashi, S., Beuthe, M., Gasca, J., Greene, D., Lee, D. S., Muromachi, Y., Newton, P. J., Plotkin, S., Sperling, D., Wit, R., & Zhou, P. J. (2007). Transport and its infrastructure. In B. Metz, O. R. Davidson, P. R. Bosch, R. Dave & L. A Meyer (Eds.), Climate Change 2007: Mitigation Contribution of Working Group III to the Fourth Assessment Report of the Intergovernmental Panel on Climate Change (pp. 323 - 386), Cambridge University Press.

Kano, N., Seraku, N., Takahashi, F., & Tsuji, S. (1984). Attractive quality and must - be quality. *Journal of the Japanese Society for Quality Control*, *14*(2), 39–48.

Kim, C., Hoon Yang, K., & Kim, J. (2008). A Strategy for Third - Party Logistics Systems. *Omega*, *36*(4), 522–534. doi:10.1016/j.omega.2006.11.011

Know Us. (2013). *About project*. Http://www.know-us.eu/2/7

Kobal, R., Dežjot, A., & Ventin, H. (2013a). EuroPacific LLC: Workshop 1. Koper.

Kobal, R., Dežjot, A., & Ventin, H. (2013b). EuroPacific d.o.o.: Workshop 2. Koper.

Kobal, R., & Dežjot, A. (2020). EuroPacific d.o.o.: Workshop 3: Follow Up. Koper.

Kohn, C. (2008). *Towards CO_2 - efficient centralized distribution* [Unpublished doctoral dissertation]. Linköping University, Linköping, Sweden.

Kondratieff, N. D. (1925). *The Major Economic Cycles. English version, 1984. Long Wave Cycle* (G. Daniels & E. P. Dutton, Eds.). Richardson and Snyder.

Kühne, B., & Böhmann, T. (2018). Requirements for Representing Data - Driven Business Models - Towards Extending the Business Model Canvas. *Proceedings of the 24th Americas Conference on Information Systems*.

Kvale, S. (2007). *Doing interviews*. Sage. doi:10.4135/9781849208963

Lam, J. S. L., & Dai, J. (2015). Environmental sustainability of logistics service provider: An ANP - QFD approach. *International Journal of Logistics Management*, *26*(2), 313–333. doi:10.1108/IJLM-08-2013-0088

Large, R. O., Kramer, N., & Hartmann, R. K. (2013). Procurement of logistics services and sustainable development in Europe: Fields of activity and empirical results. *Journal of Purchasing and Supply Management*, *19*(3), 122–133. doi:10.1016/j.pursup.2013.05.002

Lieb, K. J., & Lieb, R. C. (2010). Environmental sustainability in the third - party logistics (3PL) industry. *International Journal of Physical Distribution & Logistics Management*, *40*(7), 524–533. doi:10.1108/09600031011071984

Lin, C. Y., & Ho, Y. H. (2008). An empirical study on logistics service providers' intention on adopt green innovation. *Journal of Technology Management & Innovation*, *3*(1), 17–26.

Lin, C. Y., & Ho, Y. H. (2011). Determinants of green practice adoption for logistics companies in China. *Journal of Business Ethics*, *98*(1), 67–83. doi:10.100710551-010-0535-9

Ludvigsen, J. (1999). Freight transport supply and demand conditions in the Nordic Countries: Recent evidence. *Transportation Journal*, *39*(2), 31–54.

Maas, S., Schuster, T., & Hartmann, E. (2014). Pollution prevention and service stewardship strategies in the third - party logistics industry: Effects on firm differentiation and the moderating role of environmental communication. *Business Strategy and the Environment*, *23*(1), 38–55. doi:10.1002/bse.1759

Jørsfeldt, L. M., Hvolby, H.-H., & Nguyen, V. T. (2016). Implementing environmental sustainability in logistics operations: A case study. *Strategic Outsourcing*, *9*(2), 98–125. doi:10.1108/SO-09-2015-0023

Manners-Bell, J. (2014). *Supply Chain Risk: Understanding Emerging Threats to Global Supply Chains*. Kogan Page.

Mangano, G., Zenezini, G., Cagliano, A. C., & De Marco, A. (2019). *The dynamics of diffusion of an electronic platform supporting City Logistics services*. Operations Management Research. doi:10.100712063-019-00147-7

Marchet, G., Melacini, M., & Perotti, S. (2014). Environmental sustainability in logistics and freight transportation: A literature review and research agenda. *Journal of Manufacturing Technology Management*, *25*(6), 775–811. doi:10.1108/JMTM-06-2012-0065

Martinsen, U., & Björklund, M. (2012). Matches and gaps in the green logistics market. *International Journal of Physical Distribution & Logistics Management*, *42*(6), 562–583. doi:10.1108/09600031211250596

Modarress, B., Ansari, A., & Lockwood, D. (2009). Outsourcing logistics to third - party providers: Practitioner's perspectives. *International Journal of Logistics Systems and Management*, *6*(1), 23–38. doi:10.1504/IJLSM.2010.029719

Möller, F., Stachon, M., Hoffmann, C., Bauhaus, H., & Otto, B. (2020). Data - Driven Business Models in Logistics: A Taxonomy of Optimization and Visibility Services. *Proceedings of the 53rd Hawaii International Conference on System Sciences*. 10.24251/HICSS.2020.661

Mollenkopf, D., Stolze, H., Tate, W. L., & Ueltschy, M. (2010). Green, lean, and global supply chains. *International Journal of Physical Distribution & Logistics Management*, *40*(1/2), 14–41. doi:10.1108/09600031011018028

Osorio, J. C., Manotas, D. F., & Rivera, L. (2017). Priorización de Riesgos Operacionales para un Proveedor de Tercera Parte Logística - 3PL. *Información Tecnológica*, *28*(4), 135–144. doi:10.4067/S0718-07642017000400016

Österwalder, A., & Pigneur, Y. (2010). *Business Model Generation: A handbook for visionaries, gamechangers, and challangers.* Wiley.

Österwalder, A., Pigneur, Y., & Tucci, C. L. (2005). Clarifying business models; origins, present, and future of the concept. *Communications of the Association for Information Systems*, *15*, 1–40. doi:10.17705/1CAIS.01601

Pålsson, H., & Johansson, O. (2016). Reducing transportation emissions: Company intentions, barriers and discriminating factors. *Benchmarking*, *23*(3), 674–703. doi:10.1108/BIJ-03-2014-0025

Pazirandeh, A., & Jafari, H. (2013). Making sense of green logistics. *International Journal of Productivity and Performance Management*, *62*(8), 889–904. doi:10.1108/IJPPM-03-2013-0059

Perboli, G., & Rosano, M. (2018). A Decision Support System for Optimizing the Last - Mile by Mixing Traditional and Green Logistics. In C. Temponi & N. Vandaele (Eds.), *Information Systems, Logistics, and Supply Chain* (Vol. 262). Springer. doi:10.1007/978-3-319-73758-4_3

Prajogo, D., & Olhager, J. (2012). Supply Chain Integration and Performance: The Effects of Long - Term Relationships, Information Technology and Sharing, and Logistics Integration. *International Journal of Production Economics*, *135*(1), 514–522. doi:10.1016/j.ijpe.2011.09.001

Raut, R., Kharat, M., Kamble, S., & Kumar, C. S. (2018). Sustainable evaluation and selection of potential third - party logistics (3PL) providers: An integrated MCDM approach. *Benchmarking*, *25*(1), 76–97. doi:10.1108/BIJ-05-2016-0065

Rogers, D.S., & Tibben-Lembke, R.S. (1998). *Going backwards: Reverse logistics trends and practices.* Reverse Logistics Executive Council. www.rlec.org/reverse.pdf

Ruggiero, U. (2014). *Sviluppo di modelli di logistica sostenibile nelle città portuali* [Development of sustainable logistics models in port cities] (Thesis). LUISS Guido Carli. https://tesi.luiss.it/13812/1/ruggiero-ugo-tesi-2014.pdf

Schneider, S., & Spieth, P. (2013). Business model innovation: Towards an integrated future research agenda. *International Journal of Innovation Management*, *17*(1), 1–34. doi:10.1142/S136391961340001X

Schumpeter, J. A. (1934). Depressions: Can we learn from past experience? In J. A. Schumpeter, E. Chamberlin, W. W. Leontief, D. V. Brown, S. E. Harris, E. S. Mason, & O. H. Taylor (Eds.), *The economics of the recovery program.* McGraw - Hill.

Schüritz, R., Seebacher, S., & Dorner, R. (2017). Capturing Value from Data: Revenue Models for Data - Driven Services. *Proceedings of the 50th Hawaii International Conference on System Sciences.* 10.24251/HICSS.2017.648

Sorescu, A., Frambach, R. T., Singh, J., Rangaswamy, A., & Bridges, C. (2011). Innovations in retail business models. *Journal of Retailing*, *87*(S1), S3–S16. doi:10.1016/j.jretai.2011.04.005

Stake, R. E. (2000). Case Studies. In N. K. Denzin & Y. S. Lincoln (Eds.), *Handbook of Qualitative Research* (pp. 821–834). Sage.

Stern, N. H. (2007). The Economics of Climate Change. *The Stern Review.* http://mudancasclimaticas.cptec.inpe.br/~rmclima/pdfs/destaques/sternreview_report_complete.pdf

Tacken, J., Rodrigues, V. S., & Mason, R. (2014). Examining CO_2e reduction within the German logistics sector. *International Journal of Logistics Management*, *25*(1), 54–84. doi:10.1108/IJLM-09-2011-0073

Tang, C. S. (2006). Perspectives in supply chain risk management. *International Journal of Production Economics*, *103*(2), 451–488. doi:10.1016/j.ijpe.2005.12.006

Teece, D. J. (2010). Business models, business strategy and innovation. *Long Range Planning, 43*(2-3), 172 - 194.

UN ESCAP. (2019). *Asia - Pacific trade and investment trends: 2019/20 Trade in goods outlook*. https://www.unescap.org/our-work/trade-investment-inovation

Vannieuwenhuyse, B., Gelders, L., & Pintelon, L. (2003). An online decision support system for transportation mode choice. *Logistics Information Management*, *16*(2), 125–133. doi:10.1108/09576050310467269

Vickerman, R., & Monnet, J. (2003). Freight traffic. In *ECMT, Managing the Fundamental Drivers of Transport Demand*. OECD.

Villani, P. M. C. (2011). *Portualità, logistica, sviluppo sostenibile* [Ports, logistics, sustainable development] (Thesis). POLIMI. http://hdl.handle.net/11311/605687

Wang, G., Dou, W., Zhu, W., & Zhou, N. (2015). The effects of firm capabilities on external collaboration and performance: The moderating role of market turbulence. *Journal of Business Research*, *68*(9), 1928–1936. doi:10.1016/j.jbusres.2015.01.002

Wang, Y., Sanchez Rodrigues, V., & Evans, L. (2015). The Use of ICT in Road Freight Transport for CO_2 Reduction: An Exploratory Study of UK's Grocery Retail Industry. *International Journal of Logistics Management*, *26*(1), 2–29. doi:10.1108/IJLM-02-2013-0021

WBCSD, World Business Council for Sustainable Development and World Resources Institute. (2004). The Greenhouse Gas Protocol: A Corporate Accounting and Reporting Standard. World Business Council for Sustainable Development & World Resources Institute.

White, P. (2009). Building a sustainability strategy into the business. *Corporate Governance*, *9*(4), 386–394. doi:10.1108/14720700910984936

Winter, M., & Knemeyer, A. M. (2013). Exploring the integration of sustainability and supply chain management: Current state and opportunities for future inquiry. *International Journal of Physical Distribution & Logistics Management*, *43*(1), 18–38. doi:10.1108/09600031311293237

WTO. (2019). *Goods Trade Barometer*. Geneva: World Trade Organization. Available at https://www.wto.org/english/news_e/news19_e/wtoi_15aug19_e.pdf

Yin, R. K. (2014). *Case Study Research: Design and Methods*. Sage.

Zott, C., & Amit, R. (2007). Business model design and the performance of entrepreneurial firms. *Organization Science*, *18*(2), 181–199. doi:10.1287/orsc.1060.0232

Zott C., & Amit, R. (2010). Business model design: An activity system perspective. *Long Range Planning, 43*(2-3), 216 - 226.

KEY TERMS AND DEFINITIONS

3PL (Logistics Operator): 3PL, or third - party logistics, is essentially a variety of services and processes that are provided to company by an external company, i.e., logistic provider, in order to reduce costs, improve efficiencies and expand capabilities.

Business Model: A business model describes the rationale of how an organization creates, delivers, and captures value, in economic, social, cultural, or other contexts.

Canvas: A template with nine elements to help describe an organization's business model.

Domestic Logistic Operator: The company's strategy, when the latter acts in foreign markets as a domestic company.

Expertise: Expert (s) skills or knowledge in a particular field in this case logistics for Asian companies.

Green Logistics: Green logistics describes all attempts to measure and minimize the ecological impact of logistics activities. It is a concept to characterize logistics systems and approaches that use advanced technology and equipment to minimize environmental damage during logistic operations.

Sustainable Innovation: Is a process where sustainability considerations (i.e., environmental, social, and economic) are integrated into company systems from idea generation through to research and development and commercialization.

Chapter 3
Agile Project Management:
Experience and Adoption

Rahul Verma
https://orcid.org/0000-0002-5356-813X
Delhi University, India

ABSTRACT

This chapter presents the notion of agile project management and identifies the existing challenges in agile project management in the new millennium. It sets the scene for discussions presented by various authors too. In particular, the chapter identifies the experience and the related problems with agile project management. It also identifies the importance of adoption of agile project management and debates about the measure of agility.

INTRODUCTION

Agile Project Management

Agile Project Management is the application of the standards of Agile Project Management to different management forms, especially project management. Taking after the appearance of the Manifesto for Agile Project Management in 2001, Agile procedures begun to spread into other ranges of activity (Denning, 2020). In 2004, one of the authors of the initial manifesto, Jim Highsmith, published Agile Project Management: Creating Innovative Products (Highsmith, 2004).

The term Agile Project Management is connected to an iterative, incremental strategy of overseeing the build and design activities of information technology, engineering, and other business areas that point to supply new service or product development in a profoundly interactive and flexible way, based on the standards communicated within the Manifesto for Agile Software Development (Moran, 2015).

Agile X procedures may moreover be called extreme project management. It could be a variant of iterative life cycle (ExecutiveBrief, 2021) where deliverables are submitted in stages. The main contrast between iterative and agile development is that agile strategies complete little portions of the deliverables in each delivery cycle (iteration) (VersionOne, 2021a), whereas iterative strategies advance the complete

DOI: 10.4018/978-1-7998-7872-8.ch003

set of deliverables over time, completing them near the end of the project. Both agile and iterative strategies were created as a response to different deterrents that created in more consecutive forms of project organization. For instance, as innovation projects develop in complexity, end users tend to have trouble characterizing the long - term prerequisites without being able to see dynamic prototypes. Projects that create in iterations can constantly assemble feedback to assist refine those requirements.

Agile Project Management moreover offers a straightforward system promoting communication and reflection on past work among group members (Project Laneways, 2021). Groups who were using conventional waterfall planning and embraced the agile way of improvement regularly go through a change phase and frequently take assistance from agile coaches who help direct the groups through a smooth change. There are ordinarily two styles of agile coaching: pull - based and push - based agile coaching. Agile Project Management approaches have moreover been adapted and employed to the government and business sectors. For illustration, inside the federal government of the United States, the United States Agency for International Development (USAID) is utilizing a collaborative project management approach that centres on integrating Collaborating, Learning, and Adapting (CLA) techniques to adapt and iterate programming (USAID, 2021).

Agile strategies are mentioned within the Guide to the Project Management Body of Knowledge (PMBOK Guide) beneath the Project Lifecycle definition: Adaptive project life cycle, a project life cycle, moreover known as agile or change - driven methods, that's intended to encourage change and require a high degree of progressing stakeholder inclusion. Adaptive life cycles are moreover incremental and iterative, but differ in that iterations are exceptionally quick (usually 2 - 4 weeks in length) and are fixed in resources and time (Project Management Institute, 2021).

BACKGROUND

In Project Management, Agile (Rally, 2010) practices include developing solutions and discovering requirements through the collaborative exertion of cross - functional and self - organizing teams and their end user (s) / customer (s) (Collier, 2011). It advocates continual improvement, early delivery, evolutionary Management, and adaptive planning, and it encourages adaptable responses to change (Beck et al., 2013; Agile Alliance, 2021).

It was popularized by the Manifesto for Agile Project Management (Kent et al., 2001). The values and principles espoused in this manifesto were derived from and underpin a broad range of Project Management frameworks, including Scrum and Kanban (The Clever PM, 2021; Larman, 2004).

While there's much recounted evidence that adopting Agile practices and values improves the agility of Project organizations, teams, and professionals, the observational evidence is blended and difficult to discover (Dybå & Dingsøyr, 2008; Lee & Xia, 2010).

In spite of the fact that Agile Project Management strategies can be used with any programming language or paradigm in practice, they were initially closely related with object - oriented situations such as Smalltalk and Lisp and later Java. The initial adopters of agile strategies were usually small to medium - sized groups working on phenomenal frameworks with prerequisites that were troublesome to finalize and likely to alter as the framework was being created. This segment portrays common issues that organizations experience when they attempt to adopt Agile Project Management strategies as well as different strategies to measure the performance and quality of agile teams (Beck, 2000).

MAIN FOCUS OF THE CHAPTER

Common Agile Project Management Pitfalls

Teams and Organizations implementing Agile Project Management often face difficulties transitioning from more traditional methods such as Waterfall Management, such as teams having an agile process forced on them (Shore & Warden, 2008). These are often termed agile smells or more commonly agile anti - patterns. Below are some common examples:

Lack of Overall Product Design: A goal of Agile Project Management is to focus more on producing working Project and less on documentation. This is in difference to waterfall models where the procedure is often highly controlled and slight changes to the system require major revision of supporting documentation. Nevertheless, this doesn't justify completely doing without any design or analysis at all. Failure to pay attention to design can cause an organization to proceed swiftly at first but then to have substantial rework required as they try to scale up the system. One of the key features of Agile Project Management is that it is iterative. When done in the approved manner design emerges as the system is developed and opportunities and commonalities for re - use are discovered (Beck, 2000).

Adding Stories to an Iteration in Progress: In Agile Project Management, stories (similar to use case descriptions) are typically used to define requirements and an iteration is a short period of time during which the organization commits to specific goals (Rouse, 2015). Adding stories to an iteration in progress is disadvantageous to a good flow of work. These should be added to the product backlog and lined up for a subsequent iteration or in rare circumstances the iteration could be cancelled (Goldstein, 2011).

This doesn't mean that a story can't expand. Organizations must deal with new information, which may produce added tasks for a story. If the new information precludes the story from being concluded during the iteration, then it should be passed over to a subsequent iteration. On the other hand, it should be prioritized against all left over stories, as the new information might have altered the story's original priority.

Lack of Sponsor Support: Agile Project Management is often implemented as a grassroots effort in organizations by Project Management teams trying to optimize their Management processes and ensure consistency in the Project Management life cycle. By not having sponsor support, teams may face resistance and difficulties from management, other Management teams and business partners. In addition, they may suffer without appropriate resources and funding (Agile - Only, 2014.). This increases the chances of failure (Bourne, 2014).

Insufficient Training: A survey performed by VersionOne found respondents cited insufficient training as the most significant cause for failed agile implementations (VersionOne, 2021b). Teams have fallen into the trap of assuming the reduced processes of Agile Project Management compared to other methodologies such as waterfall means that there are no actual rules for Agile Project Management.

Product Owner Role is not Properly Filled: The product owner is responsible for representing the business in the Management activity and is often the most demanding role (Sims & Johnson, 2011).

A common botch is to have the product owner role filled by somebody from the Management team. This requires the organization to make its own decisions on prioritization without real response from the business. They try to delay work as they reach outside the team for direction or solve business issues internally. This often leads to breakdown and distraction in collaboration (Rothman, 2011).

Organizations are not Focused: Agile Project Management requires organizations to meet product commitments, which means they should emphasis only on work for that product. On the other hand, organization members who seem to have spare capacity are over and over again expected to take on other work, which makes it problematic for them to help complete the work to which their organization had committed (Fox, 2014).

Excessive Planning / Preparation: Organizations may fall into the trap of spending too much time planning or preparing. This is a common trap for organizations less familiar with Agile Project Management where the organizations feel obliged to have a complete specification and understanding of all stories. Organizations should be prepared to move forward only with those stories in which they have confidence, then during the iteration continue to prepare and discover work for subsequent iterations (often referred to as grooming or backlog refinement).

Problem - Solving in the Daily Stand - Up: A daily stand - up ought to be a timely, focused meeting where all team members spread information. If problem - solving occurs, it frequently can only include certain team members and potentially isn't the best use of the complete team's time. If amid the daily stand - up the team begins diving into problem - solving, it ought to be set aside until a sub - team can examine, usually promptly after the stand - up completes (Mountaingoatsoftware, 2021a).

Assigning Tasks: One of the aiming benefits of Agile Project Management is to enable the team to make choices, as they are closest to the problem. Furthermore, they ought to make choices as close to execution as possible, to utilize more timely information in the decision. If organization members are allocated tasks by others or too early in the process, the benefits of timely and localized decision making can be lost (May, 2014).

Being assigned work moreover constrains organization members into certain parts (for example, organization member A must continuously do the database work), which limits openings for cross - training (May, 2014). Organization members themselves can select to take on assignments that provide cross - training opportunities and stretch their abilities.

Scrum Master as a Contributor: In the Scrum technique, which is a popular technique that claims to be steady with Agile principles and values, a scrum master is the person responsible for ensuring the scrum process is taking place, and coaching the scrum team through that process. A common drawback is for a scrum master to act as a giver. Whereas not prohibited by the Scrum technique, the scrum master has to guarantee they have the capacity to act in the part of scrum master first and not work on Management tasks. A scrum master's part is to encourage the process rather than make the product (Berczuk, 2014).

Having the scrum master too multitasking may result in numerous context switches to be beneficial. Moreover, as a scrum master is responsible for guaranteeing barricades are evacuated so that the organization can make forward progress, the advantage gained by individual tasks moving forward may not outweigh barricades that are conceded due to lack of capacity (Berczuk, 2014).

Lack of Test Automation: Due to the iterative nature of Agile Management, multiple rounds of testing are often needed. Automated testing helps reduce the impact of regression tests, integration, and repeated unit and frees testers and developers to focus on higher value work (Namta, 2014).

Test automation moreover supports continued refactoring required by iterative Project Management. Permitting a tester to rapidly run tests to affirm refactoring has not modified the functionality of the application may diminish the workload and increment confidence that clean - up endeavours have not introduced new defects.

Allowing Technical Debt to Build Up: Centring on conveying new functionality may result in increased technical debt. The organization must permit themselves time for defect refactoring and remediation. Technical debt ruins planning capacities by expanding the amount of unscheduled work as production defects divert the organization from further progress (Band, 2014).

As the framework evolves it is imperative to refactor as entropy of the framework naturally increases (Shore, 2014). Over time the need of constant maintenance causes increasing Management costs and defects (Band, 2014).

Attempting to Take on Too Much in an Iteration: A common misconception is that Agile Project Management allows continuous change, however an iteration backlog is an agreement of what work can be completed during an iteration (Allaboutagile, 2021a). Having too much Work - In - Progress (WIP) domino effects in ineffectiveness such as queuing and context - switching (George, 2014). The organization must avoid feeling stressed into taking on extra work (Mountaingoatsoftware, 2021b).

Fixed Quality, Scope, Resources, and Time: Agile Project Management fixes ideally resources, quality, and time (iteration duration) in advance (in spite of the fact that maintaining fixed resources may be troublesome if testers are frequently pulled away from tasks to handle production occurrences), whereas the scope remains variable. The product owner or customer frequently pushes for a fixed scope for an iteration. However, organizations ought to be hesitant to commit to the locked scope, resources, and time (commonly known as the project management triangle). Efforts to add scope to the fixed time and resources of Agile Project Management may result in decreased quality (McMillan, 2014).

Developer Burnout: Due to the continuous nature and focused pace of Agile practices, there's an increased risk of burnout among individuals of the delivery team (Procedia Computer Science, 2021).

SOLUTIONS AND RECOMMENDATIONS

Measuring Agility

Internal Assessments: The Agility measurement index, among others, rates advancements against five dimensions of product development (interaction, effort, novelty, risk, and duration) (Datta, 2006; Jroller, 2021). Other methods are based on quantifiable goals (Peter & Henry, 2009) and one survey recommends that velocity can be utilized as a metric of agility (Kurian, 2006). There are also agile self - assessments to decide whether a group is using Agile Project Management practices (Nokia test (Joe, 2007), Karlskrona test (Mark & Mayberg, 2014), 42 points test) (Allaboutagile, 2021b).

Public Surveys: One of the early surveys announcing gains in business satisfaction, productivity, and quality by using Agile Project Management methods was a study conducted by Shine Technologies from November 2002 to January 2003 (Shine Technologies, 2021).

FUTURE RESEARCH DIRECTIONS

A comparative study, the State of Agile, is conducted each year beginning in 2006 with thousands of members from around the Project Management community. This tracks patterns on the seen benefits of good practices, lessons learned, and agility. Each study has detailed expanding numbers saying that Agile Project Management increases their productivity; improves their ability to manage changing customer priorities; and helps them deliver software faster (Stateofagile, 2021). Studies have moreover reliably appeared better results with agile product development strategies compared to classical project management (Status Quo Agile, 2021; Ambler, 2006). In balance, there are reports that a few feel that agile development methods are still too young to empower broad academic research of their success (Agilemodeling, 2021).

CONCLUSION

Agile practices can be wasteful in huge organizations and certain sorts of developments (Larman & Bas, 2009). Numerous organizations accept that Agile Project Management techniques are too extraordinary and receive a Hybrid approach (BinFire, 2021) that blends components of Agile Project Management and plan - driven approaches (Barlow et al., 2011). A few strategies, such as Dynamic Systems Development Method (DSDM) endeavour this in a taught way, without relinquishing principal standards.

REFERENCES

Agile Alliance. (2021). *What is Agile Software Development?* Author.

Agile - Only. (2021). *Project Roles and Responsibility Distribution.* Author.

Agilemodeling. (2021). *Answering the "Where is the Proof That Agile Methods Work" Question.* Author.

Allaboutagile. (2021a). *Step 4: Sprint Planning (Tasks).* Www.allaboutagile.com

Allaboutagile. (2021b). *How Agile Are You? (Take This 42 Point Test).* Www.allaboutagile.com

Ambler, S. (2006). *Survey Says: Agile Works in Practice.* Dr. Dobb's.

Band, Z. (2014). *Technical Debt + Red October.* Author.

Barlow, J. B., Justin, S. G., Mark, J. K., David, W. W., Ryan, M. S., Paul, B. L., & Anthony, V. (2011). Overview and Guidance on Agile Development in Large Organizations. *Communications of the Association for Information Systems, 29*(1), 25–44. doi:10.17705/1CAIS.02902

Beck, K. (2000). *Extreme Programming Explained.* Addison - Wesley.

Beck, K., Grenning, J., Martin, R. C., Beedle, M., Highsmith, J., Mellor, S., van Bennekum, A., Hunt, A., Schwaber, K., Cockburn, A., Jeffries, R., Sutherland, J., Cunningham, W., Kern, J., Thomas, D., Fowler, M., & Marick, B. (2001). *Manifesto for Agile Software Development.* Agile Alliance.

Beck, K. M., Beedle, M., Bennekum, A. V., Cockburn, A., Cunningham, W., Fowler, M., Grenning, J., Highsmith, J., Hunt, A., Jeffries, R., Kern, J., Marick, B., Martin, R. C., Mellor, S. J., Schwaber, K., Sutherland, J., & Thomas, D. (2013). *Manifesto for Agile Software Development.* Undefined. S2CID 109006295.

Berczuk, S. (2014). *Mission Possible: Scrum Master and Technical Contributor.* Www.agileconnection.com

BinFire. (2021). *Introduction to Hybrid project management*. Author.

Bourne, L. (2014). *What Does a Project Sponsor Really Do?* blogs.pmi.org

Collier, K. W. (2011). *Agile Analytics: A Value - Driven Approach to Business Intelligence and Data Warehousing*. Pearson Education. 10.1145/1185448.1185509

Denning, S. (2020). What Is Agile? *Forbes*.

Dybå, T., & Dingsøyr, T. (2008). Empirical studies of agile software development: A systematic review. *Information and Software Technology, 50*(9-10), 833 - 859. doi:10.1016/j.infsof.2008.01.006

ExecutiveBrief. (2021). *Which Life Cycle Is Best For Your Project?* PM Hut.

Fox, A. (2014). *Working on Multiple Agile Teams*. techwhirl.com/

George, C. (2014). *Why Limiting Your Work - in - Progress Matters*. Leankit.com.

Goldstein, I. (2011). *Sprint issues - when sprints turn into crawls*. Www.axisagile.com.au

Highsmith, J. (2004). *Agile Project Management: Creating Innovative Products*. The Agile Software Development Series.

Joe, L. (2007). *Nokia test, a scrum - specific test*. Agileconsortium.blogspot.com.

Jroller. (2021). *David Bock's Weblog: Weblog*. Author.

Kurian, T. (2006). Agility Metrics: A Quantitative Fuzzy Based Approach for Measuring Agility of a Software Process. *ISAM - Proceedings of International Conference on Agile Manufacturing'06 (ICAM - 2006)*.

Larman, C. (2004). *Agile and Iterative Development: A Manager's Guide*. Addison-Wesley.

Larman, C., & Bas, V. (2009). *Top Ten Organizational Impediments to Large - Scale Agile Adoption*. Inform IT.

Lee, G. & Xia, W. (2010). Toward Agile: An Integrated Analysis of Quantitative and Qualitative Field Data on Software Development Agility. *MIS Quarterly, 34*(1), 87–114. doi:10.2307/20721416

Mark, S. & Mayberg, S. (2014). *Karlskrona test, a generic agile adoption test*. Mayberg.se.

May, R. (2014). *Effective Sprint Planning*. Www.agileexecutives.org

McMillan, K. (2014). *Time, Resources, Scope... and Quality*. Www.adeptechllc.com

Moran, A. (2015). *Managing Agile: Strategy, Implementation, Organisation and People*. Springer. doi:10.1007/978-3-319-16262-1

Mountaingoatsoftware. (2021a). *Daily Scrum Meeting*. Www.mountaingoatsoftware.com

Mountaingoatsoftware. (2021b). *Sprint Planning Meeting*. Www.mountaingoatsoftware.com

Namta, R. (2014). *Thoughts on Test Automation in Agile*. Www.infoq.com

Peter, L. & Henry, C. T. A. (2009). *Assessing Agility*. Academic Press.

Procedia Computer Science. (2021). *Current study on limitations of Agile.*. doi:10.1016/j.procs.2016.02.056

Project Laneways. (2021). *What is Agile Management?* Author.

Project Management Institute. (2021). *A Guide to the Project Management Body of Knowledge* (5th ed.). PMBOK Guide.

Rally. (2010). *Agile with a Capital "A" Vs. agile With a Lowercase "a"*. Author.

Rothman, J. R. (2011). *When You Have No Product Owner at All.* Www.jrothman.com

Rouse, M. (2015). *Sprint (software development) definition.* Searchsoftwarequality.techtarget.com.

Shore, J. (2014). *The Art of Agile Development: Refactoring.* Www.jamesshore.com

Shore, J., & Warden, S. (2008). *The Art of Agile Development.* O'Reilly Media.

Sims, C., & Johnson, H. L. (2011). The Elements of Scrum (Kindle ed.). Dymaxicon.

Stateofagile. (2021). *2013 State of Agile report: Why Agile?* Author.

Status Quo Agile. (2021). *Second study on success and forms of usage of agile methods.* Author.

Shine Technologies. (2021). *Agile Methodologies Survey Results.* Author.

The Clever PM. (2021). *Which is better - Kanban or Scrum?* Author.

USAID. (2021). *ADS Chapter 201 Program Cycle Operational Policy.* Author.

VersionOne. (2021a). *Agile Project Management.* Author.

VersionOne. (2021b). *9th State of Agile Report.* Stage of Agile Survey. Author.

KEY TERMS AND DEFINITIONS

Agile Project Management: It is more flexible approach and promotes collaborative working with the customer.

Agility: Ability to move easily and quickly.

Manifesto: It is a published declaration.

Chapter 4
Project Success Criteria, Critical Success Factors (CSF), and Agile Projects

Canser Bilir
Istanbul Sabahattin Zaim Universitesi, Turkey

ABSTRACT

There have been major developments in project management over the years; however, the success rates of projects are still far from the desired levels. The number of studies focusing on project success has been increasing over the last decades. This chapter reviews the concept of project success, project success criteria, and CSF by narrowing the focus from generic projects to IT and then agile projects. The review revealed that client satisfaction has a critical role in the perceived success of the project, along with iron triangle (cost, budget, scope). It is widely accepted that some CSF are dependent on the context of the project. Top management support, communication, clear and linked project objectives, user involvement, teamwork, and effective planning are critical factors in IT projects. There are two differences in the evaluation of the success between agile and traditional software projects: frequency of the evaluation and a stronger emphasis on ensuring customer satisfaction. There is higher importance on people-related factors and customer involvement in agile projects.

INTRODUCTION

Projects are defined as temporary endeavors to generate a unique product, service, or result (PMI, 2017). A project is also defined as possessing the following characteristics: A defined beginning and end, a specific, predetermined goal or output, a series of interrelated activities, a limited budget (Pinto & Slevin, 1988a). To create a competitive advantage, improve their operations, and differentiate their products or services, the companies are turning to project management (Jugdev & Muller, 2005). Even though there have been major developments in project management over the years, the success rates of projects are still far from the desired levels (Chaos Report, 2021; PMI, 2020). The number of studies focusing

DOI: 10.4018/978-1-7998-7872-8.ch004

on project success has been increasing over the last few decades. Most of these studies focus on either measuring project success or identifying the CSF of the projects with different characteristics. The concept of project success is an interesting subject from an academic perspective; however, it is particularly important to help the project management practitioners understand how improving underlying success factors will lead to increased project performance. Therefore, this chapter reviews the concept of project success, project success criteria, and CSF. The following "Background" section provides an introduction to the literature on "project success." Then, the perception and the measurement of project success are defined. Next, the CSF for the projects are discussed. After that, CSF, in the current literature, specifically for the software development projects, are presented. In the last subsection of the literature, agile software development projects are defined. This subsection included the discussion of the perception of the project success for agile projects and the review of the CSF for those projects. In the next section, future research suggestions are provided, and the chapter ends with conclusions.

BACKGROUND

The number of studies on project success has been increasing over the last few decades. The majority of the research on project success falls into two categories: In the first category, many studies are dealing with the project success criteria (e.g., Ika, 2009; Prabhakar, 2008; Davis, 2018; Oseyi-Kyei & Chan, 2017; Chan, Scott & Edmond, 2002). Those studies discuss how the success of the projects should be measured and what criteria should be used to quantify the project success. The literature on the measurement of project success and how the concept of project success is evolved is reviewed under the "Project Success" title.

In the second vein of the studies on project success, many studies are dealing with the CSF (Ika, 2009). CSF are defined as the input to the management system that supports the project's success (Prabhakar, 2008). In this category of the studies on project success, many researchers (e.g., Davies, 2002; Nasir et al., 2015; Yalegama, Chileshe & Ma, 2016; Marzagao & Carvalho, 2016) discussed the CSF and their impact on project success for projects with different characteristics. The literature on the critical factors and their impact on the different dimensions of the project success is reviewed under the "Critical Success Factors (CSF)" title.

PROJECT SUCCESS, CRITICAL SUCCESS FACTORS, AND AGILE PROJECTS

Project Success

There are various similar definitions of the project. In one of the definitions, projects are defined as temporary endeavors to generate a unique product, service, or result by PMI (2017). Kerzner (2013) defines project management as the planning, organizing, directing and controlling of the required resources for a relatively short-term objective that has been defined to complete specific goals and objectives. A project is also expected to possess the following characteristics: A defined beginning and end, a specific, predetermined goal or output, a series of interrelated activities, a limited budget (Pinto & Slevin, 1988a).

On the other hand, there is no commonly accepted definition of project success and no consensus on when and how to call a project successful or failed (Ika, 2009). "Project success" may have a different meaning for different people with different perspectives. Some people may consider a project successful if it has reached its goals in terms of duration, budget, and scope. Some other people may focus on the overall objective of the project regarding the justification of the project (Palcic & Buchmeister, 2012). Therefore, a distinction between project management success and project success must be made (Figure 1). Project management success focuses more on cost, time, and quality. On the other hand, project success is more related to the success or failure of the project's outcome (Ika, 2009).

Figure 1. The meaning of project success
Source: Sudhakar, 2012

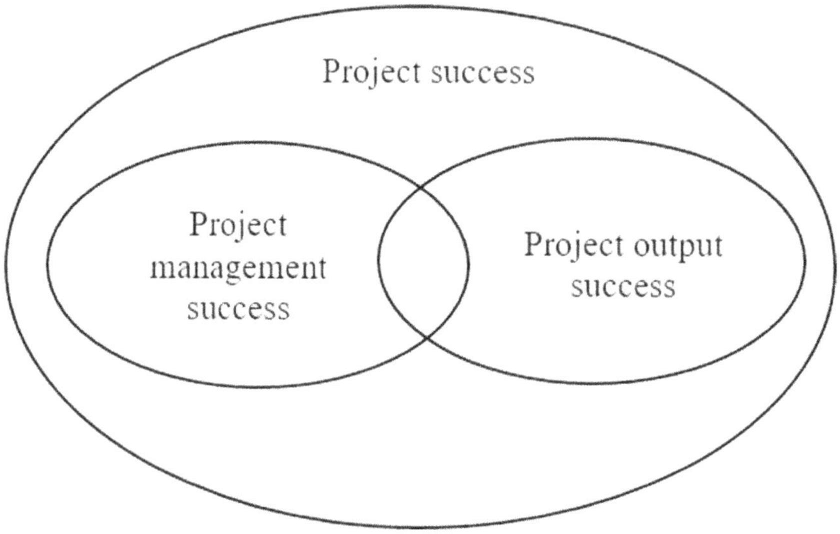

For example, a new product development project may be completed on time, on budget, with all predefined functionalities. However, the project's outcome, i.e., new product, may not have the desired success on the market in terms of sales etc. In that case, the project is considered successful from a project management success perspective; however, it is also considered unsuccessful from a project (product) success perspective. A Guide to the Project Management Body of Knowledge (PMBOK), published by the Project Management Institute in project management, considers success as achieving goals successfully within the previously drawn frame. "If a project has reached its original targets set by its client, activities are carried out as it should be, and a determined problem is resolved within the limits of time, cost and quality determined before; this project can be defined as successful (PMI, 2017)."

As mentioned in the background section, the majority of the research on project success falls into two categories: Studies dealing with the project success criteria and studies dealing with the CSF (Ika, 2009). In the first category, many studies discuss how the success of the projects should be measured and what criteria should be used. Even though the criteria used in project success measurement are quite controversial, cost, time, and quality (the iron triangle) are commonly used as the success criteria by researchers (Atkinson, 1999). Figure 2 presents the various dimensions in the iron triangle.

Figure 2. The iron triangle
Source: Atkinson, 1999

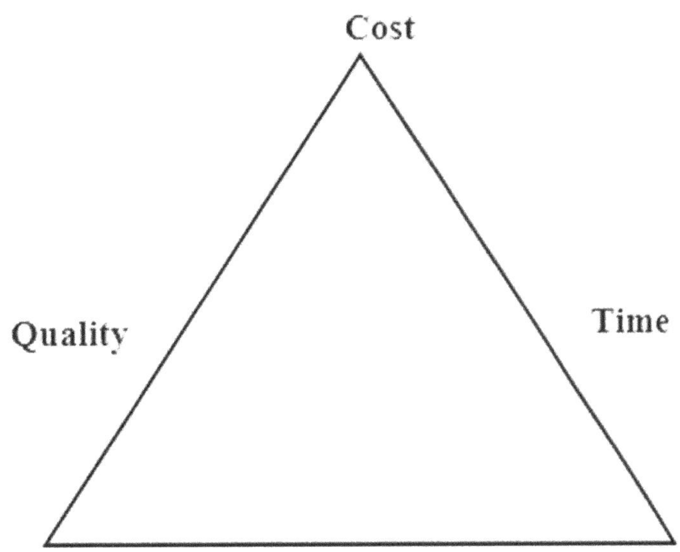

Later on, the researchers agreed that the client satisfaction with the project's output also had a critical role in the perceived success or failure of the project. Therefore, client satisfaction has been added to the definition of project success. Client satisfaction is measured by technical validity (the output of the project should work in a way it is supposed to), organizational validity (if the project is right for the intended clients), and organizational effectiveness (if the output of the project is contributing to an improved level of organizational effectiveness) of the project's output as illustrated in Figure 3 (Pinto & Slevin, 1988a).

Understanding of the project success has changed over the last 40 years. Jugdev and Müller (2005) assess the changes in the understanding of the project success and discuss CSF in their study. The authors define four consecutive periods to explain how the concept of the project success evolved throughout the years:

Period 1 - Project Implementation and Handover (the 1960s-1980s): In that period, simple metrics which the project team can easily measure, such as time, costs, specifications, were used to measure. Those metrics are easy to use and within the control of the project organization. Project teams focused on completing the project on time, on budget and with the defined functionalities. There was a gradual trend towards including customer satisfaction as a variable in measuring project success in that period.

Period 2 – Critical Success Factor (CSF) Lists (the 1980s – 1990s): The focus was on developing CSF lists which are the elements required to create where projects are managed successfully. Even though a number of CSF were defined in this period, no integrated group of factors was defined. During the period, customer satisfaction became increasingly important because of the competition and market pressures.

Period 3 – CSF Framework (the 1990s – 2000s): CSF frameworks emerged in the transition from period 2 to period 3. Several authors defined comprehensive frameworks on the conditions and elements of project success. Those elements included attitudes, project definition, external factors, finance, contract strategy, schedule, communications and control, human resources management etc.

Period 4 – Strategic Project Management (21st Century): In that period, the attention on project success is shifted from the operational and tactical level to a more holistic view of the value of project management as a strategic competency. That is, projects are increasingly used as a way towards the achievement of organizational objectives, and project success dimensions should include benefits to the organization and prepare them for the future.

Figure 3. Key factors of client satisfaction
Source: Pinto & Slevin, 1988a

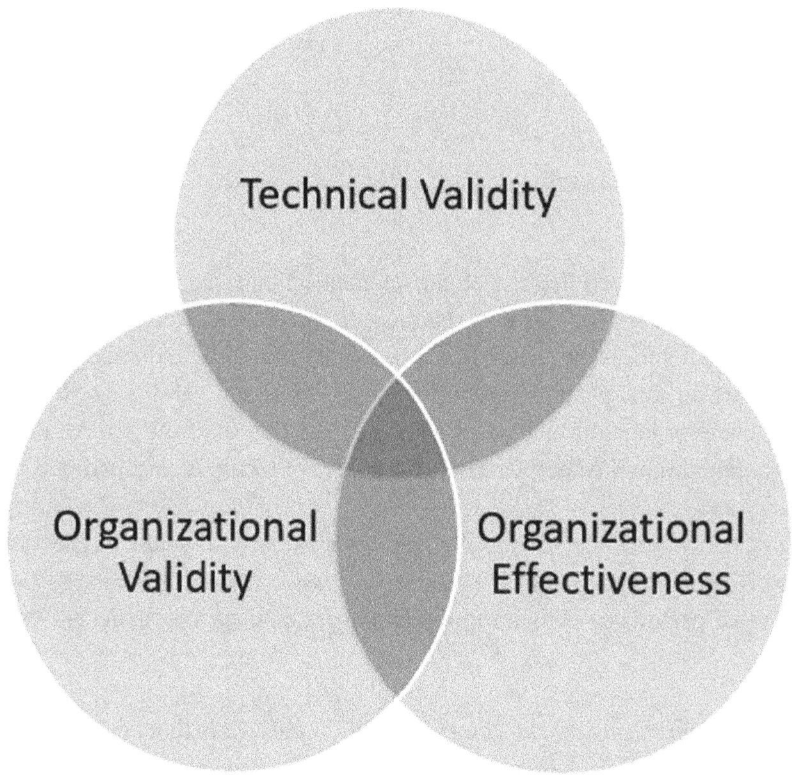

In one of the recently published studies discussing how projects' success/failure rates should be measured, Castro et al. (2021) proposed a generic measure of project success where different projects can grade differently using the same scale. The authors collected data through quantitative surveys from 264 Brazilian project managers from a range of industries and business areas with various levels of experience. Their proposed project success measurement model had five dimensions: project efficiency, organization benefits, project impact, future potential, and stakeholder satisfaction.

Davis (2018) claimed that different stakeholders do not recognize the same success dimensions for a project and have different views. Then, the author assessed different views of project success by different stakeholders and proposed a multiple stakeholder model to reconcile the different views. Results of the study showed that the perceptions of different stakeholders are significant to the final project outcome. The proposed multiple stakeholder model required input from all stakeholders to define the final project success dimensions.

In project success literature, it is also discussed that each project should be measured in a specific way reflecting the industry, type of the project, project size, project orientation etc. (Castro et al., 2021). Therefore, many researchers investigated the project success criteria for a specific type of project, e.g., Information Technology (IT) projects. Pankratz and Basten (2014) investigated project managers' views on IT project success criteria. The study identified eight commonly accepted success criteria by interviewing eleven experienced project managers in Germany:

- Adherence to budget: Conformance between planned and actual development cost
- Adherence to schedule: Conformance between planned and actual development time
- Meeting functional requirements: Conformance between specified functional requirements and their realization
- Meeting non-functional requirements: Conformance between specified non-functional requirements and their realization
- Process efficiency: Ratio of objective achievement to the expended effort (budget)
- Customer satisfaction: Customer organization's stakeholders are satisfied with the project
- Contractor satisfaction: Contractor organization's stakeholders are satisfied with the project
- The system is used by the customer: Developed system is deployed and used by end-users after the completion

However, those criteria look very similar to what were proposed by Pinto & Slevin (1998a). Client satisfaction-related criteria seem to be customized for IT projects and the outputs of the IT projects.

Critical Success Factors (CSF)

CSF are defined as "elements required to create an environment where projects are managed consistently with excellence (Kerzner, 1987). In another definition, project success factors are defined as the input to the management system that led to the project's success (Prabhakar, 2008). As briefly mentioned in the "background section," there are many studies investigating the critical success factors and their impact on the perceived performance of the project with different characteristics.

In a pioneering study, Pinto and Slevin (1988b) investigated the "critical" factors contributing most to the success of the projects. After surveying project managers and the members of PMI, the authors listed ten key success factors:

- Project mission: Clarity of goals and strategic direction.
- Top management support: Willingness of top management to provide required resources and authority/power for project success.
- Project schedules/planning: Detailed activity scheduling for project implementation.
- Client consultation: Communication, consultation and active listening to all impacted parties (stakeholder management).
- Personnel: Recruitment, selection and training of the necessary personnel for the project team.
- Technical tasks: Availability of the required technology and expertise to perform project activities.

- Client acceptance: The act of "selling" the final project to its ultimate intended users. Customer "buy-in."
- Monitoring and feedback: Timely and comprehensive control at each phase in the implementation process.
- Communication: The provision and distribution of the key information to all relevant parties throughout the project.
- Troubleshooting: Ability to handle unexpected crises and deviations from plan.

Those factors are the factors considered to be managed and controlled by the project team. Later on, the authors also added four more factors considered outside the control of the project team. These factors are:

- Characteristics of the project team leader: Competence of project leader (managerial and technical skills) and the amount of authority available to perform his/her duties.
- Power and politics: The degree of political activity within the organization.
- Environmental events: External or environmental factors impacting the operations of the project team, positively or negatively.
- Urgency: The perception of the importance of the project or the need to implement the project as soon as possible.

Belassi and Tukel (1996) also reviewed the CSF to classify them and describe their impact on project success. In the study, the factors are grouped into four areas:

- Factors related to the project
    - The size and the value of a project
    - The uniqueness of project activities vs. standard activities
    - The density of the project network
    - Project life-cycle
    - The urgency of the project outcome
- Factors related to project manager and the team members
    - Ability to delegate authority
    - Ability to tradeoff
    - Ability to coordinate
    - Perception of project manager's role and responsibilities
    - Competencies of the project manager
    - Commitment (Project manager)
    - Technical background for team members
    - Communications
    - Troubleshooting
    - Commitment (Team members)
- Factors related to the organization
    - Top management support for the project
    - Project organizational structure (functional vs. matrix organization)
    - Functional managers' support for the project
    - Project champion (project sponsor)

- Factors related to the external environment
    - Political environment
    - Economic environment
    - Social environment
    - Technological environment
    - Unique nature of the project
    - Client's attitude
    - Competitors
    - Sub-contractors

The authors also concluded that not all critical success/failure factors apply to all projects as the results varied substantially from one industry to another or from one type of project to another type of project. That is because of the unique nature of the projects. Their study also demonstrated that some factors might be critical for some industry sectors, while those factors might not be relevant for the other industries. They also concluded that environmental factors, such as political, economic, and social factors, impact the project's performance. As the political, economic, social, and cultural factors change from one geographic region to another, analyzing the impacts of those factors in different geographic regions may help both practitioners and academicians understand the underlying environmental factors behind the success/failure of the projects.

After these pioneering studies, many researchers discussed the CSF for projects with different characteristics or projects executed in a specific context and/or geographic location. In a recent study, authors conducted a descriptive and explanatory study to analyze the impact of 38 CSF compiled from the current literature on project success factors (Pacagnella et al., 2019). Compiled success factors are classified into five different groups:

- Factors related to human resources: Human resources-related factors include empowerment, project manager leadership, project team integration, project team flexibility, conflict handling, project management experience, and team experience.
- Organizational factors: These factors are related to the organizational environment in which the projects are carried out and include project management authority, organizational structure, change management, top management support, and project management office.
- Factors related to the stakeholder relationship: These factors include effective communication, incentive mechanism, disincentive mechanism, integration with suppliers, selection of suppliers, and client engagement.
- Project management related factors: These factors are related to how the project is managed and include the definition of clear objectives, clear documentation, project planning, management of requirements, prevention of multitasking, analysis of critical resources, interdependencies between projects, analysis of limiting factors, register of lessons learned, risk identification, risk analysis, responses to risks, reserves of time and money, risk control, and control of baselines.
- Factors related to technical aspects: These include communications infrastructure, information systems for projects, technical performance control, proper execution of commissioning, and use of previous technologies.

In the study, the authors used a sample of 182 respondents to identify and understand the relationship between the CSF and project performance considered in four various dimensions: efficiency, impact on consumers, impact on the team, and preparation for the future. The study concluded that the impacts of various CSF on different dimensions of project success occur in a varied and heterogeneous way; therefore, different types of projects may have different CSF, especially when considering various dimensions of project success.

Abylova and Salykova (2019) also concluded that project success factors change according to the necessities and the priorities of the projects, and they added that there is still a need for more studies investigating the CSF because of the changing nature of the projects through time.

Recently, many articles have been published to identify the CSF for the specific type of projects. For example, in a study published in the International Journal of Project Management in 2016, authors investigated the CSF and their relationship with project performance, considering Six Sigma projects. The CSF for Six Sigma projects are compiled under three categories: project management competencies, project manager competencies, and Six Sigma methodology applications. A survey-based research applying the structural equation modeling is used to review the results of 149 responses from 37 companies in Brazil and Argentina. After analyzing the responses, the authors concluded that Six Sigma project performance is statistically and positively impacted by the three measures of CSF: Six Sigma methodology applications, project management competencies, and project manager competencies. They also underlined the importance of project manager competencies as they also reinforce the Six Sigma methodology applications and Project Management competencies (Marzagao & Carvalho, 2016).

Construction projects are one of the classical types of projects, which project management techniques have been applied for decades. Williams (2016) also identified the CSF and their interaction in construction projects by presenting a case from the United Kingdom. The author categorized the success factors under six areas: company culture, single team, project setup, customer satisfaction, subcontractors, and post-handover. The author also concluded that some of the success factors are generic for different types of the projects; on the other hand, others are context-dependent for the type of the project or even the company. The study also showed that some factors played a more critical role in the success of the construction projects:

- Organizational culture including communications, stakeholder engagement and leadership styles (an example of a generic success factor).
- The company's sense of locality and size (an example of a specific success factor for the project)
- Single team approach including the subcontractors
- Creating a learning team environment pursuing continuous improvement.

IT Projects, and IT Project Success Factors

IT projects may be defined as a project which includes IT-based changes. IT projects are more complicated, and the success rates of those projects are lower (Chaos Report, 2021). Most of the IT projects include software development, and they are often poorly defined and aimed to be finished in a challenging project duration because of market pressures. Lack of constraints, invisibility, complexity and flexibility are the characteristics of complex IT projects (Sudhakar, 2012). IT projects also require a higher level of novelty than other types of projects. (Iriarte & Bayona, 2020). Software projects, maybe the most common type of IT projects, have multiple stakeholders such as team members, users, customers, top management etc. Unfortunately, each stakeholder has their own priorities and interests, those priorities and interests are poorly defined, and they often conflict with each other. Therefore, the success rates of the IT projects are not very encouraging.

Because the success rates of IT projects are even lower than the success rates of overall projects and because of the importance of the IT projects, recently many studies specifically investigated the CSF for IT projects. Iriarte and Bayona (2020) reviewed the relevant articles published until 2017 to synthesize the most referenced CSF in IT project success literature in an article focusing on IT projects. In their study, the authors conclude that soft skills and people skills are the most important critical factors for IT projects. Top referred factors include top management support, user involvement, internal communication, knowledge and technical expertise, and effective planning.

In another study, Sudhakar (2012) also reviewed and analyzed the CSF for software development projects. Then, the author proposed a conceptual model and categorized CSF under seven categories:

- Communication-related factors: Communication is an essential part of project management for any project, including IT projects. Most commonly referred communication-related CSF are identified as communication in the project, leadership skills, strong relationship between users and IT staff, reducing ambiguity, and maximizing stability.
- Technical factors: Technical factors seem to have less impact on the project success than organizational, managerial, and environmental factors. Most referred factors are technical task and capabilities, troubleshooting, technical uncertainty, technical implementation problems, integration of the system.
- Organizational factors: Five most referred organizational factors are top management support, realistic expectations, organizational politics, financial support and use of power.
- Environmental factors: Five most referred environmental factors are user involvement, customer involvement, vendor partnership, external environment events, and client acceptance.
- Product factors: Those factors are related to the output of the project. The most referred product-related factors are accuracy of output, reliability of output, timeliness of output, quality control, documentation of systems and procedures.
- Team factors: Factors in that category are mainly related to how the team is formed, the capabilities of the team members, and how the team works. The five most referred critical team-related success factors are team capabilities, teamwork, team member selection, project team coordination, and task orientation.
- Project management factors: As the name of the category implied, those are the factors related to the management of the project. That is the category including the most number of CSF. The five most referred of those CSF are project planning, project control mechanisms, project schedule, project manager's competence, and clear project goal.

In another study focusing on success factors in IT projects, the authors reviewed the literature and used the experience from 28 IT projects. Then, the authors concluded that risk analysis, user involvement, and top management support are of particular importance for the success of IT projects. Risk analysis includes the identification of risks and taking preventive or responsive actions to manage those risks. User involvement is defined as having the end-user of the project outcome consulted throughout the project. Top management support may be defined as the active support and involvement of the project sponsor in the project (Wurtemberg et al., 2011).

In a very well-known study, Standish Group measures IT projects' success and failure rates since 1985. They publish the results in Chaos Report each year. In each year's reports, the relative importance of the success factors is also reviewed and published, along with the measurements of project success rates. The latest chaos report describes three consolidated factors affecting the outcome of the project: Good sponsor, good team, and good place. Good sponsor covers the skills required by the project sponsor to support the success of the project. Good team includes the factors related to the characteristics of an effective synergy-creating team. Good place includes the organizational and environmental factors to support the project sponsor and the project team for the success of the project (Chaos Report, 2021).

To summarize, the CSF identified in the project success literature focusing on IT projects, top management support, communication in the project, clear and linked project objectives, user involvement, teamwork and creating positive synergy, and effective planning seem to be critical among other key IT projects success factors.

Agile Projects and Project Success

Despite all the studies and developments in the field of project management, the success rates of software development projects are far from the desired level. In the 21st century, agile methodologies emerged as a new way of managing projects in reaction to the low-level customer satisfaction of software projects. Some experts believe that agile project management will become the new way of managing projects. Even though the agile project management approach may be used to manage different types of projects, it is still mainly used for managing software development projects (Bergmann & Karwowski, 2019). Therefore, this section of the chapter pays special attention to the agile software development projects, specifically on the perception of project success and the CSF for agile software development projects. First, the agile software development projects are defined, and the main differences between agile and traditional software development projects are identified. Next, the measurement of project success for agile projects is briefly discussed. Finally, studies on the CSF for agile projects are reviewed to identify the most critical success factors contributing to the success of agile projects.

Agile Software Development

Even though software developments projects play a critical role in the development of the modern world, software development projects often result in delayed, failed, abandoned, or rejected results. Based on that reality, in February 2001, a group of senior software development methodologists attended a summit to develop a new and improved way of software development and then formed the Agile Alliance (Chow & Cao, 2008). As an essential output of the summit, the agile manifesto is published. The agile manifesto for software development addresses the inflexibility inherent to the traditional software development methodology and its negative impact on the project results (Tam et al., 2020). On the other hand, the word "agile" means something flexible and responsive based on the changes. Therefore, agile methods imply the "ability" to survive in a constantly changing environment such as software development projects and to emerge with success. There are many "agile" based software development methodologies depending on different viewpoints, such as Extreme Programming (XP), Scrum, Feature-Driven Development (FDD), Dynamic System Development (Method (DSDM), Adaptive Software Development (ASD), Crystal and Lean Software Development (LD) (Chow & Cao, 2008). Agile values are (Campanelli & Parreiras, 2015; Chow & Cao, 2008):

- Individuals and interactions over processes and tools
- Working software over documentation
- Customer collaboration over negotiation
- Responding to change over strictly following the plan

Compared to traditional software development methodologies, agile methodologies provide many advantages in time to market, increased quality and productivity, improved IT and business alignment, and enhanced flexibility. The agile principles are identified as follows (Campanelli & Parreiras, 2015):

- Early and continuous delivery of working valuable software
- Change in requirements definitions is welcome
- Deliver software frequently
- Constant people interaction (business and developers)
- Motivated working people
- Face-to-face communication is prioritized
- Working software is progress
- Keeping a constant working pace
- Technical excellence and good design
- Work simplicity
- Self-organized teams
- Continuous improvement throughout the project

Table 1 summarizes some differences between traditional and agile software development methodologies from a project management perspective.

Table 1. Traditional vs. agile software development

Traditional software development	Agile software development
1. Follows a top-down approach, and the changes are not welcome	1. Various techniques are experimented with by the team to arrive best possible solution gradually
2. It has a leadership style of working	2. There is a free flow of communication. Anyone can present ideas within the team
3. Pre-planning is done to carry out the various phases	3. More flexible compared to the traditional model as it can change its workflow based on any new request for modifications.
4. The customer is involved in the initial phases of requirements collection & definition	4. Customer involvement is crucial at all steps of the development process
5. Project plan is prepared before the process of system development	5. Project work is delivered incrementally. When one module is ready, it is presented to the customer for confirmation
6. The ownership lies in the project manager	6. There is a concept of shared ownership. That means every team member is equally responsible for their individual contribution
7. There is one-time delivery of the product/software	7. There is incremental delivery of the product
8. Bureaucratic and mechanical organizational structure, targeting large organizations	8. Flexible and participative organizational structure, targeting small and medium organizations and encouraging social cooperation

Source: Tam et al., 2020

Project Success Criteria for Agile Software Development Projects

Even though there are many differences between traditional and agile software development projects, and the values for agile projects are different from traditional software development projects, as discussed above, the perception of success is not entirely different for agile projects. Siddique & Hussein (2016) investigated the similarities and dissimilarities between agile-based and waterfall-based projects regarding how success is perceived and managed by interviewing 32 agile practitioners in Norway. According to the study's findings, the success criteria for agile projects are similar to those used for traditional software development projects. Agile projects success criteria include delivering the project on time, on budget and with the predefined scope (Project management success). They also include product-success-related criteria such as customer satisfaction, provided value to the customer, impact on supplier organization, creating new businesses, learning and sustaining the supplier business.

The study also identified two major interrelated differences in the perception of the success between agile projects and traditional software development projects. One of the differences is in the frequency of the success evaluation. In agile projects, performance measurement evaluation is carried out on a regular basis after each increment. This continuous assessment and evaluation of project success offers several major advantages;

- Greater commitment and involvement from the customer: Continuous measurement of the project gets the customer focused on the project and eventually increases the level of commitment.
- A higher level of mutual trust and a better sense of control with better knowledge sharing.
- Reduced task uncertainty: As there is a limited number of tasks in each increment and the results can be easily measured, continuous measurement with increments helps reduce the level of uncertainty about the direction of the project.
- Multiple and subjective assessments: The measurement of success is performed collaboratively. Thus, the decision on the success or failure of the delivery is based on a negotiated argument. This decision-making process allows multiple and subjective assessments by various stakeholders.

The second major difference in the perception of project success between agile projects and traditional software development project is related to the focus of the measurement. There is a stronger emphasis on ensuring customer satisfaction in agile projects than in traditional software development projects. Impact on the customer is measured in terms of how quickly the value is generated for the customer. Generated value includes meeting specifications, satisfying customer needs, and providing a high level of return on investment for the customer. The continuous assessment of the outcomes of the project after each iteration has a positive impact on how the customer perceives the success of the project outcome. To achieve the desired level of customer satisfaction, organizations should meet the following conditions (Siddique & Hussein, 2016):

- Customers consider themselves as an essential part of the development process through continuous feedback and prioritization of features
- The control of the project is on the customer
- The customer obtains value for money and is able to see the value created at each iteration.

CSF for Agile Projects

There is a limited number of studies explicitly investigating the CSF that help software development projects using agile methods to succeed. In a pioneering study, Chow and Cao (2008) conducted a survey study on the CSF of agile software development projects to identify the possible success factors four each of for success categories – Quality, Scope, Time, and Cost. After reviewing the relevant case studies, agile projects and practices, the authors compiled a list of 36 CSF for agile projects classified into five categories: organizational, people, process, technical, and project. Those factors are presented in Table 2.

Table 2. CSF for agile projects

Dimensions	Factors
Organizational Factors	1. Strong executive support 2. Committed sponsor or manager 3. Cooperative organizational culture 4. Oral culture placing a high value on face-to-face communication 5. Organizations where the agile methodology is widely accepted 6. Colocation of the entire team 7. Facility with an agile-style work environment 8. Reward system appropriate for agile
People Factors	9. Highly competent team members 10. Highly motivated team members 11. Managers knowledgeable in the agile process 12. Managers with an adaptive management style 13. Coherent, self-organizing teamwork 14. A good relationship with the customer
Process Related Factors	15. The agile-oriented requirement management process 16. The agile-oriented project management process 17. The agile-oriented configuration management process 18. Strong communication focus with daily face-to-face meetings 19. Honoring a regular working schedule (no overtime) 20. Strong customer commitment and presence 21. Customer having full authority
Technical Factors	22. Well-defined coding standards 23. Pursuing simple design 24. Rigorous refactoring activities 25. The right amount of documentation 26. Regular delivery of software 27. Delivering the most important features first 28. Appropriate integration testing 29. Appropriate technical training to team
Project Related Factors	30. Project nature being non-life-critical 31. Project type being of variable scope with emergent requirements 32. Dynamic accelerated schedule 33. Small team 34. No multiple independent teams 35. Up-front cost evaluation 36. Up-front risk analysis

Source: Chow & Cao, 2008

To conduct the analysis and identify the most imperative factors contributing to the success of the projects, the authors gathered data from 109 agile projects from 25 countries. After the reliability analysis on the factors, 12 factors were identified to be used for further analysis. Multiple regression analysis showed that (a) a correct delivery strategy, (b) proper practice of agile software engineering techniques, and (c) high caliber team capability were statistically significant in the success of the agile projects. Some other factors were also found to be critical to a certain extend: (a) a good agile project management process, (b) an agile-friendly team environment, (c) a strong customer involvement. On the other hand, the study could not find statistically significant relationships between agile project success and some commonly widely accepted success factors such as strong executive support, strong sponsor commitment, availability of the physical agile facility and agile-appropriate project type.

In a recent study, Tam et al. (2020) investigated the five people-factors to identify the most contributing factors to the success of the agile software development projects by surveying 216 agile practitioners from a variety of business areas. The authors measured the success in terms of cost, time, and customer satisfaction, and they selected and characterized five people factors: "personal characteristics," "training and learning," "societal culture," "team capability," and "customer involvement." Those factors were combined into a conceptual model and tested the validity of the model. Their study indicated that two factors, "team capability" and "customer involvement," can significantly explain the variation in the success of agile software development projects. This result directs agile practitioners to focus on selecting a highly capable team and promoting customer involvement and collaboration.

Bergman & Karwowski (2019) reviewed the current literature to identify the most critical success factors in the perceived success of agile projects. Their literature review indicated that the agile approach is more people-oriented rather than process-oriented. The people factors are important factors in the success of agile development projects. Those factors include a highly knowledgeable and skilled project team, supportive top management, and deeply involved customers. In addition to people factors, the organizational form and culture are also critical for the success of agile projects. That is, it is essential to have a flexible and less hierarchical organizational structure supporting a fast-changing environment to be more adaptive. Another critical factor is the process that supports iterative, test-driven development and emphasizes adaptability. The appropriate technology and tools are also crucial for the success of agile project implementation.

In conclusion, the literature review on CSF for agile projects reveals that the CSF for agile software development projects are different from the CSF for traditional software development projects to some extent. There is higher importance on people-related factors, including the competencies of the team members and executive support. Continuous customer involvement is very critical in agile projects. An agile process in place, supporting collaboration and communication is another essential critical factor in the success of agile projects.

FUTURE RESEARCH SUGGESTIONS

It is widely accepted that project success factors change according to the necessities and the priorities of the projects (Abylova & Salykova, 2019). In addition, environmental factors, such as political, economic, and social, impact the project's performance and need to be understood (Belassi & Tukel, 1996). Therefore, there is a need for more studies investigating the CSF and their impact on project success for different types and the size of the projects. As the political, economic, social, and cultural factors change from one geographic region to another, analyzing the impacts of those factors in different geographic regions may also help practitioners and academicians understand the critical factors behind the success/failure of the projects in those specific regions.

Naturally, agile projects are quite different from traditional projects from a project success perspective. Project performance is evaluated regularly, and the final output of the project is not strictly defined in agile projects. Agile methods provide flexibility to allow for an iterative planning process and to change requirements (Bergmann & Karwowski, 2019). Despite the difference in the execution of the agile projects, there are only a few studies investigating the project success factors and their impact on different dimensions of the project success. Therefore, there is also a need for more studies focusing on agile development projects and CSF.

The literature review revealed that people-related factors are important factors in the success of projects, including agile development projects (Tam et al., 2020). People-related factors include the capabilities of team members, communications, culture, personal characteristics etc. It is also known that leadership styles and the leadership capabilities of the project leaders play critical roles in the success of the projects (Shenhar & Wideman, 2020). Therefore, it may be concluded that any study investigating the leadership styles and capabilities of project leaders and their impact on the performance of agile projects would contribute to the project success literature. It is also commonly accepted that organizational cultures and the different types of organizational cultures impact the success of both IT projects and other types of projects (Yazici, 2011; Gu et al., 2014; Kendra & Taplin, 2004). However, there is no study investigating specifically the impact of the different types of organizational culture and their impact on the performance of the agile software development projects. Research investigating those relationships for agile software development projects would also substantially contribute to the project success literature.

CONCLUSION

In this section of the chapter, the results of the literature review on project success, including agile development projects, are summarized. On the perception of project success, there is a widely accepted distinction between project management success and project (product) success in the current literature. Project management success focuses more on cost, time, and quality (iron triangle) (Ika, 2009). Project success, on the other hand, focuses on client satisfaction. Recently, the researchers agreed that client satisfaction with the project result also has a critical role in the perceived success of the project. Even though there are different criteria used to measure client satisfaction, in the literature, most of the criteria are similar to those used by Pinto & Slevin (1988a). They measure client satisfaction by technical validity, organizational validity, and organizational effectiveness. Success criteria used to measure the success of the IT projects are also similar to those used to measure client satisfaction by Pinto & Slevin (1988a). The only difference is that the client satisfaction-related criteria are customized for IT projects.

CSF are defined as elements that led to the success of the projects. Many studies are investigating the CSF and their relationship with the different dimensions of project success. Understanding the success factors is critical in project management both for practitioners and academicians; however, it is widely accepted that all CSF do not apply to all projects, and some CSF are dependent on the context of the project, project size, company culture, country etc. That is even more important when the different dimensions of project success are considered (Belassi & Tukel, 1996; Abylova & Salykova, 2019; Pacagnella et al., 2019).

IT projects are defined as a project that includes IT-based changes and the most common form of IT projects is the software development projects. They are considered more complicated because of the technical complexities and the different priorities and interests of different stakeholders. There are also many studies explicitly focusing on the CSF for IT projects. Top management support, communication in the project, clear and linked project objectives, user involvement, teamwork and creating positive synergy within the team, and effective planning may be defined as very critical, among other factors in the success of IT projects (Iriarte & Bayona, 2020; Wurtemberg et al., 2011; Chaos Report, 2020).

In the 21st century, in reaction to the low level of IT projects success rates, agile methodologies emerged as a new way of managing software development projects. In agile methodologies, the focus is on flexibility and customer involvement. Even though the values for agile projects are different, success criteria for agile projects are similar to those used for traditional software development projects. They include delivering the project on time, budget and scope (Project management success), and product-success-related criteria such as customer satisfaction, value to the customer, impact on supplier organization, creating new businesses, learning and sustaining the supplier business. There are also two identified major differences in the perception of success between agile and traditional software development projects. One of the differences is in the frequency of the success evaluation. Performance measurement evaluation is carried out on a regular basis after each increment in agile projects. That helps build mutual trust and customer involvement in agile projects. Secondly, there is a stronger emphasis on ensuring customer satisfaction in agile development projects (Siddique & Hussein, 2016).

There is a limited number of studies investigating the CSF and their impact on the success of agile software development projects. In a well-known study, Chow & Cao (2008) compiled a list of 36 CSF for agile projects and classified them into five categories: organizational, people, process, technical, and project. The review of the current literature on CSF for agile projects revealed that the CSF for agile software development projects are different from traditional software development projects to some extent. There is higher importance on people-related factors and customer involvement in agile development projects. An agile process supporting collaboration and communication is another important critical factor (Tam et al., 2020; Bergman & Karwowski 2019).

REFERENCES

Abylova, V., & Salykova, L. (2019). Critical success factors in project management: A comprehensive review. *PM World Journal*, *8*(5), 1–13.

Atkinson, R. (1999). Project Management: Cost, Time and Quality, Two Best Guesses and A Phenomenon, Its Time to Accept Other Success Criteria. *International Journal of Project Management*, *17*(6), 337–342. doi:10.1016/S0263-7863(98)00069-6

Belassi, W., & Tukel, O. I. (1996). A new framework for determining success/failure factors in projects. *International Journal of Project Management*, *14*(3), 141–151. doi:10.1016/0263-7863(95)00064-X

Bergmann, T., & Karwowski, W. (2019). Agile Project Management and Project Success: A Literature Review. In J. I. Kantola, S. Nazir, & T. Barath (Eds.), *Advances in Human Factors, Business Management and Society. AHFE 2018. Advances in Intelligent Systems and Computing* (Vol. 783). Springer., doi:10.1007/978-3-319-94709-9_39

Campanelli, A. S., & Parreiras, F. S. (2015). Agile methods tailoring – A systematic literature review. *Journal of Systems and Software*, *110*, 85–100. doi:10.1016/j.jss.2015.08.035

Castro, M. S., Bahli, B., Barcaui, A., & Figueiredo, R. (2021). Does one project success measure fit all? An empirical investigation of Brazilian projects. *International Journal of Managing Projects in Business*, *14*(3), 788–805. doi:10.1108/IJMPB-01-2020-0028

Chan, A. P., Scott, D., & Edmond, W. M. (2002). Framework of Success Criteria for Design/Build Projects. *Journal of Management Engineering*, *18*(3), 120–128. doi:10.1061/(ASCE)0742-597X(2002)18:3(120)

Chow, T., & Cao, D. (2008). A Survey of Critical Success Factors in Agile Software Projects. *Journal of Systems and Software, 81*(6), 961 – 971. . doi:10.1016/j.jss.2007.08.020

Davies, T. J. C. (2002). The "real" success factors on projects. *International Journal of Project Management*, *20*(3), 185–190. doi:10.1016/S0263-7863(01)00067-9

Davis, K. (2018). Reconciling the views of project success: A multiple stakeholder model. *Project Management Journal*, *49*(5), 1–10. doi:10.1177/8756972818786663

Gu, V. C., Hoffman, J. J., Cao, Q., & Schniederjans, M. J. (2014). The effects of organizational culture and environmental pressures on IT project performance: a moderation perspective. *International Journal of Project Management, 32*(7), 1170-1181. . doi:10.1016/j.ijproman.2013.12.003

Ika, L. (2009). Project Success as a Topic in Project Management Journals. *Project Management Journal*, *40*(4), 6–19. doi:10.1002/pmj.20137

Iriarte, C., & Bayona, S. (2020). IT projects success factors: A literature review. *International Journal of Information Systems and Project Management*, *8*(2), 49–78. doi:10.12821/ijispm080203

Jugdev, K., & Müller, R. (2005). A Retrospective look at our Evolving Understanding of Project Success. *Project Management Journal, 36*(4), 19 - 31. . doi:10.1177/875697280503600403

Kendra, K., & Taplin, L. J. (2004). Project Success: A Cultural Framework. *Project Management Journal, 35*(1), 30 – 45. . doi:10.1177/875697280403500104

Kerzner, H. R. (1987). In search of excellence in Project management. *Journal of Systems Management, 38*(2), 30 - 40.

Kerzner, H. R. (2013). *Project Management: A Systems Approach to Planning, Scheduling, and Controlling* (12th ed.). Wiley.

Marzagao, D. S. L., & Carvalho, M. M. (2016). Critical success factors for six sigma projects. *International Journal of Project Management*, *34*(8), 1505–1518. doi:10.1016/j.ijproman.2016.08.005

Nasir, M. H., Sahibuddin, S., Ahmad, R., & Mohd, S. S. (2015). How the PMBOK Addresses Critical Success Factors for Software Projects: A Multi-round Delphi Study. *Journal of Software*, *10*(15), 1283–1300. doi:10.17706/jsw.10.11.1283-1300

Oseyi-Kyei, R., & Chan, A. P. C. (2017). Comparative analysis of the success criteria for public-private partnership projects in Ghana and Hong Kong. *Project Management Journal*, *48*(4), 80–92. doi:10.1177/875697281704800407

Pacagnella, A. C., Da Silva, S. L., Pacifico, O., Ignacio, P. D. A., & Da Silva, A. L. (2019). Critical success factors for project manufacturing environments. *Project Management Journal, 50*(2), 1–16. doi:10.1177/8756972819827670

Palcic, I., & Buchmeister, B. (2012). Project Success in Slovenian Companies. In *DAAAM International Scientific Book.* DAAAM International. doi:10.2507/daaam.scibook.2012.05

Pankratz, O., & Basten, D. (2014). Ladder to success - eliciting project managers' perceptions of IS project success criteria. *International Journal of Information Systems and Project Management, 2*(2), 5 – 24. doi:10.12821/ijispm020201

Pinto, J. K., & Slevin, D. P. (1988a). Project Success: Definitions and Measurement Techniques. *Project Management Journal, 19*(1), 67–72.

Pinto, J. K., & Slevin, D. P. (1988b). Critical Success Factors Across the Project Life Cycle. *Project Management Journal, 19*(3), 67–74.

Prabhakar, G. P. (2008). What is Project Success: A Literature Review. *International Journal of Business and Management, 3*(9), 3–10. doi:10.5539/ijbm.v3n9p3

Project Management Institute (PMI). (2020). *Pulse of Profession 2019.* Project Management Institute. Available: https://www.pmi.org/learning/thought-leadership/pulse

Project Management Institute (PMI). (2017). *A Guide to the Project Management Body of Knowledge (PMBOK Guide)* (6th ed.). Project Management Institute.

Shenhar, A. J., & Wideman, R. (2020). Optimizing Success By Matching Management Style to Project Type. *PM World Journal, 9*(11), 1 – 21.

Siddique, L., & Hussein, B. A. (2016). A qualitative study of success criteria in Norwegian agile software projects from suppliers' perspective. *International Journal of Information Systems and Project Management, 4*(2), 63–79. doi:10.12821/ijispm040204

Sudhakar, P. G. (2012). A model of critical success factors for software projects. *Journal of Enterprise Information Management, 25*(6), 537–558. doi:10.1108/17410391211272829

Tam, C., Moura, E. J. C., Oliveira, T., & Varajao, J. (2020). The factors influencing the success of on-going agile software development projects. *International Journal of Project Management, 38*(3), 165–176. doi:10.1016/j.ijproman.2020.02.001

The Standish Group International. (2021). *Chaos Report 2020.* The Standish Group International, Inc. Available: https://www.standishgroup.com/about

Williams, T. (2016). Identifying Success Factors in Construction Projects: A Case Study. *Project Management Journal, 47*(1), 97–112. doi:10.1002/pmj.21558

Wurtemberg, L. M. V., Franke, U., Lagerström, R., Ericsson, E., & Lilliesköld, J. (2011). IT project success factors: An experience report. *2011 Proceedings of PICMET '11: Technology Management in the Energy Smart World (PICMET)*, 1 - 10.

Yalegama, S., Chileshe, N., & Ma, T. (2016). Critical success factors for community-driven development projects: A Sri Lankan community perspective. *International Journal of Project Management, 34*(4), 643–659. doi:10.1016/j.ijproman.2016.02.006

Yazici, H. J. (2011). Significance of Organizational Culture in Perceived Project and Business Performance. *Engineering Management Journal, 23*(2), 20 - 29.

ADDITIONAL READING

Association for Project Management (APM). (2019). *APM Body of Knowledge* (7th ed.). Association for Project Management.

Bezdrob, M., Brkic, S., & Gram, M. (2020). The pivotal factors of IT projects' success – Insights for the case of organizations from the Federation of Bosnia and Herzegovina. *International Journal of Information Systems and Project Management, 8*(1), 23–41. doi:10.12821/ijispm080102

Emam, K. E., & Koru, A. G. (2008). A replicated survey of IT Software Project Failures. *IEEE Software, 25*(5), 84–90. doi:10.1109/MS.2008.107

Livesey, P. V. (2016). Insights of project managers into the problems in project management. *Construction Economics and Building, 16*(1), 90–103. doi:10.5130/AJCEB.v16i1.4600

Misra, S. C., Kumar, V., & Kumar, U. (2009). Identifying some important success factors in adopting agile software development practices. *Journal of Systems and Software, 82*(11), 1869–1890. doi:10.1016/j.jss.2009.05.052

Ozturan, M., Gursoy, F., & Ceken, B. (2019). An empirical analysis on the effects of investment assessment methods on IS/IT project success. *International Journal of Information Systems and Project Management, 7*(4), 33–52. doi:10.12821/ijispm070402

Saleh, Y., & Alshawi, M. (2005). An alternative model for measuring the success of IS projects: The GPIS model. *Journal of Enterprise Information Management, 18*(1), 47–63. doi:10.1108/17410390510571484

Sanchez, O. P., Terlizzi, M. A., & Moraes, H. R. (2017). Cost and time project management success factors for information systems development projects. *International Journal of Project Management, 35*(8), 1608–1626. doi:10.1016/j.ijproman.2017.09.007

Varajao, J., Domingues, C., Riberio, P., & Paiva, A. (2014). Failures in software project management – are we alone? A comparison with construction industry. *Journal of Modern Project Management, 2*(1), 22–27. doi:10.19255/59

KEY TERMS AND DEFINITIONS

Agile Software Development: A specific form of software development methodology focusing on providing flexibility in development processes and ensuring customer satisfaction.

Client Satisfaction: It is a measure of how the output of the project meets or surpasses the expectations.

Critical Success Factors: A management term for an element necessary for an organization or project to reach the mission.

Information Technology: The use of computers to run the operations.

Iron Triangle of Project Management: Three constraints project managers work within are also called the iron triangle of project management. Those constraints are budget, scope, and schedule.

Organizational Validity of the Project Output: Defines whether the output of the project is contributing to an improved level of organizational effectiveness.

Project: A temporary study to generate a unique outcome (product, process, building, software etc.) as a result of interconnected activities.

Project Management Success: Focuses more on cost, time, and scope.

Project Manager: A professional responsible for planning and execution of project activities and managing the project team.

Project Scope: Defines the work included and not included in the project to generate the desired output.

Project Success: Related to the success or failure of the project's outcome.

Project Team: Individuals from different groups with specific knowledge or skill set to carry out the work of the project.

Requirements: A singular documented need that a particular design, product or process aims to satisfy.

Success Criteria: A set of standards or levels by which to judge whether a project has been successful.

Technical Validity of the Project Output: Defines whether the output of the project work in a way it is supposed to.

Chapter 5
Machine Learning and Data Science Project Management From an Agile Perspective:
Methods and Challenges

Murat Pasa Uysal
https://orcid.org/0000-0002-8349-9403
Baskent University, Turkey

ABSTRACT

Successful implementations of machine learning (ML) and data science (DS) applications have enabled innovative business models and brought new opportunities for organizations. On the other hand, research studies report that organizations employing ML and DS solutions are at a high risk of failure and they can easily fall short of their objectives. One major factor is to adopt or tailor a project management method for the specific requirements of ML and DS applications. Therefore, agile project management (APM) may be proposed as a solution. However, there is significantly less study that explores ML and DS project management from an agile perspective. In this chapter, the authors discuss methods and challenges according to the background information and practice areas of ML, DS, and APM. This study can be viewed as an initial attempt to enhance these knowledge and practice domains in view of APM. Therefore, future research efforts will focus on the challenges as well as the experimental implementation of APM methods in real industrial case studies of ML and DS.

INTRODUCTION

Contemporary developments in cutting - edge technologies, along with the advances in Artificial Intelligence (AI), have paved the way for various integrated and sophisticated systems. The proliferation of AI systems has enabled new business models and brought opportunities for organizations. The successful implementations of AI can have a great impact on the activities and competitiveness of an organization. On the other hand, there is also an overestimation of their benefits, opportunities, and return on invest-

DOI: 10.4018/978-1-7998-7872-8.ch005

ment of AI projects. How to realize AI as a long - term and stable solution is difficult, and defining the required procedures is not clear. To that aim, Bughin et al. (2017) indicate the factors for transforming an organization towards AI as: a good and reasonable business case, "the adaptation of business processes to the capabilities of AI", effective and efficient AI environment, techniques and tools, solid data ecosystem, and organizational culture. Ransbotham et al. (2017) report the challenges in the adoption of AI systems as follows:

- Difficulties in the acquisition of AI - related skills and knowledge,
- "Competing of AI projects with other projects in the company",
- Safety and security aspects of systems using AI,
- Cultural and organizational barriers in the AI adoption,
- Limited technological capabilities,
- Lack of leadership and management support for AI initiatives,
- Unclear business cases for AI projects.

In this context, Machine Learning (ML), which has a close relationship with the Data Science (DS) discipline, can be viewed as one of the most popular subfields of AI. However, recent studies reveal the facts about the failure of ML and DS projects, inadequate return on investment, and unsatisfactory results. It is reported that organizations employing AI solutions with big data are at a high risk of failure and may fall short of project objectives (Kelly & Kaskade, 2013). There may be, of course, various domain / process / technology - specific causes when we view this issue from the perspectives of different disciplines, such as DS, Computer Science (CS), and Software Engineering (SE). Ponsard et al. (2017) and Saltz et al. (2019) indicate that the majority of ML or DS research studies focuses on technical aspects rather than project management issues. More than 80% of data scientist state that an explicit process model is not followed, and they note that more systematic methods would improve their performances. Therefore, one major factor has been adopting or tailoring a project management method suitable for the idiosyncratic requirements of ML and DS applications (Saltz, 2015; Cao, 2017; Nalchigar et al., 2021). Studies refer to various issues, however, there is significantly less research, which explores the DS and ML project management from an agile perspective. The objective of this chapter is, therefore, to present and discuss the findings from the literature according to the solutions, background of the ML, DS, and Agile Project Management (APM) knowledge domains.

BACKGROUND

Data Science

The term big data refers to the collection of large and complex data sets that are difficult to process by using traditional data management methods, tools, and techniques. Volume (size of data), variety (diversity and types of data), velocity (speed of data generation), and veracity (accuracy of data) are the main characteristics of big data. Therefore, it becomes more and more difficult to use big data resources for a maximum advantage when the amount of data grows, variety, and velocity increases. The types of data may be structured, unstructured, machine - generated, graph - based, streaming, and in the forms of audio, video, or image. DS has evolved from the traditional data management and statistics disciplines

(Cielen et al., 2016). As being multidisciplinary, it borrows some of its techniques from computer science, uses complex algorithms, and includes the processes to build predictive models. Thus, meaningful information can be derived to make better business decisions and valuable insights can be inferred from the knowledge extracted. The main steps of a DS project are as follows:

- **Problem Definition:** It is important to define a problem, set a research goal, and identify the organizational benefits and how a data science project can contribute to the business processes. Understanding the context of the research is highly critical for project success. Therefore, a project charter document can help to frame the mission, scope, timeline, deliverables, success criteria, data, resources, costs, risks, project team, and approval committee.
- **Data Acquisition:** Data can be defined as the observations of real - world objects and phenomena. The concept data corresponds to a collection of discrete entities, descriptions of things, events, facts, measurements, words, numbers, etc. (Zheng & Casari, 2018). Each part of data provides a small and limited aspect of reality, and thus, the collection of the data parts gives us the big picture related to the research problem. For the success of any DS and ML project, it is critical to collect and process a large volume of data. The data can also be in different forms, which may range from text files to databases, provided by various online or offline data sources. Completeness, timeliness, accuracy, and consistency are the core criteria, and thus, assuring the data quality is an important issue.
- **Data Processing (Cleansing, Transforming, and Integrating Data):** This stage mainly focuses on the processes: preparing the research data, combining the data retrieved from different sources, transforming and integrating it, cleansing, and removing possible errors. As being labour - intensive, data processing can take up much of the project time, which may be up to 80%. Therefore, it is extremely important since data is also used for other critical processes, such as, representing the research problem, exploring and analysing the data, and determining the algorithms in the form of learning models. The success of any DS and ML project is directly dependent on the quality of this process. The main purpose is to bring the data to a common standard. As the data is better, the models will perform better.

Different types of errors have to be eliminated during data processing. Data entry errors, missing values, impossible values, redundant white spaces, and outliers are among the common errors. Miss interpretation of the data, different units of measurement, deviation from a data coding base, and different levels of aggregation can also cause inconsistencies between data sets used in the project. Missing data can be omitted or imputed from a static or statistical distribution. Transforming data into a suitable form simplifies data modelling, analysis, exploration as well as estimation processes. Too many features or variables can make the data science process difficult to manage, and thus, they may not add new information or contribute to the models. In this case, it may be better to reduce the number of research variables. In any case, it is important to note that every type of data error and inconsistencies between data sources have to be corrected as early as possible.

- **Conducting Exploratory Data Analysis (EDA):** EDA, as being a preliminary and iterative data assessment process, is conducted to have a deeper and better understanding of the research data. Its main components are statistical analysis, summary statistics, data visualization tools, and techniques (Muller & Massaron, 2015). We try to describe the data, seek relations between variables, identify known and unknown situations and patterns, and report the results by means of different types of graphs, tables, plots, and various data visualization techniques. EDA produces useful information, and thus, processing this information produces useful knowledge, such as inferential and correlation statistics. It is also required for forming research hypotheses, determining and developing predictive models, and evaluating these models by calculating their accuracies. Therefore, EDA gives direction to the model development stage and helps us become more effective in the subsequent analysis and modelling processes (Mukhiya & Ahmed, 2020).

- **Building Models:** The main purpose of this stage is to use, design, or build the models for developing the best solution to the research problem by using prediction, classification, and clustering algorithms. Modelling is an iterative process, which includes the selection of suitable algorithms that can be fit to the data, execution of the models, comparison and evaluation of the results, and making decisions respectively. The model development process is very similar and has a close relation to the one included in ML projects. Visual languages or programming languages, such as Python, Java, R, and C++ can be used during the modelling process.
- **Presenting Results:** After a successful data analysis or development of a well - performing model, we may either present the results or develop a software application integrated with our prediction model. However, in the future, it is highly probable that we will have to modify the model or software application depending on the new requirements or changes in the input data. Therefore, the application of monitoring and maintenance procedures is critical for assuring the long - term success of DS projects.

Machine Learning

Machine Learning (ML) is a branch or subfield of AI and it is defined as "a field of study that gives computers the ability to learn without being explicitly programmed (Samuel, 1959)". ML studies the data and algorithms as the learning models that can learn to perform tasks by relying on patterns existing in data. While it is closely related to statistics, applied mathematics, and CS, ML can be linked to the model development of the DS projects. DS uses an algorithm as a sequence of statistical and mathematical processing steps for modelling. In ML, however, the algorithm is first trained to find features or complex patterns in a massive amount of training data. Next, this model is used to make predictions or decisions based on testing data. As the performance of an algorithm becomes better, the predictions or decisions would be more accurate. Therefore, data and an appropriate algorithm together form a model that has to be fit into the solution space. The type of learning or a ML model is often categorized into supervised learning (SL), unsupervised learning (UL), and reinforcement learning (RL).

Steps of Machine Learning (ML)

The main stages of a ML project are as follows:

- Problem definition,
- Data acquisition,
- Data processing (cleansing, labelling, transforming, and integrating data),
- Feature engineering (extraction),
- Model training,

- Model testing, validation, and evaluation,
- Deployment and monitoring.

Some of the stages of ML projects, such as problem definition, data acquisition, and data processing share the same characteristics as the stages of DS projects mentioned above. ML can also be directly linked to the modelling stages of the DS projects. Therefore, we briefly discuss the feature extraction, model training and testing, model evaluation, model deployment and monitoring stages as follows:

- **Feature Engineering (Extraction):** This stage comes after the data acquisition and data processing stages. The terms Feature Engineering (FE), feature construction, and feature extraction are sometimes used interchangeably. FE is the process of formulating the most appropriate features from raw data and making them available for the modelling, training, and testing stages of ML (Zheng & Casari, 2018). It is simply the process of transforming unstructured and raw data components or elements into suitable data formats that can be used by learning algorithms / models. FE can also be part of data acquisition and data processing as well as model building phases. Data help us to understand real - world objects, reality, events, or phenomena that have identifying features. In ML, a feature can be defined as a representation of raw data, which may be a scalar (numeric value) or an ordered list of scalars. ML algorithms can be regarded as the mathematical formulas or learning models that relate the numeric quantities to each other while they describe the relationships from various aspects of the data. ML applications try to fit these learning models to the data to make predictions and to have a deeper insight.

Features play an intermediary role between data and models. Therefore, they have to be derived from the available data carefully. However, features may be scattered among various data sources since combining multiple data inputs may improve the models' performances. Filtering, wrapping, and embedding methods are used for feature selection. Filtering removes the features that are not useful for the models. Wrapper methods allow the use of subsets of features. Embedding methods are used during model training processes. Sometimes some modelling techniques are used to derive features, which in turn whose output becomes the input of another model. Consequently, we may remove some of the data because of irrelevance, overload, or redundancy. In this case, FE methods that are performed before model training and testing can have adverse effects, which can cause problems such as over - fitting and low performance.

The procedures on the FE and data processing stages may be complicated, time and resource - consuming. Therefore, the majority of time is spent on data processing and FE activities. To that aim, an ML pipeline can be used as a method for automating ML workflows to develop effective and efficient learning models. ML pipelines can encapsulate multiple sequential steps, organization - specific practices, and best practices. They are highly critical for both maintaining multiple learning models and integrating them with different software applications. The automated ML pipelines enable the cooperation and coordination in data science and ML teams, automated model development and testing, and version control.

- **Model Training:** As a solution to a ML research problem, a model is the combination of an algorithm and data with suitable features. Therefore, models have to be correct, interpretable applicable, maintainable and represent the problem domain as precisely as possible. Every ML model is created after a training process where appropriate algorithms. They are fed with training and testing data to build the best mathematical representation between the data and target. The learning algorithms search patterns in the training data to map the input to the target, and thus, they make decisions or predictions "without being explicitly programmed to do so (Amazon, 2021)". A complex problem, data, or business case sometimes may require chaining or combining multiple models and techniques. In this case, the output of a model becomes the input for another model and this process is defined as ensemble learning. Supervised learning (SL), Unsupervised Learning (UL), Semi - Supervised Learning (SSL), and Reinforcement Learning (RL) are the main types of learning methods in ML (Muller & Guido, 2017).

- **Supervised Learning:** SL occurs when the model learns from labelled training data to make predictions. This is similar to student learning with examples of input / output pairs under the supervision of an instructor. The learning model is presented the training data with example inputs and corresponding labelled outputs, and then it maps the new testing or unseen data to new outputs (VanderPlas, 2017). The algorithm is said to have learned the task and generalized when it improves the accuracy of its predictions over time. SL algorithms are mainly employed for classification and regression problems. Predicting a discrete value or a class label from a predefined list of possibilities is the goal of classification tasks. However, if the prediction is a continuous or a floating - point number, and it has continuity between possible outcomes, then it is said to be a regression task. Build a training data set for SL often requires human effort and data processing procedures, but it pays off and thus, speeds up and automates the rest of the project work. k - Nearest Neighbour (k - NN), Linear Regression, Logistic Regression, Polynomial Regression, Support - Vector Machines, Decision Tree, Random Forest, Naive Bayes, and Neural Networks are the major SL algorithms (Muller & Guido, 2017; Fenner, 2020). For example, k - NN is easy to understand and maybe the simplest algorithm, however, the prediction can be slow if the number of features or the number of data samples is very large. Decision trees can be used for both classification and regression tasks. Ensembles are the methods that combine multiple ML algorithms to create more powerful learning models.
- **Unsupervised Learning:** In UL, the models learn from the data without reference to labels. The main purpose is to identify commonalities in the input data and then to determine the patterns, clusters, and distinct groups. These types of algorithms can also be used in the EDA processes to have a better understanding of the raw data. UL models may include the dimensionality reduction (DR) tasks for a more concise representation of fewer features that summarize important characteristics of the data. One common application of the UL algorithms would be the pre - processing of SL models to improve the SL models' accuracy and their performances. However, one important challenge is as UL is sensitive to the scaling of the training large data, and thus, we may not be sure about how well the model is or what the right output should be. Comparing outcomes between different models is another challenge. The major UL algorithms are k - Means, k - Medoids, DBSCAN, Principal Component Analysis, Hierarchical Clustering, and Hidden Markov. For example, k - Means is one of the commonly used and simplest clustering algorithms. It finds the cluster centres that represent certain regions of the raw data.
- **Reinforcement Learning:** The idea behind RL is learning by interacting with a dynamic environment (Sutton & Barto, 2015). This is similar to a computer program that has to perform various tasks to achieve a certain goal. RL is like learning by trial and error. It occurs when the model learns from labelled data through experimentation by giving negative or positive feedbacks. The system, like a software agent, gives feedback to change its status when it navigates its problem space or environment. RL models come into play when examples of desired outputs or behaviours

are not available, however, it is still possible to score examples of behaviours according to some criterion (Barto & Dietterich, 2004). In ML, RL algorithms use dynamic programming techniques and their environments may be represented by using finite Markov decision processes and Monte Carlo methods.

- **Model Testing, Validation, and Evaluation:** After training ML models, testing, validating, evaluating, and selecting the best deployment model are important tasks. Model validation can be carried out by using quantitative and qualitative methods. While quantitative techniques focus on data and models, qualitative techniques emphasize the ML process life cycle (Zheng, 2015). Different ML models, such as classification, regression, and clustering have also different performance or evaluation metrics. For instance, the accuracy, precision - recall, confusion matrix, area under the curve, and log - loss metrics are used for the classification tasks. The root - mean - square error is the most commonly used evaluation metric for regression tasks. The cross - validation strategy divides the data into parts and uses each part one time as test data while the rest is uses as training data. The hold - out strategy is based on training the data on the larger part while validation is done by using the smaller and randomly hold - out data set. Testing is conducted with separate and unused data. A good ML model should have good predictive power as well as it should generalize well to the unseen data. In the SL process, over - fitting and under - fitting may be the two common modelling errors for the classification tasks. Over - fitting occurs when the model is too complex, and thus the algorithm learns too much by memorizing the training data but displays low performance against the testing data. In the opposite case, under - fitting occurs when the model is too simple and if it cannot detect all the aspects of the data.
- **Deployment and Monitoring:** This is the last, but perhaps the most tangible part of a ML project from the viewpoint of users, customers, and all stakeholders. This stage can be as simple as producing only the reports or as complex as developing software applications and integrating the ML model with various systems. Another important issue is about how to monitor and measure the benefits from the deployed ML solution. Therefore, a detailed plan would be helpful for the day - to - day business actions as well as performing maintenance activities.

Machine Learning and Data Science Team

ML and DS teams usually deliver complex projects that may consist of the various activities belonging to the system engineering, software engineering, and data engineering knowledge domains. Although project roles may differ and mostly depend on the project management methods adopted by the teams, the roles related to system engineering, software engineering, and data engineering are the common ones. It is important to note that project stakeholders, users, business analysts, system analysts, data scientists, and data engineers exist in both ML and DS projects (Dubovikov, 2019). A business analyst acts as a business expert and helps to understand business requirements and problem domain, and may prepare the requirements document. A system analyst may define and design the system and software integration documents. A data engineer can take on the tasks, such as data preparation and data processing, especially in projects requiring the use of big data, very complicated, and large - scale data sources. A data scientist, who acts as a researcher, performs statistical analysis, uses existing algorithms and develops DS models. More complex or integrated projects may also include software architect, backend, and frontend / software developers.

Agile Project Management

In the project management knowledge domain, transparency, customer focus, adaptability, ownership, effective leadership, and continuous improvement are regarded as the important attributes of agile processes. Thus, agility requires the application of this set of agile principles to project management endeavours. APM is an iterative approach to software development that focuses on the production of working software with manageable tasks in short iterations. It attaches importance to continuous communication and customer feedback, motivated teamwork, quick response to changes or new requirements. The followings present the values that are given:

- "Individuals and interactions over processes and tools",
- "Working software over comprehensive documentation",
- "Customer collaboration over contract negotiation",
- "Responding to change over following a plan",

The APM approach is declared as a manifesto with the following agile principles (Agile Manifesto, 2001):

- "Our highest priority is to satisfy the customer through early and continuous delivery of valuable software."
- "Welcome changing requirements, even late in development. Agile processes harness change for the customer's competitive advantage."
- "Deliver working software frequently, from a couple of weeks to a couple of months, with a preference for the shorter timescale."
- "Business people and developers must work together daily throughout the project."
- "Build projects around motivated individuals, give them the environment and support they need and trust them to get the job done."
- "The most efficient and effective method of conveying information with and within a development team is face - to - face conversation."
- "Working software is the primary measure of progress."
- "Agile processes promote sustainable development. The sponsors, developers and users should be able to maintain a constant pace indefinitely."
- "Continuous attention to technical excellence and good design enhances agility."
- "Simplicity - the art of maximizing the amount of work not done - is essential."
- "The best architectures, requirements and designs emerge from self - organizing teams."
- "At regular intervals, the team reflects on how to become more effective, then tunes and adjusts its behaviour accordingly."

Scrum

Scrum is regarded as one of the most popular agile software development methods. It adopts an iterative and incremental development approach, and it organizes the overall work in cycles (Sutherland & Schwaber, 2017). Each cycle is time - boxed and called Sprint, lasts from two to six weeks with an unalterable goal. Each sprint includes all the software development activities. Sprint Planning Meeting is the first activity, in which the product features are selected from the product backlog and they are named Sprint Backlog. A Sprint goal is achieved during Sprint Execution. Short Stand - up Meetings are conducted to monitor the daily project progress. Toward the end of the Sprint, the Sprint Review and the Sprint Retrospective Meetings are held as inspect - and - adapt activities. The newly created product increment is reviewed and demonstrated to the project stakeholders in the Sprint Review. While the Sprint Review focuses on the product deliverables and product itself, the Sprint Retrospective reflects on the Scrum processes used to build the product. Product Owner, Scrum Master, and Development Team are the main roles in Scrum. The Product Owner is responsible for creating a prioritized list of requirements in the form of User Stories. The Development Team determines how to build the product features in the Sprint Backlog. The Scrum Master acts as a Scrum guide, facilitator, and coach both to the Product Owner and Development Team.

Kanban

Kanban is a simple project management method that has close links to lean thinking and just - in - time scheduling. It has no specifically defined process framework and roles, however, meetings can be on - demand (Brechner, 2015). Teams are free to use their process models as long as they support Kanban principles. Using a task board, visualizing the workflow, limiting the work - in - progress, measuring and managing the flow by implementing quick feedback loops are the core principles. Kanban aims to maximize value and minimize waste, and therefore, it balances the work demands with the team's available capacity to avoid bottlenecks.

Data - Driven Scrum

Data - Driven Scrum (DDS) is proposed as a framework for agile data science projects. It integrates the basic structure of Scrum with some of the principles of Kanban. It assumes a DS project as the sequence of iterative experimentations (DDS, 2021). The goal of each iteration should be to have an experiment in mind, conducting it, and finally observing the results. Each cycle includes three successive steps: creating experimentation, observing its performance, and analysing the results. The team - works (experiments) are executed iteratively on a product backlog with flexible deadlines until they are done. Therefore, some of the DDS's features, such as roles, events, and the use of item backlogs, are similar to Scrum. However, variable length iteration, flexible high - level task estimation, and iteration - independent meetings are the main differences. Consequently, decoupling meetings from the iteration, high - level item estimation, and capability - based execution are regarded as the core principles of DDS.

Team Data Science Process

Microsoft proposes Team Data Science Process (TDSP) as an agile and iterative method for data analytics and AI application development (TDSP, 2021). It is the combination of software engineering practices and DS methods, such as Scrum, Cross - Industry Standard Process for Data Mining (CRISP - DM), and Knowledge Discovery in Databases (KDD). Business understanding, data acquisition and understanding, modelling (feature engineering, model training, model evaluation), and deployment are the major stages of TDSP. Similar to a software engineering project, it defines these roles: solution architect, project manager, data engineer, data scientist, application developer, and project lead.

Crisp - DM

As being one of the oldest methods, but still having wide acceptance, CRISP - DM was initially proposed as a standard process model for data mining projects (CRISP - DM, 2000). It is defined with a hierarchical process model that includes four levels of abstraction. The CRISP - DM reference model provides the life cycle of a DS project, which is broken down into six phases. These are business understanding, data understanding, data preparation, modelling, evaluation, and deployment respectively. Although these phases, tasks, and their discrete steps are performed in order, the sequence of the phases and required tasks is not rigid. CRISP - DM provides comprehensive guidance and detailed descriptions of processes however, it has not defined project roles.

MAIN FOCUS OF THE CHAPTER

In terms of data processing and modelling, ML and DS projects have much in common. However, the review of literature indicates that the studies reporting various challenges can be grouped into the DS, ML, and Software Engineering (SE) fields. Current applications of ML and DS projects mostly adopt the models very similar to the KDD and CRISP - DM methods, which have not significantly evolved in the past two decades (Saltz et al. 2017). DS projects are usually task - focused and adopt the traditional step - wise or linear approaches. Although CRISP - DM may be the oldest method, there is no agreement on what type of a DS process model is suitable for the contemporary requirements of agile ML and DS applications.

ML and DS projects are usually managed by using ad hoc methods since any process maturity model is not defined. A low level of process maturity is one of the causes of incomplete or unsatisfactory projects (Kelly & Kaskade, 2013). Therefore, this situation makes the planning and coordination tasks as the main challenges for the projects (Saltz et al., 2018). Additionally, there is a clear need to have a consensus on which the critical success factors and key performance indicators would be suitable for both ML and DS projects (Gupte, 2018). In the same line, Clemmedsson (2018) pre - sets the results of case studies about the companies conducting ML projects. Thus, lack of competence, management support, stakeholder inclusion, poorly estimated budgets, and schedules are found to be the main causes of failures.

ML and DS projects naturally have a focus on the timeliness, quality, availability of data, which are different from other types of SE and information system projects (Kelly & Kaskade, 2013). Furthermore, the rapid growth in big data requires additional computing and storage resources along with the data processing environments (Larson and Chang, 2016). Having not appropriate and sufficient data, wrong data forms and feature selection, problems in model or algorithm use, model training biased, over - fitting, incomplete testing are amongst the major pitfalls of ML projects (Clemmedsson, 2018). Along with the developments in technology and big data resources, data storage and data management are the serious sources of risk affecting the overall project success. Moreover, adaptability, scalability, safety, and privacy as the additional challenges for the development of large - scale ML systems in practical industrial settings (Lwakatare et al., 2020).

The data processing terms, such as "data management", "data engineering", and "data analytics" are used interchangeably (Gartner, 2015). However, these tasks involve different skills and knowledge, and there are also no clear descriptions of the roles in the projects. Coordination within the team and project stakeholders is another issue (Espinosa and Armour, 2016). The success of projects is highly dependent on the technical skills and knowledge of individuals who are expected to be experts on data processing, algorithms, and application development at the same time. Therefore, a project team using immature ML and DS processes would be highly dependent on its senior data scientists or expert ML practitioners.

Behaviours of software systems are initially defined and specified by using various design models and programming codes. However, this is reverse in ML systems where system behaviours are continuously learned after processing the training and testing data sets. Minor changes in the system input can drastically change the system behaviours, which means that ML projects need specific techniques for testing, validation, and verification procedures. Comprehensive and detailed requirement analysis and specification may not be possible for ML at the beginning. Moreover, the black - box nature of ML algorithms, makes the explanations difficult for both technical and non - technical stakeholders, such as "what is possible and what is not" (Ishikawa and Yoshioka, 2019).

In a controlled experiment, Saltz et al. (2017) compared the DS teams using Scrum, Kanban, CRISP - DM, and baseline project management methods. Understanding the data and client requirements, task estimation were the challenges for the teams using Scrum. Requirements specifications were better and conduction of the projects were natural for the teams using CRISP - DM, however, they delayed the analytics, modelling, and coding processes. Although baseline teams were not given guidance and did not use a specific DS method, they used a management method that was similar in their previous classes. Interestingly, they also evolved to CRISP - DM and found it better than Scrum. An interesting finding was as the Scrum framework could not be fully utilized by the DS teams. For Scrum teams, estimation was difficult, and therefore, these teams did not have much confidence in how to complete tasks in the sprints. Finally, Kanban was perceived slightly better than the other project management methods due to its simplicity, visualization, continuous improvement, and flexible approach.

Estimating what can be done within a sprint may be a serious issue for ML and DS projects adopting sprint - based Scrum. A fixed - length sprint can cause to include unrelated and unrealistic backlog items (DSPM, 2021). For example, exploratory data analysis or model evaluation may require longer or smaller chunks of backlog items. Therefore, spring lengths have to be flexible and need to be modified according to the requirements of ML or DS experimentation procedures (DDS, 2021). On the other hand, Kanban does not describe project roles, process - specific guidelines, tools, and techniques. This situation may provide the teams with flexibility and using their customized process models, however, it can also cause misunderstanding and uncertainty, which may bring additional implementation problems (Brechner, 2015). Aforementioned, CRISP - DM is relatively more mature and provides a clear description of the phases and a sequence of tasks for the DS project. However, it still owns deficiencies and lacks the agile benefits needed by contemporary DS and ML projects. Therefore, Microsoft claims that TDSP leverages the fixed - length sprints of Scrum while addressing the role definition weakness of the CRISP - DM method (TDSP, 2021).

Requirement processes, team performance management, quality management, risk management, and maintenance have to be core aspects both for SE and ML. However, requirements specification for ML is much more challenging (Rahman et al., 2019). SE extends its activities beyond data processing and model development, and therefore, it focuses on the software development life cycle and system evolution. On the other hand, ML applications emphasize the enhancement of model development activities and techniques mainly related to data processing and algorithms. One important difficulty is the aligning and synchronizing data processing and model development with the software development processes (Amershi et al., 2019). Some studies indicate that the dynamic and complex context for the design, development, and maintenance of large - scale ML - based software systems highly differs from the traditional and agile software development contexts. Therefore, we need to integrate ML and DS workflow management into the SE best practices (Lwakatare et al., 2020).

A research study conducted by a Microsoft team presents the results of a case study on SE challenges for ML and AI projects (Amershi et al., 2019). Accordingly, data discovery and management can be much more difficult and complicated than the other types of SE activities. Model customization and reuse require different skills than that are found in SE teams. Since SE, ML and AI modules can be entangled in various complex ways, ML modules may be more challenging than the traditional software modules. Automating the processes, such as data aggregation, synthesizing, feature extraction, and pipeline are the common concerns for the teams. Furthermore, integrating software development infrastructure with ML development would speed up the experimentations.

In another study, Tsoy & Staples (2020) explore the critical success factors in agile analytics projects. They find that team environment, organizational environment, and management commitment form the organizational success factors. People success factors include team capability and customer involvement. Project definition and project management processes form the process success factors. Agile software techniques and delivery strategies compose the technical factors. Project nature, project type, and project schedule are also included in the project success factors. In the same line, Brasjö & Lindovsky (2019) point out the importance of organizational transformation to assure the success of ML and DS projects.

SOLUTIONS AND RECOMMENDATIONS

Hybrid Methods

When adopting the agile principles, it is possible to customize APM according to organizational needs or DS and ML project requirements. This, of course, depends on organizational culture, teams' own experiences, and the context of DS and ML projects. Brasjö & Lindovsky (2019) report that CRIS - DM, Scrum, Kanban, and TDSP have been used with various modifications in ML projects. Saltz & Suthrland (2019) propose a more structured and repeatable process model by integrating lean Kanban with Scrum - like iterations. Hybrid approaches can combine different types of PM methods, where the agile and plan - driven may be the ends of a scale. Some studies report the similar effectiveness of hybrid methods to fully APM methods (Gemino et al., 2021).

The plan - driven methods may be preferred for the projects that have predictable tasks and practices, well - understood and achievable project objectives. Adopting only a plan - driven method may be rigid or inflexible, on the other hand, using an only agile method may not be suitable for complex systems with interdependent components (Kneuper, 2018). Although there may be potential contributions, there are still some limitations of hybrid methods as well. First of all, there are no explicit guidelines, theoretical and practical background for forming the hybrid methods for the characteristic requirements of DS and ML projects. For example, Sithambaram et al. (2021) present the challenges and issues that impact the success of agile and hybrid projects, and thus, group them into four categories of organization, people, process, and technology.

FUTURE RESEARCH DIRECTIONS

This study can be viewed as an initial attempt to enhance the ML and DS project management knowledge domains in view of APM. Therefore, our future research efforts will focus on the following research topics:

- Experimental implementation of APM methods in real industrial ML and DS cases,
- Exploring and / or establishing the theoretical and practical background of hybrid project management methods designed for ML and DS projects,
- Exploring and / or establishing the process maturity models for ML and DS projects.

CONCLUSION

ML and DS are the popular subfields of AI as they have enabled new business models and brought innovative solutions to the various problems of practice areas. Although they can have a great impact on organizations, there are also some facts about the failure of ML and DS projects along with their unsatisfactory results. One major factor has been adopting or customizing APM methods for the specific requirements of ML and DS applications. Consequently, the important insights are as follows:

- There is an overestimation of the opportunities presented by the ML and DS projects.
- Organizations prefer using the project management methods that they are familiar with or similar to the ones in the domain of SE.
- Although they have similar core features, none of the APM methods has wide acceptance in ML and DS.
- Using iterative and adaptable methods helps to address the core challenges that are specific to the requirements of ML and DS projects.
- The lack of a process maturity model is one of the causes of incomplete or unsatisfactory ML and DS projects.
- DS projects are task - focused and usually managed by using ad hoc methods and techniques.
- Scrum - like methods are still popular for ML and DS projects. However, the challenges in task estimation and fixed - length of sprints are the main drawbacks.
- Establishing a manual or automated data or ML pipelines is a major challenge for the fixed - length iterative developments cycles as in Scrum.
- Although Kanban may be perceived as flexible as and easier than the other APM methods, it does not provide process - specific guidelines, tools, and techniques for ML and DS projects.
- As being a relatively new method, DDS may meet the deficiencies of Scrum with its decoupled meetings from iterations, high - level task estimations, and capability - based executions.
- CRISP - DM provides the most comprehensive guidance; however, it does not define project roles and lacks the agile benefits.
- Microsoft's TDSP method combines the SE practices with the agile methods, such as Scrum, CRISP - DM, KDD, and defines the project roles.
- Requirements specification and aligning ML and DS processes with software development are much more difficult. Therefore, there is a clear need for the integration of workflow management into SE practices.

- The terms data engineering, data analytics, and data management are used interchangeably, however, they require different skills and knowledge.
- Finally, automating the software engineering, data collecting, synthesizing, feature extraction, and pipeline processes is also a common concern for ML, DS, and SE teams.

REFERENCES

Agile Manifesto. (2001). *Twelve principles of agile software*. https://agilemanifesto.org

Amazon. (2021). *Training ML models*. https://docs.aws.amazon.com

Amershi, S., Begel, A., Bird, C., DeLine, R., Gall, H., Kamar, E., Nagappan, N., Nushi, B., & Zimmermann, T. (2019). *Software engineering for machine learning: A case study*. Microsoft Research. https://www.microsoft.com

Barto, A. G., & Dietterich, T. G. (2004). Reinforcement Learning and its Relationship to Supervised Learning. In *Handbook of Learning and Approximate Dynamic Programming*. Wiley.

Brasjö, C., & Lindovsky, M. (2019). *Machine learning project management: A study of project requirements and processes in early adoption* (Unpublished MS Thesis). Chalmers University of Technology, Sweden.

Brechner, E. (2015). *Agile Project Management with Kanban*. Microsoft Press.

Bughin, J., & Hazan, E. (2017). Five management strategies for getting the most from AI. *MIT Sloan Management Review*. https://sloanreview.mit.edu/article/five-management-strategies-for-getting-themostfrom-ai

Cao, L. (2017). Data science: Challenges and directions. *Communications of the ACM*, *60*(8), 59–68. doi:10.1145/3015456

Cielen, D., Meysman, A., & Ali, M. (2016). *Introducing data science: Big data, machine learning, and more, using Python tools*. Manning Publications.

Clemmedsson, E. (2018). *Identifying pitfalls in machine learning implementation projects: A case study of four technology - intensive organizations* (Unpublished MS Thesis). Kth Royal Institute of Technology, Sweden.

CRISP - DM. (2000). *CRISP - DM 1.0: Step - by - step data mining guide. The CRISP - DM consortium*. SPSS Publication.

DDS. (2021). *Data driven scrum framework*. https://datadrivenscrum.com

DSPM. (2021). *Data science project management*. https://www.datascience-pm.com

Dubovikov, K. (2019). *Managing Data Science*. Packt Publishing.

Espinosa, J. A., & Armour, F. (2016). The big data analytics gold rush: a research framework for coordination and governance. *Proceedings of Hawaii International Conference on System Sciences (HICSS).* 10.1109/HICSS.2016.141

Fenner, M. E. (2020). *Machine learning with python for everyone.* Pearson Education.

Gartner. (2015). *Gartner says business intelligence and analytics leaders must focus on mind - sets and culture to kick start advanced analytics.* https://www.gartner.com/newsroom/id/3130017

Gemino, A., Reich, B. H., & Serrador, P. M. (2021). Agile, traditional, and hybrid approaches to project success: Is hybrid a poor second choice? *Project Management Journal, 52*(2), 161–175. doi:10.1177/8756972820973082

Gupte, A. (2018). *Determining critical success factors for big data projects* (Unpublished Doctoral Dissertation). Purdue University.

Ishikawa, F., & Yoshioka, N. (2019). How do engineers perceive difficulties in engineering of machine - learning systems? *Proceedings of IEEE / ACM 6th International Workshop on Software Engineering Research and Industrial Practice.*

Kelly, J., & Kaskade, J. (2013). *Cios & big data what your IT team wants you to know.* Infochimps Inc. http://www.infochimps.com

Kneuper, R. (2018). *Software processes and life cycle models.* Springer Nature Switzerland AG.

Larson, D., & Chang, V. (2016). A review and future direction of agile, business intelligence, analytics and data science. *International Journal of Information Management, 36*(5), 700–710. doi:10.1016/j.ijinfomgt.2016.04.013

Lwakatare, L. E., Raj, A., Crnkovic, I., Bosch, J., & Holmström, H. O. (2020). Large - scale machine learning systems in real - world industrial settings: A review of challenges and solutions. *Information and Software Technology, 127*, 106368. doi:10.1016/j.infsof.2020.106368

Mukhiya, S. K., & Ahmed, U. (2020). *Hands - on exploratory data analysis with Python.* Packt Publishing.

Muller, A. C., & Guido, S. (2017). *Introduction to machine learning with Python.* O'Reilly Media, Inc.

Muller, J. P., & Massaron, L. (2015). *Python for data science for dummies.* John Wiley & Sons, Inc.

Nalchigar, S., Yu, E., & Keshavjee, K. (2021). Modelling machine learning requirements from three perspectives: A case report from the healthcare domain. *Requirements Engineering, 34567*, 1–18.

Ponsard, C., Majchrowski, A., Mouton, S., & Touzani, M. (2017). Process guidance for the successful deployment of a big data project: Lessons Learned from Industrial Cases. *Proceedings of IoTBDS*, 350 - 355.

Rahman, S., Rivera, E., Khomh, F., Guéhéneuc, Y. G., & Lehnert, B. (2019). *Machine learning software engineering in practice: An industrial case study.* https://arxiv.org/abs/1906.07154

Ransbotham, S., Kiron, D., Gerbert, P., & Reeves, M. (2017). Reshaping Business with Artificial Intelligence. *MIT Sloan Management Review.* https://sloanreview.mit.edu

Saltz, J. (2015). The need for new processes, methodologies and tools to support big data teams and improve big data project effectiveness. *Proceedings of the IEEE International Conference on Big Data*, 2066 - 2071.

Saltz, J., Hotz, N., Wild, N., & Stirling, K. (2018). Exploring project management methodologies used within data science teams. *Proceedings of the Americas Conference on Information Systems (AMCIS).*

Saltz, J., Shamshurin, I., & Crowston, K. (2017). Comparing data science project management methodologies via a controlled experiment. *Proceedings of the 50th Hawaii International Conference on System Sciences*, 1013 - 1022.

Saltz, J., & Suthrland, A. (2019). SKI: An agile framework for data science. *Proceedings of IEEE International Conference on Big Data (Big Data),* 3468 - 3476.

Samuel, A. (1959). Some studies in machine learning using the game of checkers. *IBM Journal of Research and Development*, *3*(3), 210–229.

Sithambaram, J., Nasir, M. H. N. B. M., & Ahmad, R. (2021). Issues and challenges impacting the successful management of agile - hybrid projects: A grounded theory approach. *International Journal of Project Management.* doi:10.1016/j.ijproman.2021.03.002

Sutherland, J., & Schwaber, K. (2017). *The Scrum Guide.* http://www.scrumguides.org

Sutton, R. S., & Barto, A. G. (2015). *Reinforcement Learning: An Introduction.* MIT Press.

TDSP. (2021). *What is the team data science process?* https://docs.mcrosoft.com

Tsoy, M., & Staples, D. S. (2020). Exploring critical success factors in agile analytics projects. *Proceedings of 53rd Hawaii International Conference on System Sciences*, 984 - 993.

Zheng, A. (2015). *Evaluating machine learning models.* O'Reilly Media.

Zheng, A., & Casari, A. (2018). *Feature engineering for machine learning.* O'Reilly Media.

KEY TERMS AND DEFINITIONS

Algorithm: A stepwise solution to a problem represented by visual, textual or computer programming codes.

Idiosyncratic: To have characteristic attributes or behaviours different from others.

Kanban: Signboard in Japanese.

Knowledge Discovery in Databases (KDD): A method for discovering valuable knowledge from various sources of data.

Model: Representation of a ML problem by using a learner algorithm, test, and training data.

Training: A process whereby a learner algorithm maps a function to the training data.

Chapter 6
Effective Agile Project Leadership Through Competency-Based Self-Reflection

Fanny Saruchera
https://orcid.org/0000-0002-2139-1966
University of the Witwatersrand, South Africa

ABSTRACT

The agile revolution and increasing cross-functionality nature of project teams imply an increasing need for effective and results-orientated project leadership. Irrespective of one's role in a project, there is a need for self-examination and self-reflection regarding how members relate during the various phases of project implementation. This chapter focuses on a theoretical review of the various elements necessary for effective agile project leadership. Through a synthesis of both old and more recent literature, the chapter identifies and conceptualizes ten determinant factors of effective agile project leadership and proposes a self-reflection framework for each of the ten project leadership competency areas. The chapter concludes by proposing a personal agile project leadership development plan (PAPLDP) template with an agility component that can be adopted for improvement and growth. This chapter challenges project managers and/or project team leaders to define their own value-based leadership competence and continuously reflect, evaluate, and improve themselves.

INTRODUCTION

As with any other managers, project managers are more likely to perform better if they match their personal characteristics and the job requirements (Müller & Turner, 2010). Such requirements include a plethora of leadership and Emotional Intelligence (EQ) qualities. These have become increasingly critical in today's dynamic and technology - driven environments, where customer requirements appear to be ever - changing. The Project Management Institute (PMI), an international professional body for

DOI: 10.4018/978-1-7998-7872-8.ch006

project management, applies what they call the "Project Manager Competency Development (PMCD) Framework" through the use of the "PMI Talent Triangle" (PMI, 2017). The PMI Talent Triangle embeds the totality of the project manager's competence in three key skill sets, including "leadership, technical project management and strategic and business management (PMI, 2017). The fact that leadership is embedded in the PMI Talent Triangle implies that leadership has become one of the key pillars of effective project management. The success of projects now rests more on the effectiveness of the leadership than the technicalities of the project. This fact has become more confirmed in the context of agile project management.

Involvement in projects entails various aspects, and individuals involved assume different roles in each project - from being a project team member right through to project management or project leadership. Regardless of the nature of the project, there remains the need for self - examination and self - reflection regarding how members relate with each other during project implementation (Du Plessis & Roelofse, 2014). As Mahatma Gandhi notes, "The best way to find yourself is to lose yourself in the service of others." This quote, though old, remains very valid in modern - day leadership, more so in modern project leadership. Through a review of more than eighty - five (85) pieces of credible research articles and books, this chapter focuses on a theoretical review of the various elements necessary for effective project leadership. It proposes a self - reflection framework for each of the identifiable leadership competence. The paper culminates with a proposal for a Personal Agile Project Leadership Development Plan (PALDP) template that can be adopted for improvement and growth.

BACKGROUND

Project management literature has been increasingly inundated with several factors impacting the success of projects and related studies (Pinto & Slevin, 1989; Lechler, 2000; Prabhakar, 2005; Doloi et al., 2011; Saruchera, 2014; Serrador & Pinto, 2015; Saruchera & Phiri, 2016; Sudhakar, 2016; Pace, 2019; Irfan et al., 2021), with some focusing on specialized projects. While such literature has increased over the years, the complexities presented by the dynamic nature of project management have continued to present new challenges that require continuous research. The global business environment presents opportunities, experiences, and challenges due to unavoidable continuous global industry transitions and disruptive technologies (Saruchera, 2021). With project agilism comes the need for flexibility, assuming simplicity, embracing change incrementally, and managing with purpose, and all these are meant to maximize project and stakeholder value. Central to all this is the need to be emotionally intelligent given the people management aspect of managing projects. The question is, "How can a project leader embrace all these requirements in a rapidly changing project environment?"

Studies on agile project management have gained momentum over the years (Highsmith, 2009; Bergmann & Karwowski, 2018; Loiro et al., 2019). Some of these studies have had a particular focus on the challenges and impact of agility on specific non - software development projects, including Information Technology (IT) projects (Azanha et al., 2017), construction projects (Truong & Jitbaipoon, 2016; Albuquerque et al., 2020), transportation infrastructure projects (Safapour et al., 2020), and academic writing projects (Eschenbach et al., 2015). Through it all, the element of leadership remains largely critical as effective project leadership is undoubtedly an essential success factor on agile projects. The key to the success of any project is the skills of the people involved in solving special situations and unforeseen problems.

However, in agile projects, the people element has had a dynamic and complex structure, which requires a continuously evolving solution, regardless of the project leadership's socio - cultural, gender and personality factors. With a rise in the migration to agile project methodologies in a globally transitioning business world (Saruchera, 2021), this study joins the ongoing discussions on agile project leadership (e.g., Hoda & Murugesan, 2016; Almeida & Simões, 2021; Sithambaram et al., 2021). The study, however, takes a self - reflection stance in proposing a framework for continuous personal development in key leadership competence necessary for effective agile project leadership. The competence and framework development are both drawn from fragmented old and current literature sources as acknowledged and discussed in the chapter. Most importantly, this chapter attempts to integrate the fragmented views by proposing a template that can be used by project managers and leaders to self - reflect and develop their personal development plans.

MAIN FOCUS OF THE CHAPTER

Theoretical Framework and Scope

There has been a surge in literature focusing on project leadership and EQ, including project leadership styles, personal leadership, and people behavioural aspects, emotional intelligence in projects, and project team dynamics, among other factors. As a result, researchers have profiled leadership competence for successful project managers for different project types (e.g., Clarke, 2010; Müller & Turner, 2010; Sithambaram et al., 2021). For instance, Müller and Turner (2010) profiled intellectual, emotional, and managerial competence such as critical analysis and judgment, communication engagement, and interpersonal sensitivity. Sithambaram et al. (2021) instead focused on generic aspects impacting agile hybrid projects.

Various other researchers have profiled elements such as application of appropriate project leadership styles (De Poel et al., 2014; Yang et al., 2011); dynamic project team leadership (De Poel et al., 2014; Hoda & Murugesan, 2016; Natvig & Stark, 2016); stress and conflict management (Berg & Karlsen, 2013; Du Plessis, 2014; Moradi et al., 2020); and the management of organizational dynamics and politics (Bruch & Ghoshal, 2003; Ferris et al., 1999; Martin et al., 2005; Highsmith, 2009; Abbasi & Ruf, 2020).

This study is built upon the deficiencies presented in the fragmented literature and views regarding project leadership. For instance, leadership has been examined over the years theoretically and empirically from multiple perspectives in various research fields (Podgórska & Pichlak, 2019). The recent effort by Podgórska and Pichlak (2019) examines the relationship between the emotional, managerial and intellectual dimensions of leadership competence and their impact on project success, moderated by the influence of project type. Despite the proven significance of leadership competence in project management, Podgórska and Pichlak (2019) admit the fragmented nature of studies revolving around the application of such competence in project leadership. Drawn from these extant literary views, Figure 1 conceptualizes the determinant factors of project leadership discussed in this chapter.

Figure 1. Conceptual framework for the determinant factors of effective project leadership
Source: Author

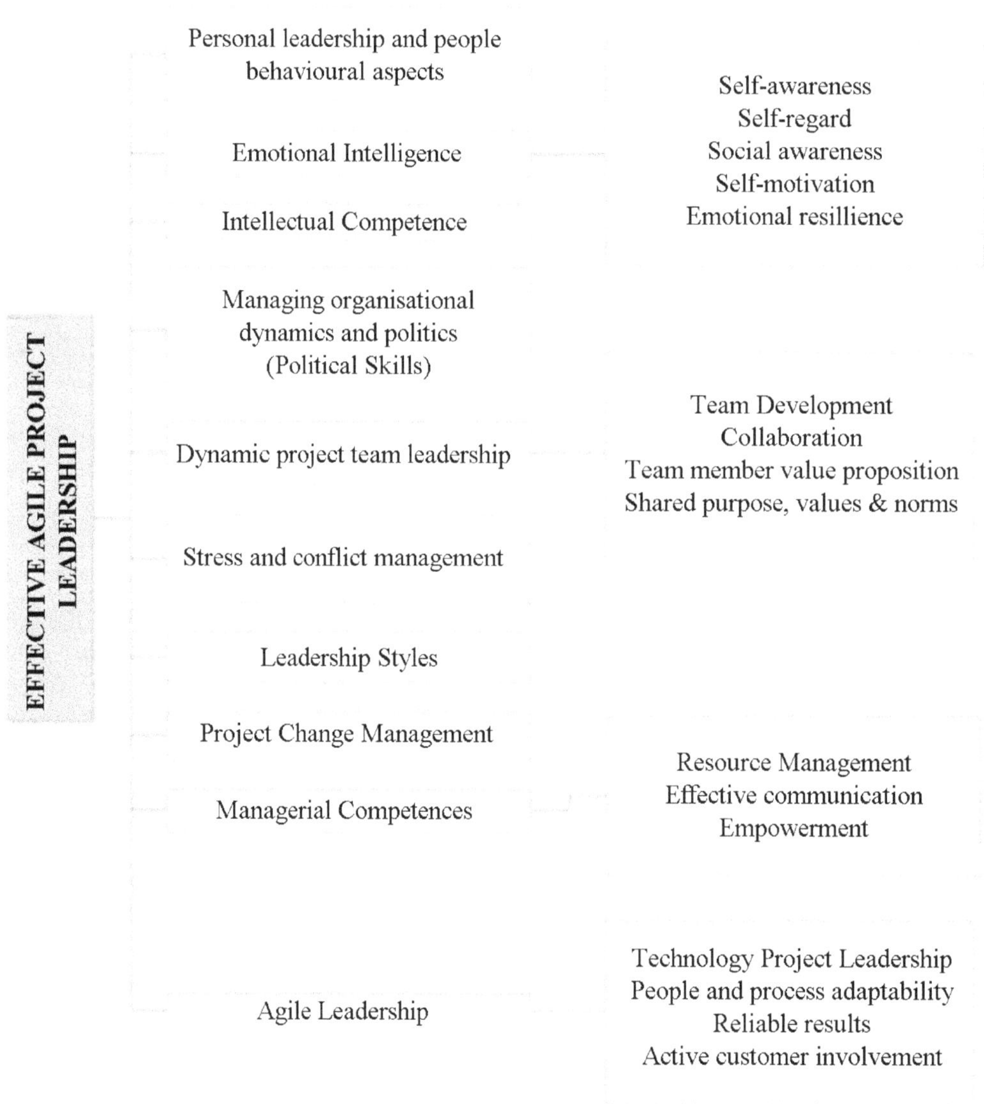

Personal Leadership and People Behavioural Aspects

Personal Leadership

The key to the success of any project is the ability of people involved in handling the different project situations, scenarios, and unpredicted complications. The success of projects thus largely relies on people's behaviour, particularly on the team leader's behaviour (PMI, 2017). It is thus imperative that the project leader appreciates and manages themselves before attempting to manage other people's behaviours. Influential or effective leaders are good followers of themselves before they can command followership. Thus, Mastrangelo et al. (2004) long established that personal leadership intermediates between professional leadership and followers' co - operation and willingness. The authors further found that professional leadership actions impact personal interactions, consequently impacting the willingness to cooperate, a view recently confirmed and supported by Abbasi and Ruf (2020) and Moradi et al. (2020).

While Mastrangelo et al. (2004) incorporated the leader's expertise, trust, level of caring and sharing, and morals as components of personal leadership, Du Plessis (2014) referred instead to EQ attributes such as self - regard, self - awareness, and self - management. However, these contributions seem to complement each other, and a self - reflection of each component contributes to personal leadership. The popular Goleman (1998) 's model views these and other social constructs as competence and expertise that can drive leadership performance, and they can be rated on a scale to ultimately measure an individual's EQ (Goleman, 2006).

In their study on praising "the incomplete leader," Ancona et al. (2007) argued that "incomplete leaders" get people within the organization to complement their strengths and compensate for their weaknesses. The authors proposed four leadership capabilities that they claim organizations need, namely: Sense - making (i.e., "interpreting developments in the business environment"); Relating (i.e., "building trusting relationships"); Visioning (i.e., "communicating a compelling image of the future"); and Inventing (i.e. "coming up with new ways of doing things") (Ancona et al., 2007). Because of this, a tool has been developed to assess one's own leadership on various aspects such as communication, involvement, empathy, and cultural diversity. Table 1 illustrates a tool that can be used for self - assessment of personal leadership for projects.

People Behavioural Aspects

On the other hand, behavioural aspects now dominate the agile project management theoretical framework instead of traditional task - oriented theories for traditional project management. Du Plessis and Roelofse (2014) established eight factors that influence human interaction and behaviour. These include individuals' perceptions, attributions, attitudes, cognitive styles, interpersonal behaviour, dyadic relationships, teamwork, and how different individuals handle conflict. Each of these has an impact on the project leader's attitude towards human interaction and behaviour. For instance, the project manager's perceptions of their team are likely to influence their exercise of power and authority.

It is thus critical to understand one's interpersonal behaviour and cognitive styles, as this will help in establishing the most appropriate approach to handling specific scenarios. A tool can also be developed based on these eight and any other relevant people's behavioural attributes. An alternative will be to embed these attributes in the template, as illustrated in Table 1. For instance, the 'teamwork', 'conflict management' and 'attitudes' variables have already been embedded in the instruments illustrated in Table 1.

Goleman (2006) and Bar - On (2006) appear to have long handled these social attributes well through their Emotional Intelligence and competence theories.

Emotional Intelligence (EQ) and EQ Competence

The significance of EQ with regard to the modern - day project manager cannot be overemphasized. The project manager is now expected to display high levels of EQ in dealing with increasingly complex human - project interactions (PMI, 2017). This has increasingly become relevant in agile projects in a globally transitioning environment. In support of Prabhakar (2005), Clarke (2010) noted that EQ facilitates especially transformational leadership, which usually characterizes the management of most projects. EQ relates to the manner in which individuals manage their own emotions and those of others (Goleman, 2006). In doing so, the following EQ elements must be reflected upon in the context of project management:

- Self - regard
- Self - awareness
- Empathy
- Social awareness
- Relationship Management

Table 1. Self - assessment instrument of personal leadership

1=Strongly Disagree; 2=Disagree; 3=Not Sure; 4=Agree; 5=Strongly Agree						
Personal Leadership Attributes		**1**	**2**	**3**	**4**	**5**
1.	***Communication***: I am an effective communicator and keep my project team informed.					
2.	***Decision-making***: I involve my project team/colleagues in decision-making processes.					
3.	***Change Management***: I have the capability to facilitate project change processes.					
4.	***Leadership and Management Skillset***: I have all the necessary leadership and management skills to lead the project.					
5.	***Resource Availability***: I ensure that the necessary and relevant resources are availed to the project team.					
6.	***Visibility and availability***: I visibly avail myself to my project team and project stakeholders.					
7.	***Cultural Diversity***: I recognize and celebrate cultural differences within my project team.					
8.	***Team Player***: I am a team player, and I lead by example.					
9.	***Conflict Management***: I can manage project conflict and keep it under control.					
10.	***Attitude towards project team members***: I treat others with respect and regard them as equally critical to the project's success.					
Interpretation of Scores: *0-10 – My personal project leadership attributes are extremely poor; I cannot lead the project.* *11-20 – My personal project leadership attributes are poor.* *21-30 – My personal project leadership attributes are fairly average. I need to develop myself personally.* *31-40 – My personal project leadership attributes are fairly good. I can improve in certain areas.* *41-50 – My personal project leadership attributes are excellent. I need to work on maintaining the momentum.*						

Source: Author

In support of Goleman's seminal contributions to the subject of EQ, Bar - On (2006) developed the widely accepted "model of emotional - social intelligence (ESI)," which helps in assessing one's level of EQ in fifteen EQ competence that is sub - grouped into five areas: "self - perception, interpersonal, self - expression, decision - making and stress management." The Bar - On EQ - I scales and an outline of what each scale assesses. The EQ concept has been contextualized in project management by Mersino (2013), demonstrating that the undoubted applicability of the scales to project management, further cemented by the more recent works of Khosravi et al. (2020), and Luong et al., (2021). The Bar - On EQ - I scales and what each of these scales assesses. Based on these scales, project managers and leaders could use these to reflect upon which areas they lack, hence working on self - improvement.

Competence from Other Forms of Intelligence

In addition to EQ, there has been a rise of multiple forms of intelligence, and it is becoming increasingly critical that project managers possess such multiple intelligences, as promoted by De Vries (2010). For instance, it has become vital that project managers should have social, physical, intellectual (IQ), spiritual (SQ), environmental (EnvQ), and cultural intelligence (CQ). Cultural intelligence (CQ) relates to one's ability to learn and understand cultural diversities and values, and norms. Ang et al. (2006) conceptualized CQ and developed a template for self - assessment of CQ, which can still be adopted in modern - day project leadership. This was followed by extensive follow - up and longitudinal studies to expand the CQ conceptualization and measurement (Van Dyne et al., 2012; Van Dyne et al., 2016). A template or tool that can be adopted for CQ self - assessment. The tool was initially developed by Ang et al. (2006) and ratified by later studies on cultural intelligence (De Vries, 2010; Van Dyne et al., 2012; Van Dyne et al., 2016).

Based on an understanding of the above - mentioned multiple intelligences, it is important to assess one's level of multi - dimensional intelligence - i.e., social, physical, IQ, SQ, EnvQ, and CQ, over and above the normal EQ.

Guided by the Bar - On (2006) EQ - I scales, project leaders should assess and reflect upon their EQ competence. They should determine their average EQ score, which can be translated and interpreted on a 1 - 20 score (Mersino, 2013; Khosravi et al., 2020). The overall score will determine how well the leader is doing and can be interpreted using the scales and interpretations provided by Mersino (2013). For instance, an overall EQ score of 14.4 implies that one is "doing well, but could improve in a few key areas" (Mersino, 2013). The results also help in establishing in which areas the leader has high or low average EQ in terms of self - perception, interpersonal competence and decision - making, stress management, and self - expression. A low score in stress management might imply a need for improvement in coping with stress and one's emotional expressions.

Project Leadership Styles and Approaches

While Prabhakar (2005) 's study reflected upon the importance of transformational leadership on project success across 28 nations, Sunindijo et al. (2007) validated the need to embed EQ in leadership styles in managing projects. Some later studies (De Poel et al., 2014; Yang et al., 2011) have proven that leadership approaches and organizational tenure diversities are critical determinants of the effectiveness of project teams. Leadership style selection is therefore not to be taken in isolation but rather embedded with EQ competence determination. Selection of the appropriate leadership styles, coupled with the application of EQ competence, is thus vital in ensuring effective project team leadership.

Project managers may lead their project teams in various styles depending on their personal preferences as well as a combination of other factors such as leader - related, organizational, environmental, and team member characteristics (PMI, 2017; Yang et al., 2011). Consequently, the traditional leadership styles available in leadership literature may be applied in project management depending on the prevailing circumstances. The common styles include laissez - faire, transactional, servant leader, transformational, charismatic, and interactional styles. This study supports the long - established view by Müller and Turner (2007) that the project manager's leadership styles must be matched to the project type. Furthermore, the study supports the need to embed such leadership matching exercises with the application of EQ competence to ensure effective agile project team leadership.

Remarkably, leadership matching is not a new phenomenon. Blanchard et al. (1985) long advocated for situational leadership as the best approach depending on the leader's personality, the task, and the circumstances. They plotted different leadership styles in four quadrants based on the extent to which the behaviour is supportive or directive. The four quadrants represent four types of leadership that project leaders can utilize. Leadership situation 1 (S1) entails highly directive and low supportive behaviour. In such a situation, the leader needs to be directive (Blanchard et al., 1985). In the leadership situation 2 (S2) quadrant, there is high directive and high supportive behaviour; hence the project leader may adopt the coaching style of leadership, which involves mentoring the subjects being lead (De Poel et al., 2014). In leadership situation 3 (S3), the leader may adopt a supportive leadership style as the situation encompasses low directive and high supportive behaviour. In a low directive and low supportive behaviour situation quadrant (S4), the project leader may delegate tasks (S4).

Yang et al. (2011) supported the model, and their study confirmed the association between various situational project manager leadership styles, project teamwork, and project success. They concluded that projects with leaders who vary their leadership styles with situations are more likely to register project success as compared to single leadership style type of leaders. The situational leadership model by Blanchard et al. (1985) is still quite relevant today as it dramatically improves how leaders do their job through motivating their followers.

Leading a Diverse Project Team

The ultimate goal for effective project teams is to achieve the intended project objectives for the benefit of the project stakeholders. However, team composition is the most fundamental aspect for teams in projects, given that project teams are often faced with time constraints (Byrd & Luthy, 2010; Hoda & Murugesan, 2016). As a result, team size, diversity, and personality are critical in project team development. De Poel et al. (2014) found out that the effectiveness of project team leadership is mainly dependent on the level of the team's diversity. A diverse project team promotes inclusiveness and acceptance of individual differences while embracing the team's strengths and opportunities.

Accordingly, diversity within the project team needs to be effectively managed so as to realize the benefits that come along with it entirely. Research has suggested various strategies to help leaders manage diversity in teams, and these include: creating inclusive policies, provision of diversity training, facilitating effective communications, encouraging interactions, building rapport, and encouraging diversity of thought (Ang et al., 2006; Buffinton et al., 2002). It is imperative to continuously engage in self - reflection in order to understand one's feelings about and attitude towards diversity. Various cultural and diversity templates are available for this exercise, including the CQ Self - Assessment Tool (Ang et al., 2006) outlined earlier.

Stress and Conflict Management

Stress Management

Stress is referred to as the "state of mental, physical and emotional strain or tension resulting from adverse or demanding circumstances" (Du Plessis, 2014). Stress emerges from environmental, workplace, and personal factors. Workplace factors include poor work relationships, failure to appreciate project team diversity, and work overload, among several other factors. With the COVID - 19 global pandemic, some project administrative work has had to be done remotely, through "TeleCheck" and teleconsultation (Linz et al., 2020). Although this study has been tackled from a medical perspective, this trend has also been witnessed in other project setups, thus mounting pressure on the remote project manager or leader whose work is better managed by working on - site. If left unmanaged, stress results in several negative physiological, psychological and behavioural consequences. There is thus a need to implement some project team interventions to manage stress, including preventive measures to eliminate stressors, encouraging task priorities, employing EQ competence, and rehabilitation of team members already under stress (Du Plessis & Roelofse, 2014; Moradi et al., 2020).

Conflict and Conflict Management

Du Plessis and Roelofse (2014) attributed conflicts to environmental uncertainties, organizational demands, and personal factors. Project team conflicts can be functional or else dysfunctional (Harrison & Lock, 2017), hence the need for conflict management. Project conflicts can be dealt with reactively and proactively. Effective leaders use both methods, though much emphasis should be put on proactive conflict management.

As a project team leader, it is crucial to minimize conflicts with team members (subordinates), clients, and other project stakeholders. However, should conflict occur, the literature suggests such reactive measures as pulling away (withdrawal), smoothing, negotiating, collaboration, and confrontation (Du Plessis, 2014; Moradi et al., 2020). The proactive approach helps to minimize or instead prevent conflicts from occurring hence minimizing the impact thereof. This can be achieved, for instance, by making the leader's expectations clear to subordinates, establishing a cooperative project work environment, maintaining close contacts with both colleagues and the project clients, and conducting regular project status and information - sharing meetings.

The leader must cordially resolve conflicts as and when they arise. The strength of project leadership is measured by the manner in which the leaders keep the team intact to achieve the business case. "Feeler" leaders are most likely to handle conflict in a more compromising manner, while "Analytics" are less likely to be accommodating towards others' views due to their cognitive analytical skills (Du Plessis & Roelofse, 2014).

Effective Communication

Popularized by Turner and Müller (2004) in their study on project communications and co - operation between the project owner (acting the "principal" role) and the project manager (playing the "agent" role), the role of communication in project management has witnessed an increased interest in the project management literature (Müller & Turner, 2010, Odhiambo, de Carvalho, 2014; Lam, 2016; Ouko, & Muhoho, 2020; Wuni & Shen, 2020). Odhiambo et al. (2020) have labelled communication "a driver of the performance of projects." The current study argues for the need for "effective" communication in projects instead of mere communication, as it impacts project delivery. Effective project communication links the project's stakeholders, provides information, and facilitates sharing of vital ideas to achieve the project's objectives. Effective communications allow the use of both verbal and non - verbal cues as they complement each other. The project leader should also engage in and facilitate stakeholder management and information sharing (Wuni & Shen, 2020). Müller and Turner (2010) called for the need for "effective dialogue," which is also influenced by judgment, listening behaviour, reflection, and questioning techniques. In an effort to ensure effective communication in agile project environments, project leaders need to establish practical communication barriers, i.e., what are the hindrances to effective communications with different project stakeholders? Establishing the root causes or hindrances will help the agile project leader to work towards avoiding the impact of such barriers through soliciting and implementing strategies for effective communication management.

Teamwork and Team Dynamics

The effectiveness of teams is primarily influenced by team dynamics such as task interdependence, contextual constraints, multi - level influences, and temporal dynamics (Byrd & Luthy, 2010). Buffinton et al. (2002) established what they termed "interpersonal dynamics" and how they serve as "potential sources of conflicts in project teams." Such dynamics thus need to be effectively managed to ensure that the business case is achieved. All these provide a base for some of the project team leadership qualities, skills, and / or competence that the project leader should possess.

Despite the team dynamics that may prevail in project teams, Verma (1997), supported by Prabhakar (2005) and Byrd and Luthy (2010), had long provided some insights into how effective diverse team leadership can be achieved. For instance, there is need for self - reflection during the predicable team development stages of forming, storming, norming, performing, and adjourning. Self - reflection during each of these team development stages can help establish the critical skills required to ensure that each of these stages becomes successful. It also helps in ensuring that individuals become compatible with the team's ethos and other team dynamics.

Secondly, Byrd and Luthy (2010) suggest several strategies for successful team development, including clarification of project scope, development of a plan of action, team and task knowledge, encouragement of creativity, team recreation, team building, and team therapy. The theory further suggests that a team charter, which defines the team's purpose, must be created so as to ensure optimal team performance and results. This idea of developing a team charter has recently been upheld by Natvig and Stark (2016), who found it to be an effective way of managing diverse and complex project groups and converting them into highly productive teams.

In support of Kujala et al. (2016), Lappi et al. (2018), and Moe et al. (2019) emphasized the importance of team empowerment as well as team autonomy. While team empowerment recognizes the need to enable the project team members to operate in particular ways hence building individual and team confidence, team autonomy affords the team some sense of self - direction and the liberty to execute tasks in their perceived best manner. However, despite these views, fundamental questions have continued to arise regarding the degree of team empowerment that is appropriate and how such empowerment can be put into practice (Lappi et al., 2018). Some of the most effective methods to manage this include the allocation of power to the project team leaders through money, i.e., by budgeting. However, the results of the analysis by Lappi et al. (2018) and other related studies seem to not suggest some transparent best practices for continuous budgeting, even though commercial frameworks such as Scaled Agile (Scaled Agile Inc., 2016) have started to consider this.

Organizational Dynamics and Politics

Power and Politics

The relationship between power, politics, and influence and their impact on the effectiveness of project leadership has been well documented. Pinto (2000) established that organizational politics particularly beset projects due to their lack of a stable power base and the need to negotiate for resources, among other reasons. Therefore, it is vital that as a leader, one obtains political skills and exercises the powers vested in the position and uses such to obtain resources and resolve any conflicts and barriers along the project path. While doing this, Martin et al. (2005) recommended that project leaders enhance their political intelligence. More specifically, it is proposed that effective project leaders should have at least "a satisfactory ability to understand people and a reasonable ability to read people's motivations and to detect any hidden agendas they may have" (Martin et al., 2005). Any gaps should be reflected in the personal development plan for necessary improvements.

Some tools and models have been developed to determine the leader's level of power, influence, and political skill. This paper proposes the adoption of the principles of influence template (Cialdini, 2001) and the political skill inventory checklist developed and validated by Ferris et al. (1999) and revisited in 2005 (Ferris et al., 2005), 2012 (Lvina et al., 2012) and more recently in 2018 and 2020 (Blickle et al., 2018; Abbasi & Ruf, 2020; González et al., 2020). The old Framework of political skills has always comprised four dimensions, i.e., Networking Ability, Interpersonal Influence, Social Astuteness, and Apparent Sincerity. However, González et al. (2020) argued that the totality of political skills requires "Innovative Work Behaviour" as a fifth dimension to measure the extent of innovativeness of one's work behaviour. Political skill can thus be measured against the following dimensions:

- Innovative Work Behaviour
- Networking Ability
- Interpersonal Influence
- Social Astuteness
- Apparent Sincerity

A Political Skill Inventory (PSI) tool for self - assessment, adopted from Ferris et al. (2005), which project managers or leaders can use to capture their ability to comprehend others at work effectively and their ability to utilize such knowledge to influence colleagues to act in ways that can enhance their personal, project and / or organizational objectives.

Organizational Energy

According to Bruch and Vogel (2011), organizational energy is "the emotional, cognitive, behavioural potential a team or organization has to pursue its goals." Bruch and Vogel (2011) established three components of organizational energy - emotional, cognitive, and behavioural energy. They further introduced "the energy matrix," in which they grouped teams into four groups (Teams A to D) according to the levels of energy they displayed. According to the Organizational Energy Matrix, Team A has 'productive' energy embedded in the positive quality of work and high intensity. Team B has 'comfortable' energy embedded in the positive quality of work but with low intensity. Team C has the negative quality and low intensity hence 'resigned inertia,' while team D has 'corrosive energy' embedded with negative quality though with high intensity.

The project team's performance is ignited through the leader's ability to boost their team's energy. Teams C and D are not desirable in any form; hence any typical project leader would avoid working with such and would also avoid creating an environment leading to such negative energies. While Team B's 'comfortable energy' may appear workable with, these are people who prefer to remain in their zones of comfort (Bruch & Vogel, 2011), hence may prove to be challenging to work with.

Thus, any project leader will desire to work with a fully - charged team (Team A) with productive energy. This is the team that will ensure that the project's objectives and timelines are met or even surpassed. Most importantly, it remains the duty of the project leader to in still productive energy within the project team and to keep resigned inertia as far as possible.

Project as Change

Integrating project and change management in modern - day leadership is now considered "a necessity" (Hornstein, 2015). However, not all change interventions succeed all the time. Change is affected by such factors as availability of resources, the attitude of team members towards the change (resistance to change), and change readiness. Regarding "change readiness," Samaranayake and Takemura (2017) stated that it is influenced by the perceived discrepancy, appropriateness, and personal valence.

Various change methodologies have been proposed, including Prosci's "ADKAR" approach (Hiatt, 2006), which provides five building blocks for change management - Awareness, Desire, Knowledge, Ability, and Reinforcement. This tool may be used to assess change management gaps existing within both individuals and organizations. This comes through the realization that the success of organizational change efforts emerges from successes in individual changes (Hiatt, 2006). The ADKAR developers proffered relevant solutions to close change gaps identified by the ADKAR templates.

Agile Leadership

Agile methodologies in project management are emerging and have fast been gaining ground and dominance, especially in high - tech, Information Technology (IT), and software development projects (Bjarnason et al., 2016; Conforto et al., 2016; Lee & Yong, 2010; Persson et al., 2012). International project management professional bodies such as PMI have also embraced Agile project management principles (PMI, 2017), and the principles are increasingly becoming applicable to other project types globally. This, coupled with the documented increasing importance placed on procurement in general (Tukuta & Saruchera, 2015) as well as specialized project procurement (de Araújo et al., 2017), has resulted in the need for effective agile project leadership. As a result, agility skills have become a requirement in ensuring effective project leadership, especially in the uncertain modern - day business environment.

According to Sidky and Smith (2009), "an agile project leader brings their soft skills together to shepherd the team versus directing them." In order to fulfil this "shepherding" role, an agile project leader is thus expected to possess analytical thinking, listening, and communication skills. The agile leader is also expected to operate as a diplomat, i.e., to ensure tactful communications without offending or touching on sensitivities, be it from the team or stakeholders' side.

A recent review of the agility construct by Conforto et al. (2016) unpacked some gaps in the theory, and the authors noted that agility should combine "rapid project planning change and active customer involvement" and that "agility has different intensities and depends on multiple organization factors". The customer involvement variable, which is aimed at prioritizing customer satisfaction early and continuous project delivery, comes as an addition to the other three determinants of agile project leadership, i.e. technology project leadership, people and process adaptability, as well as reliable results, as proffered by preceding studies (Fernandez & Fernandez, 2008; Highsmith, 2009; Owen & Koskela, 2006). As the "customer involvement" phenomenon is revisited, a study by Najafi - Tavani et al., (2020) echoed the need for relationship learning and customer involvement in new product development projects.

From a marketing perspective, despite the arguments against it, the customer remains "the king" (Fjeldstad et al., 2020). Respecting this mantra as a path to creating customer loyalty (Makasi & Saruchera, 2014) remains vital even in the context of project management. It is thus not surprising to note the customer involvement variable being embedded in the agility construct, which has been long pending in the project management discipline. The project client is central to almost everything in project management. The effective agile project leader should therefore possess some flare of customer care skills as this will go a long way in enhancing customer involvement, as advocated by Conforto et al. (2016), lately supported by Storey and Larbig (2018), and Najafi - Tavani et al. (2020).

SOLUTIONS AND RECOMMENDATIONS

Application and Self - Reflection: Growth and Development

Project leaders must do a self - assessment of each of the above competence. Such assessments could help establish the leader's areas of strength and weakness, which should be reflected in the PAPLDP. Some leaders will find it rewarding to be assessed by their peers. However, an honest self - assessment can still serve the purpose. Guided by the self - assessment and reflections, the leader should establish the areas of growth and development drawn from the project leadership competence discussed above. Scores obtained in each competency should typically guide the intended leadership development plan, ideally incorporating a plan of action and expected timelines.

For each of the skills or leadership competence in the plan, the use of the self - assessment tools and / or templates provided will help determine the level of proficiency, i.e., whether the project leader is competent, somehow competent, or not competent within a particular area. The leader then determines and sets the target proficiency. For instance, if the project leader is not competent or "lowly" competent in stress management, the goal is to be proficient in that area, hence the need to close the skills gap. For such proficiency to be achieved, there is a need to identify some development opportunities, whether internal or external to the organization; for example, training in a particular area such as project agility leading to certification in that area and / or enrolling in master classes and workshops for enhancing specific competence. In order to allow for measurement and progress checks, it is crucial to set and work with some timelines and Key Result Areas (KRAs), as these can be used to check if the target proficiency levels have been reached. Table 2 illustrates a proposed template that can be adopted for agile project leadership personal skills development (PAPLDP), inclusive of EQ development planning. Further details regarding each of the template's components are provided in the descriptors beneath the template.

Table 2. Proposed template for personal agile project leadership and eq development planning

Skill / Competence Area		Current Proficiency (CP)	Target Proficiency (TP)	Development Opportunity (DO)	Target Time Frame (TTF)	Key Result Areas (KRAs)
Personal Leadership & people behavior	Communication					
	Leadership & management					
EQ & Competence	Self-perception					
	Interpersonal competence					
	Decision-making					
	Stress Management					
	Self-expression					
Project Leadership styles	Matching leadership styles to project type					
Leading diverse project teams	Cultural Intelligence (CQ)					
	Team player					
	Promoting inclusiveness					
Conflict Management	Conflict Management					
Effective communication	Presentation skills (Eye contact)					
	Use of verbal & non-verbal cues					
Teamwork & team dynamics	Understanding team dynamics					
	Managing team development challenges					
Organizational dynamics and politics	Exercising power and influence					
	Networking ability					
	Social astuteness					
Change	Change awareness					
	Change reinforcement					
Agile Project leadership	Technology Project Leadership					
	People and process adaptability					
	Reliable results					
	Active customer involvement					

Source: Author

* The following explanations should be used with the template:

- Competence relates to the ability of the leader to action something successfully or efficiently. The plan revolves around ten competence or skills derived from the literature synthesis.

- Proficiency relates to the degree of skill or expertise - this can be simply expressed as "Low," "Average," or "High." OR "Competent", "somehow competent" or "not competent". The current proficiency (CP) will determine the target proficiency (TP). Even if the CP is high, there is always a development opportunity (DO) for development, which can be achieved by maintaining the current perceived high CP.
- Development Opportunity (DO) relates to an opportunity availed by the organization or the project environment to improve one's weaknesses or skills deficiencies. For example, a training opportunity, workshop, enrolment to a master class, interaction with a professional body, etc.
- Target Time Frame (TTF) relates to the anticipated timeframe to capitalize on the Development Opportunity (DO). It depends on the length of the opportunity and / or the target set as per individual preferences.
- Key Result Areas (KRAs) are general metrics or parameters to validate the success of the intervention methods or Development Opportunities to improve one's skills.

FUTURE RESEARCH DIRECTIONS

This study's primary limitation lies in the fact that its research process was based primarily on the review of the literature and not on empirical evidence. However, the approach adopted added value through synthesizing the existing understanding and fragmented views on determinants of effective agile project leadership. The determinants emerging from this study are thus premised on conclusions drawn from previous studies. Future studies could thus consider the application of these determinants from the perspective of different project types and / or companies. It is also possible that the generic application of the practically effective agile leadership principles and determinants discussed in this chapter might be disputed, and application may vary from one project type to the other. Therefore, future studies could also consider exposing the study's conceptual Framework to statistical tests or other acceptable tests to verify the relationships proposed and qualitatively discussed in this chapter.

CONCLUSION

The increasing significance of effective leadership and EQ in project management can never be overemphasized, mainly because of the increasing agility of project environments. Migrating to agile project management implies more than changing the organization's processes as it also demands a change in organizational culture, which can be the most challenging part. However, with effective agile project leadership skills, it is possible. Several projects have failed due to the failure to display effective leadership and EQ skills. Such failures could have been avoided through an ongoing Programme of self - reflection, self - assessment, and working with a practical personal development plan. While self - reflection helps to reveal one's leadership strengths in some areas, it is essential to note that even the best project leaders or managers also possess specific weaknesses in some aspects of communication, exercising power and influence, as well as project change management, among other weaknesses. Accordingly, a personal leadership development plan with timelines guides project leaders in improving their weaknesses while striving to maintain and / or enhance their strengths. This will see them becoming competent in most of the areas established by this paper, hence enhancing the chances of project success.

REFERENCES

Abbasi, S., & Ruf, T. (2020). Reduction of the fluctuation rate in multi - project organizations through agile leadership. *Management*, *8*(2), 128–133.

Albuquerque, F., Torres, A. S., & Berssaneti, F. T. (2020). Lean product development and agile project management in the construction industry. *Revista de Gestão*, *27*(2), 135–151. doi:10.1108/REGE-01-2019-0021

Almeida, F., & Simões, J. (2021). Leadership Challenges in Agile Environments. *International Journal of Information Technology Project Management*, *12*(2), 30–44. doi:10.4018/IJITPM.2021040102

Ancona, D., Malone, T. W., Orlikowski, W. J., & Senge, P. M. (2007). In praise of the incomplete leader. *Harvard Business Review*, *85*(2). PMID:17345683

Ang, S., Van Dyne, L., & Koh, C. (2006). Personality correlates of the four - factor model of cultural intelligence. *Group & Organization Management*, *31*(1), 100–123. doi:10.1177/1059601105275267

Azanha, A., Argoud, A. R. T. T., de Camargo, J. B. Junior, & Antoniolli, P. D. (2017). Agile project management with Scrum: A case study of a Brazilian pharmaceutical company IT project. *International Journal of Managing Projects in Business*, *10*(1), 121–142. doi:10.1108/IJMPB-06-2016-0054

Bar - On, R. (2006). The Bar - On model of emotional - social intelligence (ESI). *Psicothema*, *18*(1), 13–25. PMID:17295953

Berg, M. E., & Karlsen, J. T. (2013). Managing stress in projects using coaching leadership tools. *Engineering Management Journal*, *25*(4), 52–61. doi:10.1080/10429247.2013.11431995

Bergmann, T., & Karwowski, W. (2018). Agile project management and project success: A literature review. In *International Conference on Applied Human Factors and Ergonomics* (pp. 405 - 414). Springer, Cham.

Bjarnason, E., Unterkalmsteiner, M., Borg, M., & Engström, E. (2016). A multi - case study of agile requirements engineering and the use of test cases as requirements. *Information and Software Technology*, *77*, 61–79. doi:10.1016/j.infsof.2016.03.008

Blanchard, K. H., Nigari, P., & Nigari, D. (1985). *Leadership and the one - minute manager*. Fontana.

Blickle, G., Frieder, R. E., & Ferris, G. R. (2018). Political skill. In D. S. Ones, N. Anderson, C. Viswesvaran, & H. K. Sinangil (Eds.), The SAGE handbook of industrial, work & organizational psychology: Personnel psychology and employee performance (p. 299 - 319). Sage Reference. doi:10.4135/9781473914940.n12

Bruch, H., & Ghoshal, S. (2003). Unleashing organizational energy. *MIT Sloan Management Review*, *45*(1), 45.

Bruch, H., & Vogel, B. (2011). *Fully charged: How great leaders boost the organization's energy and ignite high performance*. Harvard Business Press.

Buffinton, K. W., Jablokow, K. W., & Martin, K. A. (2002). Project team dynamics and cognitive style. *Engineering Management Journal*, *14*(3), 25–33. doi:10.1080/10429247.2002.11415170

Byrd, J. T., & Luthy, M. R. (2010). Improving group dynamics: Creating a team charter. *Academy of Educational Leadership Journal*, *14*(1), 13.

Cialdini, R. (2001). *Influence: The psychology of persuasion*. Harper Collins.

Clarke, N. (2010). Emotional intelligence and its relationship to transformational leadership and project manager competence. *Project Management Journal*, *41*(2), 5–20. doi:10.1002/pmj.20162

Conforto, E. C., Amaral, D. C., da Silva, S. L., Di Felippo, A., & Kamikawachi, D. S. L. (2016). The agility construct on project management theory. *International Journal of Project Management*, *34*(4), 660–674. doi:10.1016/j.ijproman.2016.01.007

De Araújo, M. C. B., Alencar, L. H., & de Miranda Mota, C. M. (2017). Project procurement management: A structured literature review. *International Journal of Project Management*, *35*(3), 353–377. doi:10.1016/j.ijproman.2017.01.008

De Carvalho, M. M. (2014). An investigation of the role of communication in IT projects. *International Journal of Operations & Production Management*, *34*(1), 36–64. doi:10.1108/IJOPM-11-2011-0439

De Poel, F. M., Stoker, J. I., & Van der Zee, K. I. (2014). Leadership and organizational tenure diversity as determinants of project team effectiveness. *Group & Organization Management*, *39*(5), 532–560. doi:10.1177/1059601114550711

De Vries, F. (2010). *The rise of multiple intelligences*. Retrieved August 21, 2020, from http://scholar.sun.ac.za/handle/10019.1/5735

Doloi, H., Iyer, K. C., & Sawhney, A. (2011). Structural equation model for assessing impacts of contractor's performance on project success. *International Journal of Project Management*, *29*(6), 687–695. doi:10.1016/j.ijproman.2010.05.007

Du Plessis, Y. (Ed.). (2014). *Project management: A behavioural perspective - principles, practices, and cases*. Pearson Education South Africa.

Du Plessis, Y., & Roelofse, K. (2014). People behaviour and project management. In Y. Du Plessis (Ed.), *Project management: A behavioural perspective - principles, practices, and cases* (pp. 3–28). Pearson Education South Africa.

Eschenbach, T., Lewis, N., Nicholls, G. M., & Schell, W. J. (2015). Using Agile Project Management to maximize your and your Co - authors' Productivity. In *2015 ASEE Annual Conference & Exposition* (pp. 26 - 1654). Academic Press.

Fernandez, D. J., & Fernandez, J. D. (2008). Agile project management—Agilism versus traditional approaches. *Journal of Computer Information Systems*, *49*(2), 10–17.

Ferris, G. R., Berkson, H. M., Kaplan, D. M., Gilmore, D. C., Buckley, M. R., Hochwarter, W. A., & Witt, L. A. (1999, August). Development and initial validation of the political skill inventory. In *Academy of Management, 59th annual national meeting* (pp. 6 - 11). Academic Press.

Ferris, G. R., Treadway, D. C., Kolodinsky, R. W., Hochwarter, W. A., Kacmar, C. J., Douglas, C., & Frink, D. D. (2005). Development and validation of the political skill inventory. *Journal of Management, 31*(1), 126–152. doi:10.1177/0149206304271386

Fjeldstad, O. H., Kagoma, C., Mdee, E., Sjursen, I. H., & Somville, V. (2020). The customer is king: Evidence on VAT compliance in Tanzania. *World Development, 128*, 104841. doi:10.1016/j.worlddev.2019.104841

Goleman, D. (2006). *Emotional intelligence*. Bantam Books.

González, R. C., Blanco, P. R. Z., Gil, F., & Antino, M. (2020). Development and validation of the Spanish version of the political skill inventory. *Anales de Psicología, 36*(2), 370–377. doi:10.6018/analesps.368871

Harrison, F., & Lock, D. (2017). *Advanced project management: a structured approach*. Routledge. doi:10.4324/9781315263328

Hiatt, J. (2006). *ADKAR: a model for change in business, government, and our community*. Prosci.

Highsmith, J. (2009). *Agile project management: creating innovative products*. Pearson Education.

Hoda, R., & Murugesan, L. K. (2016). Multi - level agile project management challenges: A self - organizing team perspective. *Journal of Systems and Software, 117*, 245–257. doi:10.1016/j.jss.2016.02.049

Hornstein, H. A. (2015). The integration of project management and organizational change management is a necessity. *International Journal of Project Management, 33*(2), 291–298. doi:10.1016/j.ijproman.2014.08.005

Irfan, M., Khan, S. Z., Hassan, N., Hassan, M., Habib, M., Khan, S., & Khan, H. H. (2021). Role of project planning and project manager competence on public sector project success. *Sustainability, 13*(3), 1421. doi:10.3390u13031421

Khosravi, P., Rezvani, A., & Ashkanasy, N. M. (2020). Emotional intelligence: A preventive strategy to manage destructive influence of conflict in large - scale projects. *International Journal of Project Management, 38*(1), 36–46. doi:10.1016/j.ijproman.2019.11.001

Kujala, J., Aaltonen, K., Gotcheva, N., & Pekuri, A. (2016). Key dimensions of project network governance and implications to safety in nuclear industry projects. EURAM 2016: Manageable Co - operation.

Lam, C. (2016). Improving technical communication group projects: An experimental study of media synchronicity theory training on communication outcomes. *Journal of Business and Technical Communication, 30*(1), 85–112. doi:10.1177/1050651915602293

Lappi, T., Karvonen, T., Lwakatare, L. E., Aaltonen, K., & Kuvaja, P. (2018). Toward an improved understanding of agile project governance: A systematic literature review. *Project Management Journal, 49*(6), 39–63. doi:10.1177/8756972818803482

Lechler, T. (2000). Empirical evidence of people as project success factors. In R. Lundin & F. Hartman (Eds.), *Projects as business constituents & guiding motives* (pp. 217–227). Kluwer Academic Publishers. doi:10.1007/978-1-4615-4505-7_17

Lee, S., & Yong, H. S. (2010). Distributed agile: Project management in a global environment. *Empirical Software Engineering*, *15*(2), 204–217. doi:10.100710664-009-9119-7

Linz, D., Pluymaekers, N. A., & Hendriks, J. M. (2020). TeleCheck - AF for COVID - 19: A European mHealth project to facilitate atrial fibrillation management through teleconsultation during COVID19. *European Heart Journal*, *41*(21), 1954–1955. doi:10.1093/eurheartj/ehaa404 PMID:32379309

Loiro, C., Castro, H., Ávila, P., Cruz-Cunha, M. M., Putnik, G. D., & Ferreira, L. (2019). Agile project management: A communicational workflow proposal. *Procedia Computer Science*, *164*, 485–490. doi:10.1016/j.procs.2019.12.210

Luong, T. T., Sivarajah, U., & Weerakkody, V. (2021). Do agile managed information systems projects fail due to a lack of emotional intelligence? *Information Systems Frontiers*, *23*(2), 415–433. doi:10.100710796-019-09962-6

Lvina, E., Johns, G., Treadway, D. C., Blickle, G., Liu, Y., Liu, J., & Ferris, G. R. (2012). Measure invariance of the political skill inventory (PSI) across five cultures. *International Journal of Cross Cultural Management*, *12*(2), 171–191. doi:10.1177/1470595812439870

Makasi, A., & Saruchera, F. (2014). The impact of operational customer relationship management on customer loyalty. *Mediterranean Journal of Social Sciences*, *5*(23), 291–291. doi:10.5901/mjss.2014.v5n23p291

Martin, L. E., Nyberg, T. L., & Buckley, M. R. (2005). Political skill at work: Impact on work effectiveness. *Human Resource Planning*, *28*(4), 45–47.

Mastrangelo, A., Eddy, E. R., & Lorenzet, S. J. (2004). The importance of personal and professional leadership. *Leadership and Organization Development Journal*, *25*(5), 435–451. doi:10.1108/01437730410544755

Mersino, A. (2013). *Emotional intelligence for project managers: The people skills you need to achieve outstanding results*. HarperCollins Publishers.

Moe, N. B., Dahl, B. H., Stray, V., & Karlsen, L. S., & Schjødt-Osmo, S. (2019). Team autonomy in large - scale agile. In *Proceedings of the Annual Hawaii International Conference on System Sciences (HICSS)* (pp. 6997 - 7006). AIS Electronic Library.

Moradi, S., Kähkönen, K., & Aaltonen, K. (2020). Project managers' competence in collaborative construction projects. *Buildings*, *10*(3), 50. doi:10.3390/buildings10030050

Müller, R., & Turner, J. R. (2007). Matching the project manager's leadership style to project type. *International Journal of Project Management*, *25*(1), 21–32. doi:10.1016/j.ijproman.2006.04.003

Müller, R., & Turner, R. (2010). Leadership competency profiles of successful project managers. *International Journal of Project Management*, *28*(5), 437–448. doi:10.1016/j.ijproman.2009.09.003

Najafi-Tavani, Z., Mousavi, S., Zaefarian, G., & Naudé, P. (2020). Relationship learning and international customer involvement in new product design: The moderating roles of customer dependence and cultural distance. *Journal of Business Research*, *120*, 42–58. doi:10.1016/j.jbusres.2020.07.020

Natvig, D., & Stark, N. L. (2016). A project team analysis using Tuckman's model of small - group development. *The Journal of Nursing Education*, *55*(12), 675–681. doi:10.3928/01484834-20161114-03 PMID:27893902

Odhiambo, A. A., Ouko, R. A., & Muhoho, D. J. (2020). Communication as a driver of performance of projects in Kenyan commercial banks. *International Academic Journal of Information Sciences and Project Management*, *3*(6), 100–112.

Owen, R., & Koskela, L. (2006). An agile step forward in project management. In *2nd Specialty Conference on Leadership and Management in Construction and Engineering* (pp. 216 - 224). Academic Press.

Pace, M. (2019). A Correlational Study on Project Management Methodology and Project Success. Journal of Engineering. *Project & Production Management*, *9*(2), 56–65. doi:10.2478/jeppm-2019-0007

Persson, J. S., Mathiassen, L., & Aaen, I. (2012). Agile distributed software development: Enacting control through media and context. *Information Systems Journal*, *22*(6), 411–433. doi:10.1111/j.1365-2575.2011.00390.x

Pinto, J. K. (2000). Understanding the role of politics in successful project management. *International Journal of Project Management*, *18*(2), 85–91. doi:10.1016/S0263-7863(98)00073-8

Pinto, J. K., & Slevin, D. P. (1989). Critical success factors in R&D projects. *Research Technology Management*, *32*(1), 31–35. doi:10.1080/08956308.1989.11670572

Podgórska, M., & Pichlak, M. (2019). Analysis of project managers' leadership competence. *International Journal of Managing Projects in Business*, *12*(4), 869–887.

Prabhakar, G. P. (2005). Switch leadership in projects an empirical study reflecting the importance of transformational leadership on project success across twenty - eight nations. *Project Management Journal*, *36*(4), 53–60. doi:10.1177/875697280503600406

Project Management Institute (PMI). (2017). *A guide to the project management body of knowledge (PMBOK® Guide)* (6th ed.). Project Management Institute.

Safapour, E., Kermanshachi, S., & Jafari, A. (2020). Effective project management principles and strategies in transportation infrastructure projects. In *Creative Construction e - Conference 2020* (pp. 126–135). Budapest University of Technology and Economics.

Samaranayake, S. U., & Takemura, T. (2017). Employee readiness for organizational change: A case study in an export - oriented manufacturing firm in Sri Lanka. *Eurasian Journal of Business and Economics*, *10*(20), 1–16. doi:10.17015/ejbe.2017.020.01

Saruchera, F. (2014). *Determinants of commercialization of technological innovations in developing economies: a study of Zimbabwe's research institutes* [Doctoral dissertation]. University of KwaZulu - Natal, Pietermaritzburg, South Africa.

Saruchera, F. (Ed.). (2021). *Advanced perspectives on global industry transitions and business opportunities*. IGI Global. doi:10.4018/978-1-7998-4303-0

Saruchera, F., & Phiri, M. A. (2016). Technological Innovations Performance and Public - Private - partnerships. *Corporate Ownership & Control*, *13*(4), 549–557. doi:10.22495/cocv13i4c4p4

Scaled Agile Inc. (2016). *Scaled Agile Framework® (SAFe®)*. Retrieved from https://www.scaledagileframework.com/

Serrador, P., & Pinto, J. K. (2015). Does Agile work?—A quantitative analysis of agile project success. *International Journal of Project Management*, *33*(5), 1040–1051. doi:10.1016/j.ijproman.2015.01.006

Sidky, A., & Smith, G. (2009). *Becoming agile in an imperfect world*. Manning Publications.

Sithambaram, J., Nasir, M. H. N. B. M., & Ahmad, R. (2021). Issues and challenges impacting the successful management of agile - hybrid projects: A grounded theory approach. *International Journal of Project Management*, *39*(5), 474–495. doi:10.1016/j.ijproman.2021.03.002

Storey, C., & Larbig, C. (2018). Absorbing customer knowledge: How customer involvement enables service design success. *Journal of Service Research*, *21*(1), 101–118. doi:10.1177/1094670517712613

Sudhakar, G. P. (2016). Understanding the meaning of "Project Success.". *Binus Business Review*, *7*(2), 163–169. doi:10.21512/bbr.v7i2.1586

Sunindijo, R. Y., Hadikusumo, B. H., & Ogunlana, S. (2007). Emotional intelligence and leadership styles in construction project management. *Journal of Management Engineering*, *23*(4), 166–170. doi:10.1061/(ASCE)0742-597X(2007)23:4(166)

Truong, D., & Jitbaipoon, T. (2016). How can agile methodologies be used to enhance the success of information technology projects? *International Journal of Information Technology Project Management*, *7*(2), 1–16. doi:10.4018/IJITPM.2016040101

Tukuta, M., & Saruchera, F. (2015). Challenges facing procurement professionals in developing economies: Unlocking value through professional international purchasing. *Journal of Transport and Supply Chain Management*, *9*(1), 1–9. doi:10.4102/jtscm.v9i1.152

Turner, J. R., & Müller, R. (2004). Communication and co - operation on projects between the project owner as principal and the project manager as agent. *European Management Journal*, *22*(3), 327–336. doi:10.1016/j.emj.2004.04.010

Van Dyne, L., Ang, S., Ng, K. Y., Rockstuhl, T., Tan, M. L., & Koh, C. (2012). Sub-dimensions of the four factor model of cultural intelligence: Expanding the conceptualization and measurement of cultural intelligence. *Social and Personality Psychology Compass*, *6*(4), 295–313. doi:10.1111/j.1751-9004.2012.00429.x

Van Dyne, L., Ang, S., & Tan, M. L. (2016). *Cultural intelligence*. Oxford Bibliographies.

Verma, V. K. (1997). *Managing the project team*. Project Management Institute.

Wuni, I. Y., & Shen, G. Q. (2020). Stakeholder management in prefabricated prefinished volumetric construction projects: Benchmarking the key result areas. *Built Environment Project and Asset Management*, *10*(3), 407–421. doi:10.1108/BEPAM-02-2020-0025

Yang, L. R., Huang, C. F., & Wu, K. S. (2011). The association among project manager's leadership style, teamwork and project success. *International Journal of Project Management, 29*(3), 258–267. doi:10.1016/j.ijproman.2010.03.006

KEY TERMS AND DEFINITIONS

Agile Project: A project that can be easily managed by subdividing it into several stages or phases. An agile project involves continuous co - operation with stakeholders and continuous improvement at each stage / phase.

Agility: The ability of an individual or an organization to think, understand and react quickly and easily to environmental changes or challenges. In a business setup, agility is perceived to be dependent on the context.

Competence: The ability to action something successfully or efficiently. Also loosely referred to as 'skills'.

Development Plan: It is commonly referred to as the 'Personal Development Plan (PDP).' It is a personal action plan based on one's awareness, values, reflection, goal setting, and personal development planning in career, education, interpersonal relationships, or self-improvement.

Emotional Intelligence: The belief that one is aware and is capable of managing and controlling self-emotions and can sensibly handle interpersonal relationships.

Leadership: The ability to exercise judiciously exercise power in its different forms to direct and influence others' behaviours.

Perceived Competency: The belief that one can or has the skill to do something successfully or efficiently.

Proficiency: A high degree of skill or expertise.

Self-Reflection: A personally intrigued, careful, and/or serious thought or introspection about one's performance, character, and actions. Self-reflection is perceived to be the foundation for personal development.

Chapter 7
A Quantitative Study of Waterfall and Agile Methodologies With the Perspective of Project Management

Kenish Rajesh Halani
Manipal University Jaipur, India

Kavita Jhajharia
https://orcid.org/0000-0002-6424-2127
Manipal University Jaipur, India

ABSTRACT

Software engineering is used in order to develop larger and complex software products. As software product is needed in almost all the industries, software engineering becomes really important. Software development can be done through various software development life cycle (SDLC) models like waterfall model, agile model, spiral model, prototype model, etc. SDLC is a framework that defines the tasks that to be performed at each step in the development process. Authors are mainly focusing on two models (i.e., waterfall and agile model). Waterfall model is a serial model which follows a strict sequence. Agile methodology can be divided into scrum methodology and extreme programming. Scrum methodology mainly focuses on how to manage tasks in a team-based environment. Scrum consists of three main roles. They are scrum master, product owner, and scrum team. While comparing both the models, the main difference obtained is waterfall does not allow any customer involvement while agile does allow it.

DOI: 10.4018/978-1-7998-7872-8.ch007

INTRODUCTION

As technology has evolved immensely over the last few decades, the use of mobile phones, laptops, and computers have grown drastically; therefore, usage of apps and software increased too hence there was a need for software engineering to make sure that the applications developed are as per client's need and requirement. Software modelling does not mean demonstrating a scientific theory or an algorithm. This is what conventionally call a software model. It means software modelling is more extensive than an algorithm or a single function. It should be able to explain the entire product's design, including interfaces, cohesion between the module, and all the software functions. Generally, Software Modelling is a way of explaining software design. It is more or less a theoretical language, picture or diagram that can be used to convey software design. Modelling helps designers develop different designs, and they pick the design that meets all the customer's requirements. This also helps designers identify the problems early in the cycle and fix them without altering the code's external behaviour. Whenever a developer selects a model, it has a tremendous effect on the testing activities. It helps to explain what, where and when of our testing activity. Mostly it also helps in deciding the testing techniques (Software Design and Modelling, 2018).

Methodologies that can be used for modelling are as follows:

- Waterfall Model
- Agile Model

BACKGROUND

Excessive studies have been done to improve the efficiency of both waterfall and agile models. Youssef Bassil, in 2009 introduced a simulation tool that would help the project managers to achieve maximum productivity with a minimum number of manpower, cost and duration. This is achieved by designing the model in such a way that all the members working on the project are busy throughout, and they waste minimum time. Mohammad Samadhi Gharajeh proposed a model in which iterative and waterfall were integrated as one; the main advantage of this is that the use of the waterfall model can be done for large complex models and the experimental results show that the customer satisfaction and project success ratio is higher as compared to the waterfall and iterative model individually. There are numerous papers proposed to improve the XP model so that the project can be completed more efficiently. Musa et al. (2011) proposed an XP model in which developers and clients both identify the security concerns at the initial stage of the project. The primary focus of this model was to ensure all the security measures are taken into considerations. He introduced security checks in all the phases of XP. Ji & Sedano (2011) compared both XP and waterfall model on a three months project with at most four developers. For five years, this project was repeatedly developed by 50 teams, and the results showed that the number of lines in the code was almost the same before and after the transition to extreme programming method; therefore, the authors concluded that any of the models could be used for mentioned criteria as the outcome of the project is exact same. Di - Bella et al. (2013) executed a case study based on a data set collected from a team of IT - professional of a large Italian company, these results were validated carefully, and it showed that the usage of pair programming leads to the decrease of new defects in the project. Li - li et al. (2011) introduced the XP high - quality analysis model it was able to get the benefit of quality feature in the kano model. This model helped to improve the client's awareness and made requirements easy to understand for the developers, i.e. errors are reduced.

Similarly, there were many proposals to improve the scrum methodology. Sharma & Hasteer (2016) reviewed many research papers and journals on scrum methodology from 2010 - 2015 and analysed its state in terms of popularity and adoption. They found that software industries tend to use the scrum model relatively more as compared to other software development life cycle models. Von - Wangenheim et al. (2013) introduced a stimulation learning game that will make students aware of the concepts of the scrum as he thought that education of this model is essential for students as it will improve their productivity and cohesiveness. Jha et al. (2016) integrated the waterfall model with the traditional scrum model and proposed solutions for the problems faced during the integration of these two models. Matthies et al. (2016) introduced a tool known as ScrumLint, which analyses the development artefacts. According to him, the feedback collected by this tool will help to improve the workflow and the overall process of the scrum model. Schar et al. (2015) integrated two models: agile scrum and a combination of HERMES 5, a sequential model with the main focus on requirement engineering, security being a primary concern as scrum lacks explicit security practices. Mokhtar et al. (2014) main aim were to minimize duplication and remove redundancy so that during the time of the audit, the desired document can be retrieved easily. They implemented this concept for an online document management system. Tirumala et al. (2016) introduced a model that was a combination of scrum and FDD model, known as the hybrid SCR - FDD model. The main focus of this model is to improve quality and time for development, as the FDD model is inclined more towards the quality of the application without considering the deadlines, whereas the scrum model focuses on time and deadlines. They validated this model by executing it on a real - time project with three teams working on it, and the results were relatively better as compared to individual models.

MAIN FOCUS OF THE CHAPTER

Waterfall Model

The waterfall model was first publicly documented by Royce is 1970 (McCormick, 2012). It can also be called a Linear or serial model. The waterfall model has discrete goals for each phase. There are many distinct approaches defined and designed that can be used during the process of a product's development, and these approaches are also called Software Development Process Models. Each process model has its particular life cycle in order to guarantee success in the process of a product's development.

In software development, one such process is known as the Waterfall model. It is still followed widely to obtain the success of the project. In the waterfall model, phases do not overlap (Cusumano & Smith, n.d.). The entire process of the waterfall model is dissociated into different process phases:

1. Requirement Phase

Requirements are a set of functionality and constrain that the client or customer expects from the system. The requirements are collected from the client or the customer by the business analyst, and once it is gathered, analysed by the team. Requirement describes "WHAT" of the system.

Requirements are documented in this phase, and any clarification or changes if there should be done before the document is finalized. A workability analysis is done to check if these collected requirements are valid or not. Once the analysis is done, and the document is finalized, this document is known as the Software Requirement Specification document (SRS). This document acts as a roadmap for the next phase of the model (Mall, 2015).

When a developer builds software, the hardest part is to determine precisely what is to be built. There are mainly four processes of requirement:

a. **Requirement Elicitation:** The main aim of this process is to gather all the necessary requirements for the software. This process can only be successful if the customer and developer share an effective relationship. There many methods used to achieve this, like Interviews, Brain Storming, and Delphi Technique etc.
b. **Requirement Analysis:** All the requirements gathered in the first process are adequately analysed, and all the inconsistencies, defects, improper data are removed, and all errors, as well as doubts, are resolved.
c. **Requirement Documentation:** All the analyzed requirements need to be appropriately documented so as to use it as a roadmap, so all the documentation of the requirements is done by this process.
d. **Requirement Review:** This process is an essential process as it helps to improve the quality of SRS (Thummadi et al., 2011).

There different types of requirements:

a. **Functional Requirements:** This requirement describe what the software has to do, also called product features.
b. **Non - Functional Requirements:** These requirements are mostly quality requirements. They specify how well the software does and what it has to do - Availability, Usability, Flexibility, Testability, Portability, etc.

Problems / Difficulties of this phase:

a. **Requirements Are Difficult To Uncover:** It is complicated to collect the requirements for the first time; there are chances requirements may be incomplete.
b. **Communication Barrier:** User and developer may have different technical backgrounds.
c. **Lack of Resources:** There may not be sufficient resources to build the system.
d. **Tight Project Schedule:** Due to a tight schedule and excess work, sometimes it may be challenging to take precise requirements.

2. Software Design Phase

Before the developer starts to code / design the system, it is crucial to understand, study and analyse the SRS from the first phase. It helps to prepare the product's design. In this phase, System design is developed, which specifics the hardware and the software requirements such as coding language, network infrastructure, compilers, System UI etc. System design describes the "HOW" of the system (Meland & Jensen, 2008).

Software design should be:

a. Correct and Complete
b. Understandable
c. Simple

A good system design planning is needed to organize the program components so that they are easy to develop and change, i.e., the program's complexity should be less. The developers should use structured techniques to deal with the size of the code; even if they use pre - existing code, it needs to be understood and well - managed (Bassil, 2012).

Types of Software Design:

a. **Bottom - Up Design:** In the approach, the design starts from the lowest level of components designs and by using these components user try to create the next intermediate levels components; this process is continued until all the components or the subsystem are decomposed into a single component.
b. **Top - Down Design:** It is an approach that identifies the most significant module in the system and breaks them into smaller units, and keeps on iterating until the desired level is achieved. This is a stepwise elaboration, i.e. start from the abstract level; in each step, the design of the product is elaborated to a more concrete level, this is done until the user reaches a level where is no need for elaboration, and the design can be implemented directly.
c. **Hybrid Design:** It is a combination of both top - down and bottom - up approach. This is required because to allow common sub - modules, to increase reusability, etc.

Software design helps to define overall system architecture, which is divided into:

a. **High - Level Design Phase:** This is the first stage of system design. This phase contains information like a list of modules, the functionality of modules, cohesion among them, Database Tables etc.
b. **Low - Level Design Phase:** Software component's design is done in this phase. The design made in the first stage is disintegrated into separate modules. The low - level design phase document contains each module's pseudo - code so that the programmer can directly code from it. It also has information about the errors, input and output of each component etc.

3. Implementation and Testing Phase

In this phase, the source code is written as per requirement specification. The program is developed in small units called components, after which these components are integrated as a whole unit. All these components' functionality is tested separately before integrating them, and this testing is known as unit / component testing (Davis, n.d.).

Testing can be done in two ways, i.e. Manual Testing and Automation Testing. When all the application functions are tested manually by testers, this type of testing is known as manual testing. When any automation tool is used to test an application's functionality and no tester is manually involved, this type of testing is called automation testing.

Developers develop software according to the requirements of the user. Software testing helps in validating that all these requirements are fulfilled or not. If the product does not meet the requirements of the client, it may result in a delay or, in the worst case, failure of the project. Testing makes sure that the end product which is built meets the client's expectations.

Testing Standards for both Waterfall and Agile Methodology

Following are some testing standards that need to be followed by the tester:

a. **Test A Program To Make It Fail:** whenever testing is done, its purpose is to find errors. The main aim of testing is to show that the application is not error - free and to find as many as possible errors to make this process more effective.
b. **Start Early Testing:** Testers should start testing in the early stage of development so that the errors can be solved without any complications. It is also cost - effective, i.e. it costs more if the error is found at a later stage. If a bug related to the requirement is found at the final stage, it would cost more than the initial stage.
c. **Testing Is Context - Dependent:** Testing depends on the context, i.e. different tests are performed on different conditions; for instance, if there are two projects build on two different models, both the projects will be tested differently. The testing approach depends on various factors like the type of application, user specifications, documentation, risk etc.
d. **Define Test Plans:** It describes test scope, risk, objectives, methods and tools to be used. Its focus is to meet the needs of the company and the client. A good strategy is required to make sure all the tests are conducted properly with accurate results.
e. **Define Practical Test Cases:** The tester should be well known with the user requirements so that he can validate it with the software for accurate results. They should make practical test cases that can expose many errors in a short period of time. A test case should consist of input data, expected output data and the actual output of the system.
f. **Test For Valid And Invalid Conditions:** Test should also be performed for invalid conditions to know the system performs, and it also helps to find maximum errors.
g. **Review Test Cases Regularly:** Test cases should be reviewed regularly because using the same test cases again and again would not find new errors and bugs, so the testers should revised test cases for effective results.

Testing is the process of checking whether the actual results match the expected one. It basically evaluates whether the system designed matches the user requirement or not. There are different types of testing performed on the system they are (Sawant et al., 2012):

a. **Unit Testing:** In unit testing, all the units of the system are tested individually and independently, which helps to ensure that all the independent modules are correctly implemented. The main advantage of this testing is that it takes fewer efforts to find errors, and the disadvantage is that tester cannot test if the interface between the units / modules is working correctly.
b. **Black - Box Testing:** It is a testing method that evaluates the structure and functionality of the product without having information about the internal structure. It is also known as behavioural

testing. Here testing is not performed on the modules but on the whole system. Four methods of black - box testing are:

i. Boundary Value Analysis.
ii. Graph Bases Testing.
iii. Robustness Testing.
iv. Worst - case Testing (Tuteja & Dubey, 2012).

c. **Regression Testing:** When integration testing is done and an additional module is added, it may create problems with the functions that previously worked properly, so to check if all the implemented functions are working correctly after the addition regression testing is performed. It is basically re - performing the test cases on some subsets to ensure that changes / addition of the module does not create any new bugs or error (Sharma et al., 2013). Regression testing can be done manually or by automation tools like capture / playback; these tools enable the developer to capture the test cases that were executed before, and their results so as to play back them for subsequent events and compare it with the new results. It focuses highly on integrated modules that can be affected by the addition of new modules.

d. **Acceptance Testing:** Acceptance testing comes into the picture when the software product is developed explicitly for a particular user. The customer conducts the number of tests to validate all the requirements. This testing is not done for large public / audiences. The process of acceptance testing is such that the customer tests the software product and gives the feedback, according to the feedback if everything is perfect, then the product is delivered to the customer, and if not, then some modifications are done based on the feedback of the customer and the product is delivered (Haugset & Stalhane, 2012).

e. **Alpha and Beta Testing:** They are conducted when the user is unknown. The customer undertakes alpha testing at the developer's place / site. It is a combination of white - box and black - box testing and is conducted in an environment controlled by the developer. The test is carried out before the product's release, and the developer records the errors or the bug that are encountered. The customer does beta testing at its end. The test is conducted in a real - time environment and not in a controlled environment, and a developer is not present when the tests are conducted. This test is carried out after the product is delivered to the customer, and if any failure or error occurs, it gets reported (Mohd & Shahbodin, 2015).

f. **White - Box Testing:** It is the opposite of black - box testing, where testing is carried out according to the analysis of the product's internal structure. It is also known as Clear - Box testing, Structured Based Testing and Glass - Box testing. This test can be performed on levels of the software development cycle. Methods of white - box testing are:

i. Unit Testing
ii. Integration Testing (Nidhra, 2012).

Some of the tools used in software testing are Selenium Web Driver (Web Application) or Appium (Mobile Application). Selenium is composed of many automation tools, and one such tool is the selenium web driver. It is an advanced version of its processor selenium RC. Selenium web driver has direct communication with the browsers, and it supports a different kind of browsers like chrome, safari, Firefox, internet explorer etc. It is faster than selenium RC. The main aim of selenium web driver is to improve the testing of the modern web application. Many languages can be used for writing test scripts in selenium web driver like java, python, ruby, etc. (Razak & Fahrurazi, 2011).

4. Deployment and Maintenance Phase

In the deployment and maintenance phase, the software is tested in a real time - environment to check its efficiency. Once the software is deployed, it is now available for the client / customer to use. Sometimes in this phase, clients and customers are trained to communicate with the software and to get the maximum benefit (Bennett & Rajlich, n.d.).

Once the product is delivered to the client / customer Maintenance phase comes into the picture. In this phase, the client is provided support and maintenance of the software. This phase's ultimate aim is to fix all the bugs, defects, and errors that occur while using the software (O'Keeffe & ÓCinnéide, 2008). Maintenance is one of the most essential phases as it provides the customer with after delivery services and updates to keep the software up with ongoing trends and technology.

Categories of Maintenance:

a. **Corrective Maintenance:** It is initiated by the occurrence of defects in the software; these defects may be a logical error, coding error, design error etc. Appropriate actions must be taken to restore the correct functionality of the software system. Patching - It is a process to fix the defects in case of emergency temporarily, but it has the disadvantage of foreseen future errors due to a lack of proper analysis.
b. **Adaptive Maintenance:** This is the process of modifying the software to make it adaptable to changing environments such as any outside factor, platform changes, government policies etc.
c. **Perfect Maintenance:** This maintenance tries to improve the processing efficiency or performance of the software product. It allows the product to restructuring to improve changeability. If there is an expansion in the customer's requirements, the developers enhance the existing software product's functionality to make it cleaner, faster and better.
d. **Other Types of Maintenance:** There are many long - term side - effects of the above the maintenances, which increases the complexity of the software, and the system starts to deteriorate. Some work is required to be done to maintain and reduce the complexity of the software. This kind of work can be called preventive maintenance.

Maintenance Process is a process of different phases used to maintain the software product:

a. **Define Maintenance Objective:** The errors and systems are identified and ways to fix them. Basically, define what needs to be done on the product.
b. **Program Understanding:** It is the first phase of the process. It tries to understand and analyse the program complexity and the documentation of the system.
c. **Generating a Particular Maintenance Proposal:** It is the second phase of the process; here, the proposal is generated for each and every maintenance activity to accomplish the implementation of these activities.
d. **Ripple Effect:** It is the third phase of the process. In this phase, record all the side - effects that have occurred due to all the modifications done in the system.
e. **Testing:** This is the fourth phase of the process. It consists of testing all the modified modules or functions of the software product to ensure that they are implemented correctly, and the system is working perfectly.

Boehm's Model

In 1933, he proposed a model for the maintenance process based on economic models and principles. He believed that economic models and principles could improve productivity in maintenance, but it could help us under the process more clearly. He represented the entire maintenance process in a closed - loop. In this model, he states that the maintenance manager's decision drives the maintenance process. (Lane et al., n.d.)

He also gave a formula for calculating the maintenance process. The formula was in terms of efforts.

The ACT is related to the number of the change request,

ACT = KLOCadded + KLOCdeleted / KLOCtotal

The annual maintenance effort (AME) in person - months is measured as:

AME = ACT * SDE

Where ACT= Annual change tariff and SDE = software development efforts in person - months. This formula is widely used (Geeks for Geeks, 2020)

Problems that can occur during maintenance:

- Since some other developer can write the program, it must be challenging to understand if the same person is not doing the maintenance activity.
- Systems are not compactable to change.
- No accurate information about the system (Anquetil et al., 2007).
- Software companies sometimes do not provide maintenance service for the long - term.

Possible Solution for this kind of problems:

- Better Documentation
- Complete Replacement of the system
- Budget and effort relocation

Agile Methodology

In 2001, the agile methodology was proposed by a team of 17 people in a written form. Agile is a software methodology that builds the software gradually using short iterations of 1 - 4 weeks so that the software development is associated with the changing environments and needs. Instead of working for 6 - 12 months continuously where all the requirements and risks of the software are candid, agile allows taking feedback of the customer after every iteration so that if there are any changes or errors, they can be fixed before moving to the next iteration. The client's involvement is throughout the life cycle of the product (Erickson et al., 2005).

Both development and testing activities run simultaneously; every cycle or iteration has its testing phase. Regression testing is implemented every time a new function is created.

Table 1. Principles of agile methodology

Sr. No	Principles of Agile Methodology
1.	"Our highest priority is to satisfy the customer through early and continuous delivery of valuable software."
2.	"Welcome changing requirements, even late in the development. Agile processes harness change for the customer's competitive advantage."
3.	"Deliver working software frequently, from a couple of weeks to a couple of months with preference to the shorter timescale."
4.	"Business people and developer must work together daily throughout the project."
5.	"Build projects around motivated individuals. Give them the environment and support they need and trust them to get the job done."
6.	"The most efficient and effective of conveying information to and within a development team is face - to - face conversation."
7.	"Working software is the primary measure of progress."
8.	"Agile processes promote sustainable development. The sponsor, developers, and the user should be able to maintain a constant pace indefinitely."
9.	"Continuous attention to technical excellence and good design enhances agility."
10.	"Simplicity - the art of maximizing the amount of work done - is essential."
11.	"The best architectures, requirements and designs emerge from self - organizing teams."
12.	"At regular intervals, the team reflects on how to become more effective, then tunes and adjusts its behavior accordingly."

Source: Agile Manifesto, 2001

Agile Testing Methodology consists of (Dingsøyr et al., 2012):

- **Scrum**: Scrum is an agile methodology that mainly focuses on how to divide/manage tasks in a team - based environment.
- **Crystal Methodologies:** This methodology concentrates on individuals and their interactions. Basically, it is a guideline for all team members about team collaboration and communication.
- **Dynamic Software Development Model (DSDM):** This methodology focuses on the entire life cycle of the product, i.e., from pre to post system implementation. Its main aim is to understand the business needs.
- **Feature Driven Development (FDD):** Like all other methodologies, its main idea is to concentrate on short iterations that serve to work out for a particular feature or the function of the system.
- **Lean Software Development:** This model aims to provide the customer with maximum output with optimum efficiency.
- **Extreme Programming:** The ultimate aim of this methodology is to give quality software and higher quality of life to the team. It is most specific regarding the engineering practices of the system.

Scrum Methodology

Scrum is an agile methodology that mainly focuses on how to divide / manage tasks within a team - based environment. Basically, scrum empowers the development team (Adi, 2015). The first software scrum was built in 1993 by Jeff Shuterland, and it was based on the research done on worldwide projects. The main aim of this methodology is to add energy, focus and clarity to project planning and implementation; it will consistently:

- Increase the speed of application development.
- Align individual and corporate objectives.
- Create a culture driven by performance.
- Support shareholder value creation.
- Achieve regular and consistent communication of performance at all levels.
- Enhance individual development and quality of life (Sutherland et al., 2007).

It is has been observed that over the last decades, due to this consistency, scrum is one of the most used models in the software industry.

Process flow of scrum testing is as follows:

- Each iteration or cycle in scrum is known as a sprint, and each sprint's duration varies from 2 - 4 weeks and takes place one after the other without any break.
- During each sprint meetings, top items that are needed to be completed in a sprint are.
- Selected from the product backlog and turned into the sprint backlog.
- The team works on defined sprint backlogs and tries to complete all task within the sprint.
- Once the backlog is fixed for a sprint, it cannot be changed, and the sprint team follows a strict workflow.
- The Scrum team delivers product features at the end of each sprint (Srivastava et al., 2017).

Scrum Methodology mainly has three roles they are (Mundra et al., 2013):

1. Scrum Master: Master, is responsible for setting up the scrum team. All the scrum meetings are organized by him. He should have experience of more than 5 years.

Duties of Scrum Master are:

a. He tries to improve the efficiency or the performance of the team and promotes the team for better creativity.
b. He is responsible for removing obstruction for the scrum team.
c. He manages the scrum process with the coordination of the team.
d. He arranges daily meetings, schedule meetings, demo and decision - making process in order to ensure that everything is working correctly.
e. The scrum master helps the product owner in designing the product backlog.
f. He acts as a shield for his team.
g. He is the one who keeps the team away from distractions and problems (Baumgart et al., 2015).

Skills Required:

a. He should have good communication skills.
b. He should be a good leader in order to assist the team members and to clarify their goals.
c. He needs to be an expert in decision making and planning.

d. He should be honest and respectful towards the team members.

2. Product Owner: The product owner creates the product backlog and is responsible for the delivery of the functionality of each sprint. Product Backlog is a list that contains all the requirements of the product and tasks that needs to be completed in a sprint. Whenever a modification is required in any module, a backlog is referred for the requirements and list of existing features.

Duties of Product Owner are (Front Row Agile, n.d.):

a. He defines the goals and vision at the beginning of every sprint.
b. Creates and maintains the backlogs.
c. He should continuously remind the scrum team about their goals.
d. He is responsible for prioritizing the needs.
e. He communicates with customers and stakeholders to assure them that the team is working in the right direction and will deliver what is expected to be delivered.

Skills Required:

a. He should have technical skills.
b. He should be extremely commutative.
c. He should be an excellent analytical thinker.
d. He should have the great problem - solving ability.

3. Scrum Team: The scrum team manages their work and organizes the work in such a way that the sprint is completed on time. The size of the team can differ from 3 - 9, which does not include the scrum master and product owner. The primary duty of scrum is that they are responsible for turning the requirements in the backlog into functional pieces within the time of the sprint.

Extreme Programming

Kent Beck developed extreme Programming in 1996. It enables developers to respond conveniently to ever - changing requirements even late in the software product's life cycle. Managers, Customers, Developers are equal parts of the team. It is a proven successful methodology as it is able to reach customer's satisfaction (Grisham & Perry, n.d.).

Kent gives 12 different practices for extreme programming (Nawrocki et al., 2002):

- **Planning Game:** The main aim of this practice is to define the requirement details properly. Both customer and developer are the part of this practice, and they make plans for the releases and iteration together they also identify the roles clearly and makes story card from each customer's point of view and split the card into the task for the developers. All the planning and schedule are made according to the amount of work.
- **Small Releases:** In small releases, the team produces a quick system and, after a short time, releases a new version of the same.
- **Metaphor:** In metaphor, developers makes the team aware of how their program will work.

- **Simple Design:** The design of the system should be simple throughout, and the complexity of the code should be less.
- **Testing:** Testers perform unit testing continuously, which should run perfectly to continue forward.
- **Refactoring:** Individuals must try to improve the internal structure of the product without changing their behaviour.
- **Pair Programming:** Two developers come together to design the production code that is used in the final product.
- **Collective Ownership:** Programming code is the property of few coders, but it is owned by the entire team collectively, and anyone from the team can change it.
- **Contiguous Integration:** The components must be integrated and built many times during an iteration, i.e. whenever a new task is implemented.
- **40 - Hour week:** This is the rule of XP that the team should not work for more than 40 hours a week and should not continue the overtime for consecutive two weeks.
- **On - Site Customer:** A real - environment user is available on site for the whole project so that if there is any query, it can be solved.
- **Coding Standards:** Programmers and developers define some set of rules to standardize coding style for the team.

The process of Extreme Programming is:

- **Planning:** The identification of stakeholders and sponsors are made in this phase. System architecture design and security related information are gathered; also, service level agreement is created.
- **Analysis:** In extreme programming, business requirements are gathered/ stored in the form of stories in the parking lot. This phrase captures the stories in the parking lot, prioritises the stories according to the task, and tries to find the estimated time span of the iteration. Resource planning is done for both development and quality & assurance teams.
- **Wrapping:** This phase develops new stories according to the needs and reviews them and checks for process improvements based on the end of iteration review comments and perform regression testing simultaneously. Small releases are done in this phase.
- **Closure:** All the training of the customer about the product is done in this phase, and the product is validated, and if the customer is satisfied with it, the product gets released.

Case Study on Waterfall Model

Assume that XYZ bank wants to make a new banking application and have approached some organization (Petersen et al., 2009).

The first phase of this model is the requirement phase, so, in this phase, the business analysts visit the customer, i.e. the bank, and gathers the requirement needed for the application.

The analyst documents the requirements as per his discussion with the client; while analysing the requirements, they found that there are some questions that needs to be answered like -

- If the application was to be used in different countries or in a single country?
- Should the application support different languages?

- What is the number of users expected to use this application?
- What level of security is required?

Table 2. Differences between scrum methodology and extreme programming

Sr. no	Scrum methodology	Extreme Programming
1.	The scrum team works in iterations called sprints, and the duration is from two weeks to 4 weeks.	Teams work in an iteration that is from one week to two weeks.
2.	Scrum does not allow changes in the sprint.	Being more flexible in extreme programming allows changes in the iteration.
3.	Scrum does not lay down any engineering practices.	XP is driven by engineering practices like pair programming, refactoring etc.
4.	The scrum team decides the order of feature's execution in the sprint meeting.	The customer strictly prioritizes order of features.
5.	Scrum emphasizes self - organization.	XP stresses engineering practice constraints.
6.	Scrum is a framework for product development, a container in which other practices can be added.	XP is one such practice that can be performed within a scrum framework.
7.	Scrum can be used in the non - software product.	While XP focuses on programming.
8.	Scrum methodology does not take feedback until the sprint review.	XP seeks feedback immediately.
9.	Scrum's main aim is to get an estimation of the time that development will take.	XP is more about helping the team to get things done as quickly as possible.

Source: Blom, 2010

All these and many more questions if the customer should answer there since once the requirement phase is completed, the customer will not get to be involved again until the acceptance testing, which is nearly the end of the project (Stol & Fitzgerald, 2014).

Now move onto the next phase of the model, i.e. system design phase; in this, the developer and the senior member work on the application's architecture, i.e. the high level and low - level designs. This design is created according to the customer's requirements; all the diagrams and stuff are created too.

Now comes the implementation phase, the designing and coding team works on the project's coding part. They keep the design documents with them to ensure that their team follows the design that is finalized. As it is a banking application, the security of the application is of high importance, so all the features related to security should be implemented properly.

After the designing is completed, testing is performed on the application. A testing team with a banking domain should be hired so that proper testing can be carried out. Many different types of testing are performed on the product, such as regression testing, acceptance testing etc. The security testing team tests the security features of the application.

Once the testing is done, deploy the application on the servers procured for the application. This includes activities like installing OS, security patches, installing databases etc. The team also communicates with the Information - Technology administrative teams to set up the application and run it on the servers (Sureshchandra & Shrinivasavadhani, 2008).

Once the application is deployed, the team works in the maintenance phase, and whatever errors and bugs are reported while the application is running is fixed by the team.

The above case study dictates the working of the waterfall model.

Understand this process from the customer's perspective:

The customer gets involved with the team in the requirement phase and gives all the information needed. Once this phase is over, the customer is not able to get involved with the team and have no idea about the design or the architecture of the product. He is not able to see any progress and is clueless regarding the development of the project, and there could be several conflicts, such as: will the delivered system is exactly as it was desired, Will the product gets delivered on time, will all the features of the system provide accurate results etc.

The customer has no idea about the product until the time of delivery, i.e. till the deployment phase; after that, he gets to see the product, and if the product is not up to his requirements, developers need to follow all the phases of the model again, which is really time - consuming, and the budget of the product will be rapidly increased, so to avoid this there are significant changes that customer cancels the project, This results into the failure of the project.

The waterfall model should be used when the requirements are entirely known, and the project is small in size, so that chances of failure will be less.

Where the waterfall model is preferred:

- Since it is highly structured, the waterfall is best used in industries like manufacturing and construction because here task and deadlines should be set and maintained and these industries are rigid that relies on - time completion of dependent stages.
- It is also used in the Development of Department of Defence (DOD) and Military programs because of the strict requirement that has to follow in this industries, requirements are well known in advance, and they are very particular about the delivery of the project.
- The waterfall model can also be used in the health sector, banking sector, corporate sector and government organization for nuclear facilities.

Case Study on Agile Model

Consider a case study and try to analyse and process it with the help of the Agile Model.

In the agile model, the process is quite different from that of the waterfall model, where the project is broken into several iterations, and all the iteration should be of the same duration. In this approach, team and client with little planning can get started with the project. Unlike the waterfall model, the agile model customer is allowed to interact with the team and work with the functioning software at the end of each iteration and provide feedback on it.

This approach allows the team to take up changes easily and make corrections if needed. In the waterfall model, each team works in a particular phase - only, i.e. once the people assigned for the collection of requirements completes its task, then it is handed over to the design team as so on but in the whole agile team works together with more an entire project (Becker, n.d.).

Software is developed and released gradually in the iterations. Development, Testing, Integration all this is done in iterations according to the requirement of the customer.

Agile provides the application as per the customer's desire, and due to the involvement of the customer, the chances of failure decreases.

Where the agile model is preferred:

- Agile is preferred when the customer is ready to invest time for the project as he is one of the most influential people in the team; he needs to devote the time necessary to make sure that the team has the necessary information required for the project.
- It was also preferred when the customer and team are ready to implement changes as agile allows a change in the software anytime.
- If requirements are less at the start of the project and do not need to meet strict regulations, agile is preferred.
- If the team is attempting to build something creative and innovative that does not exist in any company today, these types of projects are well served in agile.
- Agile methodology has become very common in the IT industry; over 52% of companies practise agile development.

Reasons for Failures of a Project

Here we have taken an example of an e - commerce website and tried to discuss the reasons behind the failure of it. There are several reasons like:

1. Improper documentation of the requirements - Documenting requirements is essential for any project as it contains all the information about how the client wants the project. If this is not maintained, it can lead to the failure of the project as there are chances that the developed software is not as per users/clients requirement.
2. Choosing the wrong technology/ platform for the project - It is imperative for us to understand the technical aspects of the project so that suitable technology can be used to make the application user friendly and convenient to use.
3. Poor Onsite experience (user testing) - After completing the backhand section, the application should be tested by the user number of times so as to make sure that the final outcome is proper and executable and therefore reduces the chances of poor onsite experience.
4. Frequent change of developers in a team - Frequent change in the team leads to inconsistency and may lead to delay in the project, so while working on a project, the manager should make sure that teams are available throughout the project; therefore, this problem can be avoided.
5. Exceeding the budget - when a budget is fixed, the team should make sure that it does not get exceeded as if it increases a lot from the fixed budget; chances are that the client refuses to proceed with the project and hence the project fails.

There are many more reasons for it, but while working on a project team should consider all these points so that failure can be avoided.

Advantages of the waterfall model:

- This model is simple and easily understandable.
- The waterfall model is best for projects which are small in size, and requirements are predefined and clear.
- It is easy to manage due to the stubbornness of the model; each phase has specific deliverables and a review process.
- Makes the final product more predictable.

- The information is very well transferred from one phase to another (Barjtya et al., 2017).
- It allows the client to get an application built on a low budget.
- In waterfall, model fresher's can also work in the development team, which makes the team more prominent, and the project can be completed early.
- In the waterfall model, the documentation of the project is accurate and precise as compared to software life cycle models.

Table 3. Difference between waterfall and agile model

Sr. No	Waterfall Model	Agile Model
1.	The team needs complete requirements about the project, to begin with.	In agile, requirements continue to grow over time and are defined when they are needed.
2.	All team members have different roles and responsibilities.	Each responsibility is shared between the teams, i.e. every team member can play any role.
3.	In waterfall, quality control activity such as testing is performed at the end of the project.	All these activities are performed throughout in agile model.
4.	In the waterfall, it is challenging to measure the success/ progress of the project features in the middle of a project.	In agile, progress can be measured easily in the middle of the project, also, as working features are delivered frequently.
5.	Progress of the project is reviewed once a week.	Progress of the project is reviewed on a daily basis.
6.	The process in the waterfall model is strictly followed since this model is serial.	This model is more of people - oriented and less importance is given to processes; they can also skip the process which are of fewer values.
7.	If the project timeline is fixed and a strict waterfall model is preferred.	In the agile model, the timeline is not strict and can be moved.
8.	If the project's budget is fixed and cannot be increased, the waterfall is used since the requirement in this model is fixed and transparent.	If budget flexibility is available, the agile model can be implemented as it allows to implement features that can take extra time and money.
9.	No Client/customer involvement in this model and gets to see the product very late in the cycle.	The client/customer involves the team in this model and gets to see the application's working model.
10.	Generally used for small projects with defined requirements.	It is generally preferred for large and complex projects with no proper initial requirements.
11.	Waterfall projects follow a projects hierarchy and once.	In agile, project teams are self - governing.
12.	A sequential and linear life cycle model and no phase is overlapped.	It is a continuous iteration of development and testing in the software development process.
13.	The project manager is from IT background.	The project manager may not have an IT background.
14.	Large team size.	Teams of 3 - 9 members.
15.	Testers and developers work separately.	Tester and developers work together.
16.	One large release of the software.	Incremental release of the software.

Source: McCormick, 2012

Disadvantages of the waterfall model:

- It is not very easy to define all the requirements clearly at the initial stage of the project.
- The waterfall model does not allow the client to get involved in the process.
- The waterfall model is not suited for complex projects since it does not accommodate changes since the requirements are fixed and predefined.

- A working framework of the project can only be seen at the end of the project.
- High chances of project failure as the client get to see the application at the end of the cycle, and if he is not satisfied with the product, they need to start from the very first phase, which is very costly and hence he decides to cancel the project. (Modi et al., n.d.).
- Delivery of the project may be delayed as each phase need to be 100% completed.
- Waterfall fall requires its employees to carry out excessive research on the user's need, and hence the process becomes time - consuming.

Advantages of the agile model:

- The agile model allows customer involvement and is an essential part of the team.
- The working feature of the product is delivered frequently, i.e. at the end of each cycle.
- Even late in the project, changes in requirements are accepted.
- The software is able to adapt to changing environments.
- People and interactions are of more importance rather than process and tools (Krishnan, 2015).
- It has daily interactions between the developers and clients so that the clients get to know all the updates about his product.

Disadvantages of the agile model:

- It may be challenging for the team to develop software if the customer is not clear about the final outcome that they want.
- Since the requirement keeps changing in an agile model, it is challenging to predict the project's final outcome.
- Poor resources planning.
- Limited documentation.
- The cost of the project may be higher than expected since changes are accommodated in this model, and because of frequent changes, the cost of the project increases. (Matinnejad, 2011).
- No place for fresher in the development team as only seniors are capable of making the decisions.
- In agile, it is difficult to assess the efforts required by the team at the beginning of the software development life cycle.

SOLUTION AND RECOMMENDATIONS

According to the case studies and the advantages and disadvantages of both the models, it is apparent that the success ratio of the agile model is relatively higher than that of the waterfall model. It is observed that nowadays, companies tend to work more with agile models as it allows them to interact with the client, which results in the development of the product, which is exactly as expected by the client. This does not mean that the waterfall model should be ignored totally, it can be used when the project is small, and the requirements of the project are clear.

FUTURE RESEARCH DIRECTIONS

Agile and waterfall model both have their strength and weaknesses for implementing a project. The model selection depends on the context and requirement of a project. If the project requirements are changing rapidly, then agile is a more suitable choice but if project has fix requirements and tight deadlines, then waterfall model is better. Scrum and Extreme programming are not end of the agile model, agile is continuously evolving to deliver high quality outcomes. Waterfall model is not preferred for the large - scale project due its issues with the requirement and verification. Waterfall model has the major drawback with the customer feedback, customer has not information of the project till the end. That might cause the conflict. Waterfall model will be more suitable if it introduces the customer involvement.

CONCLUSION

It is evident that the usage of the model clearly depends on what type of project the company is working on. Every project has its own criteria, and based on that, the team decides on which model they should work on. So, therefore, to say that this particular model is best for all kind of project is not acceptable, and hence both models are of equal importance in the software industry.

REFERENCES

Adi, P. (2015). Scrum Method Implementation in a Software Development Project Management. *International Journal of Advanced Computer Science and Applications*, *6*(9). Advance online publication. doi:10.14569/IJACSA.2015.060927

Agile Manifesto. (2001). *Principles*. Retrieved from Https://Agilemanifesto.Org/Principles.Html

Anquetil, N., de Oliveira, K. M., de Sousa, K. D., & Batista Dias, M. G. (2007). Software maintenance seen as a knowledge management issue. *Information and Software Technology*, *49*(5), 515–529. doi:10.1016/j.infsof.2006.07.007

Barjtya, S., Sharma, A., & Rani, U. (2017). A detailed study of Software Development Life Cycle (SDLC). *Models.*, *6*(7), 4.

Bassil, Y. (2012). A Simulation Model for the Waterfall Software Development Life Cycle. *International Journal of Engineering*, *2*(5), 7.

Baumgart, R., Hummel, M., & Holten, R. (2015). *Personality Traits of Scrum Roles in Agile Software Development Teams - A Qualitative Analysis*. Academic Press.

Becker, C. H. (n.d.). *Using eXtreme Programming in a Student Environment: A Case Study*. Academic Press.

Bennett, K., & Rajlich, V. (n.d.). *Software Maintenance and Evolution: A Roadmap*. Academic Press.

Blom, M. (2010). Is Scrum and XP suitable for CSE Development? *Procedia Computer Science*, *1*(1), 1511–1517. doi:10.1016/j.procs.2010.04.168

Cusumano, M. A., & Smith, S. (n.d.). *Beyond the Waterfall: Software Development at Microsoft*. Academic Press.

Davis, A. M. (n.d.). A conci rent process model of software development. *ACM SIGSOFT*, *19*(2), 14.

di Bella, E., Fronza, I., Phaphoom, N., Sillitti, A., Succi, G., & Vlasenko, J. (2013). Pair Programming and Software Defects—A Large, Industrial Case Study. *IEEE Transactions on Software Engineering*, *39*(7), 930–953. doi:10.1109/TSE.2012.68

Dingsøyr, T., Nerur, S., Balijepally, V., & Moe, N. B. (2012). A decade of agile methodologies: Towards explaining agile software development. *Journal of Systems and Software*, *85*(6), 1213–1221. doi:10.1016/j.jss.2012.02.033

Erickson, J., Lyytinen, K., & Siau, K. (2005). *Agile Modelling, Agile Software Development, and Extreme Programming*. Academic Press.

Front Row Agile. (n.d.). *The role of a product owner responsibilities and characteristics*. Retrieved from Https://www.Frontrowagile.com/blog/posts/74-the-role-of-a-product-owner-responsibilities-and-characteristics

Geeks for Geeks. (2020). *Boehms software maintenance model*. Retrieved from Https://www.geeksforgeeks.org/boehms - software - maintenance - model/

Grisham, P. S., & Perry, D. E. (n.d.). *Customer Relationships and Extreme Programming*. Academic Press.

Haugset, B., & Stalhane, T. (2012). Automated Acceptance Testing as an Agile Requirements Engineering Practice. *2012 45th Hawaii International Conference on System Sciences*, 5289 - 5298. 10.1109/HICSS.2012.127

Jha, M. M., Vilardell, R. M. F., & Narayan, J. (2016). Scaling Agile Scrum Software Development: Providing Agility and Quality to Platform Development by Reducing Time to Market. *2016 IEEE 11th International Conference on Global Software Engineering (ICGSE),* 84 - 88. 10.1109/ICGSE.2016.24

Ji, F., & Sedano, T. (2011). Comparing extreme programming and Waterfall project results. *2011 24th IEEE - CS Conference on Software Engineering Education and Training (CSEE&T),* 482 - 486. 10.1109/CSEET.2011.5876129

Krishnan, M. S. (2015). Software Development Risk Aspects and Success Frequency on Spiral and Agile Model. *International Journal of Innovative Research in Computer and Communication Engineering*, *03*(01), 301–310. doi:10.15680/ijircce.2015.0301024

Lane, S., Gu, Q., Lago, P., & Richardson, I. (n.d.). *Adaptation of Service - Based Applications: A Maintenance Process?* Academic Press.

Li-Li, Z., Lian-Feng, H., & Qin-Ying, S. (2011). Research on Requirement for High - quality Model of Extreme Programming. *2011 International Conference on Information Management, Innovation Management and Industrial Engineering*, 518 - 522. doi:10.1109/ICIII.2011.132

Mall, R. (2015). *Fundamentals of software engineering*. Academic Press.

Matinnejad, R. (2011). Agile Model Driven Development: An Intelligent Compromise. *2011 Ninth International Conference on Software Engineering Research, Management and Applications*, 197 - 202. 10.1109/SERA.2011.17

Matthies, C., Kowark, T., Richly, K., Uflacker, M., & Plattner, H. (2016). ScrumLint: Identifying Violations of Agile Practices Using Development Artifacts. In *Proceedings of the 9th International Workshop on Cooperative and Human Aspects of Software Engineering - CHASE '16*, (pp. 40 – 43). ACM Press.

McCormick, M. (2012). *Waterfall vs. Agile Methodology*. MPCS, Inc.

Meland, P. H., & Jensen, J. (2008). Secure Software Design in Practice. *2008 Third International Conference on Availability, Reliability and Security*, 1164 - 1171. 10.1109/ARES.2008.48

Modi, H. S., Singh, N. K., & Chauhan, H. P. (n.d.). *Comprehensive Analysis of Software Development Life Cycle Models*. Academic Press.

Mohd, C. K. N. C. K., & Shahbodin, F. (2015). Personalized Learning Environment: Alpha Testing, Beta Testing & User Acceptance Test. *Procedia: Social and Behavioral Sciences*, *195*, 837–843. doi:10.1016/j.sbspro.2015.06.319

Mokhtar, R., Jaafar, N. H., Tahar, N. F., Sukiman, S. A., Aris, A., & Abu Bakar, N. F. (2014). An integrated document management system for managing self - programme accreditation using scrum approach. *2014 International Symposium on Technology Management and Emerging Technologies*, 102 - 106. 10.1109/ISTMET.2014.6936487

Mundra, A., Misra, S., & Dhawale, C. A. (2013). Practical Scrum - Scrum Team: Way to Produce Successful and Quality Software. *2013 13th International Conference on Computational Science and Its Applications,* 119 - 123. 10.1109/ICCSA.2013.25

Musa, S. B., Norwawi, N. M., Selamat, M. H., & Sharif, K. Y. (2011). Improved extreme programming methodology with inbuilt security. *2011 IEEE Symposium on Computers & Informatics*, 674 - 679. 10.1109/ISCI.2011.5958997

Nawrocki, J., Jasinski, M., Walter, B., & Wojciechowski, A. (2002). Extreme programming modified: Embrace requirements engineering practices. *Proceedings IEEE Joint International Conference on Requirements Engineering*, 303 - 310. 10.1109/ICRE.2002.1048543

Nidhra, S. (2012). Black Box and White Box Testing Techniques—A Literature Review. *International Journal of Embedded Systems and Applications*, *2*(2), 29–50. doi:10.5121/ijesa.2012.2204

O'Keeffe, M., & Ó Cinnéide, M. (2008). Search - based refactoring for software maintenance. *Journal of Systems and Software*, *81*(4), 502–516. doi:10.1016/j.jss.2007.06.003

Petersen, K., Wohlin, C., & Baca, D. (2009). The Waterfall Model in Large - Scale Development. In F. Bomarius, M. Oivo, P. Jaring, & P. Abrahamsson (Eds.), *Product - Focused Software Process Improvement* (Vol. 32, pp. 386–400). Springer Berlin Heidelberg. doi:10.1007/978-3-642-02152-7_29

Razak, R. A., & Fahrurazi, F. R. (2011). Agile testing with Selenium. *2011 Malaysian Conference in Software Engineering*, 217 - 219. 10.1109/MySEC.2011.6140672

Sawant, A. A., Bari, P. H., & Chawan, P. M. (2012). Software Testing Techniques and Strategies. *International Journal of Engineering Research and Applications*, *2*(3), 7.

Schar, B., Jungling, S., & Thonssen, B. (2015). Towards an Agile Requirements Engineering Process Combining HERMES 5 and SCRUM. *2015 International Conference on Enterprise Systems (ES)*, 98 - 109. 10.1109/ES.2015.17

Sharma, C., Sabharwal, S., & Sibal, R. (2013). *A Survey on Software Testing Techniques using Genetic Algorithm*. Academic Press.

Sharma, S., & Hasteer, N. (2016). A comprehensive study on state of Scrum development. *2016 International Conference on Computing, Communication and Automation (ICCCA)*, 867 - 872. 10.1109/CCAA.2016.7813837

Software Design and Modelling. (2018). Retrieved April 19, 2020, from https://sea.ucar.edu/best - practices/design

Srivastava, A., Bhardwaj, S., & Saraswat, S. (2017). SCRUM model for agile methodology. *2017 International Conference on Computing, Communication and Automation (ICCCA)*, 864 - 869. 10.1109/CCAA.2017.8229928

Stol, K. J., & Fitzgerald, B. (2014). Two's company, three's a crowd: A case study of crowdsourcing software development. *Proceedings of the 36th International Conference on Software Engineering - ICSE 2014*, 187 - 198. 10.1145/2568225.2568249

Sureshchandra, K., & Shrinivasavadhani, J. (2008). Moving from Waterfall to Agile. *Agile 2008 Conference,* 97 - 101. 10.1109/Agile.2008.49

Sutherland, J., Viktorov, A., Blount, J., & Puntikov, N. (2007). Distributed Scrum: Agile Project Management with Outsourced Development Teams. *2007 40th Annual Hawaii International Conference on System Sciences (HICSS'07),* 274a - 274a. 10.1109/HICSS.2007.180

Thummadi, B. V., Shiv, O., & Lyytinen, K. (2011). Enacted Routines in Agile and Waterfall Processes. *2011 AGILE Conference*, 67 - 76. 10.1109/AGILE.2011.29

Tirumala, S., Ali, S., & Anjan, B. G. (2016). A Hybrid Agile model using SCRUM and Feature Driven Development. *International Journal of Computers and Applications*, *156*(5), 1–5. doi:10.5120/ijca2016912443

Tuteja, M., & Dubey, G. (2012). A Research Study on importance of Testing and Quality Assurance in Software Development Life Cycle (SDLC). *Models*, *2*(3), 7.

von Wangenheim, C. G., Savi, R., & Borgatto, A. F. (2013). SCRUMIA - An educational game for teaching SCRUM in computing courses. *Journal of Systems and Software*, *86*(10), 2675–2687. doi:10.1016/j.jss.2013.05.030

KEY TERMS AND DEFINITIONS

Agile Model: Agile model mainly emphasizes on idea of iterative development where requirement and solutions throughout the development cycle.

Extreme Programming: Extreme programming's main aim is to improve the software quality and is most specific regarding appropriate engineering practices.

Scrum Model: Scrum is one of the framework of agile whose main focus is on teamwork and accountability. It is based on an iterative and incremental process.

Software Development: Software development is a collection of processes which are used to develop high quality computer software and applications.

Software Development Life Cycle: It is process which is used by software industry to develop high quality software applications that meets the user's requirement.

Waterfall Model: It is a sequential model which follows a strict order and is divided into several phases.

Chapter 8
The Role of an Agile and Lean Project Management Toolkit for Assisting E-Learning Project Management Teams in Multi-National Organisations:
Accounting for Inter-Organisational Architecture, Culture, Agility, and Change in Legacy Systems

Jonathan Bishop
https://orcid.org/0000-0002-9919-7602
Crocels Community Media Group, UK

Kamal Bechkoum
University of Gloucestershire, UK

ABSTRACT

Project management is a term for which there are endless books professing the right way to conduct it. Project management is the systematic application of a standardized approach to conducting a project that increases that project's chances of success. It is known that IT projects are some of those projects most likely to fail, and e-learning projects are no different. The aim of this chapter is to explain how it might be possible to develop a toolkit that could allow e-learning systems of any scale to be developed by those who often have to deliver learning, but may not necessarily have skills in project management or ICT development. It is intended that the proposed toolkit would be valued by other internationally focussed organisations where learning and teaching are a core part of the activities that it conducts, but on a smaller scale. To achieve this, research is proposed at the University of Gloucestershire and Crocels Community Media Group. A pilot study is conducted, and the questionnaire for the study proves to be reliable.

DOI: 10.4018/978-1-7998-7872-8.ch008

INTRODUCTION

Essential to conducting research is finding a problem to solve (Booth, 2003). In terms of this project the problem is that standardised project management or service methodologies do not have regard for the organisational architecture and working practices of those who choose to adopt them. Often choosing a methodology is therefore a battle in itself (Kerzner, 2014). This often results in project failure (ibid). The project therefore aims to develop a toolkit for managers to customise standardised methodologies for their organisation. It will do this through conducting action research in an e - learning organisation that has a strong organisational architecture as well as cultural and working practices of its own. This should better ensure project success.

Project management research can be seen to be divided into the four areas of management of a project, management of a project - based organisation, management of a project network, and management of an organisation network (Artto & Kujala, 2008). Projects are collaborative endeavours and often involve bringing people together from multiple backgrounds (De - Laat & Lally, 2003). Table 1 presents an approach to devising a project management tool based on equation modelling.

Table 1. Approaches to devising a project management tool based on equation modelling

#	Approach To Devising A Project Management Tool Based On Equation Modelling
1	An equation model adopted by an e - learning organization will be put forward and the memorandum and articles and other documents analyzed using CAQDAS based on emergent theory. An alternative model will be developed for other organizations.
2	An equation model will be utilized by an e - learning organization and evaluated through collecting data using interviews of it in action, which will be analyzed using CAQDAS based on thick description. A more detailed version will be adopted.
3	An equation model utilized by an e - learning organization will be re - evaluated through a qualitative questionnaire of those in the organization using CAQDAS based on theory building. An alternative model will be proposed and adopted if necessary or the model will be integrated with existing theoretical models.

Source: Own

There is an abundance of literature on establishing organisations, but little directly relevant to e - learning organisations. Answering question 1 in the previous section would resolve this. There is a significant amount of research in the area of project management and some emerging in e - learning. Answering question 2 above would provide a specific model for e - learning projects. There is a significant amount of research into pedagogies for learning, and this vast amount of information needs to be made directly applicable to e - learning systems so that the objectives of e - learning organisations can be met. Answering question three in the previous section would achieve this.

BACKGROUND

What is significant about this study is not only is it based around understanding the organisational context of several multi - national organisations, but it also seeks to understanding different approaches to delivering education in different nations.

Legacy Systems Reengineering

Legacy systems often pose a problem for organisations if they are not able to adopt to the changing environment of that organisation or prevent the organisation from adopting new strategies (Alderson & Shah, 1999). They can be valuable for organisations if they are able to be extended in functionality as the organisation and its staff evolve (Zhang & Yang, 2004). Some have been scathing about legacy systems, referring to them as “roadblocks to progress” (Wu et al., 1997). Whether or not legacy systems are beneficial to an organisation are dependent on that organisation’s approach to architecture, culture, agility, and change (Sommerville, 2016). Table 2 shows some of the factors that affect how a legacy system can be assessed.

Table 2. Sommerville’s factors and questions for environment assessment of legacy systems

Factor	Questions
Supplier stability	Is the supplier still in existence? Is the supplier financially stable and likely to continue in existence? If the supplier is no longer in business, does someone need to maintain the system?
Failure rate	Does the hardware have a high rate of reported failures? Does the support software crash and force system restarts?
Age	How old is the hardware and software? The older the hardware and support software, the more obsolete it will be. It may still function correctly, but there should be significant economic and business benefits to moving to a more modern system.
Performance	Is the performance of the system adequate? Do performance problems have a significant effect on system users?
Support requirements	What local support is required by the hardware or software? If high costs are associated with this support, it may be worth considering system replacements.
Maintenance costs	What are the costs of hardware maintenance and support software licenses? Older hardware may have high annual licensing costs.
Interoperability	Are there problems interfacing the system to other systems? Can compilers, for example, be used with current versions of the operating system?

Source: Sommerville (2016)

It is known that there is a difference between how users interact with head - mounted displays and desktop interfaces (Ruddle et al., 1998). If head - mounted displays proved more engaging, the question has to be asked whether one should replace legacy desktop technologies with these new devices. It has been argued that one should wait at least 6 months before adopting a new technology (Nielsen, 2000). Not so long ago one could buy Google Glass head - mounted displays from the high street and develop for them (Firstenberg & Salas, 2014). However, the original units are now themselves legacy systems, with Google having released an ‘enterprise edition’ designed for commercial environments meaning unlikely many legacy systems it is no longer even possible to use the first editions. Whist it is still possible for many websites based on Wireless Mark - up Language (WML) to work through Wireless Application Protocol (Jasma, 2001), Google Glass was not based on this open protocol (Firstenberg & Salas, 2014) and therefore as soon as the Web and smartphone applications needed to support Google Glass were dropped by Google, its heads - up displays became unusable. Compare this with a Nokia 7110 or Nintendo DS with an Internet cartridge – these devices can still run WAP applications using WML even to this day. Therefore, if one considers Table 2, even though Google Glass is a relatively new technology it would be essential to discontinue it on age, even though age would not be a factor in determining whether to keep a Nokia 7110 or Nintendo DS if one wanted to run WAP applications on it.

Agile Project Management

Agile project management is based on the principle that if an organisation designs its products for continued improvement then there will always be added value for the stakeholders that will use that product (Sohi et al., 2016). Essential to agile development is a collaborative work culture, which is often not possible with methodologies like PRINCE2, which is quite bureaucratic in nature (Berger, 2007). Agile project management and legacy systems redevelopment might appear to go and in hand. The moment one makes a change to a legacy system one has made an iteration and then if one commits to making iterations one is engaging in agile development. There are several factors to consider when deciding whether to adopt an agile approach to maintaining a legacy system, as can be seen from Table 3.

Table 3. Sommerville's approaches to legacy system management

Factor	Description
The use of the system	If s system is only used occasionally or by a small number of people, then it may have limited value. Upgrading the system may be an option if it places an important role, such as a student registration system used at the start of the academic year.
The business processes that are supported	When a system is introduced, organizational processes are usually introduced to exploit the systems capabilities. If the system is inflexible, changing the processes may be impossible.
System dependability	System dependability is not only a technical problem but also an organization problem. If a system is not dependable it can affect the whole of an organization's stakeholder base.
The system outputs	If an organization depends on the outputs of a system then it has high value, but if these outputs can be gained another way the system may have lower value.

Source: Sommerville (2016)

Lean Project Management

Many project teams do not have all the resources at their disposal that larger organisations have, including usability testing laboratories (Cunliffe, 2000). For projects that develop products that can be built in affordable stages and then assembled like one might do with manufacturing a car then lean project management can be effective (Nekoufar & Karim, 2011).

When one is working with legacy systems, lean project management and agile project management can look quite similar. This is because changing a legacy system can involve several steps, and as can be seen from Table 4 (Sommerville, 2016), showing there are many considerations in deciding whether to drop or extend a legacy system.

Table 4. Sommerville's criteria for deciding whether to drop or extend a legacy system

Option	Description
Scrap the system completely	This option should be chosen when the system is not making an effective contribution to the organization.
Leave the system unchanged and continue with regular maintenance	This option should be chosen when the system is still required but is stable and the system users make relatively few change requests.
Reengineer the system to improve its maintainability	This option should be chosen when the system quality has been degraded by change and where new change to the system is still being processed.
Replace all or part of the system with a new system	This option should be chosen when factors, such as new hardware, mean that the old system cannot continue in operation, or where off - the - shelf system would allow the new system to be developed at a reasonable cost.

Source: Sommerville (2016)

E - Learning Project Management

E - Learning project management has been traditionally thought of something that occurs within academic departments of publicly funded universities (Manford & McSporran, 2003). However, e - learning can be used to enhance any organisation (Rosenberg, 2000), yet educational technology often goes underutilised in many dedicated educational environments (Cuban, 2001).Understanding the context in which learning will occur is an important actor for utilising e - learning project management (German, 2017). E - Learning systems can quite quickly become legacy systems. The World Wide Web has changed this to some extent (Weller, 2002), however many books recommending specific uses of the Web are out of date (Slocombe, 2001; Zeid, 2000). Table 5 shows some of the factors that can help determine whether to keep and / or expand legacy systems based on whether they have high or low value for an organisation (Sommerville, 2016). As e - learning projects involve a reach of different job roles with many cross - overs between them

Table 5. Sommerville's approach to assessing whether to maintain a legacy system

Quality	Value	Description
Low	Low	Keeping these systems in operation will be expensive, and the rate of the return will be small. These systems should be scrapped.
Low	High	These systems are making an important contribution, so they cannot be scrapped. The low quality means they are expensive to maintain.
High	Low	These systems do not contribute very much but may not be very expensive to maintain / If expensive changes become necessary, they should be scrapped.
High	High	These systems must be kept in operation. However, their high - quality means investment in transformation or systems improvement is not necessary. Normal systems maintenance is required.

Source: Sommerville (2016)

THE HUMAN SIDE OF PROJECT MANAGEMENT IN FOUR MULTI - NATIONAL ORGANISATIONS

The aim of this section is to find the commonalities in the structures of four multi - national organisations in order to understand how it might be possible to develop a toolkit that could be used by any multi - national organisation to tailor established or emerging project management methodologies to their organisation. The four organisations chose are Crocels Community Media Group, University of Gloucestershire, Royal Air Force and Church of England. As the focus of the toolkit is around e - learning project, then in the case of job roles those that would fit within the definition of knowledge management are the ones that have been chosen.

1. Crocels Community Media Group

Crocels Community Media Group, which to date has tailored PRINCE2 and ITIL to its own internal approaches (Bishop, 2019a), is a Nano - conglomerate (i.e. a corporate grouping of unrelated small businesses and start - ups in several countries) and is developing its website Crocels.com as an information service so that website management is more effective (Elliott, 2007). By determining how Crocels's methodologies can be used to adapt existing project management methodologies to develop its own e - learning products the project will as a result provide insights for other organisations who have their own cultural practices and want to tailor standardised methodologies to their organisation. Each person who works for Crocels is assigned a portfolio based on their technical skills and job role, which is either consulting, content, technology, services and support (Bishop, September 09 2007). These are explained in Table 6. Understanding an organisation's human resource structure allows for a greater understanding of how that organisation operates so that it is easier to adapt to accommodate the human resource structures of other organisations (Wang & Zhu, 2017).

Table 6. Job roles at the crocels community media group

Job Role Areas (Location)	Job Role Functions (Disciplines)	Description
Consulting (London)	Dean, Deputy Dean (Knowledge); Chairman, Deputy Chairman (Executive)	The Dean and Deputy Dean are responsible for research. The Chairman and Deputy Chairman are responsible for direction of the companies. The Secretary and Deputy Secretary are responsible for legal operations and compliance.
Content (Delaware, London, Limerick)	Agent, Deputy Agent (Marketing); Clerk, Deputy Clerk (Information)	The Agent and Deputy Agent are responsible for news and media services. The Clerk and Deputy Clerk are responsible for information management.
Technology (Gloucester)	Technologist, Deputy Technologist (Technology); Webmaster, Deputy Webmaster (Communications)	The Technologist and Deputy Technologist are responsible for the development side of operations. The Webmaster and Deputy Webmaster are responsible for ensuring the operation of cyberspace communications.
Services (Pontypridd, Swansea, Limerick)	Secretary, Deputy Secretary (Compliance); Chaplain, Deputy Chaplain (Operations)	The Chaplain and Deputy Chaplain are responsible for operations involving human resources.
Support (Pontypridd, Swansea)	Treasurer, Deputy Treasurer (Finance); Safe - guarder, Deputy Safe - guarder (Security)	The Treasurer and Deputy Treasurer are responsible for financial compliance. The Safe - guarder and Deputy Safe - guarder are responsible for the security of personnel and clients.

Source: Own

Within the different job roles each person within Crocels is assigned to a pay grade that reflects the level of competence they are exercising in those roles. These are set out in Table 7. A Deputy in Table 6 is usually someone from Technician to Chief Craftsman and the Officer superior to the Deputy is someone who is a Specialist or Chief Specialist. Both groups must meet the criteria to be a "competent person" for the role they hold. The reason Engineers and Chief Engineers do not get to be an officer or deputy is because they are usually external to the company.

Table 7. Job grading at crocels community media group

Band	Job Grade	NVQ Level	Description
0	Apprentice	Entry Level 1 to Entry Level 3	A person that usually has limited experience in the area they are working in and may require supervision, such as someone on a work placement or a volunteer giving up their time without payment.
1	Assistant Technician	Level 1	A person usually performing manual or clerical work in support of others.
2	Associate Technician	Level 2	A person usually initiating manual or clerical work at a routine level.
2	Technician	Level 2 to Level 3	A person usually performing manual or clerical work at a level that requires innovation.
3	Assistant Craftsman	Level 3	A person with a level of experience that they can support solutions to problems that may occur during operations.
3	Associate Craftsman	Level 3 to Level 4	A person with a level of experience that they can initiate solutions to problems that may occur during normal operations.
4	Craftsman	Level 4	A person with a level of experience that they can innovate solutions to problems that may occur during novel operations.
4	Assistant Engineer	Level 4 to Level 5	A person with a level of expertise that usually allows them to support new projects, portfolios or programmes.
5	Associate Engineer	Level 5	A person with a level of expertise that usually allows them to initiate new projects, portfolios or programmes.
6	Engineer	Level 6	A person with a level of expertise that usually allows them to innovate new projects, portfolios or programmes.
7	Assistant Specialist	Level 6 to Level 7	A person operating under direct authority from a senior manager, usually holding delegated authority from a company director or trustee.
7	Associate Specialist	Level 7	A senior manager, usually holding the role of company director or trustee, responsible for the direction of a specific company or organisation, who may be elected by the members of that company.
8	Specialist	Level 8	A senior manager, usually holding the role of company secretary, where they may be corporate secretary of one or more companies or organisations. They are usually appointed as corporate secretary by the parent company.
9	Sponsor	Level 9	An innovator who gives financial backing to the organization through loans to the parent company. May receive dividends and honorarium payments instead of traditional remuneration.

Source: Own

2. The University of Gloucestershire

The University of Gloucestershire is "a campus university located in the county of Gloucestershire in the South West of England" (Marston, 2012). The University of Gloucestershire is located over three campuses, Oxstalls Campus in Gloucester and The Park and Francis Close Hall in Cheltenham" (Stevens, 2018). The university is "located in an area known as the Cotswolds, a region famous for its outstanding natural beauty" (Marston, 2012). The University of Gloucestershire is "committed to being an academic community with a global outlook, recognising that our stakeholders are best served by an internationally engaged institution which furthers opportunities for intercultural learning, teaching and research" (Fritchie, 2018).

Table 8. Relevant roles at the University Of Gloucestershire

Role	Description
Data and User Support Officer	Work closely with the IT department, support teams during SITS upgrades and as software updates are applied, reviewing documentation, discussing change requirements, and managing system-testing to ensure uninterrupted service delivery. Take the lead in analyzing and reviewing key business processes undertaken by the Registry Services team to ensure that they operate effectively and efficiently and, working with users, implement change processes as necessary.
Chaplain / Senior Chaplain	To manage the University Chapel and Campus faith spaces appropriately and imaginatively to make best use of those facilities. Engage in outreach both within the University and the local community. Highly motivated, flexible and adaptable, with the drive to deliver. Understanding of and able to value the University's Anglican and Evangelical foundation, yet able to relate and respond to those from other faiths and none within a contemporary academic setting.
Coach in Practice	The Coach in Practice will support both mentors and students in practice, assisting with ongoing assessment of students, quality assurance and the implementation of a student coaching model in practice. In response to staff and student feedback, the coach in practice role will be pivotal in ensuring students are as prepared as possible for practice from their first day as a student in a practice area to their graduation as a registered Social Worker. It is essential that applicants are confident in their own knowledge, skills and ability to teach in their chosen practice area. Applicants must also be able to manage their own time within agreed boundaries determined by University and Placement area.
Digital Content Officer	Manage and deliver digital projects from brief to delivered outputs under the guidance of the nominated project lead. Design, develop and implement web - based activity, continually researching and incorporating new technologies. This will include interface design, creation of animation, graphics, video and audio. It will also include data gathering.
Marketing Officer	Lead on all online and offline marketing / communications campaigns and projects across all four channels of physical, phone, online and network. Identifying and employing emerging marketing channels / tools to maximize the impact of the marketing and communications campaign. Support development and delivery of network groups in conjunction with the project manager.
Lecturer / Senior Lecturer	To contribute to the teaching and development of appointed programme, primarily; provide tutorial support through the Personal Tutor scheme; maintain professional standing and expertise through a process of continuing personal and subject development through participation in University and Faculty staff development events and through personal self - development and scholarly activity; ensure that health and safety procedures within classrooms, studio and workshop areas are adhered to; ensure that University and School policies and methodologies for quality assurance are applied; undertake assessment of student work and to ensure that University and School policies for the processes and stages of assessment, and the appropriate feedback within stated time constraints, are achieved.
Academic Services Administrator / Team Leader	To create an open, honest and vibrant working environment that is congruent with the University's People and Culture Strategy, including overseeing effective staff development and performance review. This will require managing staff fairly in line with the University's employment policies and procedures. This includes addressing formal progression and career development for staff, setting objectives and managing performance. Role holders will address capability and disciplinary matters other than the formal stages of the disciplinary / capability processes; seeking advice and support from the Head of School and HR as appropriate.

Source: Own

Table 8 sets out the job roles at the University of Gloucestershire that are relevant to this study. The roles include Data and User Support Officer (Newell, 2014), Chaplain (Dove, 2017), Coach in Practice (Jefferies, 2020), Digital Content Officer (Booth, 2016), Marketing Officer (Clark, 2020), Senior Lecturer (Fleming, 2020), Lecturer, Academic Services Administrator / Team Leader. There are also senior management positions like Head of Department / Head of School, Deans and a Vice - Chancellor.

In keeping with the other companies investigated, Table 9 sets out the pay grades that are used by the University of Gloucestershire to calculate what each member of staff gets paid.

Table 9. Job grades at the University Of Gloucestershire

Group	Description
A	PTAA and academic contract staff without holiday pay
B	PTAA contract staff holiday pay for each hour at 13.43%
C	PTAA contract staff total hourly pay including holiday pay
D	Academic contract staff holiday pay for each hour at 18.4%
E	Academic contract staff total hourly pay including holiday pay
F	Academic contract staff pay for comprehensive teaching hour with support time
G	Academic contract staff holiday pay for comprehensive teaching hour
H	Academic contract staff total pay (working hours and holiday hours) for comprehensive teaching hour with support time (2.5 hours) and accrued holiday pay

Source: Own

3. The Royal Air Force (including Royal Air Forces Association and Royal Air - Force Air Cadets)

It has been argued that the Royal Air Force's strength has been its role as auxiliary to the Royal Navy and British Army (Harvey, 2008). Operationally, the Royal Air Force's main role is to provide air bombing support to the other two forces, with other personnel existing to support operations in a non - combatant capacity (Macgregor, 1935). Indeed, the concept that the RAF is focussed mainly with air power is one that is often refuted (Ledwidge, 2012). The motto of the Royal Air Force is 'through adversity to the stars', which is meant to signify that if someone's medical condition or disability can be alleviated then one can serve, such as through personnel with normally corrected vision being permitted to serve as pilots in World War II (Pearson, 2014).

4. The Church of England (including the wider Anglican Communion)

The Church of England is an institution that is part of the wider evangelical movement of Christianity, which includes those who oppose equality between men and women and other beliefs that do not reflect the original Christian message of 'loving one's neighbour' (Sani & Reicher, 2000). Specifically, the Church of England can be seen as the parent of the wider Anglican Communion that includes the Church in Wales, with the Church of England being excommunicated from the Roman Catholic Church which itself was excommunicated from the Eastern Orthodox Church (Evans, June 13 2019).

Table 10. Relevant job groups and descriptions within the Royal Air Force (RAF)

Job Group	Description
Chaplain	An RAF Chaplain provides spiritual support, strength and guidance to service personnel and their families. Chaplains act as a valuable source of personal wellbeing and guidance in times of war and peace.
Legal Officer	Law in the RAF addresses the rules and regulations of the organisation, society at large and the international community. An RAF Legal Officer has a wide variety of legal challenges linked to the force and plays a central role in ensuring that we function smoothly. A related role is RAF Police.
Personnel Trainer / Instructor	When the Royal Air Force is not on operations, it is training. An RAF Personnel Training Officer leads, develops and manages training on RAF and MOD Units throughout the UK, on overseas bases, and on exercises and operations around the world.
Personnel Support	An RAF Personnel Support Officer works across a range of specialties: Infrastructure Management, HR, Development, Accounts Management and Media Operations, to name a few. Personnel Officers vary their roles and develop a broad set of transferable skills, making them widely employable in other, non - specialist areas.
Cyberspace Communications	A Cyberspace Communications Specialist is responsible for the technology at the heart of the RAF. It is their job to set up, operate and maintain the technology the RAF relies on to communicate.
Media Operations	An RAF Media Operations Officer is the voice of the RAF, supporting media operations officers and HQ Air Command with the delivery of national and international communications campaigns to make sure the RAF's stories are communicated correctly and fairly. A related role is RAF Musician.

Source: Wigston, 2020

Table 11. Job grades and descriptions within the Royal Air Force (RAF)

Job Grade	Title	Description
Civilian Instructor	Civ Inst	Civilian Instructors undertake a variety of roles and use their own personal interests and skill sets to assist with training in the organization's core activities.
Non - Commissioned Officer	NC Off	Non - Commissioned Officers have more responsibility than Civilian Instructors and are normally required to give at least 12 hours per month of their own time supporting the organization in their primary tasks.
Pilot Officer	Plt Off	Pilot Officer is the lowest ranked Commissioned Officer.
Flying Officer	Fg Off	A Flying Officer is a junior Commissioned Officer.
Flight Lieutenant	Flt Lt	A Flight Lieutenant is a junior Commissioned Officer. The rank originated in the Royal Naval Air Service (RNAS) in 1914 and was adopted by the RAF in 1919.
Squadron Leader	Sqn Ldr	A Squadron Leader is the most junior of all the Senior Officer Ranks. The rank was adopted in 1919, with it replacing Major.
Wing Commander	Wg Cdr	Wing Commander is a Senior Officer rank. It was adopted by the RAF in 1920.
Group Captain	Gp Capt	Group Captain is a Senior Officer rank. It was adopted by the RAF in 1919.
Air Commodore	Air Cdre	Air Commodore is a one - star Senior Appointment in the RAF. It was adopted in 1919.
Air Vice - Marshal	AVM	Air Vice - Marshall is a two - star Senior Appointment in the RAF. It was adopted by the RAF in 1919.
Air Marshal	Air Mshl	Air Marshal is a three - star Senior Appointment in the RAF. It was adopted by the RAF in 1919.
Air Chief Marshal	Air Chf Mshl	Air Chief Marshal is a four - star Senior Appointment in the RAF. It was adopted by the RAF in 1922, with Chief Marshall being adopted in 1919.
Marshall of the RAF	MRAF	Marshall of the Air Force is a five - star Senior Appointment in the RAF.

Source: Own

Table 12. Relevant ministry groups within the Church of England (And Anglican Communion)

Ministry Group (Title)	Description
Lay Preacher (Pastor)	A lay preacher is generally defined as a religious authority who lacks the formal training of a priest, but it can also be used for those who challenge the established order and who have received some formal theological training (Larsson, 2016)
Chaplain (Pastor)	A Chaplain is a religious authority who provides spiritual care through compassionate presence and active listening, being skilled in serving humanity, often educated to postgraduate level (Kelley Sr., 2009).
Reader (Elder)	A Lay Reader is a religious authority that is licenced to assist a priest, including when that priest becomes ill (Macbean, 1934)
Pioneer (Elder)	A pioneer minister is a religious authority who has the necessary vision and gifts to be a missionary entrepreneur and with the capacity to form and lead fresh expressions and new forms of church appropriate to a particular culture (Ross & Baker, 2014)
Priest (Reverend, Father, Sister)	A priest is an ordained religious authority who is responsible for conveying the contents of the Bible through the set liturgy, the absolution, and the sacrificial celebration of the "Body and Blood" (Koepping, 2002)
Senior Priest (Bishop, Archbishop)	A senior priest, such as a Bishop or Archbishop, is a person whose church is a cathedral and who is responsible for the area that cathedral falls within, called a diocese (Keene, 2000)

Source: Own

In appointing its personnel, the Church of England has been permitted to discriminate on the grounds of sex and gender (Fry & David, 2019b) as well and sexual orientation and sexuality in general (Brown, 2020). This has resulted in many of the senior grades in Table 13 being dominated by men who either are gynasexual, or keep their androsexual - based sexuality secret, especially as those members of the Anglo - Catholic 'High Church' within the Church of England openly refuse to allow women priests within the church buildings they control, regardless of sexual orientation (Fry & David, 2019a).

Conclusion

As the four different organisations have now been understood, it is now important to seek to tailor a lean and agile project management methodology to be suitable for all four organisations. Kanban is a lean project management methodology because it involves breaking a project down into smaller activities and then assembling them all together. In the case of Scrum, it is an agile project management methodology, as it involves each part a project being conducted in sprints with each new sprint improving on the previous one.

METHODOLOGICAL APPROACH

This section sets out the methodological approach that will be taken to the study. To do this the 'research onion' was used to explain the approach that will be taken (Saunders et al., 2009). The research methodology and methods to develop and test the e - learning products in order to develop and equation and toolkit is explored through using the 'research onion.'

Table 13. Ministry grades within the Church of England

Ministry Grade	Description
Non - Stipendiary	Non - stipendiary religious authorities are unpaid for the work they do and often finds this means they can blend mission and ministry with other things in their life they deem important (Murphy, 2000)
Curate	A curate serves in a supporting role to a vicar and is usually equally qualified to them but paid much less (Ganzel, 1967).
Vicar	Vicars are paid a hefty stipend, meaning they get a fixed sum regardless of how much they work. Some believe that the stipend vars are paid should be replaced with results - based payments (Hankins, 1984; Miller, 1984).
Team Vicar	A team vicar is paid a stipend somewhere between that of a vicar and a rector (Kater, 1999).
Rector	A rector usually manages a large number of churches and so are remunerated with a stipend for their skills at planning and conducting services in a large geographical area (Bennett, 1985).
Dean	A Dean is usually responsible for a large area than a rector but is usually remunerated based on another position they hold, such as team vicar (Napier, 1835).
Deacon	A deacon helps the faith community live and grow in its identity as stewards of God's love, including by reading the gospel (Siburg, 2018). A deacon is not a "mini - priest or pastor," or a "partial pastor or priest," or a "substitute pastor" or priest (Ferrari, 2016).
Archdeacon	An Archdeacon is usually understood in this second, "potential" or "dispositional," sense with the power to exercise archidiaconal functions that is, who will exercise such functions under suitable circumstances (Braithwaite, 1938).
Bishop	An Anglican bishop is consecrated in the apostolic succession by the laying on of hands (McGrath, 2005). An Anglican bishop is not an autocrat, but he can under certain defined conditions dissolve the pastoral relationship between a rector and a parish (Stowe, 1948).
Archbishop	An archbishop is the bishop of an archdiocese, which is usually a prestigious diocese with an important place in local church history (Anonymous, 2015). An Archbishop is entitled to eight chaplains (William, n.d.).

Source: Own

Research Design

Research design refers to the specific plans and techniques used to answer the research question and control for the variables or other conditions being tested (Dulock, 1993).

Ethics

In addition to the questionnaires, participants will be asked to complete a participant information sheet and consent form. The protocols from the British Psychological Society will be used throughout the project, as well as those from the British Educational Research Association and BCS – The Chartered Institute for IT. The University of Gloucestershire's ethics committee may be consulted, or otherwise the NHS's Integrated Research Application System will be used. Crocels's ethics consent form will be completed at the earliest opportunity.

Philosophy

An anthropological approach to data collection and constructivist approach to data analysis will be adopted as the philosophy with the ontological and epistemological principles used with these based on those associated with the ecological cognition framework (Bishop, 2007a; Bishop, 2007b) and equatricism (Bishop, 2011a; Bishop, 2011b). Every attempt will be made to make the religious and historical education in the workshops open to all of the Main Middle East religions and those of other religions, even if the content is approved by the Church of England, meaning the research outcomes are valuable to a range of contexts. The pedagogical approach can therefore be considered inclusive education (Thomas & Vaughan, 2004).

Time Horizons

The follow - up of, and reflection on, the standardised methodologies will result in a new methodology that will be tested and revised in three separate e - learning software contexts. The standardised methods used are / were PRINCE2 (Graham, 2008), ITIL (Farenden, 2012), Kanban (Rose, 2018; Sayer & Williams, 2012) and Scrum (Layton, 2015).

Strategies

The research project will be based upon Crocels's programme management of community initiatives of workshop - based projects that use its information service to provide historical education. The first author leads the programme management at Crocels, where it has been decided for the workshops between 2020 and 2023 to be based on educational programmes used by the Church of England, albeit delivered in as secular a way as possible.

Data Collection

Data collection is critical to the research process and the means through which the research design is implemented in the first instance (Rimando et al., 2015) is explored through using the 'research onion' (Saunders et al., 2009).

Approaches

Data will be collected from those who work directly with the project management methodologies as developers and deliverers through questionnaires and interviews (Briggs et al., 2012; James & Busher, 2009). Data will also be collected from testing on users through workshops where e - learning products containing religious and historical content will be used in a blended learning setting (such as an IT suite or religious institution) and in some cases totally by distance learning. In either case the approach will be guided inquiry.

Strategies

The data collection strategy will be action research, which is common in educational settings (Briggs et al., 2012). There will be two additional iterations to those conducted since 2009, involving the extending of Crocels IS and use of it in blended learning workshops with a theological theme to them based on making learning programmes sanctioned by the Church of England more secular to appeal to all. Reflecting on the earlier iterations involving historical education online and the new ones involving religious education in addition will make it possible to devise the software development methodology with the candidate as project manager to feed into the design of the toolkit.

Choices

The development of the project management methodologies will be tested and amended through practical e - learning software development. Online interviews and questionnaires (Briggs et al., 2012; James & Busher, 2009) will be used to gather individual feedback from those participating in the project. Data collection will take the form of web metrics, user observations, online questionnaires and interviews (James & Busher, 2009; Kuniavsky, 2003). For the workers, including self - employed workers, there will be two questionnaires - one related to organisational architecture and one related to contingent working. These workers are involved in consulting, content, technology, services and support. There will also be two questionnaires for participants in projects using the e - learning software. One will ask them for feedback on the sessions to determine the effectiveness of the e - learning, the other their degree of spirituality in the environment they are in, as one session will be in a religious institution (i.e. church, synagogue or mosque) and the other in an IT suite. This will help determine the impact situated learning has when data from the two questionnaires are combined. The workers involved in developing and delivering the e - learning products will be interviewed after the final workshop has been conducted and evaluated. After the final workshop both developers, deliverers and users will be asked to complete the Values and Lifestyles Survey (Mitchell, 1983) along with a modification of the questionnaire used for the "Alpha Course" used for the first workshop so it is generalised for both the workshops, not just the one based on the Alpha Course. More details on the Alpha Course can be found in Annex IV.

TECHNOLOGIES, TECHNIQUES, AND PROCEDURES

The development of e - learning products, including on legacy platforms, will take the form of extending its information service, Crocels IS, which will be tested at each iteration through blended learning workshops, having already been tested at two stages (Bishop, 2012; Bishop & Kommers, 2016). Those involved in e - learning product development and those involved in testing them will be administered questionnaires relating to the organisation, covering organisational agility, architecture, culture and change. The questionnaires will be administrated to those who work directly with the project management methodologies and on users taking part in workshops where e - learning products containing religious and historical content will be used in a blended learning setting (such as an IT suite or religious institution) and in some cases totally by distance learning. Data collection will also take the form of web metrics, user observations and interviews of both the project management team and users. Where possible they will be administered online (James & Busher, 2009; Kuniavsky, 2003). Qualitative data (Silverman, 2015) will be analysed using NVivo (Bazeley & Jackson, 2013; Ritchie & Lewis, 2013) and a coding framework devised during the literature review. Quantitative data will be cleaned using Microsoft Excel and analysed using IBM SPSS Statistics. From analysing the questionnaire and observational data, there will be devised an equation as well as a project management toolkit utilising it and other findings. This toolkit will assist those managing projects in their organisation, especially those developing e - learning products for use in multiple sites with a varying level of legacy and state of the art systems.

In project management there are trade - offs between time, cost and quality, scope and how this impacts project design. In the project being discussed in this article there will be a range of legacy and contemporary systems used. They will involve the use of existing and new multimedia materials for the purposes of e - learning. The e - learning products that will be developed for the workshops that users will take part in will be based on Web - Based Learning (Weller, 2002), making use of the Digital Classroom of Tomorrow (Bishop, 2004) and Clicks and Mortar Environments for Learning and Leisure Experiences (Bishop, 2012; Bishop, July 19 2012; Bishop, September 09 2007) approaches to delivering blended learning through Classroom 2.0 and School 3.0 respectively in Wales, as well as working with similar projects globally. For instance, in England it was called Curriculum and Pedagogy in Technology Assisted Learning (CAPITAL), in Italy it was Classi 2.0, and in Spain it was Escuela 2.0. Scotland were invited to join the project, but instead created Curriculum for Excellence (CfE), which had minimum use of ICT. DCOT in Wales was inspired by another project in Wales called ACE (Reddy, 1997).

Figure 1. The digital classroom of tomorrow (DCOT) approach to classroom 2.0
Source: Own

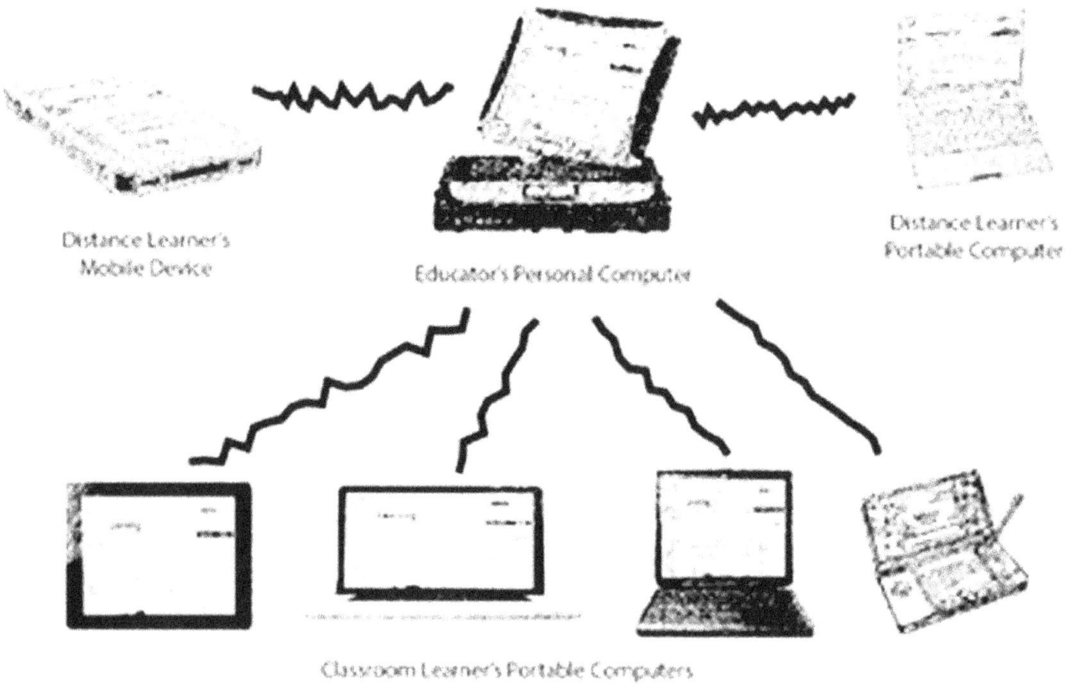

The DCOT approach to blended learning in Wales (Figure 1) relies on an educator using their computer to manage the computers or other devices of the learners they are educating. This became called Classroom 2.0 and focuses on linking up technology, including remotely through 'eTwinning'. The CAMELLE approach to blended learning on the other hand does not always take place in a classroom and is called School 3.0 as a result. An educational environment based on Classroom 2.0 will provide tailored learning materials to learners based on their ability and learning style (Bishop, 2004) whereas a School 3.0 environment will take account of the behavioural patterns of learners, such as through monitoring web metrics or tracking biometrics such as EEG and eye - movement (Bishop, 2016) and not necessarily occur in a classroom, even though it might be supported by buildings infrastructure (Bishop, 2019). An education environment based on Technologies 4.0 involves the development of educator competencies as much as those of learners. Finally, in Society 5.0 it is not necessary to have an educator, as learners can engage directly with e - learning systems that adapt to their individual circumstances, including where they are accessing the e - learning system from and the device they are using.

Figure 2. The Welsh technological approach to technologies 4.0
Source: Own

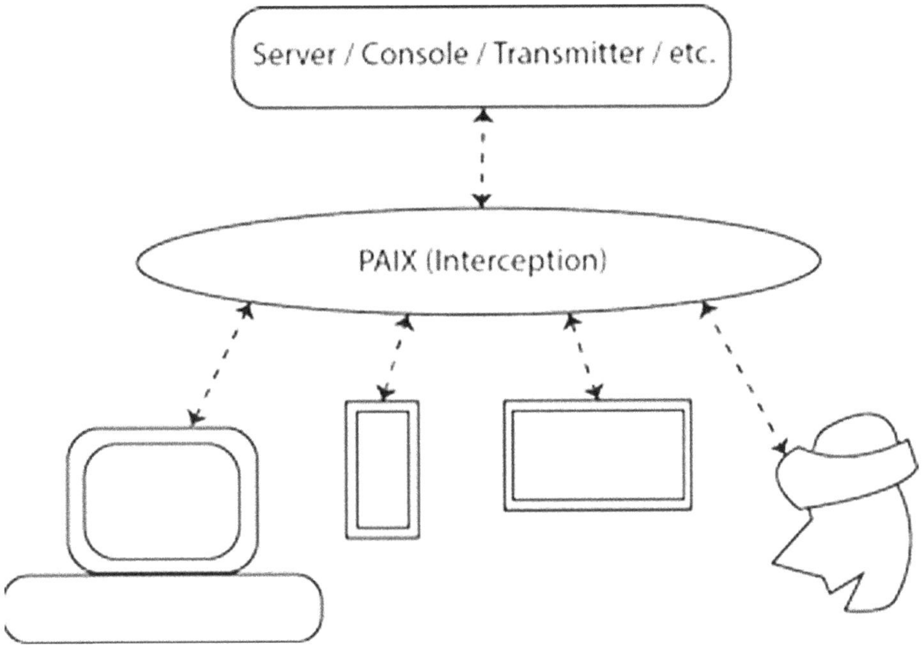

The development of e - learning products for Crocels will take the form of extending its information service, Crocels IS, which will be tested at each iteration through blended learning workshops, having already been tested at two stages (Bishop, 2012; Bishop, December 17 2016). Potential applications that could be developed / refined are in Table 14.

Those involved in e - learning productive development will be administered two questionnaires; one on organisational architecture and one on working practices. It is likely that in workshops that are not based in an IT lab that dedicated tablets (Caldwell & Bird, 2015; Cheshire, 2016; Price, 2013; Russell, 2001) will be used so as to avoid the problems that occurred during Emotivate 2017 where one participant was using his father's computer and his father had not logged out (Bishop, 2019). However, it will be essential to ensure the learning environment is designed for community for enhanced participation (Powazek, 2002). For that reason, the University of Gloucestershire's facilities, especially in terms of its C11 incubator and Chapel will be used to conduct the research.

Table 14. Potential e - learning products to be developed

Product	Description
Crocels Buddy (formerly Reseller Buddy)	An application that allows contacts one has amassed on social media platforms or in one's smart devices address book to be categorized according to emotion / sentiment in order to build further networking opportunities and reduce unwanted interactions.
Crocels Comprend	A managed learning environment that adapts based on the ability, learning style and neurological profile of the learner.
Crocels Mediat	An e - therapy system based around linking neural impulses to emotions and 2D / 3D representations of avatars or even super - imposition of the patient.
Crocels Paix	An application that allows the features of Crocels Comprend and Crocels Proteger to be available over a home or professional network regardless of platform, so long as it runs over HTTP or similar transfer protocol.
Crocels Parle	An application that allows people with communication difficulties in a specific language to become familiar with the nuances of the language, especially idioms.
Crocels Proteger	An application that can detect whether a person is being harassed on an electronic communications network, such as while taking part in e - tivities in order to support e - moderating.
Crocels Surveys (formerly QPress)	A Web - based application that allows a user to sort cards in order to determine their personality, other preferences, or to test their ability at card prediction.
Crocels Talk	A touch - screen application that makes use of audio to help people with severe learning difficulties and intellectual development disorder access education more easily accessed by others.
Crocels Vois Engine (formerly VOIS)	An application API that interfaces with smartphones, VR headsets and similar screen - based devices to provide advice at the opportune moment about how to participate in a social situation.

Source: Own

Data Analysis

Data analysis is the study of data resulting from data collection, often called observations (Nakai & Ke, 2011). The purpose of data analysis is to understand the data collected in order to answer the research questions posed (Kaplan & Maxwell, 2005). The outcome of data analysis needs to be both valid and legitimate (Collins et al., 2006).

Strategies

The questionnaires contain a mixture of quantitative questions that will rely of a deductive approach and qualitative that will rely on an inductive approach. Videos recorded at workshops will likely require an inductive approach whereas web metrics collected from the use of ICTs and advertising data will require a deductive approach as the variables in the case of the latter are fixed. Qualitative data (Silverman, 2015) will be analysed using NVivo (Bazeley & Jackson, 2013; Ritchie & Lewis, 2013) and a coding framework devised during the literature review. Quantitative data (such as from the questionnaires, advertising or page metrics) will be cleaned using Microsoft Excel and analysed using IBM SPSS Statistics (Oakshot, 2016; Field, 2017). From analysing these an equation will be developed as well as a project management toolkit to assist those managing projects in their organisation, especially those based on using e - learning in religious and historical contexts. Further details on these are in Table 5.

Approaches

A mixture of deductive and inductive approaches will be used. Whilst those self - identifying as positivists might prefer deductive approaches and those self - identifying as phenomenologists might prefer inductive approaches, the candidate takes a pragmatic approach depending on the research question and anticipated answer based on available data. For instance, after cleaning the data it might become apparent one approach is more suitable than the other. This will be done in the case of quantitative data using the Descriptive feature of SPSS after assembling the data in Excel and importing it and labelling it.

Data Collection

This section sets out the approaches to data collection by discussing the data collection setting, strategy and the techniques for collecting data. Data collection is the systematic approach to obtaining observations from a sample or other source (Cassidy, 2001).

Strategies

Through conducting a systematic project managed study it will be possible to learn lessons that will lead to the development of a toolkit for project managers in organisations like Crocels Community Media Group, the University of Gloucestershire, the Royal Air Force and Church of England to use to conduct their projects. By collecting data, during the workshops where the e - learning software developed using the project management approach is tested, it will be possible to develop an equation model through which several info - graphics can be included in the toolkit.

Approaches

By carrying out the workshops it will be possible to develop an equation for improving the likelihood of project success. This will be done through the collection of data during the workshops, such as web metrics from actual use of the e - learning systems development and participant satisfaction data from questionnaires. The equation development will first involve the development of theory using Matlab then the testing of the model using AMOS, which is based on structural equation modelling (Khine, 2013).

Choices

The equation will become part of the toolkit through info - graphics. It will be in a spiral bound format with an ISBN number from The Crocels Press Limited. To test it, personnel from the Crocels Community Media Group, University of Gloucestershire, Royal Air Force and Church of England will be invited to test it, where they will be fitted with eye - tracking and an EEG to monitor and record their usage of it. They will also be interviewed on how they found the toolkit.

Techniques and Approaches

By using the lessons learned from the development of the e - learning products and implementation of them into different environments through 'The Emotivate Project' and 'The Dogtagz Project' and the blended learning workshops associated with them, it will be possible to devise a toolkit for other project managers to tailor their organisation's culture to standardised project management methods they might come across. The toolkits will take the form of ring - bounded manuals that project managers will flip through in order to improve the management of their project. The equation that will be derived will feature in the toolkit as a flowchart, or other form of info - graphic, so that all the project manager needs is a calculator to follow the steps to implement the equation.

PILOT STUDY - TESTING OUT THE WORKSHOPS AND QUESTIONNAIRE

A pilot study was conducted with three retired persons aged between 52 and 76, all of whom were married in heterosexual relationships. Two of the participants were women and the other was a man. All were Caucasian and all took part from the same remote location with the instructor participating at a distance. Participants were asked to watch a religious video and play the same video game on a different legacy device. The video game was Fritz Chess and the platforms were the Nintendo Wii and DS and a Windows XP laptop. The instructor took part over an Apple Macintosh laptop and Apple iPhone. After taking part in various intervals of the workshop participants were asked to complete a questionnaire.

The Cronbach's alpha for the 77 items on the questionnaire that were classified as 'scale' was 0.616 with there being no missing items for the three participants. This would suggest the scale is highly reliable and if used on a greater number of participants would produce better results.

It was clear from looking at how the questionnaire was used by the three participants that it would need to be split into two questionnaires. One a registration and consent form to collect the descriptive data about the participants and the other the questionnaire consisting of the 77 items.

Tailoring of Methods

It is necessary to understand the driving forces behind risk analysis and risk management techniques on projects in order to tailor the methods.

TAILORING METHODS FOR CROCELS

There are a number of different methodologies that are available s standardised approaches to achieving project deliverables, including on a service orientated basis. The most popular include PRINCE2, ITIL, Kanban (Rose, 2018) and Scrum (Cohn, 2010; Flouri & Berger, 2010; Layton, 2015).

PRINCE2

Crocels has already run a project that has involved the tailoring of PRINCE2. Called C2 - Tech - S2, or PRINCE2 - DDE, the method integrates Crocels's three models with PRINCE2. Table 15

Table 15. PRINCE2 tailored to Crocels Community Media Group (C2 - Tech - S2 or PRINCE2 - DDE)

DDE Stage	Star Lifecycle Iteration (OCD5 Stage)	Stage Aim (MAPEL Stage)	Stage Tasks (Task Methods)
Design	**A. Consulting** (OCD5.3 Know your Stratum)	I. Identify User Goals (MAPEL Stage 1)	**1.** Starting up a project 1.1. Discuss the suitability of given systems in terms of style, ease of use and the end user (User Experience Analysis) 1.2 Produce a design concept in terms of customer, purpose and target audience (Scenario Based Design) 1.3. Prepare flow diagrams showing navigation through system (Requirements Analysis)
	B. Content (OCD5.2. Know your subject matter)	II. Identify Information Users need to Achieve Goals (MAPEL Stage 2)	**2.** Initiating a project 2.1 Collect a range of source materials (e.g. text, graphics, forms, processes) that can be used and modified in various contexts (Business Activity Modelling) 2.2 Create index of source material identifying copyright status and other Meta data of each, indicating relevance to requirements, and ensuring recognition of user participation (Current Environment Analysis). 2.3 Select the most appropriate materials, considering file size, customs and practice, and save files in appropriate format to maintain user interest (Entity Behavior Modelling) 2.4 Store files in a preparation folder for easy access in a range of contexts (Requirements Cataloguing).
Develop	**C. Technology** (OCD5.1. Know your technology)	III. Identify Mediating Artifacts Users need to Achieve Goals (MAPEL Stage 3)	**3.** Managing product development 3.1 Create a simple system that can accommodate different users (User Task Analysis and Prototyping) 3.2 Create hyperlinks as mediating artefacts to avoid dead links (Third - Party Resource Refinement and Tuning) 3.3 Create text and image based mediating artefacts to enhance participation (User Scenario Testing). 3.4 Create persuasive links for e - mail and other applications (Social Planning and Modelling).
Evaluate	**D. Services** (OCD5.4. Know your policies)	IV. Develop System (MAPEL Stage 4)	**4.** Managing product delivery 4.1 Create a homepage or menu screen and other nodes compliant with standards (Two - Tree Modelling). 4.2 Create and format system nodes to ensure compliance with policies and law (Connected - Dots Modelling). 4.3 Create tables and format cells, columns and rows that take account of accessibility and multi - platform standards (Nuts and Bolts Audit). 4.4 Set text color, font styles and heading size and size, location, borders of images, to accommodate those with disabilities and other needs (Design Matters Audit).
	E. Support (OCD5. Know your purpose)	V. Evaluate Persuasiveness (MAPEL Stage 4)	**5.** Closing a project 5.1 View results in preview environment and run testing sequences (Inspection / Walkthrough). 5.2 Collect feedback, from at least three users, in terms of suitability for purpose, ease of use and style (User Focus Groups and Interviews). 5.3 Test out system in real world, showing regard for effect on body posture, potential eyestrain and positioning of user hardware (Direct Observation).

Source: Own

ITIL

Crocels has already run a project that has involved the tailoring of ITIL. Called MOLPSL - S5 for online communities and cyber - communities or MLLPSL - S5 for e - learning and EdTech, the method that can be used for either online community or e - learning development.

Figure 3. ITIL tailored to Crocels Community Media Group for online communities (MOLPSL - S5)
Source: Own

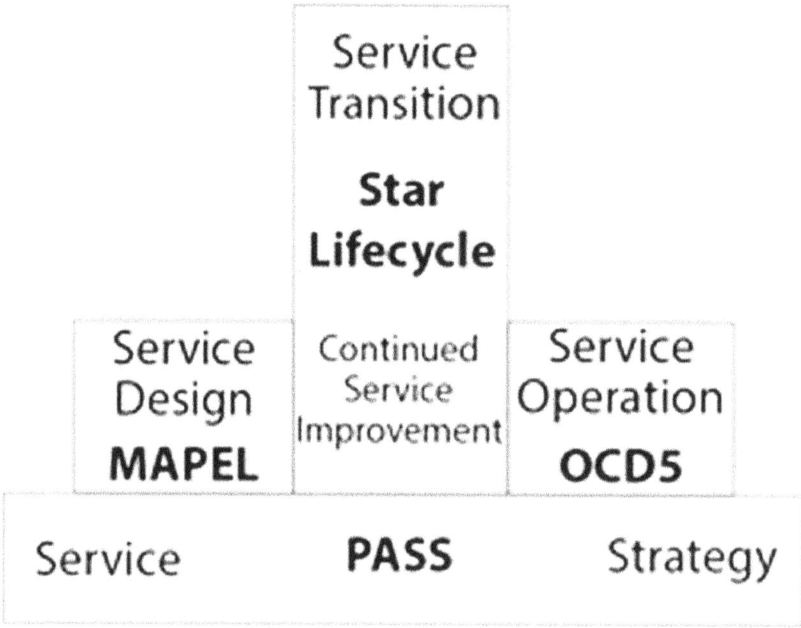

Table 16. ITIL tailored to Crocels Community Media Group (ITIL - DDE)

DDE Stage	ITIL Factor	Crocels Methodology
Design	Service Design	MAPEL
	Service Strategy	PASS
Develop	Service Transition / Continued Service Improvement	Star Lifecycle
Evaluate	Service Operation	OCD5 (Online communities) / LCC (E - Learning)

Source: Own

Kanban and Kanban - DDE

Crocels intendeds to use a modification of Kanban. Kanban is a method that recognises the need to break down a project into a set of tasks, each with an estimated duration. The Crocels adaptation is in Table 17.

Table 17. Kanban tailored to Crocels Community Media Group (Kanban - DDE)

DDE Stage	Kanban Stage	OCD5 Stage	Star Lifecycle Stage	MAPEL Stage
Design	Backing	Known Your Stratum	Consulting	Identify User Goals
	Planning	Know Your Technology / Subject Matter / Stratum	Consulting, Content, Technology	Identify Mediating Artifacts Users need to Achieve Goals
Develop	Progressing	Known Your Purpose / Stratum	Consulting	Identify Information Users need to Achieve Goals
	Developing	Know Your Technology / Purpose / Stratum	Technology	Develop System
Evaluate	Testing	Know Your Technology / Subject Matter / Stratum	Technology, Support	Evaluate Persuasiveness
	Completing	Know Your Policies / Stratum	Services, Support	Develop System and Evaluate Persuasiveness

Source: Own

Scrum

The Crocels adaptation of Scrum is in Table 18.

Table 18. Scrum tailored to Crocels Community Media Group (Scrum - DDE)

DDE Stage	Scrum Stage	OCD5 Stage	Star Lifecycle Stage	MAPEL Stage	Scrum objective
Design	Vision	Know Your Purpose	Consulting	Identify User Goals	This goals of the product and its alignment with organizational strategy
	Product Roadmap	Know Your Technology	Consulting, Content, Technology	Identify Mediating Artifacts Users need to Achieve Goals	Holistic view of the product features that create the project vision
	Release planning	Know Your Stratum	Consulting	Identify Information Users need to Achieve Goals	Release timing for specific project functionality
	Sprint Planning	Know Your Policies	Consulting	Identify Information Users need to Achieve Goals	Establish specific iteration goals and tasks.
Develop	Daily Scrum	Know Your Technology / Subject Matter	Content, Technology Services	Develop System	Establish and coordinate priorities of the day.
	Sprint Review	Know Your Technology / Subject Matter	Content, Technology Services	Evaluate Persuasiveness	Demonstration of working product.
Evaluate	Spring Retrospective	Know Your Technology / Subject Matter	Content, Technology Services	Evaluate Persuasiveness	Team refinement of environment and process to optimize efficiency
	Release Project	Know your Stratum	Support, Consulting	Identify User Goals / (Re -) Develop System / (Re -)Evaluate Persuasiveness	Release product as per the release plan.

Source: Own

The last section discussed in depth how standard project management and service delivery methods could be tailored based on the internal structures of the Crocels Community Media Group. It is not necessary to replicate the process in full for the other organisations in this study, but a brief discussion of their approaches can be easily understood in light of the previous detailed section.

UNIVERSITY OF GLOUCESTERSHIRE

The University of Gloucestershire is a higher education institution in the South West of England with campuses in Cheltenham and Gloucester as well as an incubator called 'C11' in Berkeley. The purpose of C11 is in Table 19. At its Frances Close Hall campus in Cheltenham it also has a building called 'The Chapel', where its chaplaincy is based. The purpose of the Chapel is in Table 20.

Table 19. The purpose of 'C11'

#	Purpose	Description
1	Cyber / digital training	To provide opportunities for training in cyberspace and digital technologies.
2	Access controlled, secure workspace	To provide access to controlled and secure workspaces for state - of - the - art research and development.
3	Conferences and networking	To provide conferences and networking to enhance collaboration.
4	Demo zone of latest cyber technology	To be the center - point showcase of the most recent developments in cyberspace technology.
5	'C11 Associate' Membership	To provide an alternative to academic fellowship and collaborating establishment status for start - ups and commercial enterprises.
6	Technology zone for start - up and scale - up businesses	To provide 'walk - in' access for start - up and scale - up businesses to access working space and network with similarly sized enterprises.

Source: University of Gloucestershire

Table 20. The purpose of the chapel

#	Purpose	Description
1	A space to relax and meet others	People should feel able to relax and meet people without feeling their rights to freedom of thought, conscience and religion are being compromised.
2	A space to explore together	People should feel free to assemble and associate with others without feeling their rights to freedom of thought, conscience and religion are being compromised.
3	A space to breathe not breath	People should feel able to engage in freedom of expression and discuss their private lives with others without feeling their rights to freedom of thought, conscience and religion are being compromised.

Source: Own

THE ROYAL AIR FORCE

The Royal Air Force is a division of the United Kingdom armed forces and considered junior to its partners the Royal Navy, which is most senior, and the British Army, which is second most senior. Nevertheless, it plays a number of key roles in the defence of the United Kingdom and wider world (Wigston, 2020). This six pillars of the RAF are in Table 21.

Table 21. The six pillars of the RAF

#	Purpose	Description
1	Respond to Threats	The UK and its allies face threats in an uncertain world, from unauthorized aircraft entering protected airspace, to cyber - attacks. The RAF's Quick Reaction Alert (QRA) Force based at RAF Lossiemouth in north east Scotland, RAF Conings by in eastern England, and the Falkland Islands in the south Atlantic, are ready to scramble state of the art planes in minutes to intercept threats.
2	Prevent Conflict	The RAF works with partners around the world to strengthen national and international security and to protect the interests and influence of the UK and our allies. It identifies and manages threats before they materialize through intelligence, surveillance and reconnaissance (ISR). It can rapidly deploy aircraft and personnel around the world to deter conflict and defeat adversaries if necessary.
3	Watch the Skies	The RAF uses a combination of state - of - art static radar, mobile units, aircraft, and satellites to gather minute - to - minute information on air activity. The RAF's Air Surveillance and Control Systems Force continuously compile a Recognized Air Picture of the airspace in and around the UK, providing vital early warning of potential threats such as unauthorized aircraft or missiles. We also monitor threats in space: from space weather and debris that can damage orbiting satellites, to hostile acts from our adversaries.
4	Deliver Aid	The RAF are ready to provide urgent assistance in an emergency, from floods in the UK, to the Ebola outbreak in Africa, and devastating hurricanes in the Caribbean. We have the aircraft, know - how, and the reach to get humanitarian aid, equipment, and people into affected areas quickly. We also evacuate civilians and military personnel from natural disasters and unrest. We support government agencies and emergency services on UK operations. On overseas humanitarian operations we work with the Department for International Development (DFID), and the governments of Commonwealth and partner countries.
5	Work in Partnership	The RAF collaborates with government, military, and civilian partners in the UK and overseas to promote UK security, prosperity and national interests around the world. Air power is most effective in a joint action with other military services such as the British Army and Royal Navy, and with government departments, all working towards a common national goal. We call this a full spectrum approach. Maintaining good relations with our international partners means we can operate from their bases to expand our global reach. As a world - class air force we also advise and train other air forces to build their capacity to respond to threats and prevent conflict.
6	Combat Cyber Threats	The RAF is responsible for protecting the UK's air and space capabilities against cyber - attack. Potential adversaries are growing their capability and confidence to launch cyber - attacks that could disrupt the UK's critical civilian and military air and space systems such as air traffic control. Successful cyber - attacks could prevent our ability to protect UK airspace and provide air power overseas. Our cyber - security specialists are working to combat such threats.

Source: Own

Global action by the RAF is quite wide. It is said the RAF is "currently active across four continents with significant operations in Eastern Europe, South Atlantic, and the Mediterranean" and that it's "proximity to unstable regions and potential adversaries provides the air power to curb threats and destabilising behaviour" (Wigston, 2020). It is also said that the RAF "continuously train and deploy with the armed forces of our NATO allies and global partners in places like Estonia, Romania, and in the fight against ISIS in Iraq and Syria" (Wigston, 2020).

THE CHURCH OF ENGLAND

One might think of the Church of England as an ongoing project. In contemporary terminology the organisation can be seen to be involved in the portfolio management through its geographical hierarchies a number of programmes through its churches which are subdivided into projects without those churches, or more recently via service orientated architectures like Zoom.

Table 22. The three purposes of the Church of England

#	Purpose	Description
A	Story	A place to receive the Word of God as spoken through the prophets.
B	Space	A place to discuss Scripture, the Creeds and how to witness doctrine.
C	Sanctuary	A place to feel part of a universal church.

Source: Own

Table 22 shows the strategy behind the Church of England's programmes. They seek on the one hand to provide a basis for those figures important to the faith, such as Isaiah, to be continue to be propagated in a world of 24 / 7 media. They seek through their churches and other forms of service delivery to give people the chance to discuss Scripture (i.e. the Holy Bible), the Catholic Creeds and to witness doctrine such as the 39 articles of religion.

Table 23. The three pillars of the Church of England

#	Pillar	Description
1	Scripture	Scripture is faith revealed.
2	Creeds	The creeds are a codification of Scripture.
3	Witness	One witnesses through the doctrine of the Church as it changes over time.

Source: Own

As can be seen from Table 23, the purposes of the Church of England's programmes is quite clear. It seeks to disseminate Scripture (i.e. the Holy Bible in this case) through founding its doctrine around the Catholic Creeds so that those who attend their services may bear witness to Jesus of Nazareth.

CONCLUSION

This article has looked at the research problem of developing project management methodologies that are based on how an organization functions at the same time as recognizing the relevance of standardized approached. The article has proposed a programme of research that would involve running software development projects, including with the use of legacy systems, which would as a result product data that can be turned into a project management toolkit to assist those in multi - national organisations. This can include Crocels Community Media Group, the Royal Air Force, Church of England and University of Gloucestershire. The toolkit will be composed of info - graphics and other graphical representations so that whether someone is working in a small community organization or a large multi - national company or arm of government, they can develop an approach to project management that is suited to their organisation's way of doing things, meaning the project is more likely to succeed. This article performed a pilot study to see whether the questionnaire aimed at the users of the legacy systems would be effective. With a Cronbach's alpha of 0.616 on a 77 item scale a sample size of 3 shows potential for a full - scale study with only minor amendments needed.

REFERENCES

Alderson, A., & Shah, H. (1999). Technical opinion: Viewpoints on legacy systems. *Communications of the ACM*, *42*(3), 115–116. doi:10.1145/295685.295722

Artto, K., & Kujala, J. (2008). Project business as a research field. *International Journal of Managing Projects in Business*, *1*(4), 469–497. doi:10.1108/17538370810906219

Berger, H. (2007). Agile development in a bureaucratic arena - A case study experience. *International Journal of Information Management*, *27*(6), 386–396. doi:10.1016/j.ijinfomgt.2007.08.009

Bishop, J. (2007a). Ecological cognition: A new dynamic for human - computer interaction. In B. Wallace, A. Ross, J. Davies & T. Anderson (Eds.), The mind, the body and the world: Psychology after cognitivism (pp. 327 - 345). Imprint Academic.

Bishop, J. (2007b). Increasing participation in online communities: A framework for human–computer interaction. *Computers in Human Behavior*, *23*(4), 1881–1893. doi:10.1016/j.chb.2005.11.004

Bishop, J. (2011a). *Equatricism: A new paradigm for research and practice in information technology, the arts, law and sciences*. Cardiff Metropolitan University's Annual Poster Symposium, Cardiff, UK.

Bishop, J. (2011b). The equatrics of intergenerational knowledge transformation in techno - cultures: Towards a model for enhancing information management in virtual worlds (Master's dissertation). Aberystwyth University.

Bishop, J. (2012). Lessons from the emotivate project for increasing take - up of big society and responsible capitalism initiatives. In P. M. Pumilia - Gnarini, E. Favaron, E. Pacetti, J. Bishop, & L. Guerra (Eds.), Didactic strategies and technologies for education: Incorporating advancements (pp. 208 - 217). Hershey, PA: IGI Global.

Bishop, J., & Kommers, P. A. M. (2016). *The impact of physical and virtual environments on human emotions: A pilot study in an adult and community education setting*. The 14th International Conference on Scientific Computing, Las Vegas, NV. 10.1109/CSCI.2016.0065

Booth, W. C. (2003). *The craft of research* (2nd ed.). University of Chicago Press Ltd.

Briggs, A. R. J., Coleman, M., & Morrison, M. (Eds.). (2012). *Research methods in educational leadership & management* (3rd ed.). Sage Publications Ltd. doi:10.4135/9781473957695

Cassidy, C. (2001). *Beyond numbers: Qualitative research methods for oriental medicine. Clinical acupuncture*. Springer.

Collins, K. M., Onwuegbuzie, A. J., & Sutton, I. L. (2006). A model incorporating the rationale and purpose for conducting mixed methods research in special education and beyond. *Learning Disabilities (Weston, Mass.)*, *4*(1), 67–100.

Cuban, L. (2001). *Oversold and underused: Computers in the classroom*. Harvard University Press.

Cunliffe, D. (2000). Developing usable web sites - a review and model. *Internet Research*, *10*(4), 295–308. doi:10.1108/10662240010342577

De-Laat, M., & Lally, V. (2003). Complexity, theory and praxis: Researching collaborative learning and tutoring processes in a networked learning community. *Instructional Science*, *31*(1 - 2), 7 - 39.

Dulock, H. L. (1993). Research design: Descriptive research. *Journal of Pediatric Oncology Nursing*, *10*(4), 154–157. doi:10.1177/104345429301000406 PMID:8251123

Farenden, P. (2012). *ITIL for dummies*. John Wiley & Sons Ltd.

Firstenberg, A., & Salas, J. (2014). Designing & developing for Google glass: Thinking differently for a new platform. O'Reilly Media, Inc.

German, E. (2017). Information literacy and instruction: LibGuides for instruction: A service design point of view from an academic library. *Reference and User Services Quarterly*, *56*(3), 162–167. doi:10.5860/rusq.56n3.162

Graham, N. (2008). *PRINCE2 for dummies*. John Wiley & Sons Ltd.

James, N., & Busher, H. (2009). *Online interviewing*. Sage Publications. doi:10.4135/9780857024503

Jasma, K. (2001). *WML & WMLScript: A beginner's guide* (J. Schachterle, J. McKensie, P. Schumauder, & A. Carroll, Eds.). McGraw - Hill.

Kaplan, B., & Maxwell, J. A. (2005). *Qualitative research methods for evaluating computer information systems. Evaluating the organizational impact of healthcare information systems*. Springer.

Kerzner, H. (2014). *Project recovery: Case studies and techniques for overcoming project failure*. John Wiley and Sons Ltd. doi:10.1002/9781118841617

Kuniavsky, M. (2003). *Observing the user experience: A practitioner's guide to user research*. Morgan Kaufmann Publishers.

Layton, M. C. (2015). *Scrum for dummies*. John Wiley & Sons Ltd.

Manford, C., & McSporran, M. (2003). E-Learning quality: Becoming a level five learning organization. *Proceedings of the 16th NACCQ*, 343 - 348.

Mitchell, A. (1983). *The nine American lifestyles: Who we are & where we are going*. MacMillan Publishing Co., Inc.

Nakai, M., & Ke, W. (2011). Review of the methods for handling missing data in longitudinal data analysis. *International Journal of Mathematical Analysis*, *5*(1), 1–13.

Nekoufar, S., & Karim, A. (2011). Lean project management in large scale industrial project via standardization. *Project Perspectives*, *33*, 72–77.

Nielsen, J. (2000). *Designing web usability*. New Riders.

Rimando, M., & Brace, A. M., Namageyo-Funa, A., Parr, T. L., Sealy, D., & Davis, T. L. (2015). Data collection challenges and recommendations for early career researchers. *Qualitative Report*, *20*(12), 2025–2036.

Rose, D. (2018). *Enterprise agility for dummies*. John Wiley & Sons Ltd.

Rosenberg, M. J. (2000). *E - Learning: Strategies for delivering knowledge in the digital age*. McGraw - Hill.

Ruddle, R. A., Payne, S. J., & Jones, D. M. (1998). Navigating large - scale "desk - top" virtual buildings: Effects of orientation aids and familiarity. *Presence (Cambridge, Mass.)*, *7*(2), 179–192. doi:10.1162/105474698565668

Saunders, M., Lewis, P., & Thornhill, A. (2009). Understanding research philosophies and approaches. In M. Saunders, P. Lewis, & A. Thornhill (Eds.), *Research methods for business students* (5th ed., pp. 106–135). Pearson Education Limited.

Sayer, N. J., & Williams, B. (2012). *Lean for dummies* (2nd ed.). John Wiley & Sons Ltd.

Slocombe, M. (2001). Max hits: Building successful websites. Rotovision.

Sohi, A. J., Hertogh, M., Bosch-Rekveldt, M., & Blom, R. (2016). Does lean & agile project management help coping with project complexity? *Procedia: Social and Behavioral Sciences*, *226*, 252–259. doi:10.1016/j.sbspro.2016.06.186

Sommerville, I. (2016). *Legacy systems* (9th ed.). Pearson Education Limited.

Thomas, G., & Vaughan, M. (2004). *Inclusive education: Readings and reflections. Inclusive education*. ERIC.

Weller, M. (2002). Delivering learning on the net: The why, what & how of online education. RoutledgeFalmer.

Wu, B., Lawless, D., Bisbal, J., Richardson, R., Grimson, J., & Wade, V. (1997). The butterfly methodology: A gateway - free approach for migrating legacy information systems. *Proceedings. Third IEEE International Conference on Engineering of Complex Computer Systems* (Cat. no. 97TB100168), 200 - 205.

Zeid, I. (2000). *Mastering the internet and HTML*. Prentice Hall.

Zhang, Z., & Yang, H. (2004). *Incubating services in legacy systems for architectural migration*. Paper presented at the 11th Asia - Pacific Software Engineering Conference. 10.1109/APSEC.2004.61

KEY TERMS AND DEFINITIONS

Legacy System: A legacy system is an information system that is either obsolete or requires maintenance to keep it operating.

Multinational Organisation: A multinational organisation is an organisation with a presence in a number of different towns or cities countrywide or worldwide.

Pillars: An organisation's pillars are the core activities or functions it performs.

Portfolio Management: Portfolio management is the method by which one manages a series of programmes.

Programme Management: Programme management is the method by which one manages a series of projects.

Project Management: Project management is the systematic approach to delivering a project.

Purposes: An organisation's purposes are the values and methods by which it operates.

Chapter 9
eXtreme Programming, Agile Methodologies, Software Project Management, Customer Role, Rigorous Testing

Kamalendu Pal
https://orcid.org/0000-0001-7158-6481
City, University of London, UK

ABSTRACT

Agile software development methodologies are attracting attention from academics and practitioners for planning and managing software projects. The eXtreme Programming (XP) challenges conformist wisdom regarding software system development processes and practices as agile methodologies. To work efficiently in the current software development practice, characterized by requirements fuzziness, XP moves away from document-centric operations into people-centric management. In the XP-based software project, the customers play an essential role, having multiple responsibilities such as driving the project, gathering requirements ('user stories'), and exercising quality control (or acceptance testing). Besides, the customers must liaise with external project stakeholders (e.g., funding authorities, end-users) while maintaining the development team's trust and the wider business. The success of such software project management practices relies on the quality result of each stage of development obtained through rigorous testing. This chapter describes three characteristics of XP project management: customer role, software testing feedback, and learning.

INTRODUCTION

Modern software system plays a vital role in shaping significant social challenges (Pal, 2019). Software is increasingly an essential value-adding component of most consumer products (e.g., mobile phones, music systems, automobiles). Besides, software systems are also heavily used in the aerospace industry, enterprise business process automation, and industrial control systems. In these software applications,

DOI: 10.4018/978-1-7998-7872-8.ch009

malfunction or error can cause loss of life or injury. Hence, error-free software function is crucial to the safety and wellbeing of people and succeeding with business operations. Succeeding with software systems means making the best use of analysis and design technology to fulfil the client's business goals and objectives. In this context, one can use the term technology to encompass all aspects of software engineering, from programming languages to analysis-and-design methods to productivity and quality. All these things encompass good software engineering practices.

It is worth considering the history that forms the basic understanding of good software engineering practices. This history is essential because the basics have been ignored in many 1990s business organizations seeking to build large and complex software systems. There is an increasing need for applying strict design principles like engineering disciplines (e.g., mechanical engineering, civil engineering) to the development of software systems (Pal, 2020) (Pal & Karakostas, 2021). Different software development process models (e.g., Waterfall, Spiral, Incremental) were introduced in recent decades, and these models provide a systematic and organized approach to software development (Sommerville, 2019). One of the critical phases in software process models is to test product correctness. This way, software products must be verified against their user requirements throughout the development process like any engineering product. Consequently, software development needs rigorous testing.

In recent times, rapid change has been an essential factor of both commercial and public life. The other crucial truism is that information technology (e.g., hardware, software, data communication networking protocols), specifically, is an integral part of many organizations and their regular operations. It is also evident (Pal, 2019) that the developers of this software need to consider design in a systematic way. Also, the burden to develop new application software support for rapidly changing processes is causing many problems for the software development community. In the recent past, traditional software design and development projects have failed many times to deliver what is needed at the cost and within the required timescale (Pal. 2020). The pressure to develop new software support for rapidly changing processes is causing severe problems for the software system development.

This is caused by some attitudinal and structural problems related to traditional software engineering. Academic and practitioners put forward some insights into the problems (Sommerville, 2019) (Pressman, 2005) and present a survey of traditional software engineering, which documents many current approaches. Besides, others such as Gilb (1988) and Beck (1999) are beginning to question how software engineering has been carried out in practical problems.

Software engineering practitioners such as Beck realize that everything about traditional software processes needs to organize in a new way. Also, Gilb and Beck proposed practices involve several well-established and reliable techniques that have been around for years. It is not just a matter of reorganizing around a few traditional techniques into different order; instead, it is a new combination of activities based on a new and very encouraging philosophy of *agile* software development.

The software industry has moved its production management from traditional software development practice to agile methodologies to mitigate the ever-increasing software complexity and globalization of software design and development. Many software development teams started to adopt new software development methodologies, known as *Agile methodologies*, for their software development purpose. In short, Agile methodologies are a reaction to traditional ways of developing software and acknowledge the requirement for an alternative to a document-driven, heavyweight software development process (Beck et al., 2001). The primary purpose of these methodologies is to keep close customer collaboration, provide business value as quickly as possible in an incremental way, and respond promptly to changing customer requirements (Barlow et al., 2011) (Cockburn & Williams, 2003).

Extreme Programming (XP) is a new breed of methodology, collectively part of the Agile methodologies, challenging traditional knowledge of system development processes and practices. The XP methodology was developed in the 1990s by Kent Beck when working on a Chrysler project (although its beginning stretches back to Smalltalk projects that he and Ward Cunningham worked on at Tektronix in the mid-1980s). The XP methodology emphasizes document-centric processes into practices that enable people (Beck, 2000). It represents one of the fastest-growing movements in the software world today.

XP is a software design and development methodology based on simplicity, communication, and business processes development-related feedback. The XP methodology works by bringing the whole team together in simple practices, with sufficient feedback to enable the team to assess where they are and tune the practices to their unique situation. XP recognizes that a development project's end goal is to produce a quality, appropriate business solution that can develop and maintain the ultimate software.

To operate appropriately in the world of vague and changing requirements, XP emphasizes practices that enable people (Beck, 2000). One of the critical roles within the XP team is the Customer role. Researchers (Beck & Fowler, 2001) describe the right customer with some qualities:

- The customer understands the domain well by working in that domain and by understanding how it works.
- Customers can understand, with development's help, how software can provide business value in the domain.
- Customers can decide on what is needed now and what is needed later.

The usefulness of the characteristics mentioned above is reviewed by academics and practitioners (Deursen, 2001) (Cohn & Paul, 2001) to real-world implementation-related issues. The XP method initiative's founding members have clarified this vital role in the XP team, but they (Beck & Fowler, 2001) acknowledge the risk associated with this role.

XP methodology depends heavily on user involvement. Applied scientific research (Baskervill & Stage, 1996) (Bostrom & Thomas, 1983) (Orlikowski & Gash, 1994) (Urquhart, 1998) in this area have been carried out, which cover the types of user and development team interaction issues and advantages advocated by this involvement.

One of the facts gathering initiatives the XP user-group is establishing a body of knowledge is collecting real-world experiences relating to XP projects (Marchesi et al., 2002). These experiences highlight several issues when projects implement the XP customer role, including who should be the customer (Gittins, Hope, & Williams, 2002) (Martin, 2002), how the role scales to large projects (Schalliol, 2002), and what should be done if the customer cannot be "onsite" (Martin, 2002) (Farell et al., 2002).

In this way, many questions remain unanswered regarding XP customers and their roles. As suggested by methodology research, this chapter uses descriptive studies exploring actual practice to address customer characteristics. The rest of the chapter is as follows. Section 2 introduces the Agile software development practice-related issues. Section 3 presents a review of related research work. Section 4 outlines the XP method, concentrating on the role of the onsite customer. Section 5 highlights the characteristics of a good customer. Section 6 describes a customer classification scheme and the relationship between these customers. Section 7 explains the implications of the study and future research. Finally, Section 8 provides brief concluding remarks and identifies future work.

AGILE SOFTWARE DEVELOPMENT

This section describes XP, an Agile methodology, for software development. In the early part of 2001, a group of academics and practitioners (Cockburn, 2006) (Highsmith, 2002) (Fowler, 2002) met in Utah, United States of America, for a workshop to present the growing idea that was referred to, at the time, *lightweight* or *light methods*. The workshop's result was the new term, *Agile*, to refer to these methods; and the *Agile Manifesto* (Beck et al., 2001).

Today, agile methodologies promising rapid delivery and time to market have started to dominate the software industry, removing traditional methodologies such as Waterfall from the mainstream (Schwaber & Beedle, 2002). *Agile manifesto* introduces four fundamental principles, as enumerated below in a tabular representation (Table 1). In this way, the manifesto creators uncovered better ways of developing software and helping others do it.

Table 1. Four fundamental principles

Number	Item	Value
1	Individual	Interactions over processes and tools
2	Working	Software over comprehensive documentation
3	Customer	Collaboration over contract negotiation
4	Responding	Change over following a plan

The above tabular representation presents the value in the items on the right; the creators (or the authors of the manifesto) want to value the items on the left.

The above concepts do not directly fit the conventional software development lifecycle, including deriving the specification, design, evaluation, and evolution. As a result, several methodologies have evolved from the Agile concept's basic principles, like Scrum, eXtreme Programming (XP), Lean, and Kanban, the prominent examples.

Also, academics and practitioners have provided a detailed description of the manifesto (Highsmith, 2002), (Fowler, 2002) (Cockburn, 2006). The Agile Manifesto also includes some basic principles that provide additional guidance: (i) the main priority is customer satisfaction using early and continuous delivery of valuable software. (ii) ready to accept changing requirements, agile processes harness change for the customer's competitive advantage even late in development. (iii) deliver intermediate prototype software frequently, with a shorter timescale preference, from a couple of weeks to a couple of months. (iv) requirement engineers, clients, and software implementers need to exchange views and ideas regularly. (v) a most effective and efficient method of conveying information to and within a development team is face-to-face conversation. (vi) pay attention to new technological innovation and sound design to technical excellence in agility. (vii) the team regularly reflects on becoming more effective, then tunes and adjusts its behaviour accordingly (Beck et al., 2001). The Agile Manifesto's values and principles provide the agile methodologies' standard foundations, and XP is one of these methodologies.

RELATED RESEARCH

Effective communication, collaboration, and coordination are the main contributing factors for success in agile methods. Communication is defined as imparting or interchanging thoughts, opinions, or information by speech, writing, or signs. Collaboration is defined as working together to accomplish a task and discussing to solve complex problems. The effective collaboration includes both individually focused duties and interactive group work. Coordination is defined as the harmonious adjustment or interaction of different people or things to achieve a goal or effect. Learning is impossible without communication (Lei, Slocum, & Pitts, 1999) as communication is a prime factor. Communication can take different forms - verbal or nonverbal through media like books, white papers, pictures, or observations. Employees cannot learn from other experts without information exchange, and knowledge acquisition and sharing would be inhibited (Ribbens, 1997; Schein, 1993). Duncan and Moriarty (1998) describe communication as the human activity that links people together and creates relationships.

There are various communication channels, but face-to-face communication is highlighted as the most effective as it provides instant feedback and multiple cues like expression, emotions, and personal focus. The knowledge acquired through face-to-face communication can be retained for a limited time, then it starts diminishing gradually. So, some tools like papers, whiteboards, and others may store information intended for future use. These tools are also helpful to access information about the project when many people work together on one project or when multiple teams (consisting of many people) are simultaneously working on different parts of the same project, and coordination among them is crucial. Small groups are more effective in coordination, communication, and collaboration than are large teams (Cockburn, 2000; Curtis, Curtis, & Iscoe, 1988). Small groups with two to ten people perform better than those working alone, especially while dealing with complex problems.

This view is also supported by Cockburn (Cockburn, 2000). According to Cao and Balasubramaniam (Cao & Balasubramaniam, 2007), agile development involves intensive teamwork and high task interdependence. As task interdependence increases, the requirement for coordination becomes greater (Cao & Balasubramaniam, 2007). The physical design of the workspace also plays a vital role in effective communication and collaboration. If people working on the same team are close to each other physically, it may be easier for them to communicate when required to eliminate ambiguity.

Furthermore, workspace design will be effective if it facilitates communication and collaboration and provides an environment to do individual work effectively. There are few researchers conducted so far that observed the importance of the physical design of workspace for effective communication and collaboration, which make up the backbone of software development, especially using agile methods (Beck, 2000; Cockburn, 2000; Heerwagen, Kampschroer, Powell, & Loftness, 2004; Sharp & Robinson, 2003). According to Heerwagen et al. (2004), a collaborative work environment requires spaces, furnishings, and technologies that support individual focus and group interaction while facilitating transitions between these activities. This chapter studied the physical settings of a small-scale software development organization working on a large, complex project using eXtreme Programming (XP) for a domain they had no previous experience with. XP is one of the approaches to agile methods. We examined how different people (e.g., developers, business experts, customers) who worked on this project communicated and collaborated effectively without disrupting individually focused tasks to complete the project successfully. Two small teams are working simultaneously on different parts of the product (project). This study shows how the communication with customers, within a team and across two groups, took place during the software project using agile methods.

Furthermore, we learned how the physical design of the workspace (proximity of different rooms on the same floor, arrangement of furniture, presence of whiteboards, communal area) enhanced effective communication and collaboration without compromising the ability to work alone in an effective way. This study is based on experiences, an extensive literature review of communication, collaboration, coordination, and the significance of these factors in the workplace. A survey questionnaire was developed to collect data and observe the physical environment and tools on communication, collaboration, and coordination in a small organization using agile methods. This study will provide a guideline for prospective office designers who are adopting agile practices.

Communication, Collaboration, and Coordination as Key Enablers

Software development can be considered as a cooperative game of invention and communication. There is nothing in the game but people's ideas and the transmission to colleagues and the computer (Cockburn, 2000). In complex situations, communication effectiveness is particularly critical to project success where multiple and integrated stakeholder's teams are involved and where "time to market" and project efficiency are vital drivers (Elliott, 2000). This is supported by many researchers in their studies (Beck, 2000; Bostrom and Thomas, 1983; Edstrom, 1997).

Focusing on skills, communication, and community allows the project to be more effective and agile than focusing on processes. People's skills and collaboration, conversations, and communications enhance flexibility and innovation (Highsmith, 2002). According to Heerwagen, Kampschroer, Powell, and Loftness (2004), knowledge work is highly cognitive and social. Workers need time alone to think and develop ideas, drawing on their memory, insight, and analytical skills. However, for ideas and concepts to become applicable to an organization, they must be available to others for scrutiny and further development (Heerwagen et al., 2004).

Face-to-Face is the Most Effective Means of Communication

Software development is considered a cooperative game of communication, implying that a project's appreciation of progress is related to how long it takes information to get from one person's head to the head of another (Cockburn, 2000). Media Richness Theory (Daft & Lengel, 1986; Daft, Lengel, & Trevino, 1987) suggests that the wealthiest communication channel enables instant feedback and can transmit multiple cues and has a high language variety and can transmit emotional contents. Face-to-face is the richest form of communication because it can transmit multiple cues (e.g., voice inflexion, body language) and facilitate shared meaning with rapid mutual feedback and personal focus, feelings, and emotions infusing the conversation (Daft, Lengel, & Trevino, 1987). From a functional perspective, informal face-to-face interactions aid understanding and problem-solving due to the enriched context, including facial expressions, gestures, posture, appearance, and other people's reactions (Kendon, 1990). Face-to-face interaction is also more flexible and can respond better to ambiguity and uncertainty (Allen, 1971). It is further supported by Cockburn (2000) that the most effective form of communication (for transmitting ideas) is interactive and face-to-face.

Also, Kolkata, Abrahamsson, and Kyllonen (Korkala et al., 2006) described that face-to-face communication is identified as the most efficient means of communication between participants. Moreover, the daily collaborative work of businesspeople and developers demands efficient verbal communication between the customer and developers (Korkala et al., 2006). Based on the existing literature, Kraut and

Streeter (1995) found that formal communication (e.g., structured meetings, specifications, inspections) is helpful for routine coordination. In contrast, informal communication (e.g., hallway conversation, telephone calls, workshops) is needed in the face of uncertainty and unanticipated problems, typical of software development. McLuhan (1964) has used the terms "hot" and "cool" when discussing different media for communication. Ambler (2002) and Cockburn (2002) have also adopted the use of "hot" and "cold" communication media. They argue that "hot" communication channels provide more information than "cold" media. According to Ambler (2002), face-to-face communication is the "hottest" communication channel, whereas e-mail is positioned as a "colder" communication channel. The use of "cold" communication media can either complement "hot" communication media or be used only in the absence of "hot" communication media. Face-to-face communication is not free from pitfalls, however.

OVERVIEW OF XP METHODOLOGY

XP is the most prominent new Agile methodologies for small to medium-sized teams developing systems (e.g., software, hardware) with rapidly changing requirements. The initial concept of XP methodology was introduced by Kent Beck (Beck, 2000) (Beck, 2004). XP works towards providing iterative and recurrent software release all along the project life cycle.

Table 2. Four fundamental variables in XP

Variable	Description
Cost	The cost variable relates to the number of financial resources to be spent.
Time	The time variable indicates when the software system (or a particular release) should be completed.
Quality	The quality variable defines the correctness related measures of the software system, as defined by the client or customer. It also describes the quality assurance related software testing criteria and measurement procedures.
Scope	The scope variable describes the software system's functionality. It includes what and how much will be done.

XP considers a software development related activity as a system of four control '*variables*. These variables are – Cost, Time, Quality, and Scope. A brief description of these variables is presented in Table 2.

A simple diagrammatic representation of these variables and their dependencies is shown in Figure 1. Time is the central variable in XP methodology. Enhancing the software system's quality can increase the time needed to improve software processes and the related testing for assurance. In other words, decreasing quality can reduce time to a particular degree (e.g., reduce the number of functional software test-related activities).

Sometimes increase the financial resources can reduce the length of time to complete the software development project. The increase of financial resources is attributed to hiring more software development personals and procuring better equipment. However, increasing the number of software developers can increase the time of overhead of communication. Also, decreasing financial resources can increases the project duration dramatically.

The dependable relations among these variables also highlight other properties of the XP methodology. For example, increasing scope means extra time is required because more software development-related activities are required to complete. At the same time, decreasing scope reduces the software development time. In this way, if, for example, business project management and customer increases scope (e.g., additional characteristics of the proposed software) and holds onto cost (using the same resources) and quality, project completion time must be increased.

Figure 1. The relationship between the variables

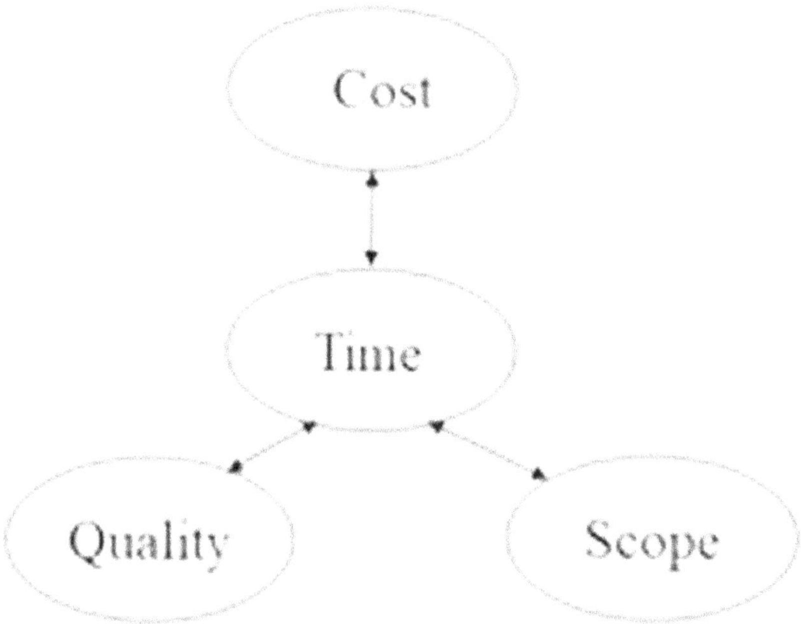

XP provides a value-added methodology. The values are based on four distinct attributes – Simplicity, Communication, Feedback, and Courage. The essential characteristics of these attributes are summarized as below:

Simplicity Encouraged: XP methodology strives for a simple software system. In this way, XP tries to deliver the most straightforward functionality that matches the business requirements. This means that the system should be as simple as possible; simultaneously, the system must work. It includes designing the most straightforward software that supports the required functionality. It also encourages building software systems for today and not for tomorrow. XP also encourages the minimum number of artefacts to an absolute minimum – the user requirements (or stories), plans (Planning Game) and the software product (i.e., code). Software coding style needs to be easy to read, understand, maintain, and modify. The XP practices and techniques can be learned in a short duration (however, mastering them, of course, takes enough time). The primary purpose for simplicity is that XP tries to manage changes and other related risks.

Accomplish Communication: Different problems can be realized to the breakdown of communication (e.g., the software engineer forgot to ask the customer an essential question). The XP methodology encourages keeping communication flowing in a variety of ways. It can be accomplished by – (i) collaborative workspaces, (ii) co-location of customer business space and software development, (iii) software develop by paired staff, (iv) alternating paired staffs frequently, (v) changing the software development tasks frequently, (vi) brief staff meetings for review the progress, and (vii) unit tests, prototype demonstrations, verbal communication is not documented.

Value of Feedback: XP based software development is heavily dependent on feedback. It is helpful for feedback at all scales (e.g., customer feedback, manager comments, developer review provision). Feedback is encouraged in – (i) incremental releases, (ii) automated unit tests, and (iii) automated software functional tests. The earlier and more frequently the software development team get feedback, the better. This way, problems are usually more minor, and hence, amendments are more accessible and cheaper.

Importance of Courage: Courage is an essential element in XP based software development. Courage is required because a considerable part of this development practices extreme in the way that go against the traditional knowledge software product development. Besides, XP based software development differs in the role of the customer in the process. For this to work, courage is needed from both the developers and the customer.

XP based software design and development follows an iterative and incremental process.

The Process XP

XP based software design and development project consists of a smaller increment of implementation, known as release. A release is a version of the software system, which describes a sub-system of the proposed software. All the functionalities of the release need to be developed thoroughly. Customer requirements are captured in natural language; informal '*user story*' cards are very similar to use cases (Cockburn, 2000) (Jacobson et al., 1992). In real applications, software developers estimate each card's times, and customers prioritize each card. In the "Planning Game", the customer selects the user stories that comprise the essential part for a short and deliverable regular interval (e.g., one month). Also, every small incremental implementation is accepted and tried by the client (or customer). The rest of the user stories are re-assessed for possible requirement and priority changes, and the project is executed for the following software incremental implementation.

In this way, the releases incrementally create the solicited functionality (assuming the software system grows over time). Releases are negotiated in the Planning Games. The customer provides what should be part of the release, and the developers determine how much time it will take to implement the software release, or the customer decides the strategic plan. The software developers assess the amount of development work that can be done within the available time. The individual release cycle is made of a few iterations. The iteration is mainly a software development facility that is used to ease the required project planning. A simple diagrammatic representation of XP based software development process structure is shown in Figure 2.

Planning Game

The Planning Game consists of three phases: (i) exploration, (ii) planning, and (iii) steering. The customer describes the system requirements in the exploration phase, and software developers estimate the complete implementation duration. In the planning phase, both the customers and developers negotiate which desired features can be completed within the given resources (time and other resources).

The steering phase negotiate plan is changed, whenever needed in response to what is learned in development while putting the plan in effect. In the exploration phase, the customer writes user stories onto Index Cards. The stories describe what the customer wants out of the system functionality.

Figure 2. Simple process structure

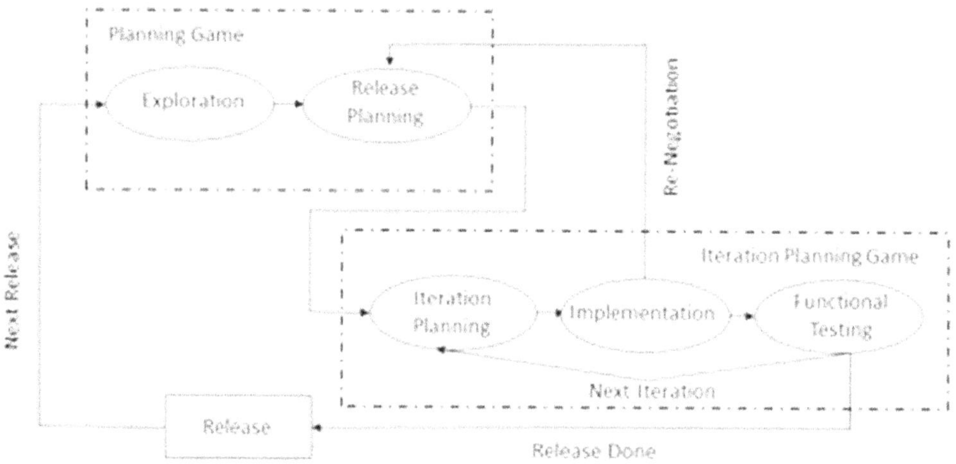

Customer Tests

The planning activities are event-oriented, and they produce excellent information and excellent steering control in the customer's hands. The XP customer defines the desired feature of a software product, and they also describe automated product acceptance tests. The software development team crafts these tests and uses them to justify that the property is implemented appropriately to themselves and customers. Automation is essential because, due to the shortage of time, manual tests are avoided.

Designing an XP based software system is neither a one-time activity nor an up-front thing, but it is an all-the-time thing. The development team follows specific design steps. These design steps are release planning and iteration planning, and development teams engage in quick design sessions and design revision through refactoring in the project's entire lifecycle. Besides, XP software project design is based on sound design principles; and one of the characteristics is 'Pair Programming.

Pair Programming

At coding phase, two programmers work side-by-side at one computer, collaborating on the same software system design and development, including coding and testing. In this way, two software programmers, sitting side by side at the same machine, build all production software. It makes sure that all production code is reviewed by at least one programmer, resulting in better design, tasting, and code. A pair of programming working areas is shown in Figure 3.

This practice does take some practice to do well, and one needs to do it well for a few weeks to see the results. In addition to providing better code and tests, Pairing also serves to communicate knowledge throughout the team.

Continuous Integration

Software development coding assignments are broken down into small tasks, preferably of no more than one day. When each task is completed, it is added to the main code collection base. In this way, there are software sub-components built regularly.

Figure 3. XP project pair programming working area

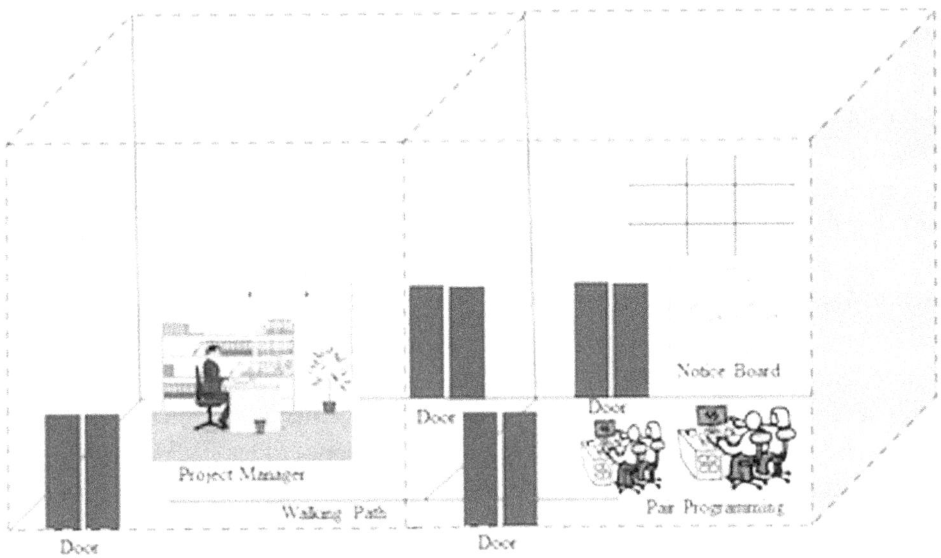

Onsite Customer

The customers are readily available and accessible to the developers to clarify and validate system requirements; preferably, customers are onsite.

The onsite customer is responsible for writing user stories and acceptance tests. Simply, a user story is a brief description of a software system requirement or feature that is:

... understandable to customers and developers, testable, valuable to the customer and small enough so that the programmers can build half a dozen in an iteration. ...A user story is nothing more than an agreement that the customer and developers will talk together about a feature. (Beck & Fowler, 2001), p. 45-46

In XP, projects are planned to use the planning game. XP projects are decomposed into small public releases of software, and within each release are iterations. Releases are small, typically two to three months. Iterations are smaller, typically one to two weeks. The planning game is run at both levels at different granularities. The planning game typically occurs as a "face-to-face" meeting, where:

- The customer prioritizes the user stories in business value order.
- The programmers sign up to estimate the user stories they will develop. They estimate the time needed to develop the story by breaking it into tasks.
- The customer confirms the final scope of the iteration or release. This step can include manipulating the stories, including breaking a story into parts, to ensure business value is delivered.
- Once the scope is determined, the programmers can enter the coding phase. This phase primarily consists of discussing the story with the customer, implementing the story, and ensuring the story passes all the customer's acceptance tests. An acceptance test proves the function works as expected by the customer.
- XP uses quick releases to maximize feedback from end-users and other business stakeholders. Therefore, regular releases are encouraged, as often as every day, but more typically every couple of months.
- Several XP practices support the coding phase, including metaphor, simple design, test-first coding, Refactoring, pair programming, collective ownership, continuous integration, coding standards and the 40-hour week. The initial text by Beck (Beck, 2001) provides an excellent overview of these practices.

There are many other agile methods like Scrum, DSDM, Crystal methods, Feature-driven development and more (Abrahamsson & Koskela, 2004). However, XP is one of the first full-featured agile methods. XP embraces the four significant values of agile methods (e.g., early customer involvement, iterative development, self-organizing teams, and flexibility) (Rico, 2006).

Advantages of user involvement in the projects have many benefits: improved product quality through a better understanding of the user requirements, improved knowledge of clients' organization, minimized risk of making unacceptable functionality, improved ability to negotiate expectations among users, improved ability to resolve conflicts regarding the design of the system, increased feeling of ownership among users, reduction in the natural resistance towards change in work practices, remedies lack decision capability in management, improved project performance and an increased willingness to experiment and improvise in search for solutions (Hanssen & Faegri, 2006). User involvement in system development success concluded that user productivity was increased, whereas training cost and user support calls were decreased with a practical user-involvement approach (Salihoglu, 2001) (William et al., 2007).

It is also highlighted that having an onsite customer can reduce errors related to business requirements. For example, one researcher estimated that with using "onsite customer" practice, rework was reduced by over 60% for the project (William et al., 2007). These onsite customers are classified as 'good customers', which need specific characteristics.

CLASSIFICATION OF CUSTOMERS

This chapter's research question focused on who was the XP customer? This question sought to clarify the types of people who undertook the role and understand if they were a single person or a team undertaking the role. In the initial reviews of the existing literature, the current findings concluded that it was always a team of people; what is more, the group of people tended to consist of up to ten distinct roles. The roles emerged as follows:

Collaboration Guides: Geek Interpreter, Political Advisor and Technical Liaison. The Geek Interpreter contributes to enhancing the collaboration within the team, particularly between the customer and programmers. The Political Advisor contributes to strengthening the partnership between the customer and the more significant organizational life of the business, ensuring the customer is better able to navigate the political dimensions necessary for the project to succeed. The Technical Liaison contributes to enhancing the collaboration between this project and other related projects and any technical specialist silos within the organizational structure. The collaboration guide roles that emerged from this research expand the collaboration facilitator role initially outlined by Highsmith (2000).

Skills Specialists: Acceptance Tester, User Interface (UI) Designer and Technical Writer. All the specialist roles support the customer to undertake their onsite customer responsibilities. The Acceptance Tester supports the customer by assisting with the acceptance testing of the software. User interface (UI) Designer supports the customer by lending their user-centre-design (UCD) skills to help them decide and design what to build. The Technical Writer supports the customer by lending their specialist writing skills to create user documentation to accompany the software when released. Each specialist skill set helps to reduce the workload of the customer and improves the resulting software released. The skills specialist roles that emerged from this research support Beck's identification of these potential roles outlined in XP second edition (Beck, 2004).

Direction Setting: Negotiator, Diplomat, Super-Secretary and Coach. Each of these roles contributes significantly to deciding what to build. The negotiator is the lead role, responsible for working with a large group of end-users and other stakeholders to create a single voice describing what to build for the development team. The Diplomats are the end-users and other stakeholders that are around that negotiating table. They provide their experiences and perceptions of what is needed and work with the Negotiator and other Diplomats to create a single voice. The Super-Secretary supports the negotiator by providing administrative support and filling in for them with the programmers when the Negotiator and Diplomats are unavailable. These roles ensure a coordinated and robust focus on understanding and communicating what to build, which Beck initially hoped to achieve with the onsite-customer practice (Beck, 2000). This research used the analogy from DeMarco (DeMacro, 1979), where he likened an analyst's role to Kissinger negotiating for peace in the Middle East to help form the emerging roles that allow Beck's initial vision to be fulfilled.

The current research is finding that a team of people implements onsite customer practice is helpful. However, we wanted to know if this finding had any bearing on the passion and overwork issues in an earlier chapter. Figure 2 depicts the interpretation of the relationship. The three corners of the figure show the roles and the interpretation of their impact on both passion and overwork depicted at the centre. Therefore, the chapter concludes that the team roles help increase the passion and decrease the customers' overwork.

The collaboration guides further enhanced the sense of team, which so many customers were passionate about retaining, and had enjoyed experiencing to a much greater degree on an XP project. The Skill Specialists tend to increase the customer's certainty (or abilities) concerning a task such as writing a story, or testing the software, improving their perception and passion for the task at hand. Establishing roles help provide a clear focus on the customer's core function and deciding what to build.

IMPLICATIONS OF THE STUDY AND FUTURE RESEARCH

The descriptions of this chapter have important implications for practitioners and academics alike. From a practical perspective, this research elucidates how various factors facilitate or impede the acceptance of XP principles. The study of two contrasting projects of similar team compositions within the same organization suggests that some characteristics may be conducive to the use of XP, while others may inhibit their acceptance. Our findings resonate with the general observation that agile methods are suitable for new projects of little scope. Since many organizations are planning to adopt agile development, quite possibly XP, the findings of this study will enable them to prepare better for the initiation, adoption, and adaptation of XP.

At the individual level, constant reinforcement of XP practices is required to ensure that developers understand the importance and value of the core principles. Suitable reward structures must be established to encourage them to follow these principles. At the team level, greater adherence to XP practices may be achieved by ensuring that team members have autonomy in choosing tasks and empowering them to make local decisions related to scope and estimates of duration. Team members should be provided incentives to choose tasks that are not in their area of expertise. As Ambler (2004) points out, team members should evolve into 'generalizing specialists.' The involvement of customers or their proxies and extensive communication among developers, customers/proxies, and testers are essential for successful acceptance. XP may be more challenging to use in some projects than in others.

When project teams are new to XP practices, the availability of appropriate tools and technologies will significantly facilitate the acceptance of XP. This study reinforces Boehm & Turner's (2004) observation that application type and size, among other things, are essential considerations in the choice of a methodology. New and small applications are more conducive to using XP than large applications that involve maintenance and code evolution. The problem is further exacerbated when integration with a large legacy codebase is required. Strict budgetary and time constraints can be barriers to the sustained use of XP. For example, pair-programming promises a better quality of code but requires additional person-hours to be expended. This can make adherence to XP practices problematic in situations involving tighter budgetary constraints. For the research community, this research adopts and extends the innovation acceptance framework proposed by Kwon & Zmud (1987) in the context of agile software development. To this end, this study offers a set of factors that may influence the acceptance of XP in an organization.

While Conboy et al. (2007) studied the assimilation of agile practices in teams across multiple organizations, this research focuses on the variations in acceptance of XP practices across teams within the same organization. Thus, the two studies complement each other and provide valuable insights into this phenomenon. More empirical research is required to understand the issues in the acceptance of agile practices. Further, there is an urgent need to evolve theoretically grounded models that can be empirically validated.

CONCLUSION

The effective management of projects in software development has attracting attention in recent decades. Software project management consists of many activities, but some essential activities are planning, monitoring and control. Projects to make software are worthwhile only if they satisfy actual needs, and so the project management team will examine how they can identify the stakeholders in a project and its characteristics. Finding those characteristics and cross-checking that they are satisfied is the means of a successful software development project. However, this cannot be accomplished unless there is accurate information and how this need to be gathered are discussed briefly in this chapter, in the context of *Agile software development.*

A software project is often connected not only with the actual writing of software. Where a software application is bought in "*off-the-shelf*", there might be no software design and writing the program as such. However, this is still a software project because so many of the other associated activities (e.g., requirement analysis, feasibility study, planning, and project execution) with this type of procurement are present.

XP software project management methods are ideal for projects that exhibit high variability in tasks, people's skills, and the technology being used. Business software systems should, therefore, carefully assess their readiness before treading the path of XP-based agility. The challenge in managing XP methodology-based software projects is to find the balance between upfront project scheduling and learning. Scheduling enacts step-by-step management practice and a finite set of activities and contingencies, which can be programmed, monitored, and executed. Learning helps adapting to unforeseen or chaotic events. The two require different management practices and project resources. Software projects with low uncertainty and complexity require much more rigorous scheduling, whereas projects with high uncertainty and complexity require a greater emphasis on learning. Openness to learning is new to many software developments projects. However, it is evident from the many spectacular project failures that the time has come to rethink some of the traditions in software project management.

The use of XP methodology has grown across software design and development practices. The current research considers the onsite practice of XP (a standard methodology in agile software development). It regards the most critical challenges in additional research, including characteristics, roles and responsibilities of the right customer, onsite customer problems, customer location, and communication with the customer.

The review process of existing XP based software development helped simplify customer roles with the project management team. The role emerged as follows: (i) collaboration guidance, (ii) skill specialists, and (iii) direction setting. Within these roles, individual customers are identified; they can be negotiators, coaches, diplomates, super secretaries, geek interpreters, political advisors, technical liaisons, acceptance testers, user interface designers, and technical writers.

REFERENCES

Abrahamsson, P., & Koskela, J. (2004). Extreme programming: A survey of empirical data from a controlled case study. *Proceedings of the Third ACM-IEEE International Symposium on Empirical Software Engineering (ISESE 2004)*, 73-82. 10.1109/ISESE.2004.1334895

Abrahamsson, P., Salo, O., Ronkainen, J., & Warsta, J. (2002). *Agile software development methods: Review and analysis*. VTT Publications.

Barlow, J. B. (2011). Overview and Guidance on Agile Development in Large Organizations. Comm. of the Ass. for Inform. *Systems*, *29*(1), 25–44.

Baskervill, R. L., & Stage, J. (1996). Controlling Prototype Development Through Risk Analysis. *Management Information Systems Quarterly*, *20*(4), 481–502. doi:10.2307/249565

Beck, K. (1999). Embracing change with extreme programming. *Computer, 32*(10), 70-77.

Beck, K. (2000). eXtreme Programming Explained: Embrace Change. Addison-Wesley.

Beck, K. (2003). *Test-Driven Development: By Example*. Pearson Education.

Beck, K. (2004). eXtreme Programming Explained: Embrace change (2nd ed.). Addison-Wesley.

Beck, K., Cockburn, A., Jeffries, R., & Highsmith, J. (2001). *Agile manifesto*. http://www.agilemanifesto.org

Beck, K., & Fowler, M. (2001). *Planning Extreme Programming*. Addison-Wesley.

Binder, R. V. (2000). *Testing Object-Oriented Systems: Models, Patterns, and Tolls*. Addison-Wesley.

Boehm, B. (2002). Get Ready for Agile Methods, with Care. *IEEE Computer*, *35*(1), 64–69. doi:10.1109/2.976920

Boehm, B., & Papaccio, P. (1988). Understanding and controlling software costs. *IEEE Transactions on Software Engineering*, *14*(10), 1462–1477. doi:10.1109/32.6191

Bostrom, R. P., & Thomas, B. D. (1983). *Achieving Excellence in Communications: A Key to Developing Complete, Accurate and Shared Information Requirements*. In Twentieth Annual Computer Personnel on Research Conference.

Chin, G. (2006). *Agile Project Management*. AEW Services.

Cockburn, A. (2000). *Writing Effective Use Cases*. Addison-Wesley.

Cockburn, A. (2006). *Agile Software Development: The Cooperative Game*. Addison-Wesley.

Cockburn, A. & Williams, L. (2003). Agile software development: it's about feedback and change *IEEE Computer, 36*(6), 39–43.

Cohn, T., & Paul, R. (2001). A Comparison of Requirements Engineering in Extreme Programming (XP) and Conventional Software Development Methodologies. *Seventh Americas Conference on Information Systems*.

Coram, M., & Bohner, S. (2005). The Impact of Agile Methods on Software Project Management. *Proceedings of the 12th IEEE International Conference and Workshops on the Engineering of Computer-Based Systems (ECBS'05)*, 363-370. 10.1109/ECBS.2005.68

Cunningham, W. (2001). *Agile Manifesto*. http://www.agilemanifesto.org

DeMarco, T. (1979). *Structured Analysis and System Specification*. Prentice-Hall.

Deursen, D. (2001). Customer Involvement in eXtreme Programming. *The Second Internal Conference on eXtreme Programming and Flexible Processes in Software Engineering.*

Farell, C., Narang, R., Kapitan, S., & Webber, H. (2002). Towards an effective onsite customer practice. *Proceedings of the Third International Conference on Extreme Programming and Agile Processes in Software Engineering*, 52–55.

Finsterwalder, M. (2001). *Does XP need a professional Customer?* XP2001 workshop on customer involvement, Cagliari, Italy. Available online at https://homepages.cwi.nl/~arie/wci2001/finsterwalder.pdf

Fitzgerald, B. (2000). Systems Development Methodologies: The Problem of Tenses. *Information Technology & People*, *13*(3), 174–185. doi:10.1108/09593840010377617

Fowler, M. (2002). *XP Customer Quotes*. WikiWikiWeb. https://martinfowler.com/articles/agileStory.html

Fraser, S., Martin, A., Biddle, R., Hussman, D., Miller, G., Poppendieck, M., Rising, L., & Striebeck, M. (2004a). The Role of the Customer in Software Development: The XP Customer – Fad or Fashion? In *OOPSLA'04* (pp. 148–150). ACM Press. doi:10.1145/1028664.1028723

Fraser, S., Martin, A., Hussman, D., Matts, C., Poppendieck, M., & Rising, L. (2004b). The XP Customer Role. In *Proceedings of Extreme Programming and Agile Processes in Software Engineering* (pp. 342–346). Springer Verlag. doi:10.1007/978-3-540-24853-8_57

Mahanti, A. (2006). Challenges in Enterprise adoption of agile methods – a survey. *Journal of Computing and Information Technology – CIT*, 197-206.

Nicoleta, C. (2005). Agile Software Project Management Methodologies. *Economy Informatics*, 1-4.

Pal, K. (2019). Markov Decision Theory Based Crowdsourcing Software Process Model. In Crowdsourcing and Probabilistic Decision-Making in Software Engineering: Emerging Research and Opportunities. IGI Publication.

Pal, K. (2020). Framework for Reusable Test Case Generation in Software Systems Testing. In Software Engineering for Agile Application Development. IGI Global Publication.

Pal, K., & Karakostas, B. (2021). Software Testing Under Agile, Scrum, and DevOps. In Agile Scrum Implementation and its Long-Term Impact on Organization. IGI Global Publication.

Pressman, R. S. (2005). Software Engineering: A Practitioner's Approach. McGraw-Hill.

Roebuck, K. (2012). *System Development Life Cycle (SDLC): High-impact Strategies – What You Need to Know: Definition, Adoption, Impact, Benefits, Maturity, Vendors.* Emereo Publishing.

Royce, W. W. (1970). Managing the Development of Large Software Systems. *Proceedings of IEEE WESCON*, *26*(August), 1–9.

Sommerville, I. (2019). *Software Engineering*. Addison Wesley.

VersionOne. (2011). *State of Agile Survey 2011 - The State of Agile Development*. Author.

Xiao-Li, L., Wei, G., Xin-Li, C., & Ke-Gang, H. (2006). Designing a test case library system of supporting sharing and reusing. *Journal of Computational Science*, *33*, 290–291.

Farell, C., Narang, R., Kapitan, S., & Webber, H. (2002). Towards an Effective Onsite Customer Practice. *The Third International Conference on eXtreme Programming and Agile Process in Software Engineering*.

Gilb, T. (1988). *Principle of Software Engineering Management*. Addison-Wesley.

Gittins, R., Hope, S., & Williams, L. (2002). Qualitative Studies of XP in a medium-sized Business. In *Extreme Programming Perspectives*. Addison-Wesley.

Grisham, P. S., & Perry, D. E. (2005). Customer relationships and Extreme Programming. In *Proceedings of the 2005 Workshop on Human and Social Factors of Software Engineering (HSSE '05)*. ACM Press.

Hanssen, G. K., & Fægri, T. E. (2006). Agile Customer Engagement: A Longitudinal Qualitative Case Study. In *ISESE'06* (pp. 164–173). ACM Press. doi:10.1145/1159733.1159759

Hansson, C., Dittrich, Y., & Randall, D. (2004). Agile processes enhancing user participation for small providers of off-the-shelf software. In *Proceedings of Extreme Programming and Agile Processes in Software Engineering* (pp. 175–183). Springer Verlag. doi:10.1007/978-3-540-24853-8_20

Highsmith, J. (2001). The Great Methodologies Debate, Part I: Opening Statement. *Cutter IT Journal*, *14*, 2–4.

Highsmith, J. (2002). *Agile Software Development Ecosystems*. Addison-Wesley.

Koskela, J., & Abrahamsson, P. (2004). Onsite Customer in an XP Project: Empirical Results from a Case Study. EuroSPI 2004, Trondheim, Norway.

Kujala, S. (2007). Effective user involvement in product development by improving the analysis of user needs. *Behaviour & Information Technology, Taylor & Francis*, *2007*, 1–16.

Marchesi, M., Succi, G., Wells, D., & Williams, L. (2002). XR: Extreme Reality - Real-life Experiences. In *Extreme Programming Practices*. Addison-Wesley.

Martin, A. (2002). *A Case Study: Exploring the Role of Customers on Extreme Programming Projects*. School of Computing and Mathematical Sciences, Victoria University of Wellington.

Martin, A., Biddle, R., & Noble, J. (2004). The XP customer role in practice: Three studies. *Proceedings of the Second Agile Development Conference (ADC 2004)*, 42-54. 10.1109/ADEVC.2004.23

Martin, A., Biddle, R., & Noble, J. (2004). The XP Customer Role in Practice: Three Case Studies. In T. Little, S. Alpert, & A. Pols (Eds.), *Agile Development Conference*. IEEE Computer Society. doi:10.1109/ADEVC.2004.23

Martin, A., Biddle, R., & Noble, J. (2004). When XP Met Outsourcing. In *Fifth International Conference of Extreme Programming and Agile Processes in Software Engineering*. Springer-Verlag. 10.1007/978-3-540-24853-8_6

Martin, A., Noble, J., & Biddle, R. (2003). Being Jane Malkovich: A Look into the world of an XP Customer. In *XP 2003*. Springer. doi:10.1007/3-540-44870-5_29

Martin, A., Noble, J., & Biddle, R. (2003). Being Jane Malkovich: A Look into the World of an XP Customer. In *Fourth International Conference on eXtreme Programming and Agile Processes in Software Engineering*. Springer-Verlag. 10.1007/3-540-44870-5_29

Myers, M., & Young, L. (1997). Hidden Agendas, Power and Managerial Assumptions in Information Systems Development: An Ethnographic Case Study. *Information Technology & People*, *10*(3), 176–191. doi:10.1108/09593849710178225

Nandhakumar, J., & Avison, D. E. (1999). The Fiction of Methodological Development: A Field Study of Information Systems Development. *Information Technology & People*, *12*(2), 1–28. doi:10.1108/09593849910267224

Orlikowski, W., & Gash, D. (1994). Technological Frames: Making Sense of Information Technology in Organisations. *ACM Transactions on Information Systems*, *12*(2), 174–207. doi:10.1145/196734.196745

Rico, D. F. (2006). *Running head: Agile Methods and the Links to Customer Satisfaction and Firm Performance.* Available online at http://davidfrico.com/rico06a.pdf

Russo, N. L., & Stolterman, E. (2000). Exploring the Assumptions Underlying Information Systems Methodologies: Their Impact on Past, Present and Future ISM Research. *Information Technology & People*, *13*(4), 313–327. doi:10.1108/09593840010359509

Salihoğlu, Y. (2001). *User Involvement in Software Project Development: A Review of Models.* Software Project Management Research Paper.

Schalliol, G. (2002). Challenges for Analysts on a Large XP Project. In *Extreme Programming Perspectives*. Addison-Wesley.

Schwaber, K., & Beedle, M. (2001). *Agile Software Development with Scrum*. Prentice-Hall.

Urquhart, C. (1998). *Analysts and Clients in Conversation: Cases in Early Requirements Gathering*. In *International Conference on Information Systems*, Helsinki, Finland.

Van Deursen, A. (2001a). Customer Involvement Experiences in a Software Product Line" *XP2001 workshop on customer involvement*. Available online at https://homepages.cwi.nl/~arie/wci2001/vandeursen.pdf

Van Deursen, A. (2001b). Customer Involvement in Extreme Programming, XP2001 Workshop Report. *XP2001 Workshop on customer involvement, ACM Software Eng*, 70-73.

Wastell, D. (1999). Learning Dysfunctions in Information Systems Development: Overcoming the Social Defences with Transitional Objects. *Management Information Systems Quarterly*, *23*(4), 581–600. doi:10.2307/249490

Williams, M., Packlick, J., Bellubbi, A., & Coburn, S. (2007). *How We Made Onsite Customer Work - An Extreme Success story. In Agile 2007.* IEEE Computer Society.

KEY TERMS AND DEFINITIONS

Agile Software Methodology: Agile software development represents a new type of approach for planning and managing software projects. It put less importance on up-front plans and strict control and relies more on information collaboration, coordination, and learning. In other words, it is an evolutionary and iterative approach to software development with focuses on adaption to changes.

Critical Software Systems: Software whose failure would impact safety or cause large financial or social losses.

Customer: The person, or persons, who pay for the software product and other services (e.g., installation, amendments, user training).

Extreme Programming: A (software development) process describes who is doing what, how, and when. It outlines practices, principles, methods for efficient production of required software development. Hence, the process serves as a template for creating projects. This way, XP is a software development methodology (or framework) try to enhance software responsiveness and quality to altering client needs. Also, it encourages frequent "releases" in short development cycles, aimed to enhance productivity and provide checkpoints at which new customer needs can be adopted.

Inputs: Identifies and describes all data needed for the appropriate processing of the function of a software system.

Outputs: Describes the results of executing the function (e.g., effect on stored data, completion status values or output parameters, screen display, or outputs that trigger other actions – such as mechanical, electrical, or other activities in process control software applications).

Scrum: An agile process framework for managing knowledge work, with an emphasis on software development.

Software Engineering: Development of software based on theoretical foundations and practical disciplines traditional to engineering.

Software Project Management: A software project can be seen as a collection of activities that create an identifiable value outcome. In its simplest form, project management consists of planning, execution, and monitoring these activities. Description of the work (tasks) and the resources (e.g., time, people, materials) needed to accomplish goals and objectives. The plan's task corresponds to the selected process model.

Software Testing: Examining a software artefact to detect differences between existing and required conditions.

Test Case Specification: A document specifying inputs, predicted outputs, and a set of execution conditions for a test item.

Test Design Specification: A document describing the specifications of the test plan for a software characteristic or combination of software characteristics and finding the related tests.

Test Plan: A document describing the objective, method, resources required, and plan of intended testing events. It finds test items, the features to be tested, the testing tasks, who do each task, and any risks requiring contingency planning.

User: The person, or persons, who uses (or operates, interacts) directly with the software product. The user(s) and the customer(s) are often not the same person(s).

Waterfall Model: A sequential design used in software development processes that progress steadily towards the end (like waterfall flows top to down) through the phases of Requirements, Specifications, Coding, Testing, and Release.

Chapter 10
Implication of Budgeting on Contemporary Project Management

Poonam Rani
J B Knowledge Park, India

Sangeeta Dharyan
K. L. Mehta Dayanand College for Women, India

ABSTRACT

It is the total sum of money allocated for the specific project for a specific period of time. The goal of the project budget is to cost control. The objective of this chapter is to give the implication of budgeting on contemporary project management. The main focus of this chapter is to discuss the introduction, history, agile approach, etc. It has a direct impact on the company's financial feasibility. The research would discuss the approaches for the projects budget estimation and various steps for cost control. There are two types of reserves against risks: one is the contingency reserve for identified risk, and the other is the management reserve for unidentified risks. The project manager needs to be aware of existing resources acquisition policies, guidelines, and procedures. The author discusses the procedures for project budgeting and methods for evaluation of project budgeting.

INTRODUCTION

A project is derived from Latin word "Pro" means Forward and "Jacerc" means throw (Project Management Institute, 2013). According to the PMBOK Guide, project management consists of five process groups; Initiation, Planning, Executing, Monitoring & Controlling and Closing (Project Management Institute, 2013). In Traditional Project Management (TPM) these are done in a linear and incremental fashion. In Agile Project Management (APM) these are done in a more iterative and adaptive way (Wysocki, 2014).

DOI: 10.4018/978-1-7998-7872-8.ch010

Project Management Institute (2013) confirmed that Project management is described as the processes where project objectives and achievement has been controlled and associated with the final result. Project management involves strategic planning and controlling of the project and the purpose of project management is:

- To prepare framework of the requirement and of the work,
- To decide the level of work,
- To allocate the required resources, and
- To plan the implementation of the work.

These people were serving their major roles of as project managers. They had to carefully think about all the processes of the project starting with planning phase to execution and monitoring phase all the way to closing of the project.

During the 1950s, Navy engaged modern project management policies in their Polaris project. During the 1960s and 1970s, Department of Defence, NASA, and biggest engineering and construction companies employed project management principles and tools to accomplish large budget, schedule - driven projects. In the 1980s, manufacturing and software development sectors started to implement and grape sophisticated project management practices / methods. By the 1990s, the project management theories, tools, and techniques were widely used by different industries and organizations.

Contemporary project management shows the tried - and - true project management techniques along with modern developments such as the most current versions of Microsoft Project Professional 2016, the Guide to the Project Management Body of Knowledge (PMBOK Guide), and many other approaches developed from adaptive (Agile) project management like Scrum, Kanban, Hybrid, and XP etc. Contemporary project management also uses many tools and techniques and considerations that come from modern approaches to quality and communications, role define, leadership principles, human strengths, and many other sources.

Budget

Budgeting is the process of preparing budgets. It is essentially a managerial process concerned with planning, co - ordination and control. It is a plan which included all the phases of operation of a business for a definite period of time. It is prepared for a future period and it expresses everything in numerical terms.

According to Koontz & O'Donnell define, Budgets are statements of anticipated results, in financial terms as in revenue and expense and capital budgets or in non - financial terms as in budgets of direct labour - hours, physical sales volume, materials, on units of production. The analysis shows that budget is:

- A statement of estimated or expected results,
- Stated in quantitative terms,
- Always for a specific future period of time, and
- Prepared to achieve specific objectives.

Project Budget

A Project Budget is the total sum of money allocated for the specific purpose of the project for a specific period of time. The main purpose of the project budget is to control project cost within the approved budget and deliver the expected project goals. A successful project is one that meets four success criteria that the project scope is delivered on schedule, it is delivered within budget and once delivered, and it meets the quality expectations of the investor and beneficiaries.

A project budget is part of a financial process that can be divided into 3 phases:

- **Cost Estimation:** established by mentioning to actual costs of similar projects if possible, it is linked to the estimated timeframe.
- **Project Budgeting:** In this phase, budget is allocated according to the breakdown of the project.
- **Cost Control**.

It is determining the total amount of money that is assigned for the use of project. It has been forecasted by the project manager or the project management team. The budget is an estimate of all type of costs that should be necessary to complete the project. They use the words "should be" because if a project is poorly estimated then the project will need more costs.

A number of constraints like political, financial, environmental and organizational, Priority / resources, Requirements, Competition, Culture, Currency, Economic climate, Customer, Inflation, Interfaces, Strike, Motivation, Ambition level may dictate the methods by which resources such as materials, services, equipment, and personnel are acquired. There are some positive and negative affect like. There are some features of project budgeting like

- Resource Requirements,
- Human or labour resources,
- Equipment and material resources,
- Budget estimate,
- Work breakdown structure,
- Standardized parameters, and
- Chart of accounts.

The Evolution of Modern Project Management Theory

The Protestants and later the Puritans introduced a number of ideas including reductionism, individualism and protestant work ethic that resonate strongly in the spirit of modern project management. In the context of modern project management these ideas were introduced into two key philosophies, liberalism and Newtonianism.

- **Liberalism:** It involved the division of labour, the ideas of capitalism that an industrious lifestyle would lead to wealthy societies.
- **Newtonianism:** It means applying scientific observations to developing the "classical school" of scientific management.

Both of these philosophies influence the scientific management theories of Taylor who published "The Principles of Scientific Management" in 1909. In this book, he advised that productivity would increase if jobs / task were optimized and simplified. Further, proposed that according to employee's skill level work should be given to employee and then give him training for a job in a specific way. They include the following:

- Hire the right person for each task, and train them to work at maximum efficacy;
- After that monitor worker performance, and provide instruction and training when it is required; and
- Distribute the work between management and worker so that management can plan and train and workers can execute the task / job efficiently.

BACKGROUND

History of the Project Management

Chiu (2010) described that both Henri Foyal and Henry Gantt are the forefathers of Project Management. While some may disagree with this statement, many will agree that both Fayol and Gantt have given significant contributions to the management field. Henri Fayol (1841 - 1925) was a French engineer in an iron and steel company (Witzel, 2003). Through observation, he classified five function of management their application to contemporary management practice. These functions are: (1) to plan, (2) to organize, (3) to command, (4) to coordinate, and (5) to control (Pugh & Hickson, 2007; Rausch, 2005; McLean, 2005). Fayol also gave 14 principles which give direction to the managers on how to execute those five managerial functions effectively. Fayol's work was criticized by many other authors because theory does not convey the true managerial complexities faced by managers in their daily routine work. In the paper Fayol stands the test of time, "says that Fayol's fundamentals principles of management are not refuted but are rather reinforced by more recent findings. Fayol has left an indelible mark on management history (Fells, 2000)".

According to Chiu (2010), the 2nd forefather of modern project management is Henry Gantt (1861 - 1919). Henry Gantt was an American engineer and a management consultant. He had best knowledge of Gantt chart. Gantt chart is used for the benefits of breaking large projects into smaller project / tasks. Gantt charts are still in use today. In 1986 Karol Adamieckic invented a novel method to visualize interdependent processes. He called it the Harmonogram. Unluckily, he only published his articles in Polish and Russian and then his invention was not widely recognized in the west (Marsh, 1975). After that, Henry Gantt designed his charts around 1910 - 1915, and the charts were later used in large projects in World War I and the construction of Hoover Dam. Therefore, the charts became associated with his name. Together with the CPM approach, this was mainly used for construction, space and aeronautics industries (Snyder & Kline, 1987).

The Four Periods of Modern Project Management

From time to time, the perception of project management kept changing. The next four decades can be seen as representing four generations in the history of modern project management: prior to 1958, 1958 - 1979, 1980 - 1994, and 1995 to present (Kwak, 2003).

Table 1. A brief History of project management

Four period	Major Project	Project Management	Technology adopted
Prior to 1958	Inter - Continental railroads, Hoover Dam, Polaris, Manhattan project	PERT / CPM (Frederick W Taylor), Gantt Chart (Henry Gantt), Monte Carlo Simulation and others	Telegraph, Telephone, First computer, Automobile, Airplane - - - First database
1958 - - 1979	Apollo 11, - ARPANET	PMI, - Inventory Control, - Material requirement planning	Xerox copier, UNIX, - Microsoft Originated
1980 - 1994	Space Shuttle Challenger, The English France Channel project, The XV Calgary Olympic Winter Games	Matrix organization, project Management software	Personal Computer, - Wireless network, First Internet browser
1995 - Present	Iridium project, - Y2K project	PMBOK (PMI)	Internet Fast Service

Source: Own

- **First Period (Prior To 1958):** During this period, project management transformed from a craft system to Human relations administration, transportation, technology advancement shortened the project schedule. Automobiles allowed for effective resource allocation and flexibility. Telecommunication system, job specification became the basis of introducing the Work Breakdown Structure (WBS) and Henry Gantt invented Gantt chart.

That time the important projects are Practical Plan for Building the Pacific Railroad, Hoover Dam, Interstate Highway and Manhattan project. After the data collection, it has been updated and analysed and then send to resident engineers, and field managers initiated the project. Project office simply functioned as an administrative office (Judah, 1857).

Gantt Charts was first used in Hoover Dam (1931 - 1936). The project hired approximately 5,200 workers, and large amount of construction resources including concrete, structural steel components, steel pipe, and so on were required (Bureau of Reclamation 1985).

The Manhattan project (1942 - 1945) on the other hand, was particularly important because many still consider it the beginning of modern project management. The Office of Scientific Research and Development (ORSD) coordinated universities and resources for the research and development of the atomic bomb. The project involved 125,000 labours, and cost nearly $2 billion. The Manhattan Project "presented the principles of organization, planning, and direction that affected the progress of standard practices for projects." (Shenhar, 2007).

- **Second Period (1958 - 1979):** During the second period, there was significant technology advancement. During that period PERT and CPM introduced as a project management tool. Simultaneously Work Breakdown Structure (WBS) approach for any projects bearing the size and scope of Polaris project (1956 - 1961).

On the other side, the world's first project management association began in 1965, now known as the International Project Management Association (IPMA). PMI is widely known as the publisher of The Project Management Body of Knowledge (PMBOK) (ITRM Guideline CPM 110 - 01, 2006).

In between 1969 to 1972, NASA successfully led six missions to explore the moon. In 1960, NASA set up the Apollo program office to provide following functions: (1) Maintain and schedule Apollo missions using PERT, (2) Procurement and contracting with suppliers such as GE, (3) Develop management system to measure the performance, (4) Set up a focal point of the Apollo program (Wolfe, 1968).

- **Third Period (1980 - 1994):** In the third era, the revolution of IT sector shifted people from using mainframe computer to multitasking personal computer that had high efficiency in managing and controlling complex project schedules (Leiner, 2000).

There were three major projects selected during the 1980s and early 1990s. These project were used the application of high technology and project management tools and practices of that time (Kwak, 2003).

- **Fourth Period (1995 - Present):** The fourth era shows is 1995 to present (in this instance the present refers to 2003). During this era internet provided fast, interactive and adapted new medium that persons to allow for purchase, sale, browse and track product and services online rapidly. This is a method of planning and managing projects developed by Eliyahu M. Goldratt. It is derived from TOC and unlike CPM and PERT the method mainly highlighted resources required to complete the project rather than the specific tasks (Goldratt, 1997). The American National Standards Institute (ANSI) and Institute of Electrical and Electronics Engineers (IEEE) recognized PMBOK as a standard in 1998.

Agile Approach

Even though, incremental software development methods go as far back as 1957, agile was first deliberated in depth in the 1970s by William Royce who published a paper on the development of large software systems. In 1957, at that time Bernie Dimsdale, John von Neumann, Herb Jacobs, and Gerald Weinberg were using incremental development, building software for IBM and Motorola. However, in the recent - days agile approach was announced in 2001, when a group of 17 software development professionals met to discuss alternative project management methodologies. These professionals gathered together to discuss flexible, lightweight and team - oriented software development approach based on their combined experience.

Some other author said that APM is based on a 1986 document published for the Harvard Business Review by Hirotaka Takeuchi and Ikujiro Nonaka entitled "The New Product Development Game." In this article, authors used rugby sport as a symbol to describe the advantages of self - organizing teams in innovative product development and distribution (Sliger, 2011).

Hastie (2004) depicted that Agile differs from traditional techniques by focusing much more on self - organization, collaboration, and team work. During the agile's achievement, believe, confidence, assurance must be present among the leader and the team members themselves.

In the English Oxford dictionary "Agility" means "moving quickly and easily". Applying this same meaning to project management, represents the sharp move away from the traditional project management methodology like the waterfall, where n number of processes to go through the last steps is finished before the project ends. Because of this mostly project delay and also impedes the easy flow of the project.

Agile Project Management (APM)

According to Vikash et al. (2012) showed that agile project management is a theoretical software framework in which software is developed. It shows comparatively less time and has various iterative and adaptive ways that result in stable software release.

According to Bustamante & Sawhney (2011) describe that agile project focusing on client value, iterative and incremental implementation, strong cooperation, tiny integrated teams, self - organization, and tiny and constant improvements. It is said to work best with tiny teams. The perfect agile project team is tiny, collocated, connect face - to - face on a daily basis and has an optimal team size that does not exceed nine individuals.

More and more companies are using agile to deliver software faster and in a smarter way (Version One, 2015; Serrador & Pinto, 2015). It found that although a lot of research has been done on agile software development and several benefits and limitations have been identified, the strength of this evidence is very low (Dyba & Dingsoyr, 2008).

In 2001, a group of 17 software development representatives from several of the most important vision of the flexible, team oriented, lightweight project management methodologies met to discuss and find common ground. They formed the Agile Alliance, and officially agile approach announced in 2001 (Agile Alliance, 2015). After the introduced agile approach, the Agile Manifesto for Agile Software Development was created (Agile Manifesto, 2019). It defined four agile values and twelve principles which all agile methodologies must conform to. The four core values given below are completely consistent with the approach to contemporary project management:

- Individuals and interactions over processes and tools,
- Working software over comprehensive documentation,
- Customer collaboration over contract negotiation, and
- Responding to change over following a plan

Agile Project Success Rate

Serrador & Pinto (2015) conducted a large - scale quantitative study to test if using agile methods has an effect on project success. It found that the use of agile methods correlated to a higher reported success rate. This was shown for 3 categories of success; overall project success, efficiency and stakeholder success (Serrador & Pinto, 2015). The most recent Standish group chaos study in 2019 showed that agile projects success rate are 2X (i.e., 42%) as compare to waterfall project and 1/3 less likely to fail than waterfall project. A failure rate of agile project is just.

With 71% of companies are using agile in 2020, it has become a standard of project management. - Agile management has helped 98% of companies. There are some specific reasons to adopted agile methodology and techniques. It showing 71% speed up software delivered, increased 51% productivity, enhance the ability to manage changing priorities, improve 42% software quality.

Agile Framework Methodology

Agile approach has been variously called iterative, incremental, adaptive, or change driven. While Agile is the umbrella name, some of the specific approaches are called SCRUM, XP, KANBAN, etc. It helped in the planning and delivery of benefits in multiple increments during project execution.

- **Scrum:** The Scrum framework is describes around a set or roles, events, and artefacts (Griffiths, 2012). It defines only three roles: Product Owner, Scrum Master, and Team Member. The Scrum Master makes sure that the Scrum process is followed and resolves obstacles. Team members are developers, testers, designers, etc. Scrum has four events: Sprint planning, daily stand - up, sprint review, and sprint retrospective. The entire work is broken down into short growth cycles i.e., Sprints. The Sprint's length is from one to four weeks. The team should strictly follow a work plan for each Sprint and constant basis follow up is required. The team involved in a project have predefined roles.
- **Kanban:** Kanban is simple, powerful approach to developing software products.
- **Hybrid:** Agile and Waterfall are two different approaches of software development management. According to the project management institute in 2019, more than 60% businesses are using hybrid project management approach like manufacturer, marketing agencies and small business and many other companies. It is the combination of the traditional Waterfall project management approach and Agile is called Hybrid.
- **Bimodal:** The term "Bimodal IT" was introduced by "Gartner" in 2014.
- **Lean:** The Lean framework promotes fast software development with less effort, time, and cost. The development cycle is as short as possible. The product delivered early is being continuously improved. Developers can also formulate the product's concept.
- **eXtreme Programming (XP):** Its focus on technical aspects of software development. **eX**treme Programming (XP) introduces engineering practices aimed at helping developers write a clear code. **eX**treme Programming (XP) is used by 9% of companies only. Extreme Programming is a set of certain practices, applied to software engineering in order to improve their quality and ability to adapt to the changing requirements. Face - to - face communications within the team and customer involvement in development are crucial.

MAIN FOCUS OF THE CHAPTER

Review of the study showed that a problem of project delays or failure in the infrastructure project is a worldwide phenomenon, project failure or delay is unacceptable for any organisation. This is due to unavoidable circumstance in the organisation and economy. Contemporary project management shows the tried - and - true project management techniques along with modern developments and many agile approaches developed from adaptive (Agile) project management like Scrum, Kanban, Hybrid, XP, etc.

Contemporary project management also uses many tools and techniques and considerations that come from modern approaches to quality and communications, leadership principles, human strengths, and many other sources. Contemporary project management is scalable, using simple versions of important techniques on projects and more involved versions on more complex projects.

"Agility" means "moving quickly and easily". Applying this same meaning to project management, represents the sharp move away from the traditional project management methodology like the waterfall, where n number of processes to go through the last steps is finished before the project ends. Because of this mostly project delay and also impedes the easy flow of the project. Agile project management is a theoretical software framework in which software is developed. It shows comparatively less time and has various iterative and adaptive ways that result in stable software release.

These days, most of the organization have adopted project budgeting as their daily work vehicle in order to accomplish their objectives, goals and strategies. Project budgeting demand and need is growing in business world. A Project Budget is the total sum of money allocated for the specific purpose of the project for a specific period of time. The main purpose of the project budget is to control project cost within the approved budget and deliver the expected project goals. On the basis of the study showed that there is very less knowledge about project budgeting.

To show the conceptual framework of the project budgeting, Author will discuss (i) Introduction (ii) History of the project management (iii) Agile approach (iv) Approaches for the project budget estimation (iv) Source of the information (v) Steps of the project budgeting (vi) Risk factors in project budgeting (vii) Methods / technologies for evaluation of project budgeting (viii) Procedures for project budgeting (ix) Conclusion.

Approaches for the Project Budget Estimation

The study has depicted that different types of projects want different approaches and competencies for their management. Large and intricate and high - risk projects require a different approach compared to smaller, simpler, low - risk projects. The main objective of a project categorization system is to support in determining the approach used for managing the project. The basic premise of a project categorization system is to provide comparability between projects (Crawford et al., 2005).

Table 2. Different types of project cost

Project cost types	Example
Material resources	Every type of items which is require for perform the work. It includes equipment, raw materials, software, and other unique materials.
Human resources	Salary, perks of full time and part time employees
Travelling Expenses	For project work, anyone who travels from one place to another place.
Training fees	Conferences, workshops, training batches, and outside contractors
Professional Services	Legal advice, consultant, market research firms, etc.
Research Expenses	Studies or data collection and analysis to support your project and deliver the best performance of the project.
Capital Expenditure	Equipment or technical upgrades, purchase of any assets to complete the project
Contingency Reserves	Contingency funds to allow for flexibility and minimize risks to budget overrun.

Source: Own

A Project Budget is the total sum of money allocated for the specific purpose of the project for a specific period of time. The main purpose of the project budget is to control project cost within the approved budget and deliver the expected project goals. There are various types of project cost.

This table with common project cost categories to help you gets started. Cost can be classified into:

- **Direct Costs** are those that you can assign directly to the core business activity, such as administrative salaries, materials, supplies, equipment, travel costs, etc.
- **Indirect Costs** are those which are supportive and allied, such can include general and administrative costs, or office space rent.

To achieve this, projects need to be classified hierarchically for the purpose of determining which project management practices are best suited to the different types of projects.

- **Bottom - Up Estimation:** Rate the individual parts of the project plan and top them up. Bottom - up estimation is one of the best way to prepare a project budget. It anticipates forecasting individual parts of the project, such as tasks, milestones, or stages, and totalling them to get project cost.
- **Top - Down Estimation:** Figure out the total and then split it into tasks or milestones. Top - down estimation is just reverse to the bottom - up approach mentioned above and a completely different game. It begins with the project budget total and involves split it into tasks or milestones. The main drawback of this approach is difficult to accurately forecast the budget before you understand the scope of work and have a project plan. This process is very challenging.
- **Analogous Estimation:** Analyse the data in similar projects to decide the cost. If you are the old person in the field of project management then you have easily managed a few projects before knowing anything about the project. You can be prepare an Auto schedule that has an algorithm which learns from past projects and applied to estimate tasks, forecast the delivery date, and determine the project budget. It is better and useful when there is limited information about the project.
- **Parametric Estimation:** Using data and applied them to the current project to advise the total. It takes cost variables or data points from precise parts of specific projects and put on them to the current project, therefore you make more decisions based on data. The advantage of this process is that it's more accurate because it employs more than one data set and uses the statistical relationship between past data and variables.
- **Three - Point Estimation:** It inspires you to think from multiple perspectives. The advantage of this approach is that you can reduce the risk but sometimes it takes longer to create budget using this approach.

Source of the Information

It can be collect from the various sources for forecasting the cost like work breakdown structure, project contract, resource cost estimate, activity duration estimates, Historical information, market conditions, investor and organization policies, chart of accounts structure. Budgeting serves as a control mechanism where actual costs can be compared with the estimated against the budget.

The project manager must also include in the budget the cost of human resources and equipment and materials required to perform the work. A number of restrictions, financial, political, and organizational, may dictate the methods by which resources such as personnel, equipment, services and material required.

Some other aspects for collecting information: Budget reports requirements, Budget management plan, Budget approval, Budget baseline, Publish budget, budget execution and budget targets, budget updates, Fundamentals of the project budgeting for development organizations, Project design monitoring and evaluation.

Steps of Project Budgeting

- **Defining the Project Budget (STEP 1):** The first steps of project budgeting is define or estimate the budget required to whole project activities. The project manager should allocate all cost to project activities, and all aspect of the project, including the cost of internal and external human resources, equipment, travel, materials and supplies, should be incorporated. The budget should be more detailed and more accurate than it was on the project proposal. It involves budget estimation, rough estimate, contract estimate, definitive estimate, analogous, top down estimate, bottom up estimate, parametric estimates.

It also includes the construction of a document that defines budget authority and responsibility. It deals chart of accounts, budget report requirements and budget management plan and budget approval.

- **Executing the Project Budget (STEP 2):** After the budget reviewed and approved the project budget to create a project budget baseline. The baseline will be used to compare with the actual cost incurred by the project as it makes progress, like expenses in personnel, purchases of goods and services and other project expenses such as shared costs and benefits. Usually the project is divided the total months / years of the project duration.

Budget implementation is the action of authorizing the expenses approved in the project budget. The project manager take steps to carry the activities that lead to hiring project staff, purchase of equipment, materials and services, all according to a project arrangement plan developed during the resource management process. This step follows after the budget has been approved and the project authorized to start participate according to the project plan.

- **Controlling the Project Budget (STEP 3):** Usually the finance department's responsibility is to record, track and monitor the budget from a cost accounting perspective and generates reports for the organizations management and the investor as part of the compliance necessities such as certifying the correct accounts are properly recorded and used.

Small projects may require only procurement and accounting unit of the organization's main financial function and larger projects may require their own finance function capability. It requires a professional accountant and a team to deal with the volume of work. Many project use the accounting software to manage the project's finances independently of the organization's overall accounting but at the end of the year data would be compile with parent organization's books.

- **Updating the Project Budget (STEP 4):** Update of budget is very important task for the project. For most projects changes to the budget need to be approved by the investor, in some instances the investor can give the project a small percentage that the project can use to cover small budget modifications. In other instances the investor may have strict limitations to allow budge changes.

It's very essential that the project manager understands the investor contract clauses and monitor with special attention the accounts or budget items that have restrictions. If there is any other types of changes come from unavoidable circumstances to the project that may limit the activities. In this situation the project manager may request that the funds originally budgeted to that activity be reallocated to another activity that the project can still work. Any other changes come caused by currency fluctuations that impact the funding available to the project.

Corrective Measures

A number of project may include a predefined limit by which a project may be over or under budget during the project implementation phase, it is usually set as a small percentage of the total, these actions may include trade - offs that will need to be discussed with management and the investor, trade - off include reducing the lowering the quality.

Corrective actions may include the use of different options to produce the similar output using different inputs, the project manager will apply the corrective actions and monitor their performance to see. It also includes consulted with the project team and the staff in charge of the activities so that changes are implemented. If there is any change in the budget need to be communicated and incorporated in the project that track cost performance.

Risk Factors in Project Budgeting

There are two types of reserves against risks: One is the contingency reserve for identified risks as a project, and the other is the management reserve for unidentified risks as changeability. However, earlier studies have depicted various methods for estimating reserves to cover the risk as an event that can only be measure as an expected uncertainty. Hence, the planned response actions could not cover the risk as changeability, which is an unexpected uncertainty that cannot be identified. The management reserve for unidentified risks must be estimated and included in the project budget, even though unidentified risks could not be accomplished by the team.

SOLUTIONS AND RECOMMENDATIONS

Methods / Technologies for Evaluation of Project Budgeting

There are some methods / techniques of the project budgeting for estimating the cost of project. They are considering various factors like risks, uncertainties, environmental changes, etc.

- **Expert Judgment:** To take expert judgment through specialist for cost estimation. When predicting costs by using this technique, you trust on specialist knowledge of the project's content and the business environment. Therefore, you get significant, important and evidence - based relation pattern between relevant cost factors / variables.
- **Delphi Method:** The Delphi method is a forecasting technique which is carried out by a group of experts. During a series of meetings, every individual member of the expert group provides their cost forecasts in the questionnaire format. Therefore, analysed the data and anonymously announced to others by a facilitator. This task is repeated for two or more each time until the ultimate goal of a final cost estimate is attained.
- **Estimation by Analogy:** It is the calculation of a new project's costs by contrasting the knowledge of its contents and features with data obtained when administering a similar project in the past. This methods based on three important key steps:
    - Determine a new project's attributes.
    - Locate any previous project with similar characteristics and retrieve all the information about its costs and financial performance.
    - Develop original cost estimates based on the acquired historical data.
- **Vendor Bid Analysis:** In this method, the services and products essential for project realization are going to be given by vendors, it is possible to calculate the cost of the complete project or its constituents by comparing suppliers' pricing proposals or bids. They can be collected in a structured way by using the request for proposal document outlining project details, including product or service and its quality to be delivered by a vendor.
- **Top - Down Estimation:** In this method, cost estimation starts with the identification of the overall scope of the project and its total cost. Therefore, the general cost is broken down into smaller components, depending on the project's contents and attributes.
- **Bottom - Up Estimation:** This method starts the cost calculation process with the identification and evaluation of separate project components as compare to the top - down estimation. After that, the expenditures for every project task or a series of tasks are then summed up to calculate the total project cost.
- **Parametric Estimation:** In this method, the total project cost is calculated based on the number and price of the project's work units. The estimation process includes just three steps:
    - Identify relevant project units (i.e., lecture hours to be delivered, square feet of pavement to be laid, number of peanut butter jars to be produced, etc.);
    - Estimate the cost of every unit by summing up the price of materials, labour, etc;
    - Calculate project expenses through this equation which is given below: Number of Work Units × Cost of a Single Unit. For define the cost of a single unit, you may refer to past project and examples thereof.
- **Three Point Estimation:** To calculate a probable project cost with the 3 - point estimating technique, the estimation project cost just create three types of estimates:
    - An optimistic estimate (The amount of money your team hopes to spend on project activities),
    - A pessimistic estimate (The project's cost in the worst - case scenario when many things go not as expected),
    - The best - guess estimate (A realistic figure, the amount of money the team will most likely spend on project activities).

- **PERT Formula:** The final project cost value is calculated by using the following equation, also known as the PERT formula, [Optimistic Estimate + Pessimistic Estimate + (4 × Best - guess Estimate)] / 6
- **Reserve Analysis:** It focuses on factors of cost uncertainty and is mainly concerned with avoiding risks that may lead to cost overruns. The purpose of this method is to determine the size of two types of backup sums:
  - Contingency reserve (The amount of money allocated for mitigation of various expected project risks (e.g., technological holdbacks, increased staff turnover, delays in supply, etc.)
  - Management reserve (The amount of money that could be utilized to handle the outcomes of unidentified risks)
- **Cost of Quality Analysis:** The purpose of the cost of quality analysis is to determine how much money is required to meet the pre - set project quality standards. The Cost of quality calculation process covers the following phases:
  - Define project quality requirements and standards;
  - Identify the Cost of Good Quality (CoGQ): cost of activities needed to prevent quality failures + costs of quality appraisal activities;
  - Identify the Cost of Poor Quality (CoPQ): The expenses of the project may incur as a result of internal quality failures (e.g., waste of time and material resources, product re - design, etc.) + expenses the project may incur as a result of external quality failures (e.g., shipping errors and damages, customer complaints, etc.);
  - Calculate the total CoQ with this simple formula: CoGQ + CoPQ.

Procedures for Project Budgeting

- **Identification of Task:** The first step is identifying the tasks and activities for the project. After that, the break - down of the project helps in cost estimation and resource allocation.
- **Cost Estimation:** Through various approaches they can estimate the cost of the project. The project activities and resources should be assigned estimated costs.
- **Contingency Planning:** The total budget should be allocated the resources and contingency resources to avoid misadventures throughout the project completion. It also helps to meet any deficiencies in the earlier stage.
- **Real - Time Management:** This step includes actual costs and expense management during the project. In this step, project cash flow is start, so this helps project manager in cost estimation also.
- **Variances:** During the project process there can be positive or negative variances found. It can be like operational variance occurs due to various reasons such as idle labour hours, machine inefficiencies, raw material shortage, etc.
- **Reconciliation:** While, the final costs of the projects can be accumulated at the end of the project completion.

FUTURE RESEARCH DIRECTIONS

A contemporary project management is scalable, using simple versions of important techniques on projects and more involved versions on more complex projects. Agile approach has been introduced as an attempt to make software developed engineering flexible and efficient. Agile project focusing on client value, iterative and incremental implementation, strong cooperation, tiny integrated teams, self - organization, and tiny and constant improvements. It is said to work best with tiny teams. The perfect agile project team is tiny, collocated, connect face - to - face on a daily basis and has an optimal team size that does not exceed nine individuals. A Project Budget is the total sum of money allocated for the specific purpose of the project for a specific period of time. The main purpose of the project budget is to control project cost within the approved budget and deliver the expected project goals. - To budget a project it is difficult that the project manager has clarity on the following points:

- Cost estimation
- Project budgeting
- Project scope
- Resource availability
- Risks

Every factor is very important for project budgeting but many are taking the project risks seriously. Therefore, Author would recommend a discussion with the risk manager to go through all ultimate risks and potential opportunities, assess them by probability and impact by monetary value. It also discuss the different strategies to handle the risk (accept, avoid, transfer, mitigate, exploit), define modification task, contingency reserve, etc. Project managers must be re - evaluate the risks on a regular basis and update the budget accordingly. For any organisation, project manager should include all the project process like scope, schedule, cost estimation, cost control, budgeting, quality, resources allocation and stakeholders' interest. It's not end of the project budgeting, even it's a starting point because very few research found in this area. So, there is a wider scope for the potential researcher in the field of contemporary project management, agile project management with budgeting.

CONCLUSION

Project management is described as the processes where project objectives and achievement has been controlled and associated with the final result. Contemporary project management shows the tried - and - true project management techniques along with modern developments and agile approaches developed from adaptive (Agile) project management. Contemporary project management is scalable, using simple versions of important techniques on projects and more involved versions on more complex projects.

With 71% of companies are using agile in 2020, it has become a standard of project management. - Agile management has been assisted 98% of companies. There are some specific reasons to adopted agile methodology and techniques. It showing 71% speed up software delivered, increased 51% productivity, enhance the ability to manage changing priorities, improve 42% software quality. Author also discussed meaning of the project budgeting. It is the total sum of money allocated for the specific project for a specific period of time. The goal of the project budget is to cost control. A history of the project management described the conceptual framework of the project management i.e., four decades can be seen as representing four generations in the history of modern project management: prior to 1958, 1958 - 1979, 1980 - 1994, and 1995 to present (Kwak, 2003). The main focus of this chapter is to discussed the contemporary project management, Agile approaches, steps, risk identified and unidentified, source of the information and methods for evaluating the project budgeting. It has a direct impact on the company's financial feasibility. There are various source of information like work breakdown structure, project contract. Some other aspects in project budgeting: Budget reports requirements, Budget management plan, etc. The Author also discussed the procedures for project budgeting and methods for evaluation of project budgeting.

REFERENCES

Agile Alliance. (2015). *Guide to agile practices.* http://guide.agilealliance.org/

Agile Manifesto. (2019). *The Agile Manifesto.* Available: www.Agilemanifesto.org

Bustamante, A., & Sawhney, R. (2011). *Agile XXL: Scaling Agile for Project Teams.* Seapine Software, Inc.

Chiu, Y. (2010). *An introduction to the History of Project Management: From the Earliest Times to A. D. 1900.* Eburon.

Crawford, L., Hobbs, J. B., & Turner, J. R. (2005). *Project categorization systems: Aligning capability with strategy for better results.* Project Management Institute.

Dyba, T. & Dingsoyr, T. (2008). Empirical studies of agile software development: A systematic review. *Information and Software Technology, 50*(9 - 10), 833 - 859. doi:10.1016/j.infsof.2008.01.006

Fells, M. J. (2000). Fayol stands the test of time. *Journal of Management History,* *6*(8), 345–360. doi:10.1108/13552520010359379

Goldratt, E. (1997). *Critical Chain. Great Barrington.* North River Press.

Griffiths, M. (2012). *PMI - ACP Exam Prep.* RMC Publications, Inc.

Hastie, S. (2004). *The Agile Mind - set: what does it take to make this stuff work?* Software Education Associates Ltd, Agile Development Conference Wellington & Sydney.

ITRM Guideline CPM 110 - 01. (2006). *Appendix C - Commonwealth.* Retrieved from vita.virginia.gov:https://www.vita.virginia.gov/uploadedfiles/vita_main_public/unmanaged/library/cpmgappendix-c.pdf

Judah, T. D. (1857). A Practical Plan for Building the Pacific Railroad. Academic Press.

Kwak, Y. H. (2003). Brief history of project management. In K. A. Carayannis (Ed.), The Story of Managing Projects. Quorum Books.

Leiner, M. (2000). *A Brief History of the Internet.* Retrieved from: http://www.isoc.org/internethistory/brief.html

Marsh, E. R. (1975). The harmonogram of karol adamiecki. *Academy of Management Journal, 18*(2), 358–364.

McLean, J. (2005). *Administrative Management in Context.* MDP UK Ltd, Gwynedd.

NASA. (1967). *Centre Responsibilities in the Apollo Program.* NASA Apollo Program Directive No. 33.
PBS. Technology Timeline: 1752 - 1990. Retrieved from: https://www.pbs.org/wgbh/amex/telephone/timeline/timeline_text.html

Project Management Institute. (2013). A Guide to the Project Management Body of Knowledge (5th ed.). Project Management Institute, Inc.

Pugh, D. S., & Hickson, D. J. (2007). *Writers on Organisations* (6th ed.). Penguin Books. doi:10.4135/9781483329628

Rausch, E. (2005). A practical focus on leadership in management - for research, education and management development. *Management Decision*, *43*(7 / 8), 988–1000. doi:10.1108/00251740510609983

Serrador, P., & Pinto, J. K. (2015). Does agile work? - A quantitative analysis of agile project success. *International Journal of Project Management*, *33*(5), 1040–1051. doi:10.1016/j.ijproman.2015.01.006

Shenhar, A. D. D. (2007). *Reinventing Project Management.* Harvard Bus. School Press.

Sliger, M. (2011). *Agile project management with Scrum.* Paper presented at PMI® Global Congress 2011 - North America, Dallas, TX.

Snyder, J. R., & Kline, S. (1987). Modern Project Management: How Did We Get Here - Where Do We Go? *Project Management Journal*, *12*(9), 56–70.

VersionOne. (2015). *9th Annual State of Agile survey.* http://stateofagile.versionone.com

Vikash, L., Somveer, K., & Sameerchand, P. (2012). People Factors in Agile Software Development and Project Management. *International Journal of Software Engineering and Its Applications*, *3*(1).

Witzel, M. (2003). *Fifty key figures in management.* Routledge. doi:10.4324/9780203402184

Wolfe, D. (1968). American Association for the Advancement of Science. *Science.* PMID:5657328

Wysocki, R. K. (2014). *Effective project management: traditional, agile, extreme.* Wiley.

KEY TERMS AND DEFINITIONS

Analogous Estimation: Analyse the data in similar projects to decide the cost.

Bottom-Up Estimation: Rate the individual parts of the project plan and top them up.

Cost of Good Quality (CoGQ): Cost of activities needed to prevent quality failures + costs of quality appraisal activities.

Cost of Poor Quality (CoPQ): The expenses of the project may incur as a result of internal quality failures (e.g., product re - design, waste of time and material resources, etc.) + expenses the project may incur as a result of external quality failures (e.g., customer complaints, shipping errors and damages, etc.).

Liberalism: It involved the ideas of capitalism, the division of labour that an industrious lifestyle would lead to wealthy societies.

Newtonianism: It means applying scientific observations to developing the "classical school" of scientific management.

Parametric Estimation: Using data and applied them to the current project to advise the total.

Three-Point Estimation: Take the best, worst, and most likely case estimates to do the average.

Top-Down Estimation: Figure out the total and then split it into tasks or milestones.

Total CoQ: CoGQ + CoPQ.

Chapter 11
Exploring the Broad Underlying Principals That Govern Project Management

Saad Darwish
Kingdom University, Bahrain

Rahul Verma
https://orcid.org/0000-0002-5356-813X
Delhi University, India

ABSTRACT

With projects becoming more complex and multifaceted than before, there arises a need for agile efficient project management. This chapter seeks to define project management efficiency. The chapter explores the five variables that influence project management efficiency. It also delves into the importance of project management efficiency. Finally, the chapter breaks down the challenges to project management efficiency and gives solutions to counter the challenges. The variables explained in this chapter are project scope, cost, time, resources, and quality. As evidenced here, each variable has a role in enhancing efficiency in managing projects. The benefits of efficiently managed projects examined are quality control, customer satisfaction, risk identification and evaluation, consistent communication, and on-schedule project delivery. The challenges expounded in the chapter are inadequate skillset, undefined goals, impossible deadlines, scope creep, resource deprivation, and poor communication.

INTRODUCTION

Agility and Project Management Efficiency

Project management is a critical aspect of every organization that ensures success in an organization's projects. It helps to unite an organization's target clients with the team and help deliver projects within the set budget and scope (Meridith et al., 2017). As a result of project management, a team has a vision

DOI: 10.4018/978-1-7998-7872-8.ch011

for successful project completion even before it is complete. Moreover, with the increasing complexity of projects, careful planning, organization, and monitoring are required. It is only through having a structured approach, relevant processes, and specific responsibilities that managers can deliver outstanding results as per the project's constraints (Jena & Satpathy, 2017). However, project management is costly and requires attention to an extensive number of details. This means that a project manager is mandated to handle multiple responsibilities at a given time, hence placing pressure on his or her performance and, in turn, affecting the project's success. Efficiency in project management is needed to avoid unwarranted stress. This Chapter seeks to address project management efficiency, its benefits, constraints, and efficiency challenges.

Project management efficiency refers to attaining the set project goals and objectives using the available resources (Zidane et al., 2017). Project management efficiency is concerned with whether the project is completed successfully using the resources made available. Project management efficiency compares the project output with the project input. The input, in this case, refers to the set scope, time, cost, and that form the scope triangle. To fully understand what project efficiency is, it is paramount that the scope triangle is explained. The scope triangle is a term used to refer to the link between scope, time, and cost (Pollack et al., 2018). These three variables depend on one another so closely that a change in one variable triggers a change in another variable to reinstate balance to the project. While the three constraints are available in every project, they are not the only project variables. In addition to scope, time, and cost, two more variables are included: quality and resources. What follows is how each variable is critical in the project management process and how each influences project management efficiency:

Constraints that Influence Project Management Efficiency and Agility

- **The Agile Project Scope:** The project scope is what is set to be achieved and the amount of work required to complete the project (Bingham et al., 2017). It outlines not only what is within the project boundaries but also what should not be done. Different industries use different terms to describe scope. For instance, in the information systems discipline, the scope is referred to as functional specification by software engineers and developers. In the engineering discipline, the scope is referred to as a statement of work. It also referred to a scoping statement, a project request form, or a project initiation document. Regardless of the name used to describe it, a project's scope creates the basis from which all project work derives (Corvello, 2017). It outlines in detail what the project management team should achieve. For instance, if the project is a website, the scope gives the project management team's requirements. The project scope will also outline the aspects that the website should not cover. It is critical that a project starts on the right track and progresses on the right track. However, the project's scope is not fixed and is subject to change during the project management process.

In determining the project scope, a record of the project goals, features, tasks, roles, deadlines, deliverables, and the total cost is documented. The project's scope influences project management efficiency in that the clearer the project scope is defined, the easier the project manager can bring the pieces together to complete the project (Fageha et al., 2016). A poorly defined project scope can lead to project failure even at the infant stage. The project manager's first step is to create a clear, specific, and attainable project scope while also accommodating any project specifications changes to increase efficiency. The project manager creates the scope by having a conversation with the client or supervisor to capture all the client's needs.

- **Cost and Agility Dimension:** The project cost is the estimated expenditure of executing a given project from start to finish (Jayaraman, 2016). Cost is usually presented as a budget with the resources' price calculated to help make decisions as to whether the project is affordable and thus decide whether to go on with it or not. Cost considerations are made throughout the project development cycle. Projects that result in the creation of products for sale require consistent cost considerations. The initial cost consideration is made at the infant stage in the project life cycle (Sanchez, 2020). For instance, a client approaches the project development team and offers an approximate figure to what the client thinks is the project's value. Project managers often deal with situations where a customer has a fixed amount that the customer is willing to spend for the project.

When a customer has a fixed budget, the project manager can only work with what is available (Khalil et al., 2017). However, in official cases, the project manager must prepare a project proposal detailing the proposed project's estimated costs. Even after the project manager presents the initial figure, the client or the supervisor can decide the better cost approximation. A higher budget, skilled personnel, better equipment, and tools can help complete the project faster (Kaim, 2019). It is challenging to get the best out of sub-standard resources for lowly funded projects. To counter this, a project manager must convince the client or the project manager's seniors by presenting reasonable demands with proper justifications for the project budget's cost. If a project manager can get the client on board and get appropriate funding, it can be easy to improve the project efficiency by acquiring superior resources.

- **Agile Timing:** Time stipulates the project's deadline and specifies the project deadline. Once a client states a time frame and the project manager agrees to it, the project manager uses time productively. Unlike other resources like money that remain intact until used, time is depleted whether used or not (Liu et al., 2016). A project manager can only trade time within or between projects. Once the clock begins, the project schedule is maintained to ensure the project development meets the deadline. A good project manager gets the project back on schedule when the need arises. Even more importantly, time and cost are closely related. The more time a project takes, the higher the price (Izmailov et al., 2016). Hence, in case the project extends past its deadline, the additional cost is incurred. The project will require more resources, and the human resources will need more compensation for the extra hours.

Additional costs can lead to frustrations due to budget cuts and low productivity due to demotivated workers. Project management efficiency is affected when workers are demotivated. To turn things around, a good project manager not only protects time relentlessly but also makes fair use of it. He or she should prioritize the tasks that need to be completed at a particular time, what job to be handled before another and what tasks can be executed simultaneously (Niazi et al., 2016). This means having superb organizational skills as well as people management skills. This is because poor management of human resources is a key factor to time wastage and underutilization of the skills at disposal. A good project manager improves project management efficiency by determining the fastest way to deliver the project on or before time. However, if the project management team cannot deliver before the set deadline, the project manager must ask the client for additional time with a reasonable explanation as to why the team could not be complete the project without losing the trust of the client as (Lotfi et al., 2020).

- Resources & Agility: Resources as assets with varied availability and used to execute tasks and realize the project possible (Ogunde et al., 2017). For instance, people, facilities, tools or equipment, and inventory. The project management team can either own the resources or get the resources for a limited time through scheduling or leasing from a third party. Regardless of their nature, resources are critical to delivering project deliverables on time. The more resources, the easier it is to attain the set goals. The better the project resources, the faster it is to get the project done. Therefore, resources have to be available reasonably and in better working conditions to increase productivity (Kadri et al., 2018). Since resources cost money, the project manager must utilize the set budget to avoid stoppages and project failure if the acquired resources exceed the budget.

Resources greatly influence project management efficiency, and therefore the project manager must ensure they acquire the best resources for the project (Paquin, 2016). This includes acquiring the most skilled personnel for the task and getting the latest project management tools and technology to handle it. This means getting in touch with suppliers and software vendors. To increase project management efficiency as far as resources are concerned, the project manager must value and not price. Furthermore, it is important that the acquisition cost stays within the set budget despite getting quality resources (Hornstein & Henry, 2015). In case the acquired resources tend to increase the overall cost, a good project manager should prioritize which resource to compromise at the expense of the others. Otherwise, he or she should convince the client to increase the budget.

- **Agility and Quality:** Quality is the degree or level of conformance of the project deliverables and processes to set industry standards or requirements (Bongiovanni et al., 2015). It is worth noting that quality, in this case, is not a requirement but rather a consequence after time, cost, and scope are put together. Quality is highly dependent on the three variables, time, cost, and scope. It is difficult to get high-quality output if the project was done in a rush, with a low budget, and with a not clearly defined scope (Taniguchi et al., 2018). In every project, two quality types exist:
    - **Product Quality:** It is the project output quality. The output can be hardware, software, or business procedures. Quality control tools like check sheets, histograms, control charts, and Pareto charts are used to measure product quality.
    - **Process Quality:** It is the project management processes quality. The focus is on the effectiveness of the procedures used is and the way of improving the effectiveness.

Quality greatly influences project management efficiency as it is directly related to the result or project deliverables (Ceptureanu et al., 2017). A project management team should always strive to improve efficiency and the quality of the product. Poor quality results can translate to customer dissatisfaction, leading to the project's termination or possible future engagements. The clients can even choose to withdraw their investment in the project even before it is completed. Poor quality results can also mean a low return on investment which can mean losses for both the client and the project management team (Taniguchi & Onosato, 2018). Therefore, the importance of quality cannot be understated. Lastly, poor quality also translates to low project management efficiency. To maintain high-quality standards, a good project manager has to ensure high process quality. In other words, the procedure used to obtain results or accomplish tasks have to be proven to work effectively and efficiently. While process quality can translate to a better product, it does not instantly guarantee product quality (Raval et al., 2015). The project management team has to ensure that the right processes are implemented to achieve the best product quality. The project management team's responsibility is to ensure consistency in the quality of the deliverables and processes used in the project development process.

BACKGROUND

History

Incremental and Iterative Project Management strategies can be followed back as early as 1957 (Gerald, 2003), with adaptive Project Management (Edmonds, 1974) and evolutionary project management (Gilb, 2021a; Gilb, 2021b) developing in the early 1970s (Gilb, 1981).

During the 1990s, a number of lightweight Project Management strategies advanced in response to the prevailing heavyweight strategies (regularly alluded to collectively as waterfall) that critics portrayed as excessively micro - managed, planned, and regulated. These included: Rapid Application Management (RAD), from 1991 (Martin, 1991; Kerr & Hunter, 1993); the Dynamic Systems Management Method (DSDM) and Unified Process (UP), both from 1994; Scrum, from 1995; eXtreme Programming (XP) and Crystal Clear, both from 1996; and feature - driven Management, from 1997. In spite of the fact that these all begun before the publication of the Agile Manifesto, they are presently collectively alluded to as Agile Project Management strategies (Larman, 2004). At the same time, comparative changes were underway in management thinking and manufacturing (Iacocca Institute, 1991; Presley et al., 1995).

In 2001, these seventeen Project engineers met at a resort in Snowbird, Utah to talk about these lightweight Management strategies: Steve Mellor, Brian Marick, Jon Kern, Ron Jeffries, Andrew Hunt, Robert C. Martin, Alistair Cockburn, Jim Highsmith, Ken Schwaber, Jeff Sutherland, Dave Thomas, Ward Cunningham, Kent Beck, James Grenning, Mike Beedle, Arie van Bennekum, and Martin Fowler. Together they published the Manifesto for Agile Project Management (Beck et al., 2001).

In 2005, a group headed by Highsmith and Cockburn wrote an addendum of Project Management standards, the PM Declaration of Interdependence (Anderson, 2005), to direct Project Management concurring to Agile Project Management strategies.

In 2009, a group working with Martin wrote an expansion of Project Management standards, the Project Craftsmanship Manifesto, to direct Agile Project Management concurring to proficient mastery and conduct.

In 2011, the Agile Alliance made the Guide to Agile Practices (renamed the Agile Glossary in 2016) (McDonald, 2016), an advancing open - source digest of the working definitions of Agile elements, terms, and practices, beside experience guidelines and interpretations from the around the world community of Agile practitioners.

The Manifesto for Agile Project Management

Agile Project Management Values

Based on their combined involvement of creating Project and helping others do that, the seventeen signatories to the manifesto broadcasted that they value (Beck et al., 2001):

- **Interactions and Individuals** over tools and processes
- **Working Project** over comprehensive documentation
- **Customer collaboration** over contract negotiation
- **Responding to change** over following a plan

That is to say, the things on the left are valued more than the things on the right.
As Scott Ambler illustrated (Ambysoft Inc., 2021):

- Processes and tools are imperative, but it is more critical to have competent individuals working together effectively.
- Good documentation is valueable in helping individuals to get it how the Project is built and how to use it, but the main point of Management is to form Project, not documentation.
- A contract is imperative but is no substitute for working closely with consumers to find what they need.
- A project plan is imperative, but it must not be too unbending to suit changes in environment or the technology, stakeholders' needs, and individual's understanding of the issue and its solution.

Some of the authors shaped the Agile Alliance, a non - profit organization that advances Project Management concurring to the manifesto's principles and values. Presenting the manifesto on behalf of the Agile Alliance, Jim Highsmith said: "The Agile development isn't anti - methodology, in fact numerous of us need to re - establish validity to the word strategy. We need to re - establish a balance. We grasp modeling, but not in order to record a few graph in a dusty corporate store. We grasp documentation, but not hundreds of pages of rarely - used and never - maintained tomes. We plan, but be familiar with the limits of planning in a dynamic environment. Those who would brand defenders of SCRUM or XP or any of the other Agile Methodologies as "hackers" are uninformed of both the methodologies and the first definition of the term hacker." (Highsmith, 2001)

Agile Project Management Principles

The Manifesto for Agile Project Management is based on twelve principles (Beck et al., 2001b):

- Customer satisfaction by continuous and early delivery of important Project.
- Welcome changing necessities, indeed in late Management.
- Deliver working Project regularly (weeks instead of months).
- Close, day by day participation between developers and business people.
- Projects are built around spurred people, who ought to be trusted.
- Face - to - face discussion is the finest frame of communication (co - location).

- Working Project is the essential degree of progress.
- Sustainable Management, able to preserve a steady pace.
- Continuous consideration to good design and technical excellence.
- Simplicity - the art of maximizing the sum of work not done - is essential.
- Best designs, requirements, and architectures rise from self - organizing teams.
- Regularly, the team reflects on how to end up more viable, and alters accordingly.

Overview

- **Iterative, Incremental, And Evolutionary:** Most Agile Management strategies break product Management work into little increments that minimize the sum of up - front design and planning. Iterations, or sprints, are brief time outlines (time - boxes) that typically last from one to four weeks. Each Iteration / sprint includes a cross - functional group working in all functions: acceptance testing, unit testing, coding, design, analysis, and planning. At the end of the Iteration / sprint a working item is illustrated to stakeholders. This minimizes overall risk and permits the item to adjust to changes rapidly (Moran, 2014). An Iteration / sprint might not include sufficient functionality to warrant a market release, but the objective is to have an accessible release (with negligible bugs) at the end of each iteration / sprint (Beck, 1999). Through incremental Management items have room to "fall flat early and often" all through each iterative stage rather than radically on a last release date (Mergel, 2016). Numerous iterations / sprints could be required to release new features or a product. Working Project is the essential degree of progress (Beck, 2001b).
- **Efficient And Face - To - Face Communication:** The guideline of co - location is that co - workers on the same group ought to be situated together to improve communication and to better establish the identity as a team (Preuss, 2006). This empowers face - to - face interaction, ideally in front of a whiteboard, that diminishes the cycle time typically taken when answers and questions are intervened through email, wiki, persistent chat, or phone (Cockburn, 2007).

No matter which Management strategy is taken after, every team ought to incorporate a consumer agent ("Product Owner" in Scrum). This individual is concurred by stakeholders to act on their sake and makes a personal commitment to being accessible for designers to reply questions all through the iteration. At the end of each iteration, the customer representative and stakeholders review progress and re - evaluate needs with a view to optimizing the Return On Investment (ROI) and guaranteeing arrangement with company goals and customer needs. The significance of stakeholder satisfaction, detailed by frequent interaction and review at the end of each stage, is why the strategy is frequently indicated as a "Customer Centered Methodology" (Jain et al., 2018).

In Agile Project Management, a data radiator is a (ordinarily large) physical display found prominently close to the Management team, where passers - by can see it. It presents an up - to - date rundown of the item Management status (Cockburn, 2008; Ambler, 2002). A build light indicator may moreover be utilized to advise a team about the current status of their item Management.

- **Very Short Feedback Loop and Adaptation Cycle:** A common characteristic in Agile Project Management is the everyday stand - up (an everyday scrum in Scrum system). In a short - term session, team individuals report to each other what they did the past day toward their team's iteration / sprint objective, what they expected to do today toward the objective, and any impediments or roadblocks they can see to the objective (Vasiliauskas, 2014).

- **Quality Focus:** Particular techniques and tools, such as code refactoring, domain - driven design, behaviour - driven Management, design patterns, test - driven Management, pair programming, automated unit testing, continuous integration, and other methods are regularly utilized to enhance product Management agility and improve quality (Jeffries et al., 2001). Typically predicated on building and designing quality in from the starting and being able to illustrate Project for consumers at any point, or at least at the end of each iteration (Lisa & Janet, 2009).

MAIN FOCUS OF THE CHAPTER

Project Management Efficiency Leads to Agile and Effective Resource Allocation

According to a survey carried out by de Carvalho et al. (2015), poor management of projects costs microbusinesses with up to 100 employees in their workforce $420,000 and over $62 million for companies with more than 100,000 employees. Therefore, project management efficiency is paramount to the success of any project-based business or organization. Below is the importance of efficiency in project management:

The most valuable resource at the disposal of any project manager is his or her team. Within the team are people with different skills and responsibilities that are key to completing the project. Efficient project management means getting the right people at the right place and on time (de Carvalho et al., 2015). In the same manner, project management efficiency ensures that other resources like tools, equipment, and machinery are acquired and made available on time to avoid project execution delays. Project managers ensure equipment is made available when required by making necessary acquisitions in advance. When tools and equipment are acquired on time, the project runs smoothly with minimal interruptions and time wastage. Resources like human resources tend to get misused, whereby a team member can be mandated to execute multiple tasks leading to overworking (Bitar et al., 2018). Overworking results in reduced morale whereby the worker feels mistreated; hence productivity is affected. A good project manager avoids overworking the employees by allocating enough personnel to work on the available tasks, delegating tasks that come up during the development process to a third party, or hiring more personnel. By allocating resources effectively, a project manager can monitor and anticipate the more demanding phases, plan, and allocate resources in advance, leading to better resource utilization.

Efficient Project Management Guarantees Customer Satisfaction

Customers always seek to get what they want, how they want it, and on time. Project management efficiency ensures that these customer needs are met. Even after the customer has laid out the project requirements, the customer will still make more demands during the project management process (Haverilla et al., 2016). If the project is software, the customer may demand that more features are added or design modifications made. A project manager's responsibility is to listen to the customer's demands and decide if the project management team can meet its needs. If the team cannot meet the customer's demands, a good project manager will explain why without leaving room for doubt. Constant reassurance to the customer by the manager is needed. If a project manager can deliver the project deliverables on time and with superior quality, what the project manager gets is a satisfied client. A satisfied client is more important than a new one since the satisfied client is likely to become a return customer in the future (Haverilla et al., 2016). A satisfied client is also likely to refer other potential clients hence a good source of word-of-mouth marketing. Interestingly, client satisfaction positively impacts the project management team as they experience improved morale due to a job well done.

Quality Control of the Procedures and Outputs

Project managers are always under intense pressure to accomplish the set project goals on time. In the event deadline are missed, timelines are tightened, and shortcuts are likely to be used, which in turn translates to poor quality outputs (Taniguchi & Onosato, 2018). Project management efficiency involves using quality processes like Agile development that ensure that every step in the development cycle is separately examined and tested. Since the project manager has total control of the quality of the processes and the output, the outcome is usually unparalleled. A project manager ensures that quality is maintained from the beginning of the project to the end. Maintenance of quality is done by developing quality standards for the processes, tools, equipment, and human resources and ensuring that they are met. For instance, quality standards for the personnel can be particular academic qualifications. Any person that does not meet the set requirements should not be hired. A project manager can also set performance quality standards so that personnel is supposed to meet a particular performance threshold (Taniguchi & Onosato, 2018). The personnel that does not meet the established performance standard can either improve or lose the job. This ensures that the team members maintain high-quality standards throughout the development period hence guaranteeing quality output. Consequently, project management efficiency directly impacts the quality and gives the project manager control over materials' quality to use and processes to apply.

Consistent Communication between Team Members

According to research carried out by Brunswicker et al. (2018), it was discovered that 57% of the projects that were studied failed due to poor communication. This is because bringing a group of people with different opinions and perspectives to work together can be hard. The more people in the project management team, the more complex and difficult collaboration among them becomes. A scenario may occur during the development process whereby one team member prefers a different methodology from another team member with neither willing to compromise. While such a scenario may seem mundane, it can result in project delays that affect timely project delivery. A project manager's responsibility is to bring people together and ensure the people work as a team. Convincing the team members to set their differences apart is a project manager's role. With efficient project management, the team works together despite the differences among the team members. Efficient project management brings in management processes that increase transparency, streamline communication among team members, and ensures accountability (Sarhadi et al., 2018). As part of improving efficiency, project managers ensure the team members are on board and have a clear vision of what they are set to achieve together. Throughout the entire development process, the project manager reminds the team members of each other's importance and ensures consistent communication.

Risks are Identified and Prepared for in Advance

Efficient project management means being on the lookout for red flags whenever there is a possibility of risks arising. A project manager can plan and identify potential risks like a task deadline that could adversely affect other deadlines if missed, a potential overspend that could skyrocket the project's budget, and other potential risks (Carvalho et al., 2015). A good project manager should not only identify these risks but also prepare for countermeasures in advance. Risks are identified by thoroughly reviewing the project plan and replaying scenarios to identify instances where things could go wrong. This enables the project manager to predict anomalies before they take place. While creating and replaying scenarios can identify some risks, other risks require prior knowledge through experience or training. Thus, a project manager must use both instincts and logic proactively to ensure that every possible threat is identified. Once the risks are identified, a project manager develops a risk management plan to minimize the risks and reduce the chances of the dangers growing into threats to the project's success (Carvalho et al., 2015). An efficient project manager can also realize when the project development process is going off track and implement course correction measures at the right moment instead of realizing anomalies when it is too late. This awareness boosts the confidence of the project management team and increases the client's trust.

Staying on Schedule While Keeping Costs and Project Resources within the Budget

A project manager's challenge is usually ensuring the project stays on schedule while maintaining the costs and ensuring project resources are not depleted. During the project management process, miscellaneous arise and raise the overall cost of the project. If they are not checked, the added expenses can derail the project from its estimated budget leading to overspending. Added financial costs can have disastrous effects like delays in the employee's salary and resource acquisition delays due to inadequate funds. This can lead to project delays, project failure, or sub-standard output delivery, all of which have disastrous results for the client and the project management team. This challenge is combatted through project management efficiency. Serrador et al. (2015) state that project management efficiency means that the project management team can properly utilize the available resources. It also means prioritization of tasks and resources to enable completion of the project tasks without increasing costs. A good project manager ensures that the team members responsible for handling funds make consultations before spending them. The project manager also ensures a good funds acquisition process so that requests for financial resources follow the appropriate chain of command before approval is made. Despite the reduced costs through the optimization of available resources, a good project manager knows that efficiency means ensuring the project outputs' quality remains up to par with the set standards and requirements (Ekrot et al., 2016).

Agile Project Management Methods

Agile Project Management strategies bolster a wide extend of the Project Management life cycle (Abrahamson et al., 2002). A few strategies center on the practices (e.g., agile modeling, pragmatic programming, XP), whereas a few center on managing the stream of work (e.g., Kanban, Scrum). A few support exercises for requirements specification and Management (e.g., FDD), whereas a few look for to cover the total Management life cycle (e.g., RUP, DSDM).

Notable Agile Project Management frameworks include:

- Adaptive Project Management (Asd) (By Jim Highsmith & Sam Bayer)
- Agile Modeling (By Scott Ambler & Robert Cecil Martin)
- Agile Unified Process (AUP) (By Scott Ambler)
- Disciplined Agile Delivery (By Scott Ambler)
- Dynamic Systems Management Method (DSDM)
- Extreme Programming (XP) (By Kent Beck & Robert Cecil Martin)
- Feature - Driven Management (FDD) (By Jeff De Luca)
- Lean Project Management (By Mary Poppendieck & Tom Poppendieck)
- Lean Startup (By Eric Ries)
- Kanban (By Taiichi Ohno)
- Rapid Application Management (RAD) (By James Martin)
- Scrum (By Ken Schwaber & Jeff Sutherland)
- Scrumban
- Scaled Agile Framework – Safe (By Scaled Agile, Inc.)

Agile Project Management Practices

Agile Project Management is upheld by a number of concrete practices, covering areas like quality, process, risk management, planning, testing, coding, modeling, design, requirements, etc. A few striking Agile Project Management practices incorporate (The Agile Alliance, 2021):

- Acceptance Test - Driven Management (ATDD)
- Agile Modeling
- Agile Testing
- Backlogs (Product And Sprint) (By Ken Schwaber)
- Behavior - Driven Management (BDD) (By Dan North & Liz Keogh)
- Continuous Integration (CI) (By Grady Booch)
- Cross - Functional Team
- Daily Stand - Up / Daily Scrum (By James O Coplien)
- Domain - Driven Design (DDD) (By Eric Evans)
- Iterative And Incremental Management (IID)
- Pair Programming (By Kent Beck)
- Planning Poker (By James Grenning & Mike Cohn)
- Refactoring (By Martin Fowler)
- Retrospective
- Scrum Events (Sprint Planning, Sprint Review, And Retrospective)
- Specification By Example
- Story - Driven Modeling (By Albert Zündorf)
- Test - Driven Management (TDD) (By Kent Beck)
- Timeboxing

- User Story (By Alistair Cockburn)
- Velocity Tracking

SOLUTIONS AND RECOMMENDATIONS

Challenges of Project Management Efficiency

While achieving efficiency in project management is paramount to a project management team, it is difficult. In achieving project efficiency, a project manager is faced with overwhelming challenges. The way a project manager deals with the challenges to achieve efficiency determines its success or failure (Hoda et al., 2016). What follows is a breakdown of the challenges and the possible solutions to maneuver the obstacles present along the way.

- **Scope Creep:** Scope creep, also known as scope changes, usually happens when the project management team lets the project's scope broaden past the original objectives. During the project development process, customers and supervisors are continually making requests for changes to the project. It requires a skilled and strong-willed project manager to listen to each request, consider it and decide whether to implement the changes while making clear communication on the effects of the changes on the set budget and set deadlines to the concerned parties (Amoatey et al., 2017). Constant requests for changes can veer the project off its original track, and a project manager's challenge is always to implement the changes while staying on track. This poses a challenge for project management efficiency.
- **Undefined Goals:** If the project goals are not well identified and defined, the entire project management team can face a hard time ensuring project efficiency. When senior management does not agree to support the project's objectives, there is minimal chance for success (Patil, 2016). In such a scenario, the project manager's solution is to prompt the client for clarity by asking the right questions. This helps in the establishment and communication of clear goals right from the beginning. With clearly defined goals, the project can now grow and take the right course. Furthermore, if the goals are crystal clear, it becomes easier to develop efficient ways to deliver the project on schedule and in the best quality.
- **Inadequate Skillset To Work On The Project:** When the required skills are not available, it becomes difficult to execute the project tasks. Some projects demand a particular skill set that the project team may not possess. To combat this challenge, the project manager's responsibility is to conduct an assessment to determine the required competencies, assess the skillset of the team members, and decide if the team can get more training, hire additional staff, or whether the project is to outsource to a qualified third party (Liikamaa, 2015). With the right skill set, project management efficiency can be made possible. Otherwise, it becomes a challenge.
- **Accountability Issues:** To successfully maintain project efficiency, accountability is paramount. A well-led project management team is evidenced when team members take full responsibility for their part in the project's success (Burga et al., 2017). A challenge presents itself when the management team is not accountable. The team members finger point and switch the blame to avoid responsibility for actions. Lack of accountability among team members is a sign of poor leadership from the project manager. Lack of accountability is a challenge to achieving project management

efficiency and project completion. The solution is for the project manager to learn how to direct his or her towards the set goal while encouraging full accountability and ownership of mistakes when they occur (Uribe et al., 2018).

- **Undefined Contingency Plans:** In every project, a project manager should always know the risks that may arise and has countermeasures in place in the event they arise (Joslin & Muller, 2015). When the contingency plan is not clearly defined, this can be disastrous to the project development process when unexpected problems arise. This also becomes a challenge to project management efficiency. A project manager needs to identify potential risk areas by gathering the right input and being aware of which areas of the project are likely to go wrong and developing a well-defined contingency plan to combat the risks when they arise (Kock et al., 2016). This leads to a smooth transition in the entire project management process and builds trust among the team members, leading to higher productivity.
- **Poor Communication:** As aforementioned, communication is a core part of the project development process as it helps build trust and increase morale among the team members. A challenge presents itself when communication is low and the team members cannot establish clear expectations. Inferior leadership skills from the project manager or poor communication skills between the team members can bring about poor communication hence making project efficiency a challenge (DuBois et al., 2015). To combat this problem, a good project manager emphasizes written and oral skills between the team members and ensures a clear communication flow and responses between senior management and the project management team leadership. Clear communication ensures that the people involved in the project management process understand each other and streamlines the development process.
- **Unrealistic Deadlines:** A project's success depends on the client's deadlines and the project manager to their team. Consistently asking the team to deliver within an impossible deadline can result in a quick decline in the team morale and overall productivity (Meredith et al., 2017). Few people can work under pressure, especially in a toxic environment where their efforts are constantly undermined. A good project manager sets clear and reasonable expectations that can be met in the set and continuously motivates the team to keep pushing significantly when the morale is declining. A good project manager paints a clear picture that it is possible to achieve and instills this confidence in the team members. A good project manager knows that completing the project within impossible deadlines is unrealistic and sets reasonable deadlines and achievable project goals. (Besteiro et al., 2015). This way, productivity is increased, which in turn improves the project management efficiency.
- **Deprivation of Resources:** For a project to be executed efficiently and effectively, management must ensure that the resources allocated are sufficient. The challenge comes in when the allocation of resources is done poorly and, in an attempt to cut expenses, resources acquired for the project become inadequate (Ogunde et al., 2017). This leads to the deprivation of resources midway before the project is complete. This stalls the project delivery and increases the chances of failure to deliver before the deadline, and can also lead to failure of the whole project, leading to wastage of the spent resources and time. In the end, it is difficult to improve efficiency if resources are scarce. A way around this is for the project manager to clearly define needs and obtain approval for resource acquisition upfront, hence avoiding future delays and ensuring the resources are well allocated on time in the project development life cycle (Li et al., 2019). A good project manager can

also encourage the team to be economical by reusing or recycling resources rather than purchasing new ones.

CONCLUSION

Project management efficiency & agility is critical for any project management team that wants to attain the set project goals and objectives while utilizing the available resources. To achieve efficiency, a project manager needs to understand the five constraints that influence project management efficiency: project scope, cost, time, resources, and quality. With these variables in mind, the agile project management team can improve project efficiency, ensure effective resource allocation, guarantee customer satisfaction, ensure quality control, maintain consistent communication, and stay on schedule while staying within the budget. However, there are challenges to realizing efficiency in project management. The challenges are scope changes that could veer the project off course, undefined goals, inadequate skillset to get the job done, accountability problems, indefinite contingency plans, poor communication, impossible deadlines, and resource deprivation. A project manager's responsibility is to notice these challenges and deal with them upfront to ensure that project management efficiency is attained.

REFERENCES

Abrahamson, P., Salo, O., Ronkainen, J., & Warsta, J. (2002). *Agile Project Management methods: Review and analysis* (Technical report). VTT. 478.

Ambler, S. (2002). *Agile Modeling: Effective Practices for EXtreme Programming and the Unified Process*. John Wiley & Sons.

Ambysoft Inc. (2021). *Examining the Agile Manifesto*. Author.

Amoatey, C. T., & Anson, B. A. (2017). Investigating the major causes of scope creep in real estate construction projects in Ghana. *Journal of Facilities Management*. https://www.emerald.com/insight/content/doi/10.1108/JFM-11-2016-0052/full/html

Anderson, D. (2005). *Declaration of Interdependence*. Academic Press.

Beck, K. (1999). Embracing Change with Extreme Programming. *Computer*, *32*(10), 70–77. doi:10.1109/2.796139

Beck, K., Grenning, J., Martin, R. C., Beedle, M., Highsmith, J., Mellor, S., Bennekum, A. v., Hunt, A., Schwaber, K., Cockburn, A., Jeffries, R., Sutherland, J., Cunningham, W., Kern, J., Thomas, D., Fowler, M., & Marick, B. (2001a). *Manifesto for Agile Project Management*. Agile Alliance.

Beck, K., Grenning, J., Martin, R. C., Beedle, M., Highsmith, J., Mellor, S., Bennekum, A. v., Hunt, A., Schwaber, K., Cockburn, A., Jeffries, R., Sutherland, J., Cunningham, W., Kern, J., Thomas, D., Fowler, M., & Marick, B. (2001b). *Principles behind the Agile Manifesto*. Agile Alliance.

Besteiro, de Souza Pinto, & Novaski. (2015). Success factors in project management. *Business Management Dynamics, 4*(9), 19.

Bitar, H., Zia, H., Bashir, M., Parava, P., Hanafi, M., Tierney, W., & Madhoun, M. (2018). Impact of fellowship training level on colonoscopy quality and efficiency metrics. *Gastrointestinal Endoscopy*, *88*(2), 378–387. doi:10.1016/j.gie.2018.04.2338 PMID:29679692

Bongiovanni, A., Colotti, G., Liguori, G. L., Di Carlo, M., Digilio, F. A., Lacerra, G., Mascia, A., Cirafici, A. M., Barra, A., Lanati, A., & Kisslinger, A. (2015). Applying Quality and Project Management methodologies in biomedical research laboratories: A public research network's case study. *Accreditation and Quality Assurance*, *20*(3), 203–213. doi:10.100700769-015-1132-5

Brunswicker, S., & Chesbrough, H. (2018). The Adoption of Open Innovation in Large Firms: Practices, Measures, and Risks A survey of large firms examines how firms approach open innovation strategically and manage knowledge flows at the project level. *Research Technology Management*, *61*(1), 35–45. doi:10.1080/08956308.2018.1399022

Burga, R., & Rezania, D. (2017). Project accountability: An exploratory case study using actor–network theory. *International Journal of Project Management*, *35*(6), 1024–1036. doi:10.1016/j.ijproman.2017.05.001

Carvalho, M. M. D., & Rabechini, R. Jr. (2015). Impact of risk management on project performance: The importance of soft skills. *International Journal of Production Research*, *53*(2), 321–340. doi:10.1080/00207543.2014.919423

Ceptureanu, E. G., Ceptureanu, S. I., Luchian, C. E., & Luchian, I. (2017). Quality management in project management consulting. A case study in an international consulting company. *Amfiteatru Economic*, *19*(44), 215.

Cockburn, A. (2007). *Agile Project Management: The Cooperative Game*. www.pearson.com

Cockburn, A. (2008). *Information radiator*. Academic Press.

Corvello, V., Javernick-Will, A., & Ratta, A. M. L. (2017). Routine project scope management in small construction enterprises. *International Journal of Project Organisation and Management*, *9*(1), 18–30. doi:10.1504/IJPOM.2017.083109

de Carvalho, M. M., Patah, L. A., & de Souza Bido, D. (2015). Project management and its effects on project success: Cross-country and cross-industry comparisons. *International Journal of Project Management*, *33*(7), 1509–1522. doi:10.1016/j.ijproman.2015.04.004

DuBois, M., Hanlon, J., Koch, J., Nyatuga, B., & Kerr, N. (2015). Leadership styles of effective project managers: Techniques and traits to lead high performance teams. *Journal of Economic Development, Management, IT, Finance, and Marketing*, *7*(1), 30.

Edmonds, E. A. (1974). A Process for the Management of Project for Nontechnical Users as an Adaptive System. *General Systems*, *19*, 215–218.

Ekrot, B., Kock, A., & Gemünden, H. G. (2016). Retaining project management competence—Antecedents and consequences. *International Journal of Project Management*, *34*(2), 145–157. doi:10.1016/j.ijproman.2015.10.010

Fageha, M. K., & Aibinu, A. A. (2016). Identifying stakeholders' involvement that enhances project scope definition completeness in Saudi Arabian public building projects. *Built Environment Project and Asset Management, 6*(1), 6–29. doi:10.1108/BEPAM-06-2014-0030

Gilb, T. (1981). Evolutionary Management. *ACM SIGSOFT Project Engineering Notes, 6*(2), 17. doi:10.1145/1010865.1010868

Gilb. (2021a). *Evolutionary Project Management (Original page, external archive).* Academic Press.

Gilb. (2021b). *Evolutionary Project Management (New page).* Academic Press.

Haverila, M. J., & Fehr, K. (2016). The impact of product superiority on customer satisfaction in project management. *International Journal of Project Management, 34*(4), 570–583. doi:10.1016/j.ijproman.2016.02.007

Highsmith, J. (2001). *History: The Agile Manifesto.* Agilemanifesto.org.

Hoda, R., & Murugesan, L. K. (2016). Multi-level agile project management challenges: A self-organizing team perspective. *Journal of Systems and Software, 117*, 245–257. doi:10.1016/j.jss.2016.02.049

Hornstein, H. A. (2015). The integration of project management and organizational change management is now a necessity. *International Journal of Project Management, 33*(2), 291–298. doi:10.1016/j.ijproman.2014.08.005

Iacocca Institute. (1991). *21st Century Manufacturing Enterprise Strategy: An Industry Led View.* Iacocca Institute, Lehigh University.

Izmailov, A., Korneva, D., & Kozhemiakin, A. (2016). Project management using the buffers of time and resources. *Procedia: Social and Behavioral Sciences, 235*, 189–197. doi:10.1016/j.sbspro.2016.11.014

Jain, P., Sharma, A., & Ahuja, L. (2018). The Impact of Agile Project Management Process on the Quality of Project Product. In *2018 7th International Conference on Reliability, Infocom Technologies and Optimization (Trends and Future Directions) (ICRITO).* Noida, India: IEEE. 10.1109/ICRITO.2018.8748529

Jayaraman, R. (2016). Project cost control: a new method to plan and control costs in large projects. *Business Process Management Journal.* https://www.emerald.com/insight/content/doi/10.1108/BPMJ-10-2014-0102/full/html?fullSc=1

Jeffries, R., Anderson, A., & Hendrickson, C. (2001). Extreme Programming installed. Addison - Wesley.

Jena, A., & Satpathy, S. S. (2017). Importance of soft skills in project management. *International Journal of Scientific Research and Management, 5*(7), 6173–6180. doi:10.18535/ijsrm/v5i7.45

Joslin, R., & Müller, R. (2015). Relationships between a project management methodology and project success in different project governance contexts. *International Journal of Project Management, 33*(6), 1377–1392. doi:10.1016/j.ijproman.2015.03.005

Kadri, R. L., & Boctor, F. F. (2018). An efficient genetic algorithm to solve the resource-constrained project scheduling problem with transfer times: The single mode case. *European Journal of Operational Research, 265*(2), 454–462. doi:10.1016/j.ejor.2017.07.027

Kaim, R., Härting, R. C., & Reichstein, C. (2019). Benefits of agile project management in an environment of increasing complexity—A transaction cost analysis. *Intelligent Decision Technologies, 2019*, 195–204.

Kerr, J. M., & Hunter, R. (1993). *Inside RAD: How to Build a Fully Functional System in 90 Days or Less*. McGraw - Hill.

Khalil, M., Qadir, J., Onireti, O., Imran, M. A., & Younis, S. (2017). Feasibility, architecture and cost considerations of using TVWS for rural Internet access in 5G. In *20th Conference on Innovations in Clouds, Internet and Networks (ICIN)* (pp. 23-30). IEEE.

Kock, A., Heising, W., & Gemünden, H. G. (2016). A contingency approach on the impact of front-end success on project portfolio success. *Project Management Journal, 47*(2), 115–129. doi:10.1002/pmj.21575

Larman, C. (2004). *Agile and Iterative Management: A Manager's Guide*. Addison - Wesley.

Li, Y., Zhang, H., Long, K., Choi, S., & Nallanathan, A. (2019). Resource allocation for optimizing energy efficiency in NOMA-based fog UAV wireless networks. *IEEE Network, 34*(2), 158–163. doi:10.1109/MNET.001.1900231

Liikamaa, K. (2015). Developing a project manager's competencies: A collective view of the most important competencies. *Procedia Manufacturing, 3*, 681–687. doi:10.1016/j.promfg.2015.07.305

Lisa, C., & Janet, G. (2009). *Agile Testing: A Practical Guide for Testers and Agile Teams*. Addison - Wesley.

Liu, C., Cheng, J., Wang, Y., & Gao, S. (2016). Time performance optimization and resource conflicts resolution for multiple project management. *IEICE Transactions on Information and Systems, 99*(3), 650–660. doi:10.1587/transinf.2015EDP7397

Lotfi, R., Yadegari, Z., Hosseini, S. H., Khameneh, A. H., Tirkolaee, E. B., & Weber, G. W. (2020) A robust time-cost-quality-energy-environment trade-off with resource-constrained in project management: a case study for a bridge construction project. *Journal of Industrial & Management Optimization*. https://www.aimsciences.org/article/doi/10.3934/jimo.2020158

Martin, J. (1991). *Rapid Application Management*. Macmillan.

McDonald, K. (2016). *How You Can Help Agile Alliance Help You*. Agile Alliance Blog.

Meredith, J. R., Shafer, S. M., & Mantel, S. J. Jr. (2017). *Project management: a strategic managerial approach*. John Wiley & Sons.

Mergel, I. (2016). Agile innovation management in government: A research agenda. *Government Information Quarterly, 33*(3), 516–523. doi:10.1016/j.giq.2016.07.004

Moran, A. (2014). *Agile Risk Management*. Springer Verlag. doi:10.1007/978-3-319-05008-9

Niazi, M., Mahmood, S., Alshayeb, M., Riaz, M. R., Faisal, K., Cerpa, N., Khan, S. U., & Richardson, I. (2016). Challenges of project management in global software development: A client-vendor analysis. *Information and Software Technology, 80*, 1–19. doi:10.1016/j.infsof.2016.08.002

Ogunde, A., Joshua, O., Amusan, L. M., & Akuete, E. (2017). Project Management a Panacea to Improving the Performance of Construction Projects. *International Journal of Civil Engineering and Technology*, *8*(9), 1234–1242.

Paquin, J. P., Gauthier, C., & Morin, P. P. (2016). The downside risk of project portfolios: The impact of capital investment projects and the value of project efficiency and project risk management programmes. *International Journal of Project Management*, *34*(8), 1460–1470. doi:10.1016/j.ijproman.2016.07.009

Patil, G. (2016). Project management challenges. *Journal of Multidisciplinary Engineering Science and Technology, 3*.

Pollack, J., Helm, J., & Adler, D. (2018). What is the Iron Triangle, and how has it changed? *International Journal of Managing Projects in Business*, *11*(2), 527–547. doi:10.1108/IJMPB-09-2017-0107

Presley, A., Mills, J., & Liles, D. (1995). Agile Aerospace Manufacturing. Nepcon East.

Preuss, D. H. (2006). *Study: Co - Located Teams vs. the Cubicle Farm*. InfoQ.

Raval, M. V., Minneci, P. C., Deans, K. J., Kurtovic, K. J., Dietrich, A., Bates, D. G., & Kenney, B. D. (2015). Improving quality and efficiency for intussusception management after successful enema reduction. *Pediatrics*, *136*(5), e1345–e1352. doi:10.1542/peds.2014-3122 PMID:26459654

Sanchez, F., Steria, S., Bonjour, E., Micaelli, J. P., & Monticolo, D. (2020). An approach based on bayesian network for improving project management maturity: An application to reduce cost overrun risks in engineering projects. *Computers in Industry*, *119*, 103227. doi:10.1016/j.compind.2020.103227

Sarhadi, M., Yousefi, S., & Zamani, A. (2018). Participative project management as a comprehensive response to postmodernism criticisms: The role of communication. *International Journal of Managing Projects in Business*, *11*(4), 935–959. doi:10.1108/IJMPB-10-2017-0119

Serrador, P., & Turner, R. (2015). The relationship between project success and project efficiency. *Project Management Journal*, *46*(1), 30–39. doi:10.1002/pmj.21468

Taniguchi, A., & Onosato, M. (2018). Effect of continuous improvement on the reporting quality of project management information system for project management success. *International Journal of Information Technology and Computer Science*, *10*(1), 1–15. doi:10.5815/ijitcs.2018.01.01

The Agile Alliance. (2021). *Guide to Agile Practices*. Author.

Uribe, D. F., Ortiz-Marcos, I., & Uruburu, Á. (2018). What is going on with stakeholder theory in project management literature? A symbiotic relationship for sustainability. *Sustainability*, *10*(4), 1300. doi:10.3390u10041300

Vasiliauskas, V. (2014). *Developing Agile project task and team management practices*. Eylean.

Zidane, Y. J. T., & Olsson, N. O. (2017). Defining project efficiency, effectiveness and efficacy. *International Journal of Managing Projects in Business*.

KEY TERMS AND DEFINITIONS

Agile Project Management: It is more flexible approach and promotes collaborative working with the customer.

Agility: Ability to move easily and quickly.

Manifesto: It is a published declaration.

Chapter 12
The Effects of COVID-19 and Disasters on Scheduling Function in Mega-Projects

Vannie Naidoo
https://orcid.org/0000-0001-8435-4348
University of KwaZulu-Natal, South Africa

ABSTRACT

Mega-projects are crucial as they strive to provide infrastructural development and support growth and sustainability of a country's economy. Scheduling is an integral part of mega-projects, and special attention needs to be given to the planning of this activity. It is important that an experienced person in the project team be responsible for scheduling activities for the mega-project. In 2020, COVID-19 appeared and had devastating consequences on the world and all sectors of society including business, industry, and the economy. Mega-projects were also affected by COVID-19, a deadly pandemic that has caused a loss of millions of lives worldwide. The scheduling of mega-projects during lock-down proved problematic, causing major delays, backlogs, and additional cost and rescheduling of activities in the project. Disasters are also another factor that can hinder project performance. This chapter will unpack scheduling in mega-projects and how it is affected by COVID-19 and other disasters.

INTRODUCTION

The area of Mega - projects is becoming increasing popular as we see the world moving towards a greater demand for mega - projects. Mega - projects are very complex and are crucial in transforming society and the economy. The manner in which it is received by the stakeholders on a mega - project is controversial. Since, Mega - projects are under the watchful high of the public, many civil rights activists and environmentalists sometimes are not in favour of a Mega-project as it can have negative effects on the physical environment and create more problems. The interesting nature of a Mega - projects is that it is continually evolving, as theorists try to unpack its complexity. Last year 2020, COVID - 19 the greatest humanitarian crisis and pandemic known to man appeared. With it, COVID - 19 brought sick-

DOI: 10.4018/978-1-7998-7872-8.ch012

ness, death, destruction and affected all facets of society worldwide. The business sector and its various components was hard hit, as lock - down brought temporary closure to businesses for many weeks or months. Mega-projects also were not spared as construction sites and other Mega - projects depend on raw materials and supplies whose deliveries were hindered or stopped, causing delays to the various Mega - projects world - wide. This chapter is on mega - projects but specifically looks at one aspect of it that of scheduling. This chapter is unique as it adds knowledge on the effects of COVID - 19, and disasters on scheduling of Mega-projects. However, before one can understand the scheduling aspects and their complexity it is important to have a brief understanding of what is mega-projects.

BACKGROUND

This chapter explores the effects of COVID - 19, natural disasters and terrorism in scheduling activities. In the study background it is important is explore what is mega - projects and what are typical mega-projects.

Mega-Projects

Many theorists writing in the area of mega-projects outlined different views and perceptions of what to their understanding are mega - projects. Mega - projects do not exist in isolation but they are closely integrated and aligned to socio - economic requirements. Mega - projects, as described by Flyvberg (2009), are initiatives that produce expensively large physical infrastructure, and are constantly under the watchful eye of the public. Brockmann (2009) define mega-projects as unique construction projects known for their complexity, vast size, expensive cost, and long time frame compared to conventional construction projects. The size and complexity are reflected by a price tag that exceeds one billion dollar and by a time frame that may exceed the five year limit. Biesenthal et al. (2018) is of the opinion that Mega - projects demand enormous amount of human, financial and technological resources. Locatelli et al. (2014) categorise mega - projects as having "extreme complexity in both technical and human terms and by far having a long record of poor delivery". Ruuska et al. (2009) define mega-projects as significant undertakings which are characterized by multi - organizations, seeking success on different objectives; subject to socio - political impacts. Oliomogbe & Smith (2012) appear to support the monetary description of mega - projects, and their estimate in that mega - projects usually have a value of greater GBP150m (British). Capka (2004) describe mega-projects as expensive projects that require the management of numerous, concurrent, and complex activities while maintaining tough schedules and tight budgets. Biesenthal et al. (2018) identify seven more characteristics that make mega-projects different form complex or large projects: reach; duration; risks and uncertainties; widely disparate actors; arenas of controversy; legal and regulatory issues. They suggest that what differentiates mega-projects is their reach and the broad impact they have on society and the environment.

Since this chapter is on scheduling issues. It is important to note that there can be many reasons why a mega - project may not come to completion or be delayed. Merrow (2011) succinctly identify and classify common problem areas in mega-projects, albeit that they are for large industrial projects. That said, the commonalities and propositions put forward prove useful, in developing a picture of issues, which are at the heart of mega-projects in general. These include:

- Greed and how this manifest in mega-projects.

- Schedule pressures—cutting corners, opportunism.
- The need to develop a business case early in the life of the mega-project.
- The need for stronger planning at the initial phases, costs to be realistically incurred
- Cost reductions without respecting the scope definition
- Rethinking the contractors obligations - issues of transferring risks to contractors
- Continuity issues - project managers changing lack of continuity (Merrow, 2011)

Typical Mega-Projects and Their Relationship to Infrastructure Development

As countries in the world, specifically emerging countries like Brazil, Russia, India, China, and South Africa emerge as economic leaders, there is a need to develop the infrastructure in these emerging nations so that economic growth can be sustained. Mega - projects thus form a significant catalyst to improve the competitive advantage for economically powerful nations. The only way for a country to remain a strong leader and economically viable in a rapidly changing and dynamic economic landscape is for countries throughout the world to enhance and grow their infrastructure in terms of Ports, roads, pipeline, airports and tunnels to name but a few.

Merrow (2011) state that in the first ten years of the 21stcentury, the world has seen more process industry mega - projects than ever before due to the current demands for energy, chemicals, and various other products. ECSA (2015) reports that the types of mega - project are vast however they are broadly categorised as infrastructure, transportation, built environment, industrial and energy. The complexity and risk profile varies with each type of mega - project hence it is important to appreciate the context in which these projects are executed when comparing the mechanisms of delivery. Priemus et al. (2016) indicate that mega - projects consist of large and complex, nuclear power plants, oil and gas plants, mineral plants. Other mega - projects consist mainly of roads and tunnels, railways, pipelines, aerospace, large sporting events, hydroelectric facilities, and marine projects. In an international global review by McKinsey (2016), it was stated that there is indications that mega - infrastructure projects are strategic investments and are increasing in complexity.

Flyvbjerg (2014) depict examples of mega-projects as high - speed rail lines, airports, seaports, motorways, hospitals, national health or pension ICT systems, national broadband, the Olympics, large - scale signature architecture, dams, wind farms, offshore oil and gas extraction, aluminium smelters, the development of new aircrafts, the largest container and cruise ships, high - energy particle accelerators, and the logistics systems used to run large supply - chain - based companies like Amazon and Maersk. Biesenthal et al.(2018) identify some examples of recent mega-projects around the world which include: the high - speed rail lines (Chuo Shinkasen Maglev Line in Japan); airports (Singapore Changi Airports); seaports (Port of Hamburg in Germany); motorways (Lamu Port South Sudan Ethiopia Transport (LAPSSET) Corridor); National Broadband (National Broadband Network in Australia); major events (London Olympics); hospitals (Chris Hani Baragwanath Hospital in Johannesburg); large - scale signature architecture (Guggenheim Museum in Bilbao); wind farms (Gansu Wind Farm Project in China); offshore oil and gas extraction (Petrobras's Floating Production, Storage and Offloading Units in Brazil); new aircraft (Boeing Dreamliner); cruise ships (Royal Caribbean's Harmony of the Seas); container ports (Shanghai); scientific projects (Cyclotron particle accelerator); bridges (Øresund bridge connecting Sweden and Denmark); supply chain systems (Amazon, USA); and even large - scale public good projects (Swachh Bharat, India's Clean India program).

Mega - projects play an important role in social development since they contribute significantly to economic growth and communities (Nijaki & Worrel, 2012). This notion is supported by Lee & Chan (2009) where they suggest that mega - projects, when viewed in a global context, have the primary goal of promoting economic growth, balancing social inequalities, and existing in harmony with the natural environment. According to PwC (2014), there is a trend in growth and infrastructure demand that has been forecasted to continue into the next two decades. This encourages the need for mega - infrastructure projects in ports, rail and cities McKinsey (2016) add that the high demand for the provision of mega - infrastructure requirements in buildings, services and ports is being driven by the high economic growth rates in the East Asian nations of China and India and developing countries in Africa and South America. PwC (2014) reports that Kenya has boosted its mega - infrastructure development projects by investing some $60 billion worth of mega - projects in East Africa. Mega - projects in the Kenyan basket of developments include a 600 kilometre railway line, 1,500 kilometres of pipelines and ports. The Lamu Port Southern Sudan Ethiopia Transport Corridor Project is driving investment because of the discovery of oil in Uganda and Kenya.

MAIN FOCUS OF THE CHAPTER

In the discussion below various themes relating to scheduling will be outlined. This will be with reference to mega-projects and specific attention in the discussion will be around COVID - 19, natural disaster and terrorism and their impact on mega-project scheduling function.

SCHEDULING TOOLS AND TECHNIQUES AND HUMAN RESOURCES

It has often been pointed out by research scholars in the area of project management that when it comes to scheduling, project scheduling tools and techniques, past project schedule data and the skill set of schedulers play an important role in the production of schedules.

1. Project Scheduling

Project scheduling consists of determining start times for all tasks such that temporal and / or resource constraints are satisfied and some objective is optimized (Jo´zefowska & Weglarz, 2006). A prerequisite for successful scheduling is the definition of all the activities required to deliver the project's scope, the correct sequencing of those activities and the addition of resources and time to create the schedule (Shash & Ahcom, 2006)

Schedules for mega - projects need to be properly planned so that delays are avoided and additional costs not incurred. There are various activities involved in scheduling. Berg & Karlsen (2014) argue that the process of scheduling commences with the identifying and defining the various activities that are required to deliver the business solution. Tilos (2012) indicate that project team specialists on work, package, discipline, and leads are usually involved in confirming the activities and the duration of time that would be required to complete the activities. Scheduling activities must be properly managed to avoid shortfall in a mega - project.

Building on this concept for a mega - project to have successful scheduling activities that are well planned and managed the past experience of the scheduler is vital. If he/she has built up a reputation in industry in managing complex schedules in a volatile and rapidly changing industry then the project organisation can be assured of success. Added to this it is important to track past schedule performance to avoid similar scheduling problems encountered in past projects. Sawyer (2012) is of the opinion that reliance should be placed on past project performance to determine the duration of the various activities but unreliable forecasting of activity durations and the absence of reliable forecasting statistics may lead to risky project schedules and challenges in managing schedule slippages.

2. Tools and Techniques Used In Scheduling

According to Arau´zo et al. (2010), classical methods based on mathematical programming can handle project scheduling when the problem complexity is low and the system stays some - what static. These characteristics is seldom true in real world projects. The most commonly used project management tools are Microsoft EPM (MP 2015) and Primavera.

Elmaghraby (1977) introduce the Multi - Mode Resource - Constrained Project Scheduling Problem (MRCPSP) as an extension of the RCPSP method. El - Abbasy et al. (2017) comment further that MRCMPSP is the extension of RCMPSP where each activity possesses different execution modes. The activities can be executed with the several combinations of modes using various construction methods, materials, crew size, and overtime policy. Under this situation, each combination will have different project performances regarding time, cost, and quality

The PMI (2013) indicates that here are two common and widely accepted formulae that are produced by namely the 'time estimate at completion' (TEAC) and the 'cost estimate at completion' (CEAC).' Narbaev & De - Marco, (2013) add that the 'Earned value management' (EVM) is also a common technique that is used for controlling schedule delays and cost overruns and EVM supports the control functions for monitoring, analysing and forecasting schedule completion and project cost. Norouzi et al. (2015) comment that common scheduling techniques are limited in their capability to estimate completion time and suggests the use of probability distribution techniques for complex schedule networks that can cause complications and make assessments difficult. Hence, he identifies the need for the "fuzzy approach" to be expanded and intensified for improved results.

Narbaev & De - Marco (2013) caution that the simple CEAC method has three limitations. They illustrate that a new regression - based non - linear CEAC methodology can be used to improve early forecasting of the final cost of completion. This method is integrated into the growth model with the earned - schedule for improved accuracy. Furthermore, they highlight that this method relies heavily on the availability of accurate schedule information as well as cost information to be produced at all levels of the project team. Norouzi et al. (2015) indicate that "unless reliable and timely reporting is established", schedules will only produce "false forecast of costs and schedules". The author recommends for future research, that factors such as "sequential relationships, schedule - changes, fast tracking and dynamic - scheduling" are incorporated into the schedule analysis for predicting project completion.

Norouzi et al. (2015) consider uncertainty as a "property of a system which is an indicative defect in human knowledge towards a system and its state of progression". Norouzi et al. (2015), adds that projects are implemented in an environment that is uncertain; thus, ambiguity is a major feature in a project environment. Common techniques do not have the capability of estimating the completion time for a project that is executed for the first time. He further explains that the use of probability distribution techniques for large, complex networks can complicate and make assessments difficult; hence the need for the fuzzy approach to be expanded and intensified for improved results. Deckro et al. (1991) offers the integer programming with decomposition approach for solving the multi - project, resource - constrained scheduling problem. Kim & Leachman (1993) propose linear programming to optimize the trade - offs of lateness costs among projects.

3. Accelerating and Compressing Schedules

Marks & Ellis (2013) explain that it is quite common on time - sensitive projects for the project team to compress schedules by accelerating and overlapping activities to arrive at an earlier project completion date. However, acceleration generally means more costs are added to an activity while overlapping tasks can cause additional schedule risks to activities that are usually undertaken in sequence. Considerations must be given to time and cost trade - off to determine if the benefits of schedule compression are worthwhile.

González et al. (2014) argue that project managers should have sufficient experience to criticise project plans in terms of resource criticality and dependencies. Hazini et al. (2013) found that the appropriate tactics for schedule compression are challenging especially if such strategies are subjective, leading to further rework, schedule slippage and cost overruns which lead to a loss situation on the project. Hazini et al. (2014) further notes that schedule compression poses a risk of further rework, schedule slippage and cost overruns sending the project into a ‘loss situation’ if such unrealistic, subjective compression strategies are implemented.

Mubarak (2010) notes that the precise loading and levelling of resources in the schedule can help interpret the trade - off between schedule outcomes (i.e., durations) and the cost of resources. In an attempt to find an optimum solution for schedule compression, Narbaev & De - Marco (2013) recommend the use of “genetic algorithms” for resolving the time - cost trade - off since genetic algorithms have the capability of running complex problems in a shorter time and optimising the “time - cost solution”.

4. Skill Requirements for Scheduling

Roe’s (2014) view that in an organisations’ commitment to delivering successful complex large projects, experienced and competent personnel must be mobilised to ensure desired investment outcomes. According to Varajao et al. (2014), construction type projects is criticised quite commonly for delays, deviations from budget, quality and production issues; thus, careful management of critical aspects is required for a project to be successful. Project planning and well - defined objectives is the top ranking criteria for both IT and Construction projects. The efficiency of the project manager is ranked 3rd and involvement of the team took 4th place. They conclude that project managers must allocate the resources that are necessary in the planning phase as project success is dependent on this key requirement. The project manager’s efficiency also ranks at the top of the critical aspects of success. Langer et al. (2008) in a study conducted in the IT sector assessing the impact of project managers’ skills found that in high complexity projects having large teams, project execution is improved when project managers demonstrate high - level skills sets in both ‘hard’ skills (technical, general) and ‘soft’ skills (tacit, non - technical). Since the nature of mega-projects are over a long duration Ziek & Anderson (2015) argue that if key personnel on project teams have excellent skills of communications, they can foster consistent engagements and well - developed relationships with team members on the project since maintaining effective communications is pivotal during complex, long - duration mega - projects. Wallace et al. (2004) support the view that the weakness in developing an appropriate team size with the relevant skills can result in issues such as unbalanced workload on disciplines, insufficient time for training and continuous professional development and failure to provide team motivation which subsequently results in poor team performance. If staff have a lack of skill and training then work can be delayed and scheduled activities can be delayed.

The aspect of emotional intelligence being a crucial skill to have in scheduling is an important consideration mega - projects. Zhang & Fan (2013) indicate there is a strong correlation between a project manager's Emotional Intelligence (EI) and project performance. They add that supportive emotional intelligence factors include, organizational awareness, empathy, cultural understanding, and self - control, and self - confidence. They also recommend that project managers with 'high cultural understanding and adaptability' be deployed to international projects while project managers with 'good organizational awareness' be retained for domestic projects. Another recommendation is that cost - plus contracts be allocated to project managers with high levels of empathy and project managers with high levels of inspirational leaders be allocated to unit price contracts.

5. Identifying Mega-Project Delays in Scheduling

Marks & Ellis (2013) define delays as the time overrun beyond the agreed completion date as stated in the contract agreed by the contracting parties for the delivery of a project.

In the state development of large housing projects in Ghana, Amoatey et al. (2015) indicate that significant delays in the project completion date were primarily related to the delayed approval of the commencing project and scope changes. Further delays occurred during construction when contractors were not paid on time due to delegated authorities in government not approving payments as per the planned timeline.

In the case of major agricultural infrastructure in Guyana, Marks & Ellis (2013) identify eight main causes of delays: access to site, weather delays, schedule being too optimistic, unforeseen ground conditions, too many change - orders, poor and incomplete site investigations prior to the bidding process, slow decisions by client, and shortages in skilled labour.

In the case of IPA's 318 mega - projects consisting mainly industrial off - shore and onshore processing plants, Merrow (2011) posit that poor engineering and poor quality control are the chief contributors to project schedule slippages. He explains that that slow engineering work mobilization drives "late and out of order equipment and engineered bulk materials". Andersen et al. (2016) argue that the complexity of mega - projects often leads to schedule overruns. Ibrahim et al. (2015) add that poor team integration of stakeholders in the early stages of the project leads to incomplete project schedules in the construction phase as a result of changing needs by the contractor.

Andersen et al. (2016) indicate that a high failure rate of international mega - projects were as a result of mega - projects not meeting their schedule targets. When mega - projects are delayed, a direct consequence is that additional funding is needed to support the extended timelines. According to Marks & Ellis (2013), it is essential that the schedule of major projects is not over - optimistic and that they have a suitable budget to match an appropriate project timeline. Furthermore, all major projects should have an appropriate funding contingency that caters for unforeseen events; otherwise it becomes difficult and time - consuming for the owner to solicit funding from government authorities, leading to further delays in completing the project.

6. The Impact of COVID-19, Natural Disasters and Terrorism on Project Scheduling

In this section, the researcher looks at COVID - 19 a pandemic, natural disasters and terrorist attacks as they give rise to situations of major disaster management in a country and would impact on the project schedule.

a. Impact of COVID-19 on Project Scheduling

During COVID - 19, in South Africa and many other countries in the world there was a lock - down imposed by the government. During this time only essential service workers were allowed to open their businesses and go to work. The rest of the country's' citizens had to stay at home so as to flatten the curve in high infections rates. Naidoo (2021) argues that the COVID - 19 pandemic brought on by the novel coronavirus, has spread across borders and reached countries throughout the world. The business arena which is a crucial component of a country's survival has also been exposed to the virus. As many countries businesses both large and small had to close down, to prevent the infection from spreading, as many governments championed Lock - down as a means to curb the spread of the virus. On the 15 March 2020, due to COVID - 19 the South African government declared a National State of Disaster.

The pandemic started in the Chinese Wuhan city. The outbreak of the case of chronic pneumonia cases in the Chinese Wuhan city of the Hubei province has been a centre of attention globally. This has been where the virus first emanated from. The unknown virus was first detected in December 2019 and subsequently identified as the 2019 novel coronavirus (COVID - 19), based on the symptoms and the laboratory test results (Huang et al., 2020). Haleem et al. (2020) posit that COVID - 19 has affected day - to - day life and is slowing down the global economy. They further argue that the economic effects of coronavirus include: the slowing of the manufacturing of essential goods, disruption of the supply chain of products, losses in national and international business, poor cash flow in the market, significant slowing down in the revenue growth while the social consequences include the cancellation or postponement of large - scale sports and tournaments, disruption of celebration of cultural, religious and festive events, undue stress among the population, social distancing with peers and family members, closure of hotels, restaurants and religious places, closure of places for entertainment such as movie and play theatres, sports clubs, gymnasiums, swimming pools and so on. Li et al. (2018) argue that Mega-projects play an important role in economic development; however, many mega-projects are considered failures or are inefficient in terms of time, schedule, and quality.

In many cases major constructions on mega-projects were halted as the country battled with the medical crisis brought on by COVID - 19. To add to this, the delays in the steady supply of materials was hindered and closure of the ports in South Africa took place during lock - down phase 5. This had devastating consequences on the management of mega-projects, especially those in the construction industry for example. According to Worldometers (2020) globally COVID - 19 has claimed to date more than a million peoples' lives. In the mega-project industry where construction takes place, site workers including technical engineers needed to be on - site, as they were required to perform activities to complete schedules tasks or to monitor the work to ensure it was being done correctly. However some new workplace policies came into being doing. Strict rules of social distancing, wearing of protective gear to shield ones nose and mouth and eyes from infection came into being. Masks had to be wore, and gloves as well. Hand sanitizers had to be present in different areas on site so that construction staff and engineers on site could sanitize their hands regularly.

According to Holland & Knight LLP (2020) workplace safety and health compliance, including advising on concerns and issues raised by the COVID - 19 pandemic are as follows:

Developing and updating plans and procedures both for office and jobsite operations compliant with applicable standards, regulations and orders, including advice and counsel regarding Occupational Safety and Health Administration (OSHA) standards governing:

i. Respirators, masks, and face coverings
ii. Other Personal Protective Equipment (PPE)
iii. Hazard communication
iv. Hand - washing or hand cleansers
v. Cleaning, disinfecting and sanitizing workplaces
vi. Blood - borne pathogens
vii. Developing and implementing jobsite best practices and working through risk exposure analyses that are driving workplace logistics, including social distancing
viii. Assisting clients with developing and implementing processes such as temperature checks and pre - access jobsite questionnaires that are compliant with U.S. Equal Employment Opportunity Commission (EEOC), Americans with Disabilities Act (ADA) and Health Insurance Portability and Accountability Act (HIPAA) guidelines, as applicable
ix. Responding to / defending OSHA complaints filed by employees, workers and third parties
x. Responding to / defending OSHA whistle - blower actions stemming from claims of retaliation based on complaints of workplace safety / health violations under OSHA or under the other nearly two dozen whistle - blower laws that OSHA oversees and is tasked with processing, (Holland & Knight LLP,2020).

To prevent the spread of the virus, construction staff had to be rotated and work in shifts, as fewer staff were allowed on site, to contain the spread of infections if any arose. If staff were infected, they had to quarantine and other staff on site who worked alongside them in that shift also had to be in 2 week isolation. During this time these staff had to get tested for COVID - 19 and seek medical attention.

Naidoo (2021) posits that since South Africa is part of BRICS, its export and demand in metals has been slow due to the COVID - 19 pandemic having economic implications on the countries GNP. South Africa also relies heavily on China and other BRIC countries for raw material and export commodities, and during Lock - down, the supply of these imports were low. Many of South African industries who rely on imports had their production and manufacturing impeded due to Lock - down. Whichever way one has to look at it, COVID - 19 has had a disastrous impact on the South African economy. Since many raw materials that come for China and other countries abroad, this has delayed mega-projects who require these urgent supplies. In many instances, these construction projects had to be reschedules and this may have created job losses for the low skilled labourers in the industry that are employed for day to day digging of trenches for example. These manual labourers were the hardest hit during COVID - 19, when mega-projects were shut down due to lack of materials. Rehiring of staff when work commenced proved difficult as some of the foreign manual labourers and artisans employed on the construction project departed to go back to their homes across the South African border. These workers went back to Zimbabwe, Malawi, Lesotho, Swaziland and Zambia. The replacement of these foreign manual labourers and artisans could impact construction quality, as the new less qualified site staff who have been brought in to complete the construction jobs on site maybe less productive or quality conscious. Some of the construction crew could have died or had health complications due to being infected with COVID - 19, so this too can impact on job delays, comprised construction quality. The rescheduling of activities and tasks, need to take place as new replacement staff are brought on to continue on the construction site and finish the project. Flyvbjerg et al. (2003) argue that Mega-projects are plagued by many underperformance problems, such as cost overruns, delays, and unqualified construction quality.

Another major consequence of lock down was that harbours in South Africa were closed, this effected goods and materials being sent in on time to the mega-project sites. There was major backlogs as South Africa battled with opening up the harbour again after lock - down stage 4. When harbours were finally opened, this caused major traffic jams as every truck came to load their goods for transit to the various sites.

Another great concern raised was the backlog created because of sick staff and not enough men being available on site to complete the task on time, thus leading to Project delays. COVID - 19 was unexpected. This lead to new schedules being drawn up to cater for COVID - 19 health crisis and the dilemmas it brought to mega-projects and rescheduling of tasks due to the pandemic.

b. Impact of Disasters on Project Scheduling

Disasters bring with it death, injuries and destruction to property and surroundings. Mega-projects can be highly affected by disasters. Sheehan & Hewitt (1969) describe disasters as the events that cause at least a hundred human deaths or a hundred human injuries or at least $1 million economic damages. In this section three types of disasters will be outline and discussed, one is natural disasters and the other are disasters due to political or social conditions and the last is due to technical faults. Blackhard (2006) is of the opinion that disasters may occur as the result of unpredictable conditions or of underestimated risks.

Natural disasters like, floods, earthquakes, hurricanes, and tornadoes are natural disasters that have been on the rise in the last few years. This is attributed to the increasing temperatures and the melting polar caps. Natural disasters have a major impact on Mega-projects. Ham et al. (2017) argue that structures under construction do not have any fire protection systems or earthquake - resistant elements, which makes them highly prone to destruction during disastrous events. Said et al. (2012) posit that during the event of fire disasters, one of the factors to be considered on a construction site is the safety of the construction crew / employers at the site. This factor must be given higher consideration when it comes to high rise building projects, as the workers have to be evacuated from each floor, which consumes a lot of time.

Mega-projects scheduling function, especially if the natural disaster occurred on the construction site. Although natural disasters are unforeseen, however as they have been occurring around the world so frequently, Mega - projects have to have in place the necessary insurance to covers loses incurred to property, equipment and lives during such catastrophic events such as natural disasters. Guha – Sapir et al. (2015) indicates that there have been around 100 natural disasters reported annually worldwide during the 1980s, and that this number has risen to over 300 since 2000. Safapour & Kermanshachi (2019) comment that one of the common issues that construction companies face following a disaster is schedule overruns. Rouhanizadeh et al. (2019) argue that various unexpected situations can occur that impact negatively on the completion of construction and reconstruction projects and might give rise to increased project costs. Nipa et al. (2020) added that disasters such as hurricanes and typhoons create serious damage to materials and machinery on construction sites, developments are emerging that will enhance the level of preparedness and reduce the amount of losses to the public. Wang et al. (2014) are of the opinion that recently, the construction industry has begun to use Radio Frequency Identification Technology (RFID), an automated tracking device that tracks materials at the site and has been shown to save 3.1% of the construction cost. This can be effectively used to track materials during certain disasters. Chavez (2016) argues that the schedule and cost of a project overruns can be significantly reduced if proper preparedness tools are considered during the planning phase. A balanced scorecard method can be adopted.

Political and social conditions prevalent in the business environment by wars, recessions or strikes and civil unrest can case disasters to occur on site on a project. Mega-projects delays, costs increases and re - scheduling of activities may occur due to strikes in South Africa for example. The strikes can cause civil unrest at times and property and equipment can get damaged when a mob decides to damage property on the site. During such civil unrests construction workers on site can get injured or the unruly mob can set alight the site, causing possible damage to property and the site crew. Once again it is prudent for the senior Project manager in charge of the mega - project to filter these costs into the initial costs and to carry insurance that can cover the, if these circumstances prevail.

Disasters due to technical faults or workplace accidents may occur on a Mega-project site. According to the New York Times (2011) The San Esteban mining company in Chile was drilling coal and gold at the San Jose mine, when on August 5, 2010 the mine was collapsed and a list of 33 miners were trapped. After a seventeen day period, the miners were determined to be alive 700m below the surface and a successful innovative rescue plan was organized. Inefficient safety plans and the total absence of an emergency plan were determined in this particular case too. The New York Times (2010) reported on the British Petroleum (BP) oil - drill platform's explosion in the Gulf of Mexico. On April 20, 2010 an explosion caused more than eleven deaths and more than seventeen injuries, while an extensive pollution to the Gulf's waters resulted. The response to this emergency was late and without a pre - defined plan, which could handle the situation and limit the disaster's implications.

When a Mega-project is affected by a disaster a set of events should take place to plan on the recovery and rebuilding the disaster ridden construction for example. There first needs to be a plan put together by the project management team, to establish injured staff, site losses to property and equipment and other losses to the project that was hit by the disaster. The first step is to make the disaster site safe, so that further injury or loss of life does not occur. Then the necessary authorities need to be called on site, namely the medical teams, fire fighters and law authorities. The injured staff or staff that incurred loss of life need to be moved after the necessary medical and law authorities provide assistance on site. The project manager of the mega - project also needs to be notified of the damages that have been incurred on site. It is prudent that the Mega - project public relations department issue a press release on the disaster that occurred on their site. During the recovery phase after the disaster, removing the debris from site is essential. Staff on site need to take proper care and preventative measures to ensure hazardous wastes are removed in the correct manner so that contamination of the site does not occur. Further to this, during debris removal staff on site must stay out of the way and ensure that they are safe during debris removal, as many accidents can happen during this stage. Maintaining safety of site workers and preventing further loss of life or injuries takes precedence during this stage.

Thereafter steps should be taken to recover the losses to equipment and property. Insurance brokers need to be notified so that pictures can be taken of the estimated damages. Claims need to be put forward to the insurance company. In times of disaster the two - stage disaster recovery model can be followed. Pardede & Tetsuo (2007) defined a two - stage model for the post - disaster recovery process: the short

- term stage where a reaction against the disaster is undertaken; and the long - term stage that concerns the activities that recover the organization's operations or the project. These two stages overlap and their duration and the initiation are not determined. The plan that controls the execution of a disaster recovery process is called disaster recovery plan or emergency plan and has several attributes for hazard detection, risk minimization, safety planning and resource capitalization.

Hallgren & Wilson (2008) classified various crises' sources, analysed a number of case studies and concluded to the following set of activities for project recovery: (a) effective risk management during project planning; (b) the existence of a dual structure in the company's organization for crisis management and for catastrophe avoidance; (c) instantaneous communication of crises between site team and project team; and (d) simultaneous operation of formally and informally developed teams. The Project Management Institute's (PMI) Body of Knowledge (PMBOK, 2007) recognizes risk and safety planning as integral parts of the construction management process, it proposes tools and techniques to deal with risks and safety but it does not provide managers with elements for disaster management. Anaya - Arenas et al. (2014) comments that from a chronological point of view, the process of emergency management can be divided into four phases, including mitigation, preparedness, response and recovery. The mitigation and preparedness phases are before the disaster, which aim at lowering the probabilities of a disaster or minimizing its effects and losses. The response and recovery phases are post - disaster phases. The response phase seeks to minimize the disaster's effects by helping people as quickly as possible and preventing any further loss, while the recovery phase supports the community in its effort to return to a normal state.

In the 4th industrial revolution great inroads have been made in technology. Certain potential natural disasters can be monitored so that steps can be taken to protect the Mega - project site with its buildings and equipment and more especially its personnel. Fung et al., (2009) defined a Risk Assessment Model (RAM) for construction safety. Their model evaluates risks and safety plans according to historical data of accidents and disasters, while they suggest principles for disaster avoidance: (a) installation of safe workstations and construction sites; (b) continuous workers' training regarding safety; (c) construction method improvement; and (d) effective safety planning for both the workers and the project. Another important issue to address is the Mega - project sites need site employees to be prepared for disasters. Spittal et al. (2006) and Nguyen et al. (2006) argue that workplace preparedness involves planning activities, such as speaking with employees about the impact and importance of preparing the company for natural hazards, having an emergency plan in place, alternative energy supplies for the company's operation following a natural disaster, insurance for this type of events, and the presence of an emergency kit in the company, among many others. The International Federation of Red Cross and Red Crescent Societies (Gospadinov, 2001) which has been involved in post - disaster situations in several countries notes that: "there has been less understanding of the part disaster preparedness must play in the setting of housing and construction standards". Thus, the Federation has committed itself to "working actively to advocate for better responses to issues like housing and construction standards [in order] … to mobilise the power of humanity for disaster prevention, preparedness, mitigation and response at local, national and international levels".

c. Impact of War or Terrorism on Scheduling of Mega-Projects

War and terrorism cause disasters of an unimaginable magnitude. When war or terrorist attacks occur, they can cause damages to a Mega - project site. Komendantova et al. (2012) advocates that poor performance of the project (time overrun and cost overrun) is due to one single factor namely and insecure environment due to insurgency and terrorism which is considered as Force Majeure.

The costs, delays, rescheduling, and rebuilding of the damaged structures can take time and millions or even billions of dollars. With the recent terrorist attacks on the rise, modern architectural monuments of a country's culture can be bombed by these terrorists. Warah (2002) is of the opinion that with globalization, the major settlements are also inter - connected and a disaster in one of them can precipitate widespread disruption in many others. Indeed, as the dramatic events of September 2001 demonstrated, while they can be symbols of national achievement and culture, particular constructed items can be the targets of attack.

During a war, bombs have caused major damage to buildings, property, equipment and surrounding areas as we know. If a terror attack or war is at hand, a Mega - project site can bear harsh consequences. If the surrounding roads or bridges are damaged due to a terrorist bombing or war, this will make it difficult for raw materials to reach the Mega - project site causing major delays to the project. Backlogs will occur and rescheduling of activities have to take place to take into account the delays. If site staff families incurred injuries during the bomb blast, then these staff would be absent from work as they need to spend time with their loved ones, and this will add to delaying the project. If staff got hurt during these attacks, they would be absent from work and this absenteeism of site staff can delay the project. If the site is damaged by acts of terrorism or war, then the project may have to be stopped until things stabilize. If the region is in war, then the project will cease as it would not be safe for site staff to endanger their lives at work. As Moor (2002) notes, human settlements are designed to protect their inhabitants against attack by intelligent hostile elements. At the same time, the technology of war aims to counteract such defences. Indeed, it would appear that with socioeconomic progress, settlements become more vulnerable as they become more reliant on their increasingly extended supply lines, and ever - expanding and vital distribution networks of water, power, gas and telecommunication systems, as well as other resources such as food. They also become dependent on community networks and government agencies at various levels. Public social and security infrastructure such as health facilities, civil defence, and the police also become crucial.

Compared to a standard project, rebuilding after a disaster is chaotic, complex, uncertain, and changing (Chang et al., 2011). After a war or terrorist attack disaster, many NGO's and Government Aid organizations both local and international come to assist in rebuilding after the disaster took place. These organizations and individuals should look at employing individuals in the local economy to help in the reconstruction of buildings damaged by war or terror attacks. By employing the local people, this will provide jobs and revive the local economy. The World Bank (2001) observes that international experience from other disaster hit areas suggests that the recovery programme should follow principles including: revival of the economy; empowering individuals and communities; affordability, private sector participation, and equity; decentralization; and communication and transparency. Consultation with, and participation by, the affected communities must be at the heart of the recovery programme, including, as far as possible, rebuilding of their own houses by individuals in their original location. Siriwardena et al. (2013) add that as construction contractors are involved with the construction of infrastructure it makes sense that they should also be involved in the event that the infrastructure is destroyed by a disaster event.

One should bear in mind that there is often great risk attached to the project and the site staff when rebuilding in disaster ridden areas that are war torn. Besides equipment and materials are hard to be delivered to these areas, another area of concern is the unsafe work environment for site staff. Contractors or project team staff can be kidnapped to stop the project from being rebuilt. Another reason is that they are kidnapped for ransom especially if the project team staff member is a foreigner. A hostile work environment is not conducive to productively and can have devastating consequences on the performance of the project.

SOLUTIONS AND RECOMMENDATIONS

- Poor project management can lead to a project not being completed on time or never at all. Taroun (2014) found that poor project management of schedules was a major reason for such failures.
- Where project schedules are unrealistic, then this may result in challenges and scheduling problems. The act of compressing schedules and unrealistic deadlines demanded from the project team requires that the project team adopts a higher schedule - risk approach.
- When owners demand unrealistic deadlines to complete projects this can cause scheduling problems. A way forward is to make sure a solid schedule is drawn up and signed by the owner and the project company. Unrealistic deadline demands should be discussed and time should be allocated in the scheduling plan to take into account these challenges, delays, strikes and other delays that can upset a project schedule.
- Rework in designs is the chief cause of schedule overruns in mega - projects. The owner changing scope as well as incomplete scope definition are associated with reworking engineering designs that require additional time and funding. A way forward is for upfront careful planning that will result in keep mega - projects on schedule. There should be a signed agreement in place that if the owner changes scope of the project, penalties can be incurred and the owner would have to pay additional costs.
- If the project team does not have a skilled, experienced scheduler there will be problems encounter in the mega - project. A way to avoid this is that skilled, experienced schedulers should be employed from the inception of the mega - projects.
- The greatest shortfall on a mega - project is if the team - leader employs project managers that are difficult to work or who are inexperienced and lack proper skill for that specific mega - project. To avoid this, having the right complement of staff will ensure that there are no delays in a mega - project.
- Strikes, load - shedding, natural disasters and COVID - 19 can have adverse effects on a Mega - project scheduling. To avoid this proper time should be allocated to take into account strikes, load - shedding, traffic - delays due to COVID - 19 road - checks and police patrols. During COVID - 19 lockdown stage 4 in South Africa, only essential services were allowed. People who were medical - staff, the municipal workers who picked up the garbage and waste, police, army and navy and food and medical supply grocery shop personnel, petrol staff and taxi and bus drivers were allowed to run businesses and work. The rest of the country had to stay indoors and could only leave their homes if they needed food and medical supplies or urgent medical assistance. This meant that many projects in the construction and infrastructure development sector had to be shut down. This caused major scheduling delays. Further to that since airports and the harbours were closed, raw materials could not reach the project and delays were incurred. The social distancing aspect made it hard for many jobs that in the infrastructure development sector. The added cost of personnel protective gear was an added cost that were not taken into account in mega - projects as no one could have foreseen the pandemic and the repercussion it would have on work and hu-

man life. Human loss and absenteeism due to being infected with COVID - 19, adds to scheduling delays. With respect to natural disasters, proper insurance should be taken, so that the business is covered as floods, hurricanes, typhoons and earthquakes can create havoc on scheduling and cause major delays.

FUTURE RESEARCH DIRECTIONS

- Socio - economic and transformation factors in mega - projects should be explored further in an attempt continuously improve social transformation, job creation and socio - economic gaps.
- Another pertinent research area is the impact of technology and its benefits in streamlining efficiencies within mega-projects more especially in the project controls domain.
- Further comparative studies of mega - projects in South Africa and the African continent are encouraged in an attempt to support successful infrastructure rollout locally and in Africa. As indicated by leading consultants, high levels of mega - infrastructure requirements are forecast on the African continent for the next few decades.

CONCLUSION

The need for scheduling is an important and distinguishing function in project management. In order for the smooth running of any Mega - project, scheduling needs to be planned and properly implemented by staff who are experienced and well trained. Due to the complexity of a Mega - project the scheduling activity can be challenging. However, a good project manager needs to plan and hire the correct people to undertake a large complex Mega - project. Since scheduling problems can be costly to a project manager, special attention needs to be placed on the staff executing these activities. There needs to be plans in place that supersede scheduling delays, this will safeguard the project management organization and ensure its continued growth and sustainability in a continually changing and volatile industry. The reality of COVID - 19 is here is stay. A good effective project management needs to learn from 2020 and plan for scheduling delays that can occur due to pandemics or disasters. The technological breakthroughs can assist project managers to plan and monitor natural disasters and take preventative measures to safeguard the site, equipment and site personnel.

REFERENCES

Amoatey, C. T., Ameyaw, Y. A., & Adaka, E. (2015). Analysing delay causes and effects in Ghanaian state housing construction projects. *International Journal of Managing Projects in Business*, *8*(1), 198–214. doi:10.1108/IJMPB-04-2014-0035

Anaya-Arenas, A. M., Renaud, J., & Ruiz, A. (2014). Relief distribution networks: A systematic review. *Annals of Operations Research*, *223*(1), 53–79. doi:10.100710479-014-1581-y

Andersen, B., Samset, K., & Welde, M. (2016). Low estimates - high stakes, underestimation of costs at the front - end of projects. *International Journal of Managing Projects in Business*, *9*(1), 171–193. doi:10.1108/IJMPB-01-2015-0008

Arau'zo, J., Pajares, J., & Lopez-Paredes, A. (2010). Simulating the dynamic scheduling of project portfolios. *Simulation Modelling Practice and Theory*, *18*(10), 1428–1441. doi:10.1016/j.simpat.2010.04.008

Berg, M. E., & Karlsen, J. T. (2014). How project managers can encourage and develop positive emotions in project teams. *International Journal of Managing Projects in Business*, *7*(3), 449–472. doi:10.1108/IJMPB-01-2013-0003

Biesenthal, C., Clegg, S., Mahalingam, A., & Sankaran, S. (2018). Applying Institutional Theories to Managing Mega-projects. *International Journal of Project Management*, *36*(1), 43–54. doi:10.1016/j.ijproman.2017.06.006

Blackhard, B. W. (2006). Hazards, Disasters and U. S. Emergency Management: An Introduction. FEMA Emergency Management Higher Education Project working draft course.

Brockmann, C. (2009). Mega - Projects: Getting the Job Done. *Proceedings - LEAD 2009 Conference.*

Capka, J. R. (2004). Mega-projects: Managing a Public Journey. *Public Roads*, *68*(1), 1–9.

Chang, Y., Wilkinson, S., Brunsdon, D., Seville, E., & Potangaroa, R. (2011). An integrated approach: Managing resources for post - disaster reconstruction. *Disasters*, *35*(4), 739–765. doi:10.1111/j.1467-7717.2011.01240.x PMID:21913934

Chavez, M. S. (2016). Hurricane preparedness in a construction site: A framework to assess the construction companies' current practices. *FIU Electronic Theses and Dissertations.*, *3047*. Advance online publication. doi:10.25148/etd.FIDC001187

Deckro, R. F., Winkofsky, E. P., Hebert, J. E., & Gagnon, R. (1991). A decomposition approach to multi - project scheduling. *European Journal of Operational Research*, *51*(1), 110–118. doi:10.1016/0377-2217(91)90150-T

ECSA. (2015). Software architecture. In *9th European Conference*. Engineering Council of South Africa.

El-Abbasy, M. S., Elazouni, A., & Zayed, T. (2017). Generic scheduling optimization model for multiple construction projects. *Journal of Computing in Civil Engineering*, *31*(4), 4017003. doi:10.1061/(ASCE)CP.1943-5487.0000659

Elmaghraby, S. (1977). *Task networks: project planning and control by network models*. John Wiley and Sons.

Flyvbjerg, B. (2009). Survival of the fittest: Why the worst infrastructure gets built - and what we can do about it. *Oxford Review of Economic Policy*, *25*(3), 344–367. doi:10.1093/oxrep/grp024

Flyvbjerg, B. (2014). What You Should Know about Mega-projects and Why: An Overview. *Project Management Journal*, *45*(2), 6–19. doi:10.1002/pmj.21409

Flyvbjerg, B., Bruzelius, N., & Rothengatter, W. (2003). *Mega-projects and Risk: An Anatomy of Ambition*. Cambridge University Press. doi:10.1017/CBO9781107050891

Fung, I. W. H., Tam, V. W. Y., Lo, T. Y., & Lu, L. L. H. (2009). Developing a Risk Assessment Model for Construction Safety. *International Journal of Project Management, 28*(6), 593–600. doi:10.1016/j.ijproman.2009.09.006

González, P., González, V., Molenaar, K., & Orozco, F. (2014). Analysis of causes of delay and time performance in construction projects. *Journal of Construction Engineering and Management, 140*(1), 1–9. doi:10.1061/(ASCE)CO.1943-7862.0000721

Gospodinov, E. (2001). *Statement by Encho Gospodinov, Head of Delegation*. The International Federation of Red Cross and Red Crescent Societies, United Nations General Assembly, 25th special session on Human Settlement (HABITAT II), New York.

Guha-Sapir, D., Hoyois, P., & Below, R. (2015). Annual Disaster Statistical Review 2014. The numbers and trends. Centre for Research on the Epidemiology of Disasters.

Haleem, A., Javaid, M., & Vaishya, R. (2020). Effects of COVID 19 pandemic in daily life. *Current Medicine Research and Practice, 1*(1), 1–2. doi:10.1016/j.cmrp.2020.03.011 PMID:32292804

Hällgren, M., & Wilson, T. (2008). The nature and management of crises in construction projects: Project - as - practice observations. *International Journal of Project Management, 26*(8), 830–838. doi:10.1016/j.ijproman.2007.10.005

Ham, Y., Lee, S. J., & Chowdhury, A. G. (2017). Imaging - to - simulation framework for improving disaster preparedness of construction projects and neighbouring communities. *Computing in Civil Engineering, 2017*, 230–237. Advance online publication. doi:10.1061/9780784480830.029

Hazini, K., Dehghan, R., & Ruwanpura, J. (2013). A heuristic method to determine optimum degree of activity accelerating and overlapping in schedule compression. *Canadian Journal of Civil Engineering, 40*(4), 382–392. doi:10.1139/cjce-2012-0380

Hazini, K., Dehghan, R., & Ruwanpura, J. (2014). An evolutionary optimization method to determine optimum degree of activity accelerating and overlapping in schedule compression. *Canadian Journal of Civil Engineering, 41*(4), 333–342. doi:10.1139/cjce-2013-0194

Holland & Knight LLP. (2020). *A Look at COVID - 19 Impacts on the Construction Industry*. Available at: C:\Users\Naidoova\Desktop\ALookatCOVID-19ImpactsontheConstructionIndustry_Insights_Holland&Knight.html

Huang, C., Wang, Y., Li, X., Ren, L., Zhao, J., Hu, Y., Zhang, L., Fan, G., Xu, J., Gu, X., & Cheng, Z. (2020). Articles clinical features of patients infected with 2019 novel coronavirus in Wuhan, China. *Lancet, 6736*(20), 1–10.

Ibrahim, C. K. I. C., Costello, S. B., & Wilkinson, S. (2015). Key indicators influencing the management of team integration in construction projects. *International Journal of Managing Projects in Business, 8*(2), 300–323. doi:10.1108/IJMPB-04-2014-0028

Jo'zefowska, J., & Weglarz, J. (2006). *Perspectives in modern project scheduling*. Springer. doi:10.1007/978-0-387-33768-5

Kim, S. Y., & Leachman, R. C. (1993). Multi - project scheduling with explicit lateness costs. *IIE Transactions*, *25*(2), 34–44. doi:10.1080/07408179308964275

Komendantova, N., Patt, A., Barras, L., & Battaglini, A. (2012). Perception of risks in renewable energy projects: The case of concentrated solar power in North Africa. *Energy Policy*, *40*(1), 103–109. doi:10.1016/j.enpol.2009.12.008

Langer, N., Slaughter, S. A., & Mukhopadhyay, T. (2008). Project manager's skills and project success in IT outsourcing. *ICIS 2008 Proceedings, 147.*

Lee, G. K. L., & Chan, E. H. W. (2009). A sustainability evaluation of government - led urban renewal projects. *Facilities*, *26*(13), 526–541.

Li, Y., Lu, Y., Ma, L., & Kwak, Y. H. (2018). Evolutionary governance for mega - event projects (MEPs): A case study of the world expo 2010 in China. *Project Management Journal*, *49*(1), 57–78. doi:10.1177/875697281804900105

Locatelli, G., Littau, P., Brookes, N. J., & Mancini, M. (2014). Project characteristics enabling the success of mega-projects: An empirical investigation in the energy sector. *Procedia: Social and Behavioral Sciences*, *119*(1), 625–634. doi:10.1016/j.sbspro.2014.03.070

Marks, M. G., & Ellis, L. A. (2013). Delays in major agricultural infrastructure projects in Guyana: Causes and proposed solutions. *The West Indian Journal of Engineering*, *36*(1), 79–85.

McKinsey. (2016). *Bridging global infrastructure gaps*. McKinsey Global Institute. Retrieved from: https://www.mckinsey.com/industries/capital-projects-and-infrastructure/our-insights/management

Merrow, E. W. (2011). *Industrial Mega-projects: Concepts, Strategies and Practices for Success*. John Wiley and Sons.

Mubarak, S. A. (2010). *Construction Project Scheduling and Control*. John Wiley and Sons. doi:10.1002/9780470912171

Naidoo, V. (2021). SME Sustainability in South Africa Post - COVID - 19. In Handbook of Research on Sustaining SMEs and Entrepreneurial Innovation in the Post - COVID - 19 Era. IGI Global.

Narbaev, T., & De-Marco, A. (2013). *Combination of growth model and earned schedule to Forecast Project Cost at Completion*. American Society of Civil Engineers.

New York Times. (2010). *BP Used Riskier Method to Seal Well Before Blast*. https://www.nytimes.com/2010/05/27/us/27rig.html?_r=1

New York Times. (2011). *Chile Mining Accident 2010*. http://topics.nytimes.com/top/reference/timestopics/subjects/c/chile_mining_accident_2010/index.html

Nguyen, L. H., Shen, H., Ershoff, D., Afifi, A. A., & Bourque, L. B. (2006). Exploring the causal relationship between exposure to the 1994 Northridge earthquake and pre - and post - earthquake preparedness activities. *Earthquake Spectra*, *22*(3), 569–587. doi:10.1193/1.2219108

Nijaki, K., & Worrel, G. (2012). Procurement for sustainable local economic development. *International Journal of Public Sector Management*, *25*(2), 133–153. doi:10.1108/09513551211223785

Nipa, T. J., Kermanshachi, S., Patel, R., & Tafazzoli, M. (2020). Disaster preparedness education: construction curriculum requirements to increase students' preparedness in pre - and post - disaster activities. *Associated Schools of Construction (ASC) International Conference.*

Norouzi, G., Heydari, M., Noori, S., & Bagherpour, M. (2015). Mathematical modelling for scheduling and determining success probability of research projects considering complex - fuzzy networks. *Journal of Applied Mathematics, 1*(1), 1–12. doi:10.1155/2015/809216

Oliomogbe, G. O., & Smith, N. J. (2012). Value in mega-projects, Organisation, Technology, and Management in Construction. *International Journal (Toronto, Ont.), 4*(3), 617–624.

Pardede, T., & Tetsuo, K. (2007). *Planning for post - disaster recovery: lesson from Aceh post - tsunami recovery.* Department of Urban Engineering, University of Tokyo. Accessed from:http://rdarc.itakura.toyo.ac.jp/webdav/ask/public/ACP2007/togu.pdf

PMI. (2013). *A guide to the project management body of knowledge, PMBOK* (5th ed.). Project Management Institute.

PriceWaterhouseCoopers. (2014). *Project success: Portfolio and change management.* Retrieved from: http://pwc.com/gx/en/service/advisory/consulting/portfolio-programme-management/global-pp.msurvey-2014.html

Priemus, H., Flyvberg, B., & van Wee, B. (2016). Introduction. In *Decision - Making on Mega - projects. Cost - Benefit Analysis, Planning and Innovation.* Edward Elgar.

Project Management Institute (PMI) Inc. (2007). *Construction Extension to the PMBOK Guide* (3rd ed.). PMI Publisher.

Roe, P. (2014). *Factors which contribute to successful projects.* Prepared for the Association for Project Management. Retrieved from: www.apm.org.uk

Rouhanizadeh, B., Kermanshachi, S., & Dhamangaonkar, V. (2019). Identification and categorization of policy and legal barriers to long - term timely post - disaster reconstruction. *Journal of Legal Affairs and Dispute Resolution in Engineering and Construction, 11*(3), 04519014. doi:10.1061/(ASCE)LA.1943-4170.0000307

Ruuska, I., Artto, K., Aaltonen, K., & Lehtonen, P. (2009). Dimensions of distance in a project network: Exploring Olkiluoto 3 nuclear power plant project. *International Journal of Project Management, 27*(2), 142–153. doi:10.1016/j.ijproman.2008.09.003

Safapour, E., & Kermanshachi, S. (2019). Identification and categorization of factors affecting duration of post - disaster reconstruction of interdependent transportation systems. *ASCE Construction Research Congress (CRC).*

Said, H., Kandil, A., & Cai, H. (2012). Agent - based simulation of labour emergency evacuation in high - rise building construction sites. *Construction Research Congress.* 10.1061/9780784412329.111

Sawyer, M. (2012). *Vico software integrating construction.* Available at: www.vicosoftware.com

Shash, A. A., & Ahcom, J. (2006). Organizational aspects of planning and scheduling subsystem. *Journal of Construction Research*, *7*(1/2), 247–265. doi:10.1142/S160994510600058X

Sheehan, L., & Hewitt, K. (1969). *A Pilot Survey of Global Natural Disasters of the Past Twenty Years*. Natural Hazard Research Publisher.

Siriwardena, M., Malalgoda, C., Thayaparan, M., Amaratunga, D., & Keraminiyage, K. (2013). Disaster resilient built environment: Role of lifelong learning and the implications for higher education. *International Journal of Strategic Property Management*, *17*(2), 174–187. doi:10.3846/1648715X.2013.806373

Spittal, M. J., Walkey, F. H., McClure, J., Siegert, R. J., & Ballantyne, K. E. (2006). The Earthquake Readiness Scale: The development of a valid and reliable unifactorial measure. *Natural Hazards*, *39*(1), 15–29. doi:10.100711069-005-2369-9

Taroun, A. (2014). Towards a Better Modelling and Assessment of Construction Risk: Insights from a Literature Review. *International Journal of Project Management*, *32*(1), 101–115. doi:10.1016/j.ijproman.2013.03.004

Tilos. (2012). *TILOS linear project*. Available at: www.tilos.org

Varajao, J., Dominguez, C., Ribeiro, P., & Paiva, A. (2014). Critical success aspects in project management: Similarities and differences between the construction and software industry. *Technical Gazette*, *21*(3), 586–587.

Wallace, L., Keil, M., & Rai, A. (2004). How software project risk affects project performance: An investigation of the dimensions of risk and exploratory model. *Decision Sciences*, *1*(35), 289–321. doi:10.1111/j.00117315.2004.02059.x

Wang, H., Hubbard, B. J., & Hubbard, S. (2014). RFID applied to supply chain logistics in disaster recovery. In *Proceedings of the 10th International Conference of the International Institute for Infrastructure Resilience and Reconstruction (I3R2) 20 - 22* (pp. 207 - 211). West Lafayette, IN: Purdue University. 10.5703/1288284315373

Warah, R. (2002). Withering heights. *Habitat Debate*, *4*(7), 7–15.

World Bank. (2001). *World Bank and Asian Development Bank Complete Preliminary Gujarat Earthquake Damage Assessment and Recovery Plan*. Available at: https://www.worldbank.org/gujarat, https://www.adb.org/

Worldometers. (2020). *COVID - 19 coronavirus pandemic*. Available at: https://www.worldometers.info/coronavirus/?utm_campaign=CSauthorbio

Zhang, L., & Fan, W. (2013). Improving performance of construction projects: A project manager's emotional intelligence Approach. *Engineering, Construction, and Architectural Management*, *20*(2), 195–207. doi:10.1108/09699981311303044

Ziek, J., & Anderson, D. J. (2015). Communication dialogue and project management. *International Journal of Managing Projects in Business*, *8*(4), 788–803. doi:10.1108/IJMPB-04-2014-0034

KEY TERMS AND DEFINITIONS

COVID-19: It is a deadly infectious disease caused by the coronavirus. It has led to the biggest world pandemic known to man in this century.

Infrastructure: Refers to roads, power-supply, harbours to name but a few that sustains the economic viability and growth of a country.

Mega-Projects: Refers to expensive, complex, large-scale projects that run into billions. Diverse public and private stakeholder involvement is prevalent.

Scheduling: Refers to a vital function in project management. Some activities include planning and developing schedules, allocating resources and times, making sure delays are managed, prevented and controlled. Make sure milestones are met.

Skills: Refers to staff on mega-projects having the necessary expertise to do their task well. There are soft skills and hard skills. It is important especially in project leadership to have both.

Terrorism: It is when a person or a group claiming to be a part of an organization use unlawful tactics, force, threats and violence against another society, state, or groups of civilians.

Training: It is about skilling project management staff with the right knowledge, attitudes, and expertise to do their job in an efficient and cost-effective manner.

War: War is a brutal armed conflict against a government, state, or society.

Chapter 13
A Case Study of Knowledge Management and Organizational Culture in an Undergraduate Software Development Team Project

Kamalendu Pal
https://orcid.org/0000-0001-7158-6481
City, University of London, UK

ABSTRACT

People work in software development projects to bundle the human resources and use the systematic approach to share system development knowledge. One can view knowledge as personalized related to facts, procedures, concepts, interpretations, ideas, and judgments. This way, knowledge is the outcome of the cognitive processing of information. Knowledge can be transferred from a source to a receiver. The collaborative knowledge-sharing mechanism is known as knowledge management (KM) in the software industry. The software developers can communicate with, learn from, and solve problems with other participating team members. The organizational culture is an essential factor in knowledge management success since it influences how team members learn and share knowledge. This chapter presents a case study that aimed to compare, in practice, the relationship between the KM cycle (SECI – socialization, externalization, combination, and internalization model) and the organizational culture through the competing values framework (CVF).

INTRODUCTION

Software system development has transitioned from a mainly individual activity of designing standalone software systems to a predominantly distributed and collaborative approach that depends on or contributes to large and complicated software ecosystems (Pal, 2020) (Pal, 2019). Many software project members

DOI: 10.4018/978-1-7998-7872-8.ch013

now contribute to multiple projects. Due to this work practice, project boundaries blur, not just in terms of their work and how they design and develop software but also their communication channels and knowledge management practice. This way, software designers want to collaborate with, learn from and co-design with other designers, creating a participatory culture within distributed software development activities. Many software designers care to bother about the programming they need to develop and the skills they gain, and their knowledge and intimacy with other participating team members. These work practices, in turn, demand more collaborative software design and development activities (Pal, & Karakostas, 2020).

Encouraging distributed and collaborative software system analysis and design requires appropriate communication mechanisms. Communication is a method of imparting or exchanging information by writing, speaking, combining, or other ways. Communication-related research issues have attracted tremendous interest from ancient time, and it has evolved considerably. One of the prominent human discourse scholars, Corax, suggested the need for "speakers to produce an effect in listeners" (Hinks, 1940) (Kennedy, 1959). Such a requirement serves through the ancient time in the views of familiar rhetoricians, logicians, philosophers, and academic books put forward a pivotal question: how does one individual communicate effectively? In answering this question, subsequent academics and practitioners add, amend, or critique the research work of predecessors. Modern researchers are also expressing their views with the traditional approaches to business communication effectiveness. For example, Monge (1973) calls for a "*dynamic*" way to assess the effectiveness and suggests that theory construction for communication in the future should focus on a new set of variables and employ a new set of analytic techniques.

This way, supporting software professionals' collaboration and communication requires new generation tools (e.g., web-based applications, telephone, email, WhatsApp, and Zoom video conferencing system) are used. A simple diagrammatic representation of some of the communication channels is shown in Figure 1. The richness and ability of these tools are enhancing today's global software development practice. Software professionals need to learn new skills to use these tools. Besides, these communication tools allow creativity in work practice, promote engagement, and help software development participation. This engagement is also demanded cultural issues of the global software development team.

Understanding global software development team-based culture is fundamental to realizing what goes on in software development teams, running them, and improving them (Schein, 1992). Team-based software development culture is defined as the shared assumptions, beliefs, and expected behaviours (norms) present in a global team. Most organization development scholars and observers recognize that organizational culture has a powerful effect on organizations' performance and long-term effectiveness. Cameron and Quinn (1999) present that what differentiates successful teams from others is their organizational culture.

Within this new dimension of software development practice, software creation combines externalized knowledge (e.g., document exchange, programming instruction, technical guidelines to tackle software design) and the tacit knowledge that resides in group-members heads (e.g., operational practices, design constraints). In real-world communication and software development, dedicated tools (e.g., Computer-Aided Software Engineering (CASE)) help developers to create and share (i.e., externalize) tacit knowledge in a highly collaborative environment.

Figure 1. Some of the communication channels in global software development

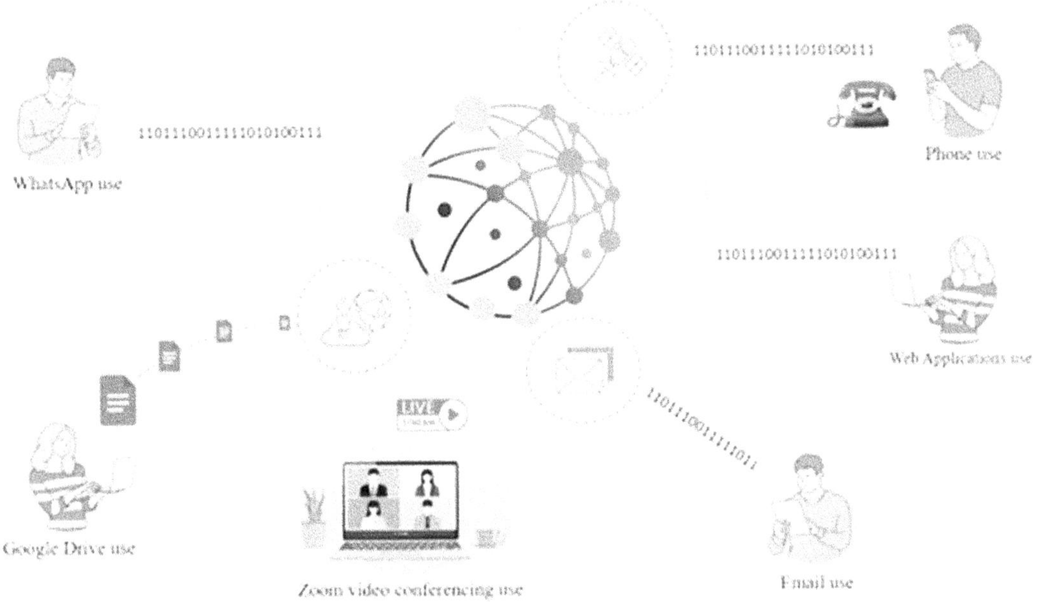

Organizations in software development practice require intensive use of knowledge in business, operations, methods, knowledge of new technologies, lessons learnt, and appropriate management of resources and times in the handling of software design and development of projects (Levy & Hazzan, 2009) (Rus et al., 2001) (Bjornson & Dingsoyr, 2008). This way, knowledge is not static in the organization; instead, it is in constant growth as diverse projects are developed, so organizations often have difficulties finding the appropriate source of knowledge and use. Software development needs a range of effort to gather the system requirements, analyze, validate the collected requirements, and design the system specifications. Simultaneously, the activities are affected by not bearing in mind the past mistakes, which increased the time and cost of implementing the previous software development projects (Corbin et al., 2007). Also, the lack of experience in software development project planning led to difficulties (e.g., taking more time than planned, abandoned projects, spiralling unpredicted cost). With these difficulties, the software system's quality may be compromised, and ultimately, the customer may be dissatisfied (Rus & Lindvall, 2002) (Bjormson & Dingsoyr, 2008).

Knowledge management is a crucial mechanism to foster improvements in software development processes. Organizational culture is an essential factor in knowledge management's success since it influences how software developers learn and share knowledge within a team. The Competing Values Framework (CVF) is a widely used method to assess organizational culture as a predictor of quality improvement implementation (Cameron & Quinn, 1999), staff and user satisfaction, and team functioning, among other outcomes. The research in this chapter used exploratory and confirmatory factor analyses to examine the underlying data structure from a CVF instrument. This research analyzed data from students' opinion surveys conducted during the delivery of a team-based software development project.

This chapter's main objectives are: (i) investigate the importance of communication channels and their use in team-based software development, (ii) address the knowledge management practice-related issues in software development, focusing on the project planning stage, so that knowledge learnt is used to benefit the software development organization (or team) and its future staff (or team-member) to utilize this acquired knowledge, and (iii) try to establish the relevance of KM on organizational culture, teamwork, enhancing learning and sharing of skills and software deployment experience.

A research-based justification is that organizational culture affects how organization staff learn, acquire, and share knowledge (Knapp & Yu, 1999). Besides, researchers (Rubenstein-Montano et al., 2000) recommend that KM practices need to affirmative the organizational culture. Academics and practitioners (Gray & Densten, 2006) (Rai, 2011) presented a theoretical model that relates the KM cycle (SECI – Socialization, Externalization, Combination, and Internalization model) (Nonaka & Takeuchi, 1995) and the organizational culture by using the Competing Values Framework (CVF) (Cameron & Quinn, 1999). This chapter presents a case study of an undergraduate software development team project to assess KM and organizational culture practices. This case study for software design and development duration was around three months. Twenty-one students expressed their views regarding team project communication channel uses, KM, and organization culture-related issues.

The remaining chapter is organized as follows. Section 2 describes global software development practice background in recent decades, an overview of knowledge management, and the CVF model. Section 3 explains the organizational culture and its relationship with knowledge management practice. It also includes knowledge management processes, the relevance of knowledge management, dynamic interaction between tacit and explicit knowledge, and coordination and communication in software development practice. 4 discusses the research method for the current case study and presents the case study results. Section 5 presents the future scope of research. Section 6 concludes the chapter with concluding remarks.

BACKGROUND OF SOFTWARE DEVELOPMENT RELATED ISSUES

In recent decades, software development practice is changing rapidly for economic and social issues. One of these critical issues is outsourcing software design and development practice. Globalization of software design and development projects (and practices) to low-cost economies has become the norm for many software developments companies. Commercial enterprises use an outsourcing strategy for their computer applications development to achieve and maintain economic advantage through different technical and commercial advantages (Herbsleb, 2007) (Grinter et al., 1999). Also, the radical innovation in the availability of various communication tools and their accessibility to use remotely located competent workforce has attracted globalization of software design and development activities (O'Brien, 2002).

The professionally skilled workforce available in low-cost countries attracts attention for outsourcing software development applications (Toaff, 2002) (Carmel & Tjia, 2005), thus allowing outsourcing companies to minimize software procurement and maintenance costs. This way, the prospect of continuous software development by leveraging temporal differences has provided the opportunity to implement the value-added corporate strategies (Toaff, 2002) (Carmel & Tjia, 2005). These strategies have ensured twenty-four hours in a day and seven days in week support between various development locations throughout the year (Espinosa & Carmel, 2003) (Deshpande & Richardson, 2009). However, outsourcing software development to organizations at different outsourcing destinations is not a simple work (Carmel, 1999) (Karolak, 1999) (Herbsleb & Moitra, 2001) (Viktor et al., 2007). The impact of global distance comprising geographic, cultural, and temporal distance introduces many challenges between software development teams and team members. These 'distance' factors can impede global software development projects (Erran, 2006) (Casey et al., 2008). Hence, globally outsourced software development management has been a complex and challenging task (Lanubile et al., 2003).

With the emergence of technologies in a world that has become increasingly globalized, the relationship between culture and management of software development remote work has become an unavoidable issue that requires to be taken into consideration (Watson et al., 1994). Globalization of software design and development works has introduced cultural and demographic diversity, preventing smooth team operation (Beise, 2004) as geographic and temporal distance shortens opportunities for direct cooperation and contact (Carmel, 1999) (Prikladnicki et al., 2003). Team operational culture is considered one of the essential issues in global software development (Carmel, 1999). Cultural diversity is often considered a limitation within distributed development teams (Baugher et al., 2000) (Larkey, 1996). This variety manifests in many forms, such as language and ethnic diversities, political and national differences, individual perceptions, work ethics, and workforce motivation related issues (Kotlarsky & Oshri, 2005) (Holmstrom et al., 2006).

Cultural distance is considered to increase with the degree of cultural differences between geographically distributed teams (Carmel & Agarwal, 2001) and consequently negatively impact the level of understanding and appreciation of remote software development teams and team members (Hayes, 2002). Linguistic distance utmost the ability for coherent communication to occur (Jensen et al., 2007) and can impact team members' formation (Pauleen & Yoong, 2001). Therefore, managing virtual software development teams whose members are geographically in different locations and linguistically dispersed is a challenging task (Ebert et al., 2001) due to the various constraints in this operation (Gurung & Prater, 2006). Cameron and Quinn (1999) present a new dimension in successful teams and their organizational culture.

Within this new dimension of software development practice, software creation combines externalized knowledge (e.g., document exchange, programming instruction, technical guidelines to tackle software design) and the tacit knowledge that resides in group-members heads (e.g., operational practices, design constraints). In real-world communication and software development, dedicated tools (e.g., CASE) help developers create and share externalized and tacit knowledge in a highly collaborative environment. Appropriate KM practice plays an essential role in team-based software design and development. This way, KM is emerging as a management responsibility and consequently software development projects are increasingly a considerable amount of resources to support the acquisition, storage, sharing, and retrieval of knowledge in their daily activities.

The research in this chapter examines how team-based software development organizational mindset – whether a business is perceived to view talent as fixed or malleable – functions as a core belief that predicts organizational culture and employees' trust and commitment. In simply, organizational culture includes a team's expectations, experiences, philosophy, and values that guide member behaviour and is expressed in team-member self-image, working practice within the team, interactions with the outside team boundary, and ultimate team achievement expectations. Culture can be defined on specific properties, including shared customs, operational norms, unwritten and written rules used for regular business practices. The definition of culture also includes the organization's vision, values, norms, systems, symbols, language, assumptions, beliefs, and habits (Needle, 2004).

CULTURE AND KNOWLEDGE MANAGEMENT

There are different types of culture (e.g., organizational, occupational, national, regional). Any of these might have immense impacts on global software development purposes. Social science researchers conducted massive research on how cultures differ, the dimensions of importance, and the resulting clustering of similar and different countries. Geert Hofstede (Geert, 1984) and Edward Hall (Edward, 1976) are among the most prominent, and they developed ten dimensions (e.g., reverting hierarchy, individualism versus collectivism, task-oriented or relation-focused, risk avoidance, long-term orientation, space, or social-distances vary by culture, material goods, friendship, time, agreement).

Most global software companies agree that knowledge is an essential asset for success and survival in an increasingly competitive and global market. Knowledge management is not a product nor a solution that organizations can buy off the shelf. Knowledge management takes a substantial amount of time to implement for an organization, and it has a lot to do with human relationships as a business practice and information technology (IT).

Knowledge Management Processes

Alavi and Leidner (2001) describe a company's knowledge management processes, based on what they call a knowledge system, the individuals and groups that share their knowledge in a company, as shown in Figure 2. In this knowledge system, the authors elaborate on the different activities related to knowledge management. This whole web of knowledge management activities is constructed on top of the modes of knowledge creation outlined by Nonaka (1994). On an individual level, every person has tacit and explicit knowledge. The knowledge is transferred back and forth through externalization and internalization within the individual or through combination and socialization between individuals. However, similarly to tacit and explicit knowledge of individuals, every group individual (e.g., team members) has two types of memory: episodic and semantic.

A group's semantic memory represents the available explicated knowledge, for example, a document on a file server. The explicit knowledge can be made available for the rest of the group by transferring it to its semantic memory. Also, an individual can increase their explicit knowledge by accessing the group's semantic memory. For this learning from the group's semantic memory, the group's episodic memory is critical.

Episodic memory represents the collection of shared experiences of the group. Every individual contributes parts of their tacit knowledge to it. Beyond the interaction of people is the utilization of knowledge. The knowledge application is always based on an individual's tacit knowledge. At the same time, when applying knowledge, the individual learns from that, which feeds back to the individual's tacit knowledge.

Additionally, the application of knowledge can also be based on the semantic memory directly, which feeds back to the group's episodic memory. This system of knowledge sharing among individuals in a group occurs in different areas of a company. Each of these groups then shares their knowledge via a group dialogue. The knowledge management process involves the following actions:

- Knowledge gathering - acquisition and collection of the knowledge to be managed.
- Knowledge organization and structuring -imposing a structure on the knowledge acquired to manage it effectively.

- Knowledge refinement - correcting, updating, adding, defining knowledge, in short, maintaining knowledge.
- Knowledge distribution - bringing the knowledge to the professionals who need it.

Relevance of Knowledge Management in Software Development

As software development is a very abstract engineering discipline, knowledge management is an important issue. When developing software, a high degree of coordination (Kraut and Streeter, 1995) and management (Sommerville, 2001; Pressman, 2000) become vital tasks. Because the focus is to solve specific problems, software projects' organization often differs enormously from one to the other (Mockus et al., 2002). Sveiby (Sveiby, 1997) points out that most companies face similar problems in administrating their intellectual capital. He explains that employees are usually highly educated and qualified professionals whose regular job is using their competence to develop software. Their primary resource is their knowledge; therefore, they are called knowledge workers.

Figure 2. Knowledge transfer among individuals in a group

Furthermore, knowledge management becomes a crucial activity because knowledge is such an essential asset in these companies, so-called knowledge organizations. It counts for software development. Hence, knowledge management for software development companies is a broad field with various approaches (Aurum et al., 2008).

Rus and Lindvall (2002) describe three aspects of software development supported by knowledge management: Core software engineering activities, product & project memory, and learning & improvement. The core activities of software engineering contain the management of documents or competencies as well as software re-use.

With product and project memory, the authors refer to the evolution of software, e.g., with the help of systems for version control, change management or design documentation. Finally, the learning and improvement include a recording of results and experiences. The reason is to learn from that and improve future decisions or activities. The desire to improve in these three areas of concern motivates knowledge management in software development (Pal & Williams, 2021).

To conduct knowledge management successfully, many different approaches are possible and documented. Liebowitz and Megbolugbe (2003) propose a framework for implementing knowledge management, which combines an activity cycle of knowledge management levels and the resulting knowledge objects. The different knowledge management levels are conceptualization, reflection, acting and review. Each of these leads to the four knowledge objects: goals, risks, constraints, or measures. The diversity of dimensions illustrates the complexity of knowledge management (Pal & Willisons, 2021).

Information systems applied to manage a company's knowledge or support managing a company's knowledge are referred to as knowledge management systems. Alavi and Leidner (2001) conducted a literature review and illustrated six perspectives on knowledge with their implications (see table 1). They identify the differences in perception of knowledge and describe a perspective on knowledge management and the knowledge management system.

Table 1. Knowledge perspectives and their implications

Perspectives		Implications for Knowledge Management (KM)	Implications for Knowledge Management Systems (KMS)
Knowledge (data and information)	Data is facts, raw numbers. Information is processed / interpreted data. Knowledge is personalized information.	KM focuses on exposing individuals to potentially helpful information and facilitating the assimilation of information.	KMS will not appear radically different from the existing information system (IS) but will be extended to help users collect data or information.
State of team member mind	Knowledge is the art of knowing and utilizing.	KM incorporate improvement of an individual's learning and understanding through the provision of information.	Information technology (IT) is to provide access to sources of knowledge rather than knowledge itself.
Object	Knowledge is an item of interest to be processed and preserved.	Key KM objective is creating and managing knowledge for the team or organization.	The role of IT involves gathering, storing, and transferring knowledge.
Process	Knowledge is a process of applying expertise.	KM focuses on knowledge flows and the process of creation, sharing, and distributing knowledge.	The role of information and communication technology is to create a link with sources of knowledge to generate and use.
Access to Information	Knowledge needs to be accessed for contextual information.	KM focuses on organized access to and retrieval of content.	The role of IT is to provide effective search and retrieval mechanisms for locating relevant information.
Ability	Knowledge is the power to influence action in a context.	KM helps to build main competencies and appreciation of strategic know-how.	The role of IT is to improve intellectual capital by supporting the development of individual and organizational competencies.

Dynamic Interaction Between Tacit and Explicit Knowledge

The knowledge management's main objective is to capture new domain-specific knowledge and use existing knowledge to make it usable in future use, preserve and spread them, and provide practical strategies for new contexts. Moreover, knowledge may be categorized into two distinct types: explicit and tacit. The tacit knowledge is subjective and domain-oriented for human perception, experience, personal values. Also, explicit knowledge is considered objective and transmittable by formal and systematic languages.

Organizational Culture and Knowledge Management

The dynamic interaction and changes between tacit and explicit knowledge proceed to a knowledge enrichment model based on SECI (Socialization, Externalization, Combination, and Internalization). The SECI model concentrate on generating, manipulating and maintaining knowledge (Levy & Hazzan, 2009): (i) socialization is the contextual experience of the collaboration process, in which a team member's tacit knowledge is distributed to another team member by observation, collaboration, cooperation or behaviour mimicking; (ii) externalization reforms tacit knowledge into explicit knowledge, and this is crucial on creation processes because concepts and ideas are generated; (iii) combination creates new explicit knowledge by putting together varieties of explicit knowledge; (iv) internalization is the process that conversions of explicit knowledge into tacit knowledge, which is also paving the way of individual learning.

Besides, software developing organizational culture is crucial to inspire interactions between team members and facilitate knowledge flow (O'Dell & Grayson, 1989). The competing values framework (CVF) is a well-known theoretical model on organizational culture-related research and its reliability and effectiveness in different application domains (Cameron & Quinn, 1999). A simple view of CVF is shown in Figure 3.

The CVF main objectives are to diagnose and trigger the changes in the organizational culture while the organizations grow and experience external environment pressure (Cameron & Quinn, 1999). Four different types of culture emerge from the CVF model (Cameron & Quinn, 1999): Clan, Adhocracy, Market, and Hierarchy, as described briefly in Table 1.

Based on the classification of the four different CVF cultures, Cameron and Quinn (Cameron & Quinn, 1999) reported and validated the organizational culture assessment mechanism. This mechanism uses a questionnaire to identify and establish an organizational culture profile. By utilizing this mechanism, it is possible to find out the current organizational profile.

Gray and Densten (Gray & Densten, 2006) and Rai (2011) proposed a theoretical model integrating the CVF and the SECI model. According to Gray and Densten (Gray & Densten, 2006), this interconnection provides an opportunity to justify and acknowledge the consequence of organizational culture on the organizational knowledge treatment process. Researchers (Gray & Densten, 2006) (Rai, 2011) conclude that: (i) organizations of clan culture are likely to focus on knowledge socialization; (ii) organizations of adhocracy culture is likely to focus on knowledge externalization; (iii) organizations of market culture are likely to focus on knowledge combination, and (iv) organizations of hierarchy culture is likely to focus on knowledge internalization.

Figure 3. Competing value framework

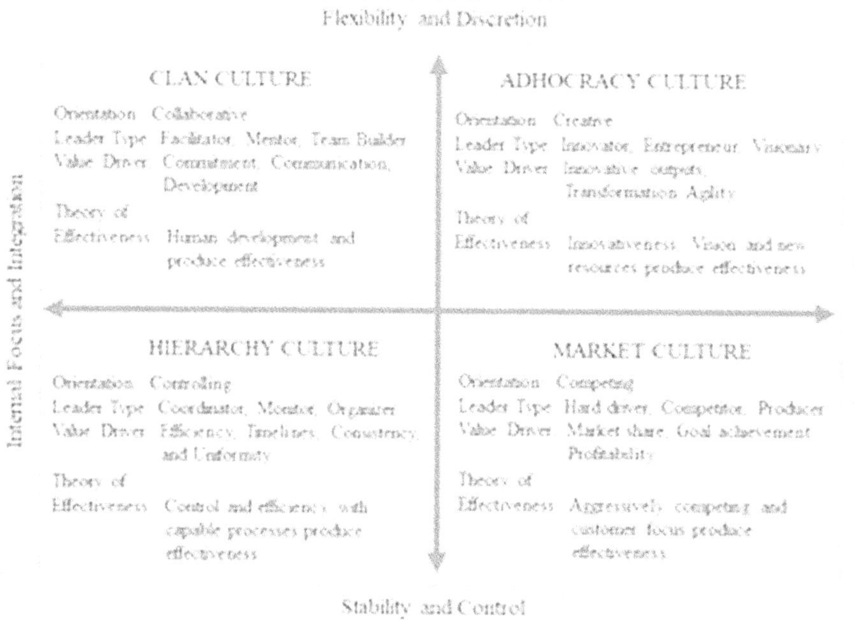

Table 2. The CVF model of cultures

Category of Culture	Description
Clan Culture	This culture is internally oriented, and it focuses on reinforcement by a flexible structure. An ideal clan culture retains its power by using trust and commitment. This culture encourages teamwork and communication among team members. Managers are treated as mentors.
Adhocracy Culture	This type of culture is externally oriented, and a very flexible organizational structure supports it. Team members are persuaded to mitigate risks and create a new strategy for innovative ideas.
Market Culture	The Market Culture is externally oriented and very much guided by organizational structure. This culture demands competitiveness to meet stakeholders' expectations and is oriented. To assist high levels of performance, clear goals and rewards are systems encouraged.
Hierarchy Culture	The Hierarchy Culture, referred to as the internal process perspective, is characterized by values that highlight predictability, control, and internal focus. Team managers maintain control through standard operating practices and procedures.

COORDINATION AND COMMUNICATION IN SOFTWARE DEVELOPMENT

Coordination between software development team members is one of the most challenging ways to improve software systems design and development. A group of researchers (Kraut & Streeter, 1995) argue that the software design and development industry has been in difficulties mode for its entire existence, and an important reason is a difficulty coordinating work between team members. Academics and practitioners have studied professional software development teams empirically to understand by analyzing software development processes, techniques, and CASE tools, and human factors in the coordination process (Herbsleb & Mockus, 2003) (Sandusky & Gasser, 2005) (Seaman & Basili, 1997)

(Wiredu, 2006). Inter-team coordination is an essential concern as software development increasingly becomes globally distributed and remains a persistent industry challenge.

In simple coordination can be viewed as decision-making and action-taking *collaboration, communication,* and *cooperation.* These three components of work practices are necessary but by themselves insufficient for coordination to take place. Collaboration is an essential part of group work. Communication is necessary because member A needs to communicate with person B, in some form, what needs to be done needed for the group. Cooperation is essential because B requires being willing to do what is required for the group. If any of the three mandatory components are lacking, the outcome will be less than ideal.

Viewing coordination through this framework leads one to ask several research questions:

1. What kinds of behaviours are associated with being helpful or unhelpful to others?
2. How do members of a software team communicate to get work done?
3. How do software teams handle dependencies on a personal level?

To understand inter-team dependencies in software development, this chapter presents a survey-based data analysis result.

Background of Survey-Based Data Analysis

The study was conducted in the context of an undergraduate team-based student software design and development project. Multiple choice questionaries were used to survey students. The study was based on three individual groups, and each group consists of pre-assigned team members. The rationale behind students' pre-assignment to teams is to ensure that teams balance talent, skills, and expertise and become aware that one must learn to establish good working relations with "*strangers*" and acquaintances in their future careers' friends.

Each team worked independently of others on the same case study. Each team's internal organization, planning the project, defining a management structure, and carrying out the work (technical or organizational) were the team members' *joint responsibilit*ies. Each team member was expected to adopt two roles in a software development project, associated job titles, and responsibility for those tasks falling within their remit.

Each team member adopts two roles (e.g., project manager, deputy project manager, system analyst, designer, programmer or coding specialist, software tester) described in the policy document. Project manager responsible for team planning, coordination, and risk management. The team manager was the central contact point to the team consultant and the client, and the role must contribute to technical work. The Deputy project manager was second in command and responsible for documentation, reports, and standards, including technical work. A system analyst was responsible for the elicitation of customer requirements. The system designer was in charge of the system design process. The programmer was dedicated to implementing the system. The software tester was responsible for writing a test plan, testing the system and its components, and recording the outcomes. Each team member had one primary role and a secondary role, e.g., project manager/systems analyst or designer/programmer. The roles were appropriately spread. It ensured that essential roles within the team were covered when members were absent.

The survey revealed that the most helpful behaviours between all the teams are related to cooperation and availability. The unhelpful behaviours are related to location (primarily felt by the distributed team members), ownership and awareness, and availability. This research finds that coordination problems in the distributed teams can be considered a superset of collocated teams' problems; distributed development adds additional difficulties caused by location (i.e., time zone), culture, and meetings mode.

EXPERIMENTAL STUDY METHOD

The online survey consisted of one-hour, semi-structured, open-ended multiple-choice questions based on the 'echo' method designed by Bavelas (Bavelas, 1942). The method is used in studies of organizations to examine task interactions in new product development (Duimering et al., 2006) and task structures of a group of professionals (Bjorn et al., 2014).

Student Survey and Results

In this step, participating students' opinions were gathered by a combination of discussions and questionnaires. The contextual information of communication and collaboration information, channel preference, and the relationship between the knowledge management cycle and organizational culture through the CVF was discussed at length. Then a multiple-choice opinion survey questionnaire was used in the opinion collection process.

In a team-based software design and development practice, groups of people are connected by the similarity of their project activities. Group members do not have to be spatially or socially connected, but they solve similar problems and learn from each other through processes like group discussion or one-to-one subject-specific matter. Members advance through a process called team-based or group-based learning and provide value to the software development community.

For example, a software designer may start acquiring knowledge by reading discussions and reporting bugs (or errors). Over time, the software designer learns from community discussions and collaborations. This way, software designers or developers may start fixing bugs and enhance their skills to the point where they can use the acquired knowledge to help other group members.

Due to the globalization of the software industry, software design and development can take place in a distributed setting, where contributors need not be in the same office or town. These global software developers often communicate on a scale and are mostly interconnected via information and communication technology (ICT) based application tools. These global communication tools can help software project management issues (e.g., sharing technological knowledge, collaboration with project members or clients). The participating students provided their opinions on the following categories: (i) coordinate with others, (ii) communicate with other members, (iii) learn with other members, (iv) learn by watching, and (v) stay up to date.

The student opinion survey also used different communication channels and resources, such as video conferencing, textbook, google search, private discussion, group discussion, and private chat facility, for project collaboration and knowledge management. This section presents more detailed information on why specific channels were considered vital to the team project management. In the student team project context, the current survey on KM practice belongs to more than one quadrant of the SECI model. Figure 4 presents some participating students' opinions in a two-dimensional visual representation.

Figure 4. Communication channels used by the respondents

	Face-to-Face	Books	Web Search	Dedicated Websites	Video Conferencing	Private Discussion	Group Discussion	Electronic mail	Telephone Conversation	Online Collaboration
	Analog		Digital							
Communicate with Others	65%				35%	11%	22%	38%	77%	
Coordinate with Others	12%				27%					
Learn	63%				21%					
Find Answers		52%	37%	29%	5%					
Learn with Other Team Members	45%									
Watch Activities				24%	31%					

Most of the team members (65%) expressed their preference for face-to-face communication for software system design. Their primary justification is that they can receive quick feedback from the team members, facilitating talking through complex problems, discussing ideas, and making software design decisions. Thus, the team uses its efforts to make explicit knowledge tacit, supporting the learning process. One example of the internalization practice identified is team members integration, which occurs after a project member learns about the team's software development process. Therefore, knowledge internalization occurs when the team's explicit knowledge (stored on Google Drive) is presented to help project team members to learn it.

The success of a software development team is the ability to coordinate successfully with one another. Private discussion (e.g., Zoom video conferencing, Email, Telephone) is essential for supporting team collaboration through single or multiple channels. Besides, effective teams contain team members who appreciate each other's ideas. If team members are ignored or belittled after providing input, they will probably stop engaging in team activities (e.g., team meetings, discussions). When this disengaging attitude prevails, collaboration is complicated. Also, some team members are not naturally driven to start communication and discussion. Taking the time to assess who is driven to talk things through compared to those who are not allowed a team member ensures everyone is given appropriate airtime.

Electronic mail (or email) is identified as an essential channel (38%) to support discussion across virtually every platform and among different stakeholders (e.g., client, team member). It is a convenient channel for disseminating information to large groups while keeping conversations private and persistent for later retrieval. This is how one can get to communicate privately and can have a proof for a later stage.

Team members can stay up to date about technologies, practices, and tools for software development (e.g., software documentation, technical articles, formal lecture handouts) using different channels (e.g., virtual learning environment – Moodle, Email, Forum, Blogs, and Dedicated websites). Within a team-based software development project, tasks consist of activities that require to be carried out by one or multiple team members. The project manager can allocate a task to multiple team members or leave it unassigned for anyone to carry out the work. Tasks need to have start dates and due dates or be left without dates to be completed anytime. Software project management tools are handy to keep the team members up to date with the progress.

Learn with other team members is an important activity in software development projects. It is part of developing a team, whether the member is a new team leader or an experienced manager. People need training and support throughout their working life, both as individuals and as teams, to develop their skills and work effectively. A substantial number of survey participants (45%) expressed their view positively on team learning.

In addition, team members learn by watching others or finding answers to a problem from books, web searches, or dedicated websites. It can be watching a video on a YouTube channel or watching a recording in a teaching and learning environment (e.g., Moodle). Web search can be a valuable tool for learners, and a bit of instruction in how to search for learning sources will help the learners become critical thinkers and independent learners. More than half of the student participants (52%) in the assessment expressed that they find problem solutions using recommended technical books in software development. At the same time, thirty-seven per cent of the participating students agreed that they get a problem solution by using a web search.

Telephone conversations have the advantage of enabling communication among software development team members and clients of a particular project. Many participants (77%) expressed their support in favour of telephone conversation.

Investigation of Knowledge Management Practices

The current investigation of the KM practices step occurred during the software project design and development initiative. Therefore, it is crucial to notice that a particular practice may belong to more than one quadrant of the SECI model. Table 3 presents some examples of practices adopted and their relationships with the SECI model. Besides, the total amount of practices of each quadrant of the SECI model is presented.

Most of the team software design and development practices (44%) focused on knowledge internalization. One example of the internalization practice identified is team members integration that happens after members returned from a short absence from team activities when those members obtain knowledge about the team's software design and development processes related to team activities. Thus, the knowledge internalization happens when the team's explicit knowledge (stored on Google Drive dedicated storage area) is presented to help absent team members learn it.

Table 3. Knowledge management practice samples and SECI quadrant totals

	Socialization	Externalization	Combination	Internalization
Web Search				
Watch				
Learn from team member				
Total	5 (28%)	4 (22%)	1 (6%)	8 (44%)

Therefore, the team uses its efforts to make explicit knowledge tacit, helping the learning process. Focusing on tacit and explicit knowledge interactions, the practices related to knowledge socialization summed 28% (e.g., training and interacting with more experienced members). Process Google Drive stored documents, and Internet use is an example of externalization practices, which occurs when the members' tacit knowledge is stored and becomes explicit and freely available to any team member with access.

Only one practice related to the combination was identified. During "lessons learned" practice execution, a combination happens when lessons related to issues that need to be improved in the subsequent development cycles are solved. Knowledge obtained from the solutions is incorporated into existing lessons learned in the organization's knowledge database.

Investigation of Organization's Profile

OCAI questionnaire application enables organizations to analyze their cultural profile, as well as to analyze in a stratified way each of the six dimensions that compose the instrument, which is: (i) dominant characteristics; (ii) organizational leadership; (iii) management of employees; (iv) organizational glue; (v) strategic emphases; and (vi) criteria of success. The detailed step by step guidance is available in the Appendix.

Twenty-one students took part in expressing their personal views regarding the OCAI questionnaire. The analysis of each dimension of the current cultural profile and how employees would like it to be eventually in the future (preferred profile) is shown in Figure 5. For example, regarding the *Dominant Characteristics*, the organization is more focused on the market culture type, meaning that the organization focuses on results and its employees are competitive and focus on achieving established goals. However, regarding the preferred profile, these employees want the organization to be dynamic and entrepreneurial, where they may feel encouraged to take risks, such as the adhocracy culture.

Concerning *Organizational Leadership* and *Organization Glue* dimensions, the organization is related to the market culture type. In this type of scenario, the leadership style is aggressive and result oriented. The employees prefer a profile related to Clan, in which leaders act as mentors, facilitating and encouraging employees' development. Finally, the current research found that employees are satisfied with the Management of Employees dimension. This dimension is related to teamwork, consensus, and participation. The current and preferred cultural profile was the same (i.e., clan profile).

Regarding the Strategic Emphases dimension, the current research verified that the Adhocracy profile is predominant. In diagnosing the current profile, this research found that the organization emphasizes acquiring new resources and creating new challenges. However, employees would like the organization to have a profile more related to Clan, emphasizing human development, levels of trust, openness, and participation.

The organization defines success based on efficiency (Criteria of Success). The noticed critical points are reliable deliveries, a well-prepared schedule and low-cost production. Preferably, the employees also wish that the organization have a Criteria of Success close to the Clan profile.

The graph based on the organization's average cultural profile is presented in Figure 5. According to Figure 5, one can observe that the most prevalent culture type in the organization is the Market. This indicates that this organization is focused on performance and values competitiveness. It is also possible to notice that the organization already tends to Clan culture.

When asked how employees would like the organization to be, the Clan type was preferred. This type of culture is characterized by a friendly working environment, emphasizing human development and teamwork.

Comparison Analysis of the Identified KM Practices as the Dominant Organization's Cultural Profile

The results of the two stages of this case study were shown in the previous subsections. These results were necessary inputs for the primary goal of this work, which is to investigate through practice the relationship between the SECI model (Nonaka & Takeuchi, 1995) and the Organizational Culture through CVF (Cameron & Quinn, 1999).

Gray and Densten (Gray & Densten, 2006) and Rai (2011) concluded that there are relationships between Socialization and Culture Clan; Outsourcing and Adhocracy Culture; combinations and Market Type Culture; Internationalization and Hierarchical Culture.

On the findings of Gray and Densten (Gray & Densten, 2006) and Rai (Rai, 2011) there is a relationship between the internalization of knowledge and hierarchical culture type. However, our case study did not observe this relationship: most KM practices were related to the knowledge internalization stage, and the predominant culture is the Market culture profile. Gray and Densten (Gray & Densten, 2006) and Rai (2011) also claim a relationship between knowledge and the cultural market profile. However, the results obtained do not infer this relationship, as this research identified only one KM practice related to knowledge combination.

According to this research, five practices were identified as part of the knowledge socialization step. This show that, after the knowledge internalization, socialization is also encouraged. The case study results also show that there is a tendency for clan culture. It is worth remembering that Clan profile core values are participation, loyalty, and commitment (Cameron & Quinn, 1999).

Creating a visual picture of the cultural profile allows the analysis results with the CVF more effectively. A picture also helps the comparisons and capture more trends than analyzing numbers alone. To create a visual representation of the results, one needs to take the average number in column A of the NOW section and plot that point in the Collaborate quadrant. This way, one needs to continue plot each column in the NOW section until all the quadrants are complete. Next, all the plotted numbers need to connect with straight solid lines until four solid lines have created a kite-like shape, as shown in Figure 5. Similarly, the averages from future (or preferred) section instead of using four solid lines of a different colour to connect the plotted numbers in each quadrant.

FUTURE WORK

In global software development, communities (or groups) of practice are based on people interconnected by their daily work-related activities. Such software project management communities can be found in many domains, including software design and development. Group members do not have to be spatially or socially connected, but they solve the same problems and learn from each other through processes like mentoring. Group members progress through a process known as 'peripheral participation': beginners watch indirectly and then participate in simple peripheral activities that are not vital but provide value to the community. For example, a potential contributor might start by only reading discussions and reporting defects in software in open-source development. Over time, these participants learn community (or group) communications through media (e.g., mailing lists, eLearning forum services). In undergraduate team-based software development, students have introduced the advantages of group communication and the use of social media. The CVF has been used in many administrative services research to assess participants satisfaction and team functioning. In the current research, the number of participants (i.e., students) was minimal. However, the underlying research data, data analysis, and satisfaction related issues need to carry out in a more significant sample of participants.

Figure 5. Organizational cultural profile

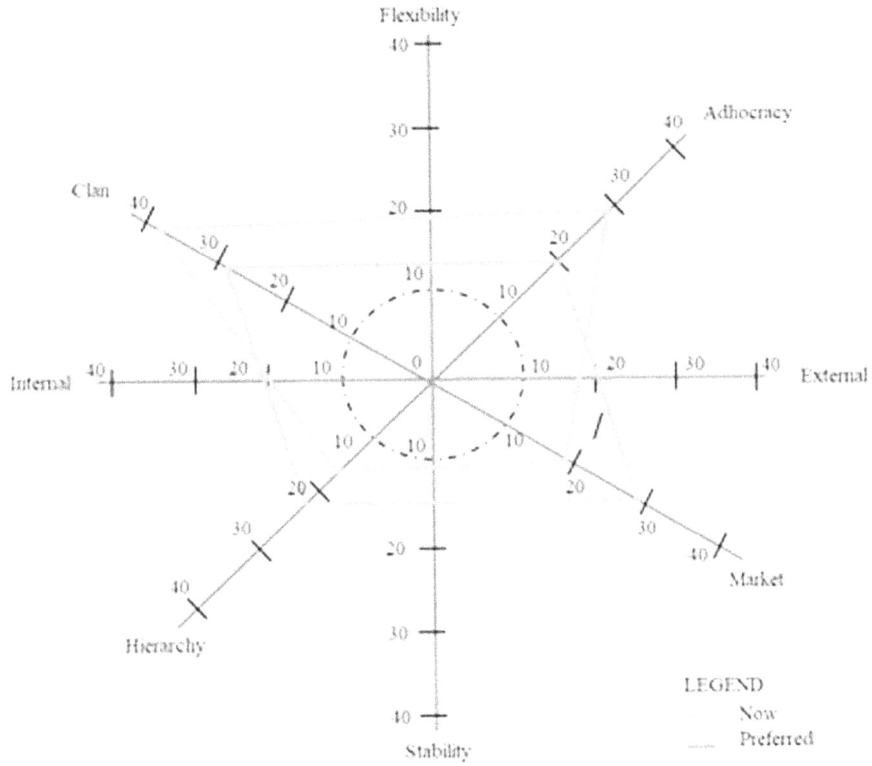

Agility at a large scale requires integrating agile and non-agile development practices into hybrid software development and delivery environments. The Agile Methodologies (e.g., Scrum, Extreme Programming, Development and Operation – DevOps) have become the preferred tools for global software design and development. The methodologies emphasize iterative and incremental development. It requires both the requirements and solutions to enhance among the collaboration teams. Besides, the success of such practices relies on the quality result of each stage of development, obtained through rigorous testing. In the future, this research will study emergent Agile software development practices, knowledge management, and collaborative communication cultures in a team-based environment.

CONCLUSION

This chapter describes an investigation of how a software development team-based project helps to foster a participatory development culture. This chapter presented a case study that aimed to compare, in practice, the relationship between the knowledge management cycle and the organizational culture through the competitive value framework. The current research collected data related to knowledge management practices adopted on one organization and requested the selected participating students answer multiple-choice questionnaires relating to organizational culture.

The chapter also describes how an undergraduate software development project help (i.e., channels) foster a participatory development culture. The global nature of the software development community has witnessed an enormous paradigm shift in recent decades in how software engineers communicate and collaborate in their daily work. The chapter provides the basic concept of knowledge management and the main issues in a team-based software development environment. Then it describes the characteristics of the team-based software development that participate in and contribute to an undergraduate students' software project. A questionary-based survey was used to ask the student about their participatory development activities (e.g., networking, learning), and their opinion regarding different communication channels (e.g., email, web-portal, telephone, video conferencing) usability in student team-project based software development. Finally, the chapter compares the advantages and challenges of using these communication and collaboration channels.

The results of this student-based software development study are limited to the context of the study performed. Context-dependent knowledge is an essential asset than theoretical knowledge. Therefore, the results obtained in this case study show the importance of investigating the proposed theories in practice. This research intends to continue investigating, through new experimental studies, the relationship between the SECI model and the framework CVF in other software development organizations.

REFERENCES

Alavi, M., & Leidner, D. E. (2001). Review: Knowledge Management and Knowledge Management Systems: Conceptual Foundations and Research Issues. *Management Information Systems Quarterly*, *25*(1), 107–136. doi:10.2307/3250961

Aurum, A., Daneshgar, F., & Ward, J. (2008). Investigating Knowledge Management practices in software development organizations An Australian experience. *Information and Software Technology*, *50*(6), 511–533. doi:10.1016/j.infsof.2007.05.005

Aurum, A., Jeffery, R., Wohlin, C., & Handzic, M. (2003). *Managing Software Engineering Knowledge*. Springer. doi:10.1007/978-3-662-05129-0

Bjorn, P., Esbensen, M., Jensen, R. E., & Mathiesen, S. (2014). Does distance still matter? Revisiting the CSCW fundamentals on distance collaboration. *ACM Transactions on Computer-Human Interaction*, *21*(5), 1–27. doi:10.1145/2670534

Beise, C. M. (2004). IT project management and virtual teams. In *Proceedings of the 2004 SIGMIS Conference on Computer Personnel Research: Careers, Culture, and Ethics in A Networked Environment (Tucson, AZ, USA, April 22 - 24, 2004). SIGMAS CPR '04*. ACM.

Bjørnson, O., & Dingsøyr, T. (2008). Knowledge Management in Software Engineering: A Systematic Review of Studied Concepts, Findings and Research Methods Used. *Information and Software Technology, Elsevier, 2008*(11), 1055–1068. doi:10.1016/j.infsof.2008.03.006

Bollinger, A. S., & Smith, R. D. (2001). Managing organizational knowledge as a strategic asset. *Journal of Knowledge Management, 5*(1), 8–18. doi:10.1108/13673270110384365

Basili, V. R., Caldiera, G., & Rombach, H. D. (1994). Experience Factory. In J. J. Marciniak (Ed.), *Encyclopedia of Software Engineering*. John Wiley and Sons.

Basili, V., Costa, P., Lindvall, M., Mendonca, M., & Seaman, C. (2001). An Experience Management System for a Software Engineering Research Organisation. *Proceedings of 26th Annual NASA Goddard Software Engineering Workshop*, 29-35. 10.1109/SEW.2001.992652

Baugher, D. V. A., & Weisbord, E. (2000). Gender and culture diversity occurring in self-formed workgroups. *Journal of Managerial Issues, 12*(4), 391–407.

Clerc, V., Lago, P., & Vliet, H. (2007). *The Architect's Mindset*. http://www.springerlink.com/content/9km6520m6027824u/fulltext.pdf

Cameron, K. S., & Quinn, R. E. (1999). *Diagnosing and changing organizational culture*. Addison-Wesley.

Carmel, E. (2006, March). Building your Information Systems from the Other Side of the World: How Infosys manages time differences. *MIS Quarterly Executive, 5*(1).

Carmel, E., & Tjia, P. (2005). *Offshoring Information Technology: Sourcing and Outsourcing to a Global Workforce*. Cambridge University Press. doi:10.1017/CBO9780511541193

Carmel, E. (1999). *Global Software Teams: Collaboration Across Borders and Time Zones*. Prentice-Hall.

Carmel, E., & Agarwal, R. (2001, March). Tactical Approaches for Alleviating Distance in Global Software Development. *IEEE Software, 18*(2), 22–29. doi:10.1109/52.914734

Corbin, R. D., Dunbar, C. B., & Zhu, Q. (2007). A three-tier knowledge management scheme for software engineering support and innovation. *Journal of Systems and Software, 80*(9), 1494–1505. doi:10.1016/j.jss.2007.01.013

Deshpande, S. & Richardson, I. (2009). Management at the Outsourcing Destination - Global Software Development in India. *IGCSE/IEEE 2009*, 217-225.

Dingsøyr, T., Brede Moe, N., & Nytro, O. (2001). Augmenting Experience reports with Lightweight Postmortem Reviews. *Third International Conference on Product-Focused Software Process Improvement, PROFES 2001*. 10.1007/3-540-44813-6_17

Espinosa, A. J., & Carmel, E. (2003). The impact of time separation on coordination in global software teams: A conceptual foundation. *Software Process Improvement and Practice, 8*(4), 249–266. doi:10.1002pip.185

Ebert, C., & Neve, P. (2001). Surviving global software development. *IEEE Software, 18*(2), 62-69.

Gray, J. H., & Densten, I. L. (2006). Towards an Integrative Model of Organization Culture and Knowledge Management. *International Journal of Organisational Behaviour*, *9*(2), 594–603.

Gurung, A., & Prater, E. (2006). A Research Framework for the Impact of Cultural Differences on IT Outsourcing. *Journal of Global Information Technology Management, 9*(1), 24-43.

Hall, E. T. (1976). *Beyond Culture*. Doubleday.

Holmstrom, H., Conchuir, E. O., Agerfalk, P. J., & Fitzgerald, B. (2006). Global Software Engineering, 2006. *IGCSE '06. International Conference on*, 3 – 11.

Hofstede, G. (1984). *Culture's Consequences: International Differences in Work-Related Values*. Sage Publication.

Herbsleb, J. D., & Moitra, D. (2001). Global Software Development. *IEEE Software*, *18*(2), 16–20. doi:10.1109/52.914732

Hayes, I. S. (2002). Ready or Not: Global Sourcing Is in Your IT Future. *Cutter IT Journal*, *15*(11), 5–11.

Nonaka, I. (1994). A Dynamic Theory of Organizational Knowledge Creation. *Organization Science*, *5*(1), 14–37. doi:10.1287/orsc.5.1.14

Nonaka, I., & Takeuchi, H. (1995). *The knowledge creating company: how Japanese company: how Japanese companies create the dynamics of innovation*. Oxford University Press.

Pressman, R. S. (2000). *Software engineering: A Practitioner's Approach (European Adaption)* (5th ed.). McGraw-Hill International.

Liebowitz, J., & Megbolugbe, I. (2003). A set of frameworks to aid the project manager in conceptualizing and implementing knowledge management initiatives. *International Journal of Project Management*, *21*(3), 189–198. doi:10.1016/S0263-7863(02)00093-5

Pal, K. (2019). Markov Decision Theory Based Crowdsourcing Software Process Model. In Crowdsourcing and Probabilistic Decision-Making in Software Engineering: Emerging Research and Opportunities. IGI Publication.

Pal, K. (2020). Framework for Reusable Test Case Generation in Software Systems Testing. In Software Engineering for Agile Application Development. IGI Global.

Pal, K., & Karakostas, B. (2020). Software Testing Under Agile, Scrum, and DevOps. In Agile Scrum Implementation and Its Long-Term Impact on Organizations. IGI Publication.

Pal, K., & Williams, I. (2021). Software Development Knowledge Management System Using Web Portal. In Digital Technology Advancement in Knowledge Management. IGI Publication.

Sveiby, K. E. (1997). *The New Organizational Wealth: Managing & Measuring Knowledge-Based Assets*. Berrett-Koehler Publishers, Inc.

Sommerville, I. (2001). *Software Engineering* (6th ed.). Addison-Wesley.

Rai, R. K. (2011). Knowledge management and organizational culture: A theoretical integrative framework. *Journal of Knowledge Management*, •••, 779–801.

Rus, I., & Lindvall, M. (2002, June). Knowledge Management in Software Engineering. *IEEE Software, 19*(3), 26–38. doi:10.1109/MS.2002.1003450

Gibbs, W. (1994, September). Software's chronic crisis. *Scientific American, 271*(3), 72–81.

Herbsleb, J. D. (2007). *Global Software Engineering: The Future of Socio-technical Coordination. In Future of Software Engineering (FOSE'07)*. IEEE.

Lasheras, J., Valencia-Garcia, R., Fernandez-Breis, J. T., & Toval, A. (2009). Modeling Reusable Security Requirements Based on Ontology Framework. *Journal of Research and Practice in Information Technology*, *4*(2), 119–133.

Kaiya, H., & Sacki, M. (2006). Using Domain Ontology as Domain Knowledge for Requirement Elicitation. *Proceedings of the 14th IEEE International Requirements Engineering Conference*, 189-198.

Sangwan, R. S., & Ros, J. (2008). Architectural Leadership and Management in Globally Distributed Software Development. *Proceedings of the 1st International Workshop on Leadership and Management in Software Architecture*, 17-22.

Korkala, M., Pikkarainen, M., & Conboy, A. (2010). A Case Study of Customer Communication in Globally Distributed Software Product Development. *Proceedings of the 11th International Conference on Product-Focused Software*, 43-46.

Rammasubbu, N., & Balan, R. K. (2008). Towards Governance Scheme for Distributed Software Development Projects. *Proceedings of the 1st International Workshop on Software Development Governance*, 11-14.

Knapp, E. & Yu, D. (1999). Understanding organizational culture: how culture helps or hinders the flow of knowledge. *Knowledge Management Review*, 16-21.

Kess, P., & Haapasalo, H. (2002). Knowledge creation through a project review process in software production. *International Journal of Production Economics, 80*(1), 49–55.

Johansson, C., Hall, P., & Coquard, M. (1999). Talk to Paula and Peter – They are Experienced. *Proceedings of the Workshop of Learning Software Organizations*, 69-76.

Kess, P., & Haapasalo, H. (2002). Knowledge creation through a project review process in software production. *International Journal of Production Economics, 80*(1), 49–55.

Kotlarsky, J., & Oshri, I. (2005). Social ties, knowledge sharing and successful collaboration in globally distributed system development projects. *European Journal of Information Systems, 14*, 37–48.

Karolak, D. W. (1999). *Global Software Development: Managing Virtual Teams and Environments*. IEEE Computer Society Press.

Rus, I., & Lindvall, M. (2002). Knowledge Management in Software Engineering. *IEEE Software, 19*(3), 26–38.

Levy, M., & Hazzan, O. (2009). Knowledge Management in Practice: The Case of Agile Software Development. *2nd Intern. Workshop on Cooperative and Human Aspects on Soft. Eng. (CHASE)*, 60-65.

O'Brien, J. A. (2002). *Management Information Systems Managing Information Technology in the Business Enterprise*. Mc Graw Hill Irwin.

Rus, I., Lindvall, M., & Sinha, S. (2001). Knowledge management in software engineering A state-of the-art-report. *Fraunhofer Center for Experimental Software Engineering and the University of Maryland, 2001*, 1–57.

Ivarsson, M., & Gorschek, T. (2012). Tool Support for Disseminating and Improving Development Practices. *Software Quality Control, 2012*, 173–199.

Jensen, M., Menon, S., Mangset, L. E., & Dalberg, V. (2007). Managing Offshore Outsourcing of Knowledge-intensive Projects - A People-Centric Approach. *International Conference on Global Software Engineering (ICGSE 2007).*

Toaff, S. S. (2002). Don't Play with Mouths of Fire, and Other Lessons of Global Software Development. *Cutter IT Journal*, *15*(11), 23–28.

Lanubile, F., Damian, D., & Oppenheimer, H. L. (2003). Global software development: Technical, organizational, and social challenges. *SIGSOFT Software Engineering Notes*, *28*(6), 1–4.

Larkey, L. (1996). Toward a theory of communicative interactions in culturally diverse workgroups. *Academy of Management Review*, *21*(2), 463–492.

Mehta, N. (2008). Successful knowledge management implementation in global software companies. *Journal of Knowledge Management*, *12*(3), 42–56.

Knapp, E. & Yu, D. (1999). Understanding organizational culture: how culture helps or hinders the flow of knowledge. *Knowledge Management Review*, 16-21.

Pauleen, D. J., & Yoong, P. (2001). Relationship building and the use of ICT in boundary-crossing virtual teams: A facilitator's perspective. *Journal of Information Technology, 16*(4), 205-220.

Prikladnicki, R., Audy, J. L. N., & Evaristo, R. (2003). Global Software Development in Practice Lessons Learned. *Software Process Improvement and Practice*, *8*(4), 267–279.

Rubenstein-Montano, R., Liebowitz, J., Buchwalter, J., & Mcgraw, D. (2000). A Systems Thinking Framework for Knowledge Management. *Decision Support Systems*, *31*(1).

Gray, J. H., & Densten, I. L. (2006). Towards an Integrative Model of Organization Culture and Knowledge management. *International Journal of Organisational Behaviour*, *9*(2), 594–603.

Rai, R. K. (2011). Knowledge management and organizational culture: A theoretical integrative framework. *Journal of Knowledge Management*, 779–801.

Nonaka, I., & Takeuchi, H. (1995). *The knowledge-creating company: how Japanese companies create the dynamics of innovation*. Oxford University Press.

Valentine, C., Deshpande, S., & Richardson, I. (2008). *Outsourcing And Offshoring Software Development: The Remote Developers' Perspective*. Global Sourcing Workshop, Val d'Isere, France.

Watson, R. T., Ho, T. H., & Raman, K. S. (1994). Culture: A Fourth Dimension of Group Support Systems. *Communications of the ACM*, *37*(10), 44–55.

KEY TERMS AND DEFINITIONS

Agile Software Development: An evolutionary and iterative approach to software development with focuses on adaption to changes.

Competing Values Framework: The competing value framework (CVF) has been recognized as one of the most important models to deal with factors that make organizations effective. The model has been applied to a variety of topics related to individual and organizational behaviour. Researchers are using this empirical technique to help thousands of organizations and tens of thousands of managers improve their performance.

Knowledge Management: Knowledge management is emerging as a critical management responsibility, and consequently, organizations are investing a vast number of resources to support the acquisition, storage, sharing, and retrieval of knowledge in software development projects.

Organizational Culture: Organizational culture can be considered as the norms that characterize a workgroup or organization. It is also suggested that the cultures of productive and economically successful organizations are often characterized by the norms of (i) collaboration, (ii) innovation, and (iii) integrity / ethical behaviour. These norms characterize successful organizational cultures, in part, by fostering greater trust and commitment among team members or employees.

Software Engineering: Software engineering is the systematic application of the engineering approach to software system development.

Software Process Development: Software design is a process to translate user requirements (or needs) into some appropriate form, which helps the programmer in software coding and implementation.

Software Project Management: A software project is the complete software development procedure from user requirement collecting to development, testing and maintenance, carried out according to the execution methodologies, in a specified period to achieve the intended software product.

APPENDIX

The Competing Values Culture Assessment

Three student groups were used for the current CVF culture assessment-related survey. In this survey, "the organization" refers to the team managed by the team manager (or the team in which individual students manage). The following six groups of questions ask the student to identify the way personal experience of the organization (i.e., team) at the time of the survey and how the student thinks it should be to accomplish its highest goals.

The instruction that pleases rate each of the statements by dividing 100 points (100 would indicate very similar and 0 would indicate not similar) between alternatives A, B, C, and D depending on how similar the description is to individual students' teams. The total scores for each question must equal 100. The assessment uses this method to better demonstrate how moving towards one profile also requires moving away from its opposite. That is, it demonstrates the inherent trade-offs of any approach to culture change.

First-rate how individual student perceives the team to be at present in the NOW column. Second, rate the team again in the PREFERRED column depending on how students think their team must accomplish its highest objectives and achieve spectacular success.

Individual participant (i.e., student) may divide the 100 points in any way among the four alternatives in each question. Some alternatives may get zero points, for example. However, remember that the total must equal 100.

Table 4. Dominant characteristics

Question Number	Alternatives	Dominant Characteristics	Now	Prefer
1	A	The team is a very personal place. It is like an extended family. Members seem to share a lot of themselves.		
	B	The team is a very dynamic and entrepreneurial place. Members are willing to sticker their necks out and take risks.		
	C	The team is very results-oriented. A notable concern is with getting the job done. Members are competitive and achievement-oriented.		
	D	The team is a very controlled and structured place. Formal procedures generally govern what members do.		
Total			100	100

Table 5. Team leadership

Question Number	Alternatives	Dominant Characteristics	Now	Prefer
2	A	The leadership in the team is simply considered to exemplify mentoring, facilitating, or nurturing.		
	B	The leadership in the team is generally considered to exemplify entrepreneurship, innovating, or risk-taking.		
	C	The leadership in the team is generally considered to exemplify an aggressive, results-oriented, no-nonsense focus.		
	D	The leadership in the team is generally considered to exemplify coordinating, organizing, or smooth-running efficiency.		
Total			100	100

Table 6. Management of team members

Question Number	Alternatives	Dominant Characteristics	Now	Prefer
3	A	Teamwork, consensus, and participation characterize the team management style in the organization.		
	B	The team management style in the organization is characterized by individual risk-taking, innovation, freedom, and uniqueness.		
	C	The team management style in the organization is characterized by hard-driving competitiveness, high demands, and achievement.		
	D	The team management style in the organization is characterized by the security of employment, conformity, predictability, and stability in relationships.		
Total			100	100

Table 7. Organizational glue

Question Number	Alternatives	Dominant Characteristics	Now	Prefer
4	A	The glue, which connects the team is loyalty and mutual trust. Commitment to this organization runs high.		
	B	The glue, which connects the team is a commitment to development and innovation. There is an importance on being on the cutting edge.		
	C	The glue that connects the team is the emphasis on achievement and global accomplishment. Aggressiveness and winning are common themes.		
	D	The glue that connects the team is formal rules and policies. Therefore, maintaining a smooth-running organization is essential.		
Total			100	100

Table 8. Strategic emphases

Question Number	Alternatives	Dominant Characteristics	Now	Prefer
5	A	The team emphasizes human development. High trust, openness, and participant persistence.		
	B	The team emphasizes acquiring new resources and creating new challenges. Trying new things and prospecting for opportunities are valued.		
	C	The team emphasizes competitive actions and achievement. As a result, hiring stretch targets and winning in the marketplace are dominant.		
	D	The team emphasizes permanence and stability. Therefore, efficiency, control, and smooth operations are essential.		
Total			100	100

Table 9. Criteria of success

Question Number	Alternatives	Dominant Characteristics	Now	Prefer
6	A	The team defines success based on the development of human resources, Teamwork, employee commitment, and concern for people.		
	B	The team defines success based on having the most unique or the newest products. Therefore, it is a product leader and innovator.		
	C	The team defines success based on winning in the marketplace and outpacing the competition. Therefore, competitive market leadership is key.		
	D	The team defines success based on efficiency. Dependable delivery, smooth scheduling, and low-cost production are critical.		
Total			100	100

Computing the Results

Transfer all your answers from the above questions onto the results key below. Flow the results key until you have the averages for A through D in both the NOW and PREFERRED columns of the assessment.

Table 10.

NOW					**PREFERR**			
1A. ____	1B. ____	1C. ____	1D. ____		1A. ____	1B. ____	1C. ____	1D. ____
2A. ____	2B.____	2C. ____	2D. ____		2A. ____	2B. ____	2C. ____	2D. ____
3A. ____	3B. ____	3C. ____	3D. ____		3A. ____	3B. ____	3C. ____	3D. ____
4A. ____	4B. ____	4C. ____	4D. ____		4A. ____	4B. ____	4C. ____	4D. ____
5A. ____	5B. ____	5C. ____	5D. ____		5A. ____	5B. ____	5C. ____	5D. ____
6A. ____	6B. ____	6C. ____	6D. ____		6A. ____	6B. ____	6C. ____	6D. ____

Table 11.

A. ____	B. ____	C. ____	D. ____		A. ____	B. ____	C. ____	D. ____

Divide Totals by 6 to get your **Average (A):**

A – represents the Collaborate Quadrant (Upper Left Corner)
B – represents the Compete Quadrant (Lower Right Corner)
C – represents the Control Quadrant (Lower Left Corner)
D – represents the Create Quadrant (Upper Right Corner)

Chapter 14
How Does Terrorism Change the Business Landscape for Firms?
A New Framework for Analyzing Risks

Luis Alfonso Dau
Northeastern University, USA

Elizabeth M. Moore
Northeastern University, USA

Max Abrahms
Northeastern University, USA

ABSTRACT

This chapter introduces a new framework for understanding firm creation and firm behavior in the face of terrorism and its ensuing risks such as institutional disruption. There is surprisingly scant theoretical or empirical research on how terrorism impacts firms and their ability to be agile in the face of risk. The extant strategic management literature is underdeveloped for making such assessments because it largely ignores the socio-cognitive impact of collective traumas on society. Building on the traditional assumptions of institutional theory from strategic management, the authors incorporate cosmopolitan memory theory from the field of international relations to offer a theoretically grounded set of testable predictions about terrorism's effects on both new and existing firms.

INTRODUCTION

There seem to be three certainties in life - not only death and taxes as the adage goes, but also terrorism. Terrorism has been a recurrent feature of the Common Era since the first century (Rapoport, 1984) though its tactical usage exploded internationally with the advent of mass communications in the late

DOI: 10.4018/978-1-7998-7872-8.ch014

19th century (Rapoport, 2004). In recent years, both the number of international terrorist incidents and fatalities has only continued to rise (START, 2016). Hardening high - value targets may reduce the utility of attacking them (Flynn, 2007), but as strategic actors, terrorists respond by gravitating to softer targets that are by definition easier to strike (Enders & Sandler, 2004). The international terrorism threat is thus expected to evolve, but not end regardless of countermeasures (Arquilla & Ronfeldt, 2001).

Given the temporal and geographical reach of terrorism, there has been surprisingly scant theoretical or empirical research on the consequences of the violence to firms (Abrahms et al., 2019; Dau et al., 2018b; Czinkota, 2010). Institutional theory within the strategic management literature supplies a useful but underdeveloped starting point for anticipating the direction of firms threatened by terrorism as well as for the ability of firms to be agile in the face of risk. When related to business, this research program emphasizes how institutions are the bedrock of firms (Meyer, 2014; North, 1990; Scott, 1987; Thornton & Ocasio, 2005) and the environments they operate in (Dau et al., 2020; Moore et al., 2019). And yet, terrorists attack in order to sow fear in the population, polarize communities, and upset the stability of societies and markets undergirding the very institutions on which businesses thrive (Heymann, 2000).

In taking the institutional environment as exogenously given, the strategic management literature is thus inadequate for making theory - informed empirical predictions about how terrorism affects either the creation or adaptation of firms to terrorism. Cosmopolitan Memory Theory (CMT) from within the constructivist tradition of international relations can fill this conceptual void by clarifying the socio - cognitive impact of traumatic events on society through an understanding of social perspectives (Guzzini, 2000; Jackson, 2001). In elucidating societal responses to collective tragedies (Hurd, 2008; Risse, 2004; Suchting, 1992), CMT is a useful complement to institutional theory for projecting how firms respond to terrorism.

As the paper explains, fusing these research programs from the strategic management and constructivist literatures yields the following set of predictions about the six major phases of the business cycle responses to terrorism. We select these phases as representations of the major strategic choices that firms make. First, informal entrepreneurship increases, while formal entrepreneurship decreases. Second, family firms gain a higher share of processes underlying supply chains. Third, corporate Social Responsibility (CSR) signalling from firms within the impacted community increases. Fourth, firms create alliances with other firms from similarly impacted areas. Fifth, firms from impacted areas become more international to hedge against future terrorist attacks in that area. Sixth, firms closest to the epicentre of the violence benefit from enhanced performance. This paradoxical development is conditional on the frequency of attacks and nature of the industry, as proximity to the violence is disadvantageous when business is tied to tourism or foreign investment, especially if attacks recur.

Beyond these testable propositions, this paper offers an important theoretical refinement to the strategic management literature. We hope to strengthen its explanatory power with a novel extension of institutional theory that takes seriously the socio - cognitive impact of terrorism on society. This paper is the first to combine the management literature with CMT, which can aid in making projections about a firm's strategic choices at different stages in the firm life cycle not only in response to terrorism, but also other global threats resulting in collective trauma. Together, insights from these fields can help to forecast how political violence will affect societal responses, specifically the strategic behaviour of firms. Thus, our insights help top - management teams and CEOs understand how to better handle the risks associated with terrorism. This enhanced framework is dynamic in the sense that it sheds light on multiple stages of a firm's life cycle from formation to adaptation and strategy, even performance. Beyond the theoretical and practical value to the study of international business, this paper contributes to resilience research (Aldrich 2012; Luthar 2006) - the burgeoning, interdisciplinary study of how society can cope with various forms of adversity for optimal recovery and development. In this vein, our paper is intended to be both descriptive and prescriptive from the firm level.

The analysis proceeds as follows. The first section describes the potential analytic value of combining concepts from CMT to institutional theory for anticipating the impact of terrorism and other collective traumas on firms. The second section demonstrates that this framework accords with extant empirical research on the societal effects of terrorism. The third section develops specific theoretically grounded propositions for how terrorism affects the creation, strategy, and performance of firms. The final section suggests fruitful avenues for future research.

BACKGROUND

Introducing Cosmopolitan Memory to Institutional Theory: A New Synergy

Institutional theory elucidates the more permanent, durable aspects of societal structures (Scott, 1995; Scott, 1987). Institutions within this theoretical framework are defined as the rules of the game (North, 1990). They provide guidelines that shape and inform firm behaviour across all stages of development from conception and creation to strategic choices and performance (Battilana et al., 2009; Dimaggio, 1988). Although the rules are sometimes breached, they are intended to create boundaries and expectations about conduct (Bernstein, 2011; Helmke et al., 2011; Karlsson & Acs, 2002; Thornton & Ocasio, 2005).

Traditionally, domestic institutions are the ones examined in the strategic management literature (Peng, 2002; Peng et al., 2008). These include the rules and regulatory frameworks put forth by the state, as well as the informal rules created at the individual and local levels (Abdi & Aulakh, 2012; Autio & Fu, 2015). In addition to the regulatory elements of institutions, there are also cognitive and normative aspects (Busenitz et al., 2000; Przeworski, 2004; Slater & Weber, 2013). Together, these three elements make up the institutions for a particular community and provide stability for the economic actors within it (Kotabe & Mudambi, 2003; Lawernce et al., 2002).

Different branches of institutional theory offer explanations as to how institutions evolve over time and either grow in power or fall into decline (Buchanan & Keohane, 2006; Rodrik et al., 2004; Slater & Weber, 2013). Although aiming to provide stability and routine to the actors (Greif & Laitin, 2004; Panke & Petersohn, 2016; Tang & Koveos, 2008), institutions are themselves subject to change, albeit usually incrementally (Beckert, 1999; Cantwell et al., 2010; Kahler, 2013). Actors within the jurisdiction of a particular set of institutions are typically able to accommodate the change conditional on the maintenance of relative normalcy (Acharya, 2004; Dacin et al., 2002; Greif & Laitin, 2004). By definition, however, terrorism strikes unexpectedly (Jongman, 1988) and is designed to suddenly disrupt societies for political gain (Frey et al., 2007). As such, institutional theory would benefit by incorporating insights from another framework that focuses on societal reactions and perspectives to collective traumas that compromise the institutions on which firms rest.

Cosmopolitan memory theory (CMT) addresses how societies respond to trauma (Guzzini, 2000; Hurd, 2008; Jackson, 2001; Risse, 2004; Suchting, 1992), which entails a rupture in normalcy often from a crisis moment (Lahad, 2005). Within this framework, traumatic events are understood as collective tragedies that require communities, or even entire nations, to grieve and mourn depending on the scope of the fallout (Kehayan & Napoli, 2005). Grief is the visceral natural reaction to a traumatic event that enables citizens to mourn by recognizing the collective loss essential for recovery (Edkins, 2003).

Traumatic events, such as terrorism or global pandemics, risk exposing the failure of the government to provide institutional stability and basic protection for its citizens and firms, frequently resulting in a loss of credibility especially in communities most directly affected (Dau & Moore, 2020 a; b; Squire et al., 1993; Young, 1994). After a traumatic event, officials may make public statements of healing, such as by commissioning commemorative sites or museums (Burnett, 2004; Freed, 1995; Ottem et al., 2007). Official symbols signal to the external world that the community is mourning, but its citizens often remain shocked, vulnerable, and distrustful of the government (Edkins, 2003; Ibreck, 2010). According to CMT, traumatized citizens "race to mourn" to compensate for the potential loss of government credibility (Davis, 2014; Freed, 1995; Kiernan, 2007; Luthans, 2006) by strengthening informal institutions independent of government initiatives (Buckley - Zitsel et al., 2006; Lahad, 2005). CMT emphasizes that most collective mourning happens at a sub - state level by small groups of friends and family, as well as within organizations in the community (Baddeley, 2012; Edkins, 2003; Squire et al., 1993).The community at the epicentre of the trauma tends to exert an especially strong sense of private ownership and initiative to collectively recover. The loss may traumatize, but ultimately strengthen the community by fostering cooperation, solidarity, and communal recovery efforts (Erdelyi, 2010; Ottem et al., 2007; Wolfgang, 2007). In attending to social perceptions of collective traumas and private responses to them, CMT offers a promising research program to better understand the impact of terrorism on society, specifically firms facing different types of strategic decisions.

MAIN FOCUS OF THE CHAPTER

Societal Responses to Terrorism

But what is terrorism? This question is essential to begin assessing its societal effects. Some researchers have likened terrorism to pornography: "You may know it when you see it, but it is impossible to come up with a universally agreed - upon definition" (Nacos, 2016; 17; see also Brill, 2008:338) Indeed, a lack of consensus over the definition of terrorism has bedevilled measuring its impact (Abrahms, 2010).

A useful distinction is between terrorism and insurgency. Terrorism typically refers to the select use of violence by non - state actors against civilian targets, whereas insurgencies denote more protracted campaigns that generally afflict illiberal countries embroiled in civil war (Jongman, 1988). Insurgencies have been found to decimate countries, including national economies. Yet only a handful of countries in the world (e.g., Afghanistan, Iraq, Nigeria, Pakistan, Somalia, Syria, and Yemen) suffer such grievous political unrest (Institute for Economics and Peace, 2016). The empirical literature suggests that outside of insurgencies, target countries are actually quite resilient to terrorism, as implied in CMT.

Because the outcome of terrorism is generally studied within the field of political science rather than economics, the focus has been on how the violence impacts political systems rather than firms (Abrahms, 2006; Berrebi & Klor, 2006; Chowanietz, 2010; Cronin, 2009; Gould & Klor, 2006). Terrorists impose economic costs to advance their political agendas (Gaibulloev & Sandler, 2009), but generally fail to frighten citizens of target countries into appeasing the perpetrators. The modal response of societies is defiance, not compliance. Berrebi and Klor (2008), for instance, find that within Israel the occurrence of a terror attack in a given locality within three months of elections causes a spike in that locality's support for the Likud and other hard - line parties opposed to concessions. Gould & Klor (2010) find that the most lethal Palestinian terrorist attacks are the most likely to induce this defiant, rightward electoral shift.

These trends do not appear restricted to Israel. Chowanietz (2010) analyses variation in public opinion within France, Germany, Spain, the United Kingdom, and the United States from 1990 to 2006. In each target country, terrorist attacks have shifted the electorate to the political right in proportion to their lethality. Related observations have been registered after al - Qaida and its affiliates killed civilians in Egypt, Indonesia, Jordan, the Philippines, Russia, Turkey, and the United States (Shapiro, 2012; Wilkinson, 2012). RAND (2009) observes in a précis of the literature: "Terrorist fatalities, with few exceptions, increase support for the bloc of parties associated with a more intransigent position. Scholars may interpret this as further evidence that terrorist attacks against civilians do not help terrorist organizations achieve their stated goals." In sum, numerous studies on the political effects of terrorism show that targeted communities do not tend to become paralyzed with fear, but resolutely resist caving in to the perpetrators.

Communities targeted by terrorism act organically to push back against the perpetrators independent of government initiatives. A recent study, for example, finds that when Palestinian terrorists attack Israeli civilians, Israeli settlers become more likely to build new outposts in West Bank districts from which the terrorists hailed (Getmansky & Sinmazdemir, 2017). As the authors conclude, "These results suggest that Israeli settlers use outpost expansion as retaliation against Palestinian communities they perceive to be involved in violence, and this shifts territorial control against Palestinians" (ibid., 31).Together, these studies on the political effects of terrorism suggest that while terrorists aim to destabilize societies with fear, localities are generally resilient, as anticipated by CMT. Accordingly, we expect most terrorism to fail against firms as well by bolstering communal solidarity, especially as they adapt to the threat environment and weakened institutional setting. In the analysis below, we develop a set of specific predictions about how firms will respond to terrorism based on the aforementioned research programs in international business and political science.

SOLUTIONS AND RECOMMENDATIONS

Predicting the Impact of Terrorism on Firms

New Venture Creation: Institutions are an important factor in new venture creation (Acs et al., 2008; Autio & Fu, 2015; Dau et al., 2015; Dau et al., 2016a; Dau et al., 2016; Stephan et al., 2015). A useful distinction is between formal and informal entrepreneurship (Dau, & Curevo - Cazurra, 2014; Moore et al., 2020; Moore et al., 2021; Sutter et al., 2013; Thai & Turkina, 2012; Williams, 2006). Formal entrepreneurs register new businesses through the codified structures put in place by the government (Acs et al., 2008; Baumol, 1993; Gries & Naudé, 2011), while informal entrepreneurs operate outside existing institutional and regulatory frameworks (Siqueira et al., 2016; Thai & Turkina, 2014; Webb et al., 2013). Each type of entrepreneur responds to institutional environments and changes in those environments in different ways (Acs, Desia, et al., 2008; Puffer et al., 2010; Stephan et al., 2015). Although there are other distinctions of entrepreneurship such as female versus male (c.f. Dau, Moore, & Abrahms, 2018a), we focus on the distinct between formal and informal entrepreneurs while also encouraging future scholars to look at other distinctions.

Formal entrepreneurs benefit from stronger institutions and clearer regulations, which signal that the government is both effective and stable (Puffer et al., 2010; Sutter et al., 2013). These qualities add security to formal entrepreneurs in many domains from intellectual property rights protection to tax rates to research and development standards as well as labour laws (Acs et al., 2008; Karlsson & Acs, 2002; Karlsson & Honig, 2009). In general, robust institutional environments afford formal entrepreneurs the luxury of reduced risk to start - up costs and operations (Khoury & Prasad, 2012).

Conversely, informal entrepreneurs flourish in weaker institutional settings (Thai & Turkina, 2012; Webb et al., 2009). Since they operate outside of the confines of the existing regulatory institutions, they are able to exploit compromised structures and frameworks (Autio & Fu, 2015; Williams, 2006). These weak structures or formal institutional voids (McCarthy & Puffer, 2016; Stephan et al., 2015) present opportunities for informal entrepreneurs because they minimize the potential negative ramifications of not formally registering a business (Mair et al., 2007; Palepu & Khanna, 2005).

As drivers of economic recovery and development (Hall et al., 2010; Schumpeter, 1946, 1947), entrepreneurs are a crucial set of actors when terrorism strikes (Frey, 2009; Shelley, 2013). Economic security is essential for resilience after an attack (Buzan, 2008; Flynn 2007). How entrepreneurs maneuver amidst the institutional disruption is thus critical to recovery. Building on the existing parameters offered by institutional theory, CMT suggests that after a terrorist attack local community's introvert to solidify their own institutions, both formal and informal, to provide immediate and visible pathways for security (Squire et al., 1993). There will be a bottom up approach to institutional rebuilding and restructuring (Berke & Campanella, 2006; Ottaway, 2002) because these communities will see the exposed failures of the government and take charge of their own narratives of recovery (Edkins, 2003; Lahad, 2005).

More specifically, informal entrepreneurship will surge initially, whereas formal entrepreneurship will initially decrease, as a result of a loss of trust in the national - level institutions and the race to recuperation. Informal entrepreneurs will be able to take advantage of the national level institutional disruptions, whereas formal entrepreneurs will be discouraged to operate within the confines of these institutions since the government failed to guarantee their validity (Autio & Fu, 2015; Thai & Turkina, 2014). Overtime, however, as the institutions are rebuilt from the bottom up and as trust in the government is restored, this relationship will invert. The preceding logic leads to the following proposition:

Proposition 1: Institutional disruptions from terrorism lead initially to an increase in informal entrepreneurship and decrease in formal entrepreneurship, while this association inverts over time.

Family Firms: Institutional theory suggests that family firms have a comparative advantage in weaker institutional environments (Aguilera & Crespi - Cladera, 2012; Burki, 2012; Dau et al., 2019; Gómez - Mejia et al., 2011). Family firms, particularly large wealthy ones, are status quo seekers who take advantage of rent seeking practices (Benavides - Velasco et al., 2013; Bertrand & Schoar, 2006; Kim & Gao, 2013). They benefit from lower levels of institutional development, particularly as it relates to shareholder rights protection, price controls, and bureaucratic red tape (Arregle et al., 2007; Morck & Yeung, 2003; Schulze et al., 2001). When national - level institutions are weak, family ties are the next best solution to augment trust and reduce uncertainty (Gedajlovic & Carney, 2010; Kotlar et al., 2014; Zahra, 2005). In these instances, family control mitigates the effects of limited formal regulatory protections (Burkart et al., 2003; La - Porta et al., 1999). By retaining ownership amongst the family connections, risk is limited from imperfect market and regulatory conditions (Gomez - Mejia et al., 2010; Miller et al., 2009; Nieto et al., 2015). In other words, family firms have unique toolkits to operate amidst less clear and stable national regulatory institutional environments.

As noted, terrorist activity can cause severe institutional disruptions (Clarke, 2015; Cronin, 2003) by sowing fear and insecurity (BrownJr. 2015; Denzin, 2007). However, more than the regulatory quality is impacted; the normative and cognitive aspects of the national level institutions are also compromised. The residual impacts of politically motivated violence and the subsequent institutional disruptions it causes result in a lack of trust and security despite the strength of the regulatory quality before the attack (LaFree & Dugan, 2009). Even environments with the strongest regulatory quality are damaged cognitively and normatively from violent institutional disruptions resulting from the failure of the government to prevent them (Cronin, 2003; Finlan, 2003; Savun & Phillips, 2009). As the social perceptions shift, simultaneously with a decline of trust in national - level institutions, family firms must reconsider their ownership strategies.

CMT suggests that in these moments following trauma, communities must heal (Baddeley, 2012; Carp, 2010) from the bottom up (Edkins, 2003; Winter, 2014). In order to carry out effective healing practices, recuperation and resiliency must be constructed from the individual level first (Boje, 1991; Wilkins, 1992). Actors introvert and seek to take care of themselves and those closest to them. The healing process becomes that of collective action, as all actors within the impacted community now share the trauma (Kuipera, 2012; Lahad, 2005). Within this framework, collective action is discussed not only across the impacted community, but within sub - groups of it (Igreja, 2008; Squire et al., 1993; Vernon, 1986).

One of the most important sub - groups is family. CMT posits that when trauma strikes, families are more likely to increase and maintain solidarity, while attending to the needs of the community around them (Burnett, 2004; Erdelyi, 2010; Young, 1994). Under external threat, family units not only become stronger, but also larger as new members get absorbed into them (BrownJr, 2015; Edkins, 2003). Family firms are extensions of families (Aguilera & Crespi - Cladera, 2012; Bertrand & Schoar, 2006; Gómez - Mejia et al., 2011)that experience many of the same concerns and advantages in crises (Chrisman et al., 2007; Kotlar et al., 2014; Schulze et al., 2001). In response to traumatic fractures and institutional disruptions brought on by a terrorist attack, family firms should experience a sense of protectiveness to safeguard their familial unit. In addition to compromising regulatory institutional quality, violent institutional disruptions shift cognitive and normative perspectives, incentivizing groups in society to become more self - reliant and prioritize survival, particularly at the organizational level (Blomberg et al., 2011; Tolbert & Zucker, 1996). When the community and family feels threatened, family firms are well situated to use their close relationships as substitutes for the disrupted institutions and government leadership (Bertrand et al., 2008; Bertrand & Schoar, 2006). As a result, we expect terrorism to have the following effect on family firms:

Proposition 2: Institutional disruptions caused by terrorism lead to an increase in the familial ownership percentage of family firms and a retention of their business interests.

Firm CSR Strategy: Firm - level CSR strategy focuses on advancing the tripartite goals of people, planet, and profit (Elkington, 1998; Gimenez et al., 2012; Hacking & Guthrie, 2008). That is, the underlying motivation of CSR strategy is to engage in business practices that not only stimulate profitability, but also benefit the community and environment surrounding the firm (Jamali & Mirshak, 2007; Runhaar & Lafferty, 2009; Voegtlin & Pless, 2014). Within institutional theory, scholars contend that a strong regulatory setting puts pressure on firms to engage in CSR signalling (Dhaliwal et al., 2011; Nikolaeva & Bicho, 2011; Srivastava et al., 2012). This theory suggests that the greater the institutional quality, the more likely firms are to participate in CSR signalling (Dau et al., 2020; Dau et al., 2016b), as a result of stronger regulatory mechanisms (Fortanier et al., 2011; Young & Marais, 2012). In other words, firms are more inclined to adhere to the rules surrounding CSR within the host environment when the government is seen as capable of enforcing CSR regulations and subsequent punishments.

Because it challenges existing regulatory institutions and government credibility (Blomberg et al., 2011; Clarke, 2015; Cronin, 2003), terrorism is likely to affect CSR signalling behaviour. Indeed, previous studies suggest that conditions associated with weaker institutions tend to result in diminished CSR signalling behaviour (Jamali et al., 2009; Jamali & Mirshak, 2007; Marano & Kostova, 2015). Based on the strategic management literature, one might therefore conclude that terrorism limits CSR activity. Yet the inclusion of CMT implies a positive relationship between terrorism and CSR.

After a terrorist attack, the local community experiences fear and begins questioning the abilities of their government to supply stability and protection (Blomberg et al., 2011). Although the local community is impacted the most, terrorism is a communication strategy that promotes insecurity beyond the immediate target area (Schmid & De - Graaf, 1982). Across the globe, observers pay attention to the response of not only the local community, but the broader national reaction (Clarke, 2015), presenting a challenge, but also an opportunity for firms. CMT suggests that non - state governmental actors, in particular firms, will assume leadership roles in society to help mourn and overcome the trauma (Erdelyi, 2010; Ottem et al., 2007; Squire et al., 1993). Leadership in this context means not only profitability, but signalling both the intent and capacity to help others impacted by the trauma (Edkins, 2003; Winter, 2014). Observers of firms, especially in targeted areas, are especially primed to receive this altruistic messaging given the erosion of trust in government to carry out its typical functions. Thus, we argue that firms from impacted areas are especially motivated to engage in CSR signalling to take care of their community and as a reputation - building tactic while their behaviour is under an international microscope. The preceding logic leads to the following proposition:

Proposition 3: Institutional disruptions caused by terrorism lead to an increase in firm - level CSR signalling.

Strategic Alliances: Firms create strategic alliances to improve capability and performance (Dau et al., 2019). Alliances are based on partnerships with other firms or other actors including individuals, non - profit organizations, or governments (Chan et al., 1997; Child, 2001; Dacin et al., 2007).Within the framework of institutional theory, scholars believe the quality of institutions affects the incentives and proclivity to form strategic alliances (Chen & Chen, 2003; Jiang & Li, 2008; Kale et al., 2000). Higher institutional quality encourages firms to take a longer - term view of alliances (Kale & Singh, 2009a; Marshall, 2015; Turley, 2010). Firms operating under these conditions are able to focus on intangible assets, knowledge flows, and technological and managerial capabilities (Das & Teng, 2000; Hamel, 1991). Conversely, lower institutional quality incentivizes firms to focus on more immediate gains and alliances given the shorter time horizon (Child, 2001; Deeds & Hill, 1996; Devlin & Bleackley, 1988). Further, firms from weaker institutional environments are encouraged to seek alliances to help them endure (Gulati & Singh, 1998; Inkpen & Tsang, 2007; Zollo et al., 2002).

As noted, terrorist attacks challenge institutions and expose the failures of the government (Clarke, 2015; Cronin, 2003). Existing theoretical frameworks suggest that firms from impacted areas would try to cultivate strategic alliances with firms from strong institutional environments for enhanced legitimacy and quicker recovery (Kale & Singh, 2009b; Li et al., 2008). Yet, some of the most lethal terrorist attacks have occurred in highly developed institutional climates from the United States to Western Europe (LaFree, 2010; START, 2015). Indeed, many scholars in international relations believe that terrorists are disproportionately attracted to liberal democracies, which generally have superior institutions when it comes to protecting firms, if not the state (Abrahms, 2007; Weinberg &Eubank, 1998).

CMT suggests that trauma has a centripetal effect on society by bringing those in mourning together for both emotional and functional reasons (Edkins, 2003; Winter, 2014). Individuals and organizations most impacted by terrorist attacks gain solidarity through a shared experience and a shift in social perceptions (Burnett, 2004; Staus, 2013) that fosters mutual empathy (Baddeley, 2012; Ibreck, 2010; Squire et al., 1993) even when the traumatic event is not entirely the same. This shared experience is an intangible asset that enables firms to learn from each other. After a firm experiences trauma from a terrorist attack, it cannot return to the same pre - attack cognitive and normative operational space. Fear of another attack becomes an enduring consideration in the firm's management strategy, forging emotional and tactical links with related firms. Such reasoning leads to the following proposition:

Proposition 4: Institutional disruptions from terrorism increase the strategic alliances between firms from similarly impacted countries.

Internationalization Strategies: Given current levels of globalization, an important consideration for firms is their internationalization strategy, including how much to keep processes and operations domestic or to expand them abroad (Melin, 1992; Pangarkar, 2008). The institutional theory literature recognizes that host country institutional quality (Lu & Beamish, 2001; Pangarkar, 2008) affects the incentives and opportunities for firms to internationalize (Cuervo - Cazurra, 2011; Kotabe & Mudambi, 2003; Luo, 2005). In general, this research suggests that firms operating in home environments with stronger institutional quality are better positioned to internationalize. Such firms may capitalize on their competitive advantage by exploiting weaker regulatory frameworks abroad (Gaffney et al., 2013; Qian et al., 2008). Firms from home environments with strong institutions also have an easier international transition if seen as previously vetted rule - followers with lower risk (Ramamurti, 2004; Xu & Shenkar, 2002).

Based on these insights from the strategic management literature, one might expect firms to curtail their internationalization strategy when terrorism disrupts their home institutions. One can even imagine some firms in extreme cases becoming too traumatized to think beyond their immediate environment, especially because international involvement is sometimes thought to elevate the risks of stoking resentment and future attacks (Savun & Phillips, 2009).CMT suggests, however, that firms may respond in the opposite fashion by losing confidence in the government and taking private initiative to circumvent it.

This post - attack self - reliance, independent of the government, extends not only to turning profits, but also to promoting survival given the absence of governmental protection. Researchers have found across many different domains that when organizations are physically threatened, they are inclined to decentralize and adopt a more networked structure (Arquilla & Ronfeldt, 2001). This strategy makes intuitive sense, as reflected in the admonition of not putting all your eggs in one basket, especially if the basket appears flawed. More formally, the resilience literature underscores the numerous benefits of decentralizing for organizational survival. Decentralization helps organizations achieve greater redundancy and participation, while lowering the risks from any part failing, including leaders (Simonsen et al., 2014). Although decentralization elevates the likelihood of incurring principal - agent problems, especially moral hazard (Hawkins et al., 2006), such concerns are presumably secondary when survival becomes paramount after a terrorist attack. Such reasoning leads to the next proposition:

Proposition 5: Institutional disruptions caused by terrorism lead firms from impacted areas to internationalize rapidly.

Firm Performance: Based on institutional theory, higher regulatory and institutional quality should positively affect local firm performance (Kotabe & Mudambi, 2003; North, 1990; Peng, 2004). More stringent regulations that monitor business transactions, intellectual property rights, and laws over research and development, labour and employment, and taxes reduce transaction and operational costs for firms (Peng et al., 2008; Poppo & Zenger, 1998; Przeworski, 2004). When regulations are clear, transparent, and effectively codified, firms are able to operate amidst market imperfections and increase profitability with reduced risk (Dau, 2013; Phillips et al., 2009).

The strategic management literature hence implies that firm performance decreases post - terrorist attack, especially in areas most directly affected (Morikawa, 2013; Peng, 2004).Insights from CMT suggest, however, that terrorism may be positively related to firm performance in geographically proximate areas, at least under certain conditions. Although traumatic events risk eroding trust in national - level institutions including the government (Edkins, 2003; Lahad, 2005; Neisser & Winograd, 1988), local communities undergo a sense of collective grief (Burnett, 2004; McGann, 2014), which fosters solidarity that helps fill the apparent void in government functions (Buckley - Zitsel et al., 2006; Erdelyi, 2010; Freed, 1995).More concretely, this cognitive and normative response may inspire the community to buy locally as part of the mourning and recovery process.

Although a single case study is insufficient for establishing trends (Bates et al., 1998), the Boston Marathon Bombing in April 2013 captures this dynamic from CMT. In killing three and wounding hundreds, the homemade bombs shook the city and exposed cracks in the national - level institutional infrastructure of the United States (Bodden, 2014). Outside of the Boston area, citizens thought twice about visiting shops, as terrorism spreads fear well beyond the targeted area (Nacos, 2016). Nevertheless, at the epicentre of the attacks, shops along Boylston Street flourished. The slogan "Boston Strong" became a rallying cry for local citizens to unify and resist the perpetrators, including with their wallets. Previous research suggests that terrorism is associated with a drop in foreign direct investment and tourism (Blomberg et al., 2011; Gaibulloev & Sandler, 2009; Sönmez et al., 1999), but CMT suggests that these setbacks may be offset by communal mourning in the form of local **patronage, leading to our final proposition:**

Proposition 6: Institutional disruptions caused by terrorism lead to an increase in firm performance in geographically proximate areas to the epicentre of the violence, except in certain industries dependent on external opinion, such as tourism.

FUTURE RESEARCH DIRECTIONS

Our interdisciplinary framework yields several testable predictions: (1) informal entrepreneurship increases, while formal entrepreneurship decreases; (2) family firms gain a larger share of supply chains; (3) firms within the impacted community increase their CSR signalling; (4) firms create alliances with other firms from similarly impacted areas; (5) firms from impacted areas become more international to hedge against future terrorist attacks in that area; and (6) most firms closest to the epicentre of the violence benefit from enhanced performance. We hope that future research will not only empirically test these propositions, but expand them to other aspects of firm strategy by leveraging interdisciplinary research outside of the traditional strategic management literature on collective traumas.

CONCLUSION

The purpose of this paper is to introduce a novel addition to institutional theory from the constructivist literature in international relations to better anticipate the reaction of firms to terrorism. In the current strategic management literature, institutional theory is ill - suited for making this assessment because it takes institutional quality as exogenous without appreciating the effects of the collective trauma and social perceptions on the local community. CMT focuses on how local communities tend to respond to collective traumas after governmental credibility is compromised. The upshot is that communities are resilient and may actually gain strength through solidarity in the course of the mourning process.

The combination of insights from both research programs supplies superior analytic leverage to begin plausibly theorizing about the effects of terrorism on firms across all stages of their lifecycles. This enhanced framework suggests that most firms not only survive terrorist attacks, but will even thrive if they can assume a leadership role in the community to help fill the perceived institutional and governmental void. As strategic actors, firms are not passive victims of terrorist attacks. Rather, they respond dynamically to post - attack changes in their institutional environments. In short, if given the proper toolkits, firms can build resilient strategies to better respond to the risks associated with terrorism.

Although political science examines the political effects of terrorism, the impact on firms has been given short shrift. Yet the survival and adaptation of firms is essential to communal and nationwide recovery. Our interdisciplinary framework yields several testable predictions: (1) informal entrepreneurship increases, while formal entrepreneurship decreases; (2) family firms gain a larger share of supply chains; (3) firms within the impacted community increase their CSR signalling; (4) firms create alliances with other firms from similarly impacted areas; (5) firms from impacted areas become more international to hedge against future terrorist attacks in that area; and (6) most firms closest to the epicentre of the violence benefit from enhanced performance. We hope that future research will not only empirically test these propositions, but expand them to other aspects of firm strategy by leveraging interdisciplinary research outside of the traditional strategic management literature on collective traumas.

Our innovative research program also highlights several critical implications for policy - makers and practitioners. From a managerial standpoint, the theoretical propositions of this article offer insights for firms at all stages of the business life cycle from conception to behaviour and strategy to performance. In addition to institutional disruptions, managers and key shareholders will understandably experience temporary fear and disorientation following a terrorist attack. Firms will not only survive, however, but even thrive if they embed themselves in the community mourning process. This embedding process will help make the firm more agile in the face of the risks associated with terrorism.

Despite substantial investment in counterterrorism (Mueller and Steward 2011), governments are unable to stop the political violence. As such, it is imperative for management scholars and practitioners to understand how this violence impacts firms. Building on the concepts of collective traumatic narratives and collective memory practices, we hope our extension of institutional theory is as helpful as it is timely.

REFERENCES

Abdi, M., & Aulakh, P. S. (2012). Do country - level institutional frameworks and inter - firm governance arrangements substitute or complement in international business relationships? *Journal of International Business Studies*, *43*(5), 477–497. doi:10.1057/jibs.2012.11

Abrahms, M. (2007). Why Democracies Make Superior Counter terrorists. *Security Studies*, *16*(2), 223–253. doi:10.1080/09636410701399424

Abrahms, M. (2010). *Lumpers versus Splitters: A Pivotal Battle in the Field of Terrorism Studies*. The New Sociology of Terrorism.

Abrahms, M. (2013). The Credibility Paradox: Violence as a Double-Edged Sword in International Politics. *International Studies Quarterly*, *57*(4), 660–671. doi:10.1111/isqu.12098

Abrahms, M., Dau, L., & Moore, E. (2019). Terrorism and Corporate Social Responsibility: Testing the Impact of Attacks on CSR Behaviour. *Journal of International Business Policy*, *2*(3), 237–257. doi:10.105742214-019-00029-6

Acharya, A. (2004). How Ideas Spread: Whose Norms Matter? Norm Localization and Institutional Change in Asian Regionalism. *International Organization*, *58*(2), 239–275. doi:10.1017/S0020818304582024

Acs, Z. J., Desai, S., & Klapper, L. F. (2008). What does "entrepreneurship" data really show? *Small Business Economics*, *31*(3), 265–281. doi:10.100711187-008-9137-7

Acs, Z. J., Desia, S., & Hessels, J. (2008). Entrepreneurship, Economic Development and Institutions. *Small Business Economics*, *31*(3), 219–234. doi:10.100711187-008-9135-9

Aguilera, R. V., & Crespi-Cladera, R. (2012). Firm family firms: Current debates of corporate governance in family firms. *Journal of Family Business Strategy*, *3*(2), 66–69. doi:10.1016/j.jfbs.2012.03.006

Aldrich, D. P. (2012). *Building resilience: Social capital in post - disaster recovery*. University of Chicago Press. doi:10.7208/chicago/9780226012896.001.0001

Arquilla, J., & David, R. (2001). *Networks and net - wars: The future of terror, crime, and militancy*. Rand Corporation.

Arregle, J. L., Hitt, M. A., Simon, D. G., & Very, P. (2007). The Development of Organizational Social Capital: Attributes of Family Firms. *Journal of Management Studies*, *44*(1), 73–95. doi:10.1111/j.1467-6486.2007.00665.x

Autio, E., & Fu, K. (2015). Economic and political institutions and entry into formal and informal entrepreneurship. *Asia Pacific Journal of Management*, *32*(1), 67–94. doi:10.100710490-014-9381-0

Baddeley, A. (2012). Working memory: Theories, models, and controversies. *Annual Review of Psychology*, *63*(1), 1–29. doi:10.1146/annurev-psych-120710-100422 PMID:21961947

Bates, R., Grief, A., Levi, M., Rosenthal, J. L., & Weingast, B. R. (1998). *Analytic narratives*. Princeton University Press.

Battilana, J., Leca, B., & Boxenbaum, E. (2009). How Actors Change Institutions: Towards a Theory of Institutional Entrepreneurship. *The Academy of Management Annals*, *3*(1), 65–107. doi:10.5465/19416520903053598

Baumol, W. J. (1993). Formal entrepreneurship theory in economics: Existence and bounds. *Journal of Business Venturing*, *8*(3), 197–210. doi:10.1016/0883-9026(93)90027-3

Beckert, J. (1999). Agency, Entrepreneurs, and Institutional Change. The Role of Strategic Choice and Institutionalized Practices in Organizations. *Organization Studies*, *20*(5), 777–799. doi:10.1177/0170840699205004

Benavides-Velasco, C. A., Quintana-García, C., & Guzmán-Parra, V. F. (2013). Trends in family business research. *Small Business Economics*, *40*(1), 41–57. doi:10.100711187-011-9362-3

Berke, P. R., & Campanella, T. J. (2006). Planning for Post disaster Resiliency. *The Annals of the American Academy of Political and Social Science*, *604*(1), 192–207. doi:10.1177/0002716205285533

Bernstein, S. (2011). Legitimacy in intergovernmental and non - state global governance. *Review of International Political Economy*, *18*(1), 17–51. doi:10.1080/09692290903173087

Berrebi, C. (2009). The Economics of Terrorism and Counterterrorism: What Matters and Is Rational Choice Theory Helpful? In P. K. Davis & K. Cragin (Eds.), *Social Science for Counterterrorism: Putting the Pieces Together* (pp. 151–202). Rand.

Berrebi, C., & Klor, E. F. (2008). Are voters sensitive to terrorism? Direct evidence from the Israeli electorate. *The American Political Science Review*, *102*(03), 279–301. doi:10.1017/S0003055408080246

Bertrand, M., Johnson, S., Samphantharak, K., & Schoar, A. (2008). Mixing family with business: A study of Thai business groups and the families behind them. *Journal of Financial Economics*, *88*(3), 466–498. doi:10.1016/j.jfineco.2008.04.002

Bertrand, M., & Schoar, A. (2006). The role of family in family firms. *The Journal of Economic Perspectives*, *20*(2), 73–96. doi:10.1257/jep.20.2.73

Blomberg, S. B., Hess, G. D., & Tan, D. Y. (2011). Terrorism and the economics of trust. *Journal of Peace Research*, *48*(3), 383–398. doi:10.1177/0022343311401641

Bodden, V. (2014). *Boston Marathon Bombings*. ABDO Publishing Company.

Boje, D. M. (1991). The Storytelling Organization: A Study of Story Performance in an Office - Supply Firm Office - Supply Firm. *Administrative Science Quarterly*, *36*(1), 106–126. doi:10.2307/2393432

Brill, E. (1998). *The Encyclopaedia of Christianity*. Eerdmans.

Brown, W. L. Jr. (2015). Promoting resiliency to address fear and terrorism challenges in the xxi century. *European Scientific Journal VO*, *1*, 348.

Buchanan, A., & Keohane, R. O. (2006). The Legitimacy of Global Institutions. *Ethics & International Affairs*, *20*(4), 405–437. doi:10.1111/j.1747-7093.2006.00043.x

Buckley-Zistel, S. (2006). Remembering to forget: Chosen amnesia as a strategy for local coexistence in post - genocide Rwanda. *Africa*, *76*(2), 131–150. doi:10.3366/afr.2006.76.2.131

Burkart, M., Panunzi, F., & Shleifer, A. (2003). Family firms. *The Journal of Finance*, *58*(5), 2167–2201. doi:10.1111/1540-6261.00601

Burki, U. (2012). Institutional Voids and Corporate Governance: A Conceptual Understanding. *International Journal of Business and Management*, *7*(10), 99–107. doi:10.5539/ijbm.v7n10p99

Burnett, M. J. (2004). Remembering Justice in Rwanda; Locating Gender in the Judicial Construction of Memory. *Seattle Journal for Social Justice*, *3*(1), 757–789.

Busenitz, L. W., Gómez, C., & Spencer, J. W. (2000). Country institutional profiles: Unlocking entrepreneurial phenomena. *Academy of Management Journal*, *43*(5), 994–1003.

Buzan, B. (2008). *People, States & Fear: An Agenda for International Security Studies in the Post - Cold War Era*. ECPR Press.

Cantwell, J. A., Dunning, J. H., & Lundan, S. M. (2010). An evolutionary approach to understanding the co - evolution international business activity : Environment of MNEs and the institutional. *Journal of International Business Studies*, *41*(4), 567–586. doi:10.1057/jibs.2009.95

Carp, J. M. (2010). Resiliency: The Essence of Survival in Chaos. *Families in Society*, *91*(3), 266–271. doi:10.1606/1044-3894.4004

Chan, S. H., Kensinger, J. W., Keown, A. J., & Martin, J. D. (1997). Do strategic alliances create value? *Journal of Financial Economics*, *46*(2), 199–221. doi:10.1016/S0304-405X(97)00029-9

Chen, H., & Chen, T.-J. (2003). Governance structures in strategic alliances: Transaction cost versus resource - based perspective. *Journal of World Business*, *38*(1), 1–14. doi:10.1016/S1090-9516(02)00105-0

Child, J. (2001). Learning Through Strategic Alliances. In Handbook of Organizational Learning & Knowledge (pp. 657 - 680). Academic Press.

Chowanietz, C. (2010). Rallying around the flag or railing against the government? Political parties' reactions to terrorist acts. *Party Politics*.

Chrisman, J. J., Sharma, P., & Taggar, S. (2007). Family influences on firms: An introduction. *Journal of Business Research*, *60*(10), 1005–1011. doi:10.1016/j.jbusres.2007.02.016

Clarke, C. P. (2015). *Terrorism, Inc.: The Financing of Terrorism, Insurgency, and Irregular Warfare*. ABC - CLIO.

Cronin, A. K. (2002). Rethinking sovereignty: American strategy in the age of terrorism. *Survival*, *44*(2), 119–139. doi:10.1093urvival/44.2.119

Cronin, A. K. (2003). Behind the Curve: Globalization and International Terrorism. *International Security*, *27*(3), 30–58. doi:10.1162/01622880260553624

Cuervo-Cazurra, A. (2011). Selecting the country in which to start internationalization: The non - sequential internationalization model. *Journal of World Business*, *46*(4), 426–437. doi:10.1016/j.jwb.2010.10.003

Czinkota, M. R., Knight, G., Liesch, P. W., & Steen, J. (2010). Terrorism and international business: A research agenda. *Journal of International Business Studies*, *41*(5), 826–843. doi:10.1057/jibs.2010.12

Dacin, M. T., Goodstein, J., & Scott, W. R. (2002). Institutional theory and institutional change: Introduction to the special research forum. *Academy of Management Journal*, *45*(1), 43. doi:10.2307/3069284

Das, T. K., & Teng, B.-S. (2000). A Resource - Based Theory of Strategic Alliances. *Journal of Management*, *26*(1), 31–61. doi:10.1177/014920630002600105

Dau, L. A. (2013). Learning across geographic space: Pro - market reforms, multi - nationalization strategy, and profitability. *Journal of International Business Studies*, *44*(3), 235–262. doi:10.1057/jibs.2013.5

Dau, L. A., & Cuervo-Cazurra, A. (2014). To formalize or not to formalize: Entrepreneurship and pro - market institutions. *Journal of Business Venturing*, *29*(5), 668–686. doi:10.1016/j.jbusvent.2014.05.002

Dau, L. A., & Moore, E. (2020). *Developing New England Business Recovery and Resilience in Response to COVID - 19*. Northeastern University's Global Resilience Institute White Paper Series (Funded by a grant from US FEMA). Available at https://globalresilience.northeastern.edu/publications-whitepaper-series-covid-19-special-investigation-report-2020-8/

Dau, L. A., & Moore, E. (2020). *A global disruption requires a global response: Policies for building international business resilience for this and future pandemics*. Northeastern University's Global Resilience Institute White Paper Series (Funded by a grant from US FEMA). Available at: https://globalresilience.northeastern.edu/whitepaperseries-covid-19-special-investigation-report-2020-11/

Dau, L. A., Moore, E. M., & Abrahms, M. (2018a). Female entrepreneurship and international organizations. In Entrepreneurship and the Sustainable Development Goals, (pp. 165 – 183). Emerald Group. doi:10.1108/S2040-724620180000008015

Dau, L. A., Moore, E. M., & Abrahms, M. (2018b). Global security risks, emerging markets, and firm responses: Assessing the impact of terrorism on firm profitability. In D. Castellani, R. Narula, Q. Nguyen, I. Surdu, & J. Walker (Eds.), *Contemporary Issues in International Business: Institutions, Strategy and Performance. Palgrave MacMillan.* doi:10.1007/978-3-319-70220-9_5

Dau, L. A., Moore, E. M., & Bradley, C. (2015). Institutions and International Entrepreneurship. International Business: Research. *Teaching and Practice*, *9*(1), 1–20.

Dau, L. A., Moore, E. M., & Kostova, T. (2020). The impact of market based institutional reforms on firm strategy and performance: Review and extension. *Journal of World Business*, *55*(4), 101073. doi:10.1016/j.jwb.2020.101073

Dau, L. A., Moore, E. M., & Newburry, W. (2020). The grass is always greener: The impact of home and host country CSR reputation signalling on cross - country investments. *Journal of International Business Policy*, 1 – 29.

Dau, L. A., Moore, E. M., Petrich, K., & Abrahms, M. (2019). Terrorism and resilience: How family businesses respond to terrorist activity. In Handbook of Global Financial Markets, (pp. 647 – 668). World Scientific Publishing.

Dau, L. A., Moore, E. M., & Robson, M. A. (2019). Strategic collaboration within competitive industries: Private sector intelligence. In T. K. Das (Ed.), Managing Inter - partner Risks in Strategic Alliances, (pp. 239 – 256). Information Age Publishing.

Dau, L. A., Moore, E. M., & Soto, M. (2016a). Informal transnational political actors and emerging markets: Understanding entrepreneurship in a changing normative atmosphere. In A. Walsh (Ed.), Entrepreneurship and Firm Performance, (pp. 19 – 41). Nova Science Publishers.

Dau, L. A., Moore, E. M., & Soto, M. (2016b). The great recession and emerging market firms: Unpacking the divide between global and national level sustainability expectations. In Lessons from the Great Recession: At the Crossroads of Sustainability and Recovery, (pp. 165 – 187). Emerald Group.

Dau, L. A., Moore, E. M., Soto, M., & LeBlanc, C. (2016). How globalization sparked entrepreneurship in the developing world: The impact of formal economic and political linkages. In Corporate Espionage, Geopolitics, and Diplomacy Issues in International Business, (pp. 72 – 91). IGI Global.

Davis, L. E. (2014). Have We Gone Too Far with Resiliency? *Social Work Research*, *38*(1), 5–6. doi:10.1093wrvu003

Deeds, D. L., & Hill, C. W. L. (1996). Strategic alliances and the rate of new product development: An empirical study of entrepreneurial biotechnology firms. *Journal of Business Venturing*, *11*(1), 41–55. doi:10.1016/0883-9026(95)00087-9

Denzin, N. K. (2007). Terrorism and the Politics of Fear. *Contemporary Sociology: A Journal of Reviews, 36*(3), 266 - 267.

Devlin, G., & Bleackley, M. (1988). Strategic alliances - Guidelines for success. *Long Range Planning*, *21*(5), 18–23. doi:10.1016/0024-6301(88)90101-X

Dhaliwal, D. S., Li, O. Z., Tsang, A., & Yang, Y. G. (2011). Voluntary nonfinancial disclosure and the cost of equity capital: The initiation of corporate social responsibility reporting. *The Accounting Review*, *86*(1), 59–100. doi:10.2308/accr.00000005

Dimaggio, P. J. (1988). Interest and Agency in Institutional Theory. In *Institutional patterns and organizations* (Vol. 1, pp. 3–22). Culture and Environment.

Dimaggio, P. J., & Powell, W. W. (1983). The Iron Cage Revisited: Institutional Isomorphism and Collective Rationality in Organizational Fields. *American Sociological Review*, *48*(2), 147–160. doi:10.2307/2095101

Edkins, J. (2003). *Trauma and the Memory of Politics*. Cambridge University Press. doi:10.1017/CBO9780511840470

Elkington, J. (1998). Partnerships from Cannibals with Forks: The Triple Bottom Line of 21st - Century Business. *Environmental Quality Management*, *8*(1), 37–51. doi:10.1002/tqem.3310080106

Enders, W., & Sandler, T. (2004). *What do we know about the substitution effect in transnational terrorism? Research on terrorism: trends, achievements and failures*. Routledge.

Erdelyi, M. H. (2010). The Ups and Downs of Memory. *The American Psychologist*, *65*(7), 623–633. doi:10.1037/a0020440 PMID:20873880

Fan, J. P. H., Wong, T. J., & Zhang, T. (2013). Institutions and organizational structure: The case of state - owned corporate pyramids. *Journal of Law Economics and Organization*, *29*(6), 1217–1252. doi:10.1093/jleo/ews028

Finlan, A. (2003). Warfare by other means: Special Forces, terrorism and grand strategy. *Small Wars & Insurgencies*, *14*(1), 92–108. doi:10.1080/09592310412331300586

Flynn, S. (2007). *The Edge of Disaster: Rebuilding a Resilient Nation*. Random House.

Fortanier, F., Kolk, A., & Pinkse, J. (2011). Harmonization in CSR Reporting: MNEs and Global CSR Standards. *Management International Review*, *51*(5), 665–696. doi:10.100711575-011-0089-9

Freed, J. I. (1995). The United States Holocaust Memorial Museum - A Dialogue with Memory. *Curator*, *38*(2), 95–110. doi:10.1111/j.2151-6952.1995.tb01044.x

Frey, B. S. (2009). How can business cope with terrorism? *Journal of Policy Modeling*, *31*(5), 779–787. doi:10.1016/j.jpolmod.2008.09.007

Frey, B. S., Simon, L., & Alois, S. (2007). Calculating tragedy: Assessing the costs of terrorism. *Journal of Economic Surveys*, *21*(1), 1–24. doi:10.1111/j.1467-6419.2007.00505.x

Gaffney, N., Cooper, D., Kedia, B., & Clampit, J. (2013). Institutional transitions, global mind - set, and EMNE internationalization. *European Management Journal*, *32*(3), 383–391. doi:10.1016/j.emj.2013.08.001

Gaibulloev, K., & Sandler, T. (2009). The impact of terrorism and conflicts on growth in Asia. *Economics and Politics*, *21*(3), 359–383. doi:10.1111/j.1468-0343.2009.00347.x

Gedajlovic, E., & Carney, M. (2010). Markets, hierarchies, and families: Toward a transaction cost theory of the family firm. *Entrepreneurship Theory and Practice*, *34*(6), 1145–1172. doi:10.1111/j.1540-6520.2010.00418.x

Getmansky, A., & Tolga, S. (2017). (in press). Settling on Violence: Expansion of Israeli Outposts in the West Bank in Response to Terrorism. *Studies in Conflict and Terrorism.*

Giménez, C., Sierra, V., & Rodon, J. (2012). Sustainable operations: Their impact on the triple bottom line. *International Journal of Production Economics*, *140*(1), 149–159. doi:10.1016/j.ijpe.2012.01.035

Gomez, D. M., Torgler, B., & Ortega, G. J. (2013). Measuring global economic interdependence: A hierarchical network approach. *World Economy*, *36*(12), 1632–1648. doi:10.1111/twec.12080

Gomez-Mejia, L. R., Cruz, C., Berrone, P., & De Castro, J. (2011). The Bind that Ties: Socio - emotional Wealth Preservation in Family Firms. *The Academy of Management Annals*, *5*(1), 653–707. doi:10.5465/19416520.2011.593320

Gomez-Mejia, L. R., Makri, M., & Kintana, M. L. (2010). Diversification Decisions in family - controlled firms. *Journal of Management Studies*, *47*(2), 223–252. doi:10.1111/j.1467-6486.2009.00889.x

Gould, E. D., & Esteban, F. K. (2010). Does terrorism work? *The Quarterly Journal of Economics*, *125*(4), 1459–1510. doi:10.1162/qjec.2010.125.4.1459

Greif, A., & Laitin, D. D. (2004). A Theory of Endogenous Institutional Change. *The American Political Science Review*, *98*(4), 633–652. doi:10.1017/S0003055404041395

Gries, T., & Naudé, W. (2011). Entrepreneurship and human development: A capability approach. *Journal of Public Economics, 95*(3 - 4), 216 - 224.

Gulati, R., & Singh, H. (1998). The Architecture of Cooperation: Managing Coordination Costs and Appropriation Concerns in Strategic Alliances. *Administrative Science Quarterly*, *43*(4), 781–814. doi:10.2307/2393616

Guzzini, S. (2000). A Reconstruction of Constructivism in International Relations. *European Journal of International Relations*, *6*(2), 147–182. doi:10.1177/1354066100006002001

Hacking, T., & Guthrie, P. (2008). A framework for clarifying the meaning of Triple Bottom - Line, Integrated, and Sustainability Assessment. *Environmental Impact Assessment Review, 28*(2 - 3), 73 - 89.

Hall, J. K., Daneke, G. A., & Lenox, M. J. (2010). Sustainable development and entrepreneurship: Past contributions and future directions. *Journal of Business Venturing*, *25*(5), 439–448. doi:10.1016/j.jbusvent.2010.01.002

Hamel, G. (1991). Competition for competence and inter - partner learning within international strategic alliances. *Strategic Management Journal, 12*(1S), 83 - 103.

Haque, M. S. (2002). The Changing Balance of Power between the Government and NGOS in Bangladesh. *International Political Science Review*, *23*(4), 411–435. doi:10.1177/0192512102023004006

Hawkins, D. G. (Eds.). (2006). *Delegation and agency in international organizations*. Cambridge University Press. doi:10.1017/CBO9780511491368

Helmke, G., Levitsky, S., & Galvan, D. (2011). Politics. *Institutions Comparative Agenda*, *2*(4), 725–740.

Herzenstein, M., Horsky, S., & Posavac, S. S. (2015). Living with terrorism or withdrawing in terror: Perceived control and consumer avoidance. *Journal of Consumer Behaviour*, *14*(4), 228–236. doi:10.1002/cb.1511

Heymann, P. B. (2000). *Terrorism and America: A common-sense strategy for a democratic society*. MIT Press.

Higgins, A. & de Freytas-Tamura, K. (2015, November 19). Attacks in Paris. *New York Times*.

Hofferberth, M., & Weber, C. (2015). Lost in translation: A critique of constructivist norm research. *Journal of International Relations and Development*, *18*(1), 75–103. doi:10.1057/jird.2014.1

Hong, J., Sun, X., & Huang, W. (2016). Local Institutions, Foreign Direct Investment and Productivity of Domestic Firms. *Review of Development Economics*, *20*(1), 25–38. doi:10.1111/rode.12204

Hurd, I. (2008). Constructivism. In The Oxford Handbook of International Relations (pp. 298 - 326). OUP.

Ibreck, R. (2010). The politics of mourning: Survivor contributions to memorials in post - genocide Rwanda. *Memory Studies*, *3*(4), 330–343. doi:10.1177/1750698010374921

Igreja, V. (2008). Memories as weapons: The politics of peace and silence in post - civil war Mozambique. *Journal of Southern African Studies*, *34*(3), 539–556. doi:10.1080/03057070802259720

Ingelaere, B. (2009). Does the truth pass across the fire without burning? Locating the short circuit in Rwanda's Gacaca courts. *The Journal of Modern African Studies*, *47*(4), 507–528. doi:10.1017/S0022278X0999005X

Inkpen, A. C., & Tsang, E. W. K. (2007). Learning and Strategic Alliances. *The Academy of Management Annals*, *1*(1), 479–511. doi:10.5465/078559815

Institute for Economics and Peace. (2016). *Global Terrorism Index 2016: Measuring and Understanding the Impact of Terrorism*. Author.

Jackson, P. T. (2001). Constructing Thinking Space: Alexander Wendt and the Virtues of Engagement. *Cooperation and Conflict*, *36*(1), 109–120. doi:10.1177/00108360121962317

Jamali, D., & Mirshak, R. (2007). Corporate Social Responsibility (CSR): Theory and practice in a developing country context. *Journal of Business Ethics*, *72*(3), 243–262. doi:10.100710551-006-9168-4

Jamali, D., Zanhour, M., & Keshishian, T. (2009). Peculiar strengths and relational attributes of SMEs in the context of CSR. *Journal of Business Ethics*, *87*(3), 355–377. doi:10.100710551-008-9925-7

Jiang, X., & Li, Y. (2008). The relationship between organizational learning and firms' financial performance in strategic alliances: A contingency approach. *Journal of World Business*, *43*(3), 365–379. doi:10.1016/j.jwb.2007.11.003

Jongman, A. J. (1988). *Political terrorism: A new guide to actors, authors, concepts, databases theories, and literature*. Transaction Publishers.

Kahler, M. (2013). Rising powers and global governance: Negotiating change in a resilient status quo. *International Affairs*, *89*(3), 711–729. doi:10.1111/1468-2346.12041

Kale, P., & Singh, H. (2009a). Managing strategic alliances: What do we know now, and where do we go from here? *The Academy of Management Perspectives*, *23*(3), 45–62. doi:10.5465/amp.2009.43479263

Kale, P., Singh, H., & Perlmutter, H. (2000). Learning and protection of proprietary assets in strategic alliances: Building relational capital. *Strategic Management Journal*, *21*(3), 217–237. doi:10.1002/(SICI)1097-0266(200003)21:3<217::AID-SMJ95>3.0.CO;2-Y

Karlsson, C., & Acs, Z. J. (2002). Introduction to institutions, entrepreneurship and firm growth: The case of Sweden. *Small Business Economics*, *19*(2), 63–67. doi:10.1023/A:1016202618249

Karlsson, T., & Honig, B. (2009). Judging a business by its cover: An institutional perspective on new ventures and the business plan. *Journal of Business Venturing*, *24*(1), 27–45. doi:10.1016/j.jbusvent.2007.10.003

Kehayan, V., & Napoli, J. C. (2005). Resiliency in the face of disaster and terrorism: 10 things to do to survive. Personhood Press.

Keohane, R., & Nye, J. (2001). *Power and Interdependence*. Longman Publishing Group.

Keohane, R. O., & Nye, J. S. (2000). Globalization: What's New? What's not? (And so what?). *Foreign Policy*, (118), 104–119. doi:10.2307/1149673

Kets de Vries, M. F. R. (1993). The dynamics of family controlled firms: The good and the bad news. *Organizational Dynamics*, *21*(3), 59–71. doi:10.1016/0090-2616(93)90071-8

Khoury, T. A., Cuervo-Cazurra, A., & Dau, L. A. (2014). Institutional Outsiders and Insiders: The Response of Foreign and Domestic Inventors to the Quality of Intellectual Property Rights Protection. *Global Strategy Journal*, *4*(3), 200–220. doi:10.1002/gsj.1079

Khoury, T. A., & Prasad, A. (2012). How do Developing Country Entrepreneurs Navigate Extreme Institutional Voids? *Academy of Management Annual Meeting Proceedings*. 10.5465/AMBPP.2012.230

Kiernan, B. (2007). *Blood and Soil: A World History of Genocide and Extermination from Sparta to Darfur. Yale*. Yale University Press.

Kim, Y., & Gao, F. Y. (2013). Does family involvement increase business performance? Family - longevity goals' moderating role in Chinese family firms. *Journal of Business Research*, *66*(2), 265–274. doi:10.1016/j.jbusres.2012.08.018

Kotabe, M., & Mudambi, R. (2003). Institutions and international business. *Journal of International Management*, *9*(3), 215–217. doi:10.1016/S1075-4253(03)00033-4

Kotlar, J., De Massis, A., Fang, H., & Frattini, F. (2014). Strategic reference points in family firms. *Small Business Economics*, *43*(3), 597–619. doi:10.100711187-014-9556-6

Krueger, A. B., & Malečková, J. (2003). Education, Poverty and Terrorism: Is There a Causal Connection? *The Journal of Economic Perspectives*, *17*(4), 119–144. doi:10.1257/089533003772034925

Kuipera, N. A. (2012). Humour and resiliency: Towards a process model of coping and growth. *Europe's Journal of Psychology*, *8*(3), 475–491. doi:10.5964/ejop.v8i3.464

La Porta, R., Lopez-De-Silanes, F., & Shleifer, A. (1999). Corporate Ownership around the World. *The Journal of Finance*, *1*(1), 471–517. doi:10.1111/0022-1082.00115

LaFree, G. (2010). The Global Terrorism Database (GTD): Accomplishments and Challenges. *Perspectives on Terrorism*, *4*(1), 24–46.

LaFree, G., & Dugan, L. (2009). Research on terrorism and countering terrorism. *Crime and Justice*, *38*(1), 413–477. doi:10.1086/599201

Lahad, M. (2005). Terrorism: The community perspective. *Journal of Aggression, Maltreatment & Trauma, 10*(3 - 4), 667 - 679.

Lange, D., Lee, P. M., & Dai, Y. (2011). Organizational Reputation. *RE:view*, *37*(1), 153–184.

Lawernce, T. B., Hardy, C., Phillips, N., Lawrence, T. B., Hardy, C., & Phillips, N. (2002). Institutional effects of inter - organizational collaboration: The emergence of proto - institutions. *Academy of Management Journal*, *45*(1), 281–290.

Li, D., Eden, L., Hitt, M. A., & Ireland, R. D. (2008). Friends, acquaintances, or strangers? Partner selection in R&D alliances. *Academy of Management Journal*, *51*(2), 315–334. doi:10.5465/amj.2008.31767271

Lu, J. W., & Beamish, P. W. (2001). The internationalization and performance of SMEs. *Strategic Management Journal, 22*(6 - 7), 565 - 586.

Luo, Y. (2005). Do Insiders Learn from Outsiders? Evidence from Mergers and Acquisitions. *The Journal of Finance*, *60*(4), 1951–1982. doi:10.1111/j.1540-6261.2005.00784.x

Luthans, F., Vogelgesang, G. R., & Lester, P. B. (2006). Developing the Psychological Capital of Resiliency. *Human Resource Development Review*, *5*(1), 25–44. doi:10.1177/1534484305285335

Luthar, S. S. (2006). *Resilience in development: A synthesis of research across five decades.* Academic Press.

Machida, S. (2009). Globalization and the Legitimacy of Intergovernmental Organizations. *International Studies*, *46*(4), 371–400. doi:10.1177/002088171004600401

Mahtaney, P. (2013). *Globalization and Sustainable Economic Development: Issues, Insights, and Inference*. Palgrave Macmillan. doi:10.1057/9781137024992

Mair, J., Martí, I., & Ganly, K. (2007). Institutional voids as spaces of opportunity. *European Business Forum, 31*(1), 34 - 39.

Marano, V., & Kostova, T. (2015). Unpacking the institutional complexity in adoption of CSR practices in multinational enterprises. *Journal of Management Studies*, *53*(1), 28–54. doi:10.1111/joms.12124

Marshall, J. (2015). New articulations in the Americas : Seizing structural opportunities. *Third*, *19*(4), 673–700.

McCarthy, D. J., & Puffer, S. M. (2016). Institutional Voids in an Emerging Economy: From Problem to Opportunity. *Journal of Leadership & Organizational Studies*, *23*(2), 208–219. doi:10.1177/1548051816633070

McCauley, C., & Moskalenko, S. (2008). Mechanisms of political radicalization: Pathways toward terrorism. *Terrorism and Political Violence*, *20*(3), 415–433. doi:10.1080/09546550802073367

McGann, J. (2014). *A New Republic of Letters: Memory and Scholarship in the Age of Digital Reproduction*. Harvard University Press. doi:10.4159/9780674369245

Melin, L. (1992). Internationalization as a strategy process. *Strategic Management Journal, 13*(2S), 99 - 118.

Melvern, L. (2001). Missing the story: The media and the Rwandan genocide. *Contemporary Security Policy*, *22*(3), 91–106. doi:10.1080/135232605123313911248

Meyer, R. E., & Hellerer, M. A. (2014). Does institutional theory need redirecting? *Journal of Management Studies*, *51*(7), 1221–1233. doi:10.1111/joms.12089

Miller, D., Lee, J., Chang, S., & Le Breton-Miller, I. (2009). Filling the institutional void: The social behaviour and performance of family versus non - family technology firms in emerging markets. *Journal of International Business Studies*, *40*(5), 802–817. doi:10.1057/jibs.2009.11

Miller, S. (2008). Terrorism and Counter - Terrorism. Terrorism and Counter - Terrorism. *Ethics and Liberal Democracy*, *579*, 1–222.

Moore, E. M., Brandl, K., & Dau, L. A. 2019. Institutional schisms in Argentina: The impact of intergovernmental organizations on country institutional environments. In International Business in a VUCA World: The Changing Role of States and Firms, (pp. 89 – 102). Emerald Group.

Moore, E. M., Dau, L. A., & Doh, J. (2020). Does Monetary Aid Catalyse New Business Creation? Analysing the Impact of Global Aid Flows on Formal and Informal Entrepreneurship. *Journal of Management Studies*, *57*(3), 438–469. doi:10.1111/joms.12552

Moore, E. M., Dau, L. A., & Mingo, S. (2021). The effects of trade integration on formal and informal entrepreneurship: The moderating role of economic development. *Journal of International Business Studies*, 1–27.

Morck, R., & Yeung, B. (2003). Agency problems in large family business groups. *Entrepreneurship Theory and Practice*, *27*(4), 367–382. doi:10.1111/1540-8520.t01-1-00015

Morikawa, M. (2013). Productivity and survival of family firms in Japan. *Journal of Economics and Business*, *70*, 111–125. doi:10.1016/j.jeconbus.2012.11.001

Mueller, J., & Mark, G. S. (2011). *Terror, security, and money: Balancing the risks, benefits, and costs of homeland security*. Oxford University Press. doi:10.1093/acprof:osobl/9780199795758.001.0001

Nacos, B. (2016). Mass - mediated Terrorism: Mainstream and Digital Media in Terrorism and Counterterrorism. Rowman & Littlefield.

National Consortium for the Study of Terrorism and Responses to Terrorism (START). (2016). Global Terrorism Database.

Neisser, U., & Winograd, E. (1988). *Remembering Reconsidered: Ecological and Traditional Approaches to the Study of Memory*. Cambridge University Press. doi:10.1017/CBO9780511664014

Nieto, M. J., Santamaria, L., & Fernandez, Z. (2015). Understanding the Innovation Behaviour of Family Firms. *Journal of Small Business Management*, *53*(2), 382–399. doi:10.1111/jsbm.12075

Nikolaeva, R., & Bicho, M. (2011). The role of institutional and reputational factors in the voluntary adoption of corporate social responsibility reporting standards. *Journal of the Academy of Marketing Science*, *39*(1), 136–157. doi:10.100711747-010-0214-5

North, D. (1991). Institutions. *Journal of Economic Perspectives*.

North, D. C. (1990). *Institutions, Institutional Change and Economic Performance*. Cambridge University Press. doi:10.1017/CBO9780511808678

North, D. C. (1991). Institutions. *The Journal of Economic Perspectives*, *5*(1), 97–112. doi:10.1257/jep.5.1.97

Ottaway, M. (2002). *Rebuilding State Institutions in Collapsed States*. Academic Press.

Ottem, E., Lian, A., & Karlsen, P. (2007). Reasons for the Growth of Traditional Memory Span across Age. *The European Journal of Cognitive Psychology*, *19*(2), 233–270. doi:10.1080/09541440600684653

Palepu, K. G., & Khanna, T. (2005). *Spotting Institutional Voids in Emerging Markets*. Harvard Business School Cases.

Pangarkar, N. (2008). Internationalization and performance of small - and medium - sized enterprises. *Journal of World Business*, *43*(4), 475–485. doi:10.1016/j.jwb.2007.11.009

Panke, D., & Petersohn, U. (2016). Norm challenges and norm death: The inexplicable? *Cooperation and Conflict*, *51*(1), 3–19. doi:10.1177/0010836715597948

Peng, M. (2004). Outside directors and firm performance during institutional transitions. *Strategic Management Journal*, *25*(5), 453–471. doi:10.1002mj.390

Peng, M. W. (2002). Towards an institution - based view of business strategy. *Asia Pacific Journal of Management*, *19*(2/3), 251–267. doi:10.1023/A:1016291702714

Peng, M. W., Wang, D. Y. L., & Jiang, Y. (2008). An institution - based view of international business strategy: A focus on emerging economies. *Journal of International Business Studies*, *39*(5), 920–936. doi:10.1057/palgrave.jibs.8400377

Phillips, N., Tracey, P., & Karra, N. (2009). Rethinking institutional distance: Strengthening the tie between new institutional theory and international management. *Strategic Organization*, *7*(3), 339–348. doi:10.1177/1476127009337439

Poppo, L., & Zenger, T. (1998). Testing alternative theories of the firm: Transaction cost, Knowledge - based, and measurement explanations for make - or - buy decisions in information services. *Strategic Management Journal*, *19*(9), 853–877. doi:10.1002/(SICI)1097-0266(199809)19:9<853::AID-SMJ977>3.0.CO;2-B

Przeworski, A. (2004). Institutions matter? *Government and Opposition*, *39*(4), 527–540. doi:10.1111/j.1477-7053.2004.00134.x

Puffer, S. M., McCarthy, D. J., & Boisot, M. (2010). Entrepreneurship in Russia and China: The impact of formal institutional voids. *Entrepreneurship Theory and Practice*, *34*(3), 441–467. doi:10.1111/j.1540-6520.2009.00353.x

Qian, G., Li, L., Li, J., & Qian, Z. (2008). Regional diversification and firm performance. *Journal of International Business Studies*, *39*(2), 197–214. doi:10.1057/palgrave.jibs.8400346

Ramamurti, R. (2004). Developing Countries and MNEs: Extending and Enriching the Research Agenda. *Journal of International Business Studies*, *35*(4), 277–283. doi:10.1057/palgrave.jibs.8400087

Rapoport, D. C. (1984). Fear and trembling: Terrorism in three religious traditions. *The American Political Science Review*, *78*(03), 658–677. doi:10.2307/1961835

Rapoport, D. C. (2001). The Fourth Wave: September 11 in the History of Terrorism. *Current History (New York, N.Y.)*, *100*(650), 419–424. doi:10.1525/curh.2001.100.650.419

Rapoport, D. C. (2004). The four waves of modern terrorism. *Attacking terrorism: Elements of a grand strategy*, 46 - 73.

Risse, T. (2004). *Social Constructivism Meets Globalization*. Freie Universität Berlin.

Rodrik, D., Subramanian, A., & Trebbi, F. (2004). Institutions rule: The primacy of institutions over geography and integration in economic development. *Journal of Economic Growth*, *9*(2), 131–165. doi:10.1023/B:JOEG.0000031425.72248.85

Runhaar, H., & Lafferty, H. (2009). Governing corporate social responsibility: An assessment of the contribution of the un global compact to CSR strategies in the telecommunications industry. *Journal of Business Ethics*, *84*(4), 479–495. doi:10.100710551-008-9720-5

Savun, B., & Phillips, B. J. (2009). Democracy, Foreign Policy, and Terrorism. *The Journal of Conflict Resolution*, *53*(6), 878–904. doi:10.1177/0022002709342978

Schmid, A. P., & Janny, D. G. (1982). *Violence as communication: Insurgent terrorism and the Western news media*. Sage.

Schulze, W. S., Lubatkin, M., Dino, R., & Buscholtz, A. (2001). Agency relationships in family firms: Theory and evidence. *Organization Science*, *12*(2), 99–116. doi:10.1287/orsc.12.2.99.10114

Schulze, W. S., Lubatkin, M. H., Dino, R. N., & Buchholtz, A. K. (2001). Agency Relationships in Family Firms: Theory and Evidence. *Organization Science*, *12*(2), 99–116. doi:10.1287/orsc.12.2.99.10114

Schumpeter, J. A. (1946). *Essays: On Entrepreneurs, Innovations, Business Cycles, and the Evolution of Capitalism*. Transaction Books.

Schumpeter, J. A. (1947). The Creative Response in Economic History. *The Journal of Economic History*, *2*(2), 149–159. doi:10.1017/S0022050700054279

Scott, R. W. (1995). *Institutions and Organizations* (2nd ed.). SAGE Publishing.

Scott, W. R. (1987). The Adolescence of Institutional Theory. *Administrative Science Quarterly*, *32*(4), 493–511. doi:10.2307/2392880

Shapiro, J. N. (2012). Terrorist Decision - Making: Insights from Economics and Political Science. *Perspectives on Terrorism*, *6*(4 - 5), 5 - 20.

Shelley, L. I. (2013). *Dirty Entanglements: Corruption, Crime, and Terrorism*. Book. doi:10.1017/CBO9781139059039

Simonsen, S. H. (2014). *Applying resilience thinking: seven principles for building resilience in social - ecological systems*. Stockholm University Press.

Siqueira, A. C. O., Webb, J. W., & Bruton, G. D. (2016). Informal Entrepreneurship and Industry Conditions. *Entrepreneurship Theory and Practice*, *40*(1), 177–200. doi:10.1111/etap.12115

Slater, D., & Weber, M. (2013). *Iron Cage in an Iron Fist of Power in and the Personalization Institutions Authoritarian Malaysia*. Academic Press.

Sloan, S. (1984). Political Terrorism: Theory, Tactics and Counter - Measures. *The American Political Science Review*, *78*(2), 552–553. doi:10.2307/1963432

Squire, L. R., Knowlton, B., & Musen, G. (1993). The structure and organization of memory. *Annual Review of Psychology*, *44*(1), 453–495. doi:10.1146/annurev.ps.44.020193.002321 PMID:8434894

Srivastava, A. K., Negi, G., Mishra, V., & Pandey, S. (2012). Corporate Social Responsibility : A Case Study of TATA Group. *Journal of Business and Management*, *3*(5), 17–27.

START. (2016). GTD Global Terrorism Database. In National Consortium for the Study of Terrorism and Responses to Terrorism (p. 63). START.

Staus, S. (2013). *The Order of Genocide: Race, Power and War in Rwanda*. Cornell University Press. doi:10.7591/9780801467158

Stephan, U., Uhlander, L., & Stride, C. (2015). Institutions and social entrepreneurship: The role of institutional voids, institutional support, and institutional configurations. *Journal of International Business Studies*, *46*(3), 308–331. doi:10.1057/jibs.2014.38

Suchting, W. A. (1992). Constructivism deconstructed. *Science and Education*, *1*(3), 223–254. doi:10.1007/BF00430275

Sutter, C. J., Webb, J. W., Kistruck, G. M., & Bailey, A. V. G. (2013). Entrepreneurs' responses to semi - formal illegitimate institutional arrangements. *Journal of Business Venturing*, *28*(6), 743–758. doi:10.1016/j.jbusvent.2013.03.001

Tang, L., & Koveos, P. E. (2008). A Framework to Update Hofstede's Cultural value Indices: Economic Dynamics and Institutional Stability. *Journal of International Business Studies*, *39*(6), 1045–1063. doi:10.1057/palgrave.jibs.8400399

Thai, M. T. T., & Turkina, E. (2012). *Entrepreneurship in the Informal Economy. Entrepreneurship in the Informal Economy: Models*. Approaches and Prospects for Economic Development.

Thai, M. T. T., & Turkina, E. (2014). Macro - level determinants of formal entrepreneurship versus informal entrepreneurship. *Journal of Business Venturing*, *29*(4), 490–510. doi:10.1016/j.jbusvent.2013.07.005

Thornton, P. H., & Ocasio, W. (2005). *Institutional Logics*. The Sage Handbook of Organizational Institutionalism.

Tina Dacin, M., Oliver, C., & Roy, J. P. (2007). The legitimacy of strategic alliances: An institutional perspective. *Strategic Management Journal*, *28*(2), 169–187. doi:10.1002mj.577

Tolbert, P. S., & Zucker, L. G. (1996). The Institutionalization of Institutional Theory. Handbook of Organization Studies, 175 - 190.

Turley, B. J. S. (2010). *Entrepreneurship and innovation in Latin America Innovation and growth — the Latin American opportunity*. Ernst and Young White Paper.

van Hoorn, A., & Maseland, R. (2016). How institutions matter for international business: Institutional distance effects vs. institutional profile effects. *Journal of International Business Studies*, *47*(3), 374–381. doi:10.1057/jibs.2016.2

Vernon, G. (1986). *Introduction to Human Memory*. Routledge International Press.

Voegtlin, C., & Pless, N. M. (2014). Global Governance: CSR and the Role of the UN Global Compact. *Journal of Business Ethics*, *122*(2), 179–191. doi:10.100710551-014-2214-8

von Schlippe, A., & Frank, H. (2013). The Theory of Social Systems as a Framework for Understanding Family Businesses. *Family Relations*, *62*(3), 384–398. doi:10.1111/fare.12010

Webb, J. W., Bruton, G. D., Tihanyi, L., & Ireland, R. D. (2013). Research on entrepreneurship in the informal economy: Framing a research agenda. *Journal of Business Venturing*, *28*(5), 598–614. doi:10.1016/j.jbusvent.2012.05.003

Webb, J. W., Tihanyi, L., Ireland, R. D., & Sirmon, D. G. (2009). You Say Illegal, I Say Legitimate: Entrepreneurship in the Informal Economy. *Academy of Management Review*, *34*(3), 492–510. doi:10.5465/amr.2009.40632826

Weinberg, L., Pedahzur, A., & Hirsch-Hoefler, S. (2004). The Challenges of Conceptualizing Terrorism. *Terrorism and Political Violence*, *16*(4), 777–794. doi:10.1080/095465590899768

Weinberg, L. B., & Eubank, W. L. (1988). Terrorism and democracy: What recent events disclose. *Terrorism and Political Violence*, *10*(1), 108–118. doi:10.1080/09546559808427446

Wilkins, B. T. (1992). *Terrorism and Collective Responsibility*. Book.

Wilkinson, P. (1986). *Terrorism and the Liberal State* (2nd ed.). Macmillan.

Williams, C. (2006). The Hidden Enterprise Culture: Entrepreneurship in the Informal Economy. *Local Economy*, *21*.

Winter, J. (2014). *Sites of Memory, Sites of Mourning: The Great War in European Cultural History*. Cambridge University Press. doi:10.1017/CBO9781107589087

Wolfgang, K. (2007). *Iconic Remembering and Religious Icons: Fundamentalist Strategies in European Memory Politics?* Berghahn Books.

Xu, D., & Shenkar, O. (2002). Institutional distance and the multinational enterprise. *Academy of Management Review*, *27*(4), 608–618.

Young, J. E. (1994). *The Texture of Memory*. Yale University Press.

Young, S., & Marais, M. (2012). A Multi - level Perspective of CSR Reporting: The Implications of National Institutions and Industry Risk Characteristics. *Corporate Governance*, *20*(5), 432–450. doi:10.1111/j.1467-8683.2012.00926.x

Zahra, S. A. (2005). Entrepreneurial Risk Taking in Family Firms. *Family Business Review*, *18*(1), 23–40. doi:10.1111/j.1741-6248.2005.00028.x

Zollo, M., Reuer, J. J., & Singh, H. (2002). Inter - organizational Routines and Performance in Strategic Alliances. *Organization Science, 13*(February), 701 - 713.

KEY TERMS AND DEFINITIONS

Corporate Social Responsibility: The management strategy by which firms actively prioritize and integrate social, environmental, and governmental concerns into their business operations and strategy.

Cosmopolitan Memory Theory: The process and experience through which global or collective concerns become localized and part of a collective memory.

Family Firms: A firm that is owned either completely or by majority share of family members.

Firm Creation: The process of starting a new business, whether formally or informally registered for the purpose of this chapter.

Institutional Theory: The rules and regulations that shape and guide firm behaviour.

Strategic Alliances: Partnerships with other firms or actors within the community.

Terrorism: The selective use of violence by non - state actors against civilian targets.

Compilation of References

Abbasi, S., & Ruf, T. (2020). Reduction of the fluctuation rate in multi - project organizations through agile leadership. *Management, 8*(2), 128–133.

Abdi, M., & Aulakh, P. S. (2012). Do country - level institutional frameworks and inter - firm governance arrangements substitute or complement in international business relationships? *Journal of International Business Studies, 43*(5), 477–497. doi:10.1057/jibs.2012.11

Abrahamson, P., Salo, O., Ronkainen, J., & Warsta, J. (2002). *Agile Project Management methods: Review and analysis* (Technical report). VTT. 478.

Abrahamsson, J., Boter, H., & Vanyushyn, V. (2018). Business model innovation of international new ventures: An empirical study in a Swedish context. *Journal of International Entrepreneurship*. Advance online publication. doi:10.100710843-018-0238-3

Abrahamsson, P., & Koskela, J. (2004). Extreme programming: A survey of empirical data from a controlled case study. *Proceedings of the Third ACM-IEEE International Symposium on Empirical Software Engineering (ISESE 2004)*, 73-82. 10.1109/ISESE.2004.1334895

Abrahamsson, P., Salo, O., Ronkainen, J., & Warsta, J. (2002). *Agile software development methods: Review and analysis*. VTT Publications.

Abrahms, M. (2007). Why Democracies Make Superior Counter terrorists. *Security Studies, 16*(2), 223–253. doi:10.1080/09636410701399424

Abrahms, M. (2010). *Lumpers versus Splitters: A Pivotal Battle in the Field of Terrorism Studies*. The New Sociology of Terrorism.

Abrahms, M. (2013). The Credibility Paradox: Violence as a Double-Edged Sword in International Politics. *International Studies Quarterly, 57*(4), 660–671. doi:10.1111/isqu.12098

Abrahms, M., Dau, L., & Moore, E. (2019). Terrorism and Corporate Social Responsibility: Testing the Impact of Attacks on CSR Behaviour. *Journal of International Business Policy, 2*(3), 237–257. doi:10.105742214-019-00029-6

Abylova, V., & Salykova, L. (2019). Critical success factors in project management: A comprehensive review. *PM World Journal, 8*(5), 1–13.

Acharya, A. (2004). How Ideas Spread: Whose Norms Matter? Norm Localization and Institutional Change in Asian Regionalism. *International Organization, 58*(2), 239–275. doi:10.1017/S0020818304582024

Acs, Z. J., Desai, S., & Klapper, L. F. (2008). What does "entrepreneurship" data really show? *Small Business Economics, 31*(3), 265–281. doi:10.100711187-008-9137-7

Acs, Z. J., Desia, S., & Hessels, J. (2008). Entrepreneurship, Economic Development and Institutions. *Small Business Economics, 31*(3), 219–234. doi:10.100711187-008-9135-9

Adi, P. (2015). Scrum Method Implementation in a Software Development Project Management. *International Journal of Advanced Computer Science and Applications*, *6*(9). Advance online publication. doi:10.14569/IJACSA.2015.060927

Agile - Only. (2021). *Project Roles and Responsibility Distribution*. Author.

Agile Alliance. (2015). *Guide to agile practices*. http://guide.agilealliance.org/

Agile Alliance. (2021). *What is Agile Software Development?* Author.

Agile Manifesto. (2001). *Principles*. Retrieved from Https://Agilemanifesto.Org/Principles.Html

Agile Manifesto. (2001). *Twelve principles of agile software*. https://agilemanifesto.org

Agile Manifesto. (2019). *The Agile Manifesto*. Available: www.Agilemanifesto.org

Agilemodeling. (2021). *Answering the "Where is the Proof That Agile Methods Work" Question*. Author.

Aguezzoul, A. (2014). Third - party logistics selection problem: A literature review on criteria and methods. *Omega*, *49*, 69–78. doi:10.1016/j.omega.2014.05.009

Aguiari, G. (2013). Che cosa intendiamo per logistica sostenibile? In G. Aguiari & R. Provedel (Eds.), *Logistica sostenibile: un'occasione di sviluppo & innovazione* (pp. 17–30). FrancoAngeli.

Aguilera, R. V., & Crespi-Cladera, R. (2012). Firm family firms: Current debates of corporate governance in family firms. *Journal of Family Business Strategy*, *3*(2), 66–69. doi:10.1016/j.jfbs.2012.03.006

Alavi, M., & Leidner, D. E. (2001). Review: Knowledge Management and Knowledge Management Systems: Conceptual Foundations and Research Issues. *Management Information Systems Quarterly*, *25*(1), 107–136. doi:10.2307/3250961

Alberti-Alhtaybat, L. V., Al-Htaybat, K., & Hutaibat, K. (2019). A knowledge management and sharing business model for dealing with disruption: The case of Aramex. *Journal of Business Research*, *94*, 400–407. doi:10.1016/j.jbusres.2017.11.037

Albuquerque, F., Torres, A. S., & Berssaneti, F. T. (2020). Lean product development and agile project management in the construction industry. *Revista de Gestão*, *27*(2), 135–151. doi:10.1108/REGE-01-2019-0021

Alderson, A., & Shah, H. (1999). Technical opinion: Viewpoints on legacy systems. *Communications of the ACM*, *42*(3), 115–116. doi:10.1145/295685.295722

Aldrich, D. P. (2012). *Building resilience: Social capital in post - disaster recovery*. University of Chicago Press. doi:10.7208/chicago/9780226012896.001.0001

Allaboutagile. (2021a). *Step 4: Sprint Planning (Tasks)*. Www.allaboutagile.com

Allaboutagile. (2021b). *How Agile Are You? (Take This 42 Point Test)*. Www.allaboutagile.com

Almeida, F., & Simões, J. (2021). Leadership Challenges in Agile Environments. *International Journal of Information Technology Project Management*, *12*(2), 30–44. doi:10.4018/IJITPM.2021040102

Amazon. (2021). *Training ML models*. https://docs.aws.amazon.com

Ambler, S. (2002). *Agile Modeling: Effective Practices for EXtreme Programming and the Unified Process*. John Wiley & Sons.

Ambler, S. (2006). *Survey Says: Agile Works in Practice*. Dr. Dobb's.

Ambysoft Inc. (2021). *Examining the Agile Manifesto*. Author.

Amershi, S., Begel, A., Bird, C., DeLine, R., Gall, H., Kamar, E., Nagappan, N., Nushi, B., & Zimmermann, T. (2019). *Software engineering for machine learning: A case study*. Microsoft Research. https://www.microsoft.com

Amoatey, C. T., & Anson, B. A. (2017). Investigating the major causes of scope creep in real estate construction projects in Ghana. *Journal of Facilities Management*. https://www.emerald.com/insight/content/doi/10.1108/JFM-11-2016-0052/full/html

Amoatey, C. T., Ameyaw, Y. A., & Adaka, E. (2015). Analysing delay causes and effects in Ghanaian state housing construction projects. *International Journal of Managing Projects in Business*, *8*(1), 198–214. doi:10.1108/IJMPB-04-2014-0035

Anaya-Arenas, A. M., Renaud, J., & Ruiz, A. (2014). Relief distribution networks: A systematic review. *Annals of Operations Research*, *223*(1), 53–79. doi:10.100710479-014-1581-y

Ancona, D., Malone, T. W., Orlikowski, W. J., & Senge, P. M. (2007). In praise of the incomplete leader. *Harvard Business Review*, *85*(2). PMID:17345683

Andersen, B., Samset, K., & Welde, M. (2016). Low estimates - high stakes, underestimation of costs at the front - end of projects. *International Journal of Managing Projects in Business*, *9*(1), 171–193. doi:10.1108/IJMPB-01-2015-0008

Anderson, D. (2005). *Declaration of Interdependence*. Academic Press.

Anderson, D. J., Concas, G., Lunesu, M. I., Marchesi, M., & Zhang, H. (2012). A comparative study of Scrum and Kanban approaches on a real case study using simulation. In *International Conference on Agile Software Development*. Springer.

Angrosino, M. V., & Mays de Pérez, K. A. (2000). Rethinking Observation. In N. Denzin & Y. Lincoln (Eds.), *Handbook of qualitative research* (pp. 673–702). Sage.

Ang, S., Van Dyne, L., & Koh, C. (2006). Personality correlates of the four - factor model of cultural intelligence. *Group & Organization Management*, *31*(1), 100–123. doi:10.1177/1059601105275267

Anquetil, N., de Oliveira, K. M., de Sousa, K. D., & Batista Dias, M. G. (2007). Software maintenance seen as a knowledge management issue. *Information and Software Technology*, *49*(5), 515–529. doi:10.1016/j.infsof.2006.07.007

Antlova, K. (2014). Agile approach in the project management of the Czech companies. *Procedia Technology.*, *16*, 929–933. doi:10.1016/j.protcy.2014.10.045

Aqlan, F., & Lam, S. S. (2015). A Fuzzy - based Integrated Framework for Supply Chain Risk Assessment. *International Journal of Production Economics*, *161*, 54–63. doi:10.1016/j.ijpe.2014.11.013

Arau'zo, J., Pajares, J., & Lopez-Paredes, A. (2010). Simulating the dynamic scheduling of project portfolios. *Simulation Modelling Practice and Theory*, *18*(10), 1428–1441. doi:10.1016/j.simpat.2010.04.008

Arquilla, J., & David, R. (2001). *Networks and net - wars: The future of terror, crime, and militancy*. Rand Corporation.

Arregle, J. L., Hitt, M. A., Simon, D. G., & Very, P. (2007). The Development of Organizational Social Capital: Attributes of Family Firms. *Journal of Management Studies*, *44*(1), 73–95. doi:10.1111/j.1467-6486.2007.00665.x

Artto, K., & Kujala, J. (2008). Project business as a research field. *International Journal of Managing Projects in Business*, *1*(4), 469–497. doi:10.1108/17538370810906219

Atkinson, R. (1999). Project Management: Cost, Time and Quality, Two Best Guesses and A Phenomenon, Its Time to Accept Other Success Criteria. *International Journal of Project Management*, *17*(6), 337–342. doi:10.1016/S0263-7863(98)00069-6

Augier, M., & Teece, D. J. (2007). Dynamic capabilities and multinational enterprise: Penrosean insights and omissions. *Management International Review*, *47*(2), 175–192. doi:10.100711575-007-0010-8

Aurum, A., Daneshgar, F., & Ward, J. (2008). Investigating Knowledge Management practices in software development organizations An Australian experience. *Information and Software Technology*, *50*(6), 511–533. doi:10.1016/j.infsof.2007.05.005

Aurum, A., Jeffery, R., Wohlin, C., & Handzic, M. (2003). *Managing Software Engineering Knowledge*. Springer. doi:10.1007/978-3-662-05129-0

Autio, E., & Fu, K. (2015). Economic and political institutions and entry into formal and informal entrepreneurship. *Asia Pacific Journal of Management*, *32*(1), 67–94. doi:10.100710490-014-9381-0

Azanha, A., Argoud, A. R. T. T., de Camargo, J. B. Junior, & Antoniolli, P. D. (2017). Agile project management with Scrum: A case study of a Brazilian pharmaceutical company IT project. *International Journal of Managing Projects in Business*, *10*(1), 121–142. doi:10.1108/IJMPB-06-2016-0054

Baddeley, A. (2012). Working memory: Theories, models, and controversies. *Annual Review of Psychology*, *63*(1), 1–29. doi:10.1146/annurev-psych-120710-100422 PMID:21961947

Bagnoli, C. (2012). Methodology of Analysis Canvas. Lecture at Faculty of Management, Koper.

Band, Z. (2014). *Technical Debt + Red October*. Author.

Bar - On, R. (2006). The Bar - On model of emotional - social intelligence (ESI). *Psicothema*, *18*(1), 13–25. PMID:17295953

Barjtya, S., Sharma, A., & Rani, U. (2017). A detailed study of Software Development Life Cycle (SDLC). *Models.*, *6*(7), 4.

Barlow, J. B. (2011). Overview and Guidance on Agile Development in Large Organizations. Comm. of the Ass. for Inform. *Systems*, *29*(1), 25–44.

Barlow, J. B., Justin, S. G., Mark, J. K., David, W. W., Ryan, M. S., Paul, B. L., & Anthony, V. (2011). Overview and Guidance on Agile Development in Large Organizations. *Communications of the Association for Information Systems*, *29*(1), 25–44. doi:10.17705/1CAIS.02902

Barto, A. G., & Dietterich, T. G. (2004). Reinforcement Learning and its Relationship to Supervised Learning. In *Handbook of Learning and Approximate Dynamic Programming*. Wiley.

Basili, V. R., Caldiera, G., & Rombach, H. D. (1994). Experience Factory. In J. J. Marciniak (Ed.), *Encyclopedia of Software Engineering*. John Wiley and Sons.

Basili, V., Costa, P., Lindvall, M., Mendonca, M., & Seaman, C. (2001). An Experience Management System for a Software Engineering Research Organisation. *Proceedings of 26th Annual NASA Goddard Software Engineering Workshop*, 29-35. 10.1109/SEW.2001.992652

Bask, A., Rajahonka, M., Laari, S., Solakivi, T., Toyli, J., & Ojala, L. (2018). Environmental sustainability in shipper - LSP relationships. *Journal of Cleaner Production*, *172*(1), 2986–2998. doi:10.1016/j.jclepro.2017.11.112

Baskervill, R. L., & Stage, J. (1996). Controlling Prototype Development Through Risk Analysis. *Management Information Systems Quarterly*, *20*(4), 481–502. doi:10.2307/249565

Bassil, Y. (2012). A Simulation Model for the Waterfall Software Development Life Cycle. *International Journal of Engineering*, *2*(5), 7.

Bates, R., Grief, A., Levi, M., Rosenthal, J. L., & Weingast, B. R. (1998). *Analytic narratives*. Princeton University Press.

Battilana, J., Leca, B., & Boxenbaum, E. (2009). How Actors Change Institutions: Towards a Theory of Institutional Entrepreneurship. *The Academy of Management Annals*, *3*(1), 65–107. doi:10.5465/19416520903053598

Baugher, D. V. A., & Weisbord, E. (2000). Gender and culture diversity occurring in self-formed workgroups. *Journal of Managerial Issues*, *12*(4), 391–407.

Baumgart, R., Hummel, M., & Holten, R. (2015). *Personality Traits of Scrum Roles in Agile Software Development Teams - A Qualitative Analysis*. Academic Press.

Baumol, W. J. (1993). Formal entrepreneurship theory in economics: Existence and bounds. *Journal of Business Venturing*, *8*(3), 197–210. doi:10.1016/0883-9026(93)90027-3

Baweja, S., & Venugopalan, N. (2015). Agility in Project Management. *PM World Journal.*, *IV*(X), 1–14.

Baz, J. E., & Laguir, I. (2017). Third - party logistics providers (TPLs) and environmental sustainability practices in developing countries: The case of Morocco. *International Journal of Operations & Production Management*, *37*(10), 1451–1474. doi:10.1108/IJOPM-07-2015-0405

Beck, K. (1999). Embracing change with extreme programming. *Computer, 32*(10), 70-77.

Beck, K. (2000). eXtreme Programming Explained: Embrace Change. Addison-Wesley.

Beck, K. (2004). eXtreme Programming Explained: Embrace change (2nd ed.). Addison-Wesley.

Beck, K. M., Beedle, M., Bennekum, A. V., Cockburn, A., Cunningham, W., Fowler, M., Grenning, J., Highsmith, J., Hunt, A., Jeffries, R., Kern, J., Marick, B., Martin, R. C., Mellor, S. J., Schwaber, K., Sutherland, J., & Thomas, D. (2013). *Manifesto for Agile Software Development*. Undefined. S2CID 109006295.

Beck, K., Beedle, M., van Bennekum, A., Cockburn, A., Cunningham, W., Fowler, M., Grenning, J., Highsmith, J., Hunt, A., Jeffries, R., Kern, J., Marick, B., Martin, R. C., Mellor, S., Schwaber, K., Sutherland, J., & Thomas, D. (2001). *Manifesto for Agile software development*. Agile Alliance. Available at: http://agilemanifesto.org/

Beck, K., Cockburn, A., Jeffries, R., & Highsmith, J. (2001). *Agile manifesto*. http://www.agilemanifesto.org

Beck, K., Grenning, J., Martin, R. C., Beedle, M., Highsmith, J., Mellor, S., Bennekum, A. v., Hunt, A., Schwaber, K., Cockburn, A., Jeffries, R., Sutherland, J., Cunningham, W., Kern, J., Thomas, D., Fowler, M., & Marick, B. (2001b). *Principles behind the Agile Manifesto*. Agile Alliance.

Becker, C. H. (n.d.). *Using eXtreme Programming in a Student Environment: A Case Study*. Academic Press.

Beckert, J. (1999). Agency, Entrepreneurs, and Institutional Change. The Role of Strategic Choice and Institutionalized Practices in Organizations. *Organization Studies*, *20*(5), 777–799. doi:10.1177/0170840699205004

Beck, K. (1999). Embracing Change with Extreme Programming. *Computer*, *32*(10), 70–77. doi:10.1109/2.796139

Beck, K. (2000). *Extreme Programming Explained*. Addison - Wesley.

Beck, K. (2003). *Test-Driven Development: By Example*. Pearson Education.

Beck, K., & Fowler, M. (2001). *Planning Extreme Programming*. Addison-Wesley.

Beck, K., Grenning, J., Martin, R. C., Beedle, M., Highsmith, J., Mellor, S., Bennekum, A. v., Hunt, A., Schwaber, K., Cockburn, A., Jeffries, R., Sutherland, J., Cunningham, W., Kern, J., Thomas, D., Fowler, M., & Marick, B. (2001a). *Manifesto for Agile Project Management*. Agile Alliance.

Beck, K., Grenning, J., Martin, R. C., Beedle, M., Highsmith, J., Mellor, S., van Bennekum, A., Hunt, A., Schwaber, K., Cockburn, A., Jeffries, R., Sutherland, J., Cunningham, W., Kern, J., Thomas, D., Fowler, M., & Marick, B. (2001). *Manifesto for Agile Software Development*. Agile Alliance.

Beise, C. M. (2004). IT project management and virtual teams. In *Proceedings of the 2004 SIGMIS Conference on Computer Personnel Research: Careers, Culture, and Ethics in A Networked Environment (Tucson, AZ, USA, April 22 - 24, 2004). SIGMAS CPR '04*. ACM.

Belassi, W., & Tukel, O. I. (1996). A new framework for determining success/failure factors in projects. *International Journal of Project Management*, *14*(3), 141–151. doi:10.1016/0263-7863(95)00064-X

Benavides-Velasco, C. A., Quintana-García, C., & Guzmán-Parra, V. F. (2013). Trends in family business research. *Small Business Economics*, *40*(1), 41–57. doi:10.100711187-011-9362-3

Bennett, K., & Rajlich, V. (n.d.). *Software Maintenance and Evolution: A Roadmap*. Academic Press.

Berczuk, S. (2014). *Mission Possible: Scrum Master and Technical Contributor*. Www.agileconnection.com

Berger, H. (2007). Agile development in a bureaucratic arena - A case study experience. *International Journal of Information Management*, *27*(6), 386–396. doi:10.1016/j.ijinfomgt.2007.08.009

Berg, M. E., & Karlsen, J. T. (2013). Managing stress in projects using coaching leadership tools. *Engineering Management Journal*, *25*(4), 52–61. doi:10.1080/10429247.2013.11431995

Berg, M. E., & Karlsen, J. T. (2014). How project managers can encourage and develop positive emotions in project teams. *International Journal of Managing Projects in Business*, *7*(3), 449–472. doi:10.1108/IJMPB-01-2013-0003

Bergmann, T., & Karwowski, W. (2018). Agile project management and project success: A literature review. In *International Conference on Applied Human Factors and Ergonomics* (pp. 405 - 414). Springer, Cham.

Bergmann, T., & Karwowski, W. (2019). Agile Project Management and Project Success: A Literature Review. In J. I. Kantola, S. Nazir, & T. Barath (Eds.), *Advances in Human Factors, Business Management and Society. AHFE 2018. Advances in Intelligent Systems and Computing* (Vol. 783). Springer., doi:10.1007/978-3-319-94709-9_39

Berg, R. V. D., & Langen, P. W. D. (2016). Environmental sustainability in container transport: The attitudes of shippers and forwarders. *International Journal of Logistics: Research and Applications*, *20*(2), 146–162. doi:10.1080/13675567.2016.1164838

Berke, P. R., & Campanella, T. J. (2006). Planning for Post disaster Resiliency. *The Annals of the American Academy of Political and Social Science*, *604*(1), 192–207. doi:10.1177/0002716205285533

Berman, S. (2012). Digital transformation: Opportunities to create new business models. *Strategy and Leadership*, *40*(2), 16–24. doi:10.1108/10878571211209314

Bernstein, S. (2011). Legitimacy in intergovernmental and non - state global governance. *Review of International Political Economy*, *18*(1), 17–51. doi:10.1080/09692290903173087

Berrebi, C. (2009). The Economics of Terrorism and Counterterrorism: What Matters and Is Rational Choice Theory Helpful? In P. K. Davis & K. Cragin (Eds.), *Social Science for Counterterrorism: Putting the Pieces Together* (pp. 151–202). Rand.

Berrebi, C., & Klor, E. F. (2008). Are voters sensitive to terrorism? Direct evidence from the Israeli electorate. *The American Political Science Review*, *102*(03), 279–301. doi:10.1017/S0003055408080246

Berrone, P., Fsfuri, A., & Gelabert, L. (2013). Necessity as the mother of 'green' innovation: Institutional pressures and environmental innovation. *Strategic Management Journal*, *34*(8), 891–909. doi:10.1002mj.2041

Bertrand, M., Johnson, S., Samphantharak, K., & Schoar, A. (2008). Mixing family with business: A study of Thai business groups and the families behind them. *Journal of Financial Economics*, *88*(3), 466–498. doi:10.1016/j.jfineco.2008.04.002

Bertrand, M., & Schoar, A. (2006). The role of family in family firms. *The Journal of Economic Perspectives*, *20*(2), 73–96. doi:10.1257/jep.20.2.73

Besteiro, de Souza Pinto, & Novaski. (2015). Success factors in project management. *Business Management Dynamics, 4*(9), 19.

Biesenthal, C., Clegg, S., Mahalingam, A., & Sankaran, S. (2018). Applying Institutional Theories to Managing Mega-projects. *International Journal of Project Management*, *36*(1), 43–54. doi:10.1016/j.ijproman.2017.06.006

Binder, R. V. (2000). *Testing Object-Oriented Systems: Models, Patterns, and Tolls*. Addison-Wesley.

BinFire. (2021). *Introduction to Hybrid project management*. Author.

Bishop, J. (2007a). Ecological cognition: A new dynamic for human - computer interaction. In B. Wallace, A. Ross, J. Davies & T. Anderson (Eds.), The mind, the body and the world: Psychology after cognitivism (pp. 327 - 345). Imprint Academic.

Bishop, J. (2011a). *Equatricism: A new paradigm for research and practice in information technology, the arts, law and sciences*. Cardiff Metropolitan University's Annual Poster Symposium, Cardiff, UK.

Bishop, J. (2011b). The equatrics of intergenerational knowledge transformation in techno - cultures: Towards a model for enhancing information management in virtual worlds (Master's dissertation). Aberystwyth University.

Bishop, J. (2012). Lessons from the emotivate project for increasing take - up of big society and responsible capitalism initiatives. In P. M. Pumilia - Gnarini, E. Favaron, E. Pacetti, J. Bishop, & L. Guerra (Eds.), Didactic strategies and technologies for education: Incorporating advancements (pp. 208 - 217). Hershey, PA: IGI Global.

Bishop, J., & Kommers, P. A. M. (2016). *The impact of physical and virtual environments on human emotions: A pilot study in an adult and community education setting*. The 14th International Conference on Scientific Computing, Las Vegas, NV. 10.1109/CSCI.2016.0065

Bishop, J. (2007b). Increasing participation in online communities: A framework for human–computer interaction. *Computers in Human Behavior*, *23*(4), 1881–1893. doi:10.1016/j.chb.2005.11.004

Bitar, H., Zia, H., Bashir, M., Parava, P., Hanafi, M., Tierney, W., & Madhoun, M. (2018). Impact of fellowship training level on colonoscopy quality and efficiency metrics. *Gastrointestinal Endoscopy*, *88*(2), 378–387. doi:10.1016/j.gie.2018.04.2338 PMID:29679692

Bjarnason, E., Unterkalmsteiner, M., Borg, M., & Engström, E. (2016). A multi - case study of agile requirements engineering and the use of test cases as requirements. *Information and Software Technology*, *77*, 61–79. doi:10.1016/j.infsof.2016.03.008

Bjorn, P., Esbensen, M., Jensen, R. E., & Mathiesen, S. (2014). Does distance still matter? Revisiting the CSCW fundamentals on distance collaboration. *ACM Transactions on Computer-Human Interaction*, *21*(5), 1–27. doi:10.1145/2670534

Bjørnson, O., & Dingsøyr, T. (2008). Knowledge Management in Software Engineering: A Systematic Review of Studied Concepts, Findings and Research Methods Used. *Information and Software Technology, Elsevier*, *2008*(11), 1055–1068. doi:10.1016/j.infsof.2008.03.006

Blackhard, B. W. (2006). Hazards, Disasters and U. S. Emergency Management: An Introduction. FEMA Emergency Management Higher Education Project working draft course.

Blanchard, K. H., Nigari, P., & Nigari, D. (1985). *Leadership and the one - minute manager*. Fontana.

Blickle, G., Frieder, R. E., & Ferris, G. R. (2018). Political skill. In D. S. Ones, N. Anderson, C. Viswesvaran, & H. K. Sinangil (Eds.), The SAGE handbook of industrial, work & organizational psychology: Personnel psychology and employee performance (p. 299 - 319). Sage Reference. doi:10.4135/9781473914940.n12

Blomberg, S. B., Hess, G. D., & Tan, D. Y. (2011). Terrorism and the economics of trust. *Journal of Peace Research*, *48*(3), 383–398. doi:10.1177/0022343311401641

Blom, M. (2010). Is Scrum and XP suitable for CSE Development? *Procedia Computer Science*, *1*(1), 1511–1517. doi:10.1016/j.procs.2010.04.168

Bocken, N., Short, S., Rana, P., & Evans, S. (2013). A value mapping tool for sustainable business modelling. *Corporate Governance*, *13*(5), 482–497. doi:10.1108/CG-06-2013-0078

Bodden, V. (2014). *Boston Marathon Bombings*. ABDO Publishing Company.

Boehm, B. (2002). Get Ready for Agile Methods, with Care. *IEEE Computer*, *35*(1), 64–69. doi:10.1109/2.976920

Boehm, B., & Papaccio, P. (1988). Understanding and controlling software costs. *IEEE Transactions on Software Engineering*, *14*(10), 1462–1477. doi:10.1109/32.6191

Boje, D. M. (1991). The Storytelling Organization: A Study of Story Performance in an Office - Supply Firm Office - Supply Firm. *Administrative Science Quarterly*, *36*(1), 106–126. doi:10.2307/2393432

Bollinger, A. S., & Smith, R. D. (2001). Managing organizational knowledge as a strategic asset. *Journal of Knowledge Management*, *5*(1), 8–18. doi:10.1108/13673270110384365

Bongiovanni, A., Colotti, G., Liguori, G. L., Di Carlo, M., Digilio, F. A., Lacerra, G., Mascia, A., Cirafici, A. M., Barra, A., Lanati, A., & Kisslinger, A. (2015). Applying Quality and Project Management methodologies in biomedical research laboratories: A public research network's case study. *Accreditation and Quality Assurance*, *20*(3), 203–213. doi:10.100700769-015-1132-5

Booth, W. C. (2003). *The craft of research* (2nd ed.). University of Chicago Press Ltd.

Bostrom, R. P., & Thomas, B. D. (1983). *Achieving Excellence in Communications: A Key to Developing Complete, Accurate and Shared Information Requirements*. In Twentieth Annual Computer Personnel on Research Conference.

Bourne, L. (2014). *What Does a Project Sponsor Really Do?* blogs.pmi.org

Brasjö, C., & Lindovsky, M. (2019). *Machine learning project management: A study of project requirements and processes in early adoption* (Unpublished MS Thesis). Chalmers University of Technology, Sweden.

Brechner, E. (2015). *Agile Project Management with Kanban*. Microsoft Press.

Briggs, A. R. J., Coleman, M., & Morrison, M. (Eds.). (2012). *Research methods in educational leadership & management* (3rd ed.). Sage Publications Ltd. doi:10.4135/9781473957695

Brill, E. (1998). *The Encyclopaedia of Christianity*. Eerdmans.

Brockmann, C. (2009). Mega - Projects: Getting the Job Done. *Proceedings - LEAD 2009 Conference*.

Brown, W. L. Jr. (2015). Promoting resiliency to address fear and terrorism challenges in the xxi century. *European Scientific Journal VO*, *1*, 348.

Bruch, H., & Ghoshal, S. (2003). Unleashing organizational energy. *MIT Sloan Management Review*, *45*(1), 45.

Bruch, H., & Vogel, B. (2011). *Fully charged: How great leaders boost the organization's energy and ignite high performance*. Harvard Business Press.

Brunswicker, S., & Chesbrough, H. (2018). The Adoption of Open Innovation in Large Firms: Practices, Measures, and Risks A survey of large firms examines how firms approach open innovation strategically and manage knowledge flows at the project level. *Research Technology Management*, *61*(1), 35–45. doi:10.1080/08956308.2018.1399022

Buchanan, A., & Keohane, R. O. (2006). The Legitimacy of Global Institutions. *Ethics & International Affairs*, *20*(4), 405–437. doi:10.1111/j.1747-7093.2006.00043.x

Buckle, P. (2003). *Empowerment, organizational commitment and job satisfaction within a chemical organization* (Unpublished master's dissertation). Potchefstroom University, Vanderbijlpark.

Buckley-Zistel, S. (2006). Remembering to forget: Chosen amnesia as a strategy for local coexistence in post - genocide Rwanda. *Africa*, *76*(2), 131–150. doi:10.3366/afr.2006.76.2.131

Buffinton, K. W., Jablokow, K. W., & Martin, K. A. (2002). Project team dynamics and cognitive style. *Engineering Management Journal*, *14*(3), 25–33. doi:10.1080/10429247.2002.11415170

Bughin, J., & Hazan, E. (2017). Five management strategies for getting the most from AI. *MIT Sloan Management Review*. https://sloanreview.mit.edu/article/five-management-strategies-for-getting-themostfrom-ai

Bunsiri, T., & Kumpron, T. (2016). Benefits of Agile Project Management. *Apheit Journal.*, *5*(1), 23–29.

Burga, R., & Rezania, D. (2017). Project accountability: An exploratory case study using actor–network theory. *International Journal of Project Management*, *35*(6), 1024–1036. doi:10.1016/j.ijproman.2017.05.001

Burkart, M., Panunzi, F., & Shleifer, A. (2003). Family firms. *The Journal of Finance*, *58*(5), 2167–2201. doi:10.1111/1540-6261.00601

Burki, U. (2012). Institutional Voids and Corporate Governance: A Conceptual Understanding. *International Journal of Business and Management*, *7*(10), 99–107. doi:10.5539/ijbm.v7n10p99

Burnett, M. J. (2004). Remembering Justice in Rwanda; Locating Gender in the Judicial Construction of Memory. *Seattle Journal for Social Justice*, *3*(1), 757–789.

Busenitz, L. W., Gómez, C., & Spencer, J. W. (2000). Country institutional profiles: Unlocking entrepreneurial phenomena. *Academy of Management Journal*, *43*(5), 994–1003.

Bustamante, A., & Sawhney, R. (2011). *Agile XXL: Scaling Agile for Project Teams*. Seapine Software, Inc.

Buzan, B. (2008). *People, States & Fear: An Agenda for International Security Studies in the Post - Cold War Era*. ECPR Press.

Byrd, J. T., & Luthy, M. R. (2010). Improving group dynamics: Creating a team charter. *Academy of Educational Leadership Journal*, *14*(1), 13.

Cameron, K. S., & Quinn, R. E. (1999). *Diagnosing and changing organizational culture*. Addison-Wesley.

Campanelli, A. S., & Parreiras, F. S. (2015). Agile methods tailoring – A systematic literature review. *Journal of Systems and Software*, *110*, 85–100. doi:10.1016/j.jss.2015.08.035

Cantwell, J. A., Dunning, J. H., & Lundan, S. M. (2010). An evolutionary approach to understanding the co - evolution international business activity : Environment of MNEs and the institutional. *Journal of International Business Studies*, *41*(4), 567–586. doi:10.1057/jibs.2009.95

Cao, L. (2017). Data science: Challenges and directions. *Communications of the ACM*, *60*(8), 59–68. doi:10.1145/3015456

Capka, J. R. (2004). Mega-projects: Managing a Public Journey. *Public Roads*, *68*(1), 1–9.

Carmel, E. (1999). *Global Software Teams: Collaboration Across Borders and Time Zones*. Prentice-Hall.

Carmel, E. (2006, March). Building your Information Systems from the Other Side of the World: How Infosys manages time differences. *MIS Quarterly Executive*, *5*(1).

Carmel, E., & Agarwal, R. (2001, March). Tactical Approaches for Alleviating Distance in Global Software Development. *IEEE Software*, *18*(2), 22–29. doi:10.1109/52.914734

Carmel, E., & Tjia, P. (2005). *Offshoring Information Technology: Sourcing and Outsourcing to a Global Workforce*. Cambridge University Press. doi:10.1017/CBO9780511541193

Carp, J. M. (2010). Resiliency: The Essence of Survival in Chaos. *Families in Society*, *91*(3), 266–271. doi:10.1606/1044-3894.4004

Carvalho, M. M. D., & Rabechini, R. Jr. (2015). Impact of risk management on project performance: The importance of soft skills. *International Journal of Production Research*, *53*(2), 321–340. doi:10.1080/00207543.2014.919423

Cassidy, C. (2001). *Beyond numbers: Qualitative research methods for oriental medicine. Clinical acupuncture*. Springer.

Castro, M. S., Bahli, B., Barcaui, A., & Figueiredo, R. (2021). Does one project success measure fit all? An empirical investigation of Brazilian projects. *International Journal of Managing Projects in Business*, *14*(3), 788–805. doi:10.1108/IJMPB-01-2020-0028

Ceptureanu, E. G., Ceptureanu, S. I., Luchian, C. E., & Luchian, I. (2017). Quality management in project management consulting. A case study in an international consulting company. *Amfiteatru Economic*, *19*(44), 215.

Cervone, H. F. (2011). Understanding agile project management methods using scrum OCLC Syst. *Serv. Int. Dig. Libr. Persp.*, *27*(1), 18–22.

Chan, A. P., Scott, D., & Edmond, W. M. (2002). Framework of Success Criteria for Design/Build Projects. *Journal of Management Engineering*, *18*(3), 120–128. doi:10.1061/(ASCE)0742-597X(2002)18:3(120)

Chang, Y., Wilkinson, S., Brunsdon, D., Seville, E., & Potangaroa, R. (2011). An integrated approach: Managing resources for post - disaster reconstruction. *Disasters*, *35*(4), 739–765. doi:10.1111/j.1467-7717.2011.01240.x PMID:21913934

Chan, S. H., Kensinger, J. W., Keown, A. J., & Martin, J. D. (1997). Do strategic alliances create value? *Journal of Financial Economics*, *46*(2), 199–221. doi:10.1016/S0304-405X(97)00029-9

Chavez, M. S. (2016). Hurricane preparedness in a construction site: A framework to assess the construction companies' current practices. *FIU Electronic Theses and Dissertations.*, *3047*. Advance online publication. doi:10.25148/etd.FIDC001187

Chen, H., & Chen, T.-J. (2003). Governance structures in strategic alliances: Transaction cost versus resource - based perspective. *Journal of World Business*, *38*(1), 1–14. doi:10.1016/S1090-9516(02)00105-0

Chen, Y. S., Lai, S. B., & Wen, C. T. (2006). The influence of green innovation performance on corporate advantage in Taiwan. *Journal of Business Ethics*, *67*(3), 331–339. doi:10.100710551-006-9025-5

Chesbrough, H. (2007). Business model innovation: It's not just about technology anymore. *Strategy and Leadership*, *35*(6), 12–17. doi:10.1108/10878570710833714

Child, J. (2001). Learning Through Strategic Alliances. In Handbook of Organizational Learning & Knowledge (pp. 657 - 680). Academic Press.

Chin, G. (2006). *Agile Project Management*. AEW Services.

Chiu, Y. (2010). *An introduction to the History of Project Management: From the Earliest Times to A. D. 1900*. Eburon.

Chow, T., & Cao, D. (2008). A Survey of Critical Success Factors in Agile Software Projects. *Journal of Systems and Software, 81*(6), 961 – 971. . doi:10.1016/j.jss.2007.08.020

Chowanietz, C. (2010). Rallying around the flag or railing against the government? Political parties' reactions to terrorist acts. *Party Politics*.

Chrisman, J. J., Sharma, P., & Taggar, S. (2007). Family influences on firms: An introduction. *Journal of Business Research, 60*(10), 1005–1011. doi:10.1016/j.jbusres.2007.02.016

Chu, Z., Wang, L., & Lai, F. (2019). Customer pressure and green innovations at third party logistics providers in China: The moderation effect of organizational culture. *International Journal of Logistics Management, 30*(1), 57–75. doi:10.1108/IJLM-11-2017-0294

Chu, Z., Xu, J., Lai, F., & Collins, B. J. (2018). Institutional theory and environmental pressures: The moderating effect of market uncertainty on innovation and firm performance. *IEEE Transactions on Engineering Management, 65*(3), 392–403. doi:10.1109/TEM.2018.2794453

Cialdini, R. (2001). *Influence: The psychology of persuasion*. Harper Collins.

Cielen, D., Meysman, A., & Ali, M. (2016). *Introducing data science: Big data, machine learning, and more, using Python tools*. Manning Publications.

Clancy, T. (2014). *The Standish Group Report - CHAOS*. Academic Press.

Clarke, C. P. (2015). *Terrorism, Inc.: The Financing of Terrorism, Insurgency, and Irregular Warfare*. ABC - CLIO.

Clarke, N. (2010). Emotional intelligence and its relationship to transformational leadership and project manager competence. *Project Management Journal, 41*(2), 5–20. doi:10.1002/pmj.20162

Clemmedsson, E. (2018). *Identifying pitfalls in machine learning implementation projects: A case study of four technology - intensive organizations* (Unpublished MS Thesis). Kth Royal Institute of Technology, Sweden.

Clerc, V., Lago, P., & Vliet, H. (2007). *The Architect's Mindset*. http://www.springerlink.com/content/9km6520m6027824u/fulltext.pdf

Cocco, L., Mannaro, K., Concas, G., & Marchesi, M. (2011). Simulating kanban and scrum vs. waterfall with system dynamics. In *International Conference on Agile Software Development*. Springer. 10.1007/978-3-642-20677-1_9

Cockburn, A. & Williams, L. (2003). Agile software development: it's about feedback and change *IEEE Computer, 36*(6), 39–43.

Cockburn, A. (2007). *Agile Project Management: The Cooperative Game*. www.pearson.com

Cockburn, A. (2008). *Information radiator*. Academic Press.

Cockburn, A. (2000). *Writing Effective Use Cases*. Addison-Wesley.

Cockburn, A. (2006). *Agile Software Development: The Cooperative Game*. Addison-Wesley.

Cohen, D., Lindvall, M., & Costa, P. (2004). An Introduction to Agile Methods. *Advances in Computers, 62*(1), 1–66.

Cohn, T., & Paul, R. (2001). A Comparison of Requirements Engineering in Extreme Programming (XP) and Conventional Software Development Methodologies. *Seventh Americas Conference on Information Systems.*

Colicchia, C., Melacini, M., & Perotti, S. (2011). Benchmarking supply chain sustainability: Insights from a field study. *Benchmarking, 18*(5), 703–732. doi:10.1108/14635771111166839

Colicchia, C., & Strozzi, F. (2012). Supply chain risk management: A new methodology for a systematic literature review. *Supply Chain Management, 17*(4), 403–418. doi:10.1108/13598541211246558

Collier, K. W. (2011). *Agile Analytics: A Value - Driven Approach to Business Intelligence and Data Warehousing.* Pearson Education. 10.1145/1185448.1185509

Collins, K. M., Onwuegbuzie, A. J., & Sutton, I. L. (2006). A model incorporating the rationale and purpose for conducting mixed methods research in special education and beyond. *Learning Disabilities (Weston, Mass.), 4*(1), 67–100.

Conforto, E. C., Amaral, D. C., da Silva, S. L., Di Felippo, A., & Kamikawachi, D. S. L. (2016). The agility construct on project management theory. *International Journal of Project Management, 34*(4), 660–674. doi:10.1016/j.ijproman.2016.01.007

Conforto, E. C., Salum, F., Amaral, D. C., da Silva, S. L., & de Almeida, L. F. M. (2014). Can agile project management be adopted by industries other than software development? *Project Management Journal, 45*(3), 21–34. doi:10.1002/pmj.21410

Cook, S. (1994). The cultural implications of empowerment. *Empowerment in Organizations., 2*(1), 9–13. doi:10.1108/09684899410054625

Cooper, R. G. (1994). Third generation new product processes. *Journal of Product Innovation Management, 11*(1), 3–14. doi:10.1111/1540-5885.1110003

Cooper, R. G. (2014). What's Next? After Stage - Gate. *Research Technology Management, 57*(1), 20–31. doi:10.5437/08956308X5606963

Cooper, R. G., & Sommer, A. F. (2018). Agile - Stage - Gate for manufacturers - Changing the way new products are developed. *Research Technology Management, 61*(2), 17–26. doi:10.1080/08956308.2018.1421380

Coram, M., & Bohner, S. (2005). The Impact of Agile Methods on Software Project Management. *Proceedings of the 12th IEEE International Conference and Workshops on the Engineering of Computer-Based Systems (ECBS'05)*, 363-370. 10.1109/ECBS.2005.68

Corbin, R. D., Dunbar, C. B., & Zhu, Q. (2007). A three-tier knowledge management scheme for software engineering support and innovation. *Journal of Systems and Software, 80*(9), 1494–1505. doi:10.1016/j.jss.2007.01.013

Corvello, V., Javernick-Will, A., & Ratta, A. M. L. (2017). Routine project scope management in small construction enterprises. *International Journal of Project Organisation and Management, 9*(1), 18–30. doi:10.1504/IJPOM.2017.083109

Council of the EU. (2019). *Stricter CO_2 emission standards for cars and vans signed off by the Council.* https://www.consilium.europa.eu/en/press/press-releases/2019/04/15/stricter-co2-emission-standards-for-cars-and-vans-signed-off-by-the-council

Crawford, L., Hobbs, J. B., & Turner, J. R. (2005). *Project categorization systems: Aligning capability with strategy for better results.* Project Management Institute.

CRISP - DM. (2000). *CRISP - DM 1.0: Step - by - step data mining guide. The CRISP - DM consortium.* SPSS Publication.

Cronin, A. K. (2002). Rethinking sovereignty: American strategy in the age of terrorism. *Survival, 44*(2), 119–139. doi:10.1093urvival/44.2.119

Cronin, A. K. (2003). Behind the Curve: Globalization and International Terrorism. *International Security, 27*(3), 30–58. doi:10.1162/016228802605536 24

Cuban, L. (2001). *Oversold and underused: Computers in the classroom.* Harvard University Press.

Cuervo-Cazurra, A. (2011). Selecting the country in which to start internationalization: The non - sequential internationalization model. *Journal of World Business, 46*(4), 426–437. doi:10.1016/j.jwb.2010.10.003

Cunliffe, D. (2000). Developing usable web sites - a review and model. *Internet Research, 10*(4), 295–308. doi:10.1108/10662240010342577

Cunningham, W. (2001). *Agile Manifesto.* http://www.agilemanifesto.org

Cusumano, M. A., & Smith, S. (n.d.). *Beyond the Waterfall: Software Development at Microsoft.* Academic Press.

Czinkota, M. R., Knight, G., Liesch, P. W., & Steen, J. (2010). Terrorism and international business: A research agenda. *Journal of International Business Studies, 41*(5), 826–843. doi:10.1057/jibs.2010.12

Dacin, M. T., Goodstein, J., & Scott, W. R. (2002). Institutional theory and institutional change: Introduction to the special research forum. *Academy of Management Journal, 45*(1), 43. doi:10.2307/3069284

Das, T. K., & Teng, B.-S. (2000). A Resource - Based Theory of Strategic Alliances. *Journal of Management, 26*(1), 31–61. doi:10.1177/014920630002600105

Dau, L. A., & Moore, E. (2020). *A global disruption requires a global response: Policies for building international business resilience for this and future pandemics.* Northeastern University's Global Resilience Institute White Paper Series (Funded by a grant from US FEMA). Available at: https://globalresilience.northeastern.edu/whitepaperseries-covid-19-special-investigation-report-2020-11/

Dau, L. A., & Moore, E. (2020). *Developing New England Business Recovery and Resilience in Response to COVID - 19.* Northeastern University's Global Resilience Institute White Paper Series (Funded by a grant from US FEMA). Available at https://globalresilience.northeastern.edu/publications-whitepaperseries-covid-19-special-investigation-report-2020-8/

Dau, L. A., Moore, E. M., & Abrahms, M. (2018a). Female entrepreneurship and international organizations. In Entrepreneurship and the Sustainable Development Goals, (pp. 165 – 183). Emerald Group. doi:10.1108/S2040-724620180000008015

Dau, L. A., Moore, E. M., & Newburry, W. (2020). The grass is always greener: The impact of home and host country CSR reputation signalling on cross - country investments. *Journal of International Business Policy*, 1 – 29.

Dau, L. A., Moore, E. M., & Robson, M. A. (2019). Strategic collaboration within competitive industries: Private sector intelligence. In T. K. Das (Ed.), Managing Inter - partner Risks in Strategic Alliances, (pp. 239 – 256). Information Age Publishing.

Dau, L. A., Moore, E. M., & Soto, M. (2016a). Informal transnational political actors and emerging markets: Understanding entrepreneurship in a changing normative atmosphere. In A. Walsh (Ed.), Entrepreneurship and Firm Performance, (pp. 19 – 41). Nova Science Publishers.

Dau, L. A., Moore, E. M., & Soto, M. (2016b). The great recession and emerging market firms: Unpacking the divide between global and national level sustainability expectations. In Lessons from the Great Recession: At the Crossroads of Sustainability and Recovery, (pp. 165 – 187). Emerald Group.

Dau, L. A., Moore, E. M., Petrich, K., & Abrahms, M. (2019). Terrorism and resilience: How family businesses respond to terrorist activity. In Handbook of Global Financial Markets, (pp. 647 – 668). World Scientific Publishing.

Dau, L. A., Moore, E. M., Soto, M., & LeBlanc, C. (2016). How globalization sparked entrepreneurship in the developing world: The impact of formal economic and political linkages. In Corporate Espionage, Geopolitics, and Diplomacy Issues in International Business, (pp. 72 – 91). IGI Global.

Dau, L. A. (2013). Learning across geographic space: Pro - market reforms, multi - nationalization strategy, and profitability. *Journal of International Business Studies*, *44*(3), 235–262. doi:10.1057/jibs.2013.5

Dau, L. A., & Cuervo-Cazurra, A. (2014). To formalize or not to formalize: Entrepreneurship and pro - market institutions. *Journal of Business Venturing*, *29*(5), 668–686. doi:10.1016/j.jbusvent.2014.05.002

Dau, L. A., Moore, E. M., & Abrahms, M. (2018b). Global security risks, emerging markets, and firm responses: Assessing the impact of terrorism on firm profitability. In D. Castellani, R. Narula, Q. Nguyen, I. Surdu, & J. Walker (Eds.), *Contemporary Issues in International Business: Institutions, Strategy and Performance. Palgrave MacMillan.* doi:10.1007/978-3-319-70220-9_5

Dau, L. A., Moore, E. M., & Bradley, C. (2015). Institutions and International Entrepreneurship. International Business: Research. *Teaching and Practice*, *9*(1), 1–20.

Dau, L. A., Moore, E. M., & Kostova, T. (2020). The impact of market based institutional reforms on firm strategy and performance: Review and extension. *Journal of World Business*, *55*(4), 101073. doi:10.1016/j.jwb.2020.101073

Davies, T. J. C. (2002). The "real" success factors on projects. *International Journal of Project Management*, *20*(3), 185–190. doi:10.1016/S0263-7863(01)00067-9

Davis, A. M. (n.d.). A conci rent process model of software development. *ACM SIGSOFT*, *19*(2), 14.

Davis, K. (2018). Reconciling the views of project success: A multiple stakeholder model. *Project Management Journal*, *49*(5), 1–10. doi:10.1177/8756972818786663

Davis, L. E. (2014). Have We Gone Too Far with Resiliency? *Social Work Research*, *38*(1), 5–6. doi:10.1093wrvu003

DDS. (2021). *Data driven scrum framework.* https://datadrivenscrum.com

De Araújo, M. C. B., Alencar, L. H., & de Miranda Mota, C. M. (2017). Project procurement management: A structured literature review. *International Journal of Project Management*, *35*(3), 353–377. doi:10.1016/j.ijproman.2017.01.008

De Carvalho, M. M. (2014). An investigation of the role of communication in IT projects. *International Journal of Operations & Production Management*, *34*(1), 36–64. doi:10.1108/IJOPM-11-2011-0439

de Carvalho, M. M., Patah, L. A., & de Souza Bido, D. (2015). Project management and its effects on project success: Cross-country and cross-industry comparisons. *International Journal of Project Management*, *33*(7), 1509–1522. doi:10.1016/j.ijproman.2015.04.004

De Poel, F. M., Stoker, J. I., & Van der Zee, K. I. (2014). Leadership and organizational tenure diversity as determinants of project team effectiveness. *Group & Organization Management*, *39*(5), 532–560. doi:10.1177/1059601114550711

De Vries, F. (2010). *The rise of multiple intelligences.* Retrieved August 21, 2020, from http://scholar.sun.ac.za/handle/10019.1/5735

Deckro, R. F., Winkofsky, E. P., Hebert, J. E., & Gagnon, R. (1991). A decomposition approach to multi - project scheduling. *European Journal of Operational Research*, *51*(1), 110–118. doi:10.1016/0377-2217(91)90150-T

Deeds, D. L., & Hill, C. W. L. (1996). Strategic alliances and the rate of new product development: An empirical study of entrepreneurial biotechnology firms. *Journal of Business Venturing*, *11*(1), 41–55. doi:10.1016/0883-9026(95)00087-9

De-Laat, M., & Lally, V. (2003). Complexity, theory and praxis: Researching collaborative learning and tutoring processes in a networked learning community. *Instructional Science, 31*(1 - 2), 7 - 39.

DeMarco, T. (1979). *Structured Analysis and System Specification*. Prentice-Hall.

Demil, B., Lecocq, X., Ricart, J. E., & Zott, C. (2015). Introduction to the SEJ special issue on business models: Business models within the domain of strategic entrepreneurship. *Strategic Entrepreneurship Journal*, *9*(1), 1–11. doi:10.1002ej.1194

Demir, S. T., & Theis, P. (2016). Agile design management - the application of scrum in the design phase of construction projects. *24th Annual Conference of the International Group for Lean Construction*, Boston, MA.

Denning, S. (2017). The age of agile. *Strategy and Leadership*, *45*(1), 3–10. doi:10.1108/SL-12-2016-0086

Denning, S. (2020). What Is Agile? *Forbes*.

Denzin, N. K. (2007). Terrorism and the Politics of Fear. *Contemporary Sociology: A Journal of Reviews, 36*(3), 266 - 267.

Deshpande, S. & Richardson, I. (2009). Management at the Outsourcing Destination - Global Software Development in India. *IGCSE/IEEE 2009*, 217-225.

Deursen, D. (2001). Customer Involvement in eXtreme Programming. *The Second Internal Conference on eXtreme Programming and Flexible Processes in Software Engineering*.

Devlin, G., & Bleackley, M. (1988). Strategic alliances - Guidelines for success. *Long Range Planning*, *21*(5), 18–23. doi:10.1016/0024-6301(88)90101-X

Dey, A., LaGuardia, P., & Srinivasan, M. (2011). Building sustainability in logistics operations: A research agenda. *Management Research Review*, *34*(11), 1237–1259. doi:10.1108/01409171111178774

Dhaliwal, D. S., Li, O. Z., Tsang, A., & Yang, Y. G. (2011). Voluntary nonfinancial disclosure and the cost of equity capital: The initiation of corporate social responsibility reporting. *The Accounting Review*, *86*(1), 59–100. doi:10.2308/accr.00000005

di Bella, E., Fronza, I., Phaphoom, N., Sillitti, A., Succi, G., & Vlasenko, J. (2013). Pair Programming and Software Defects—A Large, Industrial Case Study. *IEEE Transactions on Software Engineering*, *39*(7), 930–953. doi:10.1109/TSE.2012.68

Dimaggio, P. J. (1988). Interest and Agency in Institutional Theory. In *Institutional patterns and organizations* (Vol. 1, pp. 3–22). Culture and Environment.

Dimaggio, P., & Powell, W. (1983). The iron cage revisited: Institutional isomorphism and collective rationality in organizational fields. *American Sociological Review*, *48*(2), 147–160. doi:10.2307/2095101

Dingsøyr, T., Brede Moe, N., & Nytro, O. (2001). Augmenting Experience reports with Lightweight Postmortem Reviews. *Third International Conference on Product-Focused Software Process Improvement, PROFES 2001*. 10.1007/3-540-44813-6_17

Dingsøyr, T., Nerur, S., Balijepally, V., & Moe, N. B. (2012). A decade of agile methodologies: Towards explaining agile software development. *Journal of Systems and Software*, *85*(6), 1213–1221. doi:10.1016/j.jss.2012.02.033

Doloi, H., Iyer, K. C., & Sawhney, A. (2011). Structural equation model for assessing impacts of contractor's performance on project success. *International Journal of Project Management*, *29*(6), 687–695. doi:10.1016/j.ijproman.2010.05.007

DSPM. (2021). *Data science project management*. https://www.datascience-pm.com

Du Plessis, Y. (Ed.). (2014). *Project management: A behavioural perspective - principles, practices, and cases*. Pearson Education South Africa.

Du Plessis, Y., & Roelofse, K. (2014). People behaviour and project management. In Y. Du Plessis (Ed.), *Project management: A behavioural perspective - principles, practices, and cases* (pp. 3–28). Pearson Education South Africa.

DuBois, M., Hanlon, J., Koch, J., Nyatuga, B., & Kerr, N. (2015). Leadership styles of effective project managers: Techniques and traits to lead high performance teams. *Journal of Economic Development, Management, IT, Finance, and Marketing*, *7*(1), 30.

Dubovikov, K. (2019). *Managing Data Science*. Packt Publishing.

Dulock, H. L. (1993). Research design: Descriptive research. *Journal of Pediatric Oncology Nursing*, *10*(4), 154–157. doi:10.1177/104345429301000406 PMID:8251123

Dybå, T., & Dingsøyr, T. (2008). Empirical studies of agile software development: A systematic review. *Information and Software Technology, 50*(9-10), 833 - 859. doi:10.1016/j.infsof.2008.01.006

Easterby-Smith, M., Thorpe, R., & Lowe, A. (2005). Raziskovanje v managementu [Research in management]. Fakulteta za management, Koper.

Ebert, C., & Neve, P. (2001). Surviving global software development. *IEEE Software, 18*(2), 62-69.

ECSA. (2015). Software architecture. In *9th European Conference*. Engineering Council of South Africa.

Edkins, J. (2003). *Trauma and the Memory of Politics*. Cambridge University Press. doi:10.1017/CBO9780511840470

Edmonds, E. A. (1974). A Process for the Management of Project for Nontechnical Users as an Adaptive System. *General Systems*, *19*, 215–218.

Edwards, K., Cooper, R. G., Vedsmand, T. & Nardelli, G. (2019). Evaluating the agile - stage - gate hybrid model: Experiences from three SME manufacturing firms. *Int. J. Innov. Technol. Manag., 16*.

Ekrot, B., Kock, A., & Gemünden, H. G. (2016). Retaining project management competence—Antecedents and consequences. *International Journal of Project Management*, *34*(2), 145–157. doi:10.1016/j.ijproman.2015.10.010

El-Abbasy, M. S., Elazouni, A., & Zayed, T. (2017). Generic scheduling optimization model for multiple construction projects. *Journal of Computing in Civil Engineering*, *31*(4), 4017003. doi:10.1061/(ASCE)CP.1943-5487.0000659

Elkington, J. (1997). *Cannibals with Forks: The Triple Bottom Line of 21st Century Business*. Capstone Publishing.

Elkington, J. (1998). Partnerships from Cannibals with Forks: The Triple Bottom Line of 21st - Century Business. *Environmental Quality Management*, *8*(1), 37–51. doi:10.1002/tqem.3310080106

Ellram, L. M., & Cooper, M. C. (2014). Supply Chain Management: It's all about the Journey, Not the Destination. *The Journal of Supply Chain Management*, *50*(1), 8–20. doi:10.1111/jscm.12043

Elmaghraby, S. (1977). *Task networks: project planning and control by network models*. John Wiley and Sons.

Enders, W., & Sandler, T. (2004). *What do we know about the substitution effect in transnational terrorism? Research on terrorism: trends, achievements and failures*. Routledge.

Eng-Larsson, F., & Kohn, C. (2012). Modal shift for greener logistics - the shipper's perspective. *International Journal of Physical Distribution & Logistics Management*, *42*(1), 36–59. doi:10.1108/09600031211202463

Erdelyi, M. H. (2010). The Ups and Downs of Memory. *The American Psychologist*, *65*(7), 623–633. doi:10.1037/a0020440 PMID:20873880

Erickson, J., Lyytinen, K., & Siau, K. (2005). *Agile Modelling, Agile Software Development, and Extreme Programming*. Academic Press.

Eschenbach, T., Lewis, N., Nicholls, G. M., & Schell, W. J. (2015). Using Agile Project Management to maximize your and your Co - authors' Productivity. In *2015 ASEE Annual Conference & Exposition* (pp. 26 - 1654). Academic Press.

Eschenbach, T., Lewis, N., Nicholls, G. M., & Schell, W. J. (2015). *Using Agile Project Management to Maximize You and Your Co - authors' Productivity. American Society for Engineering Education. 122nd ASEE Annual Conference & Exposition*, Seattle, WA.

Espinosa, A. J., & Carmel, E. (2003). The impact of time separation on coordination in global software teams: A conceptual foundation. *Software Process Improvement and Practice*, *8*(4), 249–266. doi:10.1002pip.185

Espinosa, J. A., & Armour, F. (2016). The big data analytics gold rush: a research framework for coordination and governance. *Proceedings of Hawaii International Conference on System Sciences (HICSS)*. 10.1109/HICSS.2016.141

Europacific.si. (2020). *About Us*. https://europacific.si/en/about - us/

European Commission. (2015). *A European Strategy for low - emission mobility*. https://ec.europa.eu/clima/policies/transport_en

European Commission. (2018). *Transport in the European Union*. https://ec.europa.eu/transport/sites/transport/files/2018-transport-in-the-eu-current-trends-and-issues.pdf

European Union. (2019). *Energy, transport and environment statistics*. https://ec.europa.eu/eurostat/documents/3217494/10165279/KS-DK-19-001-EN-N.pdf/76651a29-b817-eed4-f9f2-92bf692e1ed9,doi:10.2785/499987 KS-DK-19-001-EN-C

Evangelista, P. (2014). Environmental sustainability practices in the transport and logistics service industry: An exploratory case study investigation. *Research in Transportation Business & Management*, *12*(1), 63–72. doi:10.1016/j.rtbm.2014.10.002

Evers, P. T., Harper, D. V., & Needham, P. M. (1996). The determinants of shipper perceptions of modes. *Transportation Journal*, *36*(2), 13–25.

ExecutiveBrief. (2021). *Which Life Cycle Is Best For Your Project?* PM Hut.

Faganel, A., Biloslavo, R., & Janeš, A. (2020). Towards an innovative ecotourism business model framework. In L. C. Carvalho & L. Calisto (Eds.), *Strategic business models to support demand, supply, and destination management in the tourism and hospitality industry* (pp. 200–215). IGI Global. doi:10.4018/978-1-5225-9936-4.ch011

Fageha, M. K., & Aibinu, A. A. (2016). Identifying stakeholders' involvement that enhances project scope definition completeness in Saudi Arabian public building projects. *Built Environment Project and Asset Management*, *6*(1), 6–29. doi:10.1108/BEPAM-06-2014-0030

Fahmi-bin-Ismail, M. & Mansor, Z. (2018). Agile Project Management: Review, Challenges and Open Issues. *Advanced Science Letters, 24*, 463 - 466.

Fan, J. P. H., Wong, T. J., & Zhang, T. (2013). Institutions and organizational structure: The case of state - owned corporate pyramids. *Journal of Law Economics and Organization*, *29*(6), 1217–1252. doi:10.1093/jleo/ews028

Farell, C., Narang, R., Kapitan, S., & Webber, H. (2002). Towards an effective onsite customer practice. *Proceedings of the Third International Conference on Extreme Programming and Agile Processes in Software Engineering*, 52–55.

Farell, C., Narang, R., Kapitan, S., & Webber, H. (2002). Towards an Effective Onsite Customer Practice. *The Third International Conference on eXtreme Programming and Agile Process in Software Engineering.*

Farenden, P. (2012). *ITIL for dummies.* John Wiley & Sons Ltd.

Fells, M. J. (2000). Fayol stands the test of time. *Journal of Management History*, *6*(8), 345–360. doi:10.1108/13552520010359379

Fenner, M. E. (2020). *Machine learning with python for everyone.* Pearson Education.

Fernandez, D. J., & Fernandez, J. D. (2008). Agile project management—Agilism versus traditional approaches. *Journal of Computer Information Systems*, *49*(2), 10–17.

Ferris, G. R., Berkson, H. M., Kaplan, D. M., Gilmore, D. C., Buckley, M. R., Hochwarter, W. A., & Witt, L. A. (1999, August). Development and initial validation of the political skill inventory. In *Academy of Management, 59th annual national meeting* (pp. 6 - 11). Academic Press.

Ferris, G. R., Treadway, D. C., Kolodinsky, R. W., Hochwarter, W. A., Kacmar, C. J., Douglas, C., & Frink, D. D. (2005). Development and validation of the political skill inventory. *Journal of Management*, *31*(1), 126–152. doi:10.1177/0149206304271386

Finlan, A. (2003). Warfare by other means: Special Forces, terrorism and grand strategy. *Small Wars & Insurgencies*, *14*(1), 92–108. doi:10.1080/09592310412331300586

Finsterwalder, M. (2001). *Does XP need a professional Customer?* XP2001 workshop on customer involvement, Cagliari, Italy. Available online at https://homepages.cwi.nl/~arie/wci2001/finsterwalder.pdf

Firstenberg, A., & Salas, J. (2014). Designing & developing for Google glass: Thinking differently for a new platform. O'Reilly Media, Inc.

Fitzgerald, B. (2000). Systems Development Methodologies: The Problem of Tenses. *Information Technology & People*, *13*(3), 174–185. doi:10.1108/09593840010377617

Fjeldstad, O. H., Kagoma, C., Mdee, E., Sjursen, I. H., & Somville, V. (2020). The customer is king: Evidence on VAT compliance in Tanzania. *World Development*, *128*, 104841. doi:10.1016/j.worlddev.2019.104841

Flodén, J. (2007). *Modelling intermodal freight transport - the potential of combined transport in Sweden* [Unpublished doctoral dissertation]. Gothenburg University, Gothenburg School of Business, Economics and Law, Sweden.

Flynn, S. (2007). *The Edge of Disaster: Rebuilding a Resilient Nation.* Random House.

Flyvbjerg, B. (2009). Survival of the fittest: Why the worst infrastructure gets built - and what we can do about it. *Oxford Review of Economic Policy*, *25*(3), 344–367. doi:10.1093/oxrep/grp024

Flyvbjerg, B. (2014). What You Should Know about Mega-projects and Why: An Overview. *Project Management Journal*, *45*(2), 6–19. doi:10.1002/pmj.21409

Flyvbjerg, B., Bruzelius, N., & Rothengatter, W. (2003). *Mega-projects and Risk: An Anatomy of Ambition.* Cambridge University Press. doi:10.1017/CBO9781107050891

Fortanier, F., Kolk, A., & Pinkse, J. (2011). Harmonization in CSR Reporting: MNEs and Global CSR Standards. *Management International Review*, *51*(5), 665–696. doi:10.100711575-011-0089-9

Forte, E. (2003a). *Logistica economica ed equilibri spazio - territoriali* [Economic logistics and spatial - territorial balances]. Working paper presented at the seminar: I fondamenti concettuali della Logistica economica, Dipartimento di Architettura e Pianificazione, Politecnico di Milano.

Fowler, M. (2002). *XP Customer Quotes*. WikiWikiWeb. https://martinfowler.com/articles/agileStory.html

Fox, A. (2014). *Working on Multiple Agile Teams*. techwhirl.com/

Fraser, S., Martin, A., Biddle, R., Hussman, D., Miller, G., Poppendieck, M., Rising, L., & Striebeck, M. (2004a). The Role of the Customer in Software Development: The XP Customer – Fad or Fashion? In *OOPSLA'04* (pp. 148–150). ACM Press. doi:10.1145/1028664.1028723

Fraser, S., Martin, A., Hussman, D., Matts, C., Poppendieck, M., & Rising, L. (2004b). The XP Customer Role. In *Proceedings of Extreme Programming and Agile Processes in Software Engineering* (pp. 342–346). Springer Verlag. doi:10.1007/978-3-540-24853-8_57

Freed, J. I. (1995). The United States Holocaust Memorial Museum - A Dialogue with Memory. *Curator*, *38*(2), 95–110. doi:10.1111/j.2151-6952.1995.tb01044.x

Frey, B. S. (2009). How can business cope with terrorism? *Journal of Policy Modeling*, *31*(5), 779–787. doi:10.1016/j.jpolmod.2008.09.007

Frey, B. S., Simon, L., & Alois, S. (2007). Calculating tragedy: Assessing the costs of terrorism. *Journal of Economic Surveys*, *21*(1), 1–24. doi:10.1111/j.1467-6419.2007.00505.x

Front Row Agile. (n.d.). *The role of a product owner responsibilities and characteristics*. Retrieved from Https://www.Frontrowagile.com/blog/posts/74-the-role-of-a-product-owner-responsibilities-and-characteristics

Fung, I. W. H., Tam, V. W. Y., Lo, T. Y., & Lu, L. L. H. (2009). Developing a Risk Assessment Model for Construction Safety. *International Journal of Project Management*, *28*(6), 593–600. doi:10.1016/j.ijproman.2009.09.006

Gaffney, N., Cooper, D., Kedia, B., & Clampit, J. (2013). Institutional transitions, global mind - set, and EMNE internationalization. *European Management Journal*, *32*(3), 383–391. doi:10.1016/j.emj.2013.08.001

Gaibulloev, K., & Sandler, T. (2009). The impact of terrorism and conflicts on growth in Asia. *Economics and Politics*, *21*(3), 359–383. doi:10.1111/j.1468-0343.2009.00347.x

Gardas, B. B., Raut, R. D., & Narkhede, B. E. (2019). Analysing the 3PL service provider's evaluation criteria through a sustainable approach. *International Journal of Productivity and Performance Management*, *68*(5), 958–980. doi:10.1108/IJPPM-04-2018-0154

Gartner. (2015). *Gartner says business intelligence and analytics leaders must focus on mind - sets and culture to kick start advanced analytics*. https://www.gartner.com/newsroom/id/3130017

Gedajlovic, E., & Carney, M. (2010). Markets, hierarchies, and families: Toward a transaction cost theory of the family firm. *Entrepreneurship Theory and Practice*, *34*(6), 1145–1172. doi:10.1111/j.1540-6520.2010.00418.x

Geeks for Geeks. (2020). *Boehms software maintenance model*. Retrieved from Https://www.geeksforgeeks.org/boehms - software - maintenance - model/

Geissdoerfer, M., Bocken, N. M. P., & Hultink, E. J. (2016). Design thinking to enhance the sustainable business modelling process. *Journal of Cleaner Production*, *135*, 1218–1232. doi:10.1016/j.jclepro.2016.07.020

Gemino, A., Reich, B. H., & Serrador, P. M. (2021). Agile, traditional, and hybrid approaches to project success: Is hybrid a poor second choice? *Project Management Journal*, *52*(2), 161–175. doi:10.1177/8756972820973082

George, C. (2014). *Why Limiting Your Work - in - Progress Matters*. Leankit.com.

German, E. (2017). Information literacy and instruction: LibGuides for instruction: A service design point of view from an academic library. *Reference and User Services Quarterly*, *56*(3), 162–167. doi:10.5860/rusq.56n3.162

Getmansky, A., & Tolga, S. (2017). (in press). Settling on Violence: Expansion of Israeli Outposts in the West Bank in Response to Terrorism. *Studies in Conflict and Terrorism.*

Gibbs, W. (1994, September). Software's chronic crisis. *Scientific American*, *271*(3), 72–81.

Gilb, T. (1981). Evolutionary Management. *ACM SIGSOFT Project Engineering Notes*, *6*(2), 17. doi:10.1145/1010865.1010868

Gilb. (2021a). *Evolutionary Project Management (Original page, external archive).* Academic Press.

Gilb. (2021b). *Evolutionary Project Management (New page).* Academic Press.

Gilb, T. (1988). *Principle of Software Engineering Management*. Addison-Wesley.

Giménez, C., Sierra, V., & Rodon, J. (2012). Sustainable operations: Their impact on the triple bottom line. *International Journal of Production Economics*, *140*(1), 149–159. doi:10.1016/j.ijpe.2012.01.035

Giri, B. C., & Sarker, B. R. (2017). Improving performance by coordinating a supply chain with third party logistics outsourcing under production disruption. *Computers & Industrial Engineering*, *103*(1), 168–177. doi:10.1016/j.cie.2016.11.022

Gittins, R., Hope, S., & Williams, L. (2002). Qualitative Studies of XP in a medium-sized Business. In *Extreme Programming Perspectives*. Addison-Wesley.

Goldratt, E. (1997). *Critical Chain. Great Barrington*. North River Press.

Goldstein, I. (2011). *Sprint issues - when sprints turn into crawls*. Www.axisagile.com.au

Goleman, D. (2006). *Emotional intelligence*. Bantam Books.

Gomez, D. M., Torgler, B., & Ortega, G. J. (2013). Measuring global economic interdependence: A hierarchical network approach. *World Economy*, *36*(12), 1632–1648. doi:10.1111/twec.12080

Gomez-Mejia, L. R., Cruz, C., Berrone, P., & De Castro, J. (2011). The Bind that Ties: Socio - emotional Wealth Preservation in Family Firms. *The Academy of Management Annals*, *5*(1), 653–707. doi:10.5465/19416520.2011.593320

Gomez-Mejia, L. R., Makri, M., & Kintana, M. L. (2010). Diversification Decisions in family - controlled firms. *Journal of Management Studies*, *47*(2), 223–252. doi:10.1111/j.1467-6486.2009.00889.x

González, P., González, V., Molenaar, K., & Orozco, F. (2014). Analysis of causes of delay and time performance in construction projects. *Journal of Construction Engineering and Management*, *140*(1), 1–9. doi:10.1061/(ASCE)CO.1943-7862.0000721

González, R. C., Blanco, P. R. Z., Gil, F., & Antino, M. (2020). Development and validation of the Spanish version of the political skill inventory. *Anales de Psicología*, *36*(2), 370–377. doi:10.6018/analesps.368871

Gospodinov, E. (2001). *Statement by Encho Gospodinov, Head of Delegation*. The International Federation of Red Cross and Red Crescent Societies, United Nations General Assembly, 25th special session on Human Settlement (HABITAT II), New York.

Gould, E. D., & Esteban, F. K. (2010). Does terrorism work? *The Quarterly Journal of Economics*, *125*(4), 1459–1510. doi:10.1162/qjec.2010.125.4.1459

Graham, N. (2008). *PRINCE2 for dummies*. John Wiley & Sons Ltd.

Gray, J. H., & Densten, I. L. (2006). Towards an Integrative Model of Organization Culture and Knowledge management. *International Journal of Organisational Behaviour*, *9*(2), 594–603.

Gray, J. H., & Densten, I. L. (2006). Towards an Integrative Model of Organization Culture and Knowledge Management. *International Journal of Organisational Behaviour*, *9*(2), 594–603.

Green, K. W. Jr, Zelbst, P. J., Meacham, J., & Bhadauria, V. S. (2012). Green supply chain management practices: Impact on performance. *Supply Chain Management*, *17*(3), 290–305. doi:10.1108/13598541211227126

Greif, A., & Laitin, D. D. (2004). A Theory of Endogenous Institutional Change. *The American Political Science Review*, *98*(4), 633–652. doi:10.1017/S0003055404041395

Gries, T., & Naudé, W. (2011). Entrepreneurship and human development: A capability approach. *Journal of Public Economics, 95*(3 - 4), 216 - 224.

Griffiths, M. (2012). *PMI - ACP Exam Prep.* RMC Publications, Inc.

Grimheden, M. E. (2013). Can agile methods enhance mechatronics design education? *Mechatronics*, *23*(8), 967–973. doi:10.1016/j.mechatronics.2013.01.003

Grisham, P. S., & Perry, D. E. (n.d.). *Customer Relationships and Extreme Programming*. Academic Press.

Grisham, P. S., & Perry, D. E. (2005). Customer relationships and Extreme Programming. In *Proceedings of the 2005 Workshop on Human and Social Factors of Software Engineering (HSSE '05)*. ACM Press.

Gu, V. C., Hoffman, J. J., Cao, Q., & Schniederjans, M. J. (2014). The effects of organizational culture and environmental pressures on IT project performance: a moderation perspective. *International Journal of Project Management, 32*(7), 1170-1181. . doi:10.1016/j.ijproman.2013.12.003

Guha-Sapir, D., Hoyois, P., & Below, R. (2015). Annual Disaster Statistical Review 2014. The numbers and trends. Centre for Research on the Epidemiology of Disasters.

Gulati, R., & Singh, H. (1998). The Architecture of Cooperation: Managing Coordination Costs and Appropriation Concerns in Strategic Alliances. *Administrative Science Quarterly*, *43*(4), 781–814. doi:10.2307/2393616

Gupte, A. (2018). *Determining critical success factors for big data projects* (Unpublished Doctoral Dissertation). Purdue University.

Gürcan, Ö. F., Yazıcı, İ., Beyca, Ö. F., Arsland, Ç. Y., & Eldemir, F. (2016). Third Party Logistics (3PL) Provider Selection with AHP Application. *Procedia: Social and Behavioral Sciences*, *235*, 226–234. doi:10.1016/j.sbspro.2016.11.018

Gurung, A., & Prater, E. (2006). A Research Framework for the Impact of Cultural Differences on IT Outsourcing. *Journal of Global Information Technology Management, 9*(1), 24-43.

Guzzini, S. (2000). A Reconstruction of Constructivism in International Relations. *European Journal of International Relations*, *6*(2), 147–182. doi:10.1177/1354066100006002001

Hacking, T., & Guthrie, P. (2008). A framework for clarifying the meaning of Triple Bottom - Line, Integrated, and Sustainability Assessment. *Environmental Impact Assessment Review, 28*(2 - 3), 73 - 89.

Haleem, A., Javaid, M., & Vaishya, R. (2020). Effects of COVID 19 pandemic in daily life. *Current Medicine Research and Practice*, *1*(1), 1–2. doi:10.1016/j.cmrp.2020.03.011 PMID:32292804

Hall, E. T. (1976). *Beyond Culture*. Doubleday.

Hällgren, M., & Wilson, T. (2008). The nature and management of crises in construction projects: Project - as - practice observations. *International Journal of Project Management, 26*(8), 830–838. doi:10.1016/j.ijproman.2007.10.005

Hall, J. K., Daneke, G. A., & Lenox, M. J. (2010). Sustainable development and entrepreneurship: Past contributions and future directions. *Journal of Business Venturing, 25*(5), 439–448. doi:10.1016/j.jbusvent.2010.01.002

Hamel, G. (1991). Competition for competence and inter - partner learning within international strategic alliances. *Strategic Management Journal, 12*(1S), 83 - 103.

Ham, Y., Lee, S. J., & Chowdhury, A. G. (2017). Imaging - to - simulation framework for improving disaster preparedness of construction projects and neighbouring communities. *Computing in Civil Engineering, 2017*, 230–237. Advance online publication. doi:10.1061/9780784480830.029

Hannola, L., Friman, J., & Niemimuukko, J. (2012). Application of agile methods in the innovation process. *International Journal of Business Innovation and Research.*, *7*(1), 84. doi:10.1504/IJBIR.2013.050557

Hanssen, G. K., & Fægri, T. E. (2006). Agile Customer Engagement: A Longitudinal Qualitative Case Study. In *ISESE'06* (pp. 164–173). ACM Press. doi:10.1145/1159733.1159759

Hansson, C., Dittrich, Y., & Randall, D. (2004). Agile processes enhancing user participation for small providers of off-the-shelf software. In *Proceedings of Extreme Programming and Agile Processes in Software Engineering* (pp. 175–183). Springer Verlag. doi:10.1007/978-3-540-24853-8_20

Haque, M. S. (2002). The Changing Balance of Power between the Government and NGOS in Bangladesh. *International Political Science Review, 23*(4), 411–435. doi:10.1177/0192512102023004006

Harrison, F., & Lock, D. (2017). *Advanced project management: a structured approach.* Routledge. doi:10.4324/9781315263328

Hastie, S. (2004). *The Agile Mind - set: what does it take to make this stuff work?* Software Education Associates Ltd, Agile Development Conference Wellington & Sydney.

Haugset, B., & Stalhane, T. (2012). Automated Acceptance Testing as an Agile Requirements Engineering Practice. *2012 45th Hawaii International Conference on System Sciences*, 5289 - 5298. 10.1109/HICSS.2012.127

Haverila, M. J., & Fehr, K. (2016). The impact of product superiority on customer satisfaction in project management. *International Journal of Project Management, 34*(4), 570–583. doi:10.1016/j.ijproman.2016.02.007

Hawkins, D. G. (Eds.). (2006). *Delegation and agency in international organizations.* Cambridge University Press. doi:10.1017/CBO9780511491368

Hayes, I. S. (2002). Ready or Not: Global Sourcing Is in Your IT Future. *Cutter IT Journal, 15*(11), 5–11.

Hazen, B. T., Cegielski, C., & Hanna, J. B. (2011). Diffusion of green supply chain management: Examining perceived quality of green reverse logistics. *International Journal of Logistics Management, 22*(3), 373–389. doi:10.1108/09574091111181372

Hazini, K., Dehghan, R., & Ruwanpura, J. (2013). A heuristic method to determine optimum degree of activity accelerating and overlapping in schedule compression. *Canadian Journal of Civil Engineering, 40*(4), 382–392. doi:10.1139/cjce-2012-0380

Hazini, K., Dehghan, R., & Ruwanpura, J. (2014). An evolutionary optimization method to determine optimum degree of activity accelerating and overlapping in schedule compression. *Canadian Journal of Civil Engineering, 41*(4), 333–342. doi:10.1139/cjce-2013-0194

Helmke, G., Levitsky, S., & Galvan, D. (2011). Politics. *Institutions Comparative Agenda, 2*(4), 725–740.

Herbsleb, J. D. (2007). *Global Software Engineering: The Future of Socio-technical Coordination. In Future of Software Engineering (FOSE'07).* IEEE.

Herbsleb, J. D., & Moitra, D. (2001). Global Software Development. *IEEE Software, 18*(2), 16–20. doi:10.1109/52.914732

Herzenstein, M., Horsky, S., & Posavac, S. S. (2015). Living with terrorism or withdrawing in terror: Perceived control and consumer avoidance. *Journal of Consumer Behaviour, 14*(4), 228–236. doi:10.1002/cb.1511

Heymann, P. B. (2000). *Terrorism and America: A common-sense strategy for a democratic society.* MIT Press.

Hiatt, J. (2006). *ADKAR: a model for change in business, government, and our community.* Prosci.

Higgins, A. & de Freytas-Tamura, K. (2015, November 19). Attacks in Paris. *New York Times.*

Highsmith, J. (2001). *History: The Agile Manifesto.* Agilemanifesto.org.

Highsmith, J. (2001). The Great Methodologies Debate, Part I: Opening Statement. *Cutter IT Journal, 14*, 2–4.

Highsmith, J. (2002). *Agile Software Development Ecosystems.* Addison-Wesley.

Highsmith, J. (2004). *Agile Project Management: Creating Innovative Products.* Addison Wesley.

Highsmith, J. (2009). *Agile project management: creating innovative products.* Pearson Education.

Highsmith, J., & Cockburn, A. (2001, September). Agile software development: The business of innovation. *Computer, 1*(1), 120–127. doi:10.1109/2.947100

Hilt, M. J., Wagner, D., Osterlehner, V., & Kampker, A. (2016). Agile Predevelopment of Production Technologies for Electric Energy Storage Systems - A Case Study in the Automotive Industry. In *Proceedings of the Procedia CIRP.* Elsevier B. V.

Hoda, R., & Murugesan, L. K. (2016). Multi - level agile project management challenges: A self - organizing team perspective. *Journal of Systems and Software, 117*, 245–257. doi:10.1016/j.jss.2016.02.049

Hofferberth, M., & Weber, C. (2015). Lost in translation: A critique of constructivist norm research. *Journal of International Relations and Development, 18*(1), 75–103. doi:10.1057/jird.2014.1

Hofstede, G. (1984). *Culture's Consequences: International Differences in Work-Related Values.* Sage Publication.

Holland & Knight LLP. (2020). *A Look at COVID - 19 Impacts on the Construction Industry.* Available at: C:\Users\Naidoova\Desktop\ALookatCOVID-19ImpactsontheConstructionIndustry_Insights_Holland&Knight.html

Holmstrom, H., Conchuir, E. O., Agerfalk, P. J., & Fitzgerald, B. (2006). Global Software Engineering, 2006. *IGCSE '06. International Conference on*, 3 – 11.

Hong, J., Sun, X., & Huang, W. (2016). Local Institutions, Foreign Direct Investment and Productivity of Domestic Firms. *Review of Development Economics, 20*(1), 25–38. doi:10.1111/rode.12204

Hornstein, H. A. (2015). The integration of project management and organizational change management is a necessity. *International Journal of Project Management, 33*(2), 291–298. doi:10.1016/j.ijproman.2014.08.005

Huang, C., Wang, Y., Li, X., Ren, L., Zhao, J., Hu, Y., Zhang, L., Fan, G., Xu, J., Gu, X., & Cheng, Z. (2020). Articles clinical features of patients infected with 2019 novel coronavirus in Wuhan, China. *Lancet, 6736*(20), 1–10.

Hurd, I. (2008). Constructivism. In The Oxford Handbook of International Relations (pp. 298 - 326). OUP.

Iacocca Institute. (1991). *21st Century Manufacturing Enterprise Strategy: An Industry Led View*. Iacocca Institute, Lehigh University.

Iannone, F. (2002a). *Territorio e nodi logistici: dagli interporti alle piattaforme logistiche, ai distripark, ai city logistics centre* [Territory and logistic nodes: from interports to logistic platforms, distriparks, city logistics centres]. working paper, Dipartimento di Scienze Economiche e Sociali, Università degli Studi di Napoli Federico II.

Iannone, F. (2002b). *Possibili applicazioni di Teoria dei giochi al mercato dei servizi logistici e di trasporto* [Possible applications of Game Theory to the logistics and transport services market]. Working paper presented at the seminar: Logistica economica e strumenti di analisi, Dipartimento di Scienze Economiche e Sociali, Università degli Studi di Napoli Federico II, June 7, 2002.

Iannone, F. (2003a). *Aspetti pubblici e privati di un modello di logistica sostenibile* [Public and private aspects of a sustainable logistics model]. working paper presented at the seminar: Trasporti e politiche economiche, University of Palermo, Facoltà di Economia, VI Riunione Scientifica SIET. Palermo.

Iannone, F. (2003b). *L'esperienza del sito* logisticaeconomica.unina.it*: pianificazione, progettazione e comunicazione Web* [The experience of the logisticseconomica.unina.it site: planning, design and Web communication]. working paper presented at the seminar: I fondamenti concettuali della Logistica economica, Dipartimento di Architettura e Pianificazione, Politecnico di Milano.

Ibrahim, C. K. I. C., Costello, S. B., & Wilkinson, S. (2015). Key indicators influencing the management of team integration in construction projects. *International Journal of Managing Projects in Business*, *8*(2), 300–323. doi:10.1108/IJMPB-04-2014-0028

Ibreck, R. (2010). The politics of mourning: Survivor contributions to memorials in post - genocide Rwanda. *Memory Studies*, *3*(4), 330–343. doi:10.1177/1750698010374921

Igreja, V. (2008). Memories as weapons: The politics of peace and silence in post - civil war Mozambique. *Journal of Southern African Studies*, *34*(3), 539–556. doi:10.1080/03057070802259720

Ika, L. (2009). Project Success as a Topic in Project Management Journals. *Project Management Journal*, *40*(4), 6–19. doi:10.1002/pmj.20137

Ingelaere, B. (2009). Does the truth pass across the fire without burning? Locating the short circuit in Rwanda's Gacaca courts. *The Journal of Modern African Studies*, *47*(4), 507–528. doi:10.1017/S0022278X0999005X

Inkpen, A. C., & Tsang, E. W. K. (2007). Learning and Strategic Alliances. *The Academy of Management Annals*, *1*(1), 479–511. doi:10.5465/078559815

Institute for Economics and Peace. (2016). *Global Terrorism Index 2016: Measuring and Understanding the Impact of Terrorism*. Author.

Irfan, M., Khan, S. Z., Hassan, N., Hassan, M., Habib, M., Khan, S., & Khan, H. H. (2021). Role of project planning and project manager competence on public sector project success. *Sustainability*, *13*(3), 1421. doi:10.3390u13031421

Iriarte, C., & Bayona, S. (2020). IT projects success factors: A literature review. *International Journal of Information Systems and Project Management*, *8*(2), 49–78. doi:10.12821/ijispm080203

Isaksson, K., & Huge-Brodin, M. (2013). Understanding efficiencies behind logistics service providers' green offerings. *Management Research Review*, *36*(3), 216–238. doi:10.1108/01409171311306382

Ishikawa, F., & Yoshioka, N. (2019). How do engineers perceive difficulties in engineering of machine - learning systems? *Proceedings of IEEE / ACM 6th International Workshop on Software Engineering Research and Industrial Practice*.

ITRM Guideline CPM 110 - 01. (2006). *Appendix C - Commonwealth.* Retrieved from vita.virginia.gov:https://www.vita.virginia.gov/uploadedfiles/vita_main_public/unmanaged/library/cpmgappendix-c.pdf

Ivarsson, M., & Gorschek, T. (2012). Tool Support for Disseminating and Improving Development Practices. *Software Quality Control, 2012*, 173–199.

Izmailov, A., Korneva, D., & Kozhemiakin, A. (2016). Project management using the buffers of time and resources. *Procedia: Social and Behavioral Sciences, 235*, 189–197. doi:10.1016/j.sbspro.2016.11.014

Jackson, P. T. (2001). Constructing Thinking Space: Alexander Wendt and the Virtues of Engagement. *Cooperation and Conflict, 36*(1), 109–120. doi:10.1177/00108360121962317

Jain, P., Sharma, A., & Ahuja, L. (2018). The Impact of Agile Project Management Process on the Quality of Project Product. In *2018 7th International Conference on Reliability, Infocom Technologies and Optimization (Trends and Future Directions) (ICRITO).* Noida, India: IEEE. 10.1109/ICRITO.2018.8748529

Jamali, D., & Mirshak, R. (2007). Corporate Social Responsibility (CSR): Theory and practice in a developing country context. *Journal of Business Ethics, 72*(3), 243–262. doi:10.100710551-006-9168-4

Jamali, D., Zanhour, M., & Keshishian, T. (2009). Peculiar strengths and relational attributes of SMEs in the context of CSR. *Journal of Business Ethics, 87*(3), 355–377. doi:10.100710551-008-9925-7

James, N., & Busher, H. (2009). *Online interviewing.* Sage Publications. doi:10.4135/9780857024503

Janeš, A., & Biloslavo, R. (2013). Preoblikovanje poslovnega modela za večjo uspešnost podjetij [Transform business model to improve company performance]. In Izzivi gospodarskega razvoja - Inovativni projektni management: zbornik prireditve, Ljubljana, GZS, Zbornica osrednjeslovenske regije.

Janeš, A., & Trnavčević, A. (2014). Dobre prakse Interreg Slovenija Italija: Projekt Know Us [Good practices Interreg Slovenia Italy: Know Us Project]. In Izzivi gospodarskega razvoja - Inovativni projektni management: zbornik prireditve, Ljubljana, GZS, Zbornica osrednjeslovenske regije.

Janeš, A., Bratkovič Kregar, T., Trnavčević, A., & Biloslavo, R. (2014). Projekt Know Us: primer povezovanja univerze in gospodarstva. In Soustvarjanje kompetenčnega znanja [Co - creation of competency knowledge] (pp. 93 - 125). Fakulteta za management, Koper.

Janeš, A., Biloslavo, R., & Faganel, A. (2017). Sustainable business model: A case study of Fonda.si. *Annales Series Historia et Sociologia, 27*(1), 175–190.

Jasma, K. (2001). *WML & WMLScript: A beginner's guide* (J. Schachterle, J. McKensie, P. Schumauder, & A. Carroll, Eds.). McGraw - Hill.

Jayaraman, R. (2016). Project cost control: a new method to plan and control costs in large projects. *Business Process Management Journal.* https://www.emerald.com/insight/content/doi/10.1108/BPMJ-10-2014-0102/full/html?fullSc=1

Jeffries, R., Anderson, A., & Hendrickson, C. (2001). Extreme Programming installed. Addison - Wesley.

Jena, A., & Satpathy, S. S. (2017). Importance of soft skills in project management. *International Journal of Scientific Research and Management, 5*(7), 6173–6180. doi:10.18535/ijsrm/v5i7.45

Jensen, M., Menon, S., Mangset, L. E., & Dalberg, V. (2007). Managing Offshore Outsourcing of Knowledge-intensive Projects - A People-Centric Approach. *International Conference on Global Software Engineering (ICGSE 2007).*

Jha, M. M., Vilardell, R. M. F., & Narayan, J. (2016). Scaling Agile Scrum Software Development: Providing Agility and Quality to Platform Development by Reducing Time to Market. *2016 IEEE 11th International Conference on Global Software Engineering (ICGSE)*, 84 - 88. 10.1109/ICGSE.2016.24

Ji, F., & Sedano, T. (2011). Comparing extreme programming and Waterfall project results. *2011 24th IEEE - CS Conference on Software Engineering Education and Training (CSEE&T)*, 482 - 486. 10.1109/CSEET.2011.5876129

Jiang, X., & Li, Y. (2008). The relationship between organizational learning and firms' financial performance in strategic alliances: A contingency approach. *Journal of World Business*, *43*(3), 365–379. doi:10.1016/j.jwb.2007.11.003

Jo'zefowska, J., & Weglarz, J. (2006). *Perspectives in modern project scheduling*. Springer. doi:10.1007/978-0-387-33768-5

Jocevski, M., Arvidsson, N., Miragliotta, G., Ghezzi, A., & Mangiaracina, R. (2019). Transitions towards omni - channel retailing strategies: A business model perspective. *International Journal of Retail & Distribution Management*, *47*(2), 78–93. doi:10.1108/IJRDM-08-2018-0176

Joe, L. (2007). *Nokia test, a scrum - specific test*. Agileconsortium.blogspot.com.

Johansson, C., Hall, P., & Coquard, M. (1999). Talk to Paula and Peter – They are Experienced. *Proceedings of the Workshop of Learning Software Organizations*, 69-76.

Jongman, A. J. (1988). *Political terrorism: A new guide to actors, authors, concepts, databases theories, and literature*. Transaction Publishers.

Jørsfeldt, L. M., Hvolby, H.-H., & Nguyen, V. T. (2016). Implementing environmental sustainability in logistics operations: A case study. *Strategic Outsourcing*, *9*(2), 98–125. doi:10.1108/SO-09-2015-0023

Joslin, R., & Müller, R. (2015). Relationships between a project management methodology and project success in different project governance contexts. *International Journal of Project Management*, *33*(6), 1377–1392. doi:10.1016/j.ijproman.2015.03.005

Joyce, A., & Paquin, R. L. (2016). The triple layered business model canvas: A tool to design more sustainable business models. *Journal of Cleaner Production*, *135*(1), 1474–1486. doi:10.1016/j.jclepro.2016.06.067

Jroller. (2021). *David Bock's Weblog: Weblog*. Author.

Judah, T. D. (1857). A Practical Plan for Building the Pacific Railroad. Academic Press.

Judi, H. M., & Beach, R. (2010). Achieving manufacturing flexibility: The role of people, technology, innovation and continuous improvement. *International Journal of Innovation and Technology Management*, *07*(2), 161–181. doi:10.1142/S0219877010001891

Jugdev, K., & Müller, R. (2005). A Retrospective look at our Evolving Understanding of Project Success. *Project Management Journal, 36*(4), 19 - 31. . doi:10.1177/875697280503600403

Kadri, R. L., & Boctor, F. F. (2018). An efficient genetic algorithm to solve the resource-constrained project scheduling problem with transfer times: The single mode case. *European Journal of Operational Research*, *265*(2), 454–462. doi:10.1016/j.ejor.2017.07.027

Kahler, M. (2013). Rising powers and global governance: Negotiating change in a resilient status quo. *International Affairs*, *89*(3), 711–729. doi:10.1111/1468-2346.12041

Kahn, R. S., Kobayashi, S., Beuthe, M., Gasca, J., Greene, D., Lee, D. S., Muromachi, Y., Newton, P. J., Plotkin, S., Sperling, D., Wit, R., & Zhou, P. J. (2007). Transport and its infrastructure. In B. Metz, O. R. Davidson, P. R. Bosch, R. Dave & L. A Meyer (Eds.), Climate Change 2007: Mitigation Contribution of Working Group III to the Fourth Assessment Report of the Intergovernmental Panel on Climate Change (pp. 323 - 386), Cambridge University Press.

Kaim, R., Härting, R. C., & Reichstein, C. (2019). Benefits of agile project management in an environment of increasing complexity—A transaction cost analysis. *Intelligent Decision Technologies, 2019*, 195–204.

Kaiya, H., & Sacki, M. (2006). Using Domain Ontology as Domain Knowledge for Requirement Elicitation. *Proceedings of the 14th IEEE International Requirements Engineering Conference*, 189-198.

Kale, P., & Singh, H. (2009a). Managing strategic alliances: What do we know now, and where do we go from here? *The Academy of Management Perspectives*, *23*(3), 45–62. doi:10.5465/amp.2009.43479263

Kale, P., Singh, H., & Perlmutter, H. (2000). Learning and protection of proprietary assets in strategic alliances: Building relational capital. *Strategic Management Journal*, *21*(3), 217–237. doi:10.1002/(SICI)1097-0266(200003)21:3<217::AID-SMJ95>3.0.CO;2-Y

Kanbanize. (2019). *Agile Project Management: A Comprehensive Guide*. https://kanbanize.com/agile/project-management

Kano, N., Seraku, N., Takahashi, F., & Tsuji, S. (1984). Attractive quality and must - be quality. *Journal of the Japanese Society for Quality Control*, *14*(2), 39–48.

Kaplan, B., & Maxwell, J. A. (2005). *Qualitative research methods for evaluating computer information systems. Evaluating the organizational impact of healthcare information systems*. Springer.

Karlsson, C., & Acs, Z. J. (2002). Introduction to institutions, entrepreneurship and firm growth: The case of Sweden. *Small Business Economics*, *19*(2), 63–67. doi:10.1023/A:1016202618249

Karlsson, T., & Honig, B. (2009). Judging a business by its cover: An institutional perspective on new ventures and the business plan. *Journal of Business Venturing*, *24*(1), 27–45. doi:10.1016/j.jbusvent.2007.10.003

Karlström, D., & Runeson, P. (2006). Integrating agile software development into stage - gate managed product development. *Empirical Software Engineering*, *11*(2), 203–225. doi:10.100710664-006-6402-8

Karolak, D. W. (1999). *Global Software Development: Managing Virtual Teams and Environments*. IEEE Computer Society Press.

Keegan, A., & Turner, J. R. (2002). The management of innovation in project - based firms. *Long Range Planning*, *35*(4), 367–388. doi:10.1016/S0024-6301(02)00069-9

Kehayan, V., & Napoli, J. C. (2005). Resiliency in the face of disaster and terrorism: 10 things to do to survive. Personhood Press.

Kelly, J., & Kaskade, J. (2013). *Cios & big data what your IT team wants you to know*. Infochimps Inc. http://www.infochimps.com

Kendra, K., & Taplin, L. J. (2004). Project Success: A Cultural Framework. *Project Management Journal, 35*(1), 30 – 45. . doi:10.1177/875697280403500104

Keohane, R. O., & Nye, J. S. (2000). Globalization: What's New? What's not? (And so what?). *Foreign Policy*, (118), 104–119. doi:10.2307/1149673

Keohane, R., & Nye, J. (2001). *Power and Interdependence*. Longman Publishing Group.

Kerr, J. M., & Hunter, R. (1993). *Inside RAD: How to Build a Fully Functional System in 90 Days or Less*. McGraw - Hill.

Kerzner, H. R. (1987). In search of excellence in Project management. *Journal of Systems Management, 38*(2), 30 - 40.

Kerzner, H. (2014). *Project recovery: Case studies and techniques for overcoming project failure*. John Wiley and Sons Ltd. doi:10.1002/9781118841617

Kerzner, H. R. (2013). *Project Management: A Systems Approach to Planning, Scheduling, and Controlling* (12th ed.). Wiley.

Kess, P., & Haapasalo, H. (2002). Knowledge creation through a project review process in software production. *International Journal of Production Economics*, *80*(1), 49–55.

Kets de Vries, M. F. R. (1993). The dynamics of family controlled firms: The good and the bad news. *Organizational Dynamics*, *21*(3), 59–71. doi:10.1016/0090-2616(93)90071-8

Khalil, M., Qadir, J., Onireti, O., Imran, M. A., & Younis, S. (2017). Feasibility, architecture and cost considerations of using TVWS for rural Internet access in 5G. In *20th Conference on Innovations in Clouds, Internet and Networks (ICIN)* (pp. 23-30). IEEE.

Khosravi, P., Rezvani, A., & Ashkanasy, N. M. (2020). Emotional intelligence: A preventive strategy to manage destructive influence of conflict in large - scale projects. *International Journal of Project Management*, *38*(1), 36–46. doi:10.1016/j.ijproman.2019.11.001

Khoury, T. A., & Prasad, A. (2012). How do Developing Country Entrepreneurs Navigate Extreme Institutional Voids? *Academy of Management Annual Meeting Proceedings*. 10.5465/AMBPP.2012.230

Khoury, T. A., Cuervo-Cazurra, A., & Dau, L. A. (2014). Institutional Outsiders and Insiders: The Response of Foreign and Domestic Inventors to the Quality of Intellectual Property Rights Protection. *Global Strategy Journal*, *4*(3), 200–220. doi:10.1002/gsj.1079

Kiernan, B. (2007). *Blood and Soil: A World History of Genocide and Extermination from Sparta to Darfur. Yale*. Yale University Press.

Kim, C., Hoon Yang, K., & Kim, J. (2008). A Strategy for Third - Party Logistics Systems. *Omega*, *36*(4), 522–534. doi:10.1016/j.omega.2006.11.011

Kim, S. Y., & Leachman, R. C. (1993). Multi - project scheduling with explicit lateness costs. *IIE Transactions*, *25*(2), 34–44. doi:10.1080/07408179308964275

Kim, Y., & Gao, F. Y. (2013). Does family involvement increase business performance? Family - longevity goals' moderating role in Chinese family firms. *Journal of Business Research*, *66*(2), 265–274. doi:10.1016/j.jbusres.2012.08.018

Kloppenborg, T. J., Anantatmula, V., & Wells, K. N. (2019). *Contemporary Project Management* (4th ed.). Cengage Learning.

Knapp, E. & Yu, D. (1999). Understanding organizational culture: how culture helps or hinders the flow of knowledge. *Knowledge Management Review*, 16-21.

Kneuper, R. (2018). *Software processes and life cycle models*. Springer Nature Switzerland AG.

Know Us. (2013). *About project*. Http://www.know-us.eu/2/7

Kobal, R., & Dežjot, A. (2020). EuroPacific d.o.o.: Workshop 3: Follow Up. Koper.

Kobal, R., Dežjot, A., & Ventin, H. (2013a). EuroPacific LLC: Workshop 1. Koper.

Kobal, R., Dežjot, A., & Ventin, H. (2013b). EuroPacific d.o.o.: Workshop 2. Koper.

Kock, A., Heising, W., & Gemünden, H. G. (2016). A contingency approach on the impact of front-end success on project portfolio success. *Project Management Journal*, *47*(2), 115–129. doi:10.1002/pmj.21575

Kohn, C. (2008). *Towards CO_2 - efficient centralized distribution* [Unpublished doctoral dissertation]. Linköping University, Linköping, Sweden.

Komendantova, N., Patt, A., Barras, L., & Battaglini, A. (2012). Perception of risks in renewable energy projects: The case of concentrated solar power in North Africa. *Energy Policy*, *40*(1), 103–109. doi:10.1016/j.enpol.2009.12.008

Kondratieff, N. D. (1925). *The Major Economic Cycles. English version, 1984. Long Wave Cycle* (G. Daniels & E. P. Dutton, Eds.). Richardson and Snyder.

Korkala, M., Pikkarainen, M., & Conboy, A. (2010). A Case Study of Customer Communication in Globally Distributed Software Product Development. *Proceedings of the 11th International Conference on Product-Focused Software*, 43-46.

Koskela, J., & Abrahamsson, P. (2004). Onsite Customer in an XP Project: Empirical Results from a Case Study. EuroSPI 2004, Trondheim, Norway.

Kotabe, M., & Mudambi, R. (2003). Institutions and international business. *Journal of International Management*, *9*(3), 215–217. doi:10.1016/S1075-4253(03)00033-4

Kotlar, J., De Massis, A., Fang, H., & Frattini, F. (2014). Strategic reference points in family firms. *Small Business Economics*, *43*(3), 597–619. doi:10.100711187-014-9556-6

Kotlarsky, J., & Oshri, I. (2005). Social ties, knowledge sharing and successful collaboration in globally distributed system development projects. *European Journal of Information Systems*, *14*, 37–48.

Krishnan, M. S. (2015). Software Development Risk Aspects and Success Frequency on Spiral and Agile Model. *International Journal of Innovative Research in Computer and Communication Engineering*, *03*(01), 301–310. doi:10.15680/ijircce.2015.0301024

Krueger, A. B., & Malečková, J. (2003). Education, Poverty and Terrorism: Is There a Causal Connection? *The Journal of Economic Perspectives*, *17*(4), 119–144. doi:10.1257/089533003772034925

Kühne, B., & Böhmann, T. (2018). Requirements for Representing Data - Driven Business Models - Towards Extending the Business Model Canvas. *Proceedings of the 24th Americas Conference on Information Systems.*

Kuipera, N. A. (2012). Humour and resiliency: Towards a process model of coping and growth. *Europe's Journal of Psychology*, *8*(3), 475–491. doi:10.5964/ejop.v8i3.464

Kujala, J., Aaltonen, K., Gotcheva, N., & Pekuri, A. (2016). Key dimensions of project network governance and implications to safety in nuclear industry projects. EURAM 2016: Manageable Co - operation.

Kujala, S. (2007). Effective user involvement in product development by improving the analysis of user needs. *Behaviour & Information Technology, Taylor & Francis*, *2007*, 1–16.

Kuniavsky, M. (2003). *Observing the user experience: A practitioner's guide to user research.* Morgan Kaufmann Publishers.

Kurian, T. (2006). Agility Metrics: A Quantitative Fuzzy Based Approach for Measuring Agility of a Software Process. *ISAM - Proceedings of International Conference on Agile Manufacturing'06 (ICAM - 2006).*

Kvale, S. (2007). *Doing interviews.* Sage. doi:10.4135/9781849208963

Kwak, Y. H. (2003). Brief history of project management. In K. A. Carayannis (Ed.), The Story of Managing Projects. Quorum Books.

La Porta, R., Lopez-De-Silanes, F., & Shleifer, A. (1999). Corporate Ownership around the World. *The Journal of Finance*, *1*(1), 471–517. doi:10.1111/0022-1082.00115

LaFree, G. (2010). The Global Terrorism Database (GTD): Accomplishments and Challenges. *Perspectives on Terrorism*, *4*(1), 24–46.

LaFree, G., & Dugan, L. (2009). Research on terrorism and countering terrorism. *Crime and Justice*, *38*(1), 413–477. doi:10.1086/599201

Lahad, M. (2005). Terrorism: The community perspective. *Journal of Aggression, Maltreatment & Trauma, 10*(3 - 4), 667 - 679.

Lam, C. (2016). Improving technical communication group projects: An experimental study of media synchronicity theory training on communication outcomes. *Journal of Business and Technical Communication*, *30*(1), 85–112. doi:10.1177/1050651915602293

Lam, J. S. L., & Dai, J. (2015). Environmental sustainability of logistics service provider: An ANP - QFD approach. *International Journal of Logistics Management*, *26*(2), 313–333. doi:10.1108/IJLM-08-2013-0088

Lane, S., Gu, Q., Lago, P., & Richardson, I. (n.d.). *Adaptation of Service - Based Applications: A Maintenance Process?* Academic Press.

Lange, D., Lee, P. M., & Dai, Y. (2011). Organizational Reputation. *RE:view*, *37*(1), 153–184.

Langer, N., Slaughter, S. A., & Mukhopadhyay, T. (2008). Project manager's skills and project success in IT outsourcing. *ICIS 2008 Proceedings, 147.*

Lanubile, F., Damian, D., & Oppenheimer, H. L. (2003). Global software development: Technical, organizational, and social challenges. *SIGSOFT Software Engineering Notes*, *28*(6), 1–4.

Lappi, T., Karvonen, T., Lwakatare, L. E., Aaltonen, K., & Kuvaja, P. (2018). Toward an improved understanding of agile project governance: A systematic literature review. *Project Management Journal*, *49*(6), 39–63. doi:10.1177/8756972818803482

Large, R. O., Kramer, N., & Hartmann, R. K. (2013). Procurement of logistics services and sustainable development in Europe: Fields of activity and empirical results. *Journal of Purchasing and Supply Management*, *19*(3), 122–133. doi:10.1016/j.pursup.2013.05.002

Larkey, L. (1996). Toward a theory of communicative interactions in culturally diverse workgroups. *Academy of Management Review*, *21*(2), 463–492.

Larman, C. (2004). *Agile and Iterative Development: A Manager's Guide*. Addison-Wesley.

Larman, C. (2004). *Agile and Iterative Management: A Manager's Guide*. Addison - Wesley.

Larman, C., & Bas, V. (2009). *Top Ten Organizational Impediments to Large - Scale Agile Adoption*. Inform IT.

Larson, D., & Chang, V. (2016). A review and future direction of agile, business intelligence, analytics and data science. *International Journal of Information Management*, *36*(5), 700–710. doi:10.1016/j.ijinfomgt.2016.04.013

Lasheras, J., Valencia-Garcia, R., Fernandez-Breis, J. T., & Toval, A. (2009). Modeling Reusable Security Requirements Based on Ontology Framework. *Journal of Research and Practice in Information Technology*, *4*(2), 119–133.

Lawernce, T. B., Hardy, C., Phillips, N., Lawrence, T. B., Hardy, C., & Phillips, N. (2002). Institutional effects of inter - organizational collaboration: The emergence of proto - institutions. *Academy of Management Journal*, *45*(1), 281–290.

Layton, M. C. (2015). *Scrum for dummies*. John Wiley & Sons Ltd.

Lechler, T. (2000). Empirical evidence of people as project success factors. In R. Lundin & F. Hartman (Eds.), *Projects as business constituents & guiding motives* (pp. 217–227). Kluwer Academic Publishers. doi:10.1007/978-1-4615-4505-7_17

Lee, G. & Xia, W. (2010). Toward Agile: An Integrated Analysis of Quantitative and Qualitative Field Data on Software Development Agility. *MIS Quarterly*, *34*(1), 87–114. doi:10.2307/20721416

Lee, G. K. L., & Chan, E. H. W. (2009). A sustainability evaluation of government - led urban renewal projects. *Facilities*, *26*(13), 526–541.

Lee, S., & Yong, H. S. (2010). Distributed agile: Project management in a global environment. *Empirical Software Engineering*, *15*(2), 204–217. doi:10.100710664-009-9119-7

Leiner, M. (2000). *A Brief History of the Internet*. Retrieved from: http://www.isoc.org/internethistory/brief.html

Levy, M., & Hazzan, O. (2009). Knowledge Management in Practice: The Case of Agile Software Development. *2nd Intern. Workshop on Cooperative and Human Aspects on Soft. Eng. (CHASE)*, 60-65.

Li, D., Eden, L., Hitt, M. A., & Ireland, R. D. (2008). Friends, acquaintances, or strangers? Partner selection in R&D alliances. *Academy of Management Journal*, *51*(2), 315–334. doi:10.5465/amj.2008.31767271

Liden, R. C., Wayne, S. J., & Sparrowe, R. T. (2000). An examination of the mediating role of psychological empowerment on the relations between the job, interpersonal relationships and work outcomes. *The Journal of Applied Psychology*, *85*(3), 407–416. doi:10.1037/0021-9010.85.3.407 PMID:10900815

Lieb, K. J., & Lieb, R. C. (2010). Environmental sustainability in the third - party logistics (3PL) industry. *International Journal of Physical Distribution & Logistics Management*, *40*(7), 524–533. doi:10.1108/09600031011071984

Liebowitz, J., & Megbolugbe, I. (2003). A set of frameworks to aid the project manager in conceptualizing and implementing knowledge management initiatives. *International Journal of Project Management*, *21*(3), 189–198. doi:10.1016/S0263-7863(02)00093-5

Liikamaa, K. (2015). Developing a project manager's competencies: A collective view of the most important competencies. *Procedia Manufacturing*, *3*, 681–687. doi:10.1016/j.promfg.2015.07.305

Li-Li, Z., Lian-Feng, H., & Qin-Ying, S. (2011). Research on Requirement for High - quality Model of Extreme Programming. *2011 International Conference on Information Management, Innovation Management and Industrial Engineering*, 518 - 522. doi:10.1109/ICIII.2011.132

Lin, C. Y., & Ho, Y. H. (2008). An empirical study on logistics service providers' intention on adopt green innovation. *Journal of Technology Management & Innovation*, *3*(1), 17–26.

Lin, C. Y., & Ho, Y. H. (2011). Determinants of green practice adoption for logistics companies in China. *Journal of Business Ethics*, *98*(1), 67–83. doi:10.100710551-010-0535-9

Linz, D., Pluymaekers, N. A., & Hendriks, J. M. (2020). TeleCheck - AF for COVID - 19: A European mHealth project to facilitate atrial fibrillation management through teleconsultation during COVID19. *European Heart Journal*, *41*(21), 1954–1955. doi:10.1093/eurheartj/ehaa404 PMID:32379309

Lisa, C., & Janet, G. (2009). *Agile Testing: A Practical Guide for Testers and Agile Teams*. Addison - Wesley.

Liu, C., Cheng, J., Wang, Y., & Gao, S. (2016). Time performance optimization and resource conflicts resolution for multiple project management. *IEICE Transactions on Information and Systems*, *99*(3), 650–660. doi:10.1587/transinf.2015EDP7397

Li, Y., Lu, Y., Ma, L., & Kwak, Y. H. (2018). Evolutionary governance for mega - event projects (MEPs): A case study of the world expo 2010 in China. *Project Management Journal*, *49*(1), 57–78. doi:10.1177/875697281804900105

Li, Y., Zhang, H., Long, K., Choi, S., & Nallanathan, A. (2019). Resource allocation for optimizing energy efficiency in NOMA-based fog UAV wireless networks. *IEEE Network*, *34*(2), 158–163. doi:10.1109/MNET.001.1900231

Locatelli, G., Littau, P., Brookes, N. J., & Mancini, M. (2014). Project characteristics enabling the success of mega-projects: An empirical investigation in the energy sector. *Procedia: Social and Behavioral Sciences*, *119*(1), 625–634. doi:10.1016/j.sbspro.2014.03.070

Loiro, C., Castro, H., Ávila, P., Cruz-Cunha, M. M., Putnik, G. D., & Ferreira, L. (2019). Agile project management: A communicational workflow proposal. *Procedia Computer Science*, *164*, 485–490. doi:10.1016/j.procs.2019.12.210

Lotfi, R., Yadegari, Z., Hosseini, S. H., Khameneh, A. H., Tirkolaee, E. B., & Weber, G. W. (2020) A robust time-cost-quality-energy-environment trade-off with resource-constrained in project management: a case study for a bridge construction project. *Journal of Industrial & Management Optimization*. https://www.aimsciences.org/article/doi/10.3934/jimo.2020158

Lu, J. W., & Beamish, P. W. (2001). The internationalization and performance of SMEs. *Strategic Management Journal, 22*(6 - 7), 565 - 586.

Ludvigsen, J. (1999). Freight transport supply and demand conditions in the Nordic Countries: Recent evidence. *Transportation Journal*, *39*(2), 31–54.

Luong, T. T., Sivarajah, U., & Weerakkody, V. (2021). Do agile managed information systems projects fail due to a lack of emotional intelligence? *Information Systems Frontiers*, *23*(2), 415–433. doi:10.100710796-019-09962-6

Luo, Y. (2005). Do Insiders Learn from Outsiders? Evidence from Mergers and Acquisitions. *The Journal of Finance*, *60*(4), 1951–1982. doi:10.1111/j.1540-6261.2005.00784.x

Luthans, F., Vogelgesang, G. R., & Lester, P. B. (2006). Developing the Psychological Capital of Resiliency. *Human Resource Development Review*, *5*(1), 25–44. doi:10.1177/1534484305285335

Luthar, S. S. (2006). *Resilience in development: A synthesis of research across five decades.* Academic Press.

Lvina, E., Johns, G., Treadway, D. C., Blickle, G., Liu, Y., Liu, J., & Ferris, G. R. (2012). Measure invariance of the political skill inventory (PSI) across five cultures. *International Journal of Cross Cultural Management*, *12*(2), 171–191. doi:10.1177/1470595812439870

Lwakatare, L. E., Raj, A., Crnkovic, I., Bosch, J., & Holmström, H. O. (2020). Large - scale machine learning systems in real - world industrial settings: A review of challenges and solutions. *Information and Software Technology*, *127*, 106368. doi:10.1016/j.infsof.2020.106368

Maas, S., Schuster, T., & Hartmann, E. (2014). Pollution prevention and service stewardship strategies in the third - party logistics industry: Effects on firm differentiation and the moderating role of environmental communication. *Business Strategy and the Environment*, *23*(1), 38–55. doi:10.1002/bse.1759

Machida, S. (2009). Globalization and the Legitimacy of Intergovernmental Organizations. *International Studies*, *46*(4), 371–400. doi:10.1177/002088171004600401

Madampe, M. A. K. G. (2017). Successful Adoption of Agile Project Management in Software Development Industry. *International Journal of Computer Science and Information Technology Research.*, *5*(4), 27–33.

Mahanti, A. (2006). Challenges in Enterprise adoption of agile methods – a survey. *Journal of Computing and Information Technology – CIT*, 197-206.

Mahtaney, P. (2013). *Globalization and Sustainable Economic Development: Issues, Insights, and Inference*. Palgrave Macmillan. doi:10.1057/9781137024992

Mair, J., Martí, I., & Ganly, K. (2007). Institutional voids as spaces of opportunity. *European Business Forum, 31*(1), 34 - 39.

Makasi, A., & Saruchera, F. (2014). The impact of operational customer relationship management on customer loyalty. *Mediterranean Journal of Social Sciences*, *5*(23), 291–291. doi:10.5901/mjss.2014.v5n23p291

Mall, R. (2015). *Fundamentals of software engineering*. Academic Press.

Manford, C., & McSporran, M. (2003). E-Learning quality: Becoming a level five learning organization. *Proceedings of the 16th NACCQ*, 343 - 348.

Mangano, G., Zenezini, G., Cagliano, A. C., & De Marco, A. (2019). *The dynamics of diffusion of an electronic platform supporting City Logistics services*. Operations Management Research. doi:10.100712063-019-00147-7

Manners-Bell, J. (2014). *Supply Chain Risk: Understanding Emerging Threats to Global Supply Chains*. Kogan Page.

Mansor, Z., Yahya, S., & Arshad, N. H. (2011). Towards the Development of Success Determinants Charter for Agile Development Methodology. *International Journal of Information Technology and Engineering.*, *2*(1), 1–7.

Marano, V., & Kostova, T. (2015). Unpacking the institutional complexity in adoption of CSR practices in multinational enterprises. *Journal of Management Studies*, *53*(1), 28–54. doi:10.1111/joms.12124

Marchesi, M., Succi, G., Wells, D., & Williams, L. (2002). XR: Extreme Reality - Real-life Experiences. In *Extreme Programming Practices*. Addison-Wesley.

Marchet, G., Melacini, M., & Perotti, S. (2014). Environmental sustainability in logistics and freight transportation: A literature review and research agenda. *Journal of Manufacturing Technology Management*, *25*(6), 775–811. doi:10.1108/JMTM-06-2012-0065

Mark, S. & Mayberg, S. (2014). *Karlskrona test, a generic agile adoption test*. Mayberg.se.

Marks, M. G., & Ellis, L. A. (2013). Delays in major agricultural infrastructure projects in Guyana: Causes and proposed solutions. *The West Indian Journal of Engineering*, *36*(1), 79–85.

Marshall, J. (2015). New articulations in the Americas : Seizing structural opportunities. *Third*, *19*(4), 673–700.

Marsh, E. R. (1975). The harmonogram of karol adamiecki. *Academy of Management Journal*, *18*(2), 358–364.

Martin, A. (2002). *A Case Study: Exploring the Role of Customers on Extreme Programming Projects*. School of Computing and Mathematical Sciences, Victoria University of Wellington.

Martin, A., Biddle, R., & Noble, J. (2004). The XP customer role in practice: Three studies. *Proceedings of the Second Agile Development Conference (ADC 2004)*, 42-54. 10.1109/ADEVC.2004.23

Martin, A., Biddle, R., & Noble, J. (2004). When XP Met Outsourcing. In *Fifth International Conference of Extreme Programming and Agile Processes in Software Engineering*. Springer-Verlag. 10.1007/978-3-540-24853-8_6

Martin, A., Noble, J., & Biddle, R. (2003). Being Jane Malkovich: A Look into the world of an XP Customer. In *XP 2003*. Springer. doi:10.1007/3-540-44870-5_29

Martin, J. (1991). *Rapid Application Management*. Macmillan.

Martin, L. E., Nyberg, T. L., & Buckley, M. R. (2005). Political skill at work: Impact on work effectiveness. *Human Resource Planning*, *28*(4), 45–47.

Martinsen, U., & Björklund, M. (2012). Matches and gaps in the green logistics market. *International Journal of Physical Distribution & Logistics Management*, *42*(6), 562–583. doi:10.1108/09600031211250596

Marzagao, D. S. L., & Carvalho, M. M. (2016). Critical success factors for six sigma projects. *International Journal of Project Management*, *34*(8), 1505–1518. doi:10.1016/j.ijproman.2016.08.005

Mastrangelo, A., Eddy, E. R., & Lorenzet, S. J. (2004). The importance of personal and professional leadership. *Leadership and Organization Development Journal*, *25*(5), 435–451. doi:10.1108/01437730410544755

Matinnejad, R. (2011). Agile Model Driven Development: An Intelligent Compromise. *2011 Ninth International Conference on Software Engineering Research, Management and Applications*, 197 - 202. 10.1109/SERA.2011.17

Matthies, C., Kowark, T., Richly, K., Uflacker, M., & Plattner, H. (2016). ScrumLint: Identifying Violations of Agile Practices Using Development Artifacts. In *Proceedings of the 9th International Workshop on Cooperative and Human Aspects of Software Engineering - CHASE '16*, (pp. 40 – 43). ACM Press.

May, R. (2014). *Effective Sprint Planning*. Www.agileexecutives.org

McCarthy, D. J., & Puffer, S. M. (2016). Institutional Voids in an Emerging Economy: From Problem to Opportunity. *Journal of Leadership & Organizational Studies*, *23*(2), 208–219. doi:10.1177/1548051816633070

McCauley, C., & Moskalenko, S. (2008). Mechanisms of political radicalization: Pathways toward terrorism. *Terrorism and Political Violence*, *20*(3), 415–433. doi:10.1080/09546550802073367

McCormick, M. (2012). *Waterfall vs. Agile Methodology*. MPCS, Inc.

McDonald, K. (2016). *How You Can Help Agile Alliance Help You*. Agile Alliance Blog.

McGann, J. (2014). *A New Republic of Letters: Memory and Scholarship in the Age of Digital Reproduction*. Harvard University Press. doi:10.4159/9780674369245

McKinsey. (2016). *Bridging global infrastructure gaps*. McKinsey Global Institute. Retrieved from: https://www.mckinsey.com/industries/capital-projects-and-infrastructure/our-insights/management

McLean, J. (2005). *Administrative Management in Context*. MDP UK Ltd, Gwynedd.

McMillan, K. (2014). *Time, Resources, Scope... and Quality*. Www.adeptechllc.com

Mehta, N. (2008). Successful knowledge management implementation in global software companies. *Journal of Knowledge Management*, *12*(3), 42–56.

Meland, P. H., & Jensen, J. (2008). Secure Software Design in Practice. *2008 Third International Conference on Availability, Reliability and Security*, 1164 - 1171. 10.1109/ARES.2008.48

Melin, L. (1992). Internationalization as a strategy process. *Strategic Management Journal*, *13*(2S), 99 - 118.

Melvern, L. (2001). Missing the story: The media and the Rwandan genocide. *Contemporary Security Policy*, *22*(3), 91–106. doi:10.1080/13523260512331391248

Meredith, J. R., Shafer, S. M., & Mantel, S. J. Jr. (2017). *Project management: a strategic managerial approach*. John Wiley & Sons.

Mergel, I. (2016). Agile innovation management in government: A research agenda. *Government Information Quarterly, 33*(3), 516–523. doi:10.1016/j.giq.2016.07.004

Merrow, E. W. (2011). *Industrial Mega-projects: Concepts, Strategies and Practices for Success*. John Wiley and Sons.

Mersino, A. (2013). *Emotional intelligence for project managers: The people skills you need to achieve outstanding results*. HarperCollins Publishers.

Meyer, R. E., & Hellerer, M. A. (2014). Does institutional theory need redirecting? *Journal of Management Studies, 51*(7), 1221–1233. doi:10.1111/joms.12089

Miller, D., Lee, J., Chang, S., & Le Breton-Miller, I. (2009). Filling the institutional void: The social behaviour and performance of family versus non - family technology firms in emerging markets. *Journal of International Business Studies, 40*(5), 802–817. doi:10.1057/jibs.2009.11

Miller, S. (2008). Terrorism and Counter - Terrorism. Terrorism and Counter - Terrorism. *Ethics and Liberal Democracy, 579*, 1–222.

Mitchell, A. (1983). *The nine American lifestyles: Who we are & where we are going*. MacMillan Publishing Co., Inc.

Modarress, B., Ansari, A., & Lockwood, D. (2009). Outsourcing logistics to third - party providers: Practitioner's perspectives. *International Journal of Logistics Systems and Management, 6*(1), 23–38. doi:10.1504/IJLSM.2010.029719

Modi, H. S., Singh, N. K., & Chauhan, H. P. (n.d.). *Comprehensive Analysis of Software Development Life Cycle Models*. Academic Press.

Moe, N. B., Dahl, B. H., Stray, V., & Karlsen, L. S., & Schjødt-Osmo, S. (2019). Team autonomy in large - scale agile. In *Proceedings of the Annual Hawaii International Conference on System Sciences (HICSS)* (pp. 6997 - 7006). AIS Electronic Library.

Mohd, C. K. N. C. K., & Shahbodin, F. (2015). Personalized Learning Environment: Alpha Testing, Beta Testing & User Acceptance Test. *Procedia: Social and Behavioral Sciences, 195*, 837–843. doi:10.1016/j.sbspro.2015.06.319

Mokhtar, R., Jaafar, N. H., Tahar, N. F., Sukiman, S. A., Aris, A., & Abu Bakar, N. F. (2014). An integrated document management system for managing self - programme accreditation using scrum approach. *2014 International Symposium on Technology Management and Emerging Technologies*, 102 - 106. 10.1109/ISTMET.2014.6936487

Mollenkopf, D., Stolze, H., Tate, W. L., & Ueltschy, M. (2010). Green, lean, and global supply chains. *International Journal of Physical Distribution & Logistics Management, 40*(1/2), 14–41. doi:10.1108/09600031011018028

Möller, F., Stachon, M., Hoffmann, C., Bauhaus, H., & Otto, B. (2020). Data - Driven Business Models in Logistics: A Taxonomy of Optimization and Visibility Services. *Proceedings of the 53rd Hawaii International Conference on System Sciences*. 10.24251/HICSS.2020.661

Moore, E. M., Brandl, K., & Dau, L. A. 2019. Institutional schisms in Argentina: The impact of intergovernmental organizations on country institutional environments. In International Business in a VUCA World: The Changing Role of States and Firms, (pp. 89 – 102). Emerald Group.

Moore, E. M., Dau, L. A., & Doh, J. (2020). Does Monetary Aid Catalyse New Business Creation? Analysing the Impact of Global Aid Flows on Formal and Informal Entrepreneurship. *Journal of Management Studies, 57*(3), 438–469. doi:10.1111/joms.12552

Moore, E. M., Dau, L. A., & Mingo, S. (2021). The effects of trade integration on formal and informal entrepreneurship: The moderating role of economic development. *Journal of International Business Studies*, 1–27.

Moradi, S., Kähkönen, K., & Aaltonen, K. (2020). Project managers' competence in collaborative construction projects. *Buildings*, *10*(3), 50. doi:10.3390/buildings10030050

Moran, A. (2014). *Agile Risk Management*. Springer Verlag. doi:10.1007/978-3-319-05008-9

Moran, A. (2015). *Managing Agile: Strategy, Implementation, Organisation and People*. Springer. doi:10.1007/978-3-319-16262-1

Morck, R., & Yeung, B. (2003). Agency problems in large family business groups. *Entrepreneurship Theory and Practice*, *27*(4), 367–382. doi:10.1111/1540-8520.t01-1-00015

Morikawa, M. (2013). Productivity and survival of family firms in Japan. *Journal of Economics and Business*, *70*, 111–125. doi:10.1016/j.jeconbus.2012.11.001

Morris, L., Ma, M., & Wu, P. C. (2014). *Agile Innovation: The Revolutionary Approach to Accelerate Success, Inspire Engagement, and Ignite Creativity*. John Wiley & Sons Ltd.

Mountaingoatsoftware. (2021a). *Daily Scrum Meeting*. Www.mountaingoatsoftware.com

Mountaingoatsoftware. (2021b). *Sprint Planning Meeting*. Www.mountaingoatsoftware.com

Mubarak, S. A. (2010). *Construction Project Scheduling and Control*. John Wiley and Sons. doi:10.1002/9780470912171

Mueller, J., & Mark, G. S. (2011). *Terror, security, and money: Balancing the risks, benefits, and costs of homeland security*. Oxford University Press. doi:10.1093/acprof:osobl/9780199795758.001.0001

Mukhiya, S. K., & Ahmed, U. (2020). *Hands - on exploratory data analysis with Python*. Packt Publishing.

Muller, A. C., & Guido, S. (2017). *Introduction to machine learning with Python*. O'Reilly Media, Inc.

Muller, J. P., & Massaron, L. (2015). *Python for data science for dummies*. John Wiley & Sons, Inc.

Müller, R., & Turner, J. R. (2007). Matching the project manager's leadership style to project type. *International Journal of Project Management*, *25*(1), 21–32. doi:10.1016/j.ijproman.2006.04.003

Müller, R., & Turner, R. (2010). Leadership competency profiles of successful project managers. *International Journal of Project Management*, *28*(5), 437–448. doi:10.1016/j.ijproman.2009.09.003

Mundra, A., Misra, S., & Dhawale, C. A. (2013). Practical Scrum - Scrum Team: Way to Produce Successful and Quality Software. *2013 13th International Conference on Computational Science and Its Applications,* 119 - 123. 10.1109/ICCSA.2013.25

Musa, S. B., Norwawi, N. M., Selamat, M. H., & Sharif, K. Y. (2011). Improved extreme programming methodology with inbuilt security. *2011 IEEE Symposium on Computers & Informatics*, 674 - 679. 10.1109/ISCI.2011.5958997

Myers, M., & Young, L. (1997). Hidden Agendas, Power and Managerial Assumptions in Information Systems Development: An Ethnographic Case Study. *Information Technology & People*, *10*(3), 176–191. doi:10.1108/09593849710178225

Nacos, B. (2016). Mass - mediated Terrorism: Mainstream and Digital Media in Terrorism and Counterterrorism. Rowman & Littlefield.

Naidoo, V. (2021). SME Sustainability in South Africa Post - COVID - 19. In Handbook of Research on Sustaining SMEs and Entrepreneurial Innovation in the Post - COVID - 19 Era. IGI Global.

Najafi-Tavani, Z., Mousavi, S., Zaefarian, G., & Naudé, P. (2020). Relationship learning and international customer involvement in new product design: The moderating roles of customer dependence and cultural distance. *Journal of Business Research*, *120*, 42–58. doi:10.1016/j.jbusres.2020.07.020

Nakai, M., & Ke, W. (2011). Review of the methods for handling missing data in longitudinal data analysis. *International Journal of Mathematical Analysis*, *5*(1), 1–13.

Nalchigar, S., Yu, E., & Keshavjee, K. (2021). Modelling machine learning requirements from three perspectives: A case report from the healthcare domain. *Requirements Engineering*, *34567*, 1–18.

Namta, R. (2014). *Thoughts on Test Automation in Agile*. Www.infoq.com

Nandhakumar, J., & Avison, D. E. (1999). The Fiction of Methodological Development: A Field Study of Information Systems Development. *Information Technology & People*, *12*(2), 1–28. doi:10.1108/09593849910267224

Narbaev, T., & De-Marco, A. (2013). *Combination of growth model and earned schedule to Forecast Project Cost at Completion*. American Society of Civil Engineers.

NASA. (1967). *Centre Responsibilities in the Apollo Program*. NASA Apollo Program Directive No. 33. PBS. Technology Timeline: 1752 - 1990. Retrieved from: https://www.pbs.org/wgbh/amex/telephone/timeline/timeline_text.html

Nasir, M. H., Sahibuddin, S., Ahmad, R., & Mohd, S. S. (2015). How the PMBOK Addresses Critical Success Factors for Software Projects: A Multi-round Delphi Study. *Journal of Software*, *10*(15), 1283–1300. doi:10.17706/jsw.10.11.1283-1300

National Consortium for the Study of Terrorism and Responses to Terrorism (START). (2016). Global Terrorism Database.

Natvig, D., & Stark, N. L. (2016). A project team analysis using Tuckman's model of small - group development. *The Journal of Nursing Education*, *55*(12), 675–681. doi:10.3928/01484834-20161114-03 PMID:27893902

Nawrocki, J., Jasinski, M., Walter, B., & Wojciechowski, A. (2002). Extreme programming modified: Embrace requirements engineering practices. *Proceedings IEEE Joint International Conference on Requirements Engineering*, 303 - 310. 10.1109/ICRE.2002.1048543

Neisser, U., & Winograd, E. (1988). *Remembering Reconsidered: Ecological and Traditional Approaches to the Study of Memory*. Cambridge University Press. doi:10.1017/CBO9780511664014

Nekoufar, S., & Karim, A. (2011). Lean project management in large scale industrial project via standardization. *Project Perspectives*, *33*, 72–77.

New York Times. (2010). *BP Used Riskier Method to Seal Well Before Blast*. https://www.nytimes.com/2010/05/27/us/27rig.html?_r=1

New York Times. (2011). *Chile Mining Accident 2010*. http://topics.nytimes.com/top/reference/timestopics/subjects/c/chile_mining_accident_2010/index.html

Nguyen, L. H., Shen, H., Ershoff, D., Afifi, A. A., & Bourque, L. B. (2006). Exploring the causal relationship between exposure to the 1994 Northridge earthquake and pre - and post - earthquake preparedness activities. *Earthquake Spectra*, *22*(3), 569–587. doi:10.1193/1.2219108

Niazi, M., Mahmood, S., Alshayeb, M., Riaz, M. R., Faisal, K., Cerpa, N., Khan, S. U., & Richardson, I. (2016). Challenges of project management in global software development: A client-vendor analysis. *Information and Software Technology*, *80*, 1–19. doi:10.1016/j.infsof.2016.08.002

Nicoleta, C. (2005). Agile Software Project Management Methodologies. *Economy Informatics*, 1-4.

Nidhra, S. (2012). Black Box and White Box Testing Techniques—A Literature Review. *International Journal of Embedded Systems and Applications*, *2*(2), 29–50. doi:10.5121/ijesa.2012.2204

Nielsen, J. (2000). *Designing web usability*. New Riders.

Niemi-Grundström, M. (2014). Developing, evaluating and managing library with agile methods. *Library Management, 35*(6/7), 481–485. doi:10.1108/LM-02-2014-0022

Nieto, M. J., Santamaria, L., & Fernandez, Z. (2015). Understanding the Innovation Behaviour of Family Firms. *Journal of Small Business Management, 53*(2), 382–399. doi:10.1111/jsbm.12075

Nijaki, K., & Worrel, G. (2012). Procurement for sustainable local economic development. *International Journal of Public Sector Management, 25*(2), 133–153. doi:10.1108/09513551211223785

Nikolaeva, R., & Bicho, M. (2011). The role of institutional and reputational factors in the voluntary adoption of corporate social responsibility reporting standards. *Journal of the Academy of Marketing Science, 39*(1), 136–157. doi:10.100711747-010-0214-5

Nipa, T. J., Kermanshachi, S., Patel, R., & Tafazzoli, M. (2020). Disaster preparedness education: construction curriculum requirements to increase students' preparedness in pre - and post - disaster activities. *Associated Schools of Construction (ASC) International Conference.*

Nonaka, I. (1994). A Dynamic Theory of Organizational Knowledge Creation. *Organization Science, 5*(1), 14–37. doi:10.1287/orsc.5.1.14

Nonaka, I., & Takeuchi, H. (1995). *The knowledge creating company: how Japanese company: how Japanese companies create the dynamics of innovation.* Oxford University Press.

Nonaka, I., & Takeuchi, H. (1995). *The knowledge-creating company: how Japanese companies create the dynamics of innovation.* Oxford University Press.

Norouzi, G., Heydari, M., Noori, S., & Bagherpour, M. (2015). Mathematical modelling for scheduling and determining success probability of research projects considering complex - fuzzy networks. *Journal of Applied Mathematics, 1*(1), 1–12. doi:10.1155/2015/809216

North, D. (1991). Institutions. *Journal of Economic Perspectives.*

North, D. C. (1990). *Institutions, Institutional Change and Economic Performance.* Cambridge University Press. doi:10.1017/CBO9780511808678

North, D. C. (1991). Institutions. *The Journal of Economic Perspectives, 5*(1), 97–112. doi:10.1257/jep.5.1.97

O'Brien, J. A. (2002). *Management Information Systems Managing Information Technology in the Business Enterprise.* Mc Graw Hill Irwin.

O'Keeffe, M., & Ó Cinnéide, M. (2008). Search - based refactoring for software maintenance. *Journal of Systems and Software, 81*(4), 502–516. doi:10.1016/j.jss.2007.06.003

Odhiambo, A. A., Ouko, R. A., & Muhoho, D. J. (2020). Communication as a driver of performance of projects in Kenyan commercial banks. *International Academic Journal of Information Sciences and Project Management, 3*(6), 100–112.

Ogunde, A., Joshua, O., Amusan, L. M., & Akuete, E. (2017). Project Management a Panacea to Improving the Performance of Construction Projects. *International Journal of Civil Engineering and Technology, 8*(9), 1234–1242.

Oliomogbe, G. O., & Smith, N. J. (2012). Value in mega-projects, Organisation, Technology, and Management in Construction. *International Journal (Toronto, Ont.), 4*(3), 617–624.

Orlikowski, W., & Gash, D. (1994). Technological Frames: Making Sense of Information Technology in Organisations. *ACM Transactions on Information Systems, 12*(2), 174–207. doi:10.1145/196734.196745

Oseyi-Kyei, R., & Chan, A. P. C. (2017). Comparative analysis of the success criteria for public-private partnership projects in Ghana and Hong Kong. *Project Management Journal*, *48*(4), 80–92. doi:10.1177/875697281704800407

Osorio, J. C., Manotas, D. F., & Rivera, L. (2017). Priorización de Riesgos Operacionales para un Proveedor de Tercera Parte Logística - 3PL. *Información Tecnológica*, *28*(4), 135–144. doi:10.4067/S0718-07642017000400016

Österwalder, A., & Pigneur, Y. (2010). *Business Model Generation: A handbook for visionaries, gamechangers, and challangers.* Wiley.

Österwalder, A., Pigneur, Y., & Tucci, C. L. (2005). Clarifying business models; origins, present, and future of the concept. *Communications of the Association for Information Systems*, *15*, 1–40. doi:10.17705/1CAIS.01601

Ottaway, M. (2002). *Rebuilding State Institutions in Collapsed States*. Academic Press.

Ottem, E., Lian, A., & Karlsen, P. (2007). Reasons for the Growth of Traditional Memory Span across Age. *The European Journal of Cognitive Psychology*, *19*(2), 233–270. doi:10.1080/09541440600684653

Owen, R., & Koskela, L. (2006). An agile step forward in project management. In *2nd Specialty Conference on Leadership and Management in Construction and Engineering* (pp. 216 - 224). Academic Press.

Pacagnella, A. C., Da Silva, S. L., Pacifico, O., Ignacio, P. D. A., & Da Silva, A. L. (2019). Critical success factors for project manufacturing environments. *Project Management Journal*, *50*(2), 1–16. doi:10.1177/8756972819827670

Pace, M. (2019). A Correlational Study on Project Management Methodology and Project Success. Journal of Engineering. *Project & Production Management*, *9*(2), 56–65. doi:10.2478/jeppm-2019-0007

Pal, K. (2019). Markov Decision Theory Based Crowdsourcing Software Process Model. In Crowdsourcing and Probabilistic Decision-Making in Software Engineering: Emerging Research and Opportunities. IGI Publication.

Pal, K. (2020). Framework for Reusable Test Case Generation in Software Systems Testing. In Software Engineering for Agile Application Development. IGI Global Publication.

Pal, K. (2020). Framework for Reusable Test Case Generation in Software Systems Testing. In Software Engineering for Agile Application Development. IGI Global.

Pal, K., & Karakostas, B. (2020). Software Testing Under Agile, Scrum, and DevOps. In Agile Scrum Implementation and Its Long-Term Impact on Organizations. IGI Publication.

Pal, K., & Karakostas, B. (2021). Software Testing Under Agile, Scrum, and DevOps. In Agile Scrum Implementation and its Long-Term Impact on Organization. IGI Global Publication.

Pal, K., & Williams, I. (2021). Software Development Knowledge Management System Using Web Portal. In Digital Technology Advancement in Knowledge Management. IGI Publication.

Palcic, I., & Buchmeister, B. (2012). Project Success in Slovenian Companies. In *DAAAM International Scientific Book.* DAAAM International. doi:10.2507/daaam.scibook.2012.05

Palepu, K. G., & Khanna, T. (2005). *Spotting Institutional Voids in Emerging Markets.* Harvard Business School Cases.

Pålsson, H., & Johansson, O. (2016). Reducing transportation emissions: Company intentions, barriers and discriminating factors. *Benchmarking*, *23*(3), 674–703. doi:10.1108/BIJ-03-2014-0025

Pangarkar, N. (2008). Internationalization and performance of small - and medium - sized enterprises. *Journal of World Business*, *43*(4), 475–485. doi:10.1016/j.jwb.2007.11.009

Panke, D., & Petersohn, U. (2016). Norm challenges and norm death: The inexplicable? *Cooperation and Conflict*, *51*(1), 3–19. doi:10.1177/0010836715597948

Pankratz, O., & Basten, D. (2014). Ladder to success - eliciting project managers' perceptions of IS project success criteria. *International Journal of Information Systems and Project Management, 2*(2), 5 – 24. doi:10.12821/ijispm020201

Paquin, J. P., Gauthier, C., & Morin, P. P. (2016). The downside risk of project portfolios: The impact of capital investment projects and the value of project efficiency and project risk management programmes. *International Journal of Project Management*, *34*(8), 1460–1470. doi:10.1016/j.ijproman.2016.07.009

Pardede, T., & Tetsuo, K. (2007). *Planning for post - disaster recovery: lesson from Aceh post - tsunami recovery.* Department of Urban Engineering, University of Tokyo. Accessed from:http://rdarc.itakura.toyo.ac.jp/webdav/ask/public/ACP2007/togu.pdf

Patil, G. (2016). Project management challenges. *Journal of Multidisciplinary Engineering Science and Technology, 3*.

Pauleen, D. J., & Yoong, P. (2001). Relationship building and the use of ICT in boundary-crossing virtual teams: A facilitator's perspective. *Journal of Information Technology, 16*(4), 205-220.

Pazirandeh, A., & Jafari, H. (2013). Making sense of green logistics. *International Journal of Productivity and Performance Management*, *62*(8), 889–904. doi:10.1108/IJPPM-03-2013-0059

Peng, M. (2004). Outside directors and firm performance during institutional transitions. *Strategic Management Journal*, *25*(5), 453–471. doi:10.1002mj.390

Peng, M. W. (2002). Towards an institution - based view of business strategy. *Asia Pacific Journal of Management*, *19*(2/3), 251–267. doi:10.1023/A:1016291702714

Peng, M. W., Wang, D. Y. L., & Jiang, Y. (2008). An institution - based view of international business strategy: A focus on emerging economies. *Journal of International Business Studies*, *39*(5), 920–936. doi:10.1057/palgrave.jibs.8400377

Perboli, G., & Rosano, M. (2018). A Decision Support System for Optimizing the Last - Mile by Mixing Traditional and Green Logistics. In C. Temponi & N. Vandaele (Eds.), *Information Systems, Logistics, and Supply Chain* (Vol. 262). Springer. doi:10.1007/978-3-319-73758-4_3

Persson, J. S., Mathiassen, L., & Aaen, I. (2012). Agile distributed software development: Enacting control through media and context. *Information Systems Journal*, *22*(6), 411–433. doi:10.1111/j.1365-2575.2011.00390.x

Peter, L. & Henry, C. T. A. (2009). *Assessing Agility*. Academic Press.

Petersen, K., Wohlin, C., & Baca, D. (2009). The Waterfall Model in Large - Scale Development. In F. Bomarius, M. Oivo, P. Jaring, & P. Abrahamsson (Eds.), *Product - Focused Software Process Improvement* (Vol. 32, pp. 386–400). Springer Berlin Heidelberg. doi:10.1007/978-3-642-02152-7_29

Phillips, N., Tracey, P., & Karra, N. (2009). Rethinking institutional distance: Strengthening the tie between new institutional theory and international management. *Strategic Organization*, *7*(3), 339–348. doi:10.1177/1476127009337439

Pinto, J. K. (2000). Understanding the role of politics in successful project management. *International Journal of Project Management*, *18*(2), 85–91. doi:10.1016/S0263-7863(98)00073-8

Pinto, J. K., & Slevin, D. P. (1988a). Project Success: Definitions and Measurement Techniques. *Project Management Journal*, *19*(1), 67–72.

Pinto, J. K., & Slevin, D. P. (1988b). Critical Success Factors Across the Project Life Cycle. *Project Management Journal*, *19*(3), 67–74.

Pinto, J. K., & Slevin, D. P. (1989). Critical success factors in R&D projects. *Research Technology Management, 32*(1), 31–35. doi:10.1080/08956308.1989.11670572

PMI. (2013). *A guide to the project management body of knowledge, PMBOK* (5th ed.). Project Management Institute.

Podgórska, M., & Pichlak, M. (2019). Analysis of project managers' leadership competence. *International Journal of Managing Projects in Business, 12*(4), 869–887.

Pollack, J., Helm, J., & Adler, D. (2018). What is the Iron Triangle, and how has it changed? *International Journal of Managing Projects in Business, 11*(2), 527–547. doi:10.1108/IJMPB-09-2017-0107

Ponsard, C., Majchrowski, A., Mouton, S., & Touzani, M. (2017). Process guidance for the successful deployment of a big data project: Lessons Learned from Industrial Cases. *Proceedings of IoTBDS*, 350 - 355.

Poppo, L., & Zenger, T. (1998). Testing alternative theories of the firm: Transaction cost, Knowledge - based, and measurement explanations for make - or - buy decisions in information services. *Strategic Management Journal, 19*(9), 853–877. doi:10.1002/(SICI)1097-0266(199809)19:9<853::AID-SMJ977>3.0.CO;2-B

Porter, M. E. (1990). The competitive advantage of notions. *Harvard Business Review, 68*(2), 73–93.

Prabhakar, G. P. (2005). Switch leadership in projects an empirical study reflecting the importance of transformational leadership on project success across twenty - eight nations. *Project Management Journal, 36*(4), 53–60. doi:10.1177/875697280503600406

Prabhakar, G. P. (2008). What is Project Success: A Literature Review. *International Journal of Business and Management, 3*(9), 3–10. doi:10.5539/ijbm.v3n9p3

Prajogo, D., & Olhager, J. (2012). Supply Chain Integration and Performance: The Effects of Long - Term Relationships, Information Technology and Sharing, and Logistics Integration. *International Journal of Production Economics, 135*(1), 514–522. doi:10.1016/j.ijpe.2011.09.001

Preez, N. D., & Louw, L. (2008). A framework for managing the innovation process. *PICMET '08 - 2008 Portland International Conference on Management of Engineering & Technology*. 10.1109/PICMET.2008.4599663

Presley, A., Mills, J., & Liles, D. (1995). Agile Aerospace Manufacturing. Nepcon East.

Pressman, R. S. (2005). Software Engineering: A Practitioner's Approach. McGraw-Hill.

Pressman, R. S. (2000). *Software engineering: A Practitioner's Approach (European Adaption)* (5th ed.). McGraw-Hill International.

Preuss, D. H. (2006). *Study: Co - Located Teams vs. the Cubicle Farm*. InfoQ.

PriceWaterhouseCoopers. (2014). *Project success: Portfolio and change management*. Retrieved from: http://pwc.com/gx/en/service/advisory/consulting/portfolio-programme-management/global-pp.msurvey-2014.html

Priemus, H., Flyvberg, B., & van Wee, B. (2016). Introduction. In *Decision - Making on Mega - projects. Cost - Benefit Analysis, Planning and Innovation*. Edward Elgar.

Prikladnicki, R., Audy, J. L. N., & Evaristo, R. (2003). Global Software Development in Practice Lessons Learned. *Software Process Improvement and Practice, 8*(4), 267–279.

Procedia Computer Science. (2021). *Current study on limitations of Agile.* . doi:10.1016/j.procs.2016.02.056

Project Laneways. (2021). *What is Agile Management?* Author.

Project Management Institute (PMI) Inc. (2007). *Construction Extension to the PMBOK Guide* (3rd ed.). PMI Publisher.

Project Management Institute (PMI). (2017). *A Guide to the Project Management Body of Knowledge (PMBOK Guide)* (6th ed.). Project Management Institute.

Project Management Institute (PMI). (2017). *A guide to the project management body of knowledge (PMBOK® Guide)* (6th ed.). Project Management Institute.

Project Management Institute (PMI). (2020). *Pulse of Profession 2019.* Project Management Institute. Available: https://www.pmi.org/learning/thought-leadership/pulse

Project Management Institute. (2013). A Guide to the Project Management Body of Knowledge (5th ed.). Project Management Institute, Inc.

Project Management Institute. (2021). *A Guide to the Project Management Body of Knowledge* (5th ed.). PMBOK Guide.

Przeworski, A. (2004). Institutions matter? *Government and Opposition, 39*(4), 527–540. doi:10.1111/j.1477-7053.2004.00134.x

Puffer, S. M., McCarthy, D. J., & Boisot, M. (2010). Entrepreneurship in Russia and China: The impact of formal institutional voids. *Entrepreneurship Theory and Practice, 34*(3), 441–467. doi:10.1111/j.1540-6520.2009.00353.x

Pugh, D. S., & Hickson, D. J. (2007). *Writers on Organisations* (6th ed.). Penguin Books. doi:10.4135/9781483329628

Qian, G., Li, L., Li, J., & Qian, Z. (2008). Regional diversification and firm performance. *Journal of International Business Studies, 39*(2), 197–214. doi:10.1057/palgrave.jibs.8400346

Rahman, S., Rivera, E., Khomh, F., Guéhéneuc, Y. G., & Lehnert, B. (2019). *Machine learning software engineering in practice: An industrial case study.* https://arxiv.org/abs/1906.07154

Rai, R. K. (2011). Knowledge management and organizational culture: A theoretical integrative framework. *Journal of Knowledge Management*, •••, 779–801.

Rai, R. K. (2011). Knowledge management and organizational culture: A theoretical integrative framework. *Journal of Knowledge Management*, 779–801.

Raj, P. & Sinha, P. (2020). Project Management in Era of Agile and DevOps Methodologies. *International Journal of Scientific & Technology Research, 9*(1), 1024 - 1033.

Rally. (2010). *Agile with a Capital "A" Vs. agile With a Lowercase "a".* Author.

Ramamurti, R. (2004). Developing Countries and MNEs: Extending and Enriching the Research Agenda. *Journal of International Business Studies, 35*(4), 277–283. doi:10.1057/palgrave.jibs.8400087

Rammasubbu, N., & Balan, R. K. (2008). Towards Governance Scheme for Distributed Software Development Projects. *Proceedings of the 1st International Workshop on Software Development Governance*, 11-14.

Ransbotham, S., Kiron, D., Gerbert, P., & Reeves, M. (2017). Reshaping Business with Artificial Intelligence. *MIT Sloan Management Review*. https://sloanreview.mit.edu

Rapoport, D. C. (2004). The four waves of modern terrorism. *Attacking terrorism: Elements of a grand strategy*, 46 - 73.

Rapoport, D. C. (1984). Fear and trembling: Terrorism in three religious traditions. *The American Political Science Review, 78*(03), 658–677. doi:10.2307/1961835

Rapoport, D. C. (2001). The Fourth Wave: September 11 in the History of Terrorism. *Current History (New York, N.Y.)*, *100*(650), 419–424. doi:10.1525/curh.2001.100.650.419

Rausch, E. (2005). A practical focus on leadership in management - for research, education and management development. *Management Decision*, *43*(7 / 8), 988–1000. doi:10.1108/00251740510609983

Raut, R., Kharat, M., Kamble, S., & Kumar, C. S. (2018). Sustainable evaluation and selection of potential third - party logistics (3PL) providers: An integrated MCDM approach. *Benchmarking*, *25*(1), 76–97. doi:10.1108/BIJ-05-2016-0065

Raval, M. V., Minneci, P. C., Deans, K. J., Kurtovic, K. J., Dietrich, A., Bates, D. G., & Kenney, B. D. (2015). Improving quality and efficiency for intussusception management after successful enema reduction. *Pediatrics*, *136*(5), e1345–e1352. doi:10.1542/peds.2014-3122 PMID:26459654

Rawat, P. S. (2011). Effect of Psychological Empowerment on Commitment of Employees: *An Empirical Study. In International Conference on Humanities, Historical and Social Sciences*. Singapore: International Association of Computer Science & Information Technology.

Razak, R. A., & Fahrurazi, F. R. (2011). Agile testing with Selenium. *2011 Malaysian Conference in Software Engineering*, 217 - 219. 10.1109/MySEC.2011.6140672

Rico, D. F. (2006). *Running head: Agile Methods and the Links to Customer Satisfaction and Firm Performance*. Available online at http://davidfrico.com/rico06a.pdf

Rimando, M., & Brace, A. M., Namageyo-Funa, A., Parr, T. L., Sealy, D., & Davis, T. L. (2015). Data collection challenges and recommendations for early career researchers. *Qualitative Report*, *20*(12), 2025–2036.

Risse, T. (2004). *Social Constructivism Meets Globalization*. Freie Universität Berlin.

Rodrik, D., Subramanian, A., & Trebbi, F. (2004). Institutions rule: The primacy of institutions over geography and integration in economic development. *Journal of Economic Growth*, *9*(2), 131–165. doi:10.1023/B:JOEG.0000031425.72248.85

Roe, P. (2014). *Factors which contribute to successful projects*. Prepared for the Association for Project Management. Retrieved from: www.apm.org.uk

Roebuck, K. (2012). *System Development Life Cycle (SDLC): High-impact Strategies – What You Need to Know: Definition, Adoption, Impact, Benefits, Maturity, Vendors*. Emereo Publishing.

Rogers, D.S., & Tibben-Lembke, R.S. (1998). *Going backwards: Reverse logistics trends and practices*. Reverse Logistics Executive Council. www.rlec.org/reverse.pdf

Rosário Cabrita, M., Duarte, S., Carvalho, H., & Cruz-Machado, V. (2016). Integration of Lean, Agile, Resilient and Green Paradigms in a Business Model Perspective: Theoretical Foundations. *IFAC-PapersOnLine*, *49*(12), 1306–1311. doi:10.1016/j.ifacol.2016.07.704

Rose, D. (2018). *Enterprise agility for dummies*. John Wiley & Sons Ltd.

Rosenberg, M. J. (2000). *E - Learning: Strategies for delivering knowledge in the digital age*. McGraw - Hill.

Rothman, J. R. (2011). *When You Have No Product Owner at All*. Www.jrothman.com

Rouhanizadeh, B., Kermanshachi, S., & Dhamangaonkar, V. (2019). Identification and categorization of policy and legal barriers to long - term timely post - disaster reconstruction. *Journal of Legal Affairs and Dispute Resolution in Engineering and Construction*, *11*(3), 04519014. doi:10.1061/(ASCE)LA.1943-4170.0000307

Rouse, M. (2015). *Sprint (software development) definition*. Searchsoftwarequality.techtarget.com.

Royce, W. W. (1970). Managing the Development of Large Software Systems. *Proceedings of IEEE WESCON*, *26*(August), 1–9.

Royce, W. W. (1970). Managing the development of large software systems. *Proceedings of IEEE Wescon.*

Rubenstein-Montano, R., Liebowitz, J., Buchwalter, J., & Mcgraw, D. (2000). A Systems Thinking Framework for Knowledge Management. *Decision Support Systems*, *31*(1).

Ruddle, R. A., Payne, S. J., & Jones, D. M. (1998). Navigating large - scale "desk - top" virtual buildings: Effects of orientation aids and familiarity. *Presence (Cambridge, Mass.)*, *7*(2), 179–192. doi:10.1162/105474698565668

Ruggiero, U. (2014). *Sviluppo di modelli di logistica sostenibile nelle città portuali* [Development of sustainable logistics models in port cities] (Thesis). LUISS Guido Carli. https://tesi.luiss.it/13812/1/ruggiero-ugo-tesi-2014.pdf

Runhaar, H., & Lafferty, H. (2009). Governing corporate social responsibility: An assessment of the contribution of the un global compact to CSR strategies in the telecommunications industry. *Journal of Business Ethics*, *84*(4), 479–495. doi:10.100710551-008-9720-5

Rus, I., & Lindvall, M. (2002). Knowledge Management in Software Engineering. *IEEE Software*, *19*(3), 26–38.

Rus, I., & Lindvall, M. (2002, June). Knowledge Management in Software Engineering. *IEEE Software*, *19*(3), 26–38. doi:10.1109/MS.2002.1003450

Rus, I., Lindvall, M., & Sinha, S. (2001). Knowledge management in software engineering A state-of the-art-report. *Fraunhofer Center for Experimental Software Engineering and the University of Maryland*, *2001*, 1–57.

Russo, N. L., & Stolterman, E. (2000). Exploring the Assumptions Underlying Information Systems Methodologies: Their Impact on Past, Present and Future ISM Research. *Information Technology & People*, *13*(4), 313–327. doi:10.1108/09593840010359509

Ruuska, I., Artto, K., Aaltonen, K., & Lehtonen, P. (2009). Dimensions of distance in a project network: Exploring Olkiluoto 3 nuclear power plant project. *International Journal of Project Management*, *27*(2), 142–153. doi:10.1016/j.ijproman.2008.09.003

Rycroft, R. W., & Kash, D. E. (1999). *The Complexity Challenge: Technological Innovation for the 21st Century*. Pinter.

Safapour, E., & Kermanshachi, S. (2019). Identification and categorization of factors affecting duration of post - disaster reconstruction of interdependent transportation systems. *ASCE Construction Research Congress (CRC).*

Safapour, E., Kermanshachi, S., & Jafari, A. (2020). Effective project management principles and strategies in transportation infrastructure projects. In *Creative Construction e - Conference 2020* (pp. 126–135). Budapest University of Technology and Economics.

Said, H., Kandil, A., & Cai, H. (2012). Agent - based simulation of labour emergency evacuation in high - rise building construction sites. *Construction Research Congress*. 10.1061/9780784412329.111

Salihoğlu, Y. (2001). *User Involvement in Software Project Development: A Review of Models*. Software Project Management Research Paper.

Saltz, J., & Suthrland, A. (2019). SKI: An agile framework for data science. *Proceedings of IEEE International Conference on Big Data (Big Data)*, 3468 - 3476.

Saltz, J. (2015). The need for new processes, methodologies and tools to support big data teams and improve big data project effectiveness. *Proceedings of the IEEE International Conference on Big Data*, 2066 - 2071.

Saltz, J., Hotz, N., Wild, N., & Stirling, K. (2018). Exploring project management methodologies used within data science teams. *Proceedings of the Americas Conference on Information Systems (AMCIS).*

Saltz, J., Shamshurin, I., & Crowston, K. (2017). Comparing data science project management methodologies via a controlled experiment. *Proceedings of the 50th Hawaii International Conference on System Sciences*, 1013 - 1022.

Samaranayake, S. U., & Takemura, T. (2017). Employee readiness for organizational change: A case study in an export - oriented manufacturing firm in Sri Lanka. *Eurasian Journal of Business and Economics*, *10*(20), 1–16. doi:10.17015/ejbe.2017.020.01

Samuel, A. (1959). Some studies in machine learning using the game of checkers. *IBM Journal of Research and Development*, *3*(3), 210–229.

Sanchez, F., Steria, S., Bonjour, E., Micaelli, J. P., & Monticolo, D. (2020). An approach based on bayesian network for improving project management maturity: An application to reduce cost overrun risks in engineering projects. *Computers in Industry*, *119*, 103227. doi:10.1016/j.compind.2020.103227

Sangwan, R. S., & Ros, J. (2008). Architectural Leadership and Management in Globally Distributed Software Development. *Proceedings of the 1st International Workshop on Leadership and Management in Software Architecture*, 17-22.

Sarhadi, M., Yousefi, S., & Zamani, A. (2018). Participative project management as a comprehensive response to postmodernism criticisms: The role of communication. *International Journal of Managing Projects in Business*, *11*(4), 935–959. doi:10.1108/IJMPB-10-2017-0119

Saruchera, F. (2014). *Determinants of commercialization of technological innovations in developing economies: a study of Zimbabwe's research institutes* [Doctoral dissertation]. University of KwaZulu - Natal, Pietermaritzburg, South Africa.

Saruchera, F. (Ed.). (2021). *Advanced perspectives on global industry transitions and business opportunities*. IGI Global. doi:10.4018/978-1-7998-4303-0

Saruchera, F., & Phiri, M. A. (2016). Technological Innovations Performance and Public - Private - partnerships. *Corporate Ownership & Control*, *13*(4), 549–557. doi:10.22495/cocv13i4c4p4

Saunders, M., Lewis, P., & Thornhill, A. (2009). Understanding research philosophies and approaches. In M. Saunders, P. Lewis, & A. Thornhill (Eds.), *Research methods for business students* (5th ed., pp. 106–135). Pearson Education Limited.

Savun, B., & Phillips, B. J. (2009). Democracy, Foreign Policy, and Terrorism. *The Journal of Conflict Resolution*, *53*(6), 878–904. doi:10.1177/0022002709342978

Sawant, A. A., Bari, P. H., & Chawan, P. M. (2012). Software Testing Techniques and Strategies. *International Journal of Engineering Research and Applications*, *2*(3), 7.

Sawyer, M. (2012). *Vico software integrating construction.* Available at: www.vicosoftware.com

Sayer, N. J., & Williams, B. (2012). *Lean for dummies* (2nd ed.). John Wiley & Sons Ltd.

Scaled Agile Inc. (2016). *Scaled Agile Framework® (SAFe®).* Retrieved from https://www.scaledagileframework.com/

Schalliol, G. (2002). Challenges for Analysts on a Large XP Project. In *Extreme Programming Perspectives*. Addison-Wesley.

Schar, B., Jungling, S., & Thonssen, B. (2015). Towards an Agile Requirements Engineering Process Combining HERMES 5 and SCRUM. *2015 International Conference on Enterprise Systems (ES)*, 98 - 109. 10.1109/ES.2015.17

Schmid, A. P., & Janny, D. G. (1982). *Violence as communication: Insurgent terrorism and the Western news media*. Sage.

Schmidt, T. S., Weiss, S., & Paetzold, K. (2018). *Agile Development of Physical Products: An Empirical Study About Motivations, Potentials and Applicability: Report*. University of the German Federal Armed Forces.

Schneider, S., & Spieth, P. (2013). Business model innovation: Towards an integrated future research agenda. *International Journal of Innovation Management*, *17*(1), 1–34. doi:10.1142/S136391961340001X

Schulze, W. S., Lubatkin, M., Dino, R., & Buscholtz, A. (2001). Agency relationships in family firms: Theory and evidence. *Organization Science*, *12*(2), 99–116. doi:10.1287/orsc.12.2.99.10114

Schumpeter, J. A. (1934). Depressions: Can we learn from past experience? In J. A. Schumpeter, E. Chamberlin, W. W. Leontief, D. V. Brown, S. E. Harris, E. S. Mason, & O. H. Taylor (Eds.), *The economics of the recovery program*. McGraw - Hill.

Schumpeter, J. A. (1946). *Essays: On Entrepreneurs, Innovations, Business Cycles, and the Evolution of Capitalism*. Transaction Books.

Schumpeter, J. A. (1947). The Creative Response in Economic History. *The Journal of Economic History*, *2*(2), 149–159. doi:10.1017/S0022050700054279

Schüritz, R., Seebacher, S., & Dorner, R. (2017). Capturing Value from Data: Revenue Models for Data - Driven Services. *Proceedings of the 50th Hawaii International Conference on System Sciences*. 10.24251/HICSS.2017.648

Schwaber, K., & Beedle, M. (2001). *Agile Software Development with Scrum*. Prentice-Hall.

Scott, R. W. (1995). *Institutions and Organizations* (2nd ed.). SAGE Publishing.

Scott, W. R. (1987). The Adolescence of Institutional Theory. *Administrative Science Quarterly*, *32*(4), 493–511. doi:10.2307/2392880

Serrador, P., & Pinto, J. K. (2015). Does Agile work - A quantitative analysis of agile project success? *International Journal of Project Management*, *33*(1), 1040–1051. doi:10.1016/j.ijproman.2015.01.006

Serrador, P., & Turner, R. (2015). The relationship between project success and project efficiency. *Project Management Journal*, *46*(1), 30–39. doi:10.1002/pmj.21468

Shapiro, J. N. (2012). Terrorist Decision - Making: Insights from Economics and Political Science. *Perspectives on Terrorism*, *6*(4 - 5), 5 - 20.

Sharma, C., Sabharwal, S., & Sibal, R. (2013). *A Survey on Software Testing Techniques using Genetic Algorithm*. Academic Press.

Sharma, S., & Hasteer, N. (2016). A comprehensive study on state of Scrum development. *2016 International Conference on Computing, Communication and Automation (ICCCA)*, 867 - 872. 10.1109/CCAA.2016.7813837

Shash, A. A., & Ahcom, J. (2006). Organizational aspects of planning and scheduling subsystem. *Journal of Construction Research*, *7*(1/2), 247–265. doi:10.1142/S160994510600058X

Sheehan, L., & Hewitt, K. (1969). *A Pilot Survey of Global Natural Disasters of the Past Twenty Years*. Natural Hazard Research Publisher.

Shelley, L. I. (2013). *Dirty Entanglements: Corruption, Crime, and Terrorism*. Book. doi:10.1017/CBO9781139059039

Shenhar, A. J., & Wideman, R. (2020). Optimizing Success By Matching Management Style to Project Type. *PM World Journal*, *9*(11), 1 – 21.

Shenhar, A. D. D. (2007). *Reinventing Project Management*. Harvard Bus. School Press.

Shine Technologies. (2021). *Agile Methodologies Survey Results*. Author.

Shore, J. (2014). *The Art of Agile Development: Refactoring*. Www.jamesshore.com

Shore, J., & Warden, S. (2008). *The Art of Agile Development*. O'Reilly Media.

Siddique, L., & Hussein, B. A. (2016). A qualitative study of success criteria in Norwegian agile software projects from suppliers' perspective. *International Journal of Information Systems and Project Management*, *4*(2), 63–79. doi:10.12821/ijispm040204

Sidky, A., & Smith, G. (2009). *Becoming agile in an imperfect world*. Manning Publications.

Simonsen, S. H. (2014). *Applying resilience thinking: seven principles for building resilience in social - ecological systems*. Stockholm University Press.

Sims, C., & Johnson, H. L. (2011). The Elements of Scrum (Kindle ed.). Dymaxicon.

Siqueira, A. C. O., Webb, J. W., & Bruton, G. D. (2016). Informal Entrepreneurship and Industry Conditions. *Entrepreneurship Theory and Practice*, *40*(1), 177–200. doi:10.1111/etap.12115

Siriwardena, M., Malalgoda, C., Thayaparan, M., Amaratunga, D., & Keraminiyage, K. (2013). Disaster resilient built environment: Role of lifelong learning and the implications for higher education. *International Journal of Strategic Property Management*, *17*(2), 174–187. doi:10.3846/1648715X.2013.806373

Sithambaram, J., Nasir, M. H. N. B. M., & Ahmad, R. (2021). Issues and challenges impacting the successful management of agile - hybrid projects: A grounded theory approach. *International Journal of Project Management*. doi:10.1016/j.ijproman.2021.03.002

Slater, D., & Weber, M. (2013). *Iron Cage in an Iron Fist of Power in and the Personalization Institutions Authoritarian Malaysia*. Academic Press.

Sliger, M. (2011). *Agile project management with Scrum*. Paper presented at PMI® Global Congress 2011 - North America, Dallas, TX.

Sloan, S. (1984). Political Terrorism: Theory, Tactics and Counter - Measures. *The American Political Science Review*, *78*(2), 552–553. doi:10.2307/1963432

Slocombe, M. (2001). Max hits: Building successful websites. Rotovision.

Snyder, J. R., & Kline, S. (1987). Modern Project Management: How Did We Get Here - Where Do We Go? *Project Management Journal*, *12*(9), 56–70.

Software Design and Modelling. (2018). Retrieved April 19, 2020, from https://sea.ucar.edu/best - practices/design

Sohi, A. J., Hertogh, M., Bosch-Rekveldt, M., & Blom, R. (2016). Does lean & agile project management help coping with project complexity? *Procedia: Social and Behavioral Sciences*, *226*, 252–259. doi:10.1016/j.sbspro.2016.06.186

Sommer, A. F., Hedegaard, C., Dukovska-Popovska, I., & Steger-Jensen, K. (2015). Improved product development performance through Agile / Stage - Gate hybrids - The next - generation Stage - Gate process? *Research Technology Management*, *158*(1), 1–10. doi:10.5437/08956308X5801236

Sommerville, I. (2016). *Legacy systems* (9th ed.). Pearson Education Limited.

Sommerville, I. (2019). *Software Engineering*. Addison Wesley.

Sorescu, A., Frambach, R. T., Singh, J., Rangaswamy, A., & Bridges, C. (2011). Innovations in retail business models. *Journal of Retailing*, *87*(S1), S3–S16. doi:10.1016/j.jretai.2011.04.005

Spittal, M. J., Walkey, F. H., McClure, J., Siegert, R. J., & Ballantyne, K. E. (2006). The Earthquake Readiness Scale: The development of a valid and reliable unifactorial measure. *Natural Hazards*, *39*(1), 15–29. doi:10.100711069-005-2369-9

Spreitzer, G. M., Janasz, S. C. D., & Quinn, R. E. (1999). Empowered to lead: The role of psychological empowerment in leadership. *Journal of Organizational Behavior*, *20*(4), 511–526. doi:10.1002/(SICI)1099-1379(199907)20:4<511::AID-JOB900>3.0.CO;2-L

Squire, L. R., Knowlton, B., & Musen, G. (1993). The structure and organization of memory. *Annual Review of Psychology*, *44*(1), 453–495. doi:10.1146/annurev.ps.44.020193.002321 PMID:8434894

Srivastava, A. K., Negi, G., Mishra, V., & Pandey, S. (2012). Corporate Social Responsibility : A Case Study of TATA Group. *Journal of Business and Management*, *3*(5), 17–27.

Srivastava, A., Bhardwaj, S., & Saraswat, S. (2017). SCRUM model for agile methodology. *2017 International Conference on Computing, Communication and Automation (ICCCA)*, 864 - 869. 10.1109/CCAA.2017.8229928

Stake, R. E. (2000). Case Studies. In N. K. Denzin & Y. S. Lincoln (Eds.), *Handbook of Qualitative Research* (pp. 821–834). Sage.

Stare, A. (2014). Agile project management in product development projects. *Procedia: Social and Behavioral Sciences*, *119*(1), 295–304. doi:10.1016/j.sbspro.2014.03.034

START. (2016). GTD Global Terrorism Database. In National Consortium for the Study of Terrorism and Responses to Terrorism (p. 63). START.

Stateofagile. (2021). *2013 State of Agile report: Why Agile?* Author.

Status Quo Agile. (2021). *Second study on success and forms of usage of agile methods*. Author.

Staus, S. (2013). *The Order of Genocide: Race, Power and War in Rwanda*. Cornell University Press. doi:10.7591/9780801467158

Stephan, U., Uhlander, L., & Stride, C. (2015). Institutions and social entrepreneurship: The role of institutional voids, institutional support, and institutional configurations. *Journal of International Business Studies*, *46*(3), 308–331. doi:10.1057/jibs.2014.38

Stern, N. H. (2007). The Economics of Climate Change. *The Stern Review*. http://mudancasclimaticas.cptec.inpe.br/~rmclima/pdfs/destaques/sternreview_report_complete.pdf

Stol, K. J., & Fitzgerald, B. (2014). Two's company, three's a crowd: A case study of crowdsourcing software development. *Proceedings of the 36th International Conference on Software Engineering - ICSE 2014*, 187 - 198. 10.1145/2568225.2568249

Storey, C., & Larbig, C. (2018). Absorbing customer knowledge: How customer involvement enables service design success. *Journal of Service Research*, *21*(1), 101–118. doi:10.1177/1094670517712613

Suchting, W. A. (1992). Constructivism deconstructed. *Science and Education*, *1*(3), 223–254. doi:10.1007/BF00430275

Sudhakar, G. P. (2016). Understanding the meaning of "Project Success.". *Binus Business Review*, *7*(2), 163–169. doi:10.21512/bbr.v7i2.1586

Sudhakar, P. G. (2012). A model of critical success factors for software projects. *Journal of Enterprise Information Management, 25*(6), 537–558. doi:10.1108/17410391211272829

Sunindijo, R. Y., Hadikusumo, B. H., & Ogunlana, S. (2007). Emotional intelligence and leadership styles in construction project management. *Journal of Management Engineering, 23*(4), 166–170. doi:10.1061/(ASCE)0742-597X(2007)23:4(166)

Sureshchandra, K., & Shrinivasavadhani, J. (2008). Moving from Waterfall to Agile. *Agile 2008 Conference,* 97 - 101. 10.1109/Agile.2008.49

Sutherland, J., & Altman, I. (2009). Take no prisoners: how a venture capital group does scrum. In *Agile Conference, 2009. AGILE'09* (pp. 350 - 355). IEEE. 10.1109/AGILE.2009.29

Sutherland, J., & Schwaber, K. (2017). *The Scrum Guide*. http://www.scrumguides.org

Sutherland, J., Viktorov, A., Blount, J., & Puntikov, N. (2007). Distributed Scrum: Agile Project Management with Outsourced Development Teams. *2007 40th Annual Hawaii International Conference on System Sciences (HICSS'07),* 274a - 274a. 10.1109/HICSS.2007.180

Sutter, C. J., Webb, J. W., Kistruck, G. M., & Bailey, A. V. G. (2013). Entrepreneurs' responses to semi - formal illegitimate institutional arrangements. *Journal of Business Venturing, 28*(6), 743–758. doi:10.1016/j.jbusvent.2013.03.001

Sutton, R. S., & Barto, A. G. (2015). *Reinforcement Learning: An Introduction*. MIT Press.

Sveiby, K. E. (1997). *The New Organizational Wealth: Managing & Measuring Knowledge-Based Assets*. Berrett-Koehler Publishers, Inc.

Szalvay, V. (2004). An introduction to agile software development. *Danube Technologies*, 1 - 9.

Tacken, J., Rodrigues, V. S., & Mason, R. (2014). Examining CO_2e reduction within the German logistics sector. *International Journal of Logistics Management, 25*(1), 54–84. doi:10.1108/IJLM-09-2011-0073

Takeuchi, H., & Nonaka, I. (1986). The new product development game. *Harvard Business Review, 64*(1), 137–146.

Tam, C., Moura, E. J. C., Oliveira, T., & Varajao, J. (2020). The factors influencing the success of on-going agile software development projects. *International Journal of Project Management, 38*(3), 165–176. doi:10.1016/j.ijproman.2020.02.001

Tang, C. S. (2006). Perspectives in supply chain risk management. *International Journal of Production Economics, 103*(2), 451–488. doi:10.1016/j.ijpe.2005.12.006

Tang, L., & Koveos, P. E. (2008). A Framework to Update Hofstede's Cultural value Indices: Economic Dynamics and Institutional Stability. *Journal of International Business Studies, 39*(6), 1045–1063. doi:10.1057/palgrave.jibs.8400399

Taniguchi, A., & Onosato, M. (2018). Effect of continuous improvement on the reporting quality of project management information system for project management success. *International Journal of Information Technology and Computer Science, 10*(1), 1–15. doi:10.5815/ijitcs.2018.01.01

Taroun, A. (2014). Towards a Better Modelling and Assessment of Construction Risk: Insights from a Literature Review. *International Journal of Project Management, 32*(1), 101–115. doi:10.1016/j.ijproman.2013.03.004

TDSP. (2021). *What is the team data science process?* https://docs.mcrosoft.com

Teece, D. J. (2010). Business models, business strategy and innovation. *Long Range Planning, 43*(2-3), 172 - 194.

Thai, M. T. T., & Turkina, E. (2012). *Entrepreneurship in the Informal Economy. Entrepreneurship in the Informal Economy: Models*. Approaches and Prospects for Economic Development.

Thai, M. T. T., & Turkina, E. (2014). Macro - level determinants of formal entrepreneurship versus informal entrepreneurship. *Journal of Business Venturing*, *29*(4), 490–510. doi:10.1016/j.jbusvent.2013.07.005

The Agile Alliance. (2021). *Guide to Agile Practices*. Author.

The Clever PM. (2021). *Which is better - Kanban or Scrum?* Author.

The Standisch Group International. (2003). *Latest Standisch Group CHAOS report shows project success rates have improved by 50%*. Author.

The Standish Group International. (2021). *Chaos Report 2020*. The Standish Group International, Inc. Available: https://www.standishgroup.com/about

Thomas, G., & Vaughan, M. (2004). *Inclusive education: Readings and reflections. Inclusive education*. ERIC.

Thornton, P. H., & Ocasio, W. (2005). *Institutional Logics*. The Sage Handbook of Organizational Institutionalism.

Thummadi, B. V., Shiv, O., & Lyytinen, K. (2011). Enacted Routines in Agile and Waterfall Processes. *2011 AGILE Conference*, 67 - 76. 10.1109/AGILE.2011.29

Tilos. (2012). *TILOS linear project*. Available at: www.tilos.org

Tina Dacin, M., Oliver, C., & Roy, J. P. (2007). The legitimacy of strategic alliances: An institutional perspective. *Strategic Management Journal*, *28*(2), 169–187. doi:10.1002mj.577

Tirumala, S., Ali, S., & Anjan, B. G. (2016). A Hybrid Agile model using SCRUM and Feature Driven Development. *International Journal of Computers and Applications*, *156*(5), 1–5. doi:10.5120/ijca2016912443

Toaff, S. S. (2002). Don't Play with Mouths of Fire, and Other Lessons of Global Software Development. *Cutter IT Journal*, *15*(11), 23–28.

Tolbert, P. S., & Zucker, L. G. (1996). The Institutionalization of Institutional Theory. Handbook of Organization Studies, 175 - 190.

Truong, D., & Jitbaipoon, T. (2016). How can agile methodologies be used to enhance the success of information technology projects? *International Journal of Information Technology Project Management*, *7*(2), 1–16. doi:10.4018/IJITPM.2016040101

Tsoy, M., & Staples, D. S. (2020). Exploring critical success factors in agile analytics projects. *Proceedings of 53rd Hawaii International Conference on System Sciences*, 984 - 993.

Tukuta, M., & Saruchera, F. (2015). Challenges facing procurement professionals in developing economies: Unlocking value through professional international purchasing. *Journal of Transport and Supply Chain Management*, *9*(1), 1–9. doi:10.4102/jtscm.v9i1.152

Turley, B. J. S. (2010). *Entrepreneurship and innovation in Latin America Innovation and growth — the Latin American opportunity*. Ernst and Young White Paper.

Turner, J. R., & Müller, R. (2004). Communication and co - operation on projects between the project owner as principal and the project manager as agent. *European Management Journal*, *22*(3), 327–336. doi:10.1016/j.emj.2004.04.010

Tuteja, M., & Dubey, G. (2012). A Research Study on importance of Testing and Quality Assurance in Software Development Life Cycle (SDLC). *Models*, *2*(3), 7.

UN ESCAP. (2019). *Asia - Pacific trade and investment trends: 2019/20 Trade in goods outlook*. https://www.unescap.org/our-work/trade-investment-inovation

Weller, M. (2002). Delivering learning on the net: The why, what & how of online education. RoutledgeFalmer.

West, J., & Bogers, M. (2017). Open innovation: Current status and research opportunities. *Innovation (North Sydney, N.S.W.)*, *19*(1), 43–50. doi:10.1080/14479338.2016.1258995

White, P. (2009). Building a sustainability strategy into the business. *Corporate Governance*, *9*(4), 386–394. doi:10.1108/14720700910984936

Wilkins, B. T. (1992). *Terrorism and Collective Responsibility*. Book.

Wilkinson, P. (1986). *Terrorism and the Liberal State* (2nd ed.). Macmillan.

Williams, C. (2006). The Hidden Enterprise Culture: Entrepreneurship in the Informal Economy. *Local Economy*, *21*.

Williams, M., Packlick, J., Bellubbi, A., & Coburn, S. (2007). *How We Made Onsite Customer Work - An Extreme Success story. In Agile 2007*. IEEE Computer Society.

Williams, T. (2016). Identifying Success Factors in Construction Projects: A Case Study. *Project Management Journal*, *47*(1), 97–112. doi:10.1002/pmj.21558

Winter, J. (2014). *Sites of Memory, Sites of Mourning: The Great War in European Cultural History*. Cambridge University Press. doi:10.1017/CBO9781107589087

Winter, M., & Knemeyer, A. M. (2013). Exploring the integration of sustainability and supply chain management: Current state and opportunities for future inquiry. *International Journal of Physical Distribution & Logistics Management*, *43*(1), 18–38. doi:10.1108/09600031311293237

Witzel, M. (2003). *Fifty key figures in management*. Routledge. doi:10.4324/9780203402184

Wolfe, D. (1968). American Association for the Advancement of Science. *Science*. PMID:5657328

Wolfgang, K. (2007). *Iconic Remembering and Religious Icons: Fundamentalist Strategies in European Memory Politics?* Berghahn Books.

World Bank. (2001). *World Bank and Asian Development Bank Complete Preliminary Gujarat Earthquake Damage Assessment and Recovery Plan*. Available at: https://www.worldbank.org/gujarat, https://www.adb.org/

Worldometers. (2020). *COVID - 19 coronavirus pandemic*. Available at: https://www.worldometers.info/coronavirus/?utm_campaign=CSauthorbio

WRIKE. (2020). *Agile Methodology Basics*. https://www.wrike.com/project-management-guide/agile-methodology-basics

WTO. (2019). *Goods Trade Barometer*. Geneva: World Trade Organization. Available at https://www.wto.org/english/news_e/news19_e/wtoi_15aug19_e.pdf

Wu, B., Lawless, D., Bisbal, J., Richardson, R., Grimson, J., & Wade, V. (1997). The butterfly methodology: A gateway - free approach for migrating legacy information systems. *Proceedings. Third IEEE International Conference on Engineering of Complex Computer Systems* (Cat. no. 97TB100168), 200 - 205.

Wuni, I. Y., & Shen, G. Q. (2020). Stakeholder management in prefabricated prefinished volumetric construction projects: Benchmarking the key result areas. *Built Environment Project and Asset Management*, *10*(3), 407–421. doi:10.1108/BEPAM-02-2020-0025

Wurtemberg, L. M. V., Franke, U., Lagerström, R., Ericsson, E., & Lilliesköld, J. (2011). IT project success factors: An experience report. *2011 Proceedings of PICMET '11: Technology Management in the Energy Smart World (PICMET)*, 1 - 10.